A
HISTORICAL COMMENTARY
ON
THUCYDIDES

A
HISTORICAL COMMENTARY
ON
THUCYDIDES

BY

A. W. GOMME

A. ANDREWES

AND

K. J. DOVER

VOLUME IV

Books V 25—VII

OXFORD

AT THE CLARENDON PRESS

1970

Oxford University Press, Ely House, London W. I

GLASGOW NEW YORK TORONTO MELBOURNE WELLINGTON
CAPE TOWN SALISBURY IBADAN NAIROBI DAR ES SALAAM LUSAKA ADDIS ABABA
BOMBAY CALCUTTA MADRAS KARACHI LAHORE DACCA
KUALA LUMPUR SINGAPORE HONG KONG TOKYO

PRINTED IN GREAT BRITAIN

ACKNOWLEDGEMENTS

THE primary responsibility for revising and supplementing Gomme's commentary on v. 25–116 belongs to Andrewes, for the commentary on vi–vii to Dover. But we have discussed one another's successive drafts very fully, to our mutual profit, and what is printed here is very much a work of collaboration. We both wish to express our warm thanks to Mrs. Gomme, who drew the maps; to R. Meiggs and D. M. Lewis for allowing us to use the numeration of their *Selection of Greek Historical Inscriptions* in advance of publication; and to the Clarendon Press for its patience and helpfulness. Andrewes wishes in addition to thank H. Lloyd-Jones and D. M. Lewis, who also read and criticized his first draft and drew attention to serious deficiencies; and Dover all those who criticized the abridged commentaries on vi–vii which were published in 1965.

A. A.
K. J. D.

CONTENTS

ACKNOWLEDGEMENTS   v

LIST OF MAPS   ix

BIBLIOGRAPHY OF SHORT TITLES   xi

NOTE ON THE MANUSCRIPTS   xv

BOOK V. 25–116   1
  EDITORIAL NOTE   3
  COMMENTARY   5

BOOKS VI–VII   193
  EDITORIAL NOTE   195
  COMMENTARY   197
  APPENDIX. The Topography of Syracuse and the Siege   466

ADDENDA   485

INDEXES   491

LIST OF MAPS

BOOK V

1. South-west Arkadia   *facing page* 34
2. The Argolid   83
3. Mantineia and Tegea   96

BOOKS VI–VII

1. Syracuse as it is today   468
2. The fortifications in 415–413 B.C.   469
3. First Syracusan counter-wall   477
4. Second Syracusan counter-wall   481
5. Athenian landings in 415 B.C.   481

BIBLIOGRAPHY OF SHORT TITLES

Reference to editions (*) of Thucydides and to commentaries (‡) on his work is made by the editor's or commentator's name only.

Reference to the other works listed below is (i) by initials alone (e.g. '*ATL*'), as stated, (ii) by the author's name alone (e.g. 'Abresch'), or (iii) when more than one work by the same author appears in the list, by the author's name and an obvious abbreviation (e.g. 'de Romilly, *Imp.*').

Abresch, F. L., *Dilucidationes Thucydideae*. Utrecht, 1755.

AFD = Meritt, B. D., *Athenian financial documents of the fifth century*. Ann Arbor, 1932.

Amit, M., *Athens and the sea*. Brussels, 1965.

Arnold, T.*‡: ed. 3. Oxford, 1847.

ATL = Meritt, B. D., Wade-Gery, H. T., and McGregor, M. F., *The Athenian tribute lists*. Cambridge (Mass.), 1939–53.

Beloch, K. J., *Griechische Geschichte*: ed. 2. Strassburg, Berlin, and Leipzig, 1912–27.

Bender, G. F., *Der Begriff des Staatsmannes bei Thukydides*. Würzburg, 1938.

Bengtson, H., *Die Staatsverträge des Altertums*: vol. ii, *Die Verträge der griechisch-römischen Welt*. Munich and Berlin, 1962.

Berard, J., *La Colonisation grecque de l'Italie méridionale et de la Sicile dans l'antiquité*. Paris, 1941.

Bétant, E. A., *Lexicon Thucydideum*. Geneva, 1843–7.

Bloomfield, S. T.*‡: ed. 2. London, 1842.

Bodin, L., and de Romilly, J.* Paris, 1955 (Books VI and VII).

Böckh, A., *Die Staatshaushaltung der Athener*: ed. 3, revised by Fränkel, M. Berlin, 1886.

Böhme, G.*‡: ed. 5, revised by Widmann, S. Leipzig, 1894.

Buck, C. D., *The Greek dialects*. Chicago, 1955.

Bursian, C., *Geographie von Griechenland*. Leipzig, 1862–72.

Busolt, G., *Griechische Geschichte*. Gotha, 1893–1904.

Busolt–Swoboda = Busolt, G., *Griechische Staatskunde*: vol. ii, edited by Swoboda, H. Munich, 1920–6.

CAH = *Cambridge Ancient History*.

Classen, J.*‡: ed. 3, revised by Steup, J. Berlin, 1905 (Book VI), 1908 (Book VII), 1912 (Book V).

Denniston, J. D., *The Greek particles*: ed. 2. Oxford, 1954.

de Romilly: see Bodin.

de Romilly, J. (tr. Thody, P.), *Thucydides and Athenian imperialism*. Oxford, 1963.

DGE = *Dialectorum Graecarum Exempla Epigraphica Potiora*: ed. 3, Schwyzer, E. Leipzig, 1923.

Doukas, N.*‡ Vienna, 1805.

Duker, C. A.*‡ Amsterdam, 1731.

Dunbabin, T. J., *The Western Greeks*. Oxford, 1948.
Ehrenberg Stud. = Ancient society and institutions: studies presented to Victor Ehrenberg. Oxford, 1966.
FGrHist: see Jacoby.
Finley, John H., Jr., *Thucydides*. Cambridge (Mass.), 1942.
Fougères, G., *Mantinée et l'Arcadie orientale*. Paris, 1898.
Freeman, E. A., *The history of Sicily*. Oxford, 1891–4.
GHI = Greek historical inscriptions: ed. Tod, M. N. Oxford, 1933–48.
Gomme, A. W., *Essays in Greek history and literature*. Oxford, 1937.
Gomme, A. W., *More essays in Greek history and literature*, Oxford, 1962.
Goodwin, W. W., *Syntax of the moods and tenses of the Greek verb*: ed. 2. London, 1910.
Grote, G., *History of Greece* (ed. 1, London, 1846–56): cited from the London, 1888, edition.
Grundy, G. B., *Thucydides and the history of his age*: ed. 2. Oxford, 1948.
GVI = Griechische Vers-Inschriften: ed. Peek, W. Berlin, 1955– .
Haacke, C. F. F.*‡: ed. 2. Leipzig, 1831.
Hatzfeld, J., *Alcibiade*: ed. 2. Paris, 1951.
Herbst, L., *Ueber C. G. Cobets Emendationen im Thukydides*. Leipzig, 1857–60.
Herbst, L., *Zu Thukydides*: posthumous papers edited by Müller, F. Leipzig, 1898–1900.
Herwerden, H. van* Utrecht, 1877–82.
HN = Head, B. V., Historia Numorum: ed. 2. Oxford, 1911.
Holden, H. A.*‡ (Book VII): ed. 2. Cambridge, 1896.
Holm, A., *Geschichte Siciliens im Alterthum*. Leipzig, 1870–98.
Hude, C.* Leipzig, 1898–1901.
Hüttl, W., *Verfassungsgeschichte von Syrakus*. Prague, 1929.
IG = Inscriptiones Graecae.
IvO = Olympia v, *Die Inschriften*, Dittenberger, W., and Purgold, K. Berlin, 1896.
Jacoby, F. (ed., comm.), *Die Fragmente der griechischen Historiker*. Berlin, 1923–30; Leiden, 1940– .
Jacoby, F., *Atthis*. Oxford, 1949.
Jeffery, L. H., *The local scripts of archaic Greece*. Oxford, 1961.
Jones, A. H. M., *Athenian democracy*. Oxford, 1957.
Judeich, W., *Topographie von Athen*: ed. 2. Munich, 1931.
Kirchhoff, A., *Thukydides und sein Urkundenmaterial*. Berlin, 1895.
Köster, A., *Das antike Seewesen*. Berlin, 1923.
Kromayer, J., and Veith, G., *Antike Schlachtfelder*. Berlin, 1903–31.
Krüger, K. W.*‡: ed. 2. Berlin, 1858–60.
Kühner, R., *Ausführliche Grammatik der griechischen Sprache*: Part I revised by Blass, F., and Part II by Gerth, B. Hanover, 1890–1904.
Leake, W. M., *Travels in the Morea*. London, 1830.
Linwood, W., *Remarks and emendations on some passages in Thucydides*. London, 1860.
Loring, W., 'Some ancient routes in the Peloponnese', *JHS* xv (1895), 25–89.

BIBLIOGRAPHY OF SHORT TITLES

LSJ = Liddell, H. G., and Scott, R., *A Greek–English Lexicon*: revised by Stuart Jones, Sir Henry, and McKenzie, R. Oxford, 1940.

Lüdtke, W., *Untersuchungen zum Satzbau des Thukydides*. Altona, 1930.

Luschnat, O., *Die Feldherrnreden im Geschichtswerk des Thukydides* (= *Philologus*, Supplbd. xxxiv/2). Leipzig, 1942.

Madvig, J. N., *Adversaria Critica ad Scriptores Graecos et Latinos*. Copenhagen, 1871–84.

Marchant, E. C.*‡ London, 1893 (Book VII), 1897 (Book VI).

Meister, C., *Die Gnomik im Geschichtswerk des Thukydides*. Winterthur, 1955.

Meritt, B. D.: see *AFD*.

Meritt, B. D., *The Athenian year*. Univ. of California, 1961.

Meyer, Eduard, *Geschichte des Altertums*: ed. 1, Stuttgart and Berlin, 1884–1902: vols. iii, iv. 1 and 2, revised by Stier, H. E. Stuttgart, 1937–56.

ML = Meiggs, R., and Lewis, D. M., *A selection of Greek historical inscriptions*. Oxford, 1969.

Müller, F.*‡ Paderborn, 1888 (Book VI), 1889 (Book VII).

Münch, H., *Studien zu den Exkursen des Thukydides*. Heidelberg, 1935.

PA = Kirchner, J., *Prosopographia Attica*. Berlin, 1901–3.

Pace, B., *Arte e civiltà della Sicilia antica*. Milan, 1935–49.

Patzer, H., *Das Problem der Geschichtsschreibung des Thukydides und die thukydideische Frage*. Berlin, 1937.

Philippson, A., *Die griechischen Landschaften*: edited by Kirsten, E. Frankfurt am M., 1950–9.

PMG = *Poetae Melici Graeci*, ed. Page, D. L. Oxford, 1962.

Popp, H., *Die Einwirkung von Vorzeichen, Opfern und Festen auf die Kriegführung der Griechen*. Diss. Erlangen, 1957.

Poppo, E. F.*‡: revised by Stahl, J. M. Leipzig, 1876–85.

Preuss, J., *Kritische-exegetische Beiträge zum VI Buch des Thukydides*. Munich, 1905.

Radford, R. S., *Personification and the use of abstract subjects in the Attic orators and Thucydides*. Baltimore, 1901.

RE = *Real-Encyclopädie der classischen Altertumswissenschaft*.

Ros, J., *Die ΜΕΤΑΒΟΛΗ (Variatio) als Stilprinzip des Thukydides*. Paderborn, 1938.

Schadewaldt, W., *Die Geschichtsschreibung des Thukydides*. Berlin, 1929.

Schmid, W., *Geschichte der griechischen Literatur*, I. v. Munich, 1948.

Schwartz, E., *Das Geschichtswerk des Thukydides*. Bonn, 1919.

SEG = *Supplementum Epigraphicum Graecum*.

SIG = *Sylloge Inscriptionum Graecarum*, ed. 3, Dittenberger, W. Leipzig, 1915–24.

Smith, C. F.*‡ (Book VII). Boston, 1888.

Spratt, A. W.*‡ (Book VI). Cambridge, 1905.

Stahl: see Poppo.

Stahl, J. M., *Kritisch-historische Syntax des griechischen Verbums der klassischen Zeit*. Heidelberg, 1907.

Steup: see Classen.

Tod, M. N.: see *GHI*.

BIBLIOGRAPHY OF SHORT TITLES

Ullrich, F. W., *Beiträge zur Erklärung des Thukydides*. Hamburg, 1846.

Vallet, G., *Rhégion et Zancle*. Paris, 1958.

van Compernolle, R., *Étude de chronologie et d'historiographie siciliotes*. Brussels, 1960.

Wade-Gery, H. T., *Essays in Greek history*. Oxford, 1958.

Weidauer, K., *Thukydides und die Hippokratischen Schriften*. Heidelberg, 1954.

Wentker, H., *Sizilien und Athen*. Heidelberg, 1956.

Widmann: see Böhme.

Woodhouse, W. J., *King Agis of Sparta and his campaign in Arkadia in 418 B.C.* Oxford, 1933.

NOTE ON THE MANUSCRIPTS

Reference is made to manuscripts and scholia in conformity with the apparatus criticus of the Oxford Classical Text, but with the following additions and modifications:

H = Parisinus gr. 1734 (s. xiv in.)

H_2 = correction or addition in H by a hand other than the hand of the copyist of the continuous text at the passage in question (cf. A. Kleinlogel, *Geschichte des Thukydidestextes im Mittelalter* [Berlin, 1965], pp. 2, 10–32, 83).

Z = Schedae Mutinenses (s. x) (cf. G. B. Alberti, *Bollettino del Comitato per la preparazione dell'Edizione Nazionale dei Classici Greci e Latini*, 1962, 27 ff.).

'*Σ*' is used for 'scholium' in place of 'Schol.', and the distribution of the scholium in question is indicated, e.g. $Σ^{Mcf}$ (cf. Kleinlogel, pp. 116–18).

The abbreviation 'recc.' (= 'unus vel plures e codicibus recentioribus') is replaced, wherever the information available makes its replacement possible, by the name of the manuscript in question or by the symbol '*ψ*', meaning any one or more of the following manuscripts: Ambrosianus A 4 inf., Athous Lavrae H 99, Basileensis E III 4, Parisini gr. 1733 and suppl. gr. 256, Trajectinus gr. 13, Urbinas gr. 92, Vaticani gr. 992 and 1292, and the second and third hands in Ottobonianus gr. 211 (cf. Kleinlogel, pp. 47–111, and Alberti, *Boll. Comit.* 1965, 15 ff.).

All quotations of Valla's Latin translation are taken from Vaticanus lat. 1801, not from Stephanus's printed edition of Valla.

BOOK V. 25–116

EDITORIAL NOTE

THE commentary on v. 25–116 is based on the following materials:

1. Gomme's work had progressed far enough for him to have a continuous text typed. For previous volumes, the typed text was close to what was eventually printed, but here there were noticeable gaps. Several topographical notes were left blank: some large questions were not treated at all: the gravest loss is that the promised appendix on the Melian Dialogue was not written. The commentary is generally less full than in the published volumes. In many places he had begun to remodel or augment his text, and it is clear that the final draft would have been widely different from the first, but we have not enough material to reconstruct it.

2. Some hundred detached manuscript notes. Many were clearly earlier than the continuous text, some later. They vary from fully worked-out sentences to mere references carrying no indication of his opinion.

3. My own contribution, which in the circumstances was necessarily substantial.

The presentation of this material was not an easy problem. The basic need was to provide an intelligible and reasonably comprehensive commentary. Many of Gomme's notes, short or long, were complete and characteristic of him, and they clearly must be printed as they stood. Equally, there was no problem where a note was wholly mine, though the authorship ought somehow to be indicated. Trouble arose where a note of Gomme's seemed, for one reason or another, to need supplement, and in the not altogether infrequent places where I found myself disagreeing with him. The solution adopted was to enclose in square brackets all passages which are wholly mine, or where I have substantially intervened. What lies outside these brackets is almost entirely Gomme's: I have not cluttered up the text by bracketing mere completion of references, or minor or consequential alterations, but I have made no change of substance without indicating it. 'Gomme (ms.)', or '(ms.)' alone, indicates that the source is a detached note, which he might or might not have wished to include in the final version.

The result is not, and could not be, wholly satisfactory. I am especially conscious that the comment sometimes becomes a dialogue in which one party is unfairly prevented from answering back. It is,

3

however, a continuous text, in which comment can be found on all points which seemed noteworthy to Gomme or to the present editors. The reader can, if he wishes, find out who is responsible for the comment; and it will be clear to attentive readers that Gomme's share in the result is much larger than the extent of bracketing might at first sight suggest.   A. A.

25–26. *Introduction to the Second Part*

25. 1. καὶ τὴν ξυμμαχίαν - - - Ἀθηναίων: (ms.) inserted later when Thucydides heard more about the alliance? See Busolt, iii/2. 1203 n., [and 27. 1 n., p. 21 below.] This is possible; for the fact that 25. 1 does not sit very well with 20. 1 does not matter, if this is a new preface. And it is that, whether completely, to a new volume after the publication of vol. i, or merely to a renewal of a narrative or an incomplete narrative.

μετὰ τὸν δεκέτη πόλεμον: see below, 26. 2 n.

ἐπὶ Πλειστόλα μέν, κ.τ.λ.: cf. ii. 2. 1 nn., and v. 19. 2 n.

Although, in the form in which we have it, there is no doubt (to my mind) that the division between the section of the *History* which covers the Ten Years' War and that which covers the subsequent years is at the end of c. 24, this particular statement, with its archon-names, derives doubtless from a projected end to a publishable work and was written, say, in 419 when it was still possible, though unlikely, that the peace would last, and when Thucydides was probably engaged in getting his story of the Ten Years' War into its final form. There will necessarily have been changes made, adaptations, *remaniements*, not only in what is now cc. 24. 2 and 25, but perhaps in 20 as well. [See also first n. above, and vol. iii, 696–8.]

It is also to be noted that in the later thirteen-books division of the *History*, neither with c. 24 nor at c. 26 did a book end. [The seventh book of that division ended at iv. 135. 2; see n. there.]

τοῖς μὲν δεξαμένοις αὐτάς: [αὐτάς refers back only to τὰς σπονδάς, not to τὴν ξυμμαχίαν in which the allies had no part. See 27. 1 n.]

πρὸς τὴν Λακεδαίμονα: [Gomme cited Graves's remark, that both πρός with acc. instead of a dative and τὴν Λακεδαίμονα for τοὺς Λακεδαιμονίους are unusual. But (a) the simple dative here would not convey clearly Thucydides' point, 'a disturbance arose among the allies in their relations with Sparta'; (b) though Greek very much more often uses the plural ethnic as the name of the state and reserves the name of the city to strictly geographical reference, the rule is not universal: cf. 30. 1 σπείσεσθαι πρὸς τὸ Ἄργος. It is not easy to detect any difference of meaning in this occasional variation.]

Stahl's punctuation and reading here may be right: τὰ πεπραγμένα· καὶ εὐθὺς ἄλλη ⟨τε⟩ - - - Λακεδαίμονα, καί, κ.τ.λ. [ἄλλη ταραχή does not introduce a fresh set of events, distinct from the trouble created by the Corinthians and others. Steup took ἄλλη to refer back to 432, when agitation among Sparta's allies had led to war: it may,

5

however, look back only to 17. 2, the objections that Corinth and others had made during the negotiation of the Peace.]

2. προϊόντος τοῦ χρόνου: [contrast 35. 2, ὑπώπτευον δὲ ἀλλήλους εὐθὺς μετὰ τὰς σπονδάς, and see n. there.]

3. ἐπὶ ἓξ ἔτη μὲν καὶ δέκα μῆνας ἀπέσχοντο, κ.τ.λ.: this precise dating suggests at once agreed or easily understood *terminus a quo* and *terminus ante quem*; yet neither is told to us, and it is not easy to discover them. For the former two possibilities are open: (*a*) from the date of the Peace of Nikias or the Athenian–Spartan alliance (early spring, 421), which is precise; but six years and 10 months brings us to midwinter 415/14, and the only thing in Thucydides' narrative that is to be placed thereabouts is the Spartan decision to think hard about capturing and fortifying Dekeleia and to send 'some help' to Sicily (vi. 93. 1–2), which by no means can be described as ceasing to 'refrain from invading Athenian territory'; and (*b*) from the date of the negotiations between Sparta on the one hand and Corinth and Boeotia on the other (below, 36. 1), which might be said to begin the period of mutual hostility and suspicion which lasted six years and 10 months (τὸ μὲν οὖν θέρος τοῦτο ἡσυχία ἦν, 35. 8), before open aggression on either side, and is perhaps suggested by προϊόντος τοῦ χρόνου, § 2 above; before that time, that is, there was real peace .The date of this is the winter of 421/20—almost certainly the beginning of winter (ἔτυχον γὰρ ἔφοροι ἕτεροι - - - ἄρχοντες ἤδη, 36. 1—they had just taken office). It has been suggested that this would take us to the Athenian landings in the Peloponnese in the summer of 414, vi. 105. 1–2, which are described there as the first open breach (τριάκοντα ναυσίν - - - - αἵπερ τὰς σπονδὰς φανερώτατα - - - ἔλυσαν: cf. vii. 18. 2–3; see also And. iii. 9).

This was W. Jerusalem's solution (*Wiener Stud.* iii (1881), 287–90), approved by Classen, Widmann, and Steup (*Thuk. Stud.* i. 87 n.), and by Busolt, iii/2. 1198 n.; and it looks the best; but it is by no means certain, for this Athenian landing took place earlier than six years and 10 months after the beginning of the winter of 421/20 (see below); and if we put back the beginning of the period of uneasy truce by a month or two to the time of suspicion preceding the Spartan approach to Corinth and Boeotia, we are, very certainly, losing that precision which we expect from so precise a statement as six years and 10 months—even the Spartan approach to Corinth not being so decisively dated as we should like it to be. It might also be thought that αὖθις ἐς πόλεμον φανερὸν κατέστησαν, below, suggests that the actual invasion of Attica at the beginning of spring 413 (vii. 19. 1, τοῦ ἐπιγιγνομένου ἧρος εὐθὺς ἀρχομένου) would be a better end to the period than the Athenian raids on the Lakonian coast in 414, for we know from book i that there was a very clear difference between αἰτίαι, even if ἀληθέσταται or φανερώταται, and the actual outbreak of war. Perhaps to this objection the use of λῦσαι τὰς σπονδάς both here and in vi. 105. 1 is sufficient answer;[1] but it may be noted at the same time that, had Thucydides chosen his two most precisely dated events—the Peace of Nikias and the invasion of 413 (as from 26. 6 we might expect)—the interval was almost exactly eight years. Yet he clearly did not mean this.

Three lines of argument are closed to us: (1) we must not make the sailing of the great expedition to Sicily the end of the period, for in that case Thucydides would not have described the period in the words ἀπέσχοντο μὴ ἐπὶ τὴν ἑκατέρων γῆν στρατεῦσαι; (2) we should not use expressions found below in 26. 2–3 to strengthen a case, because that passage may have been written at a different time from this and with a different aim—that is, Thucydides maybe was thinking of something else (see nn. there); and (3) where so much is doubtful—both the beginning and the end of the period of ἀνοκωχή—we should not emend the figures in order to make them look correct.

[The end of the period, at vi. 105, is perhaps less doubtful than the last sentence suggests, but I share Gomme's uneasiness about the beginning (see further 35. 2 n.); and about the interval, for if the six years and 10 months begin at 36. 1 with the beginning of winter, and if this is after 1 November 421 (vol. iii, 706), then the raid must be later than 1 September 414. Thucydides has not made it easy to date this exactly:

(a) The landing of the Athenian force outside Syracuse is necessarily later than its return to Katane (vi. 94. 4), to be dated to the middle of April (p. 266); and it belongs to summer (96. 1) not to spring (94. 1, 95. 1). But we have little indication how long after the middle of April it took place, or how long must be allowed for the further sequence down to the capture of the second Syracusan counter-wall (96–102).

(b) The death of Lamachos (101. 6), during the fight for the second counter-wall, is dated to the archon-year 415/14 by Σ Ar. Th. 841, τετάρτῳ ἔτει πρότερον from 412/11. Thus Lamachos died before c. 10 July 414 (Meritt, Ath. Year, 218: for the calendar of this year see also pp. 264 ff. below). We may still wonder how this was known. An Atthidographer might note Lamachos' death (cf. Androtion, FGrHist 324 F 41), and his system would compel him to assign it to a specific archon; but it is as likely that the date results from an over-confident distribution of Thucydides' narrative between the years as that, for example, a dated dispatch from Nikias survived in the

7

archives for later study. But we do not know that the calculation was bad, and the fact remains that our only piece of evidence indicates that the events of 96–102 ended at or before the beginning of July 414; and nothing in Thucydides contradicts this conclusion.

(c) ἐν δὲ τούτῳ (104. 1) Gylippos was at Leukas. The reference must be to the situation of 103, the Syracusans inactive and the Athenians pressing on with their walls. The report which reached him at Leukas, that the circumvallation was complete, indicates that the events of 96–102 were over before he crossed. He was anxious to get to Sicily quickly (104. 1), and the rest of this chapter should still belong to the first half of July.

(d) The Spartan invasion of the Argolid was κατὰ τοὺς αὐτοὺς χρόνους τούτου τοῦ θέρους (105. 1). The narrative of Gylippos' movements is interrupted to accommodate this, and there is a clear implication that the events of 105 are, roughly, contemporary with those of 104, not with those of vii. 1. The Spartans ravaged τῆς γῆς τὴν πολλήν, which might take some time: vi. 105. 3 indicates that the Athenian raid took place while they were still ravaging. If the Aristophanes scholiast can be trusted, it will not be easy to put this raid as late as September.

(e) Gylippos' next actions (vii. 1–4. 3)—landings at Himera, collection of forces, march to Syracuse, several battles, the beginning of the third counter-wall—must take some time. At this stage Nikias decided to fortify Plemmyrion (4. 4), and the description of the effects indicates a substantial period of occupation before Nikias wrote the letter, which was dispatched before the end of summer (8) and reached Athens after the beginning of winter (10). 13. 2 suggests that Thucydides did not anticipate in 4. 6–7 as he did in parts of 27–8 (see ad loc.).

It is not surprising that historians mostly place this raid in the height of summer. It is perhaps not quite impossible to put it as late as September, but if we do so we must (1) spread the narrative of vi. 94–104 over the longest period possible and (almost certainly) reject the dating of Lamachos' death to 415/14, and (2) compress the narrative of vii. 1–7 to an improbable extent.

The conclusion of the Peace of Nikias, in which the parties swore not to bear arms against one another, is intrinsically the most likely *terminus a quo* for the six years and 10 months, and the only one for which the reader has been in any way prepared.[1] If Thucydides meant

---

[1] [Gomme seems to have been increasingly dissatisfied with Jerusalem's solution. A note, which still accepts this as 'probably best', continues —'But . . . one expects that the beginning of the year 421 is one terminus; i.e. he ought to have said where he began (and in vi. 105 he does not say that his 6 years and 10 months are over).' Steup met the same difficulty by suggesting that a clause has dropped out, in which the length of the 'genuine' peace was

that, the figures in our text are wrong, but it would be merely rash to propose any particular emendation.]

It is true that for Thucydides' *History*, as we now read it, the ὕποπτος ἀνοκωχή lasts from v. 20 (or 25) to v. 116, i.e. for six years and 3–4 months,[1] because with the beginning of vi (or, if you will, vi. 26 or 30) he is no longer narrating events of an ἀνοκωχή but a continuous war (cf. τὰ ἔπειτα ὡς ἐπολεμήθη ἐξηγήσομαι, 26. 6), and one notes that there is no such summary, or explanation of method, at the end of the narrative of the ἀνοκωχή as we have at the beginning of it. This may mean, perhaps probably does mean, that vi–vii were composed in their now finished form at a different time from, and after, v. 25, though not, or not necessarily, after v. 26 (see 26. 2 n.), though Thucydides will have begun 'taking notes' of τὰ Σικελικά as soon as he heard, from Athens or from Sicily, of the preparations for it. A long time elapsed between 421 and 412, and between 412 and 404; and, however constant Thucydides was in his general political outlook, his view of his own *book*, of the shape and length of its several parts, must have changed considerably, and perhaps often, in the intervals.

ἐς πόλεμον φανερὸν κατέστησαν: cf. i. 23. 6, ii. 1.

26. 1. γέγραφε δὲ καὶ ταῦτα: for the tense, cf. γέγραπται, 24. 2; for this sentence was written after the end of the war, and intended for a completed work. He had of course his preparatory 'notes' for the whole. The aorists of i. 1 and i. 97. 2 are slightly different. Note too the future, ἐξηγήσομαι, § 6.

ἐξῆς, ὡς ἕκαστα ἐγένετο: in ii. 1 we have ἐγίγνετο, which fits ἐξῆς more closely; and Classen emended to the imperfect here.

[Gomme added, 'perhaps rightly'; and he was often ready to switch tenses by emendation. If I lean the other way, it is not from any feeling that, in such matters, the authority of the manuscript tradition is particularly great: rather, that it is hard enough to be sure one has appreciated nuances of this kind in a foreign language when that language is still spoken, and I doubt if our knowledge of Greek is always deep enough for us to understand fully the reasons why Thucydides, an author notoriously addicted to variation, should have preferred one form of expression to another. Where there is an evident and substantial difference of meaning, that must of course enter into the argument. Here there is certainly a distinction—the

given: the charm of this is that edd. can then insert whatever length of 'genuine peace' may suit their own theories.

Other possibilities are formally open. But, whatever we imagine in detail, the termini must be definite and datable events.]

[1] *Another* confusion between τέσσαρες and δέκα (see i. 103. 1)? This was Ullrich's view; but see above.

aorist looks at these things as completed actions, the imperfect treats them as a continuous developing process—but the general sense of the passage is much the same either way. Neither tense is incorrect here, or even markedly inappropriate. If Thucydides here wrote the aorist, the reason might be that the events of the war were all past by the time he wrote this sentence.]

ἔτη - - - ἑπτὰ καὶ εἴκοσι: see below, n. on τοσαῦτα ἔτη, § 3.

2. For the different dates of composition of 25 and 26, see especially 25. 1, τοῖς μὲν δεξαμένοις αὐτὰς εἰρήνη ἦν, and 26. 2, τὴν διὰ μέσου ξύμβασιν εἴ τις μὴ ἀξιώσει πόλεμον νομίζειν. (And were all of 25 and all of 26 each written at one time?)

τοῖς [τε] γὰρ ἔργοις ὡς διῄρηται ἀθρείτω: I do not myself doubt that Stahl was right to bracket τε and Böhme right in taking τὰ ἔργα as subject of διῄρηται, 'as they are severally defined' ('characterised' Graves), not, as Classen, 'wie diese (sogenannte) Friedenszeit durch die thatsächlichen Verhältnisse unterbrochen, zerrissen ist'. If we do not bracket τε, τὰ ἔργα are confined to the actions in the relative clause, ἐν ᾗ - - - ξυνέθεντο, as though the Mantinean and Epidaurian campaigns and the rest were not to be counted among τὰ ἔργα. If we do bracket τε, I incline to accept Bekker's οὐδ' for οὔτ' before ἀπεδέξαντο, making the whole relative sentence into one divided by οὔτε - - - τε (ἔξω τε τούτων: Stahl seems to have misunderstood Bekker's meaning).

[The deletion of τε is surely right: the co-ordination of τοῖς τε ἔργοις - - - ἔξω τε τούτων - - - καὶ οἱ ἐπὶ Θρᾴκης is unsatisfactory, whereas the subordination of everything after οὔτε ἀπέδοσαν to the relative ἐν ᾗ gives a better sense and runs easily. Bekker's οὐδ' would do no harm, but there is no positive call for correction. Böhme's analysis of the first clause is very much less attractive. It is entirely natural that the ξύμβασις, the object of ἀθρείτω, should be the subject of διῄρηται, and that τοῖς ἔργοις should belong to the latter as the agent which 'divides' or 'defines'. ἀθρείτω (sc. τὴν ξύμβασιν) τοῖς ἔργοις, ὡς διῄρηται (sc. τὰ ἔργα) is unnecessarily awkward. But Classen's translation of διῄρηται ('interrupted, torn apart') is certainly too strong: 'let him look at the period of the Peace, as it is divided up by the things which happened in it'.]

With τοῖς ἔργοις cf. ἀπ' αὐτῶν τῶν ἔργων σκοποῦσι, i. 21. 2.

πρὸς τὸν Μαντινικὸν καὶ Ἐπιδαύριον πόλεμον: below, cc. 53 ff. (the Mantinean campaign being more specifically that told in cc. 61 ff.; it is surely wrong to refer to c. 33, for that little war concerned Sparta and Mantineia only—was not one of the ἀμφοτέροις ἁμαρτήματα— and was hardly more a ξύγχυσις τῶν σπονδῶν than the continued Athenian siege of Skione).

The use of πόλεμος here and in § 3 below, in the context in which the unity of the whole war is being argued, should have saved us from thinking that the use of ὅδε ὁ πόλεμος for the Ten-Years' War (where it does mean that war only) implies that Thucydides had not yet thought of the whole war as one. See vol. iii, 497. We may also believe that it did not require a great measure of acumen in him to see, from the first, that the peace was very insecure.

πολέμιοι: 'at war with', a more decisive breach of the peace than the Boeotian ten-days' truce. The siege of Skione, the Olynthian capture of Mekyberna (39. 1), are cases in point, as well as the refusal of Amphipolis to re-enter the Athenian alliance. Before the winter of 416/15, however, the Chalkidians had made a ten-days' truce with Athens (vi. 7. 4).

ἐκεχειρίαν δεχήμερον: [Thucydides does not tell us what a 'ten-day' truce was; presumably a truce made in the first instance for ten days and thereafter terminable at ten days' notice by either side. A truce which needed explicit renewal every ten days would require an unconscionable amount of travelling by envoys (though this is perhaps what Gomme contemplated, 23. 1 n.); and one tacitly renewed every ten days would involve risks of miscalculation.]

3. εὑρήσει τις τοσαῦτα ἔτη, λογιζόμενος κατὰ τοὺς χρόνους, καὶ ἡμέρας οὐ πολλὰς παρενεγκούσας: for the language here, and as well the imperative ἀθρείτω in § 2, cf. c. 20, ἡμερῶν ὀλίγων παρενεγκουσῶν - - - σκοπείτω δέ τις κατὰ τοὺς χρόνους - - - εὑρήσει.

τοσαῦτα ἔτη are the twenty-seven years of § 1 and the 'thrice nine' of the oracle cited below. For the bearing of this on the composition of cc. 25 and 26, see n. on § 6 below.

καὶ ἡμέρας οὐ πολλὰς παρενεγκούσας: unfortunately we have not Thucydides' own date for the end of the whole war, and therefore no means of judging what he meant by 'a few days over' here, as we had in 20. 1. There we not only had the phrase αὐτόδεκα ἐτῶν καὶ ἡμ. ὀλ. παρ., but the precision and accuracy of his method of dating by summers and winters of each year are expressly guaranteed by the phrase; here it is only the accuracy of an oracle which is in question, for which '27 years and a bit' would be enough. Moreover, 'a few days over' 27 years need not mean the same as 'a few days over' 10 years. Plutarch tells us that the fall of Athens took place on 16 Mounychion (Lys. 15. 1). [Gomme then referred to Meritt's calculation of the Julian equivalent, AFD 176, and to Meritt, The Athenian Calendar, 108–9, and his own vol. iii, 703: for this, see below.] But the calculation is uncertain, and we do not know either what event Thucydides had in mind by 'the end of the war'. Some days elapsed between the 'taking of Peiraieus and the long walls' (§ 1) and the beginning of their destruction; and it is a matter of days that we are concerned with.

[See now Meritt, Ath. Year (1961), 218–19. (a) He here abandons 'any attempt to fix the order of full and hollow months within individual years', and gives no 'ideal' calendar of months as in *AFD* 177–9; for our problem this gives a latitude of only a day or two. (*b*) His equivalents for 1 Hekatombaion are now based on the observable new moon rather than the astronomical conjunction, and are thus for the most part two days later than those of *AFD* 176; this makes no difference to the relative chronology, for the date of the attack on Plataia (ii. 2. 1 n.) may as properly be shifted from *c.* 6–7 March 431 to *c.* 8–9 March as 1 Hek. 404/3 from 6 July 404 to 8 July. 16 Moun. should be roughly 73–4 days before 1 Hek., i.e. around 23–4 April 404. Thus if Plutarch is right the ἡμέρας οὐ πολλάς of this passage amount to some 47–9 days; and this, even with Gomme's qualifications above, is disquietingly high.

Gomme's note indeed suggests ('it is a matter of days') that he had in mind a much smaller figure, but he seems to have given less detailed attention to this than to the problem of 20. 1. There, vol. iii, 711 pays tribute to modern calculations that the Athenian year 422/1 was intercalary, but p. 712 shows sympathy with the older view that it was ordinary, and that the 'few days over' were 4 or 5; and no firm decision is given. That difficulty is resolved with the revival of the view that 422/1 was ordinary (p. 19 below). Here the difficulty is less acute, not perhaps so much because we are dealing with an oracle (Thucydides here invites calculation in the same terms as in c. 20, see preceding n.) as because we do not know the basis of Plutarch's date. Thucydides' formulation would be more natural if Athens surrendered in March 404, not towards the end of April.]

τοῖς ἀπὸ χρησμῶν, κ.τ.λ.: Thucydides, normally scornful of oracles (ii. 21. 3, 54. 2–3), and of portents (vii. 50. 4), and not very polite to them here (μόνον δὴ τοῦτο), yet does seem to attach more weight to this than, simply as a curiosity, it deserved. See also n. on § 6. **ἐχυρῶς ξυμβάν**: 'turned out securely in accordance with the facts', ἐχυρός as in i. 32. 2, ii. 62. 5 (τόλμα), iii. 83. 2 (λόγος), vii. 41. 4 (ἐλπίς), and elsewhere: 'to be relied on'.

4. τρὶς ἐννέα ἔτη: the oracular style is preserved too by Plutarch, *Nic.* 9. 8, but perhaps from Thucydides. [Cf. also vii. 50. 4.]

5. αἰσθανόμενός τε τῇ ἡλικίᾳ: [διὰ τὸ μὴ παρηβηκέναι τὴν ἡλικίαν, παρακολουθῶν πᾶσι Σ^Msc₂, but in view of the confident unfulfilled γέγραφε of § 1 we can be sure that it had not entered Thucydides' mind that he might be thought senile at the time of writing this chapter. He must mean, as he has usually been understood, that he was old enough in 432 to have adequate insight into events of that time. I agree with those (e.g. Finley, 12) who find a defensive note in the assertion: that is, Thucydides' age in 432 was such that he might have been, perhaps was, charged with immaturity. That need not mean that he was very young (cf. vi. 12. 2, with n.), but it is a reason for not putting his birth too early.

Two ancient estimates survive. (*a*) Pamphila ap. Aul. Gell. xv. 23 said he was forty at the outbreak of the Peloponnesian War. Since H. Diels, *Rh. Mus.* xxxi (1876), 47 ff., this has generally been taken to represent Apollodoros (cf. Jacoby, *Apollodors Chronik*, 277 ff.). It clearly exemplifies the practice of taking a date important for the person concerned and using this as his ἀκμή, a procedure unlikely to be adopted where there was genuine evidence and quite implausible here. Suda, s.v. Θουκυδίδης, and Eusebius seem to have had the same date for his ἀκμή. (*b*) Marcellinus 34, παύσασθαι δὲ τὸν βίον ὑπὲρ τὰ πεντήκοντα ἔτη, implies that he was not much over fifty at his death, which must then be taken to follow soon after 404. It has been suggested that Marcellinus' source assumed that he was thirty when he was appointed general in 424; but, popular as this argument is today, I know of no trace of comparable reasoning in antiquity. In view of Apollodoros' procedure it is unlikely that more solid evidence was available.

This passage and the generalship provide the only firm basis. No ancient authority tells us of a minimum age for the generalship, but such limits were common (the scanty evidence for Athens is discussed by Kahrstedt, *Untersuchungen zur Magistratur in Athen*, 18 f.), and where thirty was the qualification for councillors and jurymen it is unlikely to have been lower for strategoi. (In the 'constitution of Drakon', Arist. *Ἀθ. π.* 4. 2–3, thirty is the general minimum, but strategoi must have legitimate sons over ten, so would themselves be over thirty.) Steup, *Einl.* to vol. i, p. iii, argued from vi. 12. 2 that 37 was still young for the office: v. 43. 2 is a safer guide, where Thucydides himself describes Alkibiades as ἡλικίᾳ μὲν ἔτι τότε ὢν νέος ὡς ἐν ἄλλῃ πόλει in a year when he was about 32 (see n. ad loc.) and was certainly elected general. It is not a certain inference, but probable, that the historian was no younger when he was appointed. But his birth and his special qualifications for service in the Thraceward area would help him to early office, and the generalship does not compel us to set his birth before *c.* 455; and the present passage discourages earlier dating. If Marcellinus' source was guessing, he was not far out.]

Note that this second preface contains not only a defence of his view of the war as a unity which is comparable with his view of its magnitude in i. 1, but a reference to his opportunities for writing it and to his method which is comparable with i. 22.

φεύγειν τὴν ἐμαυτοῦ ἔτη εἴκοσι: there is no reason to suppose that Thucydides did not return soon after the fall of Athens, in the summer or autumn of 404 B.C., though some have thought that he waited till the victory of Thrasyboulos in 403, to make εἴκοσι more precise.

[Andokides i. 80 points out that the decree of Patrokleides (ibid.

77–9), passed during the siege of Athens, did not permit the return
of exiles, which followed after the formal peace. This was one of
the terms of surrender: X. *HG* ii. 2. 20; Plu. *Lys.* 14. 8. His exile was
thus formally ended, and he was free to return, in the spring of 404,
nearer 19 than 20 years after his exile (not before the start of winter
424/3: iv. 89. 1, 108. 7 nn.), but it would be natural to round the
figure off to 20 not 19 (cf. i. 18. 2, vi. 59. 4, with nn.), especially if
his actual return was later than the earliest moment possible.

The trouble lies not here, but with Pausanias i. 23. 9, discussing
a group of dedications on the Akropolis, Οἰνοβίῳ δὲ ἔργον ἐστὶν ἐς
Θουκυδίδην τὸν Ὀλόρου χρηστόν· ψήφισμα γὰρ ἐνίκησεν Οἰνόβιος κατελ-
θεῖν ἐς Ἀθήνας Θουκυδίδην, καί οἱ δολοφονηθέντι ὡς κατῄει μνῆμά ἐστιν
οὐ πόρρω πυλῶν Μελιτίδων.[1] The last clause agrees closely with the
statement of Didymos in Marcellinus 32, who also asserts that
Thucydides died a violent death soon after his return (ἥκοντα οὖν
αὐτὸν ἀποθανεῖν βίᾳ), but connects this with a recall of exiles μετὰ τὴν
ἧτταν τὴν ἐν Σικελίᾳ, for which he cites Philochoros (*FGrHist* 328 F
137) and Demetrios (i.e. Dem. of Phaleron, 228 F 3). We should also
note *IG* i². 108 (revised text, ML 89), where a second hand has
added below the first decree for Neapolis in Thrace, of Pryt. VI.
410/09, the note Οἰνοβίοι Δεκελεεῖ στρατεγõι ΤΤΤⱵΗ[- - : Meritt and
Andrewes, *BSA* xlvi (1951), 205, identify this as the payment recorded for Pryt. VIII. 12 of this year in ML 84. 28 (*IG* i². 304A;
AFD 96); cf. also *JHS* lxxiii (1953), 7–8. This is almost certainly
the same man, for the name is not common and the connection with
the Thraceward area is suggestive. Pliny's statement, *NH* vii. 30.
111, that the Athenians exiled Thucydides as a general but recalled
him in admiration of his histories, presupposes publication in exile
and is indifferent support for Pausanias' special decree.

Since the twenty years of exile run out at a date near that of the
general recall in 404, a decree special to Thucydides is an embarrass-
ment, yet Pausanias clearly means this. That rules out Gilbert's
suggestion, *Philol.* xxxviii (1879), 252 ff., that Oinobios proposed
a general decree for the execution of the surrender terms. Schöll's
solution, *Hermes* xiii (1878), 440–1, that Thucydides distrusted the
general recall and waited for an individual decree, and Steup's,
pp. xvii–xviii, that the recall of 404 was only partial, hardly fit the
situation as our sources give it: where Kritias and his like felt free to
return, Thucydides need feel no special distrust. Busolt's answer,
Hermes xxxiii (1898), 339, a decree before the surrender extending to
Thucydides the benefit of Patrokleides' amnesty, ends the formal
exile too soon. Jacoby, on Philoch. F 137, n. 4, cuts the knot by dating Oinobios' decree to 410/09 and supposing that Thucydides did

[1] [A ms. note refers to Oinobios, and to Frazer, ii. 287–8, but gives no
indication of Gomme's own view.]

not accept this recall. This is a plausible date, for reconciliation was in the air then (411/10 would be even more plausible: see *JHS* 1953, as above), and in this context Thucydides' influence in the north might be of use. (But there is no need to connect the decree with Didymos' general decree 'after the defeat in Sicily', which Jacoby less convincingly identifies as a measure passed but not executed by the Four Hundred: Krüger brought Marcellinus 32 into line with the general tradition by excising τὴν ἐν Σικελίᾳ, and Jacoby's resistance to this seems perverse.)

Jacoby's solution is the least unattractive so far proposed. The circumstances in 410, especially after the restoration of democracy (cf. Lys. xxv), were such that Thucydides might well have thought return risky. No serious objection arises from the fact that Pausanias evidently thought that he returned in virtue of Oinobios' decree and died soon afterwards; if the decree remained on record, Hellenistic scholars might well have made the mistake of connecting it with Thucydides' actual return.]

καθ' ἡσυχίαν: cf. ii. 93. 3 n. 'Not distracted by troubles or other activities', rather than 'at leisure'.

αἰσθέσθαι: there is something to be said for Classen's defence of αἴσθεσθαι as a form of the present tense, here and elsewhere in Thucydides. [For this, see Steup and Classen, ii. 93. 3 Anh. Gomme found the aorist improbable, and the present might seem more suitable for a general statement; but the τι particularizes and allows one to see this as a series of single perceptions, for which the aorist is appropriate. Cf. 26. 1 n.]

6. διαφοράν τε καὶ ξύγχυσιν τῶν σπονδῶν καὶ τὰ ἔπειτα ὡς ἐπολεμήθη ἐξηγήσομαι: the previous sentences seem to make it clear that this means all the events (of the 27-years' war) from the Peace of Nikias to the end, divided into two parts, the uneasy ἀνοκωχή, 'suspension of fighting', and the open warfare of books vi–viii (the slight inconsistency by which the open warfare seems to begin with the Sicilian expedition—see 25. 3 n., ad fin.—is of no importance in this connection, but it has significance for the dates of composition of the *History*: see below). So, for example, Classen: 'mit diesen Worten (διαφοράν - - - σπονδῶν) charakterisiert Thuk. die Zeit des unsicheren Friedens, ähnlich wie er am Schluss des ersten Buches die schwankenden Zustände vor dem Ausbruch des Krieges σπονδῶν ξύγχυσις nennt' (i. 146). But the comparison makes at least a verbal difficulty; for in i. 146 the σπ. ξ. (and the αἰτίαι καὶ διαφοραί) are expressly put outside the war, here the argument has been the opposite, that the years of 'confusion¹ of the treaty' must be treated as part of the war. Doubtless a 'confusion' before a war begins is not the same as one in

¹ [ξύγχυσιν is rather the 'breaking' of the treaty; but Gomme's point about the 'confusion' is of course nevertheless valid.]

a very unstable period between two wars; but the contradiction of language is nevertheless notable. There the 'Peloponnesian War' does not begin till the Peloponnesians are fully engaged; here it goes on for nearly seven years before the Peloponnesians are again, at least formally, engaged, though fighting on a large scale had of course taken place in the Argolid and at Mantineia. Had the thrice nine years anything to do with this? For the prophecy is only true on the assumption of one war that lasted from 431 (not from 433 or 435) to 404.[1]

We may at this moment express some preliminary thoughts about the composition of the *History* that are immediately suggested by these two chapters, separated as they are (as originally *thought*, to use Mme de Romilly's valuable distinction) by a long period of time —by perhaps 8 or 9 years, 412 to 403 B.C. If, as is possible, Thucydides died suddenly (*perhaps* by violence, as the unreliable *Life* has it: see § 5 n.) not long after the restoration of democracy at Athens in 403,[2] it is interesting and important that he could write this c. 26 so soon after the end of the war; for it shows not only that he could now see—at whatever distance in his own timetable of work (however far off was 'the end of the tunnel')—in what manner and in what year his *History* would end, but that he could easily contemplate its completion (26. 1, γέγραφε, as well as ἐξηγήσομαι here). It will mean that he had already collected material for the whole—though doubtless not all the material he was looking for for each and every part of it—but, for the last seven years, not in a form in which, in the opinion of his 'editors', his 'literary executors', it could be published; that is, it was in the form of disconnected notes. (Let us not be afraid, in *this* context, of the word 'editor', or of *éditeur*: someone saw to it, after Thucydides' death, that his work reached the public —ἠνέχθη ἐς τὸ κοινόν.) Thus, in discussing the composition of the *History*, we have to bear in mind three (at least three) different, though doubtless often overlapping, stages subsequent to the first collection of material (οὐκ ἐκ τοῦ παρατυχόντος πυνθανόμενος, κ.τ.λ., i. 22. 2): (1) disconnected notes, now lost because 'unpublishable' in the sense used above, unless some of them have found their way into our text by mistake (see, e.g., nn. on iii. 17 and 84, though I do not myself share such a view in these cases); (2) notes put into order, properly connected one with the other, but not intended to be the last word, as, presumably, most of bk. viii and perhaps of v. 25–116;

---

[1] [A ms. note draws attention to the interpolation in X. *HG* ii. 3. 9–10: 28½ years (29 ephors) to the end of summer 404.]

[2] On this I hope to have something to say later. [The hope was not fulfilled, except to the extent that his article on Thucydides for the *Encyclopaedia Britannica* covers some of this ground. (My thanks are due to the editors for allowing me to see this in advance of publication.)]

and (3) the finished narrative: though, of course, not all of the separate 'notes' were of equal fullness and length, nor all of (2) equally 'rough'; nor need we suppose that all of (3) would have been left untouched had Thucydides lived longer.

That is to say, we must imagine, for this second part of the *History*, some such stages as these: (i) (*a*), at least as early as 419 B.C., 'I have not for certain finished my task; I must go on collecting material and making notes, if only for new διαφοραί and ξύγχυσις τῶν σπονδῶν; it does not look as though the peace will last'; and (*b*), from early summer 415, 'I must collect material for the Sicilian expedition', as well as (*c*), next year, 'I must go on with this work for Aegean Greece as well as for the West'. (ii) 'Working up' this material, as circumstances permitted, e.g. bks. i–v. 24 almost completed and ready to be published (hence a second preface, v. 25–6), the Mantineia and Melos campaigns in bk. v, Sicily, and perhaps parts of viii, as full as he wished them to be. (iii) Deciding the major divisions of his work (into three parts—Ten Years' War, confused peace, and the rest?—or into four, with the Sicilian expedition separate from the Ionian War?), and (*a*) writing the preface to the whole (i. 1, I think, was written first for the Ten Years' War, then rewritten for the whole: how much of the rest of i. 2–23, 89–118, was early it would be hard to say), and (*b*) the second preface, 'this was all one war, lasting, as indeed was prophesied, twenty-seven years. I was able, in a special way, to observe the whole.'

27–31. *Diplomatic Exchanges: (a) Defensive Alliance between Corinth, Argos, Mantineia, and Elis*

27. 1. ἡ ξυμμαχία: all MSS. have αἱ ξυμμαχίαι, but most editors accept Cobet's correction. [Gomme had reservations, citing Graves, who pointed out the variation between singular and plural in 46. 5 and 48. 1. The plural could only stand if it were well attested with a singular meaning, which is not the case: certainly only one alliance is in question here. Probably, both here and at 48. 1, the singular has been corrupted in consequence of the neighbouring plurals σπονδαί, πρεσβεῖαι, etc.]

καὶ αἱ - - - πρεσβεῖαι: since the MSS. here vary between καὶ αἱ and αἱ καί, and at § 2 init. some of the recc. omit καί before οἱ μὲν ἄλλοι, it seems justifiable, in the interests of lucidity, to bracket one or the other καί, preferably the first.

αἵπερ παρεκλήθησαν ἐς αὐτά: [for αὐτά cf. vi. 10. 2, αἳ ἡσυχαζόντων μὲν ὑμῶν ὀνόματι σπονδαὶ ἔσονται (οὕτω γὰρ ἐνθένδε τε ἄνδρες ἔπραξαν αὐτὰ καὶ ἐκ τῶν ἐναντίων), with n. there. If this passage had ἐς αὐτάς, the reference of παρεκλήθησαν would clearly be to the conference which debated the peace terms (17. 2, τότε δὴ παρακαλέσαντες τοὺς ἑαυτῶν ξυμμάχους): the neuter should have a wider meaning, 'the complex of which the peace was the central element', or, more concretely, 'the various matters which needed discussion'. This raises the question whether there was one continuous conference of Sparta's allies lasting down to this point, as Gomme took it (nn. to 22. 1, 22. 2 ἀπέπεμψαν, 24. 2 οὐ πολλῷ ὕστερον), or a series of separate meetings. This in turn opens wider questions, especially the problem about Thucydides' year-divisions (vol. iii, 711–12), and this is perhaps the place in which to state my grounds for dissenting from some of Gomme's conclusions.

On the main point, Thucydides' seasonal year:

1. I agree with Gomme that the words αὐτόδεκα ἐτῶν διελθόντων καὶ ἡμερῶν ὀλίγων παρενεγκουσῶν in 20. 1 constitute, at least at first sight, a claim to high precision which must be looked at seriously; and I assume that παρενεγκουσῶν means '*plus* a few days' (20. 1 n., and Pohlenz, NGG 1920, 62). The termini are not seriously in doubt. No sense can be made of the phrase unless the ten years start from the attack on Plataia (20. 1 n.). The obvious end is the date named in the treaty, 25 Elaphebolion 422/1 (19. 1): Thucydides might conceivably have thought of the day when the Athenian or Spartan assembly voted to accept the terms, or when one or the other party swore to them, but none of these fits so easily with αἱ σπονδαὶ ἐγένοντο; and any of these alternatives would curtail the interval between the ratification and the coming into force of the treaty, which is probably important (19. 1 n., 21. 3 n.). The problem is, by what sort of year Thucydides is reckoning.

(a) Since the attack on Plataia came after the beginning of spring 431 (ii. 2. 1), and the peace came into force before the beginning of summer 421 (v. 24. 2), he cannot be using his own seasonal years, since the interval would then be 'ten years *less* some days'; and this follows equally, whether or not Thucydides' spring was tied to a fixed point in the solar year. Gomme partly met this by saying, of the note of time τελευτῶντος τοῦ χειμῶνος ἅμα ἦρι, that 'Thucydides probably by the combined phrase means a certain passage of time during which the last discussions about the terms of the peace were held' (20. 1 n.), and that this is 'an instance of Thucydides overrunning, so to speak, the boundaries he has set for himself' (24. 2 n.). Apart from the fact that to speak so undermines faith in the fixed beginning of Thucydides' spring, the phrase under discussion is meaningless unless he had a particular day in mind for αἱ σπονδαὶ ἐγένοντο; and that day was still within his winter.

(b) Lunar years and months are on the face of it unlikely. I do not indeed think that, when Thucydides told his readers to disregard τὴν ἀπαρίθμησιν τῶν ὀνομάτων (20. 2: see below), his mind was on the irregularities of the lunar calendar as managed by city magistrates, but he certainly knew all that we do and more about these irregularities. Further, the interval from the end of Anthesterion to 25 Elaphebolion is more than 'a few days'.

(c) Calculation in terms of the solar year is, to the modern mind, the most natural way to the precision which Thucydides' phrase seems to claim; and in Thucydides' day the length of the solar year had been worked out with a close approximation to accuracy, though we do not certainly know how widespread the knowledge of a Meton or Euktemon was, in detail, among educated Athenians. It is likely that a man of Thucydides' calibre would be interested, and, if he was, the required calculation was possible (W. K. Pritchett and B. L. van der Waerden, *BCH* lxxxv (1961), 17–52). The attack on Plataia took place *c.* 8–9 March 431 (ii. 2. 1 n., as amended v. 26. 3 n.). The approximate equivalent for 25 Elaph. 422/1 varies by a month, according as this Attic year was ordinary or intercalary (vol. iii, 712). If it was ordinary, 1 Hek. 421/20 should be determined by the observable new moon of 16 June 421, the previous 25 Elaph. should be around 14 March 421, and the 'few days' are of the order of five. If it was intercalary, 1 Hek. is tied to 16 July (Meritt, *Ath. Year*, 218), and the few days are of the order of 35. Recent opinion has been that it was intercalary, producing the result which Gomme found unacceptable. Meritt and McGregor, *Phoenix* xxi (1967), 85–91, now argue that it was ordinary, on the quite independent ground that both Prepis (*IG* i². 311. 8) and Menekles (370. 5–6) are named as first secretary of the council—Menekles for the whole year, and Prepis as defining a single date of payment—in the year when Aristion was archon, 421/20, which suggests that the conciliar year of Prepis, 422/1, ran over into the archon-year 421/20; and this is possible only if the archon-year 422/1 was ordinary. If this is accepted, even as a possibility, the way is open to give a satisfactory sense to Thucydides' phrase, and the case is that much strengthened for regarding the calculation as based on the solar year.

2. Thucydides certainly claimed in 20. 2–3 that a reader who looked at his dating by seasons, not at a list of magistrates, could see for himself that the war lasted ten summers and ten winters. Gomme interpreted this—he was not of course alone, but the appendix to vol. iii presents the implications with unusual clarity and thoroughness—as a claim that the system of organizing the narrative by summers and winters provided, by its own virtue, the precision implied in 20. 1, the divisions between summer and winter being tied to fixed points in the solar year. This seems to me unlikely, for the following reasons:

(a) The system would work only if it 'was one familiar to and accepted by his readers' (705); but the examples given in the following pages (esp. 707) show that it is most unlikely that any one scheme was thus accepted. If it were not, it would be necessary for Thucydides to state the terms of his own system, which he conspicuously does not do.

(b) Thucydides has not stated his result in the form of a precise number of 'days over', and the reader is not invited to share in or to verify this calculation. He is invited instead to count the seasons, and to verify that there were ten summers and ten winters; this he can do from the narrative provided, but he cannot tell from the narrative that there were 'a few days over'. The point of 20. 2–3 is surely much simpler, that ἀπαρίθμησις of, e.g., Athenian archons or Spartan ephors would give eleven names, whereas the seasonally organized narrative shows that there were only ten summers and winters (Pohlenz, NGG 1920, 63; Jacoby, FGrHist IIIb (Suppl.) i. 19; Meritt, Historia xi (1962), 437; and indeed Gomme, 710). The demonstration is greatly helped by the fact that both the critical events occurred close to the division between winter and spring (for the further question about the time of year of the surrender of Athens in 404, see 26. 3 n.).

(c) If Thucydides could fix the dates of the attack on Plataia and the peace, he could have fixed at least some other events as precisely, but the system as a whole is not used in this way. (A ms. note draws attention to the fact that there are only three astronomical dates in the narrative, ii. 78. 2 περὶ ἀρκτούρου ἐπιτολάς, vii. 16. 2 and viii. 39. 1 περὶ ἡλίου τροπάς: these are familiar seasonal landmarks, neither the basis nor the product of calculation.) He may date an event to the beginning or the end of a season (twice to the middle period of the summer, v. 57. 1, vi. 30. 1: for the vagueness of this indication, see p. 271 below), but we constantly find ourselves unable to place the event precisely: for the awkward example of vi. 105, see pp. 7–8 above—this is a case where the modern inquirer would be much better off if Thucydides had noted in his narrative the point at which the Athenian archon changed. In spite of Gomme, 702, this indeterminacy must be significant. For a narrative of war, his method is more suitable than reckoning by archons, but it is not in detail more exact (οὐ γὰρ ἀκριβές ἐστιν, οἷς καὶ ἀρχομένοις καὶ μεσοῦσι καὶ ὅπως ἔτυχέ τῳ ἐπεγένετό τι), and he cannot be boasting that it is.

(d) The indications of season which he does give for the crucial events (ii. 2. 1, v. 20. 1 and 24. 2) do not confirm the detail of the calculation in 20. 1, but weaken it: see (1) (a) above. A similar problem arises in connection with the late beginning of Thucydides' summer in 411, viii. 60. 3 (Gomme, 711). This has recently been treated by W. K. Pritchett, CP lx (1965), 259–61, and Meritt, CP lxi (1966), 182–4, and will be discussed ad loc.: I do not at present see any way, other than emendation, by which it could be brought under Gomme's system. The problem presented by v. 17–24 is equally intractable for this system, and the seasonal indications given here can only be reconciled with it by speaking of 'Thucydides overrunning . . . the boundaries he has set for himself'—which amounts to saying that the system breaks down at the only point where anyone has ever found a use for it.

I conclude therefore that v. 20 presents two quite distinct points. 20. 1 gives us, in imprecise terms, the result of an exact calculation made for this occasion only: the basis of it is not disclosed, and the reader is neither invited nor given the means to verify it. 20. 2–3 invite the reader to verify, from the disposition of the narrative he has read, that the calculation is approximately correct, ten years and not eleven. The large controversy over this passage has arisen from not keeping these two points distinct.

On smaller issues:

3. Kirchhoff (155 ff.) plausibly suggested that Thucydides' account of the alliance between Athens and Sparta, and the references to it in 25. 1 and 27. 1, are later additions to a text which originally dealt only with the peace. In 25. 1, καὶ τὴν ξυμμαχίαν disrupts the connection between τὰς σπονδάς and τοῖς μὲν δεξαμένοις αὐτάς; in 27. 1, καὶ ὕστερον ἡ ξυμμαχία still more obviously, since fewer words intervene, breaks the connection between αἱ - - - σπονδαί and ἐς αὐτά, suggesting that Sparta's allies were somehow concerned in the Athenian alliance, though we have just been told that they were dismissed before the Spartans turned to Athens. If these are additions, then καὶ ξυμμαχίαν in 27. 2 is another, though these words create no offence in themselves. Kirchhoff's own solution, that Thucydides did not see the documents till after 404, is subject to the objections set out in vol. iii, 680–1: that of Schwartz (57–9), that the editor cooked up, out of a draft which had fallen into Thucydides' hands, an imperfect account of an alliance never made, shows the 'editor' at once too active and too negligent: Steup's bracketing of ἐς αὐτά does not solve the difficulty in 25. 1. I can offer no fresh explanation, how Thucydides came first to omit, then to insert, the alliance and these references to it; but it seems likely that he did so. In that case, the original text might have presented winter as ending at or soon after 25 Elaphebolion, in the middle of March; but that is still too late for Gomme.

4. 17. 2 n. There seems no reason why the threat of ἐπιτειχισμός should not have been made at the last moment, and the order to the allies would naturally come at the approach of spring. If this precipitated agreement, it is quite in order that the threat and its effect should be joined by τε - - - καί, whereas Gomme's pause after ἤδη is not at all natural. The main problems are not made appreciably easier by pushing this threat further back into winter.

5. 22. 1 n. ἔτι is only 'clearly . . . required' if we take this to be

the same conference that met at 17. 2, still in session now. This does not seem likely. The result of that meeting must be reported to the cities, and we should expect the several embassies, content or protesting, to go home to do this; that they (or their successors— it is reasonable to suppose that the personnel would be much the same) should be in Sparta again some 2–3 weeks later is not surprising, for there was plenty to discuss, and this first year of the peace is full of embassies. ἥπερ καὶ τὸ πρῶτον below reads as if it referred to a separate earlier occasion, not to an earlier phase of the same continuing conference. It is not easy to make anything of αὐτοί, and Krüger's αὐτοῦ, as Gomme says, is not needed: Lloyd-Jones suggests αὖθις, a very light change which would give a satisfactory sense.

It is a minor, but still troublesome, consequence of Gomme's view that ἀπέπεμψαν in 22. 2 'does not mean that the delegates left Sparta'. In 22. 3, the addition of ⟨ἔτι⟩, and of ⟨τῶν⟩ before πρέσβεων, brings in an avoidable complication: there is no need to identify these Athenian envoys with those who took the oath for the peace treaty, much less (24. 2 n., following Busolt, iii/2. 1202 n. 2) to suppose that they had remained in Sparta to negotiate the alliance. It is simpler, and avoids disrupting the narrative sequence, to suppose that the embassy of 22. 3 is a separate mission, whose primary purpose Thucydides did not feel that he needed to explain, as in the more notorious instance of i. 72. 1: cf. also the very vague description of the conference at Mantineia in 419, v. 55. 1–2.

The order of events, as I understand them, is as follows:

Middle to late February (17. 2, πρὸς τὸ ἔαρ ἤδη): conclusion of the negotiations for the peace.

End of February and beginning of March (10–13 Elaph.): Dionysia at Athens. (If a reason is needed for Thucydides' mention of the Dionysia, a possible answer is that Spartan envoys came to Athens at that time to swear to the treaty (cf. 23. 4). 13 and 25 Elaph. are close enough to justify ἐκ Διονυσίων εὐθὺς τῶν ἀστικῶν.)

Middle of March (25 Elaph.: 20. 1 τελευτῶντος τοῦ χειμῶνος ἅμα ἦρι): treaty comes into force.

Soon after: Klearidas arrives in Sparta (21. 3). Allied envoys in Sparta, of whom some refuse to accept peace: envoys dismissed (22. 1–2). Negotiation of alliance with Athens (22. 3).

Late March: conclusion of the alliance. Beginning of summer (24. 2 καὶ τὸ θέρος ἦρχε). Proclamation of Argive alliance (27. 2–28).

The insertion of the passages relating to the Spartan–Athenian alliance has to some extent cut the connection between 27. 1 and 22. 2 ἀπέπεμψαν. Without these passages (I am not suggesting that a clean cut is possible: 22 will have been in some degree remodelled to accommodate the alliance), there would be no difficulty in taking these embassies as the same that were dismissed in 22. 2. I take it that they left soon after 25 Elaph., and that the Corinthian negotiations with Argos in fact overlap with the negotiations for the Athenian–Spartan alliance.]

2. τῶν ἐν τέλει ὄντων: [the meaning of this phrase is clear, but confusion can arise when τὰ τέλη is taken as an equivalent expression, as Busolt–Swoboda, ii. 687 n. 4, who see only a difference of view-point, 'those in authority' as opposed to 'the authorities'. For τὰ τέλη, see 77. 1 n. For this phrase: (a) οἱ ἐν τέλει (ὄντες) always means those in office or authority as opposed to the mass of soldiers or citizens; whereas τὰ τέλη at Sparta can in a suitable context mean the whole assembly. (b) It is usable anywhere: i. 10. 4, the Greeks before Troy; iii. 36. 5 (here plainly the prytaneis, not, as Gomme suggested, the generals), iv. 65. 2, viii. 50. 4, Athenian city or army; i. 90. 5, ii. 10. 3, v. 60. 1, vi. 88. 10 (see n.), Spartan city or army; v. 27. 2, Argos; vii. 73. 1, Syracuse; cf. Hdt. ix. 106. 3, Peloponnesian commanders; X. *HG* iii. 5. 23, Spartan army. τὰ τέλη in Thucydides is only used of Sparta. (c) It is usable for any kind of constitution.] Argos was in fact now a democracy (29. 1).

ὁρᾶν τοὺς Ἀργείους ὅπως σωθήσεται ἡ Πελοπόννησος: a reminder to Argos of her old ambitions, which had been frustrated by Sparta (see 28. 2). Corinth appears not to have aimed at leadership of the Peloponnese for herself.

ἥτις αὐτόνομός - - - δίδωσι: [only allies capable of independent action would be of use; and, as Steup notes, this formula would exclude the subjects of Athens. But the formula may be simply a Peloponnesian convention (cf. 59. 5, 79. 1), not specially meaningful for this occasion : the language of this passage is quasi-documentary.]

ἐπιμαχεῖν: a defensive alliance only. See 48. 2. [This is the only known occurrence of the verb ἐπιμαχεῖν, and the noun ἐπιμαχία is not common. From the late fifth century onwards new alliances were normally defensive in form, so that the specialized term was no longer needed, and the wider term συμμαχία had, in the fourth century, the meaning which Thucydides explains here, τῇ (sc. γῇ) ἀλλήλων ἐπιμαχεῖν.]

αὐτοκράτορας: the power was qualified expressly by the exclusion of Sparta and Athens from possible alliance (28. 1). [For the meaning in general, see i. 126. 8 n., vi. 8. 2 n.]

28. 2. ἐπ' ἐξόδῳ γάρ, κ.τ.λ.: see 14. 4, 22. 2. [The treaty was near expiry when the Spartans tried to renew it, in the previous winter, and it has not run out now. In his description of the negotiations of spring 420 (40–1) Thucydides does not make it quite plain whether it had then expired, though 40. 3 might suggest that the Argives had allowed it to run out. This is important also for the history of the years 451 and 450 (cf. vol. i, 328, 366), and it is unfortunate that it is not made clearer here.]

κακῶς ἤκουσε: 'had come into disrepute'. [Gomme, with Krüger, expected imperfects for ἤκουσε and ἔσχον, but the slightly different sense given by the aorists is acceptable: cf. 26. 1 n.]

It is significant that the successes of Brasidas in Thrace had done little to restore the prestige of Sparta in the Peloponnese. They were too distant. Cf. 75. 3 below, and Nikias' words vi. 11. 6. And in addition, Spartan policy was tortuous in the extreme, not only in the Thraceward district, as the Corinthians do not fail to imply (30. 2–3), but in the Peloponnese (29. 2, τοὺς Λακ. ἅμα δι' ὀργῆς ἔχοντες, κ.τ.λ.). We must remember that there had been no invasion of Attica since 425, and that the reason for this was Spartan anxiety for the lives of the Sphakteria prisoners, men who, by Spartan tradition, should never have surrendered; that, in consequence, many of Sparta's Peloponnesian allies must have felt that the last chance of ending the war favourably was being thrown away.

We may be sure too that Thucydides did not write, or think, any of these passages with iv. 81. 2–3 in mind. The latter is explicitly written after 413, and is concerned with the feelings of the Athenian allies. Our present passage belongs to the Peloponnese and to a time immediately after the peace of Nikias.

ἀμφοτέροις δὲ μᾶλλον ἔνσπονδοι ὄντες ἐκκαρπωσάμενοι: cf. Ar. Pax 475–7:

> οὐδ' οἵδε γ' εἷλκον οὐδὲν ἀργεῖοι πάλαι
> ἀλλ' ἢ κατεγέλων τῶν ταλαιπωρουμένων,
> καὶ ταῦτα διχόθεν μισθοφοροῦντες ἄλφιτα.

29. 1. καὶ οἱ ξύμμαχοι αὐτῶν: [these were presumably small Arkadian communities, subjects of the kind mentioned in the next sentence. See iv. 134. 1 n.; and for the westward expansion of the cities of eastern Arkadia, 33. 1 n. below.

A ms. note summarizes the argument of H. B. Mattingly, *Phronesis* iii (1958), 31–9, on Pl. *Smp.* 193 a, that Plato had in mind the suppression, in 418, of this incipient Arkadian power. On this, see Dover, *Phronesis* x (1965), 2–20. Gomme did not give his own view, though his note that Plato was about 11 in 418 suggests scepticism.]

τοῖς γὰρ Μαντινεῦσι, κ.τ.λ.: see iv. 134, and below.

[In 378 a decree of Sparta's alliance was in force, forbidding private wars while the League army was abroad (X. *HG* v. 4. 37: Kleitor, at war with Orchomenos, had built up a mercenary force which Agesilaos wished to borrow, τοῖς δ' Ὀρχομενίοις εἶπεν, ἕως στρατεία εἴη, παύσασθαι τοῦ πολέμου· εἰ δέ τις πόλις στρατιᾶς οὔσης ἔξω ἐπὶ πόλιν στρατεύσοι, ἐπὶ ταύτην ἔφη πρῶτον ἰέναι κατὰ τὸ δόγμα τῶν συμμάχων). Larsen, *CP* xxviii (1933), 261, said 'there is nothing to indicate that it was new at the time': I should rather deduce from the wording that this *was* a recent δόγμα, needing the support of Agesilaos' proclamation, not something traditional that could be taken for granted. Earlier instances are indecisive: the League was not formally involved when Corinth was fighting with Megara, i. 103. 4; the battle of iv. 134 might be excused by the current truce with Athens.

Unlike Athens, Sparta needed militarily efficient allies, but they must not individually grow too strong, and the building up of larger units in Arkadia would be especially dangerous. Mantineia's fears were well grounded.]

δημοκρατουμένην: see below, 31. 6; [and for the date and nature of the democracy, 47. 9 n.]

2. ἀποστάντων: 'break away from'; see n. on iii. 9. 1.

πλέον τέ τι εἰδότας: [inside information about something which the rest of the Peloponnese did not know, presumably about the real intentions of Sparta. It is not very clear what this could be, but maybe the Peloponnesians were not very clear about it either.]

εὔορκον εἶναι προσθεῖναι καὶ ἀφελεῖν, κ.τ.λ.: these *words* are found not in the peace treaty but in the treaty of alliance, 23. 6, in which only Sparta and Athens were, on paper, concerned, and this provision is a natural one. In the former the word used is μεταθεῖναι (ὅπη ἂν δοκῇ ἀμφοτέροις, Ἀθηναίοις καὶ Λακεδαιμονίοις, 18. 11). In practice this amounts to the same thing, and note the use of τὴν μετάθεσιν below; and we must not argue that Thucydides when he wrote this had not seen the documents of the treaties. At the most it means that he did not have them in front of him when he wrote this chapter— he may well have written it in the Peloponnese, and we need not suppose that he carried all his manuscript about with him on his travels. See too n. on c. 47 (pp. 62–3).

3. δουλώσασθαι: cf. iv. 20. 4, ἡμῶν γὰρ καὶ ὑμῶν ταῦτὰ λεγόντων, κ.τ.λ., and my note there.

30. 1. καὶ ᾐτιῶντο, κ.τ.λ.: there is something to be said for the view accepted by Graves that εἰ - - - ἔσονται is not the second object of ᾐτιῶντο, but subordinate to παραβήσεσθαί τε - - - τοὺς ὅρκους, this being the second object, and τε only pointing forward to καὶ ἤδη ἀδικεῖν.

[But εἰ in the sense of ὅτι is no difficulty, cf., e.g., E. *Andr.* 205–6, οὐκ ἐξ ἐμῶν σε φαρμάκων στυγεῖ πόσις, ἀλλ' εἰ ξυνεῖναι μὴ 'πιτηδεία κυρεῖς.]

εἰρημένον, κ.τ.λ.: [the agreement to which the Spartans appeal is not a temporary arrangement special to the negotiations of 422/1, but a standing order to which the allies had sworn long since (§ 3, τοὺς τῶν ξυμμάχων ὅρκους; § 4, τῶν παλαιῶν ὅρκων).

This is a key text for the organization of the Peloponnesian

League, for which see Busolt–Swoboda, ii. 1330–7; Larsen, *CP* xxvii (1932), 136–50, xxviii (1933), 257–76, xxix (1934), 1–19. From the time these oaths were instituted, the League was not, as it may once have been, simply an agglomeration of separate alliances of its members with Sparta: it may be premature to speak of a 'League constitution', but the adoption of this clause created regular arrangements for deciding the League's common policy by the majority vote of a conference. This was long before 421. Larsen (140 ff.) argues stoutly against the view that nothing so systematic could have been evolved by the late sixth century, and makes a good case for a date between the break-up of the expedition against Athens in 506 (Hdt. v. 75) and the first recorded conference a few years later (ibid. 91–3): it is significant that a Spartan proposal was voted down on that occasion.]

2. οὐ δηλοῦντες ἄντικρυς: this was the ἀληθεστάτη πρόφασις. Cf. 17. 2 n.

[For Sollion, see ii. 30. 1; for Anaktorion, iv. 49. Both were now in Akarnanian hands, and the Akarnanians were still in some sense Athens' allies (cf. vii. 57. 10, where the wealth of explanation for their presence at Syracuse suggests that the formal alliance would not by itself have brought them there). We are not, however, told that they were a party to the Peace of Nikias (Gomme's reference to this passage in iii. 114. 3 n. takes this too easily); and iii. 113. 6–114 shows that Athens would have had some difficulty in persuading them to surrender their gains. Compulsion was hardly practicable, and these places form another exception to the principle invoked by Elis at 31. 5 (see n. there). For the position at Anaktorion later, see vii. 31. 2 with n. (it is hard to see how αὐτοὶ εἶχον in that passage could mean less than an Athenian garrison, but we have no idea when or why it was installed).]

ἰδίᾳ τε: [see i. 66, with Gomme's note. ἰδίᾳ there is taken, following Steup, to mean that Aristeus' expedition was a private venture and not an act of the Corinthian state. If so, the oaths here sworn ἰδίᾳ must be the oaths of individual Corinthians; but the alternative is far more probable, that ἰδίᾳ in both places refers to state action (as in vi. 13. 2) taken by Corinth independently, before the League declared war. Cf. ξυμμαχίαν ἰδίαν in 39. 3, 40. 1. There is no difficulty in supposing that Corinth formally committed herself to Poteidaia in 432. This was strictly an act of war, and Thucydides so describes Corinth's action in i. 66, ἀπὸ τοῦ προφανοῦς ἐμάχοντο; in the next sentence, οὐ μέντοι ὅ γε πόλεμός πω ξυνερρώγει, he was of course thinking of the League war. Cf. *CQ* N.S. ix (1959), 228 n. 1.]

31. 1. Λεπρέου: see Leake, i. 49–68; [Bursian, ii. 277–8; Fiehn, *RE* Suppl. v. 550–5. It lay in the southern part of the coastal strip of

Triphylia, between the Alpheios and the Neda, some miles inland (Str. viii. 3. 16, 344).] (ms.) Cf. H. L. Bisbee, *Hesperia* vi (1937), 537, with n. 5.

2. πολέμου γὰρ γενομένου ποτέ, κ.τ.λ.: [if Thucydides had dated this transaction, and described it more fully, we might understand more clearly what our other sources imperfectly record.

(*a*) In 479, a contingent of 200 Lepreates fought at Plataia (Hdt. ix. 28. 4; ML 27. 11), whereas the Eleans arrived too late (Hdt. ix. 77. 3): for the politics of this, see *Phoenix* vi (1952), 2; W. G. Forrest, *CQ* N.S. x (1960), 229. Lepreon here appears independent of Elis and friendly with Sparta, and, though these are special circumstances, it seems likely that the relation described by Thucydides arose after 479.

(*b*) Hdt. iv. 148. 4 enumerates six cities of this area, including Lepreon, of which τὰς πλεῦνας (i.e. not all) ἐπ' ἐμέο 'Ηλεῖοι ἐπόρθησαν; probably after 479, and after the συνοικισμός of Elis in 471/70 (Diod. xi. 54. 1), an act which Sparta can hardly have approved (for the question whether Elis' democracy also dates from this time, see 47. 9 n.). It has been supposed (e.g. Beloch, ii². 1. 140 n. 4) that Pausanias refers to these same campaigns when he says (v. 10. 2) that the temple and statue of Zeus at Olympia were made ἀπὸ λαφύρων, ἡνίκα Πίσαν οἱ 'Ηλεῖοι καὶ ὅσον τῶν περιοίκων ἄλλο συναπέστη Πισαίοις πολέμῳ καθεῖλον. In the present state of our knowledge, this seems the most likely context for Lepreon's special arrangement with Elis.

But for Thucydides, this record of aggression would suggest that Elis was in the wrong. But he knew more about the facts, and will have heard the arguments; and since he chose to present only the Elean side of the case we can probably conclude that he thought poorly of the Spartan side. It would help us if he had told more, but we can understand that he might think the detail unimportant.

Sparta still held Lepreon in 418 (c. 62). When Aristophanes in 414 refers to τὸν 'Ηλεῖον Λέπρεον (*Av.* 149: for the gender, Fraenkel, *Studien zur Textkritik und Textgeschichte* (*Festschrift Jachmann*, 1959), 11–12), this is probably for identification, not a statement about its current status—but the line might be taken to mean that Lepreon was in fact open for colonization at this time (cf. 34. 1 n.), provided we are prepared to say the same for Opous (152–3). Elis must then have regained it, in circumstances unknown to us, for, when Sparta attacked Elis after the fall of Athens, Xenophon records (*HG* iii. 2. 25) that Lepreon at once revolted from Elis and joined the Spartans.]

καὶ λυσάντων: Krüger's καταλυσάντων is probable: [the simple verb is used in this sense in verse, but not in Classical prose. Gomme did not say whether he would then keep the καί, with Classen and others. Steup pointed out that, with the καί, 'Ηλείων is the subject of καταλυσάντων, and Ἠλεῖοι - - - ἔταξαν follows awkwardly on this: without a καί, and with Steup's comma after γῆς, we can take Eleans and Lepreates as the unexpressed subject of καταλυσάντων, and the sentence runs more easily.]

τάλαντον: [evidently (cf. the next sentence) an annual rent, and it looks high for half the Lepreatis. But we do not know how much of the fertile coastal strip Lepreon owned at this time, nor do we know enough of the circumstances of the agreement. c⟨G⟩ τάλαντα opens the possibility of a still higher sum, which is still less likely.]

3. τοῦ Ἀττικοῦ πολέμου: the war seen from the Peloponnesian side. So αἱ Ἀττικαὶ σπονδαί, 29. 2, 36. 1. The Athenian name has prevailed.

καὶ δίκης Λακεδαιμονίοις ἐπιτραπείσης: it is odd that Elis should have agreed to Sparta being chosen as arbitrator. [But Lepreon had appealed to Sparta, and to refuse her arbitration might well seem dangerous: if, as seems likely (though the wording does not make it certain), Elis' change of mind is very recent, she will have been emboldened by Sparta's general loss of prestige (28. 2 n.) and the current agitation against her leadership. The Eleans may have expected a favourable decision, and backed out only when they saw how Sparta was going to act.]

5. τὴν ξυνθήκην: [Grote understood this to mean that the Peloponnesians made a formal agreement with one another in these terms at or before the outbreak of war, and he is followed by Classen and others. This presupposes a quite extraordinary distrust between the members, and alternatives must at least be considered. Steup, assuming that members of the League must always have been safeguarded against seizure of their territory by another member (this is surely wrong, cf. 29. 1 n.), took ξυνθήκην to refer to the ancient oaths of 30. 1, 4, and excised ἐν ᾗ - - - ἐξελθεῖν as the addition of a reader who thought it referred to the Peace of Nikias. Steup excluded a real reference to this peace, because the text contains no such provision, and Elis had not accepted the peace. This last is no argument, for Elis could use against Sparta a document to which Sparta had subscribed; but it is a serious question, whether the words following εἴρητο have to be a quotation from, or a close equivalent of, the words of the ξυνθήκη referred to.

εἰρῆσθαι in comparable contexts regularly refers to the text of a formal document (i. 35. 2, 40. 2, etc., the Thirty Years' Peace; it need not be a text inscribed on stone, cf. iv. 23. 1, the Pylos truce of 425). It is natural that this should be the normal reference, since it was mainly about such texts that question arose. But (*a*) εἰρῆσθαι is also used where no document is in question (iv. 77. 1, the day agreed between Hippokrates and Demosthenes; iv. 111. 2, the signal agreed between the Toronaians and Brasidas; frequently of military orders); (*b*) great difficulties arise if we take v. 39. 3 εἰρημένον and 46. 2 εἴρητο to refer to the treaty texts quoted by Thucydides (see 39. 3 n.). The usage of other authors gives no very clear guidance, but, e.g., A. *Ag.* 301, 1620 are cases where no written text is in question. It seems that εἴρητο might retain its literal meaning and need not, in itself, imply verbal quotation from a fixed text. On the other hand, ξυνθήκη and ξυνθῆκαι elsewhere in Thucydides (16 instances) refer to an actual (or in i. 37. 3 a potential) formal agreement. The looser use of ξυντίθεσθαι (e.g. 32. 7) perhaps opens the possibility that ξυνθήκη might refer to a less formal understanding; but one would certainly expect τὴν ξυνθήκην - - - ἐν ᾗ εἴρητο (for the combination, cf. vii. 18. 2) to introduce at least the paraphrase of a text.

But 17. 2, ὥστε ἃ ἑκάτεροι πολέμῳ ἔσχον ἀποδόντας τὴν εἰρήνην ποιεῖσθαι, propounds, as between the opposing parties, the same principle which the Eleans now propound as between members of the League; and Diod. xii. 74. 5, Plu. *Nic.* 10. 1, use almost identical formulas in their brief summaries of the terms. It thus seems possible that the Eleans are bringing forward not a term of the peace as it was eventually formulated, but the (surely much discussed) principle on which it was supposed to be based; and are giving this principle a fresh twist by attempting to apply it between the allies of their own side. If this is not acceptable, we can only revert to Grote's interpretation; and remark, with Gomme, that 'it is a characteristic detail of Thucydides' manner that we hear of the ξυνθήκη now for the first time'.]

6. οἱ ἐπὶ Θρᾴκης Χαλκιδῆς: [Gomme (21. 3 n.) suggested that the ambassadors who came with Klearidas to Sparta had stayed in the south to negotiate this alliance; which may well be right, though they must at some time have returned home for authority to conclude it.] **Βοιωτοί:** cf. 17. 2, 32. 5.

τὸ αὐτὸ λέγοντες: certainly 'in agreement with each other' (as iv. 20. 4), not 'with the Corinthians and Argives'. περιορώμενοι is surely middle, 'watching events', its usual meaning in Thucydides, not passive, whether 'left to do as they pleased by Sparta', as Crawley and (in different words) Warner, or 'watched closely by Sparta', as some edd. and LSJ; there was neither reason nor opportunity for a close watch on Boeotia when nothing was done to prevent the secession of Corinth. If this is correct, ὑπὸ τῶν Λακ. is a difficulty (it can hardly be taken with ἡσύχαζον, 'under the influence of Sparta'); but it may well arise from an ancient editor who took περιορώμενοι for passive, and to mean 'despised' (Dobree, Stahl, Classen); or else, as Graves says, Haase's τὰ ἀπό for ὑπό is attractive and may be right. [The nearest parallels are vi. 93. 1, vii. 33. 2, where, however, the word is used without an expressed object; but Haase's suggestion gives a good sense, and the alternative theory of an insertion is not very plausible.]

(ms.) All this does not suggest much truth in Alkibiades' claim, vi. 16. 6, that *he* made the Peloponnesian alliance against Sparta. The whole of 27–31 explains, though, Nikias' view that Sparta did not really welcome the peace of 421.

αὐτοῖς ὀλιγαρχουμένοις: for Boeotia see iii. 62. 3, where we read between the lines, [and *Hell. Oxy.* 16 Bart. (11 G–H)]; for Megara, iv. 74. 3–4 n.

32. 1. *Surrender of Skione*

32. 1. Σκιωναίους: see iv. 122, 123. 4, v. 2. 2, 18. 8. The women and children had been removed to safety, though some women doubtless remained, as at Plataia (cf. iii. 68. 2). Thucydides clearly did not have iv. 123. 4 in mind when he wrote this, and was probably not in Thrace when Skione fell; he is remembering only the terms of Kleon's resolution.

The treatment of Skione, with that of Melos, was especially remembered afterwards by Athens' traducers: see Isoc. iv. 100, 109, xii. 62 ff.

(ms.) See also Paus. i. 15. 4.

Πλαταιεῦσιν: (ms.) For the Plataians and their rights in Athens, see iii. 55. 3 n., and Busolt, iii/2. 1038 n. 2. (He does not emphasize enough that citizens of another city could be given πολιτεία *en masse* without losing their original identity; and that the Plataians from 427 always hoped that an Athenian victory would re-establish an independent Plataia. Hence so many would be ready to settle in Skione—it helped to prevent them being individually lost in Athens.)

Δηλίους: see c. 1. The Athenians are nearly as superstitious as the Spartans (vii. 18. 2–3).

2. Φωκῆς καὶ Λοκροί: nothing more is told us, by Thucydides, of *this* little war. This is a very brief 'note', of something which he had heard, from a distance, one which he would have either supplemented or deleted in a final revision.

See, however, below, 64. 4 with n. [Both are thought to be available as Spartan allies in 418, though neither contingent actually appeared. Diod. xii. 80. 4 mentions briefly a victory of Phokis over Lokris, under the year 418/17 and after describing the aftermath of the campaign of Mantineia; and his language suggests that he thought this war began at this time. He may, however, have misplaced it: xii. 80. 5 is not reassuring (cf. 116. 3 n.).]

32. 3–7. *Diplomatic Exchanges: (b) Sparta, Tegea, Corinth, and Boeotia*

4. ἀνεῖσαν τῆς φιλονικίας καὶ ὡρρώδησαν: for a similar quick change from optimism to anxiety, cf. the Athenians at Rhegion when they heard there was but little wealth in Segesta, vi. 46. 2. [For the attitude of Tegea, see also c. 62 below.]

5. τὰς τε δεχημέρους ἐπισπονδάς: see 26. 2, with n. It is interesting that we are not told about this immediately after c. 19, especially as ἐπισπονδαί should mean rather 'additional clauses to a treaty' (or a renewed treaty, as the verb in 22. 2) than 'another, subsequent treaty with a different state'; but it belongs to the period of the uneasy peace, the Boeotians having in the interval presumably had an ἀνοκωχὴ ἄσπονδος with Athens, like the Corinthians (§ 7 below).

6. εἴπερ Λακεδαιμονίων εἰσὶ ξύμμαχοι: i.e., 'if you belong to the Peloponnesian League, for it was Λακ. καὶ οἱ ξύμμαχοι who made peace with us' (18. 1). The Boeotians had also been allies of Sparta during the war, but of a different kind; and the difference was much the same as that between on the one hand Athens and *her* allies, i.e. the Delian League, and on the other such allies as Akarnania or Kerkyra, and, very soon, Argos. Cf. 36. 1.

[Gomme's view, that Boeotia was not a regular member of the Peloponnesian League, seems to be based mainly on the different treatment Athens here accorded to Boeotia and Corinth; but I am not sure he was right. No Greek writer distinguishes different levels inside the group called Λακ. καὶ οἱ ξύμμαχοι, but differentiation was clearly possible: not all allies need swear the oaths referred to in 30. 1–4, as Athens did not in 421 (c. 23). The only test we can apply, as regards membership of the League whose machinery is referred to in 30. 1–4, is whether the state in question attends conferences of the allies and votes at them; and this the Boeotians seem to do (17. 2; X. *HG* ii. 2. 19; perhaps also Phokis, D. xix. 65). Cf. 39. 3 n., and vii. 18. 2 with n.

Athens' different treatment of Corinth and Boeotia here may have other causes. The retort to Corinth makes the point that she was in some degree in revolt against Sparta (30, 38. 3), while Boeotia was at least less so (31. 6, 38. 3). Also, Athens had a vulnerable land frontier with Boeotia, but not at this time much to fear from Corinth.]

7. ἀνοκωχὴ ἄσπονδος: either a truce by verbal agreement, not fortified by oath and accompanying libations to the gods, or, as Grote, a simple *de facto* truce without any agreement.

33. *Sparta Frees the Parrasioi from Mantineia*

33. 1. Πλειστοάνακτος τοῦ Π. Λακ. βασιλέως: the formal title though he has been mentioned more than once before, as often in Thucydides; see, e.g., n. on ii. 19. 1.

ἐς Παρρασίους: [see Bursian, ii. 225 f., 235 ff. They occupied the western side of the plain of the Alpheios, and their territory ran up into Mt. Lykaion, where a temple of Apollo Parrasios was neighbour to the important shrine of Zeus Lykaios (Paus. viii. 38. 8).

This passage, with iv. 134, strikingly demonstrates the extent of the westward expansion of the cities of eastern Arkadia, but we know little of the detail. (See map opposite p. 34.)

(*a*) Pausanias' list of the communities which coalesced into Megalopolis includes (viii. 27. 4) ἐκ δὲ τῶν συντελούντων ἐς 'Ορχομενόν, Θεισόα (south of Dhimitsána) Μεθύδριον (58. 2 n.: south of Vytína) Τεῦθις (Dhimitsána). This was the natural direction for Orchomenos, round the north of the main mountain mass. We cannot be sure they had come so far by 421: the silence of 58. 2, which makes no connection between Methydrion and Orchomenos, is not decisive.

(*b*) The natural route for Tegea was the relatively level corridor past Pallantion and down the upper Alpheios. To reach Laodokeion (iv. 134. 1: for the location, just south of the later Megalopolis, see 64. 3 n.) the Tegeates must have had at least a working arrangement with Pallantion and Asea, but no community or area is explicitly called 'subject' to Tegea, as Parrasia is here to Mantineia. (On Arist. fr. 592 Rose, see Wade-Gery in *Ehrenberg Stud.* 297–8, with the postscript on p. 302; for doubts of its relevance, Beloch, i². 1. 334 n. 3.)

(*c*) In competition with Tegea, Mantineia could not use this southern route, but there was a manageable alternative through the mountains. They had access to the plain of the upper Helisson, the northern part of which may regularly have been Mantinean territory (Fougères, 116). From there they could descend past Dipaia and (probably: cf. Fougères, 384 n. 4) Trikolonoi into the Alpheios plain. A Mantinean army using this route and a Tegeate army coming down the upper Alpheios could easily collide at Laodokeion.

The inhabitants of the mountain region and those of the Alpheios corridor were alike Mainalioi. Pausanias' list of the communities ἐκ Μαινάλου (viii. 27. 3) does not differentiate Mantinean and Tegeate spheres of influence. For Mantineia's allies or subjects, see 29. 1, 58. 1, 67. 1–2 with nn.; and Bölte, *RE* xiv. 1321–2.]

ἐπικαλεσαμένων: the genitive is doubtless due to the fact that only some of the Parrasioi had invited their help, κατὰ στάσιν.

τὸ ἐν Κυψέλοις τεῖχος, κ.τ.λ.: [there is no other evidence for the site, and the notion that a fort in Parrasia threatened Skiritis raises topographical questions. This area was vital for Spartan communications. For their route up the Eurotas valley and into the Alpheios plain, see 64. 3 n. The easy route into Messenia, for an army with wagons, then leads round the northern offshoot of Taygetos and over a low saddle to the west, joining the line of the modern Megalopolis–Kalamata road. The political configuration of the district was radically altered by the foundation of Megalopolis, and this affects all evidence later than 370. (See map opposite p. 34.)

For the whole area, and Sparta's interest in it, see especially Bölte, *RE* iiiA. 1308–12. We may distinguish:

1. Lykosoura is the most southerly community which was certainly Parrasian.

2. Next to the south, up the Alpheios, is Maleatis, for which see Bölte, *RE* xiv. 867–9 and 942–7 (with map). Whatever the true reading in Paus. viii. 27. 4 (below), Malea was not reckoned as Parrasian when his list was composed.

3. Paus. viii. 34. 5 puts the source of the Gatheatas river in Kromitis, that of its tributary Karnion in Aigytis. These streams are identifiable, and the territory of Kromoi must lie near or across the road to Messenia, to the west of

4. Aigytis, which must include the narrow valley which runs up to the south along the west side of the beginnings of Taygetos. But its early and late importance shows that it cannot be confined to this valley: cf. Ephoros, *FGrHist* 70 F 117, Paus. iii. 2. 5 on the alleged early city of Aigys, of which there is no later trace; Plb. ii. 54. 3 (below).

5. Belmina (variously spelt) lay somewhere west of the mouth of the Eurotas gorge (64. 3 n.), at the foot of Mt. Khelmós, on which stood the Athenaion of Plutarch (*Cleom.* 4. 1) and Polybios (see Loring, 37–41). Belminatis, in effect a continuation of the main Eurotas valley, presumably extended NNW. as far as the watershed, but there is no direct evidence to show if it went beyond that towards the Alpheios. Polybios (ii. 54. 3: see Walbank's n.) speaks of Antigonos Doson in 224 expelling the garrisons of Kleomenes III κατά τε τὴν Αἰγῦτιν καὶ Βελμινᾶτιν χώραν. The latter will be the Athenaion (ibid. 46. 5); the former is not specified, but Plutarch (*Cleom.* 6. 3) says he had fortified Leuktra, which may thus lie in Aigytis, but its location is not secure enough to assist us in defining the latter (see 54. 1 n.).

6. The rough location of Skiritis is not in doubt: the mountainous triangle between the Eurotas and Oinous rivers, with its apex near Sparta and its base towards the upper Alpheios; cf. Bursian, ii. 117 f., Leake, iii. 28 ff. The Skiritai formed a separate corps in the Spartan army (67. 1, with n.), and are in this respect distinguishable from the ordinary perioikoi who were incorporated into the regular units of the army. The only place explicitly ascribed to Skiritis is Oion (X. *HG* vi. 5. 24–6, which leaves no doubt about its approximate position: see Loring, 61–2); Xenophon's wording tells against the suggestion, not supported by any ancient source, that Karyai belonged to it. In the upper Eurotas valley Pellana, a member of the Lakonian Tripolis (Plb. iv. 81. 7; Liv. xxxv. 27. 9), was presumably an ordinary perioikic town: the other two members are not known (Bölte, 1319, shows that Belmina was not one). Again, one would

suppose that some of the apex of the triangle, between Pellana and Sellasia, was ordinary perioikis. To the north Eutaia, Mainalian in Paus. viii. 27. 3, is placed by Leake and Loring (50–1) in or against the hills to the south of the plain of Asea, on the strength of X. *HG* vi. 5. 12, 20–1. The rough limits are clear, and it seems likely that the Skiritai from whom the special corps was drawn belonged entirely to the mountain area enclosed by these points.

Paus. viii. 27. 4, παρὰ δὲ Αἰγυπτίων καὶ Σκιρτώνιον καὶ Μαλαία καὶ Κρῶμοι καὶ Βλένινα καὶ Λεῦκτρον, is certainly corrupt. Αἰγυπτίων must be Αἰγυτῶν: the following καί is anomalous, and Curtius inserted ⟨Αἴγυς⟩ before it, but see (4) above. Niese, *Hermes* xxxiv (1899), 540 n. 1, suggested παρὰ δὲ Αἰγυτῶν καὶ Σκιριτῶν Οἶον καί - - -, abolishing Skirtonion, which is cited by Steph. Byz. s.v. from Pausanias but is not found elsewhere. This is very plausible, and it implies that for the purpose of building up Megalopolis in 369 Aigytai and Skiritai could be taken (perhaps a little artificially, see Bölte, 1311) as a unit comparable to the others of the list, which include Mainalioi and Parrasioi. Steph. Byz. Σκίρος· Ἀρκαδίας κατοικία πλησίον Μαιναλείων καὶ Παρρασίων may possibly refer to a sub-section of Megalopolis, there being no place elsewhere called Skiros. If one were to distinguish, the westerly communities probably count as Aigytai, viz. Malea, Kromoi, Leuktron; Oion is certainly Skirite, and perhaps Belmina.

For the terminology before 370, we can only follow the hints given in Thucydides and Xenophon. The latter names Skiritis (*HG* vi. 5. 24–5, vii. 4. 21) and Malea (*HG* vi. 5. 24; probable emendation, vii. 1. 28), but not Aigytis: the former only Skiritis. It is quite possible that in 420 the part of the plain south of Parrasia and south and west of the Alpheios was reckoned to Skiritis. In any case, we are bound to suppose that the Mantineans' fort was directed, not against the mountains where the Skiritai mainly lived, but against Sparta's regular communications, especially with Messenia.]

2. ξυμμαχίδα: [ξυμμαχίαν, the unanimous reading of the MSS., can have a virtually territorial sense (e.g. iv. 118. 4), and there was no need for emendation. For 52. 2, see n. there.]

34. *Internal Events at Sparta*

34. 1. οὓς ὁ Κλεαρίδας, κ.τ.λ.: see 21. 3.

τοὺς μὲν μετὰ Βρ. Εἵλωτας μαχεσαμένους: seven hundred in number, iv. 80. 5, less casualties.

οἰκεῖν ὅπου ἂν βούλωνται: the helots were slaves, *adscripti glebae*; these men were freed. It might appear that this freedom was in practice considerably restricted if they were soon after settled, by the Spartan authorities, in Lepreon; we are probably to suppose that

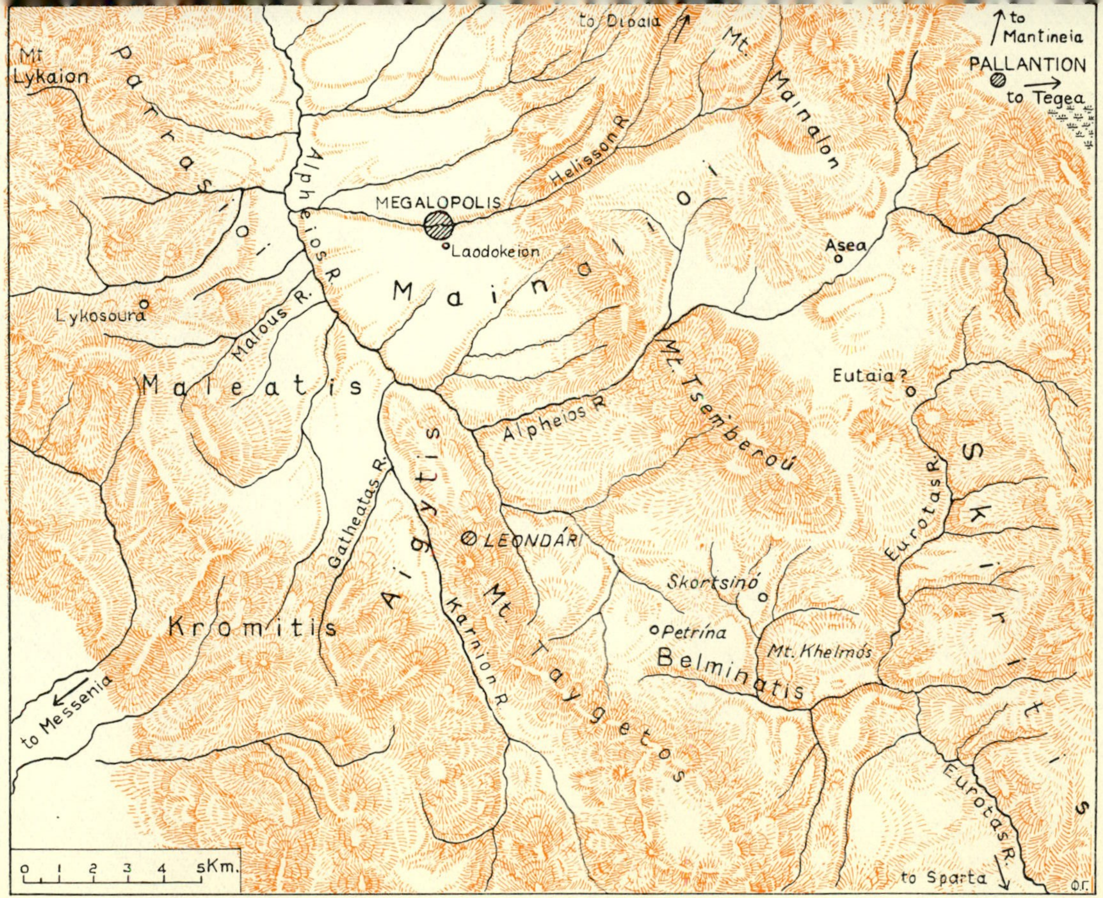

MAP I. SOUTH-WEST ARKADIA

they were offered land there (they might have difficulty in finding land elsewhere). They were not of course citizens, even of inferior status.

μετὰ τῶν νεοδαμώδων: [Thucydides writes as if we knew about them already, and they were a familiar feature of the period of Spartan domination, to 371. But they have not been mentioned before, and it looks as if the creation of this class was a recent and important development. Possibly he intended to explain, not here but at the point when the force was instituted, and never fulfilled this intention.

These are liberated helots (οἱ κατὰ δόσιν ἐλεύθεροι ἀπὸ τῆς εἰλωτίας, Hesych. s.v.: cf. Pollux iii. 83; Σ^GMsc₂, Σ Patm.). Unlike Brasidas' helots, who receive their freedom only now on their return, these seem to be freed before or at their enrolment: cf. the gloss at vii. 58. 3, ἐλεύθερον ἤδη εἶναι (the not very clear distinction made in Myron, FGrHist 106 F 1, possibly refers to this point). Hesych. δαμώδεις· δημόται (cf. Tyrt. fr. 3. 5 Diehl: some form of δαμώδης should probably be restored in the corrupt passage of the Rhetra, Plu. Lyc. 6. 2) ἢ οἱ ἐντελεῖς παρὰ Λάκωσι suggests that νεοδ. means in some sense 'new citizens', cf. Σ^recc· νέων πολιτῶν, Σ^recc· 67. 1 νεοπολῖται: but nothing in the other evidence supports Kahrstedt's contention, Griechisches Staatsrecht, i. 46–7, that they became full citizens. Their situation, like that of μόθακες and other intermediate categories, remains obscure. Hesychios' κατὰ δόσιν does little to illustrate the process of their liberation, which must of course be a public act not a matter of private generosity.

The war service of helots referred to in iv. 80. 3–4 (ἐν τοῖς πολέμοις γεγενῆσθαι σφίσιν ἄριστοι) was not necessarily hoplite service. But Brasidas' 700 (iv. 80. 5) were hoplites, apparently on a level with his paid Peloponnesians: for Sicily in 413 (vii. 19. 3) the Spartans chose out of the best of the helots and νεοδ., 600 hoplites altogether: after that we hear of no more helot soldiers till Epameinondas' invasion of 370/69, when they were offered freedom εἴ τις βούλοιτο ὅπλα λαμβάνειν καὶ εἰς τάξιν τίθεσθαι (X. HG vi. 5. 28). But we hear increasingly of νεοδ., in considerable numbers: Thibron took 1,000 to Asia in 400 (X. HG iii. 1. 4), Agesilaos 2,000 in 396 (iii. 4. 2). With the Peloponnesian mercenaries, for whom Aristeus and Brasidas provide precedent (Th. i. 60. 1, iv. 80. 5), they formed a force which could be used on detached expeditions, especially on long-term service overseas, for which the regular army was not suited. Sparta could not have fought the Ionian war, or the Asiatic campaigns of the early fourth century, without them.

These developments may not have been precisely foreseen in the 420s, but the expeditions of Knemos, Eurylochos, and Brasidas already showed the need for some such force. Somehow, in the ordinary course of Spartan life, some helots could acquire enough experience to be usable as hoplites: cf. Brasidas' 700, and Xenophon was told that over 6,000 volunteered in 370/69. But a force systematically trained would be far more effective, and it looks as if the νεοδ. were instituted for just this purpose. Their creation must have been a deliberate act of state.

This was probably late in the Archidamian War. νεοδ. were apparently not available for Brasidas in 424, and it was perhaps the performance of his helots that encouraged Sparta to institute them. With the peace, and withdrawal from the distant north, they could be settled where they could at need be called out again (67. 1). But there were not enough for Gylippos in 413: perhaps recruitment had stopped (cf. also 57. 1 n.), but if so it was soon resumed. They are not heard of after 370/69 (X. *HG* vi. 5. 24), perhaps because Xenophon's narrative stops soon after, more probably because Sparta no longer conducted the kind of campaign for which they were needed.

It would have helped our understanding of Sparta's organization and war-effort if Thucydides had said something about their creation.]

ἐς Λέπρεον - - - κείμενον, κ.τ.λ.: one would not have guessed from this geographical note that the dispute between Elis and Sparta over Lepreon had been recounted a page or two back (31. 2–5)—no geographical note there, and only the barest reference to the dispute here. Lepreon had been declared 'autonomous' by Sparta (31. 4), in dubious circumstances; it looks as if many Lepreatai had refused the gift of autonomy and migrated to Elis, leaving land to be settled by these enfranchised helots and νεοδαμώδεις. It would have thrown light on the position and policy of Sparta in the Peloponnese if Thucydides had given us more detail of this dispute.

This part of ἡ Λακωνική had been called ἡ Μεσσηνία ποτὲ οὖσα γῆ in iv. 3. 1, 2.

2. δείσαντες μή τι - - - νεωτερίσωσιν: it is notable how fearful the reputedly stable and well-governed Sparta was of στάσις, whether from brave helots (iv. 80) or her own disgruntled citizens. They would take no 'security risks'. Athens had claimed to be freer (ii. 37, 39, etc.); and it needed a great public crime, the mutilation of the Hermai, to shock her into such fears (vi. 53. 3).

ἀτίμους: for other Spartan ways of treating those who had failed to reach the highest standard of Spartan honour, see Hdt. vii. 231–2; X. *Lac. Pol.* 9. 4–5; Plu. *Ages.* 30 (Grote, v. 425).

πριαμένους τι: presumably real property, the right of possession in this being normally confined to citizens in the Greek states.

35. 1. *Athens Loses Thyssos in Akte*

35. 1. τὴν ἐν τῇ Ἄθω Ἀκτῇ Διῆς: see app. crit. here and at 82. 1. These very brief notes of Thucydides often leave the event obscure to us

(cf. 32. 2); yet the fact that Dion repulsed Brasidas in winter 424/3 (iv. 109. 3–5), the implication that, by contrast with Thyssos, it was not in alliance with Athens now, though it is not said to have seceded from that alliance till 417 (82. 1)—all this is in favour of Poppo's correction Χαλκιδῆς (or οἱ Χ.). The reading of cG at 82. 1 may be a reminiscence of the corrupt reading here.

[Ἄθω Ἀκτῇ Διῆς, however, is much closer to the MSS., and still closer is Meineke's Ἀθωΐδι Ἀκτῇ Διῆς, taken into the text by Steup but not noticed by Stuart Jones or Powell (for the form Ἀθωΐς, cf. Steph. Byz. s.v. Ἄθως). If Διῆς is correct, the words Ἀθηναίων οὖσαν ξύμμαχον cannot be meant to distinguish Thyssos as an Athenian ally from an aggressor outside the League. Steup excised them, but they are an unlikely interpolation. The point may simply be to stress that the victim was an ally of Athens, a fact which is not less significant if the aggressor was also an ally: this would be a symptom of the changed attitude of Dion, foreshadowing her revolt a little later.

For Thyssos, see iv. 109. 3 with n., v. 18. 5 n. For argument in favour of Poppo's correction, see West and Meritt, *AJA* xxix (1925), 66 n. 3.]

35. 2–48. *Diplomatic Exchanges: (c) Sparta, Athens, Corinth, Boeotia, and Argos*

2. ὑπώπτευον δὲ ἀλλήλους εὐθὺς μετὰ τὰς σπονδάς: [this is in sharp contrast with 25. 2, προϊόντος τοῦ χρόνου ὕποπτοι ἐγένοντο. No doubt both statements could be justified, as different ways of looking at the same facts, but these sentences were not thought at the same time, and one imagines Thucydides would have removed the contradiction if it had come to his attention. § 8 below has been held to support Jerusalem's thesis, that the end of this summer marks the beginning of the six years and 10 months of 25. 3 (see n. there), but § 2 militates against this view.]

3. τἄλλα: Panakton, held by the Boeotians, was the most important of these (18. 7).

λέγοντες αἰεί - - - ἄνευ ξυγγραφῆς: [that is, they kept putting forward definite dates, but orally, without a written agreement which might, even without oaths, be felt to tie them down effectually; but as each date approached it was replaced by another. These oral assurances are, I believe, the reference of εἰρημένον in 39. 3: see n. there.]

4. τά τε ἄλλα χωρία: see 18. 7—Kythera, Methana, etc.

5. Πάνακτον: for the identification of the fort see n. on v. 3. 5, and vol. iii, 735.

7. κατῴκισαν αὐτοὺς ἐν Κρανίοις: presumably by agreement with the Kranioi (cf. ii. 30. 2, 33. 3) The helots were soon to be sent back to

Pylos, 56. 2–3. [According to Diod. xiv. 34. 2, there were Messenians in Kephallenia after the war: either not all the original garrison was sent back, or those whose release is described in X. *HG* i. 2. 18 returned to Kephallenia.]

8. ἔφοδοι: see i. 6. 1 for ἔφοδος = peaceful approach, and n. on ἐπήρχοντο, iv. 120. 1.

36. 1. ἔτυχον γὰρ ἔφοροι ἕτεροι, κ.τ.λ.: a valuable indication that the ephorate began its year of office not long before the beginning of Thucydides' winter, i.e., [at latest,] at some time in October (see Appendix to vol. iii).

[For a clear discussion, see Beloch, ii². 2. 270 ff. This is our firmest piece of direct evidence. The list in X. *HG* ii. 3. 9–10 gives 29 ephors from (inclusive) Ainesias, under whom war broke out in 431, to Eudios, under whom Lysander sailed home τελευτῶντος τοῦ θέρους in 404; which shows that new ephors came into office between spring and the end of summer. From Plu. *Agis* 15. 4, 16. 1, it seems that Agesilaos' ephorate was drawing to an end at a point after the harvest in 241.

Indirect evidence comes from the annual nauarchs. (*a*) Knemos starts before the end of summer 430 (ii. 66. 2, 67. 1) and ends after the beginning of winter 429 (93. 1). (*b*) Alkidas starts before winter 428 (iii. 16. 3, 18. 5); his end in 427 is less clear (69. 2, 86. 1). (*c*) Astyochos seems to start well before the end of summer 412 (viii. 20. 1, 25. 1). (*d*) Mindaros' arrival is also well before the end of summer 411 (viii. 85. 1). These instances imply a year beginning in the late summer, Knemos ending rather late, Astyochos and Mindaros beginning rather early. For a while thereafter the Spartans seem to have gone over to a system whereby the nauarch retained his command till spring, probably overlapping the *de jure* term of his successor: we find an autumn takeover again in 400 (X. *An.* vii. 2. 5, 7) and 395 (*Hell. Oxy.* 19 Bart. (14 G–H) 1).

Since so many Greek calendars seem to begin their year from solstice or equinox, it is likely enough that the Spartan new year began theoretically at the new moon next after the autumn equinox—but with all the factors of uncertainty that beset Greek lunar calendars.]

Spartan policy at this time is changeable and capricious. There is no reason to suppose it would have been any different if peace had been made in 425 (see my note on iv. 20. 4: vol. iii, 458–60).

We learn the name of the Spartan ephor 'eponymos', successor to Pleistolas, from X. *HG* ii. 3. 10: it is Kleinomachos.

Κλεόβουλος καὶ Ξενάρης: [in the reverse order 37. 1, in this order 38. 3, but 46. 4 suggests that Xenares, if either, was the more important. He is probably the same as the Xenares of 51. 2, see n. there.]

ταῦτά τε γιγνώσκειν: I prefer Reiske's ταὐτά, whether it is to be interpreted 'agree together' (so Poppo, and others: cf. 38. 1) or 'agree with them (the two ephors)'. [ταῦτα, if retained, would refer to the policy of the two ephors just enunciated, and thus mean the same as ταὐτά in the second alternative above. ταὐτά in the sense 'agree with one another' seems more pointed.]

πειρᾶσθαι Βοιωτούς, κ.τ.λ.: Βοιωτούς is 'Boeotia', τοῖς Βοιωτοῖς (above) the Boeotian ambassadors, whose own opinions may have differed from the official Boeotian as widely as those of Kleoboulos and Xenares did from the official Lacedaemonian (Sparta was an *ally* of Athens at this moment); but the whole sentence is so clumsy —μετὰ Βοιωτῶν with Βοιωτούς the subject of the verb, and with an αὐτούς between them—that Stahl with reason suspected the text. Graves says that μετὰ B. is for μεθ' ἑαυτῶν 'to avoid misunderstanding'; but there is no need for μεθ' ἑαυτῶν either: the sentence in 32. 5 which he cites as a parallel is much easier, even if we keep ὥσπερ Βοιωτοὶ εἶχον in the text. What one expects is that the ambassadors should be the subject of πειρᾶσθαι as of γιγνώσκειν with some such meaning as 'attempt, first to persuade Boeotia to join the alliance with Argos, and then to bring Argos, with Boeotia, into alliance with Sparta'—⟨πείθειν⟩ after Βοιωτούς (as Hude). Or, with Stahl's μετὰ τούτων for μετὰ Βοιωτῶν, 'then, with the help of Corinth, to bring Argos', etc. Even so it is not strictly logical, for both the Corinthian and the Boeotian ambassadors should be the subject of πειρᾶσθαι.

[Ullrich's μετὰ Κορινθίων, adopted by Steup, makes this latter interpretation easier, and the scribe's confusion is still intelligible. If the received text is to be defended, we must give the wider subject, the Boeotian and Corinthian ambassadors, to γιγνώσκειν only, and make Βοιωτούς the subject of πειρᾶσθαι, and excuse μετὰ Βοιωτῶν on the ground that this is virtually reported speech, what they are eventually to say to Argos; but Gomme's insertion produces a much less tortured sentence. He also wished to change αὖθις to εἶτα, but αὖθις may mean 'as the next step', cf. 76. 2, and iii. 106. 2.]

ἑλέσθαι γάρ, κ.τ.λ.: [the Boeotians will be saved from the peace only if Sparta can be turned against Athens. This is what Kleoboulos and Xenares want, and the Corinthians too—this plot confirms the general impression of the narrative, that Corinth had no positive enthusiasm for her new alliance but would return to her old loyalty as soon as Sparta gave up the peace policy. We thus expect this clause to explain how the proposed manœuvre will fit such a purpose.]

Stahl objects that πρό cannot be taken to mean 'at the price of'; but his remedy, to bracket Ἀθηναίων, in order to make the clause mean 'chose the friendship of Argos rather than her enmity and the end of the (just expiring) treaty between them', is not at all convincing. [Classen's attempt to give πρό a temporal sense has found no followers: the reader could not naturally take it so. Steup characteristically bracketed all from ἐλέσθαι to ῥᾴω ἂν εἶναι, but this compressed tangle cannot be attributed to an interpolator, though conceivable for Thucydides in his first draft.

This is unlike many of the difficulties in Thucydides in that the reader is likely at first sight to take the sense required, that 'Sparta will choose the Argive alliance even if it means enmity with Athens and dissolution of the treaty': it is the critic analysing the sentence at leisure who will say that 'ἐλέσθαι A πρό B' ought to mean 'prefer A to B'. The interpretation which the context requires can be got from these words if we take it as a matter of priority—the Argive alliance *would matter more than* the enmity of Athens. The convergence of πρό and ἀντί in expressions such as vi. 10. 4 πρὸ πολλῶν τιμᾶσθαι makes this sense of πρό easier.]

ἠπίσταντο - - - ἡγούμενοι: [the subject of ἠπίσταντο can only be Kl. and Xen., expounding Spartan policy to the ambassadors: the latter might know the fact and express it in these terms, but the context gives them no opportunity to speak. As the text stands, ἡγούμενοι must also be Kl. and Xen., thinking that it will be easier to re-start this particular extra-Peloponnesian war if there is no danger of war with Argos within the Peloponnese. To reach back thus for ten lines over a long parenthesis is harsh, but there is no alternative, for this participial clause is not a reason why they understood Spartan policy to be what it was, and it cannot be taken inside the parenthesis. With Krüger's ἡγουμένους there need be no parenthesis, or at most (as Gomme wished) a brief one ending at ἐσελθεῖν: the Spartans always wanted Argos' friendship because they thought this would make their extra-Peloponnesian war easier. ἡγουμένους makes for easier reading and more satisfactory sense.

Even with these alterations the sentence is still harsh and full of obstacles that look to be avoidable. Though one cannot say what revision might have made of it, this looks like a first draft.]

καλῶς σφίσι φίλιον: 'friendship on honourable terms', 'the right kind of friendship', with καλῶς used much as in iii. 32. 2.

2. ἐδέοντο Βοιωτούς: I would bracket the unnecessary and anomalous Βοιωτούς. The subject of παραδώσουσι is sufficiently clear from the previous sentence, as well as because only Boeotia could hand over Panakton to Sparta. [Alternatively we might consider Stahl's insertion of ⟨παρασκευάζειν⟩.]

How can Sparta, or two Spartan ephors, have hoped that the Boeotians, holding as they thought a valuable asset to use for themselves against Athens, would hand it over to her so that *she* could use it for her purposes? [Gomme offered no answer, but as regards the ephors it is not surprising that they should treat Spartan interests as paramount and expect others to do the same. The problem is, why the Boeotians were ready to consider the surrender. No doubt some Boeotians thought Sparta's re-entry into the war more important: and in the event Boeotia was ready to do without Panakton (if not to restore it intact) in return for a new alliance with Sparta (39. 2–3).

We should also consider the prospects for the success of this involved plan. (*a*) For Boeotia cf. *Hell. Oxy.* 17 Bart. (12 G–H), whose analysis of the internal division reaches back into this war. The pro-Spartan group, to which these ambassadors (and the current Boeotarchs, cf. 37. 4) clearly belong, increased its influence while Boeotia profited from the war and Spartan forces were close at hand, but it would be in danger whenever Sparta showed either weakness or a tendency to favour Boeotia's enemies. At this moment the federal Councils were at least not anxious to offend Sparta (38. 3: but cf. 52. 1, just over a year later), and it is implied that they would have accepted the plan if it could have been explained to them in full. (*b*) There is no trace as yet of internal division at Corinth, where the normally pro-Spartan oligarchy seems to be in full control and to switch the city's policy as convenient (cf. G. T. Griffith, *Historia* i (1950), 239): there would be no trouble there. (*c*) But at Argos, though the Boeotian alliance would be welcome in itself (37), alliance with Sparta needed open discussion in full assembly (28. 1), and feeling at Argos was such (28. 2, 37. 2, cf. 37. 3 n.) that the plan was not likely to have an easy passage there. The Boeotians might have found themselves entangled in the Argive alliance without attaining their further object, a possibility which does not seem to strike any of the conspirators. (*d*) At Sparta, it is clear that the war party was not yet in a majority, but the logic of the situation created by the peace worked in their favour, and Sparta would presumably have accepted the Argive alliance if it were ever offered on these terms. It does not seem an altogether hopeful plot: but no doubt Kl. and Xen. thought that they would profit by any trouble they could stir up.]

37. 2. τῆς ἀρχῆς τῆς μεγίστης: see 47. 9 n.

καθ' ὁδόν: [whatever circuitous routes might be necessary in wartime (cf. 64. 3 n.), the peacetime road, for both, lay past Argos.]

3. κατὰ τύχην γὰρ ἐδέοντο τούτων, κ.τ.λ.: 'as it happened, they were asking just what their friends from Sparta had bid them do'; but in a very different spirit—both thought they were getting out of their difficulties (ῥᾴω, 36. 1; ῥᾳδίως, 37. 2), but Argos was seeing herself at the head of a powerful coalition able to talk on more than equal terms with Sparta or anyone else, while Sparta was only trying to get out of a very awkward situation brought about by her own vacillating and disingenuous policy. Hence the two Argives could promise immediate official action.

4. τοῖς βοιωτάρχαις: [see iv. 91 n.]

5. καὶ αὐτοὺς ἀπέπεμψαν, κ.τ.λ.: 'they themselves were thanked and the conference ended'; i.e. they did not get what they had hoped and expected, immediate acceptance of the proposals. 'We will have a second conference in Argos', say the Boeotarchs, 'after consideration among ourselves'; and they begin (38. 1) with a proposed special alliance with Corinth, Megara, and the Chalkideis and other seceding states from the Thracian district of the Delian League.

38. 1. τὸ γὰρ αὐτὸ ἐποίουν: [Megara has not been mentioned till now, but the plan has evidently been explained to them, and they are ready to follow the same line as the Boeotians.]

2. ταῖς τέσσαρσι βουλαῖς: Thucydides has told us a little about the Boeotarchs at iv. 91, but nothing about the four boulai other than what he says here, that they possessed the ultimate authority (in foreign affairs, at least). [From *Hell. Oxy.* 16 Bart. (11 G–H) 2 we know that in each individual city there were four councils, one of which in rotation acted as probouleutic body to the other three sitting as an assembly; so that a combined session of all four was needed for decision. The author does not describe the procedure of the federal council, saying only (§ 4) that each of the eleven μέρη appointed sixty councillors, and that they met on the Kadmeia. From this passage it appears that the federal council operated on the same system as the city councils. This was a joint meeting of all four sections, so the use of the singular τὴν βουλήν in § 3, and of the plural again in § 4, is intelligible.]

ὅσαι βούλονται, κ.τ.λ.: a purposely vague and wide-reaching phrase, for the Boeotarchs hoped to be able, with this authorized, to conclude the alliance with Argos (Grote, v. 429). But the boulai were nervous even of a special treaty with Corinth, because of her recent quarrel with Sparta and sudden friendship with Argos (§ 3); much more would they have been antagonized if the proposed treaty with Argos had been boldly set before them. [See also next n.]

3. οὐ γὰρ εἶπον, κ.τ.λ.: [the secret could not be revealed without alarming the Argives, who were not a party to the plot in c. 36 and might not accept Boeotia and Megara if their ulterior purpose were known: for the Argive point of view, see 37. 2–3 with nn.]

μετὰ τῶν Λακεδαιμονίων: Stahl's conjecture, μετ' αὐτῶν Λ., adopted by Classen, is surely right; for the advice was just this, to enter first into an alliance with Corinth and Argos, and thereby, with Argos, become allies of Sparta herself (36. 1). [The received text is unsatisfactory, since 'join with Sparta' would more naturally be expressed by μετὰ Λ. γίγνεσθαι, without the article. Steup thought one could not supply ξυμμάχους with Λ., since Boeotia was already the formal ally of Sparta, but this is unrealistic, as 39. 3 immediately shows.]

τὴν βουλήν: [for the singular, see § 2 n. The expectation of the Boeotarchs, that the councils would tamely accept whatever they proposed, is an interesting example of that dominance of the executive
which Athens took such pains to avoid, but which was probably
characteristic in general of oligarchies.]

4. ἀμέλεια δέ τις ἐνῆν, κ.τ.λ.: [cf. Corinth's reaction to the earlier
rebuff at Tegea, 32. 4 with n. Thucydides' language perhaps betrays
impatience with the inefficiency with which the manœuvre was
carried out.]

39. 1. *Athens Loses Mekyberna*

39. 1. Μηκύβερναν: see 18. 6 n. This is another reminder how weak
were Athenian forces in Thrace, and in the Chalkidian peninsula in
particular, and how remiss their policy—or how exhausted and reluctant to fight they were.

(ms.) It is not only, and not principally, the incidents told in
short sentences, as this and 35. 1, which distinguish this part of book
v, but most of all cc. such as 38, 40–1, stories of complex and involved
diplomacy told very differently from ii–v. 24 (a quite different time).
v. 17, e.g., is different.

39. 2–3. *Story of Negotiations Resumed*

2. οἱ Λακεδαιμόνιοι - - - ἦλθον ἐς τοὺς Βοιωτούς: Spartan diplomacy
becomes yet more tortuous, so clearly double-faced that both the
opposing factions in Sparta support this move. [Gomme's insistence
on the tortuous character of Spartan policy in these years is amply
justified: but in this instance it is at least natural that all Spartan
parties should want to recover Pylos. On πρεσβευόμενοι, see vi.
104. 2 n.]

κομίσασθαι ἂν αὐτοὶ Πύλον: [the Spartan reason for wanting Boeotia
to restore Panakton has been stated already at 36. 2, and is repeated
at the end of this sentence and in the middle of § 3, in almost identical
words. If this was all written at one time, the repetition is somewhat uneconomic. One might imagine an earlier stage at which the
point about Sparta 'wronging' Athens had not been fully developed
or the Spartan–Athenian alliance brought into the story (§ 3), and
a later stage when these considerations were more present to his
mind: but no such division of c. 46 is possible, and the repetition
still seems excessive. It must presumably be put down to imperfect
revision.]

3. ξυμμαχίαν ἰδίαν: [Boeotia, though rejecting the peace, had committed no further act of revolt and clearly wished to remain inside
the Spartan alliance (31. 6, 38. 3): an ambiguous position, and the
new alliance deepens the formal uncertainty. It was argued above

43

(32. 6 n.) that Boeotia was probably bound to Sparta by the type of alliance standard in the Peloponnesian League, which obliged her to accept the majority decision of a conference (30. 1 with n.). This passage supports that argument: an ἰδία ξυμμαχία (cf. 30. 2 n.) means one outside the standard framework—ὥσπερ Ἀθηναίοις, just as Athens' alliance of the previous spring was outside it. The gain to Boeotia was great, since in effect this condoned her disobedience and made it impossible *de facto* for Sparta to join Athens in compelling her to accept the peace.]

εἰρημένον ἄνευ ἀλλήλων, κ.τ.λ.: see 23. 1 n. No such clause is to be found in c. 23, but the provision may have been understood to be included in 23. 1 (Ed. Meyer, *Forschungen zur alten Geschichte*, ii. 290 ff.); or a new clause may have been subsequently agreed, as Thirlwall suggested (*History of Greece*, iii. 332 n. 1).

[For Stahl's proposed insertion in 23. 1, see n. there: it would be an odd coincidence if our text of c. 23 were defective at the precise point to which Thucydides referred back. Wilamowitz's suggestion (*Sb. Berl.* 1919, 954) is no more probable, that this clause had stood in the treaty but was dropped at its renewal (46. 4): revision is improbable in that situation, and Thucydides' copy would more naturally be of the original text. Meyer took this as an implied term, or a condition implicit in the mere fact of the alliance: but 23. 1–2, the relevant clauses, relate to cases where the territory of Sparta or Athens has already been invaded, and there is no formal reason why either should not make a defensive alliance with a third party on the same terms, provided (but this of course is not realistic) it was ready to act in all cases against the aggressor. Thirlwall (above) compared the joint decrees of Sparta and Argos in 80. 1 (which included καὶ μὴ ξυμβαίνειν τῳ μηδὲ πολεμεῖν ἀλλ' ἢ ἅμα) subsequent to their treaty in c. 79; similarly Pohlenz, *NGG* 1920, 79–82, drawing attention to 35. 3 and surmising a lacuna there after ἀναγκάσουσιν. Momigliano, *Riv. Fil.* lvii (1929), 272, suggested an oral agreement subsequent to the treaty; De Sanctis, ibid. 439–40, objected that an oral agreement would not be binding, at least at Athens, without a decree of the assembly, but the objection holds only if εἰρημένον here must refer to a text formally fixed in writing. For the meaning of εἰρημένον, see 31. 5 n.: in my belief, it might refer to a looser understanding, ἄνευ ξυγγραφῆς (35. 3).

For the fact, it has also been doubted (especially Steup, ad loc.) if Sparta or Athens would thus restrict themselves to an agreed foreign policy. But 80. 1, cited above, is an adequate parallel, on the face of it a still more surprising surrender of Sparta's freedom of action. The answer is, presumably, that restrictions of this form would be understood to apply to matters of common interest, or the matters which preoccupied the parties at the time, whether such limitation were expressed or not. Athens' attention is in this case concentrated (42. 2, 46. 2) on the Spartan promise to compel the Boeotians and others to adhere to the peace. Sparta had clearly given at least an oral undertaking (35. 3, 42. 2), which could have had the form given in 39. 3 and 46. 2, and I take it that this is the reference of εἰρημένον here and εἴρητο in 46. 2. The treaty text would thus be irrelevant.]

τοῦ χειμῶνος τελευτῶντος ἤδη καὶ πρὸς ἔαρ: see 17. 2, with my n., and vol. iii, Appendix, 705. [See also 27. 1 n., p. 18 above: events which occur before Thucydides' formal division must be taken to belong to his winter, even if πρὸς ἔαρ.]

καθῃρεῖτο: see 40. 1, 42. 1. As Stahl notes, this statement is here very abrupt when we are expecting to hear that Panakton was handed over to Sparta; and the excuse for the demolition is not stated till 42. 1, nor the Spartan reaction to it.

YEAR 12: 420–419 B.C. (CC. 40–51)

40–48. *Diplomatic Exchanges Continued*

40. 1. ὡς οἵ τε πρέσβεις, κ.τ.λ.: [(1) see 38. 4. Thucydides does not make it clear how far the Corinthians (or any other party) had reported the reason for the failure: the full story could not easily be told (38. 3 n.), and the non-arrival of the Boeotians would naturally give rise to speculation about their general intentions. (2) Argive knowledge of the destruction of Panakton (strictly, that it is in process of demolition, whereas the alliance is complete) seems premature: the Spartan ambassadors, who set out (42. 1) during the negotiations of 40. 3–41, appear to discover the fact only when they reach Boeotia. (3) 42. 2 πυνθανόμενοι does not make it clear whether the Athenians first heard of the Spartan–Boeotian alliance from these Spartan ambassadors, or knew of it already: rumour would no doubt spread quickly.

(2) looks like a slip (but see also § 2 n.). In his summary of the Argives' situation, Thucydides has allowed them to know at least the external aspect of the events narrated in 38. 4, 39. 3, but has overlooked a small anachronism.]

ἐς Λακεδαιμονίους - - - χωρήσῃ: [Steup objected that the Spartan–Boeotian alliance would not of itself cause the defection of Argos' existing allies; and Stahl oddly took the clause to refer to prospective not actual allies. But if Sparta, Athens, and Boeotia had come to the kind of understanding adumbrated in § 2, the Argives had every reason to fear a landslide. They could not, for instance, count on Corinth's loyalty.]

2. πεπεῖσθαι - - - καθελεῖν: (ms.) we want παραδοῦναι, especially with τούς τε Ἀθηναίους εἰδέναι to follow. [It is not indeed easy to imagine why the Spartans should positively persuade the Boeotians to an act which was bound to exasperate Athenian feeling and make the return of Pylos much less likely; and 42. 1 shows that they had done no such thing. If Thucydides wrote παραδοῦναι or the equivalent, καθελεῖν is due to καθαιρούμενον and καθῃρεῖτο above, either as deliberate correction or as psychological error; and this is perhaps not more remarkable than other cases where the MSS. are unanimous in error. In that case, what the Athenians know is that they are to gain Panakton and Boeotia's adherence to the peace; and this is alarming enough for the Argives. With the MSS. text, the Athenians know of the destruction, and are presumed to have condoned it for the sake of Boeotian adherence to the peace, which is still more alarming as evidence of their good understanding with Sparta. Perhaps Thucydides did write καθελεῖν, and its subordination to πεπεῖσθαι (which is needed for καί - - - ἐσιέναι) is due to over-hasty compression.

If we emend καθελεῖν, we should also consider emending καθαιρούμενον in § 1.]

ἐκ τῶν διαφορῶν: [given the whole context, there is no difficulty in understanding this to mean the differences between Sparta and Athens, the main subject of the book from c. 25 onwards. If the two great powers are agreed, neither will make separate alliances to the detriment of the other; if they quarrel, Athens will be as ready to 'wrong' Sparta (cf. 46. 3) as Sparta to wrong Athens.

Steup's rearrangement—comma after ἐλπίζοντες, ἐκ τῶν διαφορῶν belonging to the εἰ-clause but taken out of it for emphasis, αὐτοῖς to mean the Athenians—produces an awkward sentence for no great gain. But see next n.]

μείνειαν: [edd. compare X. An. ii. 3. 24, but that is the maintenance of an existing truce, whereas here, unless we follow Steup (above), it is a matter of negotiating a new treaty to replace an old one which, very possibly, has already expired. (Cf. 28. 2 n. In view of πρότερον, this clause cannot be used to show that the old treaty was still in force; and the language of 40. 3–41 is at least consistent with its having already expired.)]

3. Τεγεάταις: [they are not recorded as having any part in the present round of negotiations. The reasons why they are singled out for mention are, presumably, their old enmity with Argos' ally Mantineia, the fact that they have a common frontier with Argos, and the part they had played in the preceding summer (32. 3–4).]

ἡγήσεσθαι: [Gomme favoured reading ἡγήσασθαι, and these terminations are easily corrupted; but the future may stand, on the analogy of the fut. inf. with διανοεῖσθαι.]

ἡγούμενοι ἐκ τῶν παρόντων, κ.τ.λ.: 'thinking it in the circumstances to be most advantageous to make peace with Sparta, as might be agreed, and remain neutral'. ἡσυχίαν ἄγειν is the negative of ἐν φρονήματι εἶναι τῆς Πελοποννήσου ἡγήσεσθαι, 'confidently hoping[1] for the leadership of the Peloponnese'. ὅπη ἂν ξυγχωρῇ not only offers a unique case of the impersonal use of ξυγχωρεῖν, but does not give a very satisfactory sense; see LSJ, who translate 'as may be agreed'. [In X. Eq. 9. 11, which edd. cite as a parallel, A has ἐγχωροίην, the rest συγχωροίη; and if the latter is read, the context there makes the required sense easier than it is here.]

κράτιστα is to be taken as in i. 85. 2.

41. 2. τῆς Κυνουρίας γῆς - - - Θυρέαν: see ii. 27. 2 and iv. 56–7, with my notes. (There is no mention of the Aiginetai here—who were not all killed in 424 B.C.; we might indeed have had here νέμονται δὲ Θ. Αἰγινῆται). Anthene is mentioned by Pausanias, ii. 38. 5, where he mentions the old battle of the 300 fought c. 550 B.C. (described in Herodotos (i. 82) and referred to by Thucydides below), and says that at some later time Kynouria was allotted to Argos by arbitration and was Argive in his day. [For the identification of the site, see Leake, ii. 486–94; Bursian, ii. 68–72.]

ἐπηγάγοντο: we certainly expect the imperfect, for Sparta takes some time before agreeing (§ 3). [But this is only true if the process described in § 3 (τὸ μὲν πρῶτον ἐδόκει, κ.τ.λ.) is to be thought of as succeeding the introduction (sc. ἐπήγοντο) of the proposition eventually accepted: it is equally possible that Thucydides announces the provisional acceptance of it as a completed fact in § 2, then goes a little back in § 3 to describe the process.]

Λακεδαίμονι καὶ Ἄργει: surprising for μήτε Λ. μήτε Ἄ. (or better, μηδετέροις), for it does not mean a war between Sparta and Argos, but 'if either is at war with a third party'. Perhaps a marginal note explaining ὁποτεροισοῦν?

3. μωρία: [almost 'childishness', 'naïvety'.]

πάντως φίλιον: πάντως is not quite 'on any terms', as Classen and Graves, for Sparta has just decisively rejected the first terms proposed by Argos; but 'were in any case desirous of having Argos friendly'.

Ὑακίνθια: see 23. 4 n., and viii. 10. 1 n. [See Addenda.]

42. 1. Ἀνδρομένης: [see app. crit., here and to οἱ περὶ τὸν Ἀνδρομένη below. The name Ἀνδρομέδης is attested for Lakonia (IG v. 1. 1232, Tainaron, early 4th c.): the corruption of this to the common Ἀνδρομένης is far more likely than the reverse process.]

---

[1] [The translation is tame: for φρόνημα cf. 43. 2, vi. 18. 4. Perhaps 'fired with ambition for . . .'.]

ὑπὸ τῶν Βοιωτῶν αὐτῶν: they had acted without consulting Sparta (cf. 40. 2 n.); and their explanation—ὡς ἦσάν ποτε, κ.τ.λ.—was not one which Thucydides wishes us to accept. For καθηρημένον see καθῃρεῖτο, 39. 3.

νομίζοντες καὶ τοῦτο ἀποδιδόναι: [Dobree, followed by Classen, understood εἶναι, i.e. 'thinking that this too was restitution'. Gomme did not decide between this and the alternative, 'that they were handing it back just as they were handing back the prisoners': but, as Steup argues, the reference of τοῦτο to Panakton is easy and natural, as the sentence stands, whereas on Classen's rendering there is no such easy point of reference.]

2. φάσκοντες πρότερον: see 35. 3, with n., and 39. 3 n.

43. 2. Ἀλκιβιάδης ὁ Κλεινίου: it is a good instance of Thucydides' manner of not explaining, or not explaining fully, a man's position or his character on the first mention of him, that he says nothing here of the general lawlessness of Alkibiades' behaviour. Such a characteristic would certainly be relevant here; but it has more point at vi. 15. 2–4, not only because Alkibiades' support for the Sicilian expedition was more important than his opposition to the peace-treaty (which was in danger of collapsing without his help) in 420, but because we are there shortly to hear of his implication in the affair of the Hermai and the Mysteries. Contrast the modern manner. Grote, v. 433–44, has a long passage on Alkibiades' character and conduct on this occasion of his first introduction into Greek history, anticipating quite a lot of the later story. Similarly W. S. Ferguson in *CAH* v. 262–4 gives on the same occasion what is almost a summary of his whole career.

[On Thucydides' introductions of important individuals, see G. T. Griffith, *PCPhS* N.S. vii (1961), 21–33; on 'double introductions', vi. 72. 2 n.]

It is to be noted, as well, that vi. 15. 2–4 was written, at least in its present form, after 404 B.C.; our present passage might be almost contemporary with the event, written soon after 420 B.C.

[Alkibiades' age will have been 32 or a little more at this time. (1) His father Kleinias was killed at Koroneia (Plu. *Alc.* 1. 1; Isoc. xvi. 28), early in 446 or perhaps in 447 (vol. i, 409; *ATL* iii. 178 n. 65), leaving a younger son Kleinias (Pl. *Prt.* 320a) as well as Alkibiades. (2) He served as a hoplite at Poteidaia, with Sokrates. The contradictory evidence (Pl. *Smp.* 219 e–220 e, *Chrm.* 153 a–b; Isoc. xvi. 29; Plu. *Alc.* 7. 3–5) is sorted out by Hatzfeld, 27 f., 62 ff., who concludes that we must trust the more extensive account in Pl. *Smp.* and Plutarch, who say that he took part in the battle late in 432 (i. 62, cf. n. on 5–6 there), not Isokrates who says that he went out with Phormion, i.e. after the battle (i. 64. 2). He therefore went out with

Archestratos (i. 57. 6) or Kallias (i. 61. 1) in 432, and since he cannot then have been less than twenty he was born not later than 452; but also not much earlier, since Isokrates says he went immediately after his *dokimasia*, and Plutarch calls him μειράκιον. (3) Nepos' statement (*Alc.* 10. 6), that at his death he was *annos circiter xl natus*, cannot be literally true and must be disregarded.]

At 32–33 he would have been thought young, in any state but Athens, and in Athens by an older opponent (as Nikias, vi. 12. 2, 17. 1), to be taking so prominent a part in politics; he had already for some years made himself notorious by his private life and was a figure in comedy. [The first known mention is Ar. *Daitaleis* (fr. 198. 6) of 427; then *Ach.* 716 of 425. And. iv. 11 says that he persuaded the Athenians to double the tribute in 425, and was one of the ten *taktai* appointed then; this is hardly possible in view of his age, but his cultivation of the Sphakteria prisoners and his hope that the Spartans might deal with him rather than with Nikias show that his public ambitions began early.]

Athens was a democracy, but Alkibiades' distinguished ancestry made it easy for him to step into a position of some importance, though not yet into high office. [(For this, cf. perhaps the advice attributed to Hagnon in *Frag. Vat. de eligendis magistratibus*, p. 21 Aly, on the advantage of giving younger men experience in the generalship, with a hunting analogy: this would be specially relevant to Alkibiades' position in 415, cf. vi. 17. 1, 18. 6.)]

φρονήματι: as in 40. 3.

διὰ Νικίου καὶ Λάχητος: cf. 16. 1, iv. 118. 11.

τὴν παλαιὰν προξενίαν: see Alkibiades' speech at Sparta, vi. 89. 2–3, where this is repeated. [A ms. note refers to E. Vanderpool, *Hesperia* xxi (1952), 1–8. The ostraka there discussed show that the grandfather, also named Alkibiades (ὁ παλαιός, Pl. *Euthd.* 275a), was the son of a Kleinias, not of the Alkibiades who helped Kleisthenes to expel the tyrants: Kirchner's stemma (*PA* ii. 442) must be amended as follows, Alkibiades I (Kleisthenes' ally)—Kleinias I (fought at Artemision)—Alkibiades II (ὁ παλαιός)—Kleinias II (killed at Koroneia)—Alkibiades III. They also show that the grandfather's ostracism (Lys. xiv. 39; And. iv. 34) belongs not to 485 (Arist. Ἀθ. π. 22. 6) but well after the Persian War. The only other known activity of Alkibiades II is his decree for Aristeides' children (Plu. *Arist.* 27. 2; D. xx. 115) after the latter's death. This probably belongs to the 460s: if any reliance can be placed in Nepos' statement (*Arist.* 3. 3), *decessit autem fere post annum quartum quam Themistocles Athenis erat expulsus*, 468/7 may be the date, cf. M. E. White, *JHS* lxxxiv (1964), 146. The renunciation of the Spartan proxeny will thus most probably be a consequence of the quarrel between Sparta and Athens in 462 (vi. 89. 2, κατά τι ἔγκλημα, covers this up for the

Spartan audience). The ostracism will then be later than Kimon's in 461.

The Spartan connection is mentioned again in viii. 6. 3. Since Alkibiades is there said to be a Spartan name, the relationship goes back at least to the father of Alkibiades I, born in the middle of the sixth century. This is likely enough at a time when the Peisistratidai too were ξεῖνοι of the Spartans (Hdt. v. 90. 1).]

θεραπεύων: cf. i. 55. 1, ἐν θεραπείᾳ εἶχον πολλῇ, the Corinthians' treatment of their prisoners from Kerkyra.

3. ἵνα Ἀργείους σφίσι σπεισάμενοι ἐξέλωσι: I believe this means, not to destroy, crush Argos, as most edd., but to isolate her—to separate, a special case of the common meaning, to remove; as Hobbes translates, 'only to get the Argives by that means away from them'. [viii. 46. 3 is a possible parallel: see n. there.]

αὖθις: αὖτις codd. See n. on i. 100. 3.

44. 1. τῶν - - - ἐν Λακεδαίμονι πρέσβεων: [those of 40. 3, whose negotiations covered a long time, while the action of 42–3 proceeds.]

πόλιν τε σφίσι φιλίαν ἀπὸ παλαιοῦ: tragedy often alluded to this ancient friendship. [A ms. note refers to J. S. Morrison, *CQ* xxxv (1941), 15, who assumes that Euripides' *Supplices* was 'intended to further the Argive–Athenian alliance for which Alcibiades was working'. Gomme remarked that *Supp.* was not necessarily to be dated to c. 420; and G. Zuntz, *The Political Plays of Euripides* (1955), 71–8, firmly dissociates the play from this alliance, eventually (88–92) dating the play to 424. The plots of *Heraclidae*, which Zuntz (81–8) for rather more positive reasons dates to 430, and of *Supplices* invite the poet to allude to the recompense Athens might expect for the services rendered by Demophon and Theseus. But *Hcld.* certainly, and *Supp.* very probably, belong to the time when Argos was still covered by her treaty with Sparta (28. 2, 40–1) and was neutral in the Archidamian War; the tone is here quite different from that of Aeschylus in *Eum.* 287 ff., in the very different circumstances of 458 (cf. i. 104. 2 n.), where Orestes promises Argive help with a generous flourish. There is no clear allusion in plays after 420 to alliance or co-operation with Argos. It does not seem that the subject much preoccupied Euripides.]

Comedy was at times more realistic, as Aristophanes in *Peace* (28. 2 n. above).

3. Φιλοχαρίδας καὶ Λέων καὶ Ἔνδιος: for the first named see 21. 1, as well as iv. 119. 2 and v. 19. 2. Leon may well be the same as the oikistes of Herakleia, iii. 92. 5, and perhaps the father of Pedaritos, viii. 28. 5: [but this was a fairly common name at Sparta as at Athens, for instance Pedaritos' successor (viii. 61. 2) was also named Leon.] Endios and his family had ancient ties of friendship with Alkibiades, viii. 6. 3.

45. 1. ἦν ἐς τὸν δῆμον ταῦτα λέγωσιν: Plutarch retells this story in *Nic.* 10, following Thucydides cc. 43 and 45 closely; whence Stahl would read ταὐτά here, from Plutarch's μὴ καὶ τὸν δῆμον ἀπὸ τῶν αὐτῶν λόγων ἐπαγάγωνται (10. 4). In *Alc.* 14 Plutarch elaborates part of Thucydides' narrative, in particular giving us Alkibiades' arguments to the Spartans why it would be better to deny in the ekklesia that they had come with full powers (14. 8–9, see below). Some explanation of the advice, by what reasoning the Spartans were persuaded, is indeed required. Nor is it clear that he would succeed *both* in causing a rift between the Spartans and Nikias *and* in upsetting Spartan plans (§ 3). Plutarch's further estimate of Alkibiades' action on this occasion in the *Comparison with Coriolanus*, 2, is influenced by Alkibiades' boast in Thucydides vi. 16. 6.

[Stahl and others took the καί before ἦν to mean 'also', implying that the council had received the Spartans favourably: the reader should understand ὥσπερ καὶ τὴν βουλὴν ἐπηγάγοντο. Steup found this hard and preferred Classen's punctuation - - - μή, καὶ ἦν - - -, taking καὶ ἐς τὸν δῆμον together, with καί alone taken out of the subordinate clause and placed before ἦν: this is harder still, and his instances do not support this form of separation, whereas vii. 85. 1 (see n. there) gives an apt parallel for the OCT punctuation. This latter does not compel us to suppose that the council had approved the Spartan proposals, for the καί might as easily, or more easily, mean 'even' or 'actually'. (It makes no difference whether we read ταῦτα or ταὐτά, for the reference will be the same; nor is it decisive that Plutarch (above) says the council was persuaded, for he or his source is consciously supplementing Thucydides.) The council's approval (as Steup remarks) was of no great moment, provided they at least gave the envoys access to the assembly, and there is no great reason for Thucydides to say anything about it.]

2. πίστιν αὐτοῖς δούς: [there can be no question of a material pledge which Alkibiades forfeited; this must be simply a verbal assurance, as iv. 51. πίστις and ὅρκοι are often joined in the same phrase, but the instances show that an oath was not a necessary element in πίστις: these words add little, beyond extra solemnity, to what is already conveyed in πείθει.]

2–4. [The difficulties in this story are brought out by Hatzfeld, 89 f. (1) Why should the Spartans listen at all to their enemy Alkibiades rather than to Nikias their friend? (2) How did Alkibiades persuade them that their denial would help their cause? (3) How, after this, could Alkibiades and Endios collaborate so closely in 413/12 (viii. 6. 3, 12)? The last is the least serious—they could be useful to one another in very different circumstances eight years later—and (1) would not greatly matter if we had a convincing answer to (2). Here Plutarch (above, § 1 n.) supplies an argument: the assembly, unlike the council, was unreasonable, and would press for further concessions if it knew they were empowered to make any. But (*a*) Plutarch's non-Thucydidean matter does not suggest genuine fresh information: the Spartan agreement with Corinth, *Alc.* 14. 5, is not reconcilable with Thucydides (it reappears more clearly in Diod. xii. 77. 3, and may be the product of a misleading summary in Ephoros), and Alkibiades' election to the generalship just after this meeting (*Nic.* 10. 9, *Alc.* 15. 1) is chronologically embarrassing, cf. 52. 2 n., and Hatzfeld, 94. (*b*) Plutarch, to make his point, has to stress the just and reasonable character of the Spartan proposals, but neither he nor Thucydides indicates any proposal that would meet Athens' complaints. (*c*) Alkibiades would have to be very careful to guard the Spartans from further contact with Nikias, after his conversation and before the meeting. (*d*) Alkibiades' proposition involved reference back to Sparta and a delay which the Spartans could only afford if they were very sure of a good result. Plutarch's supplement to Thucydides will not bear the weight which the story puts on it.

Hatzfeld concluded (91 ff.) that the Spartans had really nothing new to offer (as he adds, 'nous connaissons ces arrangements où l'une des parties, en échange d'une concession substantielle, ne reçoit que le maintien de ce qu'elle possédait déjà'), and that Alkibiades exposed this fact to the assembly. This raises the question, how far the powers claimed by the envoys in § 1 really extended (περὶ πάντων ξυμβῆναι τῶν διαφόρων). Such 'full powers' need not amount to much, as in the case of the Peloponnesian ambassadors of iv. 118. 10, τέλος ἔχοντες, who might complete the formalities if Athens accepted their proposition, but amendments would have needed a fresh embassy. Nor could such ambassadors commit their city to a really unwelcome concession: Andokides iii. 33 claims that he and his colleagues in winter 392/1 might have sworn to the peace in Sparta without referring back to the assembly, but he does not sound confident about this (34), and in the end four of them were exiled for having offered, at the conference in Sparta, concessions which the assembly was not prepared to make, Philoch. *FGrHist* 328 F 149. In our passage, in spite of Plutarch (*Alc.* 10. 4), Thucydides' wording may mean only that the envoys were empowered to swear to certain proposals if Athens accepted them. Hatzfeld deduced from the fate of Nikias' embassy in 46. 2–4 that no concession was ever intended. This may not be quite fair, for the scene in the Athenian assembly and the harsh instructions given to Nikias (46. 2) will have strengthened the hand of Xenares' party and reduced the chances of accommodation; but it is still unlikely that the original embassy could have satisfied Athens on the points raised in 46. 2, or even reached a compromise.

Hatzfeld's case is built on facts taken from Thucydides and on probabilities which Thucydides could estimate better than we can. Nevertheless it is a fairly strong case, and it seems possible that Thucydides' judgement was seduced by a touched-up version of the story, which admirably illustrated the qualities and defects of Alkibiades.]

4. σεισμοῦ δὲ γενομένου, κ.τ.λ.: another 'note' of an incident which was, in its effect, of no importance. [Minor tremors are not uncommon in Greece, and were naturally taken as portents, to break off a meeting (e.g. 50. 5) : even a drop of rain might break up an assembly (Ar. *Ach.* 170–1). But no one could tell that the small tremor was not the precursor of a serious earthquake.] Attention to it was not simply superstition. [For military expeditions broken off by earthquakes, see iii. 89. 1, vi. 95. 1, with nn.]

46. 1. τῇ δ᾽ ὑστεραίᾳ: it would be interesting to know how many citizens could or would spend another morning on the Pnyx, even on so important an occasion as this.

ἠπατημένων - - - ἐξηπατημένος: [there seems to be no distinction of meaning. The compound verb is in general the more common in prose, and though Thucydides has eight instances of the simple verb to four of the compound, these four do not suggest that he felt the preposition to intensify the meaning. Stahl and others bracket τῶν Λακεδαιμονίων αὐτῶν ἠπατημένων, mainly because they feel the phrase stylistically awkward; but that leaves us with καίπερ καὶ αὐτός, which is not attractive. The sentence would, however, be more elegant without αὐτῶν, which slightly blunts the point that Nikias was deceived because the Spartans had been deceived.]

ἐν μὲν τῷ σφετέρῳ καλῷ, κ.τ.λ.: referring to the general situation at the time of the peace in 421, as at 28. 2 and as Nikias repeated in 415, vi. 11. 6, rather than to the particular moment of this meeting ; that is, Nikias does not mean by ἀναβάλλεσθαι that war will at once begin if the Spartan embassy is sent empty away. ἀναβάλλεσθαι will mean rather 'avoidance of war', which is the best possible thing for Athens; Sparta is looking for some 'lucky discovery' which will give her the occasion to run the risk of going to war again ('it would be a positive godsend to risk her hand as soon as she could'— Warner) : an immediate treaty between Athens and Argos would be such a εὕρημα. For this estimate of the situation in 421—Athenian success and Spartan disgrace—see n. on 28. 2.

2. Πάνακτόν τε ὀρθὸν ἀποδιδόναι, κ.τ.λ.: the terms are in fact stiff, in the circumstances, and Nikias could hardly hope for success at Sparta ; he is trying to play the strong man before his own countrymen.

καθάπερ εἴρητο: see 39. 3 n.

3. εἰπεῖν τε - - - ὅτι - - - πεποιῆσθαι, ὡς παρεῖναί γ' αὐτούς: [the anomaly of εἰπεῖν ὅτι + inf. is not to be removed by emending ὅτι away, since σφεῖς (which would have to be changed to σφᾶς) would then refer to persons who are not the subject of εἰπεῖν; it may be regarded (as Gomme suggests) as a variety of εἰπεῖν ὅτι followed by the speaker's words in the first, not the third, person. This passage has been used to justify iv. 37. 1 γνοὺς ὅτι διαφθαρησομένους αὐτούς, but Gomme was surely right to reject this (and Π² there omits ὅτι).] ὡς παρεῖναί γ' αὐτούς means 'indeed, you may add, the Argive ambassadors are here for that very purpose'.

εἰ ἐβούλοντο ἀδικεῖν: [in general, it would be a 'wrong' to adhere to an alliance which was clearly hostile to Sparta; in particular, Elis was one of the cities which Sparta and Athens should jointly compel to join the Peace.]

4. ταῦτα γίγνεσθαι: [i.e., that they should *not* make the required declaration. For the negative reference of ταῦτα, see vi. 74. 1 n.]

τοὺς δὲ ὅρκους - - - ἀνενεώσαντο: Nikias was content with very little. Presumably this was a special oath, not the normal renewal laid down in the treaties, 18. 10 and 23. 4. [According to this latter clause, the Spartans should have come to Athens at the Dionysia to swear to the alliance, and presumably also to the peace (cf. 24. 1 n.). It is not clear what time of year we have now reached, but by 49. 1 we have come to the Olympic festival without any substantial event intervening, which suggests that these negotiations were spread over some time and that the Dionysia are now past, possibly also the Hyakinthia (23. 4). We are not told that the Spartans had come to the Dionysia, but the fulfilment of the formality would hardly be worth a note: Thucydides would be more likely to have mentioned it if they had failed to keep this obligation.]

5. παραγαγόντος Ἀλκιβιάδου: [a ms. note shows that Gomme would have preferred to take these words inside the parenthesis, as Steup and other edd. This makes it clear that παρόντες refers to the Argives' presence in the assembly: if Thucydides had meant only that they were still in Athens, he might be expected to have inserted ἔτι. (This is presumably the point to which Gomme refers forward in 22. 1 n.)]

47. *Treaty between Athens and Argos, Mantineia, and Elis.*

It is of this document that we possess a fragment of the official Athenian copy on stone—from the right-hand edge, about 12 letters of each line at the top to about 6 at the bottom (out of 77), as far as § 8 init.—from the south slope of the Akropolis, near the Theatre of Dionysos, *IG* i². 86 (*GHI* 72, not in ML). For discrepancies between this and our text of Thucydides, see the app. crit.; none is

serious. It is possible that, quite apart from variations due to translation into different dialects, strict verbal identity of the several
official copies, on papyrus and on stone, was not aimed at, any
more than, apparently, in the copies of the English *Magna Carta*
(see A. J. Collins, 'The Documents of the Great Charter of 1215',
Proc. Brit. Acad. xxxiv (1948), 234–79, esp. 266 ff.); and that we are
wrong, therefore, to correct Thucydides' text from the inscription,
instead of simply recording the variations. In form there seem to
have been three separate treaties, between Athens and each of the
three Peloponnesian cities named at the beginning (1–2), these three
being already allies among themselves (48. 2); hence ἑκάτεροι in § 1
(but ἕκαστοι in § 5; and see § 10 n., and 48. 1, the MSS. reading αἱ
ξυμμαχίαι).

[Gomme later queried this explanation and added the alternative
in a later note (to § 1), that the two parties are Athens and the three
cities acting as a unit. This accounts equally well for ἑκάτεροι (cf.
ὁπότεροι in the King's Peace, X. *HG* v. 1. 31) and ἕκαστοι. §§ 2 and
3–4 deal with the cities' obligations to Athens and Athens' to them,
but not with their obligations to one another: this is intelligible on
either supposition, since the cities were already allies of one another;
nor is § 10 decisive. The second explanation is the simpler, but it
makes little practical difference.]

The text inscribed on stone had a title, thus restored: [**ΑΡΓΕΙΟΝ
ΜΑΝΤΙΝΕΟΝ ΕΛ**]**Ε**[**Ι**]**ΟΝ**, this being the Attic copy, or rather
a copy on stone of the Attic copy. When and where did Thucydides
see a copy in Attic script? A final draft would of course have been
taken, one to each of the three cities, by their delegates, who had
agreed the terms in Athens, and would have been preserved in their
archives. Its title would have included **Α⊙ΕΝΑΙΟΝ**. (It is possible
that the copy in bronze set up in Olympia by the four allies con-
jointly (§ 11) was in Attic script, and was seen by Thucydides.) Cf.
vol. iii, 606–7.

[Bengtson, *Staatsverträge*, no. 193, adds little but bibliography.
The concern of commentators that Thucydides should have seen the
Athenian copy, or a copy in Attic script, seems unnecessary, though
he would surely have had no difficulty in procuring a copy from
Athens. D. Cohen, *Mnemosyne* 1956, 289–95, argues for an alternative,
but not substantially different, restoration of the heading and the
first clause.]

47. 1. ἑκατὸν Ἀθηναῖοι ἔτη: [the explanation of this abnormal word-
order is far from clear. If the intention was to separate Athens from
the three cities with whom the treaty was made, this was not maintained in § 3.]
ἑκάτεροι: see above. (Busolt, however, iii/2. 1228 n. 1, follows Herbst,

55

Hermes xxv (1890), 376, in taking the two parties to be Athens and the Peloponnesian 'Dreibund'—cf. § 2—and ἔκαστοι in § 5 to mean each of the four cities.)

3. ἐπὶ τὴν γῆν: the codd. all have ἐς, which has a good meaning (*invade* the land, cross the frontier), and should perhaps be retained in spite of ἐπὶ τὴν γῆν in the next section. [But in favour of the alteration, the corresponding line (8) of the inscription should be restored ἴοσι ἐπί (Kirchhoff), not ἴοσιν ἐς (*IG* i²), since the text uniformly has no ν ἐφελκυστικόν before a vowel.] See Tod's comment.

4. ⟨μηδεμιᾷ τῶν πόλεων⟩ - - - [ταῖς πόλεσιν]: see app. crit. Clearly either alternative is possible, and both phrases might have been used (cf. § 3 ad fin., § 4 ὑπὸ ἀπασῶν τούτων τῶν πόλεων, § 7, § 12); i.e. official copies may have differed (see above); but it is interesting that some of the *recentiores* have μηδεμιᾷ τῶν πόλεων, more probably taken from an older MS. now lost than a happy emendation.

5. μηδὲ κατὰ θάλασσαν: [see 56. 2, with n.]

6. ἐπὴν ἔλθωσιν - - - καὶ ἀπιοῦσι κατὰ ταὐτά: [the thirty days begin from the arrival of the troops at the city which has summoned them. The city of origin must provision them for the journey as well as for the thirty days; and it must provide for the return journey too (ἀπιοῦσι). Thus the city which needs help gets a full month's service at its ally's expense.]

τρεῖς ὀβολοὺς Αἰγιναίους: [approx. 4·3 Attic obols, an adequate allowance. It would not be fair to compare rates of *pay* (1 Attic dr. to a hoplite, iii. 17. 4, or to a sailor, vi. 31. 3; 3 Attic ob. to a sailor, viii. 45. 2; the same for a juryman, after 425), since this is explicitly a ration-allowance, σῖτον; nor allowances which are supplementary to pay, like the extra ob. given to an Athenian councillor εἰς σίτησιν while his tribe held the prytany, Arist. Ἀθ. π. 62. 2. Demosthenes (iv. 28) reckons 2 Attic ob. a day for food alone, which is on the low side, and he expects the soldiers to supplement this from booty. Closer in time and perhaps in circumstances is X. *HG* v. 2. 21, 3 Aeginetan obols per man per day for those cities which did not wish to take part in the expedition against Olynthos in the late 380s.]

Note that hoplite, light-armed, and archer all get the same grant, [and that nothing is provided for the hoplite's servant, as it is in iii. 17. 4.] Note also that a month is thought to be a reasonable length of time for a campaign (vol. i, *Introduction*, 10–12).

7. ⟨τῇ στρατιᾷ⟩ τὴν ἡγεμονίαν ἐχέτω: a not uncommon privilege. Cf., [e.g., X. *HG* vii. 5. 3; *IG* ii². 112 (= *GHI* 144). 34–5, another case where Athens allied herself with a group of Peloponnesian states. For other possible arrangements, see, e.g., X. *HG* vii. 1. 2, 14. If Greek history does not show frequent disaster arising from such unpractical divisions of command, the reason is that most military operations were carried out either by a single city, or by an alliance whose hegemon (Sparta, Athens, Thebes) exercised command in the field without question.]

Sometimes the privilege was the post of honour in the right wing, as below, 67. 2. [See n. there: it is not clear how command in the field was exercised during the Mantineia campaign.

Here edd. have for once attributed to Thucydides a substantial divergence from the text of the inscription, in form if not in meaning. After [μεταπεμφσαμέ]νε the stone has ΤΕΙΣ, almost inevitably τêι σ[τρατιâι]; and with this addition Thucydides' text exactly fills out the line. Qualms about the dative led Kirchhoff to restore in the inscription not τὲν hεγεμονίαν ἐχέτο but χρέσθο hεγεμονεύοσα, a phrase of identical length. The simpler form of words given by Thucydides should be retained if it is not clearly impossible. Steup thought of an error on the stone, ΤΕΙΣ written for ΤΕΣΣ (i.e. τês σ[τρατιâs); Stahl thought the dative tolerable, citing X. *An.* vii. 1. 40, *HG* iv. 2. 9, and, though these are both instances of an individual leading an army, this seems the right solution.]

ἐν τῇ αὐτῆς: [Duker's αὐτῆς (for the codd. αὐτῇ) is certainly right: the reflexive is not needed, and the stone has no room for hεαυτές, or even ἑαυτές.]

8. κατὰ πόλεις: this is not in contrast with Ἀθ. μὲν ὑπέρ τε σφῶν αὐτῶν καὶ τῶν ξυμμάχων, giving the right to the several 'allies' of Argos, of Elis, and of Mantineia, to a part in the decision that was denied to those of Athens; it is only 'each one of the three cities separately' (see next section, and § 1 n.).

τὸν ἐπιχώριον ὅρκον: [each city is to swear by the god(s) whom it locally regards as providing the most weighty sanction. The content of the oath, which to us might seem the more natural meaning of ὅρκος, is, on the other hand, prescribed by the treaty.]

9. Ἀθήνησι μέν - - - αἱ ἔνδημοι ἀρχαί: [Aristotle, Ἀθ. π. 24. 3, for the period of the empire, distinguishes ἀρχαὶ δ' ἔνδημοι μὲν εἰς ἑπτακοσίους ἄνδρας, ὑπερόριοι δ' εἰς ἑπτακοσίους, where one number is almost certainly wrong and both have been suspected (cf. Wilamowitz, *Aristoteles und Athen*, ii. 202 ff.); Aischines makes the same distinction in i. 19. Most edd., with their eyes on Thucydides' language and especially on i. 70. 4, have understood a distinction between magistrates whose duties kept them at home and those whose service might take them abroad, as the strategoi: cf. Σᴬᴮᶠᴹᶜ² οἱ ἐπιδημοῦντες ἄρχοντες. But on the analogy of other treaties, e.g. iv. 119. 2, we expect here precisely the strategoi, as Gomme objected; and Aristotle's distinction is far more probably between officials whose seat of office was at Athens, including strategoi as well as archons, and those whose post was by its nature wholly abroad, the archons in allied cities, phrourarchs, etc. The number of ἔνδημοι ἀρχαί was certainly large, even if not 700, and Gomme found this

57

a difficulty. But it is already a large undertaking to have 500 councillors swear; a number of fourth-century treaties were to be sworn
to by the whole body of Athenian hippeis, the first being *IG* ii². 16
(= *GHI* 103) of 394; and in *IG* i². 90. 9, of roughly the period of our
treaty, the council is certain, though alternatives could be found
for the restoration τ[ὸς στρατεγὸς καὶ τὰς ἄλλας ἀρχάς].]

ἐν Ἄργει δὲ ἡ βουλή, κ.τ.λ.: [there was more than one change of
system at Argos in the fifth century: W. G. Forrest, *CQ* N.S. x
(1960), 221–9; M. Wörrle, *Untersuchungen zur Verfassungsgeschichte
von Argos im 5. Jahrh. v. Chr.*, Diss. Erlangen [1967]. See also
Busolt–Swoboda, esp. 349 f.; W. Vollgraff, *Mnem.* 1930, 26–8, and
Le décret d'Argos relatif à un pacte entre Knossos et Tylissos (1948),
84 ff. We must be cautious in using material from other periods:
this boule may be very different from that of Hdt. vii. 149. 1 (481)
or *IG* iv. 554 ('*c.* 480?', Jeffery, 169, no. 20). *SEG* xiii. 239 ('*c.* 475?',
Jeffery, 169, no. 22) is the earliest surviving decree of the assembly
called ἀλιαία; the council called βωλά appears with it in ML 42. 45,
from the middle of the century, and both are regular features thereafter. We have no detail of the council's numbers or composition:
it was presumably probouleutic, though the preambles of Argive
decrees record only the decision of the assembly.

The conspicuous absentees from our text are the damiorgoi, who
appear on two early inscriptions, *SEG* xi. 336, 314 (and on the more
fragmentary 302: all '*c.* 575–550?', Jeffery, 168, nos. 7–9). *EM* 265. 46
says that magistrates with this title were special to Argos and
Thessaly, though they certainly occur elsewhere (p. 59). They were
important at Mycenae (*IG* iv. 493: '*c.* 525?', Jeffery, 174, no. 1), and
are found at Epidauros and Troizen. It has been suggested that the
'Eighty' are the damiorgoi, but this is an impossibly high number
for such a magistracy. They are better taken as a smaller council,
possibly a pre-democratic relic like the Athenian Areopagus (Wörrle,
56). They reappear only once, in a third-century decree, Vollgraff,
Mnem. 1916, 221. 29–30, ἐπιμεληθῆμεν δὲ τούτων (sc. the publication
of the decree) τὸν ταμίαν κα[ὶ τὸν]ς ὀγδοήκοντα: which does not help
to determine their main function in 420 or earlier. They could have
been drawn from the four tribes (72. 4 n.), twenty from each.

Epidauros had once councillors called ἄρτυνοι, Plu. *QG* i. 291 d–e;
Hesych. ἄρτυνος· ἄρχων shows that this could also be the title of a
magistrate. *IG* iv. 554 exempts from prosecution, in respect of the
treasures of Athena, [ἐ τὰ]ν βολὰν τ[ὰν] ἀνφ' Ἀρίστονα ἐ τὸν(ς) συναρ-
τύοντας [ἐ ἄ]λλον τινὰ ταμίαν, which is far from clear, but it establishes
the existence of an important board of artynai (or artynoi) at an
early stage of the democracy. Their relation to the council is not
clear: the wording rather suggests that Ariston both presides over
the council and belongs to the artynai, but from ML 45 onwards

the office regularly mentioned with the council is that described by
the formula ἁϝρέτευε βολᾶς, and the disjunction in *IG* iv. 554 con-
vinces Wörrle (73–5) that Ariston was not an artynas; this may
be too rigid, and the procedure of *c.* 480 may differ from that of
c. 450. In the fragment, Vollgraff, *Mnem.* 1919, 160 (also *IG* iv². 1,
p. xix: '*c.* 450–425?', Jeffery, 170, no. 41), the restoration of line 2 as
]ι δ' ἐπ' ἀρ[τ]υ[νόντον is too fragile to build on. The democracy may
have replaced the damiorgoi by artynai, perhaps immediately after
Sepeia. If so, the artynai will be the ἀρχὴ ἡ μεγίστη of 37. 2.

The MSS. reading αἱ ἀρτῦναι has been defended, mainly on grounds
of our ignorance, which is undeniable. ἀρτύνα might be a collective
term for the artynai: the plural would be a general term equivalent
to the ἀρχαί of Athens and Mantineia, and is retained as such by
Steup. Duker's οἱ, which makes this a particular board of magistrates, suits the Argive evidence; and Elis (below) is given no
general ἀρχαί.]

ἐν δὲ Μαντινείᾳ οἱ δημιουργοί, κ.τ.λ.: [there is still less material
for a constitutional history of Mantineia, but synoikismos and democracy will have brought changes. These have been dated around 470
and connected with the synoikismos of Elis (Busolt, iii/1. 118); or
to the late 460s (Fougères, 372 ff.); Bölte, *RE* xiv. 1319–21 (1930),
supposed that territorial expansion (29. 1, 33) and democratic reform
had gone hand in hand in the later years of the Archidamian War.
The basis for this is Aelian's account (*VH* ii. 23) of the boxer and
lawgiver Nikodoros, for whom Diagoras of Melos wrote a poem
(fr. 2 Diehl): see Jacoby, *Abh. Akad. Berl.* 1959, 3. 14, 18–19, with
n. 136. Thucydides accounts adequately for the quarrel with Sparta
without mentioning constitutional change at Mantineia, but his
silence is hardly decisive. There may of course have been more than
one reform. It is natural to refer to this period the agrarian constitution praised by Aristotle, *Pol.* 1318ᵇ23 ff., in which the demos did
not elect the magistrates directly; but though this was some time
before Aristotle wrote (27 ὥσπερ ἐν Μαντινείᾳ ποτ' ἦν) it could be
referred to the time after the dioikismos of *c.* 385.

Damiorgoi as magistrates are not specifically Dorian (Hesych.
s.v. δημιουργός), nor special to Argos and Thessaly (*EM* 265. 46),
but are found elsewhere in the Argolid, in Arkadia, Elis, Achaia,
in several areas of Central Greece, and in Thera and Cyrene: see
K. Murakawa, *Historia* vi (1957), 385 ff. They seem often to be the
chief magistrates, and are often eponymous. For epidemiourgoi, see
i. 56. 2 with n. For Mantineia they are attested by *IG* v. 2. 261. 9
('*c.* 460–450?', Jeffery, 216, no. 28), but we have no details of their
powers, nor about the council. αἱ ἄλλαι ἀρχαί will mean literally all
the other magistrates, cf. n. on Athens above. See also Busolt–
Swoboda, esp. 505 ff.

59

Aristotle, *Pol.* 1310ᵇ21–2, mentions demiourgoi and theoroi as examples of κυρίας ἀρχάς which in old times were held for long terms and sometimes formed the basis for tyranny. Theoroi (except in religious contexts) are less common than damiorgoi, but are found in Aigina and Thasos, and near at hand in Tegea (X. *HG* vi. 5. 7, in 370). See Busolt–Swoboda, 508. We cannot distinguish the functions of theoroi and damiorgoi: polemarchoi are presumably military officers.] ἐν δὲ Ἤλιδι οἱ δημιουργοί, κ.τ.λ.: [historians of Elis have concentrated on Olympia and the number of Hellanodikai at various periods: a slippery basis, since some of the essential figures are corrupt (Paus. v. 9. 5; Σ Pind. *Ol.* iii. 12(22)a: cf. Jacoby on Aristodemos, *FGrHist* 414 F 2), and there is no necessary connection between a change in this number and political change at Elis. Our other main source is the series of documents inscribed in bronze at Olympia, *Olympia*, vol. v (*IvO*), which have been very variously dated. Miss Jeffery (218–21) has provided a more secure basis, and she dates the earliest (boustrophedon) fragment *IvO* 1 to '*c.* 525?', spreading the rest over the fifth century.

Aristotle, *Pol.* 1306ᵃ14 ff., describes a tight earlier oligarchy with 90 gerontes, but it is generally assumed that a democratic revolution took place in the fifth century, though democracy is not explicitly attested for Elis in this book, as it is for Argos and Mantineia at 29. 1. This has often been associated with the synoikismos which Diod. xi. 54. 1 dates to 471/0 (so Busolt, iii/1. 116). A democratic constitution, perhaps in conscious imitation of Kleisthenes of Athens, is suggested by the formula used in *IvO* 7. 4, σὺν βολᾶι ⟨π⟩εντακατίον ἀϝλανέος (cf. Hesych. ἀλανέως· ὁλοσχερῶς. Ταραντῖνοι) καὶ δάμοι πλεθύοντι, and the negative version in *IvO* 3. 8, ἄνευς: βολὰν: καὶ ζᾶμον πλαθύοντα. But Miss Jeffery (218–20) dates the former '*c.* 500?' and the latter '*c.* 475?', with persuasive arguments from the letter-forms; and if this is correct it looks as if democracy was instituted in Elis before the Persian Wars, which is unexpected but not impossible. Elis' loyalty to Sparta was doubtful in 479 (Hdt. ix. 77. 3), and the story of Hegesistratos (ix. 37. 1) may suggest bad relations at an earlier date.

The machinery of government is illustrated in *IvO* 2 ('*c.* 475–450?', Jeffery, ibid.), where certain penalties are to be enforced by ὀρ (= Attic ὃς) μέγιστον τέλος ἔχοι καὶ τοὶ βασιλᾶες, otherwise the Hellanodikas must exact a fine from them; and other penalties are to be dealt with by the damiorgia. For damiorgoi, who are found on other Elean inscriptions, see preceding note. οἱ τὰ τέλη ἔχοντες puzzled commentators by its apparent generality (cf. 27. 2 n.), till this inscription showed that such a periphrasis might in the official language of Elis designate some precise person; it is still not clear why the periphrasis is used, or whether it would always designate the same official(s). The 'Six Hundred' are most likely the council, raised from 500 (above) to 600 in the course of the century, for whatever reason. Thesmophylakes, like nomophylakes, occur in various places: their function was perhaps in origin to preserve the city's law-code, as the thesmothetai of Athens according to Arist. *Ἀθ. π.* 3. 4; the nomophylakes of Paus. vi. 24. 3 (cf. 23. 6), whose duties include instructing the annual Hellanodikai in their business, may be descendants of those called here thesmophylakes.]

10. ἀνανεοῦσθαι δὲ τοὺς ὅρκους: the oaths to this 100-year alliance were to be repeated every four years; but already, before the first four years had elapsed, it was in pieces.

[Gomme commented (cf. p. 55) that 'Athenian delegates must go to the three cities in turn, which suggests a separate treaty (in form) with each; but the delegates of all three come to Athens together, which suggests only one treaty': but the procedure, on either side, seems compatible with either possibility. It is noticeable that no provision is made for renewing the obligations of the three cities to one another, but that had presumably been taken care of in the treaty mentioned, but not exactly dated, in 48. 2.

One might expect (Gomme here refers to Arnold) that the Athenians would go first to Argos, the nearest city, and finish at Elis for the Olympic festival. The names are, however, given in the reverse order, an order not found elsewhere in the text: but cf. vi. 72. 1, with n.: possibly Elis comes first because the ceremony there was felt to be the most important,] cf. § 11, ad fin. The two festivals were separated from each other by two years, as the great Panathenaia were held in the third year of an Olympiad.

11. τὰς δὲ ξυνθήκας, κ.τ.λ.: [the distinction between the agreement and the alliance, etc. is cumbrous, but cf. the oath in § 8, where κατὰ τὰ ξυγκείμενα is apparently needed to define the alliance to which the cities are to swear. There is no need to excise καὶ τῶν ὅρκων with Kirchhoff, though the order σπονδῶν—ξυμμαχίας—ὅρκων would have been more logical.]

Ἀθηναίους μὲν ἐν πόλει: [i.e. on the Akropolis, cf. ii. 15. 6 with n. *IG* i². 86 was in fact found at the bottom of the south slope.]

Ἀργείους δὲ ἐν ἀγορᾷ, κ.τ.λ.: [the temple of Apollo Lykeios, Paus. ii. 19. 3 ff. For its importance, and its position in the agora, cf. Soph. *El.* 6–7 with *Σ*, and Jebb's appendix.]

Μαντινέας δὲ ἐν τοῦ Διὸς τῷ ἱερῷ: [probably the temple of Zeus Soter, Paus. viii. 9. 2: cf. Frazer ad loc., and Bölte, *RE* xiv. 1337.]

[Gomme thought there must be a lacuna, for the record of Elis' obligation to set up a copy. But it was Elis' practice throughout the fifth century (§ 9 n.) to set up bronze plaques at Olympia to record treaties and laws, and it seems unreasonable to expect two such stelai at Olympia.] *IG* i². 86 does not help here.

Pausanias saw this stele over 500 years later: v. 12. 8.

'Ολυμπίοις τοῖς νυνί: see 49. 1. [This suggests that we are now well on in the summer, see 46. 4 n.]

12. ἐὰν δέ τι δοκῇ ἄμεινον εἶναι, κ.τ.λ.: [cf. 18. 11, 23. 6, where the structure of the clauses supports the excision here of δ' after ὅτι.]

On the question of Thucydides' use of documents in his history, and of this one in particular, it is worth while quoting one of the most careful of modern scholars, M. N. Tod. After giving the correct view about the small divergencies between Thucydides' text and *IG* i². 86, 'that verbal divergencies were tolerated even between two copies of a decree engraved for public and permanent exhibition', e.g. *IG* i². 76 (*GHI* 74, ML 73: the Eleusinian copy and the small fragment of the Athenian copy of the decree about first-fruits at Eleusis; cf. iv. 118. 1 n., and Wilhelm, *Oest. Jh.* vi (1903), 14), he continues (p. 178), 'literal accuracy was not demanded of the ancient historian'; and 'in those parts of Thucydides' work which underwent his final revision documents are always summarized and never quoted *in extenso*' (with a reference to J. B. Bury, *The Ancient Greek Historians*, 109, on the 'canon' of 'homogeneity in style'). 'If, then, "we have here (v. 47) material which was to be wrought in during a final revision", it is no wonder if Thucydides at the outset omitted from his copy of the treaty a few words and phrases unnecessary to its sense and changed others into the forms which he uses elsewhere throughout his work.' But, except for changes of θάλαττα to θάλασσα, ἐάν to ἤν and the like, this is just what Thucydides has not done: see, for instance, the repetitions of ἑκατὸν ἔτη §§ 1 and 3, and the names of the cities and αὗται αἱ πόλεις ἅπασαι so frequently repeated. (It is the *modern* historian who omits repetitions —see, e.g., Grote, v. 452, in the course of a narrative more copious than that of Thucydides, and Busolt, iii/2. 1228–9.) And, of course, if we can say at all that some parts of the *History* were finally revised, one of these parts is ii–v. 24 (not just ii–iv), and this includes three documents, as well as a longish quotation from a Homeric hymn, *in extenso*. See Carl Meyer, *Die Urkunden, etc.*, and my review of it in *CR* N.S. vi (1956) 220–1.

For all that, however, we may well ask ourselves whether Thucydides would have kept this particular document in full in a final revision; for it is exceptionally wordy and repetitive: contrast iv. 118–19 and v. 18, which have, by comparison, little 'padding'. He might (or he might not) have reduced it to something like the form of iv. 16 (the terms of the truce at Pylos), which is, though 're-written', yet left in a documentary style, not in what is characteristically Thucydides' own. Chapter 47 is too long for the narrative in which it is imbedded, as we have it.

This brings us to a further problem. It is a commonplace that book v, as we have it, was not finally revised; yet cc. 27–48, the story of the diplomatic interchanges during the eighteen months that succeeded the peace (excluding the episodes, 35. 1 and 39. 1), are detailed, and may easily be as long and as full as ever Thucydides intended. It is perhaps the nature of the events to be narrated, not the moment, or opportunity, of the narration within the composition of the whole work, that has determined the scope and length of this section, just as, to take the obvious examples from this book, the narratives of the Mantineia and Melos campaigns are comparable, in their length and fullness, with similar narratives elsewhere. It is not exact to say that any part of the *History* received Thucydides' *final* revision; we do not know what he might yet have added or altered—he might have wanted more about the internal politics of Athens; but this particular section was, perhaps, as nearly finished as most others (though see below on 48. 2).

[As regards the degree of finish, Gomme has nowhere argued out his thesis that the end of iv and v. 1–24 are as near final revision as the bulk of ii–iv; and many (e.g. Wade-Gery in *OCD*, 'Thucydides') have held that they are not. At the end of iv Brasidas' exploits are finished work, stage (3) of Gomme's classification in 26. 6 n. (pp. 16–17), but there is relatively little about affairs in the south: in v. 25 ff. reference to the north is scrappy, as Gomme has noted. Thucydides might well have wished to redress these proportions; and though 27–48 are full enough he might well have wished them more tidy. It cannot be taken as established that verbatim documents occur in 'finished' parts of the work. (For another view of Carl Meyer's book, see *JHS* lxxvii (1957), 328–9.)

Further, the proposition that 'it is the *modern* historian who omits repetitions' is largely contradicted by what is said of iv. 16 in the next paragraph, and the repetitions and unexplained detail in the verbatim documents remain a serious reason for thinking that Thucydides would not have left them as they stand. If 47 is too long for its narrative context, as I would agree, the same could be said of 77 and 79: see 76. 3 n.]

48. *Corinth Abstains from the New Alliance*

48. 1. ἡ ξυμμαχία: [as at 27. 1, Gomme considered the possibility of retaining the MSS. reading, αἱ ξυμμαχίαι (Graves), and referred to 47. 1 n. for the possibility that there were, formally, not one but three alliances. The singular in 46. 5 is against this, and cf. 78, 80. 1.]

2. γενομένης πρὸ τούτου: this treaty, one of full alliance between the three cities which Corinth had refused to join, content as she was with the ἐπιμαχία (ὥστε τῇ ἀλλήλων ἐπιμαχεῖν, 27. 2), has not been

expressly mentioned before, but it is implied by the language of
44. 2, 46. 5, the joint action of the three cities. Similarly the absence
of Corinth from these negotiations at Athens implies that her treaty
with 'Argos and her allies' had been an ἐπιμαχία only. (The general
term, ξυμμαχία, of course includes the other.) Such unevennesses of
narrative are not, of course, unknown in ii–v. 24.

3. πρὸς τοὺς Λακεδαιμονίους: [the apparently fluctuating policy of
Corinth is consistent enough, if we suppose that the object of her
leaders was not to do damage to Sparta, but to change the foreign
policy which had led to the peace (36. 1 n.); as the chances of this
increase, she turns back towards her old alliance.]

49–50. 4. *The Olympic Festival of* 420 B.C.

49. 1. παγκράτιον: see iii. 8. 1 n. Diodoros xii. 77. 1 records that
Hyperbios of Syracuse won the stadion. [See also Jacoby's introduction to the historians of Elis and Olympia, *FGrHist* IIIb. 222–4,
esp. nn. 11, 30. He assumes, reasonably enough, that the custom of
identifying Olympiads from the winner of the stadion dates from
the publication of Hippias' list; the date of that is not exactly
known, but we may fairly take it to be later than the writing of this
passage. Gomme (ms.) thought that this passage and iii. 8. 1 suggested that Thucydides had seen a list of some kind.

For Androsthenes son of Lochaios the Mainalian (Gomme, ms.,
noted that he is here called Ἀρκάς not Μαινάλιος), who twice won the
pankration and dedicated a statue made by his countryman Niko-
damos, see Paus. vi. 6. 1.]

τὸ πρῶτον: his second victory was, in the nature of things, probably
in 416. More important, Thucydides could not have written the words
before 416 at the earliest.

εἴρχθησαν: i.e. their official *theoria* was not admitted, nor any Lacedaemonian competitor for the games; but individuals might be
present as spectators (50. 4). It might indeed have been difficult to
keep them out.

ἐν τῷ Ὀλυμπιακῷ νόμῳ: the law was that of the panhellenic sanctuary; the Eleans administered it. The state of Elis had 'won a
verdict of condemnation of Sparta from the court' (κατεδικάσαντο,
middle); the court was composed of Eleans, but this was according
to the custom of all Greece and by general consent. [The meaning
of ἐν τῷ - - - νόμῳ does not seem to be different from that of the
commoner κατὰ τὸν νόμον: cf. i. 77. 1.]

⟨ἐς⟩ σφᾶς: [Classen attempted to justify σφᾶς as referring to the
Spartans, with no reflexive sense, but this was rightly rejected by
Steup. ⟨ἐς⟩ σφᾶς (Shilleto) or σφίσιν (Stahl) enable us to refer it to the

Eleans: the latter would be the more normal with ἐπενεγκεῖν, and the same change is needed at vi. 61. 5 where ἐς σφᾶς would not be possible. σφῶν (Göller) is a good deal more awkward.]

Φύρκον τε τεῖχος: clearly in Lepreatis, and in that half of it which had come to Elis by the pact made before the Peloponnesian War began, 31. 2; but its site is unknown. [It is natural to assume that Sparta's two offences are connected; and that the attack on Phyrkos also took place during the truce, in spite of the placing of the words ἐν ταῖς Ὀλυμπιακαῖς σπονδαῖς. The sending of the troops is the main charge in § 2 and § 4, and must be the reference of λαθεῖν in § 3; the attack is treated throughout as a subsidiary charge, and is only glanced at again in § 4.

Hesych. φύρκος· τεῖχος is not a mere reflection of this passage, but a genuine dialect word: cf. the further entries φούρκορ, φυρκηλίτοι. This does not of course prevent Phyrkos from being a proper name here.]

αὐτῶν ὁπλίτας: whether αὐτῶν is possessive, to be taken with Lepreon, and so the Eleans, or partitive with ὁπλίτας and so the Lacedaemonians, is uncertain; probably the former, which gives it more point. [It is hard indeed to see what point it has if it refers to the Spartans: if to the Eleans, it is probably necessary to add ⟨ὅν⟩ after αὐτῶν.]

Classen's proposal to read ⟨χιλίους⟩ before ὁπλίτας, in order to explain at once δισχίλιαι - - - δύο μναῖ, seems right.

δύο μναῖ: there is some evidence that this was the usual figure, at least in the Peloponnese, for a hoplite's ransom who had been made prisoner-of-war (Hdt. vi. 79. 1: see n. on iii. 70. 1).

2. μὴ ἐπηγγέλθαι πω: again a question of dates is involved, as in the case of Skione, iv. 122; but here, presumably, Elis by her reply meant, 'even if our heralds had not reached Sparta when your hoplites left, you could have discovered on reaching the boundaries of Lepreon that the truce had been announced in Elis'.

3. παρ' αὐτοῖς: παρ' αὐτοῖς seems clearly right. [Most edd. print it without comment.]

4. καὶ ὅπλα - - - ἐπενεγκεῖν: [the Spartan argument is clear enough to this point—if the Eleans thought the Spartans were already in the wrong, there was no point in proclaiming the truce at Sparta: but they had done this, showing that they did not think Sparta in the wrong. Gomme asked why the Spartans did not add, 'and by our decision of last year (31. 4), Lepreon is an autonomous state (and our troops are not invading it, but were invited)'. The Spartan claim, ὡς οὐκ ἀδικοῦσι (§ 5), in effect covers this, and deals with the major charge of sending troops into Lepreon during the truce (on which alone the fine is calculated, § 1). ὅπλα - - - ἐπενεγκεῖν clearly echoes the phrase used in § 1 of the attack on Phyrkos, the subsidiary offence, and it would make sense if the Spartans here said, 'and in fact we are no longer attacking you anywhere'. The change of subject is abrupt (though not unparalleled, cf. nn. to vi. 18. 6, 86. 2). The alternative is even less attractive, to continue the Eleans as the subject of the infinitive. The Spartans would then be arguing that Elis by not counter-attacking implicitly admitted the Spartans' right: but the ἔτι would imply that the Eleans had in fact previously counter-attacked somewhere, whereas there is no suggestion in the text that they had done anything of the kind, and § 3 ἡσυχαζόν-των σφῶν almost denies that they had. (The choice of the aorist ἐπενεγκεῖν, where one might have expected ἐπιφέρειν, is probably determined by the echo of § 1; in § 4 it must be translated as a pluperfect.)

The matter has not been set out very clearly.]

5. τοῦ αὐτοῦ λόγου εἴχοντο: this sophistic arguing between two grave Peloponnesian states is very like what we are told to expect in Athens, and to the dispute between the Athenian and Boeotian delegates after Delion, iv. 97–9.

50. 2. πλὴν Λεπρεατῶν: presumably because they had invited, or at least accepted, Lacedaemonian armed assistance.

3. ἐν Ἁρπίνῃ: Michaelis's correction of the MSS. Ἄργει has been accepted by all modern editors. It does not seem to me certain: ὑπέμενον τὴν ἑορτήν (if this is said of the Athenian cavalry only) seems to suit a distant place better: [(ms.) 'they were waiting for the end of the festival?'] See also Graves. [If we keep Ἄργει, the relative clause refers only to the Athenians, for the others must be west of Argos. ἦλθον δὲ αὐτοῖς presumably means that they went to Olympia or near it: it must then mean something different for the Athenians, who would be guarding Argos (as the Argives guarded Mantineia in 421, 33. 2) or ready to threaten a Spartan force if it moved out. With Ἁρπίνῃ, the relative clause can refer to all contingents, and the sentence is easier and more informative.]

Harpine was in the Alpheios valley, one of the eight towns of the Pisatis (i.e. in the Elean perioikis), upstream and not far from Olympia (Str. viii. 3. 32, 357).

These armed forces who move (if Harpine is right) a good deal nearer to Olympia than were the Spartans in Lepreatis, were, it must be supposed, not breaking the truce because they had been invited by the Eleans, who administered the festival, 'in order to prevent Sparta from further violation of it'.

4. Λίχας: a prominent figure, first mentioned in 22. 2: see n. there. ῥαβδούχων: [attendants to the authorities (here the Hellanodikai), who enforce discipline: cf. Ar. *Pax* 734; and there is perhaps a hint of discipline in Pl. *Prt.* 338 a. Later the standard translation of the Latin *lictor*.]

πληγὰς ἔλαβεν: [X. *HG* iii. 2. 21, followed by Paus. vi. 2. 2, speaks of whipping—μαστιγοῦντες αὐτόν, ἄνδρα γέροντα, ἐξήλασαν—which would increase the fear of Spartan intervention, especially if Xenophon means that he was a member of the gerousia. (If so, he was already over 60 in 420, and probably in his seventies when he went to Ionia in winter 412/11, viii. 39. 2, where he died soon afterwards νόσῳ, 84. 5.)]

Βοιωτῶν δημοσίου: [the certain instances of a state stable are Argive: *POxy* ii. 222 (*FGrHist* 415). 6, 31, Isoc. xvi. 1 (Plu. *Alc.* 12. 3, etc.); less certain, the Eleans of Dyspontion in 672, Phlegon, *FGrHist* 257 F 6 (Jacoby assumes a lacuna). Here we have a fiction, and cannot firmly deduce that the Boeotian League maintained such a stable: but for the fiction to be plausible, the practice must have been more widespread than the instances suggest. X. *HG* iii. 2. 21 has παραδόντος Θηβαίοις (but he sometimes has 'Thebes' where he should have 'Boeotia', e.g. *HG* iii. 5 *passim*): Paus. vi. 2. 3 cites Θηβαίων τὸν δῆμον from his 'Elean records': Thucydides may have made a mistake in writing Βοιωτῶν.]

προελθών - - - ἡνίοχον: [this passage is cited by Suda s.v. ἀγών, with *Od.* viii. 200, as an instance of ἀγών used to designate a place, τὸν τόπον ἐν ᾧ ἀγωνίζονται.]

ἡσύχασάν τε: Graves notes that the aorist, 'became quiet', or 'were pacified', suggests that they had actually made some threatening movement. The arrival of troops in Lepreatis was recent enough perhaps to justify this tense. I agree with those who take αὐτοῖς in the next clause to refer to Sparta.

It was not till 402 B.C. that the Spartans took their revenge on Elis, X. *HG* iii. 2. 21–3. [This slight was then remembered among other grievances; cf. Diod. xiv. 17. 4–12, 34. 1; and Paus. iii. 8. 3, who confusingly gives his account of this war before telling us about Agis' occupation of Dekeleia in 413. For the date of the Elean war see Beloch, i². 2. 185 f., iii². 1. 19 with n. 1.]

As Grote points out, v. 453, this was the first Olympic festival since the Peace of Nikias, by which among other things free access, ἰέναι ἀδεῶς, was guaranteed to all Greeks to the panhellenic shrines (18. 2); this was not a good omen for the future, and in fact δέος ἐγένετο τῇ πανηγύρει μέγα μὴ ξὺν ὅπλοις, κ.τ.λ.

50. 5. *Conference at Corinth*

5. δεησόμενοι αὐτῶν, κ.τ.λ.: [for the attitude of Corinth see c. 48, with nn.] The earthquake may only have served as an excuse for ending a seemingly endless conference.

51–52. 1. *Fighting at Herakleia Trachinia: the Boeotians Take Possession*

51. 1. Ἡρακλεώταις τοῖς ἐν Τραχῖνι: for Herakleia in Trachis, and its neighbours, see iii. 92–3 (foundation of the colony in 426 and brief summary of its later history).

[The Ainianes in historical times occupied the valley of the Spercheios, inland from the Malians (Scyl. 62), north and west of Oita. The Dolopes were still further inland, the extreme corner of Phthia given by Peleus to Phoinix (*Il.* ix. 484), up against Pindos (Str. ix. 5. 3, 430); they extended west of this, to the upper Acheloos, Thuc. ii. 102. 2, and there was a detachment on Skyros, i. 98. 2. For the Malians, on whose land Herakleia stood, see iii. 92. 2: Thucydides does not say whether the Trachinioi were involved in the present trouble, but they were the victims of a later Spartan purge *c.* 399 (Diod. xiv. 38. 4–5, cf. 82. 7, Polyaen. ii. 21). All three tribes were members of the Delphian amphiktiony, and in some degree subject to the Thessalians. One might have expected to hear also of the Oitaioi, the original oppressors of Trachis (iii. 92. 2), who bore the main brunt of Agis' attack in winter 413/12, viii. 3. 1.] On Θεσσαλῶν τινάς, see n. on αἴτιον δὲ ἦν, κ.τ.λ., iii. 93. 2, ad fin.

2. Ξενάρης ὁ Κνίδιος: whether this 'son of Knidis' was the same as the Xenares who has been mentioned for his anti-Athenian activities when ephor in 421/20 (36. 1, etc.), we do not know. [It is likely enough, and the fact that his patronymic is given here, but not in the earlier passages, must not be taken as an indication that this is a new character: cf. G. T. Griffith, *PCPhS* N.S. vii (1961) 21–33.]

YEAR 13: 419–418 B.C. (CC. 52–56)

52. 1. παρέλαβον: not κατέλαβον, but in the friendliest manner. [Diod. xii. 77. 4 says the Herakleotai sent for help, and the Thebans sent them 1,000 chosen hoplites. The concrete detail suggests a non-Thucydidean source, rather than mere muddle: cf. xii. 70. 1, 5, which also suggest that Ephoros had non-Thucydidean sources for Boeotia; *FGrHist* 70 T 17, and Jacoby's introduction, IIc, p. 31.]

This is another case in which an episode is carefully dated between one year and the next (vol. iii, 703–4).

Ἀγησιππίδαν: [very possibly the same as the commander sent to Epidauros at the beginning of the next winter, 56. 1. (Alkidas, iii. 92. 5, is another example of a Spartan officer who continued to be employed in spite of what looks like incompetence.)]

ὡς οὐ καλῶς ἄρχοντα: so iii. 93. 2.

68

δείσαντες - - - μή - - - Ἀθηναῖοι λάβωσιν: [this may seem thin, but the Boeotians had suffered much from Athenian enterprise in the last forty years, and may genuinely have feared that Athens would intervene now that Herakleia was weakened by defeat.] We are expressly told (iii. 93. 1) that nothing came of the expected threat to the Athenian interests in Euboea: [but the foundation had been made in part as a move against Athens, and the threat might be renewed.

The anger of the Spartans is understandable, even if we accept Diodoros' story. Herakleia must have been in Spartan hands again, and the Boeotians were once more on good terms with Sparta, by winter 413/12 when Agis made his expedition to the north (viii. 3. 1): but Thucydides tells us nothing about Herakleia in the interval.]

52. 2. *Alkibiades with an Allied Force in the Peloponnese*

2. στρατηγὸς ὤν: the first mention of Alkibiades as strategos in Thucydides. [At 54. 2 we are still in the month before Karneios, so early in the Attic year, probably Hekatombaion (54. 2 n.): Alkibiades' excursion belongs to the spring, before the usual campaigning season. He was thus general for 420/19. It can hardly be true that he was elected immediately before the conclusion of the alliance of c. 47, as Plutarch says (p. 52, and 46. 4 n.): but he may have entered on office at that point.]

μετ' ὀλίγων Ἀθηναίων ὁπλιτῶν: Isokrates xvi (περὶ τοῦ ζεύγους). 15 says that Alkibiades διακοσίους ὁπλίτας ἔχων τὰς μεγίστας πόλεις τῶν ἐν Πελοποννήσῳ Λακεδαιμονίων μὲν ἀπέστησεν, ὑμῖν δὲ συμμάχους ἐποίησε. This may refer, very inaccurately (Argos, Mantineia, and Elis are presumably the cities), to this expedition; and 200 may be the right figure for the few Athenian hoplites of Thucydides.

περὶ τὴν ξυμμαχίαν: [Steup put a comma after ξυγκαθίστη and attached these words to διαπορευόμενος, mainly because Patrai was not a member of the alliance and its walls were therefore not allied business. But clearly any arrangement that could be made with Patrai was an advantage to the allies; and Steup's awkward punctuation does not produce good sense even from his point of view. περί here refers to 'behaviour towards', as in, e.g., κακουργεῖν περὶ τοὺς γονέας. It would perhaps be an improvement to insert ⟨τά⟩ before περί.]

διαπορευόμενος Πελοπόννησον τῇ στρατιᾷ: how did he go? By sea, with his small Athenian force, as far as Argos (cf. 53, below), thence to Mantineia, to Elis, and, continuing by land, through Dyme in western Achaia to Patrai; or, perhaps, by the mountainous country of north Arkadia from Mantineia, and descending from there (by the road from the modern Kalávryta?) to Patrai direct.

Πατρέας: the modern Patras, at this time apparently occupying only the higher ground away from the sea, on the top of which are the remains of a Frankish castle (see [Leake, ii. 132, Ernst Meyer, *RE* xviii. 4. 2197]). The town became more important in Roman times (hence perhaps the mention in Paus. vii. 6. 4), with the increase of traffic, political as well as commercial, between Italy and the east, as it also revived with the Frankish conquest of the Peloponnese in the Middle Ages.

The Achaioi were nominally allies of Sparta, ii. 9. 2, 90. 1. [But cf. 82. 1 below, and Paus. loc. cit. On this, and on the expedition as a whole, see J. K. Anderson, *BSA* xlix (1954), 84.]

τείχη καθεῖναι - - - ἐς θάλασσαν: for the Athenian policy, see i. 103. 4 (Megara), 107. 1 (Athens and Peiraieus), and below, v. 82. 5 (Argos). καὶ αὐτὸς ἕτερον - - - ἐπὶ τῷ 'Ρίῳ: i.e. it was intended to be an Athenian (not an Achaian) station on the south coast of the narrow entrance to the Gulf of Corinth, with Naupaktos not far away on the opposite shore. See ii. 86. 3 n. The two would not 'completely command the entrance', as is often asserted;[1] but they would be a considerable hindrance to Corinth and Sikyon; see, e.g., ii. 90. 1–4 and 92. 6, the Peloponnesian approach to Naupaktos along the Achaian shore and the retreat to Corinth, before and after the second battle off Naupaktos. Also vii. 34.

Corinth acts directly against Argos and her allies on this occasion; but there was no fighting—her protest and threatened opposition were sufficient to deter Alkibiades.

Plutarch, *Alc.* 15. 6, who (like Isokrates, above) confuses the events of these years, quotes a supposed quip of Alkibiades in answer to a man of Patrai who feared the power of Athens.

For all these exaggerations, it was a grandiose scheme for an Athenian general at the head of a mainly Peloponnesian army to march through the Peloponnese, cocking a snook at Sparta when her reputation was at its lowest. Its daring, such as it was, its theatricality, and its small practical value, were alike characteristic of Alkibiades.

(ms.) Thucydides does not make anything like so much of Alkibiades' 'triumphant' march through Peloponnese ('triumphant' is my word, not his), as a mark of Spartan depression (28. 2), as he does of the consequences of Pylos and Kythera, iv. 55–6. Because book v is unfinished? or because he thought Alkibiades' success superficial, and shown to be so by Mantineia? The success of Pylos did not *last* longer—Brasidas in Thrace succeeded that, as Mantineia this; but he may well have thought that it went deeper, certainly that it

---

[1] [Not, indeed, in the manner of a modern fort with artillery; but when both naval stations were occupied, they could exercise so much control that 'command' is not a great exaggeration.]

impressed men's minds more, because it was the first time since men could remember that Sparta was thus cowed: Alkibiades was therefore only a flash in the pan at the end of this grey period of Spartan history. We need not agree with him if we do not want to; but the playing-down of Alkibiades may be deliberate, may (that is) be the result of deliberate judgement, not of his never having 'written up' book v.

οἷς ἦν ἐν βλάβῃ τειχισθέν: [edd. compare i. 100. 3, οἷς πολέμιον ἦν τὸ χωρίον κτιζόμενον: which is different to the extent that the building there was actually under way, whereas here τειχισθέν refers to the fort Alkibiades was only contemplating. The different tense is no great matter, for in either case the objection is to the completed work, if it is completed. This instance does not fit comfortably into the categories given by Kühner–Gerth, i. 215–16, for the omission of ἄν with an indicative; but it is not quite a conditional—'the fortification fell within the sphere of βλάβη'.]

53–56. *War between Argos and Epidauros*

53. προφάσει μέν: a clear case in which πρόφασις is the 'occasion' of an action, as well as the 'excuse', and this πρόφασις is referred to as τῆς αἰτίας ('the cause of complaint') in the second part of the sentence. τοῦ Ἀπόλλωνος τοῦ Πυθαέως: [see Bacchylides' paian, as now printed in Snell's 1961 (8th) edn., fr. 4; and W. S. Barrett, *Hermes* lxxxii (1954), 421–44, who has put the interpretation on a much more secure basis. Two points are clear from Thucydides: (*a*) there was a single shrine which could be called 'the' shrine of Apollo Pythaieus (for the spelling see Barrett, 434), and the reader would know which was meant; (*b*) if the Argives were κυριώτατοι τοῦ ἱεροῦ, others had some share in it. Barrett argues that the shrine was the one at Asine (Paus. ii. 36. 5, already picked out by Poppo as the most probable), which was spared when the Argives destroyed Asine at the end of the eighth century and maintained by them thereafter; and not the one on the way up to the Larisa at Argos (Paus. ii. 24. 1). It has often been supposed, following K. O. Müller, that Argos' religious rights in the NE. Peloponnese were based on this shrine at Argos and exemplified in our passage; but though the rights were real (Hdt. vi. 92. 1–2) there is no strong reason to connect them with this cult, and even Telesilla's assertion that Pythaieus first appeared at Argos (Paus. ii. 35. 2) may merely reflect later Argive pretensions. The Asinaians were Dryopes (a people who were thought to have left the Parnassos area when the Dorians entered it, Hdt. viii. 43, 73. 2), and specially proud of their origin (Paus. iv. 34. 9–11); if the cult was originally theirs it was specifically not Dorian, though it was later adopted at Sparta (Paus. iii. 10. 8, 11. 9) as well as at Argos.]

ὑπὲρ βοταμίων: not yet explained, either βοτάμια or the meaning here of ὑπέρ.

[Commentators have mostly thought in terms of dues arising from pasture on land belonging to the god. (But Stahl's emendation βοτανῶν was unwise, for in such a context an otherwise unknown word from a local religious vocabulary is only too likely.) The difficulty of this type of explanation is that ὑπέρ in connection with a sacrifice should mean 'on behalf of' some person(s) or cause, i.e. 'in order to make the god well-disposed towards' the object of the preposition. It is far from easy to construct anything suitable out of βοταμίων, and we may have to allow a weaker sense of ὑπέρ, 'on account of'. If so, serious consideration should be given to the idea which Wilamowitz threw off, without argument, in *Hermes* xxxvii (1902), 307 (= *Kl. Schr.* iv. 149), that this was 'a sacrifice of atonement for the castration of bulls': this at least gives a tolerable etymology (the original form was presumably βου- or βω-, written by Thucydides as *BO-*, and left so because it was not understood), and Gomme (ms.) seemed to favour it.]

τῆς τε Κορίνθου ἕνεκα ἡσυχίας: ['to keep Corinth quiet', a fairly bold phrase; the following acc.+fut. inf. is in effect a transition to *oratio obliqua*—for the combination of a statement of purpose and a statement of prospective fact, cf. vi. 99. 2 with n. There is no doubt, in general, what is meant, but it is another matter what practical steps the Athenians envisaged with respect to Corinth. Though the mountains are not high, the country between Epidauros and Corinth is tangled and broken, and a military force operating against Corinth would land directly on the Corinthian coast, as Nikias in 425 (iv. 42. 2), rather than march from Epidauros.

Thucydides' comparative readiness to explain Athenian policy here is in marked contrast with his silence about the strategic purpose of the Athenian attack on Epidauros in 430 (ii. 56. 4), a silence which drew no comment from Gomme. At that time Argos was neutral, and in treaty with Sparta, though it may have been hoped that Argos could be drawn into the war if Athens had acquired Epidauros. As regards Corinth, the operations of the First Peloponnesian War show Corinth's interest at that time in the eastern Argolid. (It would have been easier to appreciate this if i. 105 had opened less abruptly: we want to know why the Athenians landed at Halieis, whether the Corinthians and Epidaurians marched out only when they heard of the landing—a long and awkward march, especially for the Corinthians—or were there already; and, if the latter, why.) The movement of Corinthian ships out of the Saronic Gulf, in wartime, must always have been risky after the Athenian capture of Aigina, and the capture of Epidauros (or Methana) would not make matters appreciably worse. But Corinth and Epidauros were old friends, and the loss of Epidauros would inevitably be felt as a severe blow by Corinth. It does not look as if Athens on her side had much to fear from Corinth, as things were: but cf. 115. 3 below, with n.

Thucydides' reticence in ii. 56 is a symptom of that polarization into speeches and bare record of fact which characterizes ii–iv (as a general rule, not completely), but not to the same degree vi–vii. Cf. Wade-Gery in *OCD* 903: many readers feel 'that the narrative of the 10 years is a compromise between the methods of tragedy and of a laboratory notebook, so that between the profoundest issues and the particular detail the middle ranges (e.g. an intelligible account of strategy) are neglected'. When he wrote book v, Thucydides had a clearer idea what needed communicating, and how to do it. (The proportions of the excursus, i. 98–117, whenever it was written, are harder to excuse: we need not wholly regret i. 106, but it compares oddly with the dismissal of the battle of the Eurymedon in four lines.)]

καὶ ἐκ τῆς Αἰγίνης, κ.τ.λ.: cf. nn. on ii. 27. 1 and 56. 4. [The only easy road out of Epidauros is the low pass which leads, past the Asklepieion, towards Argos. Otherwise, the external communications of this region were all by sea till very recent times.]

Σκύλλαιον: [the SE. promontory of the peninsula (Str. viii. 6. 1, 368), in the territory of Hermione (ibid. 13, 373).]

54. 1. ἐς Λεῦκτρα: for Lykaion in W. Arkadia, see 16. 3 n. [This general indication of their direction shows that they went by the upper Eurotas valley and over the watershed towards the later Megalopolis: for this route see 64. 3 n., and for the topography of the region in which Leuktra must lie, 33. 1 n.

Paus. viii. 27. 4 gives Leuktron among the communities which took part in the foundation of Megalopolis; X. *HG* vi. 5. 24, on Epameinondas' invasion of winter 370/69, mentions a Spartan force ἐπὶ Λεύκτρῳ ὑπὲρ τῆς Μαλεάτιδος. The precise site has not been found, but was very probably near the modern Leondári: see Leake, ii. 322–3; Bölte, *RE* xiv. 867–9 (Malea 4).]

ᾔδει δὲ οὐδείς, κ.τ.λ.: [this implies that the initial move, to a point above the Alpheios somewhere south of Megalopolis, did not make it clear that the army would continue in the same direction, towards Elis; Spartan practice left open the possibility that it would turn east towards Tegea or Mantineia (64. 3 n.).]

Edd. think that αἱ πόλεις are those of the Lakonian perioikis, as the others, members of the Peloponnesian League, are specifically mentioned in the next sentence; but it is probable that καὶ οἱ ξύμμαχοι αὐτῶν has dropped out of the text after πανδημεί above. [Gomme did not pursue this further: the insertion he proposes would confuse the

reference of ἑαυτῶν, and Σ^recc· πόλεις· αἱ Λακωνικαί makes it unlikely
that the words he desiderated were in the text when this scholion
was first formulated. But Gomme's interpretation is probably right
even if we refrain from making the insertion. αἱ πόλεις ἐξ ὧν ἐπέμφθησαν
is appropriate for members of the league sending their separate contingents, less so for the perioikic towns (we are lamentably ignorant of
the mechanism for calling up the perioikoi, but it is clear that the men
were individually integrated into the framework of the Spartan army,
not organized in city contingents) ; and it is not obviously noteworthy
that the perioikic cities should not have been told the destination.

The situation is as obscure as the procedure. (a) If no one knew
the destination, this expedition had not been decreed in open assembly but was ordered out by executive action. (This was not
necessarily, or even probably, Agis' own intervention: Hdt. vi. 56,
relied on by Gomme and others, cannot mean that the king had a
right to 'declare' war on any land he chose, for Herodotos is speaking
of his own time, when such decisions were conspicuously taken by
the assembly. The ephors, who controlled the actual call-up of an
army, may have been responsible, or ephors and gerousia: cf.
Ehrenberg Stud. 11.) Such executive action is on the face of it more
likely when the state is formally at war; but we have not been told
that Sparta was so. (b) Once the league was formally at war, Sparta
might summon her allies at will, but we have not been told of any
conference to discuss war. The answer is, no doubt, that the Argive
threat to Epidauros was felt to be a sufficient *casus foederis*—cf.
§ 4, the Epidaurian summons to 'the allies'—and that the Spartan
authorities saw some advantage in a quick stroke against Argos, not
stopping to complete the formal procedures.]

2. τὰ διαβατήρια θυομένοις: see X. *Lac. Pol.* 13. 2–5. [Though
other Greeks were very ready to sacrifice before an important
military decision, the term διαβατήρια is attested (before the Roman
period) only for Sparta. Cf. Popp, 42–6, who argues forcefully that, in
view of the other evidence on Sparta, genuine religious feeling is
a more probable cause for the Spartan withdrawal, here and at 55. 3,
than the military or political considerations proposed by some
modern historians.]

Καρνεῖος δ' ἦν μήν: the month which in more than one Dorian city
was sacred, and during which military campaigns, or their initiation,
were avoided. It corresponded generally [that is, provided the
correspondence was not thrown out by divergent intercalation] with
the Attic Metageitnion, the second month of the Attic year (Plu.
Nic. 28. 2) and so, very roughly, with August.

[Gomme wished to insert ⟨μῆνα⟩ after μέλλοντα, but did not argue
this: cf. Σ^recc· μετὰ τὸν μέλλοντα· μῆνα δηλονότι, and the late instances
of τὸ μέλλον sc. ἔτος given by LSJ, μέλλω IV.]

3. ἄγοντες τὴν ἡμέραν ταύτην πάντα τὸν χρόνον: 'keeping this day, the 26th or 27th of the month, throughout', so that the advent of the sacred month Karneios was postponed, as Grote (v. 466 n.) and Madvig first explained this. (The explanation, among other advantages, also accounts for the mention of the date by the lunar calendar (cf. n. on διελέλυντο μέχρι Πυθίων, v. 1): it was not only four days before the beginning of Karneios, but it was remembered because, during the whole time of the invasion, days were intercalated by naming each successive one the 27th.)

All that this petty device achieved was to satisfy the piety of the *Argives*; if Corinth and Phleious would not move during Karneios, they were inhibited anyhow. [More was achieved by the opposite procedure, which according to Xenophon (*HG* iv. 7. 2–3, v. 1. 29) the Argives employed in the Corinthian War, that is, to juggle with the months so as to proclaim a sacred truce every time the Spartans invaded the Argolid; till Agesipolis obtained a ruling at Olympia and Delphi that he need not be bound by such tricks.] As Grote says, where intercalation of months was irregular and intercalation of days sometimes necessary, in order to preserve the proper relation of month and moon, and the moon's cycle with the sun (see vol. iii. 713–15), it would be, comparatively, easy to intercalate dishonestly. Yet we hear very little of such juggling, any more than of false διοσημίαι, in Greek history, before the times when foreign monarchs had to be placated and flattered; and the proverb that Grote quotes from Hesychios at the end of his footnote, ἐν Κέῳ τίς ἡμέρα; ἐπὶ τῶν οὐκ εὐγνώστων· οὐδεὶς γὰρ οἶδεν ἐν Κέῳ τίς ἡμέρα, ὅτι οὐχ ἑστᾶσιν αἱ ἡμέραι, ἀλλ᾽ ὡς ἕκαστοι (ἕκασται, the four cities of Keos?) θέλουσιν ἄγουσιν [see Krates fr. 29], is itself evidence for regularity elsewhere. [See also pp. 264 ff. below.]

4. τοὺς ξυμμάχους ἐπεκαλοῦντο: [in the absence of any other indication, we must take these to be the other members of the Peloponnesian League, who could be called out directly since an attack on a member was already in progress. Cf. § 1 n.]

ὧν τινες οἱ μέν, κ.τ.λ.: [from 55. 1 it is clear that some allies did come to the help of Epidauros, in spite of the month, and Steup thought that this should be mentioned in the text, before Thucydides proceeds to make distinctions among those who did not come; but he was mainly concerned here with the effect of the Argive device, and the text is probably in order.]

55. 1. ἀπὸ τῶν πόλεων: [this in itself unrevealing phrase ought to be made intelligible by its context. Since the conference met in Mantineia and was summoned by Athens, one expects that the 'cities' will be those of their alliance; and the presence of the Corinthians has been explained (e.g. Busolt, iii/2. 1235 n. 1) by supposing an attempt to bring them into the alliance. 55. 1 περὶ εἰρήνης shows that the object, and presumably the membership, of the conference was wider. Steup thought that a definition of the 'cities' and a statement of purpose had fallen out of the text: but the vagueness may be due to a lack of interest in the ostensible aims of the meeting (see next n.). Thucydides probably had the allies of Epidauros (54. 4) still in mind, and did not realize that the reader's attention was not still directed towards them.]

Ἀθηναίων παρακαλεσάντων: one supposes that Nikias had initiated this pacific and apparently moderate move by Athens, and that it was directly contrary to Alkibiades' plans (53). Thucydides was not in Athens, and was perhaps unable to get information direct from there (cf. below, 56. 3); but this seems a singular example of reticence.

[The reticence is undeniable, and it is impossible to believe that Thucydides had no more information than the one detail he gives. The answer is, presumably, that he thought this inconclusive meeting unimportant, except as a temporary interruption to the war in Epidauros: note that he tells us nothing about the main business of the conference of 36. 1 above. Without knowing what was proposed and discussed, it is not even possible to be sure that the intention was pacific. The first half of the fourth century saw numerous conferences about κοινὴ εἰρήνη, but it was not the innocent peace-loving states that summoned them, rather the leading state of the day playing for its own ambitious purposes on Greek love of peace and weariness with war. Here, if the Athenians carried on in the manner of 46. 2–3, the conference would serve to advertise their complaints against Sparta and prepare for the declaration, which they made during the winter at Alkibiades' instigation, that the Spartans had broken their oaths (56. 3). In other words, the invitation to this conference may as easily be due to Alkibiades as to the pacific Nikias.]

Εὐφαμίδας ὁ Κορίνθιος: [a Εὐφαμίδας Ἀριστωνύμου swore on behalf of Corinth to the truce of 423, iv. 119. 2.]

ἀφ' ἑκατέρων: g's reading, ἐφ' ἑκατέρων, adopted by Stahl and Steup, seems preferable: 'to go to each side and end the hostilities'. [Gomme did not argue this further, and Steup's reasons are less than adequate: there is no difficulty in dividing the conference, like the combatants, into two sides and saying that delegates were to go 'from each side'.]

3. ἐς Καρύας: on the more direct road to Arkadia and thence to the Argolid. See Bursian, ii. 118; [and 64. 3 n. below. Paus. iii. 10. 7, going in the opposite direction, says it was to the right (i.e. to the west) of the road, before you came to Sellasia. This time there could be no doubt where the army was going: contrast 54. 1, with n.]

4. πυθόμενος δέ, κ.τ.λ.: [Gomme accepted Fr. Portus's deletion of δέ, and rejected Hude's substitution of δή (for which it is not indeed

easy to find a parallel in Thucydides). He also preferred to read πυθόμενοι (B) and ἀπῆλθον (codd.). If we keep δέ, the participle must go with the following verb, and we can only make sense of this by taking ἐξεστρατεῦσθαι, with Arnold and others, to mean 'had finished the campaign and gone home': Gomme rightly rejected this, comparing especially ii. 12. 2 ἐξεστρατευμένων. Without δέ, the participle goes with the preceding verb and explains the Athenian expedition; but Steup with reason objected that in that case it is the Athenians in general, not just the thousand hoplites and Alkibiades, who should have learnt of the Spartan movement. Steup's own more complicated remedy is unnecessary, for πυθόμενος, agreeing with Alkibiades, makes good sense: he learnt the fact, no doubt from his Argive friends, and (as Thucydides did not feel it necessary to mention) communicated it to the assembly, who decreed the expedition. πυθόμενοι and ἀπῆλθεν will then be alternative attempts to reduce the sentence to order, after the δέ had been, for whatever reason, interpolated. For the question of intrusive δέ, cf. vii. 57. 4 n.]

καὶ τὸ θέρος οὕτω διῆλθεν: 'without much done', said Müller–Strübing to explain the unusual διῆλθεν for ἐτελεύτα; without approval by most edd. [Gomme himself suspected διῆλθεν so soon after ἀπῆλθον: but cf. ii. 47. 1, iv. 116. 3 (the end of a far from uneventful winter).]

56. 1. Λακεδαιμόνιοι - - - κατὰ θάλασσαν: unaccustomed daring by Sparta. They had just allowed themselves to be twice put off from land-expeditions in the summer; now, in winter and by sea, they brave the Athenians.

Ἀγησιππίδαν: [see 52. 1, with n.]

2. γεγραμμένον ἐν ταῖς σπονδαῖς: 47. 5. [The Argive complaint cannot mean that the Athenians were seriously expected to prevent any and every enemy passage by sea (Classen compared Perikles' boast in ii. 62. 2, but Steup rightly objected), only passage through waters that might reasonably be reckoned Athenian. By the Athenian occupation of Aigina (and Methana) this part of the Saronic Gulf could certainly be so reckoned. Agesippidas presumably took the shortest route, from Kenchreai along the coast to Epidauros (παραπλεῦσαι, but one would not hug too closely this inhospitable and thinly inhabited shore), and for the latter part of his voyage he would normally be visible from Aigina, if he had not been seen before. The Athenians do not seem to disclaim responsibility. Cf. the proceedings of both sides in summer 412, viii. 7 ff.]

ἀδικήσεσθαι αὐτοί: the Spartans might complain of being wronged if Athens brought the helots back to Pylos after the recent agreement (35. 6–7), but Argos would be really wronged if she did not.

3. τῇ μὲν Λακωνικῇ στήλῃ ὑπέγραψαν: Krüger compared Ar. *Lys.* 513, τί βεβούλευται περὶ τῶν σπονδῶν ἐν τῇ στήλῃ παραγράψαι; It shows some restraint in the Athenians that they had not taken this step before. How much we wish that Thucydides had been in Athens to observe the political forces at work just at this time!

[The Athenians did not denounce the treaty altogether (in which case they might well have taken down the stele, as Arnold says, comparing D. xvi. 27; cf. also *GHI* 147. 39–40), but recorded Sparta's breach of faith to justify their own somewhat dubious action. The Spartan breach is not, as Steup thought, the passage of Agesippidas through Athenian waters, but their general failure to execute important provisions in the peace, as Athens had complained in 46. 2. Neither side is yet quite ready for full-scale war, but the raids from Pylos come very near to a formal breach of the peace, and were sometimes so regarded by the Spartans: see vi. 105. 1 n.]

ἐκ Κρανίων: [see 35. 7, above.]

5. τελευτῶντος τοῦ χειμῶνος πρὸς ἔαρ ἤδη: see 39. 3 n.

ὡς ἐρήμου οὔσης: see nn. cited in vols. ii–iii, index, s.v. ἐρῆμος. [The point here is presumably that διὰ τὸν πόλεμον—the scattered sort of war described in § 4—the troops of Epidauros were not concentrated in the city.] Once again a small number of men, if determined and awake, could hold a wall against a much larger force.

YEAR 14: 418–417 B.C. (CC.57–81)

57–59. *Spartan Invasion of Argos*

57. 1. τοῦ δ' ἐπιγιγνομένου θέρους μεσοῦντος: [Spartan invasions usually begin τοῦ ἐπιγιγνομένου θέρους, and the further qualification μεσοῦντος—otherwise only vi. 30. 1, where the same point is being made—means that this was appreciably later than the usual season.]

It has been shrewdly asked, if Epidauros was so hard pressed and Sparta in such haste (εἰ μὴ προκαταλήψονται ἐν τάχει, below), why did the latter not move before midsummer? (Müller–Strübing, *Aristophanes*, 402; Beloch, *Die attische Politik seit Perikles*, 53, *Gr. Gesch.* ii². 1. 348; Busolt, iii/2. 1237); and the clever answer has been found that 'obviously' Sparta waited till the Athenian elections in the spring of the year, at which the 'peace-party' won a decisive victory, Nikias, Laches, Nikostratos, and Autokles being elected and Alkibiades not re-elected (61. 2), took effect at midsummer. That is to say that, when Athens was in a hostile mood (56. 3), Sparta held her hand; when 'the new government entered on office' at Athens, and the pacifists and pro-Spartans could control policy, she immediately took the offensive in the most provocative way (and this without any change in her own ephorate). I do not know which is the more exasperating assumption, that Sparta followed so inconsequent[1] a policy, or that a peace-party had 'won an election' in Athens but could not affect policy till they took office, and that Alkibiades could persuade so long as he was in office, but not when he was elected ambassador (61. 2, where see n.). I prefer Steup's view that the Spartans may have waited till they were convinced, by the growing coldness of their friends or by their urgent persuasions, that they could wait no longer. There was also some gain in waiting till their grain harvest was over. We may complain that Thucydides tells us so little of the political feeling in Athens in this year (below, p. 125); but we are not entitled to fill the gap which he left. He left it presumably because he did not know; and we should follow his example.[2] At most we might guess (if we like) that, if Alkibiades failed to be re-elected (perhaps through some lawless prank that temporarily lost him his popularity), the Spartans hoped in the spring that Athens would be peacefully inclined; and took action in the summer when she found that her hopes were ill-founded.

αὐτοὶ καὶ οἱ Εἵλωτες: here and in 64. 2 only does Thucydides use this unexpected combination. Nearest is καὶ οἱ Εἵλωτες οἱ περὶ αὐτούς, iv. 8. 9, and that is a special case—the tally of men cut off on Sphakteria. There the helots are, expressly, those normally expected in any Spartan army, servants to the hoplites. Here and in 64. 2 it presumably means a larger and, perhaps, a special force.

[For helot soldiers, and νεοδαμώδεις, see 34. 1 n. If recruitment of νεοδ. had temporarily ceased, there may have been a reserve of trained but not liberated helots (cf. vii. 19. 3): but the order of battle at Mantineia (67. 1) discloses no force of helot origin except the Brasideioi and νεοδαμώδεις. Perhaps Thucydides refers to these.]

2. ὅσοι ἄλλοι Ἀρκάδων: [at Mantineia (67. 1) only Heraies and Mainalioi are named, with no numbers given; but that was the result of a hurried summons (64. 2–3), and at this stage the Spartans still had Orchomenos on their side.]

ἄμιπποι: [codd. ἄνιπποι, as in X. HG vii. 5. 23–4 and Arist. Ἀθ. π. 49. 1, but the correction is certain in these texts (cf. Harp. s.v.), and probable in Hdt. i. 215. 1 (Aristarchos' note in PAmh. 12). The relevant texts are collected and discussed by Jacoby, on Philochoros,

---

[1] [While I would endorse the general line of this argument, I doubt if 'inconsequent' is quite the right word here. The Spartans might well calculate that there was less chance of retaliation when 'pacifists' were influential at Athens.]

[2] [These repressive sentiments reflect Gomme's indignation at the false basis of the speculations he is attacking. His practice shows that he did not mean to ban all guesses which go beyond the text; his own guess, in the next sentence, is soundly based on the view that the elections show only the mood of Athens at the time of election, and that we must allow for changes of mood thereafter.]

FGrHist 328 F 71: those which speak of one rider with two horses can be discarded (the correct term for these was probably ἄμφιπποι), since it is clear, especially from Xenophon, that our ἄμ. are on foot.

Xenophon says that Epameinondas at Mantineia in 362 used his cavalry as a kind of ram (ἔμβολον ἰσχυρόν) to punch a hole in the enemy line, καὶ ἀμίππους πεζοὺς συνέταξεν αὐτοῖς, whereas the enemy had drawn up their cavalry like a hoplite line and had no ἄμ. In *Hipparch*. 5. 13 he remarks on the weakness of cavalry unsupported by infantry against cavalry with ἄμ., and adds that it is possible to conceal infantry not only among but behind cavalry, thus making it clear that the normal ἄμ. were stationed in amongst the cavalry. We have no very clear description of their mode of operation, but Caesar's description of Ariovistus' Suebi (*BG* i. 48. 5, cited by most edd.) may give some idea: *pedites velocissimi* of equal number with the cavalry, like our ἄμ., one assigned to each horseman. Cf. also *BC* iii. 84. 3.

In 362 it is again the Boeotian cavalry who have ἄμ., and it is stated explicitly that the other side had none: but Athens at least had adopted the system by the time of Ἀθ. π. 49. 1, perhaps before the death of Isaios (Harp. s.v.). It was, as Jacoby notes, familiar, so that Athenian writers did not feel a need to explain, as Caesar does.]

οἱ δ' ἄλλοι: from Epidauros, Pellene, Sikyon, and Megara (58. 4).

58. 1. καὶ ἐπειδὴ ἐς τὸν Φλειοῦντα, κ.τ.λ.: I find no difficulty in the construction ('getting prior information both of the first preparations at Sparta and now that they were making for Phleious'). [The Argives would have no difficulty in learning that Phleious was the rendezvous: preparations to receive so large an army could not be hidden.]

Μαντινῆς: Diodoros, xii. 78. 4, gives the number of the Mantinean forces too, but as 'not far short' of the 3,000 Eleans. This looks like a guess, because Thucydides gives none.

[There are serious defects in Diod. xii. 78. The statement (78. 1) that Argos blamed Sparta for not rendering the sacrifice to Apollo Pythios could be careless condensation of an original which said that the quarrel with Sparta arose out of the Epidaurian quarrel; it is less easy to guess how Diodoros then came to describe (78. 2) Argive campaigns against Troizen, which clearly correspond to those against Epidauros in Thucydides; and the campaign of this summer is summarized with a deplorable carelessness (78. 3–4). But it is always possible, and often likely, that Diodoros' crasser mistakes are entirely his own work. They do not automatically invalidate all his details, and we must allow the possibility that Ephoros had access to genuine non-Thucydidean material: cf. 52. 1 n., 67. 2 n. The only other evidence on Mantinean numbers is Lys. xxxiv. 7, where the citizen total is given as οὐδὲ τρισχιλίους ὄντας in 403 : the speaker has an interest in keeping the number low.]

τοὺς σφετέρους ξυμμάχους: [cf. 67. 2 (with n. on 67. 1 Μαινάλιοι), 81. 1. These are the remains of Mantineia's Arkadian empire (33. 1 nn.) : no names are given.]

2. ἐν Μεθυδρίῳ: some 20 miles NE. of Megalopolis (Paus. viii. 35. 5, 36. 1 ; Plb. iv. 10. 10), [between two streams.] See Leake, ii. 57–8; [Ernst Meyer, RE xv. 1387 ff. The Spartans did not want to fight before they joined their northern allies, so they avoided Mantineia and went west of Mainalon, no doubt picking up their W. Arkadian allies somewhere west or south-west of Methydrion. The Argives and Mantineans would also be safer if they joined the Eleans as soon, i.e. as far west, as they could ; and in view of their eventual inferiority in numbers and quality (60. 3) it was much to their advantage if they could catch the Spartans before they made their junction with their allies at Phleious (μεμονωμένοις : cf. the advice of Timolaos in 394, X. HG iv. 2. 11–12).]

3–4. τὴν κατὰ Νεμέαν ὁδόν: [this is the obvious way from Phleious to Argos, from the eastern end of the Phleiasian plain over a low pass to join the main road from Corinth and Kleonai to Argos, the Tretos road described in Paus. ii. 15. 2, a narrow defile through overhanging mountains but then as now open to wheeled traffic. For the road taken by Agis, commentators have been tempted to think of the best known alternative to the Tretos, the 'Kontoporeia' (Paus. ibid. ; the name is given by Plb. xvi. 16. 4 and Ptolemy Euergetes II, FGrHist 234 F 6) which was a short cut from Kleonai to Argos, east of the Tretos, coming down into the plain at Mycenae. But it is wildly unlikely that Agis made a detour round to the east of the forces guarding the Nemea road: we should look rather for more direct routes through the mountains west of the Tretos. Leake, ii. 415, deals only cursorily with this region: E. Curtius, Peloponnesos, ii. 479, 582–3, is clearer (but he opts for the Kontoporeia); Ernst Meyer, RE xvi. 2315, gives the most likely answer (below); cf. also Fougères, 396 n. 4, and H. Lehmann, Argolis (1937), i. 108.

The obvious western alternative is the way which leads up from Phleious to the pleasant small plain of Yimnó and the springs of the Asopos, west of Mt. Keloussa (Str. viii. 6. 24, 382, now Megálo Vounó) : this will be the pass where Agesipolis wanted to build a fort in 388, X. HG iv. 7. 7 ἐπὶ ταῖς παρὰ Κηλοῦσαν ἐμβολαῖς. But the ascent from the Phleiasian side is gradual and easy, and though the descent into the valley of the Inachos is steep the route as a whole is hardly χαλεπή. Agis may have expected to find it guarded (Orneai must be somewhere near it, 67. 2 n.), and he probably went by some steeper path east of the main summit of Keloussa: there are several possibilities, with no way to choose between them or decide exactly where he came down into the plain. Meyer's suggestion is as likely as any, that he came by way of Malandréni, while the Corinthians, etc. went to Fikhtiá further east, on the main road opposite Mycenae.]

4. παραγγείλας: there is no such awkwardness in this participle as Steup found; it is of course to be taken with the following datives, which correspond with καὶ Κορίνθιοι, κ.τ.λ. in the next clause. [See also next n.]

ὄρθιον: [so recc., adopted by most edd. ; the meaning 'steep' is amply attested, and the Corinthians' route led them over high ground. Gomme, however, noted Graves's opinion that ἡμέρας ἤδη, 59. 1 below, supports the emendation ὄρθριοι here ; and noted, but did not discuss, the MSS. reading ὄρθριον. This would be an adverb, as Ar. *Eccl.* 377, 526 (cf. Hdt. ii. 173. 1 τὸ ὄρθριον), and there seems no reason not to retain it if the sense is adequate.

ὄρθριον would mean that the Corinthians, etc. set out during the period of some two hours before sunrise. Agis must have started earlier: the Argives' move ἡμέρας ἤδη shows that he must have marched by night, and the sequence of tenses ἐχώρησε - - - κατέβη - - - ἐπορεύοντο suggests that his march and descent were completed while the Corinthians were on their way (see further 59. 1). The timing seems to be right, but it is still odd that Thucydides should tell us explicitly when the Corinthians moved and leave us to infer the time of Agis' start. Steup's proposal of a lacuna after παραγγείλας was partly due to his belief that the time of Agis' movement ought to be stated.]

ἐς τὸ πεδίον: [even if they had early information of Agis' movement and of his route, the Argives could not reach him before he got down into the plain.]

5. Σάμινθον: the site is not known. [There is no other mention of the place, and our guesses must be based on our view of Agis' route. If he came down near Malandréni (§§ 3-4 n.), Saminthos should probably be sought in the neighbourhood of Koutsopódhi, some 2 miles north of Argos, as Leake suggested.]

59. 1. ἡμέρας ἤδη: [see 58. 4 n.]

τῷ Φλειασίων καὶ Κορινθίων στρατοπέδῳ: [see § 3 n.]

2. ἀλλὰ καταβάντες: [the change of subject, from the Boeotians, etc. to the Argives, is somewhat harsh ; but there is no need, with Steup, to see in what follows a sign of incomplete revision. γνόντες in § 1 means that the Argives were told of Agis' move, so they marched down: here they could see him ravaging, which they could not have done from Nemea, and they form up for battle.]

3. ἐν μέσῳ δὲ ἀπειλημμένοι ἦσαν οἱ Ἀργεῖοι: [one of the main puzzles of this episode is that the rank and file of both armies were convinced

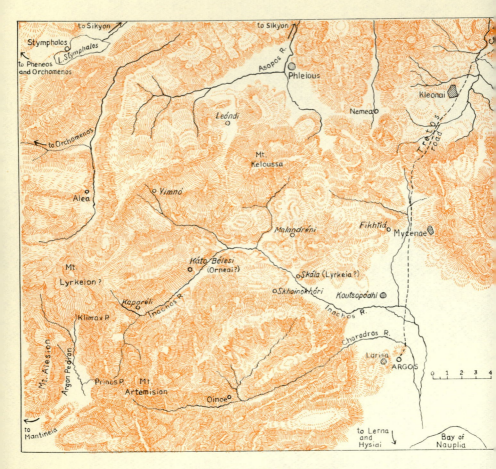

MAP 2. THE ARGOLID

that their own forces were in a position to win a clear victory, whereas the leaders avoided battle. Thucydides here commits himself firmly to the Spartan view, that the Argive position was desperate; and the wording of §§ 4–5 implies that the Argive leaders saw more clearly than the mass of their forces.

Agis' contingent was on the plain, but we cannot be sure how far north he was operating, i.e. how far away from the city towards the mouth of the pass. καθύπερθεν, of the Corinthians, etc., can only mean literally 'on higher ground'—'behind' or 'further inland', as, e.g., Hdt. iv. 8. 1, would be equally true of the Boeotians, etc.— so they were presumably on the foothills above Fikhtiá and the mouth of the pass, either just arriving when the Argives issued from the defile or already drawn up for the intended battle: they were not strong enough by themselves to prevent the Argives brushing past them. The phrase used here suggests that the Argives did not advance much further into the plain, but drew up still quite close to the Corinthian position. The Boeotians, etc. found the Argives already gone when they reached Nemea, in which case their cavalry were ordered to pursue (58. 4); but we are not told how near they were at this critical moment, and this seems to be the element of doubt that accounts for the divergent views the armies took of the situation. If Agis' force could have been crushed before the Boeotians arrived, then the Argives were justified in supposing that their generals had lost a very favourable opportunity. Thucydides judged that they were wrong: the informants whom he most trusted must have told him that there was time for the Boeotians to come up.

Ferguson in *CAH* v. 270 puts the main point clearly; Henderson, *The Great War between Athens and Sparta* (1927), 307–16, also sees it, but in supposing that the Boeotians never appeared at all he contradicts what Thucydides implies, and his map on p. 308 is very misleading.]

ἵπποι δὲ αὐτοῖς οὐ παρῆσαν: it is noteworthy that Ἄργος ἱππόβοτον, so well known in Homer, had no cavalry, and that Athens, less favoured for horses by nature, had.

μόνοι τῶν ξυμμάχων: 'the only allies who had not arrived'; but Thucydides does not say why. See 74. 1, 3, 75. 5 nn.

[These nn. refer to the uneven quality of Thucydides' information from Athens; Gomme did not comment on the actual timetable. There had been time for a messenger to go to Elis, and for the Eleans to collect their army and march right across the Peloponnese; but the Athenians had to come by sea round Skyllaion (53), and the events of the campaign move fast, so their late arrival may be due only to the fact that sea transport, especially of horses, takes longer to arrange.]

4. πρὸς τῇ πόλει: [repeated at 60. 5, which suggests that this was an important point for the indignant Argives. There may have been

83

a substantial body of troops in the city, though Thucydides has said nothing of this: Gomme (ms.) suggests that the Argives perhaps sent a two-thirds levy into Arkadia, and then to Nemea, leaving one-third of their good troops in the city, plus the oldest and youngest.]

5. τῶν πέντε στρατηγῶν: connected, [almost inevitably], with the five *lochoi* of 72. 4: see n. there.

60–63. *Four Months' Truce; Capture of Orchomenos*

60. 1. τῶν Ἀργείων: 'partitive genitive dependent on οἱ ταῦτα εἰπόντες', Graves, followed by Steup, arguing that the words should not be bracketed. [Gomme in the end inclined to agree with Stahl that the words are unnecessary: but in the structure of the whole chapter there seems to be an intention of taking together, first the negotiators on each side (here καὶ ὁ Ἆγις), then the rank and file who criticized them (cf. § 5 καὶ αὐτοί, which serves to link the Argive objectors with the Spartan); and in that case τῶν Ἀργείων here is justified, even if it is clear, without these words, who is meant.

Similarly, Gomme doubted Graves's contention that οἱ μέν here is answered by οἱ δὲ Λακεδαιμόνιοι in § 2, and preferred to call it μέν *solitarium*, with Haacke and Stahl (it might here be due to association with ταῦτα εἰπόντες, since μέν is so common in the first words after the end of a speech); and indeed, if Graves is right, Thucydides allowed himself to be extensively diverted from the contrast he was making. Nevertheless it still seems to be in his mind at the beginning of § 5.]

ἀφ' ἑαυτῶν: [these two took the initiative, and had no authority except Thrasylos' powers as general. (πλῆθος in 59. 4 is the main body of the army: here it must be the assembly, which had indeed had no opportunity to express an opinion, but lasting peace could not be promised without its authority.) The phrase cannot mean that they acted wholly on their own, for the other generals must at least provisionally have consented (cf. the attitude of 'the Argives' of 61. 1), or the disengagement of the armies would have been impossible. Agis will have extricated his force sideways, towards the hills through which he had marched earlier, and he could rely on his own men's obedience (§ 2), but he had to be sure that the Argives would not attack him as he moved. If the position is correctly analysed in 59. 3 n., the time consumed in these parleys will have served to improve Agis' own position.]

τῶν ἐν τέλει ξυστρατευομένων: [for the general meaning of this, see 27. 2 n. Xenophon, *Lac. Pol.* 13. 1, speaks of consultation with the polemarchs as normal; and in 13. 5 of the ephors who accompanied an expedition, not interfering but ready at the king's call (cf. *HG* ii. 4. 36).]

84

οὐδενὶ φράσας τῶν ἄλλων ξυμμάχων: ξυμμάχων was quite unnecessarily bracketed by Krüger and Stahl: Agis had not only not consulted any of his own advisers, except one, but not any of the allies either—which in such a case as this, a resolve to stop a campaign and make peace, he should have done (cf. 61. 2 on the other side).

2. διὰ τὸν νόμον: [a very clear instance of the unassailable right of the king to give orders, once he is in charge of an army beyond the borders; cf. 66. 3, viii. 5. 3, Hdt. vi. 56, Arist. *Pol.* 1285ᵃ5.]

ὑπὸ ἱππέων: [this clearly assumes that the Boeotians would have arrived in time, cf. 59. 3 n.]

3. στρατόπεδον γὰρ δὴ τοῦτο κάλλιστον: one of many such statements in Thucydides, from i. 1. 2 on: cf. iii. 17, and v. 74. 1 below, as well as the more obvious vi. 31. 1. In view of ii. 9, 11. 1, however, it is surprising. [Many edd. stress κάλλιστον and maintain that the army of 431 may have been more numerous but this was better appointed. κάλλιστον is a striking word to use, and cannot be divorced from the army's appearance (cf. Sappho 16 LP); but Thucydides, in the preceding sentence and through most of this, is concerned with its strength.]

πανστρατιᾷ belongs only to Λακεδαιμόνιοι, though strictly it should be said of Φλειάσιοι too (57. 2), the rest being represented by select troops. The Epidaurians are omitted (58. 4), as likely as not by MS. error, unless there is a special point in ὤφθη - - - ἐν Νεμέᾳ (below) and this contingent had gone home by another route: [their nearest way was eastwards past the Asklepieion, but they must have come to Phleious more circuitously.]

By what route did Agis return? The ordinary route was southwards and then westwards up to the south end of the Arkadian plain to Tegea; but ἕως ἔτι ἦν ἀθρόον ἐν Νεμέᾳ suggests not the time before the army divided into three groups for the purpose of attack (58. 4), but before the dispersal of the armies each to its own city— the Corinthians, Megarians, and Boeotians, perhaps the Epidaurians too, would separate from the rest at Nemea. If that is correct, Agis went back by the same or nearly the same circuitous route by which he had come; this would of course help him to control all his allies till he had got them away from the Argolid. It would also probably take them past Orchomenos; see 61. 5. [Agis must also have left at Phleious baggage which would have hampered his march over the mountains; and the same should be true of the Epidaurians.]

Σᴹˢᶜ² in a long note poses an ἀπορία: ἐν Νεμέᾳ is inaccurate if the reference is to the army before the march from Phleious to the Argolid, for only one division went by Nemea (58. 4; and the Argives were at Nemea itself, 58. 4, 59. 1); and gives as λύσις the view stated here.

ὤφθη - - - ἐν Νεμέᾳ has suggested to some that Thucydides

85

actually saw this fine army on the march; certainly he knew a good deal about it.

ἀλλὰ κἂν ἄλλῃ ἔτι προσγενομένῃ: Graves, followed by Steup, objects to Bekker's correction of the MSS. καί to κἄν, which has been adopted by most edd.; he compares 52. 2, οἷς ἦν ἐν βλάβῃ τειχισθέν. [As Gomme then noted, the comparison is not exact; 52. 2 is easier, see n. there.]

5. μετὰ πολλῶν καὶ ἀγαθῶν ξυμμάχων: but without the Athenians and so without any cavalry (59. 3); and the Eleans proved wilful (62. 2).

6. ἐν τῷ Χαράδρῳ: the bed of a watercourse (which has water only after heavy rain) which runs along the north and east sides of the city, forming a natural defensive trench. [Cf. Paus. ii. 25. 2: this is the watercourse which runs down through a long and narrow valley from Oinoe and emerges into the plain on the north side of the Larisa, and then joins the (equally dry) bed of the Inachos.

Nothing further is known of the procedure mentioned here. From Athens we know of special provision for charges of desertion in the field (they were heard, after return, by a jury of soldiers: Lys. xiv. 5, cf. Pl. *Lg.* xii. 943 a–b), but no exact parallel is known for this Argive procedure. The Charadros, no doubt, just seemed an appropriate place for a lynching: it is less likely that a general had regularly to answer for his conduct of a campaign in such a court, and it was probably a later trial that ended in the confiscation of Thrasylos' property. At least at first, the authorities tried to maintain his truce (61. 1).]

Thucydides does not make sufficiently clear the process of Argive action and inaction. The Athenian delay doubtless hindered decision; and we may suppose that the two groups of citizens, which we might, for this period of the uncertain truce, label the pro-Athenian and the pro-Spartan parties, were fairly evenly matched (in energy and intelligence, if not in numbers): but we should have liked much more detail, to make the narrative live.

[Thrasylos must mainly have justified his truce as an urgent military necessity; but the issue is confused by the fact that the proposed settlement with Sparta is just what the pro-Spartan group would want for its own sake, and no doubt there was a higher proportion of pro-Spartans in the class from which generals and magistrates were drawn. But it must be remembered that Agis, if his military advantage was real, would hardly have settled for less.]

61. 1. Ἀθηναίων βοηθησάντων: [Diod. xii. 79. 1 adds κατὰ θάλατταν, an easy guess; and ἱππεῖς δὲ διακοσίους is a type of variant common in Diod., for which we need not postulate a non-Thucydidean source (cf. 58. 1 n.). The accounts for 418/17 (ML 77 = IG i². 302) show no payment for this expedition, so it was presumably ordered and paid for in 419/18, i.e. before *c.* July 9 (Meritt, *Athenian Year*, 218). For Laches and Nikostratos, see § 2 n.

A ms. note refers to V. Ehrenberg, *JHS* lxvii (1947), 55–6, and so to Eupolis' lines from the *Demoi* (fr. 8. Ib. 8 Dem. = Page, *Greek Lit. Papyri*, p. 208, ll. 28–30), which have something to say of unfavourable omens before this force set out and of a demagogue nevertheless pressing the plan through; but there is no indication of Gomme's own interpretation of this far from easy passage.]

οἱ Ἀργεῖοι: [not the πλῆθος of 60. 1, 5, but the body which received ambassadors in the first instance and decided whether they should be given access to the assembly; at Athens this would have been the boule, and in view of Hdt. vii. 148. 3 ff. it may have been the same at Argos. The name of the state is used for the organ of state relevant to the case, which here gives a slightly misleading impression. As we know nothing of the composition of the boule, we cannot say whether it was likely to be more pro-Spartan than the δῆμος, or merely thought that Thrasylos' action had been justified by the circumstances.]

ὅμως γάρ, κ.τ.λ.: 'in spite of this reinforcement', the arrival of the Athenians, not 'in spite of their anger with Thrasylos', or even 'in spite of everything' (Warner).

πρὶν δὴ Μαντινῆς - - - κατηνάγκασαν: the MSS. reading, πρὶν ἤ (supported by Π[13]), is defended by Classen; [and by Steup, comparing Lycurg. 128 and the decree of 418/17 now numbered *IG* i². 94. 9. The construction is rare in Attic (Kühner–Gerth, ii. 445, with n. 2). Of the alternatives, Gomme preferred Hofmann's οἵ ('in later times pronounced the same as ἤ') and found Haase's δή 'unnecessarily emphatic': but the emphasis is not so very heavy, and πρὶν δή gives an appropriate sense, 'till in the end'. But emendation is not necessary.]

κατηνάγκασαν δεόμενοι: a phrase to be remembered when we try to force the meaning of ἀνάγκη and its derivatives to mean literally inevitable necessity. See ii. 70. 1 n., and vol. iii, 726.

2. Ἀλκιβιάδου πρεσβευτοῦ παρόντος: see 57. 1 n. Two further points may be noted: (1) that there is no *evidence* that Laches and Nikostratos belonged to a 'peace-party' in Athens; see iv. 119. 2 with n. Nikias was the only man we know who was consistently in favour of peace, and he for personal reasons rather than from political conviction (v. 16. 1; see *JHS* lxxi (1951), 74–80 = *More Essays*, 101–11). (2) Without express evidence, we should not believe that the Athenians at one and the same time sent two men in command of a military force to follow a policy friendly to Sparta, and Alkibiades, not in command but as ambassador, to frustrate them; they sent both him and Nikias together to Sicily, but in the fond hope that their different qualities would produce well-balanced action (cf. vi. 17. 1), not in order that the one should conquer Sicily and the other return home after a military display.

We cannot indeed be certain that Alkibiades was not one of the ten strategoi[1] of this year: he may have been refused a military command on this occasion (we can guess a reason) and retained as ambassador, because he was so eloquent. (Diodoros' statement, xii. 79. 1, that he was ἰδιώτης, is a false inference; [or at least, there is no strong reason for thinking it has independent authority, cf. § 1 n., and 58. 1 n.])

οὐκ ὀρθῶς - - - καὶ γένοιντο: 'it was wrong that it had been concluded *at all* without the allies' agreement'. καί does not mean 'both', and is not 'displaced', as Stahl (comparing iii. 67. 6) and Classen (cf. ii. 46. 1). So Krüger. The wording of the treaty of alliance, 47. 4, seems to support the argument of the allies, though the Argives might have answered that they had only concluded a four months' truce, not 'ended the war'. The allies on both sides were scurvily treated.

ἐν καιρῷ γὰρ παρεῖναι σφεῖς: the orator is aware of the weak point in the *Athenian* case. [This presumably refers to their late arrival, which Gomme throughout treats as wilful; but see 59. 3 n. It seems more likely that this phrase means that the allies had the chance of important gains, now that they were reinforced and the powerful enemy army had for the moment disbanded.]

4. ὅμηροι: nothing is known of these, or why the Spartans should have placed hostages with Orchomenos, which is out of the way for them. Perhaps they had only taken these hostages, from 'untrustworthy circles' in Parrasioi and elsewhere, at the beginning of this campaign, and left them at Orchomenos on the way to Phleious.

5. ὁμήρους - - - Μαντινεῦσι: [see 77. 1 n.]

62. 1. Ἠλεῖοι μὲν ἐπὶ Λέπρεον: [naturally the Eleans' prime object (cf. 31, 34, 49–50), but strategically an aberration. The loss of Tegea would gravely weaken Sparta, and might be expected to lead to further defections, whereas nothing much could follow from a success at Lepreon; and this move to the west would leave Mantineia and Orchomenos open to a Spartan counter-attack.]

2. αὐτῶν τῶν ἐν τῇ πόλει: Steup defends the MSS. reading Τεγεατῶν against Stahl's τῶν, probably rightly ('some of the Tegeates themselves were working inside the city for surrender'). For the omission

---

[1] [Wade-Gery, *CQ* xxiv (1930), 34 n. 2, observed that Ἀλκιβιάδει Σκαμβονί]δει would fill the gap in *IG* i². 302 (ML 77). 17, and this was printed by Meritt, *AFD* 160; but he supposed that Nikostratos was from the same tribe IV and that Alkibiades was elected after Nikostratos' death (74. 3) to fill the vacancy. See further D. M. Lewis, *JHS* lxxxi (1961), 119; D. M. MacDowell, *CQ* N.S. xv (1965), 41–51.]

of τῶν he compares i. 27. 2, αὐτῶν δὲ Κορινθίων, which is not convincing; [but τῶν is not required if ἐν τῇ πόλει is taken with the verb
(Schütz, cited by Steup). A simple remedy is to add ⟨τῶν⟩ after
Τεγεατῶν: Steup's objection, that there is no contrast between two
groups of Tegeates, is pedantic. (Gomme, doubtfully, thought that
Σ^recc· ἠμέλουν τῶν κατὰ τὴν πόλιν πραγμάτων implied a text without
τῶν.)]

63–74. *The Campaign of Mantineia*

63. 1. ὡς οὔπω πρότερον αὐτοὶ ἐνόμιζον: this seems unlikely Greek
to me; but neither Krüger's bracketing of αὐτοὶ ἐνόμιζον nor Hert-
lein's ὡς before αὐτοί (Classen) is convincing. The repetition too of
the statement in 60. 2–3 in similar words seems to argue lack of
revision; and αὐτοί especially is out of place. [Stahl thought that
αὐτοί referred to the contrast between the Spartan view and the
view of the mass of the Argives, though that has been sufficiently
stressed, cf. 60. 1 n.

The basic difficulty is that, as the sentence runs, the reader will
think he has reached the end of it at πρότερον. Perhaps two alternative formulations have been superimposed, ὡς οὔπω πρότερον and
ὡς αὐτοὶ ἐνόμιζον: or a word may have been lost after πρότερον, e.g.
καθότι.]

2. ἐπειδὴ δέ - - - ἠγγέλλετο - - - ἐβούλευον: [that is, on the first return of the army, angry as they were, they took no steps against
Agis; but now they did. The point is rightly stressed by D. Kagan,
CP lvii (1962), 215, and it is logical enough. Peaceful settlement with
Argos had long been an object of Spartan policy (36. 1, 41. 3), and if
this could be obtained without a battle so much the better. At first it
seemed as if the truce might hold (61. 1), and if it had led on to the
further settlement promised in 59. 5 Agis would have been justified,
however much his army resented the truce at the time. He over-
estimated the solidity of his Argive friends' position—he had better
have made his military advantage plainer, by allowing at least a
limited battle, but he was perhaps reluctant to incur casualties—
and now his policy had been proved wrong.

ἐβούλευον is the deliberation of the assembly, not the sentence of
a court. Paus. iii. 5. 2 describes the standard form of court for the
trial of a king (28 gerontes, the other king, five ephors); but clearly
here, and probably in the case of Kleomenes I after Sepeia (Hdt.
vi. 82. 2, see *Ehrenberg Stud.* 19 n. 15) the assembly decides. Possibly
it always kept control, referring only such cases as it wished to this
court (Hdt. vi. 85. 1, of Leotychidas, δικαστήριον συναγαγόντες
ἔγνωσαν could be taken in this sense). The possibilities are again illustrated in the irregular proceedings which ended with the execution

of Agis IV, Plu. *Agis* 19: first the ephors sent for those gerontes whom they knew to be on their side, ὡς δὴ κρίσεως αὐτῷ γινομένης ('as if this were a real trial'); later, Agis' mother and grandmother demanded τὸν βασιλέα τῶν Σπαρτιατῶν λόγου καὶ κρίσεως τυχεῖν ἐν τοῖς πολίταις, which in all the circumstances cannot refer to a small court.]

παρὰ τὸν τρόπον τὸν ἑαυτῶν: [so also i. 132. 5. But there were political reasons for proceeding carefully against Pausanias, and the Spartans could be precipitate enough when the case seemed clear, as here, or in the case of Leotychidas, Hdt. vi. 85.]

τήν τε οἰκίαν αὐτοῦ κατασκάψαι: [the same penalty was inflicted on Leotychidas at his second trial, Hdt. vi. 72. 2 (a ms. note refers to the discussion by H. W. Parke, *CQ* xxxix (1945), 111). Herodotos does not say that a fine was also inflicted, but the result was that he fled to Tegea and lived there till he died, though he seems to have remained titular king (J. Johnston, *Hermathena* xlvi (1931), 110).]

δέκα μυριάσι δραχμῶν: presumably of the Aeginetan standard, so some 140,000 Attic (over 23 tal.), an immense sum (see vol. ii, 45–7). Miltiades is said to have been fined 50 tal. (Hdt. vi. 136. 3); doubtless such large fines were intended to mean, in practice, permanent disqualification for office—[or indeed the crippling of a whole political group. No ordinary Spartan citizen could pay such a fine in money, but the kings were probably exempt from the restriction on owning silver.]

3. ῥύσεσθαι: not found elsewhere in Attic prose, and not exactly in this sense in Homer, and only rarely in tragedy. It has been suggested that ῥ. τὰς αἰτίας was a Spartan usage, and perhaps (Stahl) Agis' own words: [cf. 65. 2, and vi. 41. 3 n.]

4. ἐν τῷ παρόντι: [in relation to § 3 τότε, and § 4 ἐπέσχον. They were ready to give Agis the chance to redeem his promise, but took some precaution meanwhile. Mantineia did redeem the promise: nothing more is heard of the sentence or of the ξύμβουλοι, and] Agis appears in full command at Dekeleia in 413, viii. 5. 3.

ξυμβούλους: we hear of such an officer attached to unsuccessful nauarchoi (who exercised an authority at sea similar to that of the kings on land: ii. 66. 2 n.): ii. 85. 1, iii. 69. 1, and viii. 39. 2.

[But it was another matter to restrict the traditional power of the king, which was absolute once the army had crossed the border (60. 2 n.). On the nature of the restriction, see next n.]

ἀπάγειν στρατιὰν ἐκ τῆς πόλεως: [ἀπάγειν is to lead troops back, or home, or away from the objective for which they have been making; so often in Thucydides, e.g. 65. 3. It is very odd indeed here, nor can I see that Thucydides makes any special point (Stahl, Steup) by not using the normal ἐξάγειν.

Haase proposed to read ἐκ τῆς πολεμίας, which gives ἀπάγειν its normal sense, and very exactly restricts the advisers to cases like that of cc. 59–60; and maybe this is all that the Spartans intended by their temporary regulation. They did not want a divided command in the field (cf. 66. 3): note also that Thucydides was told (iii. 79. 3) that Brasidas as 'adviser' could not press his own plan against Alkidas, ἰσοψήφου οὐκ ὄντος.

Diod. xii. 78. 6 is very different, προσέταξαν μηδὲν ἄνευ τῆς τούτων γνώμης πράττειν, and he has one of the advisers intervene during the battle (79. 6). This is part of the story of the Argive Thousand, which Ephoros developed and certainly in some degree romanticized (67. 2 n.): it is a deliberate alteration or addition, not Diodoros' carelessness, but this general restriction seems a less likely alternative.]

64. 2. αὐτῶν τε καὶ τῶν Εἱλώτων: see 57. 1 n.

ὀξεῖα καὶ οἷα οὔπω πρότερον: the last words only explain ὀξεῖα: they do not mean that in some other respect too the expedition was unparalleled. The urgent order to their Arkadian allies and the return of one-sixth of the force from Orestheion, when they found that things in Tegea were not so desperate as they had feared (§ 3), are both signs of this haste.

[This is the third οὔπω πρότερον in 18 lines, which Classen took as a sign of imperfect revision. Steup (his n. to 63. 1) claimed that Thucydides did not object to such repetition, citing 35. 4–5, but there the two occurrences of δεσμώτας are logically connected.]

3. ἐς Ὀρέσθειον τῆς Μαιναλίας: Agis, in spite of his haste, did not march by the shortest route to Tegea (by way of the modern road to Tripolis), but up the Eurotas valley, NNW. from Sparta. It may well be that this was the easier way for an army (the other is certainly steeper; in modern times we have become accustomed to it because the road goes that way), and was a better way to get into touch with his Arkadian allies. [We have also to keep Agis' ἅμαξαι in mind (72. 3). The basic discussions are by W. Loring, *JHS* xv (1895), 47 ff. (to which a ms. note refers), and Ernst Meyer, *RE* xviii. 1014–16. See map opposite p. 34.

There is no record of the more direct road by Karyai towards Tegea before 419 (55. 3), but it was used by Epameinondas in 370/69 (X. *HG* vi. 5. 25), and in the early second century (Plb. xvi. 37. 4; Livy xxxiv. 26, xxxv. 27). It took a much less direct course than the modern road (see Loring, 52–60), so there was not so much saving in time over the western route by Orestheion, which was used in 479 (Hdt. ix. 11. 2; Plu. *Ar.* 10. 9), in 419 (54. 1 above), on this occasion in 418, in 370 (X. *HG* vi. 5. 10–11), and in 362 (ibid. vii. 5. 9). Paus. iii. 20. 8–21. 3 does not make it clear how high above the Eurotas the road went past Pellana and Belmina (from 21. 1 it is clear that it did not stick close to the river throughout), but it is likely that it went much lower than the modern route, which serves the large villages just under the cliffs of Taygetos and then drops into the valley under Mt. Khelmós, in the area where we should look for Belmina. Just east of Khelmós the stream which the ancients regarded as the main stream of the Eurotas (cf. Paus. viii. 44. 3–4) enters the main valley from the NE. by a deep gorge. There can never have been a road for wagons up the gorge, but just north of Khelmós there is a practicable way, steep at first from the Spartan side but easy enough above the village of Skortsinó and over into the plain SW. of Asea. North of this the summit of Mt. Tsemberoú blocks the way, and if the Spartans did not go by Skortsinó they must have continued NNW. along the line of the main valley and over the low watershed into the plain of Megalopolis. After crossing a corner of the Megalopolis plain, they had a choice of easy passes, between the modern road to Tripolis and the higher reaches of Tsemberoú, into the plain of Asea; and from Asea the road is easy to Pallantion and the eastern plain.

Again, there is no easy way out of the Eurotas valley to the left, over the northern offshoots of Taygetos towards Messenia (33. 1 n.), till well beyond Khelmós and up on to the watershed over to Megalopolis.

Loring thought the Spartans should not go too far west, so he assumed they went by Skortsinó, and located Orestheion east of Tsemberoú, at the western end of the plain in which Asea lies. Meyer replied that the gradients on the other route are easier, and located Orestheion, on this and other grounds, very close to Megalopolis. Either route could without great trouble have been made practicable for wagons, and the choice between them must be made on other grounds. It is in Meyer's favour that the Spartans in 419 could go as far NW. as Leuktra (54. 1) without it being clear where they meant to go: this strongly suggests that it was not unusual for them to go NNW. to the Megalopolis plain, and yet turn east towards Tegea.

The advantage of Meyer's location is that Oresthasion, Orestheion, Oresteion can be identified as the same place and as the centre of the Oresthis of iv. 134. 1, ἐν Λαοδοκείῳ τῆς ᾿Ορεσθίδος. To take Oresthis first, Paus. viii. 44. 1 has a Ladokeia in the suburbs of Megalopolis, on the road to Pallantion; and Ladokeia is named in Plb. ii. 51. 3, 55. 2, as the site of the victory of Kleomenes III and of Lydiadas' death (Plu. *Cleom.* 6, *Arat.* 37, does not give the name but places the battle just outside the city). Steph. Byz. s.v. Μεγάλη πόλις says that half the city was called Orestia, after Orestes. The double coincidence makes it certain that we should look for Oresthis here, SE. of Megalopolis and including part of the site of the city.

Pausanias' Oresthasion cannot be far from here; it is in the same direction from Megalopolis, off to the right of the road to Pallantion, before you reach Asea (viii. 44. 2), but he does not tell us how much before. He uses this name throughout, deriving it from Oresthes son of Lykaon (viii. 3. 1–2), but he says that it changed its name to Oresteion, ἀπὸ 'Ορέστου κληθεῖσα. Tellon, who won the boys' boxing at Olympia in 472, is Oresthasios in Paus. vi. 10. 9 and on his monument, IvO 147–8 (but Mainalios in POxy. ii. 222 (FGrH 415). 1. 29, which gives the date). The change of name must be later than this, and when Euripides sends Orestes to an eponymous Oresteion in Arkadia one would naturally conclude that he meant Pausanias' Oresthasion/Oresteion and that the change of name began in the second half of the fifth century. Euripides' Oresteion indeed appears to be too far west: El. 1273–4, on the Alpheios but Λυκαίου πλησίον σηκώματος: Or. 1643–7, on the Parrasian plain (whereas Oresthasion is Mainalian, POxy. above and Paus. viii. 27. 3) and somehow of concern to the Azanes (who belong to northern Arkadia). Euripides' geography is perhaps confused: ancient commentators showed disquiet, Σ Or. 1645 (Pherekydes, FGrHist 3 F 135) τὸ δὲ 'Ορέστειον τῆς Παρρασίας κεχώρισται. Pausanias' identification of Oresthasion and Oresteion may be allowed to stand, and it is most unlikely that the Orestheion of Hdt. ix. 11. 2 and Thucydides is a different place.

It thus seems likely that Meyer is right, that Orestheion is to be sought close to Megalopolis, and that Spartan armies marching north did more often than not go by way of the upper Eurotas and cross the SE. corner of the plain of Megalopolis.]

τοῖς μὲν Ἀρκάδων - - - ξυμμάχοις: see 67. 1.

τὸ ἕκτον μέρος - - - τὸ πρεσβύτερόν τε καὶ τὸ νεώτερον: see ii. 13. 6 n. (vol. ii, 38–9) for the significance of this for Thucydides' calculation of relative numbers of different age-groups.

In 75. 1 we are told that these men (the over-forties and, probably, those of 18–19) were called up again. In 72. 3 there is mention of οἱ πρεσβύτεροι on the field at Mantineia; but they are older men (perhaps perioikoi and helots only) already detailed, from the beginning when the march out of Sparta began, to look after the 'train'. The oldest and youngest in our present context had been mustered to fight in the ranks, if necessary. (The 'older man' of 65. 2 may have been one of the ξύμβουλοι of 63. 4, or a senior officer; for strategoi and others were often over military age.)

τὰ οἴκοι φρουρεῖν: [this was not for fear of anything the Eleans might do (62. 2)—if they, e.g., moved against Lepreon, the Spartans could deal with this more easily from Orestheion—nor, surely, for fear that the allies might anticipate Epameinondas and march by the other road towards Sparta. Presumably this is yet another symptom of their perennial nervousness about their internal situation, the helot danger.]

4. καὶ Φωκέας καὶ Λοκρούς: when we last heard of these, 32. 2, they had begun a war on their own. [For Diod. xii. 80. 4, see 32. 2 n.]

ξυνέκλῃε γὰρ διὰ μέσου: especially through the capture of Orchomenos by Mantineia and her allies. The normal route for these allies of Sparta to come would be by lake Stymphalos. [This is easily accessible from Sikyon, and so far friendly territory: thereafter the easiest way is over the pass to the plain of Pheneos, and south by way of Kaphyai to Orchomenos. This is the reverse of the way the Spartan army had to take when, as was normally the case, the easier road through the Argolid was closed to it; and provision must have been made for the passage of wagons over the relevant passes. If Orchomenos had been friendly, they still had the territory of Mantineia itself between them and Tegea, unless they made a long circuit through western Arkadia.]

5. πρὸς τῷ Ἡρακλείῳ: Thucydides does not say where this was in Mantinike, how far from the city, any more than he tells us about the heroön of Androkrates and other places near Plataia (iii. 24); but he might reasonably have assumed[1] a wider knowledge of the country round Plataia than of Mantineia. Pausanias does not mention the Herakleion in his list of noteworthy places on the two roads south from Mantineia to Pallantion and Tegea (viii. 10. 1, 11. 1–6). [It has often been placed on the western edge of the plain, on the assumption that the enemy were on Mt. Alesion opposite (65. 1 n.): it should not be too far north, but anywhere north of Mýtikas (below) it would probably lie away from the Pallantion road, which would help to account for Pausanias not noticing it. Of course, it may simply have been of no interest.]

For a detailed account of the battle see Kromayer–Veith, iv. 207–20 (cf. i. 47 ff. for the topography). A quite different, and perverse, explanation of what happened will be found in W. J. Woodhouse's article in *BSA* xxii (1916–18), 51–84, and his book, *King Agis of Sparta* (Oxford, 1933): on which see Kromayer (vol. iv) and my chapter in *Essays*, 132–55. [See map opposite p. 96.

Gomme's own (not very extensive) comment on the topography and on the movements leading up to the battle was given at the end of his n. on 74. 1; and, after considerable hesitation, I have left this out. His view was substantially that given in his *Essays* (above), except that here he took no account of the wood Pelagos, and accounted for the Spartans' surprise (66. 1) more decidedly in terms of an Argive movement at night (cf. *Essays*, 140 n. 1, 141). There are

---

[1] [The grounds of this assumption are not stated, but (*a*) Plataia was on the way to Delphi for most inhabitants of S. Greece, (*b*) the annual festival of iii. 58. 4 (cf. *ATL* iii. 101) will have attracted visitors; whereas Mantineia was less in the ordinary paths of Greek travel, and was not the site of a famous joint Hellenic victory.]

serious objections to this (66. 1 n.), and the alternative possibility ought at least to be discussed, but it would not have been easy to do this by adjusting or augmenting his note. I have therefore started afresh, with a topographical note here—mostly about the wood, which enters into the argument so much that it must be discussed in advance—and notes on the various details as they arise. I have freely used Gomme's notes; and have tried at all stages to make it clear where he held a different view.

The plain of Tegea and Mantineia is today featureless, except for minor inequalities; for its slight tilt downwards towards the north, see 65. 4 n. About a third of the way from Mantineia to Tegea it contracts to a waist, between Mýtikas, a ridge projecting into the plain from the mountains to the west, and Kapnístra, a ridge running north and south along the eastern side. The gap leaves a good two miles of ground level enough for fighting: modern maps, in their zeal to depict the foothills, make it look too narrow. It has generally been assumed that this, the nearest thing to a natural division in the plain, marked the frontier between the two cities. As Gomme several times insists, we do not positively know this, and the boundary might have altered from time to time (*Essays*, 141–2); but there is no positive reason for placing it anywhere else.

It might have been expected that there would be one main road south from Mantineia, at least as far as the waist, dividing thereafter to go SW. to Pallantion and south to Tegea. But Pausanias makes it plain that there were two roads from the start (Plb. xi. 11. 4 speaks of three gates on this side of the city: one must be the western gate). These must have kept to opposite sides of the plain: Bury's map, reproduced in *CAH* v. 274, vi. 102, is misleading here. The Tegea road (called Xenis, Plb. xi. 11. 5) ran below Mt. Alesion, and by the end of the mountain was a temple of Poseidon Hippios, οὐ πρόσω σταδίου Μαντινείας (Paus. viii. 10. 2: the distance must be corrected from Plb. ix. 8. 11, seven stades from the city, cf. Fougères, 103–6). After this (Paus. viii. 11. 1) you come to a place full of oaks, called Pelagos, and the Tegea road goes through the oaks; then an altar which marks the frontier, but no distances are given, and there is no sign whether the altar is still inside the wood.

About 30 stades along the Pallantion road (which would take one roughly to Mýtikas) the wood Pelagos touches that road (11. 5): somewhere near this is Epameinondas' tomb (he was buried on the battlefield, 11. 7), and a stade further on is a temple of Zeus Charmon. The description stops there, probably (as in other cases) because Pausanias has now reached the frontier; though, as Gomme remarks (cf. *Essays*, 142), this would only tell us that the temple was the last object of interest before the frontier, not how much further the frontier was.

Taking Pausanias' evidence as it stands, we seem to have a wood whose northern edge, on the eastern side of the plain, was appreciably further south than Mt. Alesion and the Poseideion, and which reached across nearly to the western side in the neighbourhood of Mýtikas. It need not have been large, indeed it would not contradict Pausanias if the wood stopped before the waist. The question is whether it was there in the fifth century.

Gomme (*Essays*, 140–1) thought it might have increased later, as population and cultivation declined, which is not very likely (cf. A. Philippson, *Das Klima Griechenlands*, 161–2, for the difficulties of re-afforestation) ; and that 'its extent and density and therefore its signification for this campaign are all very uncertain', but even a small thin wood might matter. Its association with Epameinondas is late and partly disreputable (Paus. viii. 11. 10 tells how Epameinondas received an oracle from Delphi, πέλαγος - - - φυλάσσεσθαι, and so took care not to embark on board ship—an all too familiar theme in stories of prophecy), and no earlier account of the battle in 362 mentions the wood. However, Pausanias does not claim that the wood played any part in the battle, and if Kromayer is right (i. 47–76) the fighting was wholly south of the narrows and the wood, but Epameinondas planned to break through the gap between the wood and Mýtikas and come round north of the wood to cut the enemy off. Again, Polybios gives a careful topographical account of Philopoimen's battle against Machanidas in 207 (xi. 11–18 : cf. Gomme, *Essays*, 141 n. 1) without mentioning the wood. But in this case the battle was wholly north of any area the wood could be supposed to cover ; and the only relevant point is that Machanidas at first (12. 4) looked as if he meant to charge Philopoimen's right head on, then deployed his forces eastwards—that is, in his approach march he clung to the western side of the plain, like Epameinondas in 362 (X. *HG* vii. 5. 21). If Pausanias' wood was there, it is natural that armies should use the gap on this side of the plain.

The silence of Xenophon and Polybios is not decisive, and we have to consider carefully the difference its presence or absence would make to the battle of 418—with some slight bias in favour of its presence, since it was certainly there later, at least by Pausanias' own time. In my belief the wood helps to explain the main crux in Thucydides' narrative, at 66. 1 : but of course, to the extent that it helps to explain the narrative, it becomes more striking that Thucydides should not even hint at its existence.]

65. 1. χωρίον ἐρυμνόν: [the λόφος of §§ 4, 6.] Thucydides does not specify it further. Since the plain is quite flat, it must be somewhere on the lower slopes of the surrounding hills, in all probability on Mt. Alesion just east of the city of Mantineia, sufficiently high up

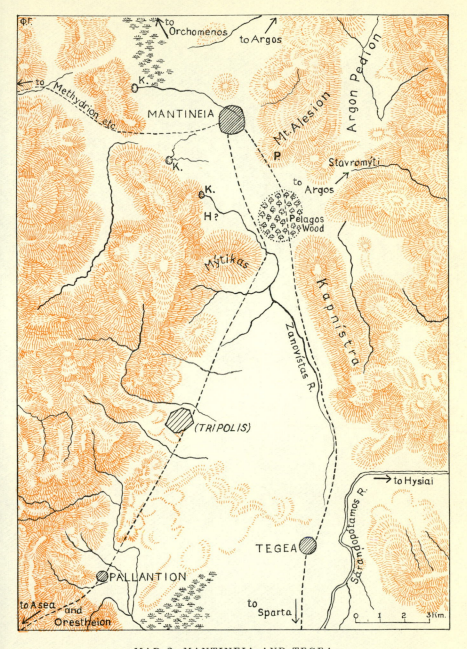

MAP 3. MANTINEIA AND TEGEA

K. = Katavothres   H? = Herakleion?   P. = Temple of Poseidon

the slope to break the cohesion of an attacking hoplite force, not so high as not to tempt it. [See also Kromayer, iv. 208, who is certainly correct in arguing that only Alesion gives room for a hoplite force of this size; and that other neighbouring hills are too steep for hoplite assault, including Stavromýti which Gomme wanted to include in the allied position.

Gomme also raised here, as in *Essays*, 137 n. 1, the question whether the allies, by taking this position, left Agis free to attack the city in the plain below. But, as he says, a small garrison could hold the walls for a long time: and the attack would have been dangerous with a hoplite force on higher ground so near at hand.]

2. ἐπεβόησεν: another lively touch, from an eyewitness. For κακὸν κακῷ ἰᾶσθαι, cf. Hdt. iii. 53. 4 and Soph. *Aj*. 362; [also Aesch. fr. 349 N² (= 695 Mette), Soph. fr. 77, and the passages cited in Pearson's n. there. This is clearly a proverbial phrase, though not taken up by the paroemiographers.]

βουλόμενον: so Plu. *an seni, etc.* (Mor. 797 c). All our MSS. have βουλομένην; if this is the right reading, as Steup, Graves, and others have maintained, and as I think preferable,[1] it too will be a reminiscence of the actual words. As Graves says, τοῦτο φρονεῖ ἡμῶν ἡ - - - ἀγωγή, 85, is similar. [But βουλόμενον, surrounded as it is by fem. accusatives, has some claim as a *lectio difficilior*.]

3. εἴτε καὶ αὐτῷ ἄλλο τι ἢ κατὰ τὸ αὐτὸ δόξαν: 'or because he himself had suddenly changed his mind' must be the meaning (so Warner), but 'because he too decided otherwise than on the same lines' is not easy. Campe's ἢ καὶ τὸ αὐτό, rejected by Stahl (who himself bracketed ἤ), is preferable—'or he himself had an apprehension (different from or the same as that of his mentor)'. [Or Dobree's deletion of ἢ κατὰ τὸ αὐτό might be justified, excising what is certainly a very odd phrase.

Thucydides' narrative, and even his anecdote, leave open the possibility that Agis never intended to press this assault seriously. Woodhouse's suggestion (45) that he was only concerned 'to cover the withdrawal of the train' (the ἁμάξας of 72. 3) will not do, for (as Kromayer says, iv. 209 n. 1) he could achieve this merely by forming up on the plain. But he may have calculated that the assault so suddenly called off, followed by an apparent retreat, would have the effect which in fact it did.]

4. τὸ ὕδωρ ἐξέτρεπεν: Arnold's account of the plain of Arkadia and of this manœuvre (based on a misunderstanding of Leake, iii. 44, 153?), quoted or referred to by many edd., has to be corrected in one major matter. Nearly all the streams (mostly mountain torrents) that enter the plain empty their water into βέρεθρα (or ζέρεθρα in

---

[1] But that Plutarch's MSS. have also ἐπετείου for ἐπαιτίου is not a reason for doubting his testimony, as Steup thinks; for it may only be a case of a very common mis-spelling.

Arkadian, Str. viii. 8. 4, 389; now called καταβόθρες), caverns in the limestone at the foot of the mountain slopes, most of them to the NW., W., and S. of the city of Mantineia; but there is a gentle slope of the plain downwards from near Tegea, 656 m. above sea-level, to near Mantineia, 626 m. It was not then a case of stopping a channel flowing from Mantineia into the Tegeatis, as Arnold says, but of diverting the water of the one considerable stream in the plain, the Sarandopótamos, which flows eastwards from Tegea, into the channel of the Zanovístas, which flows north from Tegea into the Mantinike. Hence ἐξέτρεπεν, not ἀπέτρεπεν. See Fougères, c. ii, and the map (above, opp. p. 96).

These *katavóthres* are easily choked and but inadequately deal, in the rainy season, with the water coming from the hills round Mantineia itself; and land round their mouths is marshy except towards the end of summer.

ὁποτέρωσε ἂν ἐσπίπτῃ: Mantineia of course would damage Tegean territory by blocking the Zanovístas channel.

βοηθοῦντας ἐπὶ τὴν τοῦ ὕδατος ἐκτροπήν: the flooding of Mantinean territory (because the *katavóthres* would be unable to accept this new supply of water) would not be immediate (now, in late summer); but the Mantineans must do all they could to prevent it at once, or it would stop the autumn sowing of their crops (in this high plain, from the middle of October onwards, earlier than in Attica). The break in the summer weather begins there about the middle of September, not many days after the time of this campaign, [which is roughly fixed by τοῦ - - - θέρους μεσοῦντος, 57. 1, of Agis' earlier invasion of the Argolid; and the fact that the Karneia was cele-brated as soon as the Spartans returned home from Mantineia, 75. 2 (cf. 54. 2 n.)—the battle was probably late in August.]

We must also remember that Agis did not have to dig a trench from the Sarandopótamos to the Zanovístas, which would take a long time (it would be about 2½ km. long, if the line of it suggested by Fougères is correct); the trench was already there, it was only the barrier which had to be broken down. [Whatever the mechanism, it is clear from Thucydides that the operation took no long time (§ 5 n. below).

Further, Agis' manœuvre did not compel the Mantineans to come and fight on the scene of his waterworks, as βοηθοῦντας ἐπί, κ.τ.λ. has suggested to some edd.; it meant only that they could not stay on the defensive, but must come down and fight a battle somewhere, victory in which would enable them to reverse what he had done. It is perfectly natural that Agis, having made his point, should march back towards the allies; if 66. 1 is correct and he was making for the Herakleion again, he expected to fight in the plain north of the narrows.]

5. τὴν ἡμέραν ταύτην: [that is, Agis' interrupted attack on the allied position was early in the day, leaving him time to march to Tegea and complete his waterworks the same day.]

ἐξ ὀλίγου: of time, I think, rather than of space, [as most edd. take it, on the ground that if time was meant it would double αἰφνιδίῳ.] A departure may be sudden after a long stay or a short one; this was the latter.

ἀπέκρυψαν: sc. ἑαυτούς. ἰδίως δὲ ἐπὶ τῶν πλοϊζομένων καὶ οὐκέτι ὁρωμένων λέγεται ὡς ἀπέκρυψαν, Σ^Msc2—'disappeared over the horizon'; so here 'were lost to view'. [Gomme compared Sappho 34 LP, and the reverse usage in Pl. *Prt.* 338 a; but he did not comment on the fact.

The plain is not flat in the manner of the alluvial plains of lowland Greece, but the undulations are slight. For an observer on the plain they are enough to conceal an army, indeed small orchards and scattered trees today prevent one from seeing far in any direction, and a wood on the scale Pausanias gives (64. 5 n.) would be an effective obstacle to sight. But one need climb only a few feet up Alesion to see clear over trees and folds in the ground to the slightly higher ridge just north of the Tripolis–Argos road. At that distance and at that time of year, haze normally precludes observation of detail, but an army of some thousands would raise a dust which could not be mistaken. Agis would disappear when he entered the wood (or, if he first went back to the Herakleion, when he passed behind it), but from Alesion he would soon reappear and his movements would be visible as far as the ridge just mentioned. He must in fact have passed beyond the ridge, for otherwise the allies could be in no doubt where he was. (From the map it might appear that the small ridges which project westwards from Kapnístra could conceal him from observers on Alesion, but in fact Alesion can be seen from almost any point on the probable line of the ancient Mantineia–Tegea road.)]

τό τε πρότερον, κ.τ.λ.: 60. 5–6. 'The sense is "as formerly . . . so now"', Graves, comparing 43. 3. Not quite: they now renewed the earlier accusation and began another as well.

6. ἐθορυβήθησαν: 'were confused'—by the enemy's action as much as by the outcry from their own troops; very much as ἐθορυβοῦντο in iii. 22. 6 (Stahl). What attitude was taken by Laches and Nikostratos?

ὡς ἰόντες ἐπὶ τοὺς πολεμίους: [their intention, that evening, was to follow up Agis' supposed retreat and attack him; or, if he retired further, presumably to try Tegea again, with a higher prospect of success. But better information in the morning may have changed their plans: see next n.]

66. 1. ξυνετάξαντο, ὡς ἔμελλον μαχεῖσθαι, ἢν περιτύχωσιν: [they had camped the night before after coming down to the level, προελθόντες ἐς τὸ ὁμαλόν (65. 6), which should mean still close to the foot of Alesion, for if they had advanced much further Agis could not have failed to know where they were. ἢν περιτύχωσιν rather suggests that they were going to look for their enemy, but Greek armies did not normally march any distance in the formation in which they proposed to fight. Nor would they normally advance through a wood in line of battle, though this could be done when necessary, cf. X. *HG* iv. 2. 19; and Pausanias' words in viii. 11. 1, χωρίον - - - δρυῶν πλῆρες, suggest widely spaced trees (as are common in highland Arkadia) rather than thick-set wood. This is the passage which tells most heavily against the presence of the wood. The alternative is to suppose that the allies knew by now, as they would be likely to do, that Agis was on his way back, and that they planned to fight somewhere near their camp. This makes a reasonable story, but it is not quite what Thucydides says; see further next n.]

ὁρῶσι δι᾽ ὀλίγου, κ.τ.λ.: [this is the most intractable puzzle in all these manœuvres. I quote first Gomme's note.]

Another question that we would naturally ask is, did not the Spartans place observers on Mýtikas and Kapnístra when they retreated to the Tegeatis, to watch the enemy movements?[1] Or, if they did, we should have been told why they did not get warning when the enemy left their defensive position on the mountain slopes. As a night (of nearly twelve hours) passed between the manœuvring of the first day and the battle (65. 3–5, 66. 1), and as the Argives so greatly surprised the Lacedaemonians, their march must have been made during the night, unobserved by enemy watches; but it is curious that Thucydides does not expressly say so. There is no feature of the *landscape* that we know, or can guess, that could explain the surprise; by day a march would have been seen, a long way off. A night march is the only possibility.

[This is more uncompromisingly stated than the similar conclusion in his *Essays*, and the note gives no hint why Gomme here excluded the wood so completely from his argument. The basic difficulty of his solution is that, if night could conceal the enemy movement down from Alesion, it could not conceal their position in the plain next day, and if Agis had scouts on the heights they should have told him of this, for he certainly marched by day, τῇ ὑστεραίᾳ. The same objection may be made against Kromayer's solution, iv. 212–13, that the wood Pelagos hindered observation, and that folds on Alesion might make it difficult to see if it were still occupied (it was also partly wooded, Paus. viii. 10. 1): it is not a question of scanning Alesion but of observing the plain. I agree with Gomme that Agis could not have failed to keep a watch on his enemies' movements.

---

[1] [Cf. *Essays*, 140 n. 1, where he goes further into the question, who occupied these heights.]

Greek military history is full of scouts, from the long-distance ἡμεροσκόποι on the heights of Euboea in 480, Hdt. vii. 183. 1, to the short-range climbers on towers and monuments in the Maiandros plain in 397, X. *HG* iii. 2. 14–15. Surprise encounters (as opposed to contrived ambushes) are rare, and the Spartan army is the least likely of all to neglect standard precautions.

The alternative is the solution which made Woodhouse (51–2) so scornful, that Agis knew that the allies had come down into the plain, but did not know their exact position or expect to find them so near and already in battle formation. But round what sort of corner could he come on them so suddenly? If he came from the general direction of Tegea no mountain would have hidden them, as Mýtikas might have done if he was coming from Pallantion; and scouts a little way uphill could see over minor obstacles. Pausanias' wood may provide a solution, though again it does not exactly fit what Thucydides says and implies. Agis, making for the Herakleion again, should leave the Tegea–Mantineia road and march towards the gap between the wood and Mýtikas. If the enemy then began their forward movement, watchers on the heights could give him notice, but that could not shorten the process of getting his army through the gap and deploying it north of the wood, a process which he must go through if he was to fight a battle at all. That is not so dangerous a manœuvre as it might look to modern eyes: while an ancient army was in a mountain defile it was vulnerable enough if it had not secured the heights above, but emergence from a defile did not then involve presenting an easy target to concentrated fire from a distance—the worst that Agis had to fear was that the two armies might meet before his own was tidily drawn up. In fact there was time enough, even for hortatory speeches (69), and the armies had still so much ground to cover before they met that the Spartans could edge away to the right to a dangerous extent (71: cf. *Essays*, 143 ff. on the degree of the surprise).

Thucydides certainly gives a different impression, of the Spartan army wholly unaware of the enemy's position till they suddenly saw one another. But it is evident from the following narrative that his informants somewhat exaggerated the shock of surprise; and there is a gap in his story somewhere, since he offers no explanation at all of the fact that the Spartans were so much surprised, indeed it seems not to have struck him that there was anything that needed explanation. There is no hint in his text either of a night march (as Gomme noted) or of a wood, but the wood offers the more plausible explanation.

I conclude that the battle was fought in the plain of Mantineia itself, well south of the city but north of the Mýtikas–Kapnístra narrows, and north of the wood; and that Thucydides probably worked from verbal descriptions of it, and had not inspected the site himself.]

ἀπὸ τοῦ λόφου προεληλυθότας: [they had moved forward from the site of their night's camp (65. 6); probably while Agis was already on the march, and probably no great distance (cf. p. 100).]

2. μάλιστα δή: Stahl and others are surely right in finding the absence of a connective most improbable here. [Gomme favoured reading δὲ δή, and compared 72. 2. But this is a most appropriate occasion for dramatic asyndeton, cf. Denniston, *Greek Prose Style*, 112 ff., 121 f.]

ἐς ὃ ἐμέμνηντο: [probably, as Steup suggests, 'as far as their memory went back', not as Σ^{Msc₂}, μετὰ τὴν τῶν ἀνθρώπων μνήμην; i.e. the Spartans are the subject. But what sort of thing were they remembering? There were occasions in the fifth century when the Spartan army might well have been 'dismayed', but faced an adverse situation with discipline and courage, as here: Thermopylae certainly, perhaps the hard-fought battle of Tanagra: but none of these involved any sudden shock of surprise, nor is it easy to think of any occasion which did, except perhaps the fighting on Sphakteria (iv. 32. 1, 34. 2, 36. 2), and that is hardly comparable to the standard hoplite battle. This is perhaps the phrase of a combatant to whom Thucydides talked: 'nothing in our experience matched this sudden emergency'.]

ἐξεπλάγησαν, κ.τ.λ.: in spite of Hude and Stuart Jones, I think it impossible to keep the MSS. reading here, because γάρ has no place, whether in explanation of Spartan action or of the statement about the action. We need ὅμως somewhere in the second sentence. [A ms. note compares the sequence viii. 1. 2 μὲν γάρ - - - 1. 3 ὅμως δέ.] This is true even if, with Graves (who compares iv. 14. 3, ὑπὸ προθυμίας καὶ ἐκπλήξεως), we weaken the sense of ἐξεπλάγησαν to '"were excited, startled" out of their usual slow and deliberate ways'. (LSJ exaggerates the force of ἐκπλήσσεσθαι, 'to be panic-struck, amazed'; but we must not weaken it either, especially in the aorist and perfect passive, and in its derivatives. It conveys the sense of 'bewilderment': 'dismay' is at least near the meaning.) Hude's putting διὰ βραχείας γάρ - - - ἐγίγνετο into parenthesis makes things worse—it helps γάρ, but leaves ἐξεπλάγησαν - - - καὶ εὐθύς, κ.τ.λ., in impossible sequence. Stahl and Steup are right in supposing a lacuna, containing a negative. [Steup indeed suggested that Σ^{Msc₂} χωρὶς ἀναβολῆς καὶ μελλήσεως implied a text containing a negative. Gomme went on to discuss various supplements, and himself suggested, e.g., ⟨ἀλλ' οὐδὲ ὡς ἐς θόρυβον κατέστησαν⟩ between ἐξεπλάγησαν and διά.

This interpretation assumes that in the clause διὰ βραχείας, κ.τ.λ., the emphasis is on the fact that the Spartans did, after only a short delay, get themselves organized: Gomme quoted Stahl, '*quae enim causa subsequitur, ea non probat perturbatos esse Lacedaemonios, sed non perturbatos.*' But Hude's interpretation (cited in Steup's appendix) is at least as likely, and calls for no alteration of the text: they were perturbed, because they had only a short time to make their preparations. LSJ, translating 'at short notice', treat this as a branch of the meaning 'delay', and Hude also understood the word in this sense. The other well-marked sense of μέλλησις in Thucydides, 'intention' or 'being about to do' (116. 1; i. 69. 4), seems more relevant—'they had only a short time for what they were going to do'—and this deals with most of Steup's not very impressive objections against Hude. (It does, however, involve a 'weakening' of the sense of ἐξεπλάγησαν, of the kind Gomme objected to: but since the Spartans did quickly recover themselves this is inevitable on any interpretation.) Rather than make the clause a parenthesis, I would put a colon after ἐξεπλάγησαν and a full stop after ἐγίγνετο. There is then no difficulty in going on καὶ εὐθύς, κ.τ.λ.]

ὑπὸ σπουδῆς: 'under the influence of speed', as in ὑπ' ὀργῆς, etc. (cf. iii. 33. 3), because they had so little time; not the usual Spartan way (cf. 70 below), yet even so they preserved their cohesion and discipline.

Ἄγιδος - - - ἕκαστα ἐξηγουμένου κατὰ τὸν νόμον: [the ξύμβουλοι of 63. 4 do not interfere in actual operations; see n. there.]

3. τοῖς μὲν πολεμάρχοις, κ.τ.λ.: on the organization of the Spartan army, see 68. 3 n. αὐτὸς φράζει shows that the polemarchs were with Agis, not each with his *mora*, until the moment of ξύνταξις began.

ἐνωμοτάρχοις: [so Stahl, and all edd. since, for codd. ἐνωμοτάρχαις, mainly because of the analogy of πολεμάρχοις. The first-declension form is guaranteed by GHI 204. 26: see Tod's note, ii, p. 307, and to his references add Arr. *Tact.* 6. 2, where there is no doubt about the reading ἐνωμοτάρχην.]

4. καὶ αἱ παραγγέλσεις: i.e. orders passed down the line, as opposed to those intended to be heard by all at once, given out by trumpet or herald; [or to the orders given in advance by the king through the polemarchs (§ 3).] Grote of course exaggerates when he says (v. 478) that this system of passing orders was peculiar to the Spartan among Greek armies, that at Athens, for example, the ταξίαρχοι never received orders from the strategos for their own τάξεις; it is the extreme subdivision and chain of command in Sparta, and the efficiency, that were unique.

ταχεῖαι ἐπέρχονται: cf. ii. 11. 9. Where speed was desirable, the Spartans had it. It is not unreasonable to suppose that Thucydides had seen the Spartan army at work—at least on manœuvre—himself at some time.

67. 1. Σκιρῖται: [for the location of the Skiritis, see 33. 1 n. The Skiritai were Arkadians (Hesych. s.v. Σκιρίτης; cf. SIG³. 665. 31–5,[1]

¹ For l. 32. see Bölte, *RE.* iiiA. 1312, whose restoration is to be preferred to Dittenberger's.

a second-century arbitration which decided that both Skiritis and Aigytis were Arkadian). After Leuktra they achieved their independence of Sparta: X. *HG* vii. 4. 21, cf. vi. 5. 26. If Thucydides includes them here among the Lakedaimonioi, that is because the whole army was Lacedaemonian, and the Skiritai were a regular element in it. They were employed mainly as scouts or in conjunction with cavalry (X. *Lac. Pol.* 12. 3, *HG* v. 4. 52; cf. *Cyrop.* iv. 2. 1, an important passage for their relations with Sparta). X. *Lac. Pol.* 13. 6 says that no one marched ahead of the king except the Skiritai and cavalry scouts, but says nothing of their place in a set hoplite battle: Diod. xv. 32. 1 says their place was with the king, as a reserve to be sent to any part of the line which was in trouble, but from the way his sentence continues it looks as if he has telescoped a reference to the Skiritai with one to the 300 'hippeis' (72. 4 n.).]

οἱ ἀπὸ Θρᾴκης Βρασίδειοι - - - καὶ νεοδαμώδεις: see 34. 1, with n.

Ἡραιῆς: [on the right bank of the Alpheios, a mile or so above the point where the Ladon joins it, in the extreme west of Arkadia near the borders of Elis. This is the lowest point at which the Alpheios is regularly fordable (in Hellenistic times there was a bridge, Plb. iv. 77. 5): Heraia's territory was fairly extensive, since Strabo, viii. 3. 2, 337, records a synoikismos of nine demes. Only fragments of its history survive: a hundred-year treaty with Elis, ML 17, dated '*c.* 500?' by Jeffery, 220, no. 6; a relatively early coinage interrupted early in the fifth century, when Heraia perhaps became the mint of an Arkadian league founded by Kleomenes *c.* 490 (W. P. Wallace, *JHS* lxxiv (1954), 33–4; some reservations about the dates, Jeffery, 210 with n. 3); evidently loyal now, and remained so after Leuktra (X. *HG* vi. 5. 11, 22), perhaps for fear of Elis. See Bölte, *RE* viii. 407–16.]

Μαινάλιοι: [no doubt most communities of Mainalioi, at least those in the south and west, were now loyal to Sparta, after the Spartan campaign in 421, c. 33 above. But as Bölte says, *RE* xiv. 1322, it is hard to see who the Mantinean allies and subjects of 58. 1, 67. 2, 81. 1 can be, if they are not the northern Mainalioi; cf. also the Mainalian hostages held by Argos, 77. 1.]

ἐπὶ τῷ δεξιῷ κέρᾳ Τεγεᾶται: see Hdt. ix. 26, [where the Tegeates claim a traditional post on the left wing, but the Athenian counterclaim prevailed. Thucydides says nothing of a traditional privilege (though he does assert a traditional post for the Skirites on the left of the Spartan contingent), but places the Tegeates on the right with the 'few' Spartans. We need not make too much of the contradiction between Herodotos and Thucydides: the 'traditional' honour claimed might well vary with the circumstances: for another variation, cf. the battle near Corinth in 394, X. *HG* iv. 2. 19–21, where the Spartans take the right wing with the Tegeates next to them. If the Spartans, even intermittently, recognized some Tegeate (and Skirite) privilege, that would help, as Gomme argued, to cement loyalty.]

Λακεδαιμονίων ὀλίγοι τὸ ἔσχατον ἔχοντες: the right being the post of honour. [The Spartans are at least represented here, though not by one of their regular formations, see 71. 3 n.]

καὶ οἱ ἱππῆς αὐτῶν: [Thucydides does not specify which states provided this cavalry. Sparta herself maintained a cavalry force in Xenophon's time (*Lac. Pol.* 11. 2), but it was not well thought of in 371 (X. *HG* vi. 4. 10–11). This must be distinguished from the τριακόσιοι ἱππῆς καλούμενοι of 72. 4, who were not cavalry at all (see n. there). It may indeed be that for much of the fifth century Sparta maintained no regular cavalry force, or a very small one: it was an innovation when they established a force of 400 cavalry in 424, iv. 55. 2.]

2. ὅτι ἐν τῇ ἐκείνων τὸ ἔργον ἐγίγνετο: these words are exact for what they mean—'the campaign was being waged in Mantinean territory', as it was, by contrast with Argive or Elean or Athenian territory—but do not mean that the allies, on their march towards the Tegeatis, had not crossed the boundary (*Essays*, 142). [If, however, my argument in 66. 1 n. is correct, the battle itself was fought literally in Mantinean territory.

The treaty between the allies provided (47. 7) that the city which sent for help should have the command, while the war was in its own territory. Thucydides says nothing about this in his narrative of the campaign—65. 5–6 do not read as if anyone was exercising unitary command—but he tells us here that the Mantineans had the post of honour on the right; that would be more easily conceded than genuine subordination.]

οἱ ξύμμαχοι Ἀρκάδων: [see § 1 n., on Μαινάλιοι.]

Ἀργείων οἱ χίλιοι λογάδες, κ.τ.λ.: since this regiment of select troops had been instituted, or at least continued, by the democracy at Argos, there is no reason to suppose it an aristocratical body, though in modern times everybody has asserted that it was; but it was a privileged body of men and, as such, they might come to think themselves something apart from, and superior to, the general run of fellow citizens. Thucydides does not say either that it was the select thousand who next spring overthrew the democracy, though 1,000 Spartan and 1,000 Argive troops together established an oligarchy friendly to Sparta at Argos (81. 2: see n. there).

[Ephoros evidently made much more of the thousand. Diod. xii. 75. 7, under 421/20 in his summary of the situation created by the peace, tells us of the installation of the thousand, young men remarkable for their property (καὶ ταῖς οὐσίαις) as well as their strength, who were relieved of all other public duties to train for war.

(Institution in 421 is not far enough back to suit Thucydides' ἐκ πολλοῦ: Ephoros, in his summary of the position of Argos in 421, probably reached back further into their history: he was apt to proceed in this way, and it sometimes confused Diodoros.)] In the course of a narrative of the campaign of 418 B.C. which in the main follows Thucydides, with characteristic confusions and misdating, xii. 78–80, Diodoros says that οἱ ἐπίλεκτοι τῶν Ἀργείων, 1,000 in number and specially trained, routed the enemy in front of them and made great slaughter (79. 4: afterwards being allowed a safe passage for retreat, see n. below on Th. v. 73. 4); and that, next year, after peace was made, τῶν Ἀργείων οἱ κατ' ἐκλογὴν κεκριμένοι τῶν πολιτῶν χίλιοι agreed among themselves to overthrow the democracy; ἔχοντες δὲ πολλοὺς συνεργοὺς διὰ τὸ προέχειν τῶν πολιτῶν ταῖς οὐσίαις καὶ ταῖς ἀνδραγαθίαις, arrested and killed the prominent leaders of the demos, frightened the rest, and accomplished their purpose (80. 2–3). Plutarch, *Alc.* 15. 3, just says that οἱ χίλιοι overthrew the Argive democracy, without having given any account of the fighting at the battle of Mantineia. Aristotle, in a list of cases in which special distinction in war had aided constitutional changes (a list which includes, for Athens in the Persian wars, both the Areopagus in one direction and 'the sailor crowd' at Salamis in the other), says that the *gnorimoi* at Argos, εὐδοκιμήσαντες περὶ τὴν ἐν Μαντινείᾳ μάχην τὴν πρὸς Λακεδαιμονίους ἐπεχείρησαν καταλύειν τὸν δῆμον (*Pol.* v. 3. 5, 1304ᵃ25). He may have got his general picture of the battle from Ephoros.

[There is great probability that all this should be derived from the single account of Ephoros; and also the lurid story of the counter-revolution in Paus. ii. 20. 2, for which see 82. 2 n. It is not at all impossible that Ephoros should have had genuine non-Thucydidean information; nor (*pace* Gomme) that the *corps d'élite* of a democracy should be drawn from a wealthier class which was out of sympathy with that democracy. But Gomme's distrust of the Ephoran version is justified: (*a*) Diodoros' account of the part played by the thousand in the battle (above) is not reconcilable with Thucydides, and there is no reason at all to throw the latter over in Ephoros' favour; (*b*) Pausanias' story is also irreconcilable with Thucydides in detail, and its romantic character is not in its favour. The non-Thucydidean version does not inspire confidence in detail, but it is still possible that the thousand did have a hand in the revolution, a point which Thucydides does not contradict.]

Κλεωναῖοι: [near the end of the long valley which from the Corinthian side approaches Nemea and the low pass over into the Argolid. Strabo, who saw it from the top of Acrocorinth, reckons 80 stades from Kleonai to Corinth, 120 to Argos (viii. 6. 19, 377). See Bursian, ii. 35–9; Bölte, *RE* xi. 721–8.

In spite of later Argive claims, Kleonai appears to have been

independent, and in control of the sanctuary at Nemea, down to the
fifth century: Pindar treats the Nemean festival as Kleonaian, *Nem.*
iv. 17, x. 42. The process by which it fell into Argos' hands is not
clear. Plu. *Cim.* 17. 2 refers to an attack by Corinth, undated but
probably not long before Kimon's time, which may be relevant. In
the 460s Kleonai both joined Argos and Tegea in their attack on
Mycenae (Str. loc. cit.; Diod. xi. 65. 2 says that Mycenae was asserting a claim to control Nemea), and afterwards gave a refuge to part
of the population of Mycenae; this is not necessarily a sign that
Kleonai's allegiance had altered during the siege, but see the argument of W. G. Forrest, *CQ* N.S. x (1960), 230–1. By the time of Tanagra,
when a Kleonaian contingent came with the Argives to help Athens
and its dead were buried in the Kerameikos (Paus. i. 29. 7), Kleonai
was firmly attached to Argos, as it was thereafter; but it retained
some separate existence, and was not one of the minor cities which
the Argives at one time or another demolished, bringing their inhabitants to Argos (Paus. viii. 27. 1).]

'Ορνεᾶται: [the position of Orneai is given roughly by Paus. ii. 25. 5–6;
it was about 60 stades from Argos to Lyrkeia (up the Inachos), and
as far again to Orneai; and beyond that is Sikyonia and Phleiasia.
60 stades should take one roughly to the point where the Inachos
emerges from its enclosed valley into the plain. Lyrkeia must not be
too far inside the valley, since Pausanias' story, and the festival for
which it supplied the *aition*, require that a beacon in or near Lyrkeia
should be visible from the Larisa of Argos; and the high ground
WNW. of the Larisa cuts it off from any site deep into the valley,
or from the hills above such a site. For this reason, and because it is
much more than 60 stades away, the modern renaming of Káto
Bélesi as Lyrkeia is certainly wrong. W. Müller's suggestion of Skála
or Skhoinokhóri, *RE* xiii. 2498–9, is entirely plausible.

From there most investigators have turned to the route over into
Phleiasia beside Mt. Keloussa (58. 3–4 n.: Curtius, *Peloponnesos*,
ii. 479; Bursian, ii. 63–4), but there are no clear reports of ancient
remains in this area (Ernst Meyer, *RE* xviii. 1123–4). Curtius placed
Orneai near Leóndi, but that is very far north for Pausanias' 120
stades from Argos. The plain of Yimnó might support a city of some
minor importance and suits the measurements better, but this valley
descends gently toward Phleious and is separated from the Inachos
by an abrupt slope; as a matter of topography and communications
one would expect the whole valley to belong rather to Phleious. If
that is right, we can look for Orneai only in the Inachos valley and its
offshoots, and the only plausible site is Káto Bélesi/Lyrkeia; which
might be somewhat short of 120 stades from Argos but is otherwise
perfectly suitable. The boundary with Phleious would then be the
watershed south of Yimnó which separates the head-waters of the

Asopos from the Inachos. But neither here nor elsewhere could Orneai have a common frontier with Sikyon.

Strabo presents other problems. Having run through the cities assigned to Argos in the Catalogue (*Iliad*, ii. 559–62), he remarks at viii. 6. 17, 376 that Homer did not mention Thyreai, and did not know Hysiai and Kenchreai on the road from Tegea to Argos, οὐδὲ τὸ Λυκούργιον (probably Λύρκειον), οὐδ᾽ Ὀρνεάς· κῶμαι δ᾽ εἰσὶ τῆς Ἀργείας, ἡ μὲν ὁμώνυμος τῷ ὄρει τῷ . . . . (probably Λυρκείῳ), αἱ δὲ ταῖς Ὀρνεαῖς ταῖς μεταξὺ Κορίνθου καὶ Σικυῶνος ἱδρυμέναις. Kramer excised all the words here cited in Greek, believing that this second Orneai was the invention of an interpolator. But 6. 24, 382 is clear enough: Ὀρνεαὶ δ᾽ εἰσὶν ὁμώνυμοι τῷ παραρρέοντι ποταμῷ, νῦν μὲν ἔρημοι πρότερον δ᾽ οἰκούμεναι καλῶς, ἱερὸν ἔχουσαι Πριάπου τιμώμενον - - - κεῖνται δ᾽ ὑπὲρ τοῦ πεδίου τοῦ Σικυωνίων, τὴν δὲ χώραν ἔσχον Ἀργεῖοι: and this Orneai is mentioned again at xiii. 1. 12, 587, in connection with the cult of Priapos, as Ὀρνεῶν τῶν περὶ Κόρινθον. Strabo evidently believed in the existence of an Orneai above Sikyon, and decided that the Orneai of the Catalogue (ii. 571, in the Mycenaean section) was this city and not the Argive Orneai.

The Argive Orneai could not overhang the plain of Sikyon, though in Roman times, when Stymphalos had voluntarily joined with Argos (Paus. viii. 22. 1), Argive territory might conceivably have reached down further north towards Sikyon. No such excuse can be found for Pausanias' statement (ii. 25. 6 above) that an Orneai 120 stades from Argos had a common frontier with Sikyon; and there seems to be a similar confusion in Paus. x. 18. 5, a dedication at Delphi by Ὀρνεᾶται οἱ ἐν τῇ Ἀργολίδι for the repulse of Sikyonians who had oppressed them in war (cf. Plu. *Pyth. Orac.* 15, 401 d). All this would be easier to understand if there was in fact, or had once been, an Orneai in the neighbourhood of Sikyon and Corinth.

Our Orneai, like Kleonai, is described as an ally of Argos, and the city survived till the Argives destroyed it in winter 416/15 (vi. 7. 2). Questions have been raised about its status because of Hdt. viii. 73. 3, on the races of the Peloponnese, οἱ δὲ Κυνούριοι αὐτόχθονες ἐόντες δοκέουσι μοῦνοι εἶναι Ἴωνες, ἐκδεδωρίευνται δὲ ὑπό τε Ἀργείων ἀρχόμενοι καὶ τοῦ χρόνου, ἐόντες Ὀρνεῆται καὶ [οἱ] περίοικοι. Since the familiar Kynouria is in the south on the Spartan border (41. 2 above) while Orneai is somewhere in the extreme north of the Argolid, it has been conjectured that in this passage Orneatai and perioikoi both designate status not geographical position, the former being a term extended from Orneai, perhaps the first to be thus subjected, to others in the same position (much as the term Πλαταιῆς was extended at Athens). Larsen, *RE* xix. 822, followed by F. Gschnitzer, *Abhängige Orte im griechischen Altertum* (1958), 79 n. 23, recommends the straightforward translation 'the people of Orneai and the neighbourhood', but does not comment on the difficulty of the distance between Orneai and Kynouria.

The likely answer is that there was another Kynouria in the north, in and near the Inachos valley. This is required still more clearly for Str. viii. 6. 7, 370, ὁ "Ιναχος χαραδρώδης ποταμὸς τὰς πηγὰς ἔχων ἐκ Λυρκείου τοῦ κατὰ τὴν Κυνουρίαν ὄρους τῆς Ἀρκαδίας. Kramer thought that all after Λυρκείου should be deleted, on the ground that Kynouria is out of place here and that Lyrkeion is elsewhere called Argive. But Kynouria and names like it are widespread: besides the Thyreate district, there is another in western Arkadia north of Lykaion (Paus. viii. 27. 4 Κυνουραῖοι, but IG v. 2. 1. 40 Κυνούριοι); cf. also Steph. Byz. Κυνόσουρα· ἄκρα Ἀρκαδίας, and Kynosoura or the like in Sparta and Megara. If the name belonged to a pre-Dorian race, the upper Inachos and its tributary valleys form a remote and separate district where another such remnant might well have been preserved, Orneai being their chief settlement. In favour of this is the fact that Herodotos' Kynourioi had been dorized under Argive rule: the Argives held Orneai in his day, whereas the Thyreatis had long been in Spartan not Argive hands. Finally, another Ionic link with this district is provided by Paus. ii. 25. 6: Orneai took its name from Orneus, son of Erechtheus. Larsen's literal interpretation of Hdt. viii. 73. 3 is fully justified, and we need not take Orneate as a description of status.

The location of Mt. Lyrkeion is less easy. Paus. ii. 25. 3, viii. 6. 6, makes the Inachos rise from Mt. Artemision, and anyone who goes as far as the bend above Kaparéli would inevitably take the valley running northwards from below the summit of Artemision to be the main valley. Accordingly Bölte, RE xi. 249, assigned the name Lyrkeion to the ridge along the west side of this upper valley, running north from the western shoulder of Artemision and dividing the territories of Argos and Mantineia. But those who said that the river rose from Lyrkeion (Str. above, Kallimachos fr. 307 Pfeiffer, Σ Ap. Rhod. i. 125, cf. Soph. fr. 271 Pearson) may as easily have meant the separate mountain now locally called Lyrkeion, north of Bölte's ridge and of the pass called Klimax (Paus. viii. 6. 4, now Pórtes): this is the mountain which closes the eastern plain (Argon Pedion) of Mantineia at its northern end, and the valley of Alea at its southern end. If one looks into the Inachos valley from the Argive plain, the bend towards Artemision is not visible and the river looks as if it rose from this mountain, as indeed much of it does.

No help can be got from the only other evidence, Demetrios' Peloponnesian campaign of 295, when Plu. Demetr. 35. 1 says that he defeated Archidamos περὶ Μαντίνειαν. Polyainos iv. 7. 9 tells how he set fire to the woods of a mountain which lay between him and the enemy, and a north wind blew the fire and smoke towards the

Spartans: the text has ὅρος Ἀρκαδικὸν Λυκαῖον, but the easy emendation Λύρκειον (Melber) is no doubt right, bringing us back to the neighbourhood of Mantineia. Demetrios could have come up the valley of Alea, and thus have reached the northern side of the mountain now called Lyrkeion, but it is not easy to imagine what he did next: the cliffs which close the head of the valley are not an inviting path for an army. No alternative position for Lyrkeion makes the story easier, and it is not worth speculating further. Fortunately the exact location of Lyrkeion makes no difference to the argument about Orneai and Kynouria above. See map opposite p. 83.

For the further fate of Orneai, see vi. 7. 1–2, with n.]

68. 1. τάξις μὲν ἥδε καὶ παρασκευὴ ἀμφοτέρων ἦν: as before the first hostile act of the whole war, ii. 8–12, and before other set battles, e.g. Delion, iv. 91–5, so here, at one of the most significant of such battles, Thucydides gives an elaborated account of the παρασκευή and γνώμη (in the speeches, mostly); there are still two more paragraphs before the clash of arms in c. 70.

τὸ δὲ στρατόπεδον τῶν Λακ. μεῖζον ἐφάνη: [this is an important element in the calculation of the numbers engaged, see § 3 n. It might be decisive, if we had been given numbers for the Spartan allies.]

2. οὐκ ἂν ἐδυνάμην ἀκριβῶς: sc. εἰ ἐπεχείρουν or εἰ ἐβουλόμην, for those who keep the MSS. reading (Hude, as well as Stuart Jones). But 'try' or 'wish' is just what Thucydides did; the unreal condition is wrong here, and Steup's οὐκ ἐδυνάμην seems preferable to Stahl's οὐκ ἂν δυναίμην. [But the text may stand if we supply, e.g., εἴ τίς μ' ἠρώτα or εἴ τίς μου ἐδεῖτο γράψαι: Pl. *Prt.* 335 e–336 a is not dissimilar.]

The frankness of this statement 'enhances the value of his testimony wherever he gives it positively'—Grote, v. 480.

διά - - - τὸ κρυπτόν: cf. iv. 80. 2–4.

ἐς τὰ οἰκεῖα πλήθη: cf. vi. 17. 5, though here the boast is more precise —'we had so many troops in the battle, and so played a larger part than we are sometimes given credit for'. It will be remembered that even for his own city Thucydides does not give an estimate for the whole population, or even for the total of citizens: cf. iii. 87. 3, iv. 94. 1.

3. λόχοι μὲν γάρ, κ.τ.λ.: I have never understood the difficulty that some have felt in the exactness of the calculation that follows here after the doubt expressed in § 2. Thucydides gives the official numbers of the *lochoi* and their subdivisions, and the number of those in the front rank. He adds that the number of ranks varied (see n. on p. 117), though 'over all', 'by and large', they were drawn up (as were most Greek hoplite armies) eight deep. The exact figure (and calculation in this sense, ἐκ τοιοῦδε λογισμοῦ, cannot help being exact) is 3,584, which makes a Lacedaemonian force, with the Skiritai, of 4,184. We might ask ourselves, why did not Thucydides here, without any of this elaborate to-do, state simply that the Lacedaemonians numbered 'about 4,000', or 'more than 4,000, without their Arkadian allies', a figure, that is, comparable with the 1,000 select Argive corps, and the 1,000 Athenian hoplites and 300 cavalry; for this would be valuable information, and elsewhere, notably in the narrative of the Peloponnesian invasions of Attica, he gives no figures at all.[1] But the answer must be, that he had been able to get some precise information about the organization of the Spartan army, but was not sure that 4,000 was the (approximately) accurate figure for the total at Mantineia (cf. 74. 1 n.) ; when he enquired further, one may suppose,—'so that would make, would it not? with the usual age-groups called up for foreign service, πανστρατιᾷ, something more than 4,000 hoplites?'—silence fell, and he got no more; and, in Sparta, he got no more than a shrug of the shoulders when he said, 'the Heraies, or the Mainalioi, or the Tegeatai, say their troops numbered so many'. All this suggests once more that he was in Lakonia during this campaign or soon after. It also shows that, when he says else-where that the Athenian or the Theban or some other force num-bered so many, he means that it numbered so many, not that this was a rough guess based on paper figures.

The Athenian figures here, and the Argive, are not strictly com-parable with the calculated Lacedaemonian. In those cities adminis-tration was not secret; a decree of the assembly would order that named generals would have so many men in this expeditionary force; and Thucydides had means of finding out what the numbers were, just as he learnt who the Athenian commanders were.

For a comparison of this account of the Spartan army with that of Xenophon, *Lac. Pol.* 11. 4 and elsewhere, see Busolt–Swoboda, ii. 708–13, [with Busolt's article, *Hermes* xl (1905), 387–449; Kromayer, *Klio* iii (1903), 173–200; Beloch, *Klio* vi (1906), 58–78; A. J. Toynbee, *JHS* xxxiii (1913), 262–72; Wade-Gery, *Essays*, 71–3, 80–5. Our two main authorities conflict over the detail, and both accounts have disquieting features: the field for speculation is wide, and not all theories can be discussed at length here.

A. *Thucydides.*

1. The system is clearly set out. There were seven *lochoi*, each of four *pentekostyes*, each of four *enomotiai*; and four men in the front rank of each *enomotia* (see X. *Lac. Pol.* 11. 4 for the ways in which an *enomotia* could be drawn up, though a front of four is not one of his examples). Thus the whole front is $4 \times 4 \times 4 \times 7 = 448$, the figure given in the text, so at least Thucydides' items are correctly transmitted.

---

[1] [Note also that he gives no figures for the Syracusan forces in vi–vii.]

By and large they were eight deep: the scholiasts do the sum for us, and it comes out at 3,584.

Only the 600 Skiritai are excluded, so the Brasideioi and *neodamodeis* form one of the seven *lochoi*. The Λακεδαιμόνιοι αὐτοί of 67. 1 are then six *lochoi*, and it is this army that we have to compare with that of other occasions. It may be tabulated as follows:

> 4 *enomotiai* of *c.* 32 each   = 1 *pentekostys* of *c.* 128
> 4 *pentekostyes* of *c.* 128 each = 1 *lochos* of *c.* 512
> 6 *lochoi* of *c.* 512 each   = *c.* 3,072.

This is five-sixths of the maximum levy (64. 3): the maximum strength of the *lochos* is thus *c.* 614, and of six *lochoi c.* 3,686.

There is one uncertain factor, whether Thucydides has included in this calculation the 300 'hippeis' of 72. 4 who fought around the king. It is a large number for him to have neglected, and Beloch (64) may be right in supposing that they were included in the main framework, and were the ἄγημα τῆς πρώτης μόρας of *Lac. Pol.* 13. 6, directly under the king in battle (and apparently taken away from their own unit for the battle, to judge from Xenophon's words). 300 is an awkward number to fit into Thucydides' scheme, and their internal organization (three *hippagretai, Lac. Pol.* 4. 3) is also abnormal; but it might be argued that these are just the ways of a *corps d'élite*. This uncertainty remains; but there is little doubt that Thucydides has disregarded the Λακ. ὀλίγοι on the extreme right wing (67. 1): I agree with Woodhouse and Gomme that these cannot be the two *lochoi* of 71. 3 (see n. there).

2. Thucydides' totals are surprisingly low.

(*a*) For our battle, we have on the Spartan side the seven *lochoi*, the Skiritai, and perhaps the hippeis, 3,584 + 600 (+ 300?) = 4,184 (or 4,484?), *plus* the unnumbered contingents of Tegea (presumably πανδημεί), Heraia, and the Mainalioi. On the other side, 1,000 Athenians and the 1,000 select Argives, *plus* the main Argive army, Kleonai, Orneai, Mantineia and her allies. This is a formidable array of unknowns. But there is some indication that the Mantinean number should be of the order of 3,000 (58. 1 n.: here they will be at maximum strength). If we call them 2,500 and the Argive main body 3,000, and allow (say) 500 for Kleonai, etc., we can keep the total down to some 8,000. Agis' army was perceptibly the larger (§ 1), and this means that the unnumbered Spartan allies amount to well over 3,500. This is not at all impossible; but to reach this result we have to keep the Argive numbers very low, whereas Thucydides' account calls for a full turn-out from Argos (74. 3, 75. 4 nn.), and 74. 1 calls for high numbers on both sides, challenging comparison with Tanagra (see 74. 1 n.). It might also be noted that the Brasideioi and *neodamodeis* should have been able to produce more than *c.* 512 hoplites:

there were 700 Brasideioi originally (iv. 80. 5) and there is no reason
to set their casualties in the north especially high; and if there were
any *neodamodeis* at all, there would probably be some hundreds.

(*b*) At the Nemea River in 394 there were ὁπλῖται Λακεδαιμονίων
μὲν εἰς ἑξακισχιλίους (X. *HG* iv. 2. 16). Of these, 600 might be Skiritai,
as in 418, or a few more; and there may be some *neodamodeis*, as
Busolt supposed, but hardly a great number, for there were then
some 3,000 in Asia (*HG* iii. 1. 4, 4. 2), and it is not likely that Sparta
liberated and armed helots in numbers much exceeding those of her
own army. Making all reasonable allowance, this still implies a
regular force in 394 larger than Thucydides' scheme permits.

(*c*) There are other indications that one-sixth of the Spartan levy
should come to more than *c.* 614. By the summer of 403, at latest,
the largest units of the army were called *morai* (X. *HG* ii. 4. 31), and
there were certainly six of them (*HG* vi. 4. 17 with vi. 1. 1; Arist.
fr. 540 Rose). Here the crucial example is the *mora* destroyed by
Iphikrates in 390, *HG* iv. 5. 11–17. One would not expect a high call-up
for garrison duty at Lechaion in 390, and there is no sign that hoplites from outside the *mora* were involved: the members from Amy-
klai had already left, and they were more than a mere handful: yet
Xenophon says that the hoplites were about 600, near the maximum
strength of Thucydides' *lochos*. The *mora* (or *lochos*) naturally varies
in strength with the number of age-groups called up. Hence the
variations in Plu. *Pel.* 17. 4, on the two *morai* defeated at Tegyra in
373, where Plutarch quotes (i) Ephoros (*FGrHist* 70 F 210) as saying
that the *mora* was 500 men (Diod. xv. 32. 1 has the same for Agesilaos'
campaign in Boeotia in 377); (ii) Kallisthenes (124 F 18) as giving 700,
possibly in his account of Tegyra, and possibly trying to enlarge the
Boeotian achievement; (iii) Polybios (fr. 60 B-W) and others as
giving 900. Polybios (disregarding the unnamed others) has been
taken to refer to the unverifiable arrangements of Machanidas or
Nabis; but if this were a possible strength for a fourth-century *mora*,
the 600 of the reduced Lechaion *mora* would be less mysterious.

3. In 66. 3 Thucydides gives the chain of command: king—polemarch—*lochagos*—*pentekonter*—*enomotarches*. The last three are
clearly connected by their names with the three types of unit given
in 68. 3. The polemarchs are thus left somewhat in the air: but two
of them had charge of *lochoi* in the battle (71. 3), though the *lochagoi*
also had some responsibility, since they determined the depth of
formation of their *lochoi* (68. 3). The apparent discrepancy is easily
resolved by supposing that the *lochagos* was the polemarch's deputy:
since the polemarchs were often in attendance on the king (X. *Lac.
Pol.* 13. 1) there would be need for deputies. Thucydides himself must
have supposed some arrangement of this kind, unless we are to con-
vict him of mere incoherence. But it must be noted that in the army

known to Xenophon the polemarch had his own unit, the *mora* (*HG* iv. 4. 7 is a clear case).

B. *Xenophon.*

1. *Lac. Pol.* 11. 4 gives us six *morai*; and each *mora* had one polemarch, four *lochagoi*, eight *pentekonteres*, sixteen *enomotarchai*. If the number of units corresponds to the number of officers (but see C. (1) below), this may be tabulated as follows (for comparison, I take the figure for the *enomotia* which Thucydides gives for Mantineia):

2 *enomotiai* of *c.* 32 each	= 1 *pentekostys* of *c.* 64
2 *pentekostyes* of *c.* 64 each	= 1 *lochos* of *c.* 128
4 *lochoi* of *c.* 128 each	= 1 *mora* of *c.* 512
6 *morai* of *c.* 512 each	= *c.* 3,072.

2. The total of *enomotiai*, and the total strength of the army, are the same as for Thucydides, and cause the same difficulties (A. (2) above). But the structure is different, not only in the addition of the *mora* on top of the *lochoi*; and this is disquieting. But for the difficulty over the total numbers, it would be comparatively easy, with, e.g., Ed. Meyer, *Geschichte des Altertums*, iii[1]. 470, to suppose that there had been no more than some redistribution and some switching of the names of units between 418 and the date to which Xenophon's description applies; and in favour of a mere change of name at the top, from *lochos* to *mora*, is Hesych. μόρα· - - - οἱ πάτρι⟨οι⟩ λόχοι μόρα αὖθις ὀνομασθέντες, and Bekker, *Anecd.* i. 279. 14, μόρα· - - - ὄνομα λόχου τινός. There would be no difficulty in principle in positing a more radical reorganization, for in warfare the Spartans were τεχνῖται (*Lac. Pol.* 13. 5) and should move with the times. But Xenophon ascribes the institution of the *mora*, like almost everything in *Lac. Pol.*, to Lycurgus; and, though the ascription may be light-hearted enough and we need not credit him with deep research, it must be doubted if even Xenophon would attribute to Lycurgus an organization which had been created in his own lifetime. (This argument tells especially against the hypothesis of an extensive reorganization after Leuktra.)

3. (*a*) The only passage of Xenophon which throws any light on the size of a *mora* is *HG* iv. 5. 11–17, discussed above, A. (2) (*c*).

(*b*) *HG* vii. 4. 20, 5. 10 gives twelve *lochoi*, not 24 as in the scheme tabulated above, B. (1); in the latter passage Xenophon is running over the force available to Sparta, and τῶν λόχων δώδεκα ὄντων οἱ τρεῖς certainly means that there were no more than twelve *lochoi*. This was in 368, after Leuktra and the loss of Messenia, and it could be that a reorganization after these disasters had halved the number of *lochoi*: but it is at least as probable—see B. (2) above—that twelve was the regular number before as after Leuktra, and that the scheme above needs amendment; see C. (1) below. Earlier in *HG* there is no mention of *lochoi*, only of *morai*, and there are no *lochagoi* anywhere in *HG*: at iii. 5. 22 Pausanias, and at iv. 5. 7 Agesilaos, call together their polemarchs and *pentekonteres* but not their *lochagoi*. In face of *Lac. Pol.* 11. 4, 13. 4, it can hardly be maintained that the army of the early fourth century had no *lochagoi*: either (Beloch) Xenophon took it for granted that the *lochagoi*, or some of them, went with the polemarchs; or it was the rule at that time that they stayed with the troops during such conferences.

(*c*) On *pentekostyes*, see Wade-Gery, 80–5. Neither a unit of fifty men, nor one which is one-fiftieth of the whole army, can be fitted into the classical system, though in Xenophon's scheme the *pentekostys* is one-forty-eighth, which is as near to one-fiftieth as the system can get. The term may well be carried over from some earlier system, and may be only approximately correct here.

(*d*) On *enomotiai*, see Toynbee. As he argued (263), the order sometimes given to τὰ δέκα (or some other number) ἀφ' ἥβης to charge out from the line implies that the age-groups concerned were more or less evenly distributed along the line, i.e. that all ages were represented at the lowest level, in the *enomotia*. We are only twice given numbers for an *enomotia* in action: *c.* 32 at Mantineia, for five-sixths of the total army; at Leuktra (*HG* vi. 4. 12) a front of three, not more than twelve deep, i.e. a total of not more than 36, with a call-up μέχρι τῶν πέντε καὶ τριάκοντα ἀφ' ἥβης (vi. 4. 17). These instances strongly suggest that the *enomotia* consisted in principle of one man from each age-class called up—not exactly, as Toynbee (264) noted: the system seems to operate in multiples of five—and this would produce the required distribution of ages along the line. (Toynbee, and others, have pointed out that the 420 hoplites cut off on Sphakteria, chosen by lot ἀπὸ πάντων τῶν λόχων (Th. iv. 8. 9) could well be one *enomotia* of 35 men from each of twelve *lochoi*.) This analysis of the *enomotia* fits the known figures and explains what it set out to explain, and is as secure as any hypothesis about the Spartan army can hope to be. We must not then try to improve Xenophon's scheme (or Thucydides') by raising the numbers in the smallest units: the fault, if there is one, lies in the structure above the *enomotia*.

C. *Should the numbers be doubled?*

1. It has long been proposed that in *Lac. Pol.* 11. 4 we should read λοχαγοὺς δύο for λοχ. τέτταρας, a comparatively easy change, which would mean that there were twelve *lochoi* throughout Xenophon's time; and this would bring Xenophon and Thucydides into line to the extent that each would have four *pentekostyes* to the *lochos*. Alternatively we might suppose that four is the correct number of

lochagoi, but there were two to each *lochos*: for instance, one might stay with the *lochos* while the other attended the polemarch elsewhere. Stobaeus' quotation of the text has τέτταρας, which is some reason for retaining it. (Suda ἐνωμοτία· - - - οἱ δὲ τὸ τέταρτον τοῦ λόχου ἐνωμοτίαν φασί, καὶ ἐνωμοτάρχης ὁ αὐτῆς ἄρχων has also been thought to refer to Xenophon, but this is less certain.)

2. The two systems would be brought closer again if we could double the number of *enomotiai*, 32 not 16 to the *mora*. It is not so easy to imagine one *enomotarches* commanding two *enomotiai*: in this case we must alter the number, and not as a matter of textual corruption: we should have to suppose that Xenophon had accidentally given the number of *enomotiai* in a *lochos* when he meant to give the number in a *mora*, a degree of carelessness which would not be incredible in him. Both systems would then have four *enomotiai* to the *pentekostys*, as well as four *pentekostyes* to the *lochos*; and, for Xenophon at least, the total numbers of the army would be doubled, *c.* 6,144 at five-sixths strength, *c.* 7,372 at maximum.

3. Postponing for the moment the question whether we can tolerate this degree of manipulation of our texts, we may note that the difficulties discussed under A. (2) would virtually disappear if this doubling were permissible.

(*a*) At Mantineia the Spartans would have five-sixths of the regular army (*c.* 6,144), the Brasideioi and *neodamodeis* (probably *c.* 1,024), the Skiritai (600), and perhaps we should add the 'hippeis' (300): a total of *c.* 7,768 (or *c.* 8,068), to which we must add their allies, making in all 11,000 or more. On the other side we could allow the main Argive army some 5,000, the whole body 10,000 or more. That is a more reasonable figure for Argos, and the totals would fully justify Thucydides' expression in 74. 1.

(*b*) The 6,000 in 394 will then be something less than a five-sixths call-up, without *neodamodeis*, which is acceptable.

(*c*) Polybios' *mora* of 900 is again less than five-sixths; and the Lechaion *mora* in 390 will be weaker, which is not unexpected for a garrison in a desultory war. The anomaly, now, would be Ephoros' *mora* of 500 in Boeotia in 377 and 373, which would be down to half-strength, if his estimate and not Kallisthenes' were correct. In general, it is easier to account for low figures by supposing a low call-up or other special circumstances, than to account for high figures by supposing that the nominal maximum was somehow exceeded.

4. Toynbee, followed by Wade-Gery, conjectured that the *morai* existed already in 418, and contained two *lochoi* each; and that Thucydides somehow contrived to miss the *mora* out of his calculation. The mechanism of Toynbee's hypothesis is not in detail acceptable; and, where Thucydides has so evidently taken trouble, we must treat the result with respect. It is to be noted that his

complaint of Spartan secrecy relates to their refusal to tell him the number outright (§ 2 ἀριθμὸν δὲ γράψαι, cf. Gomme at the head of this note), whereas his language at the end of § 2 (ἔξεστί τῳ σκοπεῖν) suggests that he believed he had discovered what he needed to know about the organization of the army. He may nevertheless have been misled, and if there was a mistake it is clear that it took the form which Toynbee supposed; but since, as is his custom, Thucydides presents us only with the result of his researches and tells us nothing of his sources, it is fruitless to speculate how such a mistake can have arisen.

That, then, is the dilemma with which this passage faces us. A special hypothesis can be framed to account for every troublesome number, from Thucydides to Polybios; but a text which calls for this amount of special pleading is necessarily suspect. On the other hand, it is very disagreeable to have to suppose that both our authorities are in error: Thucydides, whose claims to accuracy we normally allow and who took special trouble here; and Xenophon, who was more familiar with Sparta than any contemporary. There can be no doubt that Gomme would have preferred to retain Thucydides' scheme intact. In his *Essays* (153 n. 2) he cited with approval Kromayer, 192 n. 5, to the effect that to modify Thucydides' evidence is to saw off the branch on which we are sitting; and a ms. note adds, 'certainly the careful calculation of Thucydides should not be changed'. For myself, with misgiving, I incline the other way and believe that we should double Thucydides' figures.]

ἀλλ' ὡς λοχαγὸς ἕκαστος ἐβούλετο: there is no great difficulty in this. On any one occasion the six *lochoi*, though based on more or less equal division of the Spartan population, did not each muster exactly the same number of hoplites, of the same age-groups, fit to go on a campaign. The differences may have been considerable, and it was left to the discretion of each *lochagos* to arrange his troops as he would, provided, presumably, his front row numbers were 'correct'.

[The call-up was unusually hurried (64. 2), and there may not have been time for the remoter perioikoi to arrive: so Kromayer, 190–1, trying to account for Thucydides' figures here. But comparison of the figures for the *enomotia* here and at Leuktra (p. 115) suggests that the number of absentees was not after all high, though it may have affected the *lochoi* unequally. We have no idea how the various perioikic communities allotted their soldiers to particular units.]

69. 1. δουλείας: in the usual political sense, 'subjection': vol. iii, 646. ὑπὲρ τῆς τε παλαιᾶς ἡγεμονίας, κ.τ.λ.: cf. Hdt. vii. 148. 4, and i. 82; and above, [28. 2, 40. 3. Steup and others may be right in distinguishing ἡγεμονία, the kingdom of Agamemnon, from ἰσομοιρία, the equality of the three original Dorian kingdoms of the Peloponnese.]

μετὰ πολλῶν καὶ ἀγαθῶν ξυμμάχων: returning the compliment of 60. 5 (but the Athenians were then absent!).

ἐν Πελοποννήσῳ: emphatic, 'if they but defeated Sparta in the Peloponnese'. Cf., with Graves, both the sentiment and the language of iv. 95. 2, the address of Hippokrates to the Athenians before Delion.

2. **Λακεδαιμόνιοι δὲ καθ' ἑκάστους**: καθ' ἑκ. should mean Sparta and her allies (Heraies, Mainalioi, and Tegea), as above § 1, init., to which ἐν σφίσιν αὐτοῖς is the contrast; [i.e. on the Spartan side Thucydides makes a distinction between the separate encouragement of each contingent and the Spartans' own practice, which is different, or has a different emphasis. What follows καὶ μετά, κ.τ.λ. belongs only to the Spartans, and Gomme was inclined to agree with Steup that some such words as καὶ αὐτοὶ βραχέως παρῄνουν had fallen out after καθ' ἑκάστους τε: but the ellipse is not difficult after what we have had in § 1.

The involved clause relating to the Spartans means roughly, 'among themselves, good men that they were, according to their customs in war they were making their (usual) exhortation, (which consisted) of reminder of the things they knew'.] (The sentence does not mean, as Grote thought, v. 482, that there were no exhortations on the Spartan side, only mutual encouragement by individuals, *because* they all knew their duty.)

μετὰ τῶν πολεμικῶν νόμων: [νόμους πολεμικοὺς λέγει τὰ ᾄσματα, ἅπερ ᾖδον οἱ Λακεδαιμόνιοι μέλλοντες μάχεσθαι· ἦν δὲ προτρεπτικά, ἐκάλουν δὲ ἐμβατήρια, Σ^Msc², followed by edd. Music played a large part in Spartan life and education, cf. Plu. Lyc. 21; and the subject-matter Plutarch describes (21. 2) would fit this context. But this would be an odd way of saying that the Spartans substituted song for verbal encouragement, and ἐμβατήρια are specifically marching-songs, which are not appropriate. The ancient commentator has probably been seduced by his knowledge that νόμος can mean a tune. 'In accordance with their practice in war' would suit better; the sense of μετά in 103. 2, μετ' ἐλπίδων, is not very different.]

εἰδότες ἔργων, κ.τ.λ.: this well-worn contrast was not especially Spartan: cf. iv. 95. 1 or vi. 68. 1 for Athenian examples. But Thucydides *may* be implying here that Spartans needed, or liked, less talk than their enemies. [It is interesting that this is, in form, Thucydides' own comment.]

70. ἐντόνως καὶ ὀργῇ: with, so to speak, their muscles taut and their feelings at a high pitch. Cf. vii. 68. 1.

ὁμοῦ: see crit. n. (where, it should be noted, [νόμου rather than νόμῳ is probably the correct reading in Gellius i. 11. 5; and, as Steup says, nothing in Gellius' own discussion warrants the belief that he read νόμῳ]). νόμῳ (with ἐγκαθεστώτων) seems to give better sense

than ὁμοῦ. Steup keeps νόμου [(with ὑπό) ; but there is some awkwardness in a text where ὑπό is followed by a genitive which it could easily
govern but does not, whereas the genitive which it actually governs
is postponed.] For the many references in later authors to this
Spartan practice, see Stahl's note.

[προέλθοιεν, MSS. and Σ^sc², fits both the context and Gellius' paraphrase (*proruerent*) rather better than προσέλθοιεν, from Gellius' quotation and Σ^M.]

This again, and 71. 1, seem to indicate a fresh personal experience,
in that in both mention is made for the first time of features of warfare which might have been explained for almost every land battle
of the war. On the other hand it is characteristic of Thucydides to
narrate or explain certain things not when they happened, but when
their significance is most to the purpose; and 71. 1 especially he may
have written because this battle of Mantineia was the grand example
of straightforward hoplite fighting. Cf. n. on iii. 21. 1, and my Sather
Lectures, 132–3; [also vi. 69. 2, with n.]

71. 1. Ἆγις ὁ βασιλεύς: again he is given the full responsibility for
the plan; the ξύμβουλοι seem to play no part on the battlefield (cf.
63. 4 n.).

τὰ στρατόπεδα ποιεῖ μὲν καὶ ἅπαντα τοῦτο: [Gomme found the order
unexpected; 'the more usual would have been ἅπαντα μὲν τὰ στρ. to
show at once that this is generalization, the particular for this occasion following with καὶ τότε in § 2'. But this is achieved by the order
in our text: τὰ στρατόπεδα comes first, to show that something is
being said about armies; there is then the antithesis, within the
general subject of armies, between their general behaviour and that
of this army on this occasion.]

This shows how wrong Stahl was to bracket ποιεῖ - - - τοῦτο, for
both μέν and ἅπαντα are essential. (Stahl also objected that ποιεῖ
τοῦτο requires γάρ in the next sentence: [but see Steup's note.])

εὐσκεπαστότατον: should we not read ⟨διὰ⟩ τὴν πυκνότητα, and take
the adjective as masculine, not feminine or neuter? ἕκαστον
is still the subject. [But τὴν πυκνότητα can be retained as subject,
whether the adjective has an active sense (affording the best protection) or a passive sense (best protected).]

2. ἔτι δὲ πλέον οἱ Λακ. καὶ Τεγ.: see 67. 1.

3. ἀπὸ τοῦ δεξιοῦ κέρως: I agree with Woodhouse (94 ff.) that this
means the right of the Lacedaemonian force in the centre, not the
Tegeates and the few Lacedaemonians of the right wing; and the two
lochoi must be only Spartan troops, not, as Graves, Spartan and
Tegeate, for the two polemarchs are Spartans, and, though a Spartan,
Agis, commanded the whole force, the Tegeates had of course their
own strategoi.

Graves thinks that the Skiritai were ordered further to the left because they were entitled to that position (67. 1), and 'it was impossible to order round a division from the extreme right to the extreme left, and apparently impracticable to move the whole line to the left'. The Greeks were not quite so simple in their battletactics. The Skiritai had to move left because immediate prevention of outflanking was required, and they could do this while the whole line was advancing, by wheeling half left. The two *lochoi* who must fill the gap were to have halted for a moment while the rest of the line moved forward, then turned left and moved behind the other *lochoi*. These last and the right wing were to close the new gap as they advanced, the latter to resist the tendency to diverge to the right, and not to attempt a wide outflanking of the enemy's left. Doubtless Agis felt that he could only be sure of his Spartans in this somewhat complicated manœuvre. To incline the whole line to the left would have been a more difficult operation in the time available. Ἀριστοκλεῖ: some have thought that he may be the brother of Pleistoanax (16. 2). [Gomme judged it unlikely, especially in view of his trial and exile (72. 1), that Thucydides could have passed over the fact that it was a king's brother who was involved. It is not, however, quite certain that Pleistoanax had a brother of this name. At 16. 2 Cobet proposed to read Ἀριστοκλέους τοῦ Δελφοῦ in place of τοῦ ἀδελφοῦ, and this has some plausibility; one could indeed imagine circumstances in which the king might employ his brother to negotiate for him, but a Delphian citizen would be more obviously useful, and the emendation is easy. (M. E. White in an important article, *JHS* lxxxiv (1964), 140–52, argues, from the fact that Pleistoanax had two younger brothers (Kleomenes, iii. 26. 2, and this Aristokles), that their father Pausanias must have lived on into the 460s: even with the loss of Aristokles, her argument would still stand.)]

72. 1. κελεύσαντος αὐτοῦ, ἐπὶ τοὺς Σκιρίτας: Campe was right in objecting that (1) we need an object to κελεύσαντος [but this would surely not be difficult to supply] and (2) we do not need the emphatic position of ἐπὶ τοὺς Σκ. before ὡς. He therefore bracketed ἐπί and transposed the comma after Σκιρίτας: Steup accepted the argument, but preferred to read ἔτι for ἐπί, an easy but not an attractive suggestion—[ἔτι - - - πάλιν αὖ is disagreeably tautologous.]

2. τῇ ἐμπειρίᾳ: it is certainly remarkable to find the Spartans worsted in ἐμπειρία (whether 'professional skill' or 'experience') in hoplite battle; nor indeed does Thucydides' narrative prove that they were: their slow and steady approach against the enemy, their refusal, in the crisis, to let themselves be disturbed by the break-through of the Argive select troops, illustrate their ἐμπειρία—in its normal sense— as clearly as their ἀνδρεία. (Indeed, we might add that Thucydides does not describe their ἀνδρεία in sufficient detail; against the enemy centre, it appears, no great courage was required.) What broke down was (probably) Agis' handling of a difficulty (which was not a very serious one, as events proved) at the beginning of the action, and the discipline of two of the polemarchs: as at Plataia the army did not show itself as the perfect machine which the Greeks were accustomed to think it was. The two aorists, of course, ἐλασσωθέντες and περιγενόμενοι, do make it clear that this breakdown was on this occasion only. [Gomme adds: 'It would have been easier if τότε had preceded κατὰ πάντα, and if for κατὰ πάντα a phrase for 'to some degree' had been substituted.' κατὰ πάντα is indeed striking: it means perhaps not 'in every detail', but 'upon which everything turned'.]

We must at the same time remember what it was that Thucydides had in mind: through the surrender on Sphakteria the Spartans had suffered a sharp fall in their age-old reputation for ἀνδρεία, not for ἐμπειρία (that had been well shown on Sphakteria): they had been defeated before 425, as at Thermopylai, and they had retreated from battlefields; but they had not been known to surrender. It was this reputation, not one for tactical skill, which they now recovered.

3. τῶν πρεσβυτέρων: [see 64. 3 n.]

4. οἱ τριακόσιοι ἱππῆς καλούμενοι: Hdt. viii. 124. 3 and X. Lac. Pol. 4. 3. They fought as hoplites. [See also 67. 1 n., and 68. 3 n., p. 112.

Herodotos' description shows that they existed in this form as far back as the Persian wars, and the earlier hippeis of Hdt. i. 67. 5 are probably the same. The name must once have had its more literal meaning: maybe the king had a young cavalry bodyguard in pre-hoplite days, and they retained the name when Sparta concentrated on hoplite fighting and neglected her cavalry.]

τοῖς πρεσβυτέροις: only by contrast with the select 1,000, not the same sort of older men as the Lacedaemonians guarding the wagons.

πέντε λόχοις ὠνομασμένοις: nothing more is known of these. [Σ^Msc₁ says we should read the name as one word, πεντέλοχοι, which is possible enough: if the information is genuine, it is interesting and important that so much detail should have been available. 'The older men, those that are called the five companies' is a very curious way of describing the main body of the Argive army; but it is hard to see where on the battlefield the main body was, if not here.

The number recalls the five strategoi of 59. 5, and suggests a division of the army, and therefore probably of the citizen body, into five. In the first half of the fifth century Argos had four tribes, the traditional Dorian three, Hylleis, Dymanes, and Pamphyloi, and a fourth, Hyrnathioi, peculiar to Argos but paralleled by the similar fourth at Sikyon (Hdt. v. 68) and comparable additions elsewhere (Busolt–Swoboda, 131–2): in Steph. Byz. s.v. Δυμᾶνες the words καὶ προσετέθη ἡ 'Υρνηθία can only refer to Argos, and mention only one additional tribe. *IG* iv. 517 ('*c.* 460–450?', Jeffery, 170, no. 32) is a stele set up in the Heraion by four hieromnemones, one from each of these four tribes, and there are other dedications by four hieromnemones. The gravestone of the Argives who fell at Tanagra, ML 35, shows by the heading ὑλλέες that the army was organized in the old tribes in the 450s. Thereafter they do not reappear till *SEG* xi. 293, 4th/3rd cent., a dedication by cavalry commanders, two *ilarchoi* from each of these tribes. They are found again in the Roman imperial period, passing honorific decrees (*IG* iv. 596–602).

There is, however, some evidence of a change in the middle of the fifth century, which may well be relevant. The earliest surviving decree of the ἁλιαία, *SEG* xiii. 239 (*c.* 475?—see 47. 9 n.), ends with the formula ἀϝρέτευε·'Επικράτες·Πανφύλας; and *SEG* xi. 339 (very fragmentary: '*c.* 450?', Jeffery, 170, no. 40) has the same tribe-name, probably in a similar formula. Thereafter Argives are identified by their phratry, not by their tribe. Over thirty of these phratry-names are now known: cf. M. Guarducci, *Mem. dei Lincei*, 6. viii (1938–9), 87; there is no comprehensive up-to-date list, but see P. Amandry, *Hesp.* xxi (1952), 215–19, P. Charneux, *BCH* lxxxii (1958), 7–8; and for a general discussion, M. Wörrle (47. 9 n. above). ML 42 (relations between Argos, Knossos, and Tylissos, '*c.* 460–450?', Jeffery, 170, no. 39) occupies a border-line position: (*a*) The clause (43–4) which dates the publication of the decree has the formula ἀϝρέτευε Λυκοτάδας ὑλλεύς. Amandry (215–18), having identified Λυκωτάδαι as a phratry, tentatively suggested that the formula meant that the presidency was held by this phratry, further identified by its tribe, and compared the naming of the tribe holding the prytany at Athens. To this there are serious objections: elsewhere the subject of ἀϝρήτευε is an individual, and the phratry-name is elsewhere used to identify an individual. The alternative, to suppose that this is an individual whose name is the same as that of the (later) phratry, need not too much alarm us: these phratries may well be an artificial creation of this time, and some of those with patronymic names might be named from families of contemporary importance. (*b*) The additional clause which follows has the formula (45) ἀ(ϝρέτευε) βολᾶς Ἀρχίστρατος Λυκοφρονίδας, the combination of personal name and phratry-name that was to be the rule. The provisional conclusion is that about 450 Argos changed from nomenclature by tribes to nomenclature by phratry; and this may have been a change of substance.

Later Argives also identified themselves by their *komai*, the first known instance being *GHI* 179 late in the fourth century. *Komai* are certainly territorial units (and some phratries have names suggesting a local connection). They were hardly new at the time of *GHI* 179.

Thucydides' five strategoi and five *lochoi*, which cannot be fitted straightforwardly into the four-tribe scheme, strongly suggest a substantial change taking place before 418. The economical conclusion is that Argos changed over, about 450, from a fourfold division based on the old tribes[1] to a fivefold division based on locality, in which *komai* and phratries were ingredients. We do not know what these divisions were called or how they were built up in detail, but the change in general is of a type which most Greek states went through at some time. The old tribes seem to have lived on at Argos, more effectively than at Athens. Whatever the explanation of the inscription of the *ilarchoi*, SEG xi. 293 (above)—and one would be reluctant to believe that the Argive cavalry was organized in tribes after the time when the infantry was reorganized on a local principle—this naming of the tribes early in the Hellenistic period suggests that their reappearance in the time of the Roman empire is not a mere antiquarian revival.]

τοῦ μὴ φθῆναι τὴν ἐγκατάληψιν: they were trodden underfoot 'in their anxiety to avoid the clutches of the enemy'. [This must indeed be the general meaning, but to get this from the Greek we must, with Steup and others, take ἐγκατάληψιν as the subject of φθῆναι, 'to avoid capture overtaking them', a curiously contorted phrase. Σ^recc. ὅτι μὴ ἔφθασαν τὸ ἐγκατειλῆφθαι ὑπ' αὐτῶν τῶν Λακεδαιμονίων has suggested a reading τῷ μὴ φθῆναι, (see Arnold's note) not a statement of purpose but an explanation of the fact that they were trodden underfoot. Early disturbance of the text at this point is indicated by Π²⁴.]

I have suggested in *Essays*, 153 n. 1, that we should perhaps doubt Thucydides' statement of the immediate panic of the allied centre. His Spartan informants were doubtless contemptuous enough—after their victory; he will later have got some information from both Argive and Athenian sources—but the Argives may have been among the pro-Spartan refugees who told how the *canaille* had thrown away all chances in the battle, and the badly-mauled Athenians, attacked on three sides after the centre's retreat, would be in no mood to sympathize with allies who had received the chief weight of the Spartan attack. As for the Mantineans, with their heavy losses, and the select 1,000 of the Argives, *they* thought that the victory which they had won had been lost by the feebleness of the rest of the army: 'our allies let us down'.

73. 1. παρερρήγνυντο ἤδη ἅμα καὶ ἐφ' ἑκάτερα: [the subject should be the whole allied force, Mantineans, Argives, and Athenians; the previous clause could be taken to mean that the Argives and their

---

[1] It is not necessary, for this argument, to discuss the date when the tribe Hyrnathioi was first established.

immediate allies of Kleonai and Orneai had given way as described
in 72. 4, but 'the Argive and allied army' more easily means the
whole line, which 'had given way at this point'. παραρρήγνυσθαι is
used of a breach in a wall, e.g. Arr. *Anab.* iv. 26. 5, and at *Anab.*
ii. 11. 1 τὸ παρερρωγὸς τοῦ Περσικοῦ στρατεύματος is the breach in the
Persian line: for Thuc. iv. 96. 6 see n. there, but there and at vi. 70. 2
the meaning 'broken up' looks at least as likely. This sense would be
appropriate here only for the narrower subject, the defeated centre,
but then there is no particular point in ἐφ' ἑκάτερα: but there is
a point, if he means that a breach had been made on both sides of
the centre, to the right by the advance of the Mantineans and the
Argive *logades*, to the left by their own retreat (so Arnold). The
basic sense is perhaps 'had had pieces broken off it', and in that case
the subject can be the whole line. Thucydides' eye is mainly on the
position of the Athenian contingent, whose special dangers are linked
by the doubled ἅμα, and τῇ μέν - - - τῇ δέ below.] ἤδη ἡσσημένους are
the Athenians of 72. 4.

οἱ ἱππῆς: typical cavalry action, *harassing* the enemy (never attempting a break through on their own, for the infantry to take
advantage of). Cf. i. 111. 1. [Gomme also considered—but the ms.
note does not show how seriously—reading παριόντες for παρόντες.]

2. παντὶ τῷ στρατεύματι: he was evidently confident that neither the
Athenians nor the centre could re-form, and attack in their turn.
[If both Athenian generals (74. 3) had already fallen, as Gomme
suggests, this would make a lot of difference.]

3. παρῆλθε: as παρελθεῖν in 71. 3.

καθ' ἡσυχίαν ἐσώθησαν: 'they got away', not 'at leisure' (not 'had
plenty of time to escape', Warner), but 'unharassed', just as in 26. 5.
τῶν Ἀργείων - - - τὸ ἡσσηθέν: the centre had not literally fled from
the field; [the disorderly flight of 72. 4 (cf. Gomme's n.) was just
enough to take them out of the immediate reach of the Spartans.]

4. καὶ πλείους: Stahl's ⟨οἱ⟩ πλείους was a mistaken conjecture, and
should not be recorded (see Steup: [if the total losses of the Mantineans were only 200 (74. 3), Stahl's text means that their whole
army amounted to less than 400). In view of these numbers, πλείους
here must be said very strictly in comparison with the Argive *logades*,
very few of whom can have been killed. This in its turn implies that
the latter's flight (§ 3) was in good order, and that they did not lose
their formation.]

τὸ πολὺ ἐσώθη: Diodoros xii. 79. 5–7 has a foolish story of valiant and
desperate fighting begun between Agis, fighting bravely with his
Spartans, and the equally brave Argives, which would have resulted
in terrible slaughter, had not Pharax, one of the ξύμβουλοι (who suddenly come thus to life in the midst of the battle—see 63. 4, 66. 2 nn.),
advised Agis not to drive brave men to desperation; so a passage

was made for them to extricate themselves. Such a reason for not following up a victory was a commonplace: see Hdt. viii. 108. 3, 109. 2.

[But however commonplace, the advice was sometimes needed in practice: see X. *HG* iv. 3. 19. The objection to Diodoros' story is not so much any intrinsic improbability as that it gives us no reason for rejecting Thucydides' version. Gomme indeed somewhat exaggerated the incompatibility of the two accounts, treating § 3 ἐς φυγὴν ἐτράποντο as a complete refutation of any claim that the *logades* had distinguished themselves in the battle; but it is true that Diodoros' story is not easily fitted into Thucydides' framework. For all we know, the ξύμβουλοι may throughout have played a large part in Ephoros' account of the campaign: see Diod. xii. 78. 6, quoted in 63. 4 n. above.]

οἱ γὰρ Λακ. μέχρι μὲν τοῦ τρέψαι: so Plu. *Lyc.* 22. 9–10, with a lofty humanity and a practical aim added as motives. Cf. Thuc. i. 70. 5. But the Spartans had achieved their aim by victory in the field; more was not needed and perhaps could not be achieved without risk of breaking the cohesion of the hoplite force and exposing it to some unnecessary loss, especially from the enemy's cavalry.

74. 1. καὶ ἡ μὲν μάχη τοιαύτη, κ.τ.λ.: Thucydides is not pretending that he had every detail of the battle fully and correctly narrated. It is remarkable that so many have taken τοιαύτη καὶ ὅτι ἐγγύτατα τούτων to mean that Thucydides is emphasizing, almost guaranteeing, the accuracy of his account, and can quote i. 22. 4, τοιούτων καὶ παραπλησίων in support, as though he were there asserting that events would exactly repeat themselves.

I have noted above the passages which seem most surely to suggest Thucydides' presence in the neighbourhood of this campaign (I mean, so to speak, the political rather than the military neighbourhood, Tegea or Sparta rather than the battlefields) at the time of the battle or soon after: 60. 3, 63. 3, 65. 2, 68. 2–3, 70; and see below, 74. 2. Thucydides' lack of precision about the other side—the vacillation of the Argives, 60. 6, the policy of the Athenians, 57. 1 n. and 75. 5, the preliminaries in 58. 1–2 and the attack on Orchomenos, 61. 4—makes a marked contrast, though we must note that he gives as lively an account of the soldiers' dissatisfaction with their commanders (65. 5–6, 'the enemy is quietly getting away and *we* are being betrayed, without anybody doing anything about it') as of Agis and his companion shortly before, 65. 2–3. This in general causes no surprise; it is clear everywhere that for the period after his exile opportunities for getting information from the Athenian side came unevenly to him; sometimes he got it, often not. With this proviso in mind, and his own qualified statement, we can accept his account of the campaign; the one thing that is still lacking is the determination of the site of the great battle. I would not now say as I did in my *Essays*, 154–5, that Thucydides had not seen it; he may indeed have thought that, once he had said it was fought in the plain, between Mantineia and Tegea, he had said enough; for the plain is quite flat . . . [Gomme's note on the topography of the campaign followed: see 64. 5 n., p. 94.]

πλείστου δὴ χρόνου, κ.τ.λ.: see 60. 3 n. [The double superlative adds an extra dimension of difficulty. The note of time must in general be intended to increase our sense of the striking character of the phenomenon, but it works differently according to the case. Thus at iv. 74. 4, on the Megarian oligarchy set up in 424, πλεῖστον δὴ χρόνον αὕτη ὑπ' ἐλαχίστων γενομένη ἐκ στάσεως μετάστασις ξυνέμεινεν, the basic surprise is that a revolution so flimsily based should have survived at all, and it is the more surprising that it should have lasted any length of time: hence, we can tolerate a comparatively short time for πλεῖστον χρόνον, and indeed we have no more than the interval between 424 and the writing of the passage, putting that as late as we dare. Here we have the opposite situation. Set hoplite battles between opposing Greek alliances were, down to this date, rare (such alliances only developed during the fifth century, and only the growth of opposition to Sparta by land produced the quite exceptional series of alliance battles in the period 394–362), so that if our wonder is to be appreciably increased we need here a much longer πλεῖστον χρόνου. Forty years is the most that can be claimed. There is no difficulty in eliminating Delion from the comparison, for there only 7,000 hoplites were engaged on either side (iv. 93. 3, 94. 1), less than the lowest possible estimate for Mantineia (68. 3 n., p. 112); and only Athens and the Boeotian cities were involved. The Archidamian War produced no other comparable battle, but Tanagra cannot be passed over: there the Peloponnesians had 11,500 hoplites, at least at the start of the campaign (i. 107. 2), and all the main cities engaged at Mantineia were engaged at Tanagra, and the Boeotians as well.

This, then, is the limit of πλεῖστου χρόνου. No translation could sound logical in English, but we may paraphrase: 'this was an exceptionally large-scale battle, involving an exceptional number of important cities; and it was a very long time since a comparable battle had been fought.' The passage clearly demands that exceptional numbers of troops were engaged, and this must affect our interpretation of c. 68.]

2. οὗπερ ἐτάφησαν: where perhaps Thucydides saw the tomb. In accord with the usual Greek custom the dead were buried on or near the battlefield (ii. 34. 1 n.).

3. Ἀργείων - - - ἑπτακόσιοι, κ.τ.λ.: [the proportion between the dead is no indication of the proportion between the whole forces—the

Argive casualties were heavy, because the worst slaughter was in the defeat of the allied centre, 72. 4—but 700 suggests a fairly large force to start with, and this again affects our interpretation of c. 68.]

ξὺν Αἰγινήταις: the Athenian ἔποικοι there. See ii. 27. 1, vii. 57. 2. But it is curious that they are thus mentioned here and not earlier. Perhaps the information came to Thucydides later, from an official list of the dead [a ms. note refers to Paus. i. 29. 13, the stele at Athens with the names of the dead of this battle], and he made a note of it, without integrating the whole.

[The name is not qualified here, as vii. 57. 2 οἳ τότε Αἴγιναν εἶχον. If that passage was written after 405 (see n. ad loc.), this may have been written earlier; but Thucydides may simply have felt that the catalogue of vii. 57 required more formality.]

αὐτῶν δὲ χαλεπόν: the usual secrecy (68. 2). περὶ τριακοσίους shows that the Spartans had to fight hard, though their losses were not so great as those of the enemy centre.

75. 1–3. *Sparta's Recovery*

75. 1. ὁ ἕτερος βασιλεύς: Hdt. v. 75. 2 tells us that it was forbidden for both kings to be on campaign at once; [or rather, to go out from Sparta with the same army, ἕπεσθαι ἀμφοτέρους τοὺς βασιλέας ἐξιούσης στρατιῆς. It has been held that the rule prevented the two kings being abroad at once, on the strength of X. *HG* v. 3. 10, ἡ δὲ τῶν Φλειασίων πόλις - - - νομίζουσα δ᾽ ἔξω ὄντος Ἀγησιπόλιδος οὐκ ἂν ἐξελθεῖν ἐπ᾽ αὐτοὺς Ἀγησίλαον, οὐδ᾽ ἂν γενέσθαι ὥστε ἅμα ἀμφοτέρους τοὺς βασιλέας ἔξω Σπάρτης εἶναι. But this was just the expectation of the Phleiasians, and they were proved wrong (ibid. 13–14). Cf. also the junction of Agis and Pausanias in Attica in autumn 405, X. *HG* ii. 2. 7–8, Diod. xiii. 107. 2: here again the two kings met in the field, but had not set out together from Sparta at the head of a single army.]

τούς τε πρεσβυτέρους, κ.τ.λ.: 64. 3. [Thucydides does not tell us why these troops were now recalled; perhaps because of the news of reinforcements on the way to the enemy, § 5 below.]

2. τοὺς ἀπὸ Κορίνθου, κ.τ.λ.: 64. 4.

Κάρνεια γὰρ αὐτοῖς ἐτύγχανον ὄντα: cf. 54. 2. Sparta's confidence is remarkable: by one victory, they were sure, that had re-established their position in the Peloponnese, the pretensions of Argos had disappeared, and that stability (in the Peloponnese, at least, to some degree also in continental Greece as a whole) which depended on her leadership and which had been so rudely shattered by the events of Pylos and Sphakteria, was now restored. They were indeed fortunate that the Peloponnesian cities thought mainly of themselves (cf. the Corinthian warning, i. 120. 2), and were not concerned with the betrayal of the cities of the Delian league in the north and in Ionia; but they could depend upon this.

Moreover, they had won this victory not by the enterprising genius of a Brasidas (indeed, as at Plataia in 479, their strategy and their tactics had both gone astray), but by their traditional virtue, βραδυτής, slowness: they had not been confused into hurry by the first surprise, they had not lost their steadiness by the mistakes of the two polemarchs, and they were not excited by victory into following it up by rapid pursuit. They had done enough; it was the month Karneios; they would march back to Sparta and celebrate the festival. Is it surprising that they won so much admiration?

(ms.) The only gain to Athens by the alliance of v. 23 was the rift between Sparta and her allies, especially in the Peloponnese. This had in some ways widened between 421 and 418, in some (cf. Corinth) narrowed. It practically closed after Mantineia. So much for Alkibiades, that mischievous man—a clear case of 'only success would justify the policy'.

3. βραδυτῆτα: cf. i. 71. 4, 72. 1, 78. 1, 84. 1 (with my nn.); also cf. v. 64. 2, 66. 2 (ὑπὸ σπουδῆς), and 70.

τύχῃ μέν - - - κακιζόμενοι: 'worsted by fortune', LSJ (after Stahl); 'reproached on account of their ill-fortune', Böhme, Classen. Rather 'maligned for what was only ill-fortune'. See i. 105. 6 and ii. 21. 3 for Thucydides' use of the word. ['Maligned' is certainly closer than 'worsted'; but the reference here may be rather to the sense of κακός discussed by A. W. H. Adkins, *Merit and Responsibility*— 'depressed to the status of κακοί', i.e. lowered in the esteem of others, and in their own.]

γνώμῃ δὲ οἱ αὐτοὶ ἔτι ὄντες: cf. ii. 87. 3 for a close parallel, and my note there.

75. 4–6. *Fighting at Epidauros*

4. ἐρῆμον: 56. 5 n.

ἐξελθόντων αὐτῶν: 'their main force having left the Argolid' for the Mantineia campaign; τῶν Ἀργείων is genitive with τοὺς φύλακας, and αὐτῶν is therefore necessary. [See Steup's n. This passage, once more, suggests that the Argive force at Mantineia was substantial.]

5. Ἠλείων - - - βοηθησάντων: their momentary pique (c. 62) cost the allies much, and perhaps saved the day for Sparta. Their repentance now served the allies very little.

Ἀθηναίων χιλίων: we should have learnt a lot if Thucydides had been in Athens at this time (74. 1 n.). Presumably this piecemeal policy of sending too small a force in the first instance and following it with another was due to the struggle between Nikias and Alkibiades. Cf. 55. 4. In 415 the Athenians determined at least not to repeat *this* mistake—with fatal results.

[But we should also compare the case of Kerkyra in 433, i. 45. 1–2 and 50. 5; and Naupaktos in 429, ii. 85. 4–6, 92. 7. Both are before Thucydides' exile, but he does not hint at political struggle and leaves us with the impression that this was an aspect of Athens' over-confidence, first thinking the job could be done with a small force, then realizing too late that more was needed. Alkibiades in vi. 16. 6 (see n. there) claims that he achieved what he did ἄνευ μεγάλου ὑμῖν κινδύνου καὶ δαπάνης, and he may in fact have recommended his policy, before the event, by saying that the war could be won on the cheap by sending relatively small forces to encourage the allies.

A ms. note draws attention to *IG* i². 302 (ML 77), but does not disclose Gomme's own view. The first payment in the Attic year 418/17, during the first prytany of the year and therefore not far in time from the battle of Mantineia (cf. Meritt, *Ath. Year*, 218, and 65. 4 n. above), was made in the first instance to]ος τοῖς μετὰ Δεμο- σθένος, which has been variously restored as τριεράρχοις ἐπὶ Ἄργ]ος (Dittenberger; Tod, *GHI* 75) or ἐπὶ ᾽Εϊόν]ος (Meritt, *AFD* 160); but the money was then transferred to στρατεγοῖς ἐπὶ Θ]ράικες Εὐθυδέμοι Εὐδέμο [- - -, an expedition not mentioned by Thucydides or any other source; the politics of this, or the military necessity, remain obscure. The second payment, in Pryt. II and not at the beginning of it, so roughly in September, was certainly connected with Argos, τοῖς τριεράρχοις ἐπὶ Ἄ]ργος τοῖς μετὰ Δεμ[οσθένος. In both cases τριεράρχοις is of course conjectural, but it is certain that the money was not paid directly to Demosthenes as strategos, in the normal way. Thucydides names no successor to Laches and Nikostratos, nor any general in charge of these 1,000 Athenians, and mentions Demosthenes only at 80. 3, as being sent from Athens specifically to withdraw the garrison from outside Epidauros. Either, then, the Athenians had intended to send a further force to Argos near the time of the battle, but diverted it to Thrace for reasons unknown to us; or, Demosthenes' connection with a force proceeding to Eïon was for some reason severed and the money paid to Euthydemos instead (the suggestion of West and McCarthy, *AJA* xxxii (1928), 350–1, that Demosthenes was withdrawn from the expedition to Eïon because he was needed to replace Laches and Nikostratos, would be more plausible if the evidence suggested, as it does not, that Demosthenes actually went to Argos). Finally, the thousand men were sent, ὕστερον τῆς μάχης and, as the record of ML 77 suggests, some time after it.]

οἱ ξύμμαχοι οὗτοι: some have queried οὗτοι; but it means '*these* allies', i.e. Eleans and Athenians with the Argives, not the Mantineans.

ἕως οἱ Λακ. Κάρνεια ἦγον: [Thucydides does not tell us whether the Argives salved their consciences in the same way as in the previous year, 54. 3, by juggling with the calendar; on that occasion it seemed to matter to them whether they technically kept the month holy.]

διελόμενοι, κ.τ.λ.: cf. ii. 78. 1–2; vii. 19. 1.

6. ἐξεπαύσαντο: 'took their rest', according to LSJ; but it appears to mean 'took a complete rest from their task', i.e. gave it up (ἀπέκαμον, Σ^Ms). So Stahl. See 80. 3.

τὴν ἄκραν τὸ Ἡραῖον: τὸ δὲ πρὸς τῷ λιμένι (sc. ἱερόν) ἐπὶ ἄκρας ἀνεχούσης ἐς θάλασσαν λέγουσιν Ἥρας εἶναι, Paus. ii. 29. 1; [see Bursian, ii. 74.] It juts out into the sea from Old Epidauros northwards.

The Athenians made of this promontory a τείχισμα, a fortress perhaps separate from the encircling wall begun, but apparently never completed, by the Argives and Eleans (but see 80. 3 n.), to serve as a base for the troops occupying this wall, as well as an additional threat to the city. Cf. the situation at Mende, where the citizens had occupied a hill just outside the town and the attackers tried to capture this first before attempting a siege, iv. 129–30; and at Skione, iv. 131.

76–81. *Sparta and Argos Make Peace*

76. 1. τοῦ δ' ἐπιγ. χειμῶνος ἀρχ. εὐθύς: i.e. the beginning of November (Appendix, vol. iii).

This date is incompatible with ἐπειδὴ τὰ Κάρνεια ἤγαγον, if the latter means 'as soon as the Karneia had been celebrated', for it seems established that the month Karneios (54. 2, with n.) corresponded to the Attic Metageitnion, the second of the civil year; i.e. at latest the end of Karneios would be near the beginning of autumn, about six weeks before winter began; [and, as several edd. point out, 54–5 show that in the previous year there had been time for further operations after the end of Karneia and before the beginning of winter.] That Sparta might wait six weeks before making this move, as Classen thought, it is easy enough to suppose; we could indeed fill the interval with Argive politics and tentative approaches to Sparta; but it is hardly the natural implication of Thucydides' words. There is no other reason to follow Krüger in bracketing ἐπειδὴ τὰ Κ. ἤγαγον; [and perhaps Thucydides meant to remind us simply that there was not at that stage, as there had been earlier, a religious obstacle. But it is likely enough, as Krüger suggested, that these words have crept in from a note by someone who took εὐθύς to mean that the Spartans moved as soon as they were free of the festival.]

2. πρῶτον σπονδάς - - - ὕστερον καὶ ξυμμαχίαν: [in fact we get first a quite informal agreement (78), then simultaneous σπονδὰς καὶ ξυμμαχίαν (79. 1). There is some lack of co-ordination here.]

130

3. Λίχας: 22. 2, 50. 4. Spartan deeds (and, doubtless, promises, as in Athens, iv. 17–20) were now more eloquent than Alkibiades' words. τὸν μὲν καθ' ὅτι εἰ - - - τὸν δ' ὡς εἰ: [if the text is correct and complete, the ellipses are harsh. Steup ascribed them to the 'official language', and thought we could supply ἔσται. Wilamowitz, *Hermes* xxxvii (1902), 308 (= *Kl. Schr.* iv. 150), followed by Schwartz, 70, supposed these to be gaps deliberately left by Thucydides, not yet certain of the precise nature of the two λόγω and leaving space for a summary of their contents; the editor then left the gaps, but inserted the documents. But it is doubtful (see next n.) if Thucydides needed to wait long to discover the terms of the λόγω; and while the ξυμβατήριος λόγος was a long and detailed document, the same can hardly have been true of the other; indeed no commentator has yet given it more than the vague character of 'a powerful threat of war' (Wilamowitz).]
ἔστι δὲ ὅδε: this and the next document (c. 79) are of importance for the consideration of two problems, the one whether Thucydides intended to leave the documents, especially those in another dialect, as they are, in his history, or would have 'translated' and abbreviated them had he lived to complete his work (as he 'translated' speeches, if he did not invent them); the other, the dates of composition of the different parts of his history. I have said something of this latter problem in my notes on the three documents recorded in the second part of the *History*, iv. 118–19, v. 18–19, 23–4; and I discussed the opinion that Thucydides could only have seen these after his return to Athens in 404. The same opinion is arguable for the document recorded in v. 47, where we can test the accuracy of Thucydides' copy; but it is not arguable at all for these two agreements between Sparta and Argos; he will have seen copies before the end of the war, and there is no reason to doubt that he saw them soon after the treaties were concluded—the most natural time for him to inquire about them and the easiest for him to see them. He thought it of sufficient interest to transcribe them, preserving the Doric; and he put them in their place among the 'notes' that he was making at the time. Whether he would later have altered it all will be discussed later [(this promise was only partly fulfilled: see below)]; but his narrative of the battle of Mantineia itself is not at all a series of detached notes; it is fully written, and the treaties follow it, as easily as the document of the truce of 423/2 follows the story of Delion and Brasidas' campaign in Thrace, and that of the Peace of Nikias the story of the Athenian defeat.

[Three ms. notes supplement this: (*a*) 'Thucydides saw the written document of a peace, which was not to be important. So saw it at the time or soon after?' This reinforces the argument of the preceding note (to τὸν μὲν καθ' ὅτι, κ.τ.λ.). (*b*) 'The two documents together, not being so important as 18–19 and 23, do perhaps look like something Thucydides would have omitted in stage (3)'—for this see 26. 6 n., p. 17—'but this proves nothing for iv. 118–19, v. 18–19, 23, 47.' (c) The third remarks on the unnecessary detail, and refers to cases where 'Thucydides has translated into his own language'—cf. Gomme's and my notes to 47. 12, pp. 62–3—adding a reference to the unexpected detail about Morgantine in iv. 65. 1, with n.

These notes suggest that Gomme was moving towards the conclusion which I would regard as inevitable, that Thucydides was not likely to have retained the full text of 77 and 79. The truce of 423 was almost as short-lived, and iv. 118–19 contain even more unexplained and apparently unnecessary detail than 77. 1; but it is easier to persuade oneself that Thucydides might have wanted to keep the full text for 423. But in both cases a summary of the essential features would follow the narrative as easily as a verbatim text. See also Bengtson, *Staatsverträge*, no. 194.

The dialect of these chapters raises some question about Thucydides' procedure in transcription, and about what the editor should print. So much unmistakable West Greek has survived in transmission that we can be sure that Thucydides, or his agent, meant in general to reproduce the original wording; and, dialect being specially liable to corruption, there is more to be said for Ahrens's whole-hearted attempt to restore dialect forms than for the retreat of Steup and others towards the MS. tradition.

We should assume that 77 was composed and circulated in Lakonian: there was no need to translate it for the Argives, as iv. 118. 1–10 have been translated into Attic, presumably for the benefit of the debate at Athens. 79, the product of negotiation between Sparta and Argos, might be in the dialect of either, or in a mixture. The formal inscriptions of both states use, till well after 418, the local alphabets which do not distinguish between ϵ and η, o and ω, but these signs for the long vowels appear, on a small scale, in private inscriptions before the end of the fifth century; see Jeffery, 183–4, 151. It is thus doubtful what a Spartan would have written on papyrus in 418; and also how Thucydides would have transcribed from an alien alphabet, i.e. whether, when faced with, e.g., ποττὸς Ἀργεῖος, he would have reproduced that or written ποττὼς Ἀργείως: but eventually the choice was made for the latter—even if only by an Attic copyist after Thucydides' death. In 77. 2, 5, 79. 1 the reading of almost all MSS. points to εἶμεν for the inf. of the verb 'to be', while recc. (and 77. 5 H₂) have ἦμεν, the correct form for Lakonian, and this might be accounted for by supposing that the text had once had εμεν, misunderstood by Attic copyists unfamiliar with Lakonian; but this is a doubtful and meagre indication. Once the text was fixed in the Ionic alphabet, the two main possibilities of corruption arise, from the tendency to substitute familiar for unfamiliar forms, and the tendency of learned editors to import what they believed to be the proper dialect forms.

For the Lakonian dialect, see Thumb–Kieckers, i. 77 ff.; D. L. Page, *Alcman: The Partheneion* (1951), 102 ff.; C. D. Buck, *The Greek Dialects* (1955), 161. The chief materials are: *IG* v. 1; Alkman; the Spartan speakers in Ar. *Lys.*; the inscriptions of Herakleia in S. Italy, founded from Spartan Tarentum, have sometimes to be taken into account. Most of the very numerous minor variations in the MSS. of Thucydides have been disregarded in what follows.

1. Numerous W. Greek, but not specifically Lakonian, features appear without serious variation: τοί, etc.; αἰ δέ κα, 77. 2, etc.; -μεν in 77. 3 ἀποδόμεν, etc.; -ντι in 77. 2 εἴκωντι, etc.

2. Imperfectly or doubtfully preserved features include:

(a) Enough instances of gen. sing. -ω and acc. pl. -ως to justify general restoration of Ἐπιδαύρω, πολεμίως, etc.

(b) 77. 5 πόλιας, 79. 1 πόλιες, 79. 4 πολίων, justify restoration of 79. 4 πόλι for the Attic πόλει. For 77. 3, 79. 4 πολίεσσι cf. παναγυρίεσσι in *SEG* xii. 379. 22 (Kamarina) and 380. 22 (Gela–Phintias), both 242 B.C.

(c) 79. 2 ὅσσοι ACF justifies restoration of 77. 7 ὅσσοι.

(d) 77. 8 ἀπιάλλην AB gives the Lakonian form, and may justify restoring 79. 4 ἐλθῆν. 77. 6 ἀλεξέμεναι is an aberration due to the frequency of this particular form in epic (Stahl cited in favour of the MSS. Alkman 42 (*PMG*) νέκταρ ἔδμεναι, but this is presumably also epic). In post-Homeric Greek the middle is much more common, but X. *Cyr.* iv. 3. 2 has ἀλέξειν, and we do not know which the dialect preferred: ἀλέξεσθαι (Herwerden) is perhaps less likely to have been corrupted than an unfamiliar ἀλέξην (Ahrens).

3. No specifically Lakonian feature is unequivocally preserved:

(a) 77. 4 τῶ σιῶ σύματος exhibits the Lakonian substitution of σ for θ. Inscriptions retain θ down to the fourth century, when *IG* v. 1. 255 and 1317 have ἀνέσηκε, and 1317 adds σιῶ: but Ar. *Lys.* already in 411 puts σ for θ whenever the speaker is a Spartan. Wilamowitz's explanation (cf. Page, 143) is surely correct: θ was written at Sparta, but its pronunciation as a spirant began there earlier than elsewhere, and Aristophanes represents this by σ for an Athenian audience, just as he underlines some oddity in the Spartan and Megarian pronunciation of ζ by writing it δδ, which local inscriptions did not adopt till much later. Xenophon's ναὶ τὼ σιώ (*HG* iv. 4. 10) is similarly a piece of deliberate local colour. But Thucydides had no reason to concern himself with pronunciation: unless we treat this as an exceptionally early case of the change at Sparta, this reading was intruded later by an editor who knew σιός as a standard Lakonism. At 77. 2, where the original cannot have had Ἀθηναῖοι, H has Ἀσαναῖοι in the margin, but this again could be a learned conjecture: at 77. 6 the various readings ἀμόθι, etc. show no trace of σ; 79. 4 διακριθῆμεν, ἐλθεῖν are only relevant if 79 was in Lakonian.

(b) Change of ε to ι before a vowel, early but not universal in Lakonian, appears in 77. 4 σιῶ, but see above. The anomalous 79. 4 δοκείοι might arise from δοκέοι or δοκίοι: the ε is apparently retained in 79. 1 κοινανεόντων. The Attic contraction in 77. 1 ἀναιροῦντας needs correction, but there is nothing to show whether it should be -έοντας or -ίοντας. 77. 7 and 79. 2 (twice) have ἐσσοῦνται or ἐσοῦνται. West Greek in general has futures in -σέω not -σω. But Herakleia is an exception, with contracted forms in 3rd sg. med. (ἐσῆται, etc.) but forms from -σω in 3rd pl. act. and med. (ἐάσοντι, ἔσσονται, etc.): and that this variation goes back to Lakonian is suggested (see Page, 123–5) by Alcm. 1. 12 παρήσομες: IG v. 1. 3]σσονται: Ar. Lys. 168 πείσομες, 1013 πωτάομαι (i.e. πωτάσομαι). If the MSS. pointed to an original ἔσσονται, that could be claimed as Lakonian: ἐσ(σ)οῦνται, with the Attic contraction, does not belong to the original document, but we cannot say what it replaced.

(c) The replacement of intervocalic σ by h (which is also Argive) occurs early in Lakonian (see Page, 142), and is found in Aristophanes (e.g. Lys. 1013, above), but it is not found in our text; nor is there any trace of ϝ.

4. There is no trace of any specifically Argive form (a conspicuous example would have been the retention of final -νς, which Argive shares with Cretan and some other dialects; but 79. 3 has -ως not -ονς).

5. Specifically Attic intrusions, apart from those already mentioned, are ξυμ- in 77. 1, 8 ξυμβαλέσθαι, and ξύμμαχοι, etc. throughout; and the final -ν of 79. 1 κοινανεόντων.]

77. 1. τᾷ ἐκκλησίᾳ: [no other document is available in which the Spartan assembly refers to itself by name, and this creates a strong presumption that it was called, as here, *ekklesia*. Xenophon, though more inclined than Thucydides to use local Spartan terms, habitually writes ἐκκλησία, but in three places (*HG* ii. 4. 38, v. 2. 33, vi. 3. 3) he uses the concrete term οἱ ἔκκλητοι, otherwise found only in Eur. *Or.* 612, 949 (of the Argive assembly); this is not familiar Attic, so Xenophon probably reflects Spartan usage: see Wade-Gery, 190 with n. 3. ἐκκλησίαι in ML 5. 24 (copy of the Theran decree, probably at least in part genuine, for the foundation of Kyrene) may also be relevant. For doubts about the conventional view that the Spartan assembly was called *apella*, see Wade-Gery, 44–7: the texts are collected in Busolt–Swoboda, 691 n. 4.

But in this connection we must also consider another formula, τὰ τέλη τῶν Λακεδαιμονίων (to be distinguished from the formula οἱ ἐν τέλει (ὄντες), for which see 27. 2 n.). The meaning of τὰ τέλη varies with the context:

1. Where only the assembly is competent to decide, it can mean the whole assembly: (a) in X. *HG* iii. 2. 23, the decision of the assembly (ἔδοξε τοῖς ἐφόροις καὶ τῇ ἐκκλησίᾳ) is announced to Elis in the terms ὅτι τοῖς τέλεσι τῶν Λακεδαιμονίων δίκαιον δοκοίη, κ.τ.λ. (b) *HG* vi. 4. 2, Kleombrotos before Leuktra asks for instructions, ἐπερωτῶντα τὰ οἴκοι τέλη τί χρὴ ποιεῖν, and he gets his answer (§ 3) from the assembly. (c) Th. i. 58. 1, τὰ τέλη τῶν Λακ. promised Poteidaia that, if the Athenians attacked them, they would invade Attica; and this is taken up by the Corinthians in i. 71. 4, addressing the Spartan assembly, in the words καὶ Ποτειδεάταις, ὥσπερ ὑπεδέξασθε, βοηθήσατε by an immediate invasion of Attica, thus suggesting that the original promise was made not, as is often assumed, by the ephors but by the assembly.

2. Sometimes it is clear that a smaller body is meant, as Th. iv. 15. 1, ἔδοξεν αὐτοῖς - - - τὰ τέλη καταβάντας ἐς τὸ στρατόπεδον (sc. at Pylos) βουλεύειν, where it cannot be contemplated that the whole assembly should migrate.

3. More often it is not clear who is meant, as in the other case in Thucydides, iv. 86. 1, 88. 1, the oaths which Brasidas said he had taken from τὰ τέλη to respect the autonomy of the allies he brought over. Cf. X. *An.* ii. 6. 4, vii. 1. 34; *Ages.* 1. 36; *HG* iii. 2. 6, 4. 26, 27, v. 3. 23, vi. 5. 28: in many of these cases it is quite likely that the assembly is meant.

In view of all this, it is likely that the document in Plu. *Lys.* 14. 8, laying down the surrender terms for Athens in 404, which begins τάδε τὰ τέλη τῶν Λακ. ἔγνω, is again a decree of the assembly: Plutarch indeed, contrasting it with a spurious story, calls this τὸ ἀληθινὸν δόγμα τῶν ἐφόρων, but (a) it is most improbable that a decision of this moment would be taken merely by the ephors, (b) Plutarch may easily have been deceived by the formula τὰ τέλη, as probably also the interpolator in X. *HG* vi. 4. 3—see (1) (b) above—who has Kleombrotos seek orders from the ephors. If so, then τάδε τὰ τέλη, κ.τ.λ., can be the opening formula of a Spartan decree (cf. also *Inscr. de Délos*, 87, the liberation of Delos in 403, ἱάλε τὰ τέλε τὸν Λακεδαιμονίον ἐς Δᾶλον κατὰς συνθέκας, κ.τ.λ.). The formula of our passage is different, but it may be that this is not in form a decree of the assembly, fully ratified. More evidence would be most welcome.

The diplomatic procedure resembles that of iv. 118, that is, proposals sent by one side to the other which might be ratified as they stood or referred back for amendment; except that Sparta's allies have not yet been consulted.]

τὼς παῖδας τοῖς Ὀρχομενίοις, κ.τ.λ.: there is a similar lack of complete agreement in detail between narrative (61. 4–5) and document in this case as there is in the two documents of 421 B.C. τὼς παῖδας, by contrast with τὼς ἄνδρας, means children, not servants (see § 3): and these will be the hostages given by Orchomenos—ὁμήρους σφῶν αὐτῶν δοῦναι Μαντινεῦσι—of 61. 5. For children taken as hostages, cf. Hdt. i. 64. 1–2 (Peisistratos from his Athenian enemies); [for an example closer in time, cf. [Herod.] π. πολ. 33 (Archelaos from Larisa, shortly before 404)]. 'The men in Mantineia' who are to be returned to Sparta will be those hostages deposited (for an unknown reason) in Orchomenos by Sparta (61. 4). The men to be returned to the Mainalioi have not been mentioned before: it has been conjectured that they were prisoners taken at the battle of Mantineia: but the position of the Mainalioi in the Spartan line (67. 1) and the narrative of the battle (72. 4) does not support the view that any Mainalioi were taken prisoner. [The situation in Mainalia was complicated, and some Mainalioi were probably still under Mantinean control, see 67. 1 n., and 81. 1. There is no difficulty in supposing that the allies had taken hostages from places in Mainalia, or that these had been deposited, as the wording here suggests, in Argos.]

τὸ τεῖχος: τὸ τείχισμα, 75. 6; not only the fort built by the Athenians on the headland, but the wall surrounding Epidauros as well.

2. εἴκωντι: [we should not emend to ἐκβῶντι, with Cobet, on the ground that this use of εἴκειν is unfamiliar: we know so little of the technical vocabulary of Doric treaties that we need not hesitate to accept εἴκωντι here. Cf., e.g., ἐφενέποντι in *SEG* xii. 371. 3.]

3. παῖδα: this also must mean children, in accord with § 1. [Steup argued that, if παῖδα here refers to hostages, there is no mention anywhere of return of prisoners by Sparta; and therefore παῖδα must refer to adults. He produced no better parallel than Hdt. i. 27. 3 Λυδῶν παῖδας, and his interpretation makes the distinction παῖδας/ ἄνδρας meaningless. This clause, like the first, refers only to hostages, and there is no need to find a reference to prisoners: if any special arrangement was made about them it was concluded separately.]

4. περὶ δὲ τῶ σιῶ σύματος: see 53. The sentence, corrupt in the MSS. (at some stage in the tradition, perhaps quite early, Doric forms had been misunderstood), has been variously emended, but not satisfactorily.

[For the forms σιῶ, σύματος, see p. 133: θύματος is used of the obligation in 53. Thucydides himself apparently thought it was due (ὃ δέον ἀπαγαγεῖν οὐκ ἀπέπεμπον), but Sparta, by taking Epidauros' side, by implication denied this; or at least, held that Argos had gone too far in her measures against the defaulter. Now the Spartans must in some way come to terms with Argos over this, either by inducing Epidauros to comply, or by finding a face-saving formula. The variegated readings of the MSS. then hover round ἐμε(ν)λην: Ahrens's αἰ μὲν λῆν is hardly a change at all. τοῖς Ἐπ. ὅρκον δόμεν, if that is the text and if these words go together, would most naturally mean that someone is to swear an oath to the Epidaurians: but, in contrast with the usual meaning (e.g. ML 64. 18–20), D. xxxiii. 13 is a clear case where δίδωσιν - - - ὅρκον τούτῳ means challenging the other party to an oath, and οὗτος ἐδέξατο means acceptance of the challenge; our phrase could then mean 'tender an oath to the Epidaurians'.[1] Unnecessary trouble has been made about the subject of the infinitives. If the context were indeterminate, Steup could properly argue that an unexpressed subject in a Spartan decree must be the Spartans, but we cannot be sure that the context did not here imply another subject; this brief clause may indeed be only the conclusion of a longer negotiation, familiar to the parties but unknown to us, a possibility which gravely adds to our difficulties. αὐτώς, with ὀμόσαι, either marks a change of subject, or indicates that it was somehow noteworthy that this party, and not some other, should be swearing.

In Ahrens's text, adopted by Stuart Jones, αἰ μὲν λῆν compels ⟨αἰ⟩ δέ, which must be understood as αἰ δὲ μή, on the analogy of εἰ δέ in Pl. Smp. 212 c, Alc. I 114 b: 'Argivi, si placet, iusiurandum in Epidaurios transferant; sin minus, ipsi iurent.' Admittedly the infinitive serving as verb of a protasis appears to be confined to protases within reported speech (Kühner–Gerth, ii. 550 ff.) and is not paralleled in a decree or the like—Steup pointed out that no other αἰ-clause in 77 or 79 is treated in this way—but Dover suggests that λῆν might have an alternative (athematic) optative *λῆιεν or *λεῖεν (cf. οικειη = οἰκοίη in BCH xxxiii (1909), 452 (Argos, 4th/3rd cent.); or (Elean) συλαιε = συλῴη in DGE 415. 6). If we read αἰ μὲν λῆεν (for the syntax cf. Buck, 138 f.), αἰ δέ presents no great difficulty: the two Plato passages (above) are conversational, not 'elevated' literary, language, and it is perfectly possible that αἰ δέ (sc. μή) was a recognized, though for us unattested, formula in Doric documents. In that case, ὅρκον δόμεν must be taken in Ahrens's sense; in the alternative (αἰ δέ), the Argives are perhaps to make a solemn affirmation of their right, which would help to save the Spartans from feeling too much guilt about their desertion of Epidauros' cause.

However, Stahl and Steup both proposed solutions which avoid the conditional altogether, in terms not of a judicial oath, but of a promise by Epidauros to perform the sacrifice. Steup looked for a verb with the meaning 'impose' to replace εμε(ν)λην, 'impose an oath on the Epidaurians, and they shall swear to give (the sacrifice)': this produces a stronger and less awkward sentence than Stahl's μέλην τοῖς 'Επ., ὅρκον δόμεν δὲ αὐτὼς [ὀμόσαι]. Solution along these

---

[1] [Footnote to Gomme's comment.] In my version of iii. 82–3 (vol. ii, 384) there is probably a mistranslation of ὅρκοι - - - πρὸς τὸ ἄπορον ἑκατέρῳ διδόμενοι, 82. 7, which is rather 'oaths offered to either party to meet a difficult situation'.

lines is certainly less complicated. It involves the complete submission of Epidauros, but for this the removal of the enemy forces would be some compensation, and Epidauros could hardly stand out in these new circumstances.

But no solution can be more than tentative, while we are so doubtful about the background of the clause, and so uncertain what to expect of it.]

5. αὐτονόμως ἦμεν πάσας καττὰ πάτρια: see 81 below. [Such conventional clauses did little to restrain dominant powers: if necessary, it could always be discovered that the current government of the city concerned was not really καττὰ πάτρια.]

6. αἰ δέ κα τῶν ἐκτὸς Πελοποννάσω τις, κ.τ.λ.: [it is interesting that it should have been thought worth while to introduce here this expression of Peloponnesian solidarity against outside enemies. The Spartan alliance, as it was built up in the sixth century, was directed as much against Argos as against outside powers; now that Sparta and Argos are united, defence of the Peloponnese becomes the convenient slogan, directed of course at Athens. In consequence a separate and express clause (§ 7) is needed to bring extra-Peloponnesian allies under the terms of the proposed treaty.

The protasis here, in contrast with the less clearly defined protasis of the corresponding clause in the main treaty, 79. 3, envisages a situation easily seen and recognized when it arose; in practice, a renewed Athenian aggression against a member of the new alliance. In this case, no question arises of the rights of members of the existing Spartan alliance to discuss and vote on their policy: this would be a *casus foederis* automatically calling for armed resistance, cf. 54. 1 n.]

ἀλεξέμεναι ἁμόθι βωλευσαμένως, κ.τ.λ.: [for ἀλεξέμεναι, see p. 133. For ἁμόθι,] see app. crit. It is interesting that *Anecd. Ox.* i. 124. 21 has διὰ τῆς ει διφθόγγου γράφονται οἷον ἀμοθεί, τὸ ἄνευ μάχης παρὰ Θουκυδίδῃ, ἀμοχθεί, a meaning which it so obviously cannot have here. ('To consult without fighting' would be relevant if a dispute between the parties to the treaty were in question.) ἁμόθι itself seems to be ἅπαξ λεγόμενον (LSJ), but its formation seems an easy one. [Edd. compare 47. 12, and i. 87. 4, viii. 54. 4, κοινῇ βουλευσάμενοι.

Though the previous clause (§ 5) dealt with the autonomy of all Peloponnesian cities, great and small, this is a new clause dealing with a different question, and the unexpressed subject can only be the parties to the treaty, Sparta and Argos. Whatever the machinery of consultation in their own alliances, or overriding that machinery, they are to consult together, ὅπα κα, κ.τ.λ. Here δικαιότατα shows that we are dealing with the question of 'fair shares', the distribution of the burden of defence; and, since Sparta and Argos apparently take the decision, τοῖς Πελ. must go with δικαιότατα rather than with δοκῇ, i.e. Sparta and Argos decide what is the fairest distribution for them, *not* a joint conference of all Peloponnesian cities decides what is fairest.]

7. τοὶ Λακεδαιμόνιοι, κ.τ.λ.: [the MSS. text can hardly stand, for to equate Sparta's extra-Peloponnesian allies with 'the allies of Sparta and of Argos' is both clumsy and vague. Steup's proposal, to insert τοὶ ἐν Πελοποννάσῳ before the second ἐντί, involves less alteration than Kirchhoff's insertion: but the present is wrong here, and Steup's argument against Kirchhoff, that we need to have the external allies equated with the Peloponnesian allies, not with Sparta and Argos themselves, is shown to be fallacious by 79. 2.

The 'allies of Argos' here contemplated cannot, of course, now include Athens. The separate alliance with Elis and Mantineia (48. 2) could hardly continue under the treaty here proposed, and was in fact given up (78): and in any case these allies, as also Kleonai and Orneai (67. 2), are excluded if, as seems almost inevitable, the qualification ἐκτὸς Πελοποννάσω applies to the allies of Argos as well as those of Sparta. From literary sources we know indeed of no allies of Argos outside the Peloponnese, unless we count the Chalkidians (31. 6, 80. 2); but the inscriptions of *c.* 450 dealing with the relations between Argos, Knossos, and Tylissos (ML 42: cf. W. Vollgraff, *Le décret d' Argos relatif à un pacte entre Knossos et Tylissos*; A. J. Graham, *Colony and Mother City in Ancient Greece*, 154–8, 235–44) show surprisingly close and solid links in matters of war and sacrifice—for instance, in the conclusion of a new treaty with an outside party the Argives are to have a third share of the votes. These Argive alliances in Crete are not so extensive or weighty as those of Sparta inside and outside the Peloponnese, and it is largely a matter of politeness to write as if the two alliances were comparable; but the Argive alliance is not merely negligible.]

8. ἐπιδείξαντας δὲ τοῖς ξυμμάχοις, κ.τ.λ.: [the difficulties of this last clause arise mainly from the final words οἴκαδ' ἀπιάλλην, and from the fact that Thucydides in 78 says nothing of the procedure of the negotiations.

The Spartans had marched out to Tegea on their own (76. 1), with a preliminary proposition which had been agreed only by their own assembly. To produce the consolidated result of 79. 1, all Peloponnesian cities embraced in the peace and alliance, their allies must be consulted, and this could have been done in the period of ἐπιμειξία that follows in 78 (but see 79. 3 n.). ταὶ δὲ ἄλλαι πόλιες ταὶ ἐν Πελ. means, almost entirely, Sparta's allies, and accordingly it is most natural to take the Spartans as the subject of συμβαλέσθαι, as they are in § 1: having stated, in the participles of § 1, the conditions Argos must fulfil, and then roughed out the general terms, the Spartan assembly goes back to the beginning and states that agreement is possible only with the consent of the allies. This first sentence creates no great difficulty.

We then turn, with αἰ δέ τι δοκῇ τοῖς συμμάχοις, to the possibility that the allies may have suggestions of detail to make, their general assent being presumed for purposes of this stage of the negotiation: the phrase is brief and vague, but intelligible, and does not call for emendation (see Graves). The next stage should be consideration of such amendments by the Spartan assembly, and the question is whether οἴκαδ᾽ ἀπιάλλην fits that. (Σᴹˢᶜ² ἐπιπέμπειν, στέλλειν, led Stahl to conjecture that the original reading was ἐπιάλλην, comparing viii. 38. 4 ἐπιστέλλει, iv. 108. 6 ἐφιέμενος, and this is worth considering: but the main problem is, what meaning we should give to οἴκαδε.)

This turns on the procedure we are to envisage:

(a) There is clearly not a conference of Sparta's allies now in session, so we cannot understand this as a simple proposal to send the allied delegates home to their own cities.

(b) Sparta might intend to summon a conference to which allied delegates should bring their cities' amendments. If they arrived thus instructed, nothing would be gained by sending them home again 'for further instructions' (but this seems to be what Gomme contemplated): nor is οἴκαδε likely in this case to mean 'to Sparta', for the natural course was to hold the conference there anyway.

(c) Sparta might assume that the allies would consent in general (the question whether alliance with Argos was desirable must have come up before), and so content herself with sending a copy of the proposition round the cities (Steup), no doubt with the Argive answer to the present message, and asking if they had any comment or amendment. If they had, it should be sent οἴκαδε, i.e. to Sparta as the place where the proposition originated; if we take the subject of ἀπιάλλην to be the individuals who travelled round with the documents (ἐπιδείξαντας), the reference of οἴκαδε is immediately clear. A conference would then be necessary only if radical amendments or total rejection were widely supported. (For the questions which might arise for the allies, see especially 79. 3 n.)

This third interpretation fits the situation well and, as Steup claimed, it does away with the need for emendation. The obscurity resides in the document having οἴκαδε when it would be clearer (to us) if it had ἐς Λακεδαίμονα: but for all we know this sense of οἴκαδε may have been familiar to the allies in communications from Sparta. ἐπιάλλην would perhaps fit slightly better than ἀπιάλλην, but if the Spartans are sending a message out to the cities, to 'send back' the answer is entirely natural.]

78. οὐ πολλῷ ὕστερον - - - αὖθις: [this is not a wholly separate transaction, but the completion of the negotiation begun in 77.]

καὶ τὴν Ἀθηναίων καὶ Ἠλείων: because a treaty was concluded between Argos on the one hand and Mantineia and Elis on the other (48. 2), before Athens joined to make the quadruple alliance (47), Classen adopted the reading of M, which puts καὶ Ἠλείων before καὶ τὴν Ἀθηναίων, and this seems right.

79. 1. αὐτοπόλιες: a word found here only in Greek (as αὐτοπολῖται also in X. *HG* v. 2. 14, the Akanthians speaking). It is compared with αὐτοτελεῖς καὶ αὐτοδίκους of the Peace of Nikias document, 18. 1, which are also combined with αὐτονόμους. There is a slight distinction: αὐτοπόλιες here emphasizes 'each city in itself' (no nonsense about Parrasia, e.g., being *part* of Mantineia). Cf. below, 81. 1, 2, 82. 1.

2. τὰν αὐτῶν ἔχοντες: [Steup noted that this qualification was not added after τοὶ Λακεδαιμόνιοι, and took this as a sign of imperfect drafting; but there is no difficulty in thinking of it as qualifying both parts of the clause. For Argos' allies outside the Peloponnese, see 77. 7 n.]

3. αἰ δέ ποι - - - κοινᾶς: [common, that is, to Sparta and Argos, for this is a treaty between these two, however much the other cities of the Peloponnese are invited to share it; and these two decide the issue. This clause is more widely framed than the corresponding clause in the first message, 77. 6, and on the face of it it overrides completely the right of Sparta's older allies to decide by majority vote whether they should go to war or not. It might, however, be envisaged that, after Sparta and Argos had jointly decided that they wished to make war, a conference of the Peloponnesian League should still meet in the old way (and, at least in theory, that Argos should consult her allies in whatever way was customary).]

βουλεύεσθαι, κ.τ.λ.: [the bearing of this is perhaps clarified by the presence, this time, of the aor. part. κρίναντας, though the tense of this has been regarded as a difficulty (see Steup's note). Edd. have, inevitably, taken the clause to mean that Sparta and Argos are to decide the contributions to be made by the allied cities. This is an abnormal meaning for κρίνω, which is used of giving judgement in a dispute or a contest but not of laying down regulations: here it may be a technical term special to the Peloponnese, for which, e.g., *Il.* ii. 362, 446 might offer a parallel. The decision about fair contributions precedes the consultation referred to as βουλεύεσθαι: the latter, then, perhaps refers to the actual conduct of the campaign. (There would be no difficulty in taking 77. 6 βωλευσαμένως in the same sense, a similar κρίναντας, or the like, being understood there.)

Thus we have, as Gomme put it, 'these two cities taking the lead, over the heads of their allies'. This has two surprising aspects:

(*a*) Almost all the cities covered by the (no doubt deliberately) neutral formula of § 1 were in fact members of the Peloponnesian League, with its long-established procedure of decision by conference. They had been acutely suspicious three years earlier about the intentions of Sparta and Athens (27. 2, 29. 2–3), and it is not easy to imagine them tamely surrendering the whole direction of the new alliance to Sparta and Argos. Indeed in the course of these negotiations, if 77. 8 is any guide to what actually happened, they were still being consulted in the familiar way.

(*b*) It is equally surprising that Sparta should agree to anything like a joint command: contrast their attitude in 480, Hdt. vii. 148–9.

However, the anti-Spartan movement of 421–418 began at a time when Sparta's prestige was low, and when she was concerned about her future relations with Argos (36. 1, 41. 3): now she had amply retrieved her reputation and Argos had agreed to an alliance. The Spartans were excited by the new prospect (80. 2 θυμῷ ἔφερον), and may well have thought that they could now carry the Peloponnese with them as never before: cf. their actions in regard to Sikyon (81. 2) and Achaia (82. 1). They need not be afraid of nominally shared command in the field—not, indeed, that the treaty specifies quite that—for the position of the Argive oligarchs in their own city was anything but secure and they would always heavily depend on Sparta.

It may be, as suggested in the preceding note, that some of the old procedures of the Peloponnesian League were to continue within the framework of the new alliance. Alternatively, since c. 78 leaves it far from clear what had happened since the Argives accepted the ξυμβατήριος λόγος and the Spartans returned home, it may be that the document given in c. 79 represents only a framework propounded by Sparta and Argos which the other cities had not yet accepted, as they are invited to do in § 1; and that in the event they never had time to declare their attitude. After the Argive counter-revolution we find a conference of the Peloponnesian League in the old style (82. 4).

The wording of 81. 2 (see n. there) leaves it uncertain whether any joint enterprise was actually undertaken except the oligarchic revolution in Argos itself.]

4. αἱ δέ τινι τᾶν πολίων, κ.τ.λ.: [the cities seem to be already committed to peaceful settlement of disputes by § 1, καττὰ πάτρια δίκας διδόντες τὰς ἴσας καὶ ὁμοίας, and the question arises, what new element is added in § 4. Two types of dispute may be relevant: (1) disputes between cities, a frequent subject in treaties; (2) disputes between citizens of different cities, in which one party needs access to the courts of the other's city. These latter were often the subject of special agreement, the ξυμβολαί (later σύμβολα) familiar in Attic (ML 31. 13, etc.) and known elsewhere (e.g. Lokris, *GHI* 34. 15), though we have seldom much idea of their content in detail; it cannot be doubted that such arrangements were long familiar in the Peloponnese, under whatever name.

The formula of § 1, δίκας διδόντες, constitutes an offer to settle peacefully, by negotiation or arbitration, with another city which has a grievance. This is the regular meaning in Thucydides: cf. particularly iv. 118. 8, δίκας τε διδόναι ὑμᾶς τε ἡμῖν καὶ ἡμᾶς ὑμῖν κατὰ τὰ πάτρια, τὰ ἀμφίλογα δίκῃ διαλύοντας ἄνευ πολέμου, where τὰ ἀμφίλογα recurs, and there is no doubt that inter-city disputes are the subject.[1] For δίκας - - - τὰς ἴσας καὶ ὁμοίας cf. 27. 2, 59. 5, which suggest that this was a traditional formula in the Peloponnese; the apparent overlap between § 1 and § 4 may be due simply to the conventional nature of the formula in § 1. An alternative meaning for δίκας διδόναι, to allow a foreigner access to the city's courts, is suggested by A. *Supp.* 701–3, ξένοισί τ' εὐξυμβόλους, πρὶν ἐξοπλίζειν Ἄρη, δίκας ἄτερ πημάτων διδοῖεν, where LSJ translate 'grant arbitration'; ML 20. 41–2 is a clearer case, τὸνκαλειμένοι : τὰν δίκαν : δόμεν τὸν ἀρχόν. But it would be rash to suggest, on the basis of these passages, that δίκας διδόντες in § 1 means something basically different from δίκας διδόναι in iv. 118. 8, and we may take it that both § 1 and the first two sentences of § 4 refer to disputes between cities. Since the third sentence (see next n.) simply reasserts traditional usage, without specifying it in any way, as regards the litigation of private persons, the innovation in § 4 must lie in the first two sentences, regarding inter-city disputes.

As this is usually understood, διακριθῆμεν represents a first stage, 'let them settle it between themselves' (so Steup, comparing Pl. *Euthyphr.* 7 c): if they cannot settle it so, then they must agree on a third city as arbitrator. However, on this interpretation the first sentence hardly performs any function, nor does the form of the second produce the required stress on ἐρίζοι: indeed, the clause αἱ δέ - - - ἐρίζοι does not express the sense Steup wants, and it would have been altogether simpler to say explicitly, e.g., αἱ δὲ μὴ δύνωνται διακρίνεσθαι. Nor is it self-evident why the subject is re-stated, or why the text here specifies τῶν συμμάχων πόλις, as if the preceding sentence concerned only Sparta and Argos.

The basic distinction in § 4 is between the machinery for settling disputes between states and that for settling disputes between individuals; attempts to distinguish varieties of inter-state disputes have not been very successful. The distinction between the subjunctive ᾖ ἀμφίλλογα and the optative ἐρίζοι has suggested possibilities,

[1] κατὰ τὰ πάτρια, as between the Peloponnesian League and Athens, is a shade unexpected, and hardly to be justified as a reference to the Thirty Years' Peace: either 'the traditional usages of Greece', or a reference to some clause in the alliance of 480 (or some consequential agreement of the Kimonian period).

but cf. Buck, 138 f., § 176. 1. Arnold made another kind of distinction by taking the first sentence to refer to quarrels between a member state and an outsider, and taking διακριθῆμεν as a neutral term not excluding war. This does at least account for τῶν συμμάχων, but the first sentence is now more otiose than ever, and the neutral sense proposed for διακριθῆμεν is most unlikely. This does, however, suggest that the root of the trouble is the fact that διακριθῆμεν is not qualified in any way (in *Euthyphr.* 7 c the means of settlement is specified). Dover suggests διακριθῆμεν ⟨ἇδε⟩· αἰ [δέ] τις: 'let them settle it thus: if any allied city . . .' (ἇδε = ὧδε is attested from Crete, ML 2. 1 of the 7th cent., and from Delphi, *DGE* 322, late 5th cent.) This does away with the need to make distinctions, which are inevitably unsatisfactory, between the reference of the two sentences, and gives a more rational structure to the clause about inter-city disputes as a whole (cf., e.g., the added clause at the end of ML 42), though it does not quite account for the degree of repetition between the two αἰ-clauses.

Arbitration between cities was of course nothing new (cf. Kerkyra's offer, i. 28. 2), and the innovation must lie in making it obligatory. There had been recent examples of war between allies of Sparta, within the Peloponnese Tegea and Mantineia (iv. 134), outside it Phokis and Lokris (v. 32. 2).]

τὼς δὲ ἔτας καττὰ πάτρια δικάζεσθαι: [the interpretation of Σ^recc., τοὺς δὲ πολιτευομένους ἐν μιᾷ ἑκάστῃ πόλει δι' ἀλλήλων λύειν τὰ διάφορα, carries no authority and can hardly be right. The only comparable instance of a treaty referring to litigation inside an independent city is the provision of the Peace of Nikias, 18. 2, that the Delphians should be αὐτοδίκους: but there was a particular history behind that (see Gomme ad loc. and on iv. 118. 3), and it would be quite another matter for a treaty between Sparta and Argos to tell, e.g., Corinth that litigation within that city might go on as before.

If this clause arises out of what precedes and asserts that in some related field the traditional procedures are to continue without modification, it most probably deals with the question of private citizens who need to have recourse to the courts of another allied city. The sense would then be that the procedure in disputes between cities is to be modified as in the preceding clause, but this last clause reassures individual litigants by telling them that they may proceed according to the traditional conventions. We do not indeed know what these were, but it may be assumed that there were in the Peloponnese arrangements similar to the Attic ξυμβολαί (see preceding n.).

In post-Homeric Greek ἔται are private citizens, as opposed to rulers or magistrates or states. This is clear for the treaty between Elis and Heraia (ML 17: 'c. 500?', Jeffery, 220, no. 6), A. *Supp.* 247

and fr. 530. 28 Mette, Eur. fr. 1014 N², *SIG³* 141. 13 (Black Corcyra);
the word survived in Tegea till the beginning of the Roman period,
IG v. 2. 20. 5, where the meaning is not so clear.

The MSS. all have τοῖς δὲ ἔταις, which would require δικάζεσθαι
to be passive; but this is unlikely, since the passive of the construction δικάζειν τινί is not found elsewhere, whereas the middle δικάζεσθαί
τινι is common. Classen's ingenious τοῖς δὲ ἔτας—the disputes referred to in the preceding clause are to be judged by private citizens
of the arbitrating city—would require the active, δικάζειν.]

80. 1. καὶ ὁπόσα - - - διελύσαντο: [ὁπόσα ἀλλήλων πολέμῳ εἶχον would
naturally mean territory or prisoners. We do not know of any
territory either party could thus claim (the insecure Argives would
hardly choose this moment to raise the question of Kynouria; see
14. 4, 41. 2), but there may have been some; prisoners from the
recent battle are probable, cf. 77. 3 n. ἢ εἴ τι ἄλλο would be merely
mysterious if it meant things acquired by some method other than
war, and it no doubt refers vaguely to other sorts of disagreement:
hence, as edd. remark, διελύσαντο rather than ἀπέδοσαν. There is
a similar but slightly less violent telescoping in vi. 105. 2 ἀποβάντες
ἐς ᾽Επίδαυρον τὴν Λιμηρὰν καὶ Πρασιὰς καὶ ὅσα ἄλλα ἐδῄωσαν τῆς γῆς
(if ὅσα ἄλλα is the correct reading: see n. there).]

ἐκ Πελοποννήσου - - - τὰ τείχη ἐκλιπόντες: [Πελοποννήσου in general
rather than ᾽Επιδαύρου in particular, and plural τείχη whereas the
fortifications at Epidauros are τὸ τεῖχος in § 3 below and in 77. 1;
this suggests that Athens is now being called on to evacuate Pylos
too (Steup), and no doubt Kythera.

§ 1 contains (*a*) the execution of the treaty, (*b*) two joint resolu-
tions subsequent to the treaty. There is no ground here to conclude,
with Kirchhoff, that documents and narrative are in conflict (but cf.
76. 2 n., 77. 1 n. on τὼς παῖδας). For the refusal to receive κήρυκα
καὶ πρεσβείαν except under conditions, cf. ii. 12. 2. For μὴ ξυμβαίνειν
τῳ μηδὲ πολεμεῖν ἀλλ᾽ ἢ ἅμα, see 39. 3, with n. on εἰρημένον.]

2. θυμῷ ἔφερον: with all the eagerness (in Argos) of minority leaders
and (in Sparta) of recent converts. They felt that they could not
afford not to be very energetic in the new policy. [In Sparta the
party for war against Athens must have been strengthened by the
victory at Mantineia, but it is likely that opposition remained. We
should like to know what part Agis took in all this, for the treaty
is very much in line with the policy he adopted in the middle of
summer 418, cf. 59. 5–60. 1, and 63. 2 n.; but we do not hear of him
again till 83. 1.]

ἀνέπεισαν Περδίκκαν: this happened to him frequently. He was last
heard of in v. 6. 2, where he was called upon to fulfil a clause of his
treaty with Athens, iv. 132. 1.

διενοεῖτο: [he must eventually have carried it further than this, for his ξυνωμοσία with Argos and Sparta was made a charge against him by Athens, 83. 4, at a time when the Spartan–Argive alliance had long collapsed.]

ἦν δὲ καὶ αὐτὸς τὸ ἀρχαῖον ἐξ Ἄργους: as Hdt. viii. 137 had already told his readers, and as Thucydides himself noted, ii. 99. 3, though not in connection with Argive policy. ii. 99 could indeed be an insertion written later than v. 80.

[Considerations of race and origin are often advanced by ancient writers as motives for political action, and they may have been more effective than we are inclined to imagine: Thucydides certainly here suggests that the attitude of Argos helped to determine that of Perdikkas, though there can have been few other occasions when Argos was relevant to his designs. His quarrel with Brasidas, and no doubt the feeling that Spartan presence might hamper him as much as Athenian, had driven him to the Athenian alliance of iv. 132. 1. The removal of Brasidas and Sparta's willingness to surrender Brasidas' gains will have played their part in his present change.]

καὶ τοῖς Χαλκιδεῦσι - - - ἀνενεώσαντο: Sparta had probably been allied with the Chalkideis (Olynthos) and Bottiaioi (cf. 30. 2–3, [where only the first oaths taken at the time of the revolt of Poteidaia were confined to the Corinthians]) since the beginning of the war, and the alliance must certainly have been renewed by Brasidas (cf. iv. 122. 2). Argos became their ally in 421 B.C., 31. 6, but as part of a move against Sparta; and of course had been a close ally of Athens since. [Since in the next sentence it is specified that the embassy to Athens was sent by Argos, without Sparta, it is probable that both states act together as regards the Chalkideis.]

3. τὸ - - - τεῖχος: see 75. 6 n., where also the ξυμφύλακες are referred to; and 77. 1. If the latter did not finish the circumvallation, they nevertheless shared in the work of the garrison.

Δημοσθένη τοὺς σφετέρους ἐξάξοντα: [Demosthenes disappears for a time after the disastrous Boeotian campaign of 424, where his personal part had included a minor defeat near Sikyon, iv. 101. 3–4. Since then he has appeared, in the literary record, only as one of those who swore to the Peace of Nikias and the Spartan alliance, v. 19. 2 and 24. 1, on which see Andrewes and Lewis, *JHS* lxxvii (1957), 180. For his appearance in the Athenian accounts for Aug.–Sept. 418 and his somewhat equivocal connection with the troops sent to Argos after the battle of Mantineia (ML 77 = IG i². 302), see 75. 5 n. On this occasion he seems to be sent out specially from Athens, so he had not actually accompanied the troops sent to Argos, and it is not clear why the commander(s) of this contingent could not bring the troops out themselves; but see end of this n.]

All of Alkibiades' fine plans for completing the humiliation of Sparta had gone astray. Athens, though she had sent out the reinforcement, showed herself singularly ineffective in saving the Argive democracy and therewith the alliance; a strong pacific feeling at Athens is certain. Perhaps finance was a difficulty, for these several expeditions by sea to Argos would be expensive; and doubtless Nikias was saying that, if they must go to war, they should attempt to recover Olynthos and Amphipolis first: cf. 83. 4, vi. 10. 5, 12. 1. Especially would he not wish to provoke Sparta further.

[But short of sending a really large force to Argos, difficult on any pretext and impossible to maintain for long, Athens had no recourse but persuasion; and Alkibiades was duly present at the critical debate in the Argive assembly (76. 3). The basic fact of the present phase was the momentary apathy and discouragement of the Argive demos after the defeat at Mantineia; with Argos in Spartan hands and their own numerical inferiority, the Athenians might reasonably decide there was nothing they could do for the moment. Had they known certainly that Argive democracy would revive so soon, it might have been worth their while to try to hang on at Epidauros, which is so close to Athens that reinforcement is easy. The reason for the special dispatch of an officer of Demosthenes' standing and experience, and for his manœuvre described in the next sentence, may have been to see whether this was practicable.]

ἀγῶνά τινα πρόφασιν - - - ποιήσας: what was the object of this little trick? Apparently simply in order that the Athenians might hand over the fort themselves rather than in conjunction with their ex-allies (with whom indeed they must have been on bad terms). It is not that Demosthenes tried at first to avoid handing it over; for that would have required μέν - - - δ' ὅμως clauses. It is a curious little detail told Thucydides by some Argive or Elean or Mantinean present, but not explained. Argos and her allies were of course due to evacuate the fort, and demolish it, by the agreement with Sparta, 77. 1.

[For a possible reason, see preceding n. By securing control of the fortification, Demosthenes secured his freedom of action; but, if he thought of holding it, he changed his mind later, or received fresh orders from Athens. We do not know how long an interval is covered by ὕστερον, though it cannot last till the Argive counter-revolution.]

Ἐπιδαυρίοις ἀνανεωσάμενοι τὰς σπονδάς: i.e. the Peace of Nikias, as rightly explained by Steup and Graves.

[Epidauros had presumably sworn to the Peace (18. 1, 9), so that there were oaths to be renewed after the recent breach; but I doubt if we ought to exclude the possibility of a local and temporary truce, not mentioned in its proper place by Thucydides.]

81. 1. οἱ Μαντινῆς - - - ξυνέβησαν καὶ αὐτοί: apparently a truce, rather than an alliance, for thirty years—X. *HG* v. 2. 2 ἐλέγοντο δὲ καὶ αἱ σπονδαὶ ἐξεληλυθέναι τοῖς Μαντινεῦσι τούτῳ τῷ ἔτει αἱ μετὰ τὴν ἐν Μαντινείᾳ μάχην τριακονταετεῖς γενόμεναι.

[These σπονδαί are evidently a separate treaty between Sparta and Mantineia, distinct from the Spartan–Argive alliance, which Mantineia might join under the terms of 79. 1 ; and somehow additional to the ordinary conditions of the Peloponnesian League which, from Xenophon's record, Mantineia certainly rejoined. There were some specific matters which had to be regulated, and Mantineia's submission might reasonably be embodied in special σπονδαί, but it remains a little odd that a long-term truce should be included, and that its expiry should be felt to make a substantial difference in Mantineia's relations with Sparta.

Xenophon also presents a chronological puzzle. The Spartan attack on Mantineia is the first event he records after the King's Peace, so that 386 is the earliest year in which this truce could have run out ; and Diod. xv. 5. 3 οὐδὲ δύο ἔτη φυλάξαντες τὰς κοινὰς σπονδάς would date it to 385, so 33 not 30 years after the agreement here recorded. Perhaps Xenophon's 30-years' truce was a separate agreement made a little later, in 415; alternatively, he may have confused the information he received. His expression, ἐλέγοντο, is odd (as if the parties were in doubt about the count) : it means, presumably, 'there was much talk about the expiry of the truce in this year', and Xenophon may have attached the talk to the wrong year.]

τὴν ἀρχὴν ἀφεῖσαν τῶν πόλεων: cf. 29. 1, 33, 47. 1, 58. 1, [and esp. n. on 67. 1 Μαινάλιοι: the reference is presumably to what was left of Mantineia's empire in northern Mainalia.] For the bearing of this, and of the changes made in Sikyon, Argos, and Achaia (82. 1), on the clause of the just-concluded treaty, 79. 1, αὐτόνομοι καὶ αὐτοπόλιες, see n. there and 77. 5 n.

We are not told that anything special happened at Elis. [Different opinions have been held about Elis' position from now until 402 (or, less probably, 399) when Sparta demanded that Elis should liberate her perioikic cities, and declared war. Xenophon on this occasion (*HG* iii. 2. 21) traces Sparta's anger back to the alliance of 420 with Athens, Argos, and Mantineia and to the incident at the Olympia of 420, 50. 4 above ; Diod. xiv. 17. 5 adds a demand that the Eleans should pay their share of the expenses of the war against Athens. J. S. Morrison, *CQ* xxxvi (1942), 72 n. 4, argues that Elis must have rejoined the League when Mantineia did ; Wade-Gery, 277 with n. 2, deduces from Th. viii. 3. 2 that Elis was not in the League in 413 ; see further vi. 88. 9, vii. 31. 1 with nn. What happened to Lepreon is also obscure ; in 402 it was in Elean hands, but revolted as soon as the Spartans invaded, X. *HG* iii. 2. 25. It would be interesting to know what happened to the Elean contingent at Epidauros, 76. 5.]

2. καὶ Λακ. καὶ Ἀργ., χίλιοι ἑκάτεροι, ξυστρατεύσαντες: [this statement of the subject leads us to expect joint action outside the borders of the two cities; but then the explicit narrowing of the subject to αὐτοὶ οἱ Λακ. excludes the Argives from any share in the action at Sikyon and leaves them only with their share in the enforcement of the revolution in Argos. The placing of ξυστρατεύσαντες in the sentence almost demands some joint action which is not in fact recorded here; the layout of the sentence does not in itself suggest a lacuna after ξυστρατεύσαντες, but the sense appears to require one. (The comma after ἑκάτεροι should in any case be deleted, and χίλ. ἑκάτ. ξυστρ. taken closely together.)]

On the thousand Argives see 67. 2 n., where I note that Thucydides does not identify them with the select force that attacked to so little purpose at the battle of Mantineia; nor say that the select troops were aristocrats. [Ephoros clearly did both; and, whatever we think of his account in other respects, he does not positively contradict Thucydides in identifying the revolutionaries with the *logades* of 67. 2.]

Busolt, iii/2. 1255 n. 5, followed by Steup, notes the unreliability of Diodoros' account of the revolution, xii. 80. 2–3, and says that, in view of Thucydides' silence, we must not believe that in this revolution in Argos there was any loss of life. I should have thought that this was a case in which we can have no opinion, one way or the other; the only thing which is certain is that the view (Müller–Strübing's, but still to be heard) that Thucydides, with his oligarchic bias, deliberately suppressed the execution of the democratic leaders, is wrong. If necessary, read a little further, 83. 2. [This is the action of the Spartans, not of the Argive oligarchs, and it is not heavily emphasized (see n. there); but it acquits Thucydides of systematic suppression of the execution of democrats.]

ἐς ὀλίγους μᾶλλον: [since Sikyon was presumably an oligarchy already, this is not 'oligarchy rather than democracy' as viii. 53. 3, but 'narrower oligarchy than before'.]

ἐπιτηδεία τοῖς Λακ.: [cf. i. 19.]

πρὸς ἔαρ ἤδη ταῦτα ἦν τοῦ χειμῶνος λήγοντος: i.e. at the very end of the fourteenth year of the war, *c.* 1 March 417 B.C., if my arguments in the Appendix to vol. iii are sound. For the expression πρὸς ἔαρ ἤδη, cf. 17. 2, and vol. iii, 704. Steup notes that this is the only time that Thucydides says τ. χ. λήγοντος instead of τελευτῶντος, and that λήγειν only occurs once elsewhere (vii. 6. 2).

YEAR 15: 417–416 B.C. (CC. 82–83)

82–83. *Dion Secedes from Athens. Counter-revolution in Argos.*
Athens Quarrels with Perdikkas

82. 1. Διῆς τε οἱ ἐν Ἄθῳ: iv. 109. 3, v. 35. 1 nn.

Λακ. τὰ ἐν Ἀχαΐᾳ: [see ii. 9. 2 with n., and J. K. Anderson, *BSA* xlix (1954), 83–5, for the attitude of Achaia in the Pentekontaetia and during the war. Alkibiades' activities in the summer of 419 (52. 2 ; cf. Paus. vii. 6. 4, which does not look as if it simply depended on Thucydides) showed that Sparta could not count on the loyalty of Achaia when there was no Peloponnesian force present; and only Pellene sent a contingent to the Peloponnesian army in 418 (58. 4, 59. 3). Anderson suggests that the Achaian oligarchies, first attested for 367 (X. *HG* vii. 1. 42–3) were established at this time. In 413 as in 429 the Peloponnesian navy used the Achaian coast as friendly territory (vii. 34), but only Pellene was brought into the ship-building programme of 412 (viii. 3. 2).]

See 79. 1 n. on αὐτοπόλιες.

2. κατ' ὀλίγον ξυνιστάμενος: cf. the story in Paus. ii. 20. 2 of the brutal insult offered to a bride, at her wedding, by Bryas, commander of the thousand select corps, as the immediate occasion of this revolt by the people. [This clearly belongs to Ephoros' account of the thousand (see 67. 2 n.).] Grote took the story seriously and in detail: [but, as Busolt, iii/2. 1263 n. 2, and Steup point out, it is not reconcilable with Thucydides' version, in which the revolt is planned to break out at a particular moment, to coincide with the Gymno-paidiai at Sparta.] Cf. n. on iii. 2. 3 for a similarly motivated story from Aristotle.

αὐτὰς τὰς γυμνοπαιδίας: 'the very day of the festival': cf. ii. 3. 4, αὐτὸ τὸ περίορθρον.

[The Gymnopaidiai were held in the heat of high summer, cf. Pl. *Lg.* 633 c; a precise date, for 371, may be obtainable from the fact that the messenger with the news of Leuktra arrived in Sparta on the last day of the festival, X. *HG* vi. 4. 16, the battle having been fought, according to Plu. *Ages.* 28. 7, *Cam.* 19. 4, on Hek. 5 of the Attic calendar. In other years the correspondence between Attic and Spartan months may have been different. Diod. xii. 80. 3 says that the oligarchic regime lasted eight months. This is defended by Meritt, *CP* xxvi (1931), 80–1: the end of winter (81. 2 above) might mean Anthesterion, the Gymnopaidiai of 417 might have been as late as Boedromion, thus eight months reckoned inclusively. This is to put the Gymnopaidiai very late, and it may be, as Gomme and others have supposed, that Diodoros 'confused the time of the first

agreement with Sparta after Mantineia with that of the revolution' :
early winter (76. 1 with 78), perhaps Posideion, to Hekatombaion.]

3. οὐκ ἦλθον ἐκ πλέονος : I agree with Stahl and others that this cannot stand, and with Steup that the best remedy is to transpose ἐκ
πλέονος to the previous clause, before (Steup prefers after) μετε-
πέμποντο ; but, if that is allowed, we still badly need ⟨τότε⟩ δὲ ἀναβαλόμενοι, as Campe saw.

[The need for this further alteration casts doubt on Steup's solution ; and the effect of the transposition itself is uncomfortable—
'so long as from a long time back their friends were sending for them'.
The text, 'so long as their friends were sending for them, from a long
time back they had not come', makes inelegant English but is
possible Greek : οὐκ ἦλθον is in effect a single notion. If the MSS. text
is right, the emphasis in the next clause must be on the participle—
'but they postponed the festival in order to come'—the antithesis
being between the expected action that was not performed and the
unexpected action that was. But even then we still need Campe's
⟨τότε⟩.]

ἀναβαλόμενοι δὲ τὰς γυμνοπαιδίας : (ms.) did they intercalate some
days and pretend they were still holding the Gymnopaidiai on the
*n*th day of the month? [Cf. 54. 3 with n.]

4. διατριβαὶ δὲ καὶ μελλήσεις ἐγίγνοντο : [for the reluctance of
Sparta's allies to campaign in the latter part of the summer cf. iii.
15. 2 ; for Sparta's own capacity for delay, e.g. viii. 96. 5.] This year
an invasion of Argos in the winter was carried out (83. 1).

5. τὴν τῶν Ἀθηναίων ξυμμαχίαν πάλιν προσαγόμενος : [a ms. note
draws attention to *IG*. i². 96, six fragments of an alliance between
Athens and Argos for fifty years made in the archonship of Euphemos,
417/16 ; and to Meritt, *Hesp.* xiv (1945), 122–7, who adds a new fragment and improves the restorations ; cf. *SEG* x. 104, *ATL* iii. 357 n. 45,
and Bengtson, *Staatsverträge*, no. 196. The treaty was ratified in the
prytany of Aiantis, in which also the first payment was made to
Teisias and Kleomedes for the expedition to Melos (84. 3 ; ML 77.
29–30 = *IG* i². 302) ; the formal conclusion of the treaty thus belongs
to the spring of 416, cf. Kolbe, 92–103.]

(ms.) Note that war between Athens and Sparta is openly referred
to.

τειχίζει μακρὰ τείχη ἐς θάλασσαν : Plutarch, *Alc.* 15. 4–5, says that
this was at the instigation of Alkibiades, an easy guess after his
activity in Patrai, 52. 2 ; but perhaps correct. It is a characteristic
piece of Plutarch : he mentions the τέκτονες καὶ λιθουργοί whom
Athens sent (technical, as well as political, assistance was well known
to the Greeks), which would appear to be direct from Thucydides ;
but he goes on ἔπεισε δὲ (sc. Alkibiades) καὶ Πατρεῖς ὁμοίως, as though
he thought that the long walls of Patrai were the later. [On this see

D. A. Russell, *PCPhS* N.S. xii (1966), 45, who argues that the arrangement is by subject, not chronological. For the technical assistance, cf. the help given by Thebes and other cities to Athens for the rebuilding of her walls in 394, X. *HG* iv. 8. 10, Diod. xiv. 85. 3; or the help given by the Boeotian cities to Chalkis for the causeway to the mainland in 410, Diod. xiii. 47. 3–5.]

Thucydides does not comment on the length of the walls and therefore the minimum number of men required to defend them in relation to Argive numbers, as he does so carefully for Athens, ii. 13. 7. The distance of the sea from Argos is about five miles, as Pausanias says, ii. 36. 6 (from the city to the sea near Lerna).

6. ξυνῄδεσαν - - - καὶ τῶν ἐν Πελ. τινὲς πόλεων: [an obvious guess is Mantineia, resentful of the agreement forced on her at the end of the previous winter (81. 1) and hoping to escape if the Argives could hold out. It may be noted that the Mantinean contingent is prominent in the Athenian expedition to Sicily, generally joined with the Argive, and its presence is twice (vi. 29. 3, 61. 5) ascribed to the influence of Alkibiades; some of it may have consisted of volunteers who came with the city's covert consent, cf. nn. to vi. 29. 3, vii. 57. 9. Another possibility is Corinth, whose abstention from the campaign against Argos this winter (83. 1) and the following winter (vi. 7. 1) is specifically noted. But Corinth had sent a contingent for the first campaign of 418 (57. 2) and one was summoned for the second (64. 4, 75. 2), and 115. 3 does not suggest that she was otherwise out of line with Spartan policy at this time; and it is not easy to see why the Corinthian oligarchy should now feel tender towards the Argive democracy. Evidently there were under-currents now lost to us. For other Peloponnesian states our completer ignorance prevents even guesswork.]

ἐκ τῶν Ἀθηνῶν: [since the formal alliance was, for whatever reason, not completed till the next spring, this may be unofficial assistance.]

83. 1. πλὴν Κορινθίων: [see 82. 6 n.]

ἐκ τοῦ Ἄργους - - - πρασσόμενον: [cf. 84. 1. There were still Spartan sympathizers left: 82. 2 means only that some were killed and some exiled, nor can Diod. xii. 80. 3 τούτων ἀναιρεθέντων be made into a total massacre.]

2. Ὑσιὰς χωρίον τῆς Ἀργείας: on the road to Tegea from Argos near the border, Paus. ii. 24. 7, viii. 6. 4, 54. 7; [some remains are still to be seen near Akhladókambos, cf. Leake, ii. 337, Frazer on Paus. ii. 24. 7.] It was the scene of the famous victory of Argos over Sparta in 669 B.C. (Paus. ii. 24. 7).

τοὺς ἐλευθέρους - - - ἀποκτείναντες: [the Argive democrats had certainly killed some oligarchs during the counter-revolution (82. 2; and the oligarchs perhaps some democrats in the previous winter, cf.

81. 2 n.), but if this is a reprisal it seems unfair and heartless. Thucydides comments on it no more than on Kleon's decree about Skione (iv. 122. 6) and its execution (v. 32. 1), or on the massacre of the Melians (116. 4). It was not remembered against Sparta by ancient critics (they concentrated on her performance in the first quarter of the fourth century), and modern historians do not moralize over the degeneration of Sparta under the stress of war; indeed, most pass over this incident even more lightly than Thucydides (e.g. Busolt, iii/2. 1266; Beloch, ii². 352; Glotz and Cohen, ii. 673; Ferguson in *CAH* v. 278).]

3. οἱ γὰρ πολλοὶ αὐτῶν ἐνταῦθα κατῴκηντο: [conveniently close, and Phleious' fear of Argos kept her loyal to Sparta: on both counts it had been the natural starting-point for Agis' campaign in 418 (58. 2).]

4. κατέκλησαν - - - καὶ Μακεδόνας Ἀθηναῖοι, Περδίκκᾳ, κ.τ.λ.: [the MSS. have *Μακεδονίας - - - Περδίκκαν*. Göller read *Μακεδόνας*, which appears to have been the reading of Σ^Msc₂ *τούτεστι τῶν εἰσαγωγίμων ἢ τῆς θαλάττης αὐτοὺς ἀπέκλεισαν*, and consequently *Περδίκκᾳ*, and this has generally been accepted. For the sense, Stahl compared i. 117. 1–2, the Samians in 440, *ἐσεκομίσαντο καὶ ἐξεκομίσαντο ἃ ἐβούλοντο. ἐλθόντος δὲ Περικλέους πάλιν ταῖς ναυσὶ κατεκλῄσθησαν.*

Some doubt is bound to arise. Thucydides uses the verb of the close siege of a restricted locality (i. 109. 4, the Athenians in Prosopitis; i. 117. 2 as above; iv. 57. 2, the Spartans afraid of being caught in Thyrea) and this seems to be the general usage. The difficulties of naval blockade with Greek warships are known (cf. Gomme, *Essays*, 201): it is true that Macedon at this period had a short coastline and that Athens had bases very near at hand, but even a complete blockade of Macedon would be very much less effective than blockade of an island, or than the blockade of a state of the southern Greek mainland.

Athens seems, however, to have had forces available in the north, though Thucydides mentions none: see the accounts of 418/17 and 417/16 (ML 77 = IG i². 302, to which a ms. note refers). (*a*) For the payment to Euthydemos late in Pryt. I of 418/17, see 75. 5 n. (*b*) For the payment to Nikias and others, perhaps early in May 417, see below, n. on *παρασκευασαμένων αὐτῶν*. (*c*) The first payment of 417/16, on the 22nd day of Pryt. I or III, was to generals ἐς] τὰ ἐπὶ Θράικες. We can imagine orders sent to, or with, any of these squadrons that actually went north (for (*b*) see below) to intercept what shipping they could; or indeed a general decree in the style of the Megarian decrees before the war, not necessarily dependent on the presence of forces in the north. But for this, or for anything we can imagine actually being done, κατέκλησαν is a curiously strong word. (S. Schechter, *CP* lviii (1963), 118–19, proposed to read ⟨ἐς⟩ *Μακεδονίαν - - - Περδίκκαν*, which in some ways runs more easily than Göller's text; but to speak of 'shutting Perdikkas up into Macedon' is still odder than to speak of 'blockading the Macedonians'.)]

τὴν - - - ξυνωμοσίαν: see 80. 2, with n.

παρασκευασαμένων αὐτῶν, κ.τ.λ.: [Busolt, iii/2. 1262 n. 1, followed Müller–Strübing in supposing that this expedition actually arrived in Thrace, and took ἀπάραντος below to mean Perdikkas' withdrawal of his contingent from a joint force; but Grote, Steup, and most others are certainly right to deduce, from the fact that Thucydides says παρασκευασαμένων - - - στρατιὰν ἄγειν and not, e.g., στρατευσάντων, that the expedition was given up before it set out. For διαλύειν used of an enterprise that never got under way, Steup compares iii. 3. 1. μάλιστα probably implies that there were other difficulties besides Perdikkas' attitude: hopes of counter-revolution in Argos may have inclined the Athenians to turn their attention to the Peloponnese again.

80. 2 οὐ μέντοι εὐθύς γε ἀπέστη, of Perdikkas' position in winter 418/17, practically rules out overt opposition to Athens' plans in 419 or 418, and we may take it that the expedition was to have sailed in summer 417. In that case the last payment of 418/17, ML 77. 20–1, to Nikias, Kallistratos, and another, was for this projected campaign. The date must almost certainly be restored as Pryt. IX. 13, probably early in May. That is well before the outbreak of the counter-revolution at Argos, whatever the exact date of that (cf. 82. 2 n.): Perdikkas made his breach with Athens while the Spartan–Argive alliance was still in being, as might be expected. The preparations went far enough for money to be voted and actually paid over: we are not told that the payment was cancelled, as the first payment of the year was (cf. 75. 5 n.), and we do not know what happened.

If Thucydides could mention the revolt of Dion in its chronological place (82. 1), he could have done the same for this abortive expedition, which even if it never sailed had results he thought worth relating. We should have welcomed a more explicit statement about the blockade of Macedon (above), or indeed more reference, however bare, to Athenian activities in the north in these years, such as we find again at vi. 7. 3. These must count among the grounds for regarding book v as not fully finished (cf. 47. 12 n.).]

†ἀπάραντος†: this is itself impossible, [even on Busolt's assumption (see preceding note), since Thucydides uses this word only of the departure of a fleet]. Σ^Msc² ἀντὶ τοῦ ἀναπεισθέντος is neither an explanation of the MSS. reading nor of a reasonable alternative to it. ἀποστάντος, ἀπατήσαντος, and ἀπαρνηθέντος seem the best suggestions made. [Of these, ἀποστάντος seems much the best: the sense, 'hold off from', 'stand away from', is just what is required, and could easily give rise to the scholiast's comment: the corruption would be psychological, induced by the mention of preparations for an expedition.]

Year 16: 416–415 b.c. (cc. 84–vi. 7)

84–116. *Alkibiades in Argos. The Expedition against Melos*

84. 1. Ἀλκιβιάδης: Diodoros xii. 81. 2 expressly says that he was elected strategos, which is probable enough. [(Diodoros' habit of writing as if the Athenians elected their generals individually *ad hoc* for particular expeditions (e.g. xii. 60. 1, 65. 1, 73. 2), however misleading, does not by itself discredit his information.)] Characteristically he dates this in the fifteenth year of the war (in the archonship of Euphemos which was 417/16) in spite of Thucydides' words at the end of the previous chapter; but the archonship of Euphemos is correct: see below.

[These are matters that concern the study of Diodoros rather than that of Thucydides, but it may be worth remarking (*a*) that Diod. xii. 81. 5–82. 1 ταῦτα μὲν οὖν ἐπράχθη κατὰ τὸ πεντεκαιδέκατον ἔτος τοῦ Πελοποννησιακοῦ πολέμου. τῷ δ' ἐκκαιδεκάτῳ, κ.τ.λ., a formula he uses nowhere else, shows that he sometimes looked into Thucydides' text, whereas, e.g., xii. 65 cannot have been written directly out of Thucydides; (*b*) that on Diodoros' own reckoning, by which the archonyear 431/30 is the first of the war (xii. 38. 1), 417/16 is correctly counted as the fifteenth; (*c*) that he has run together under this year three items concerning Argos, Th. v. 83. 2, 84. 1 (both 417/16), and vi. 7 (416/15), whereas his one brief reference to Melos comes at the end of a curious miscellany in xii. 80. 5 under 418/17.]

τοὺς δοκοῦντας - - - τὰ Λακ. φρονεῖν: [cf. 83. 1 with n.]

κατέθεντο αὐτοὺς Ἀθηναῖοι: cf. iii. 72. 1; and for the fate of these men, vi. 61. 3.

ἱπποτοξόταις εἴκοσι: see ii. 13. 8 n. for the mounted archers. It is not explained what use was made of this small force on Melos—for raiding isolated farms and hamlets perhaps.

τῶν δὲ ξυμμάχων καὶ νησιωτῶν: [Stahl, Steup, and others understand this as 'allies, and islanders into the bargain', which must be right. The alternative is to separate these two as distinct components of the *c.* 1,500 hoplites, and Gomme doubtfully suggested that ξυμμάχων might be allies from outside ('Argives, Thessalians and such'), νησιωτῶν ordinary members of the Delian confederacy: but no reader could take ξυμμάχων in this way in this context, and there is no hint that Argives or others in fact took part. Thucydides' form of words (including the echo νῆσον - - - νησιωτῶν) underlines the fact that hoplites from the islands took part in this operation, indeed they outnumbered the Athenian hoplites present. Cf. § 2 n.

In the mouth of an opponent, especially a Dorian speaking to Dorians, νησιῶται is almost a term of abuse: cf. particularly Gylippos,

vii. 5. 4. But on the other side cf. vi. 68. 2, which suggests that something like an *esprit de corps* was growing up.]

On *IG* i². 97, which has generally been thought to be a decree relating to the sending of this force against Melos, but which Meritt now thinks was for a tribute-collecting fleet in the early years of the Archidamian War (*Robinson Studies*, ii. 298–303), see *SEG* xii. 26, and above, vol. iii, 727–8.

We possess the partly preserved record of two payments for this expedition on *IG* i². 302 (ML 77. 29–33), one of ten talents (the other figure is lost): it belongs to the archon-year 417/16 B.C., so early summer 416, but the exact date is lost. [(The restoration in l. 29 must be either Pryt. VIII or Pryt. IX, in l. 31 IX or X.)]

2. Λακεδαιμονίων - - - ἄποικοι: see Hdt. viii. 48.

οὐκ ἤθελον ὑπακούειν: on the position of Melos in relation to the Athenian ἀρχή see ii. 9. 4, iii. 91. 1, with my notes, also iii. 29. 1, 32. 2 nn. It will be remembered that Melos was assessed for tribute in the τάξις φόρου of 425 B.C. (vol. iii, 503): but it is clear from this passage that according to Thucydides it had not in fact paid tribute, unlike Thera with which it is coupled in ii. 9. 4. M. Treu, however, *Hist.* ii (1954), 253/73 and iii. 58–9, believes that Melos became an ally of Athens in 425. [This was mainly on the general ground that Athens could not possibly include Melos in the assessment of 425 unless she had joined the empire; and he was adequately answered by W. Eberhardt, *Hist.* viii (1959), 284–314, with a careful survey of the areas where the assessment must be regarded as unrealistic. A. E. Raubitschek, *Hist.* xii (1963), 78–83, revived Treu's view with the doubtful help of Σ Ar. *Av.* 186, 363 (for which see 116. 3 n.) and Diod. xii. 80. 5, but did not comment on Eberhardt's arguments. The brief summary given here of Melos' relations with Athens is not easily interpreted in Treu's sense, and the thesis that Melos was an ally in revolt is inconsistent with parts of the following dialogue. To maintain this thesis we have to suppose that Thucydides positively falsified the facts.

If we decline to do that, we may still complain of insufficient information. τὸ μὲν πρῶτον - - - ἡσύχαζον can only refer to the early years of the war. ἔπειτα - - - δηοῦντες τὴν γῆν could refer to iii. 91. 3, but not to this stage of the present operation (§ 3 πρὶν ἀδικεῖν τι τῆς γῆς): if it is not a reference to Nikias' attack in 426,[1] Thucydides

---

[1] Gomme devoted little space to these operations, remarking (iii. 91. 1 n.) that 'this was a considerable force, and Nikias does little with it'. iii. 91. 4 seems to me to imply that Nikias had arranged his meeting in Boeotia with Hipponikos and Eurymedon, including the precise date, before he left Athens. If so, he could not spend too much time at Melos, indeed a surrender might seriously have dislocated his time-table. The assembly, then, was ready to authorize a campaign against Melos in 426, which is very natural if Melos had helped Alkidas in 427 (iii. 32. 2 n.): but for Nikias and his colleagues

must have passed that over here, and the brief reference is to some other operation which he did not record in its place. That is much less likely, and I take it that ἐς πόλεμον φανερὸν κατέστησαν refers to the situation after 426. In the dialogue the Melians (a) do not claim that they are now allies of Sparta, (b) do not complain that Athens' action is in breach of the Peace of Nikias. That is, the πόλεμος φανερός was never formally concluded by a treaty, though neither side did anything and it was quietly forgotten till now. In all this we find no reason why Athens should attack Melos in 416 rather than in any other year, unless we take the general ground that they were restless after the collapse of their plans in the Peloponnese and ready to take up anything that offered; which is no doubt true, and relevant for the mood in which they took up the opportunity to intervene again in Sicily next year.

On balance, however, it seems unlikely that the attack in 416 was due solely to an Athenian whim, without any immediately antecedent quarrel. (a) The topic is excluded from the dialogue in terms which suggest that there was something to be said about it. In 89 the Athenians say they will not claim that they were punishing a wrong, and the Melians must not say that they have done Athens no harm. The Athenians cannot simply be saying that there was nothing under this head to discuss—Melos either had or had not done Athens some harm—and to raise the topic serves only to raise in the reader's mind a question which Thucydides did not propose to answer, a procedure which is most easily explicable if the issue were a real one, and had been raised in fact. (b) The fact that hoplites from other islands took part (§ 1 n.) is no doubt in large part due to their expectation that Athens would in any case win: cf. iii. 5. 1, 6. 1 on the allies' attitude at the start of the revolt of Mytilene, and Melos in peacetime was a much less formidable antagonist for Athens than Mytilene during the war and with the hope of Peloponnesian support. But the fact that these island hoplites at Melos were from the start a majority of the force suggests a degree of confidence on Athens' part that the operation would have their goodwill. This must not be overstressed. In *PCPhS* N.S. vi (1960) 1–2 I rashly asserted that Athens employed allied hoplites only at moments of high confidence: the use of allied hoplites is commoner than that, as T. J. Cadoux has pointed out to me, especially of allies near the scene of operations, and especially in the north. But the fact that the Athenian hoplites at Melos were in a minority arouses the suspicion that the attack was not just an evidently monstrous outrage.

If there were specific grounds for an attack in 416, we cannot now expect to discover what they were. (The notion, never very plausible,

Melos may have been no more than an excuse to take out a force whose real (and necessarily secret) use was to be against the Boeotians.

that Melian coinage constituted a provocation to Athens, is exploded
by C. M. Kraay's re-examination of the numismatic facts, *Num. Chr.*
7. iv (1964), 1–20.) The subsequent massacre, which early became
a standing charge against Athens, monopolized attention, and no
one was interested in re-examining the reasons for sending the expedition in the first place: they must have been discoverable (e.g.)
for Isokrates, but his defence of Athens (iv. 100 ff., in 380) relates
only to the massacre. But though Thucydides must have had the
massacre present to his mind, his dialogue is formally about the
question whether Melos should submit without fighting, and for our
judgement of this the current relations of Melos with Athens, and
with other islands, are not irrelevant. For all Thucydides has told
us, III. 4 μέτρια προκαλουμένης might be entirely justified, or not at
all; a more detailed introduction would have been helpful.]

3. Κλεομήδης - - - Τεισίας: neither is mentioned again in Thucydides,
nor is either father, unless Lykomedes father of Archestratos, i. 57. 6,
is the same man; but all four, the first pair of the deme Phlya, the
second from Kephale, are confirmed by *IG* i². 302 (= ML 77. 29–33),
recording Athenian expenditure for the expedition to Melos in
417/16 B.C. (§ 1 n., and cf. 83. 4 n.). The Lykomedes who was killed
in battle in 425 or 424 (*IG* i². 949. 14) may have been Kleomedes'
father, or his brother (so *PA*); he was of the Kekropid phyle to
which Phlya belonged. The Lykomedes son of Aischraios who as
trierarch was the first Greek to capture an enemy ship in the Persian
War (Hdt. viii. 11. 2, at Artemision; Plu. *Them.* 15. 3, at Salamis) and
dedicated his trophy to Apollo Daphnephoros at Phlya (Plu. loc. cit.),
was doubtless of the same family and perhaps Kleomedes' grandfather. [These are probably all members of the *genos* Lykomidai,
which controlled the important mystery-cult of Ge at Phlya (Toepffer,
Att. Genealogie, 208–15; cf. Plu. *Them.* 1. 4 for its most famous
member, Themistokles, who, however, belonged to a branch living
in Phrearrhioi). The Daphnephoreion at Phlya is mentioned also in
Ath. x. 424 f.] A Teisimachos son of Teisias of Kephale was *tamias* of
the Goddess, one of those responsible for payments for the gold and
ivory statue of Athena, in 444 or 443 (*IG* i². 359. 15–16; cf. *SEG* x.
260).

[As regards Kleomedes, D. M. Lewis points out to me that his name
would fit ML 77. 21, the payment early in 417 to Nikias, Kallistratos,
and another general of whose name only the initial *K* remains (cf.
83. 4 n.); and no other contemporary general beginning with *K* is
known.]

πρὶν ἀδικεῖν τι τῆς γῆς: somewhat as Brasidas at Akanthos (iv. 84. 2;
cf. τά τε ἴδια μὴ βλαφθῆναι 87. 6), but that good speaker was admitted
to the assembly and addressed the multitude. History might have
been very different if the Athenian ambassadors had been given

the same privilege at Melos; for Brasidas' words were ἐπαγωγά, indeed ἐφολκὰ καὶ οὐ τὰ ὄντα (iv. 88. 1, 108. 5), as the Athenians' might have been (85).

ἐν δὲ ταῖς ἀρχαῖς καὶ τοῖς ὀλίγοις: [ἀρχαί in Greek would include the council, often the most powerful organ in an oligarchy, as well as magistrates in the more familiar sense; and ὀλίγοι will be the privileged voters. As we know nothing of the constitution of Melos, we cannot say what the qualifications for voting were, or how the council, etc. were composed. Since it is contemplated that the Athenians might have been brought before the πλῆθος, there may also have been a formal assembly of all citizens, but probably, as Gomme said, 'summoned rarely and only for certain purposes or at the will of the council'.]

85. ἐπαγωγὰ καὶ ἀνέλεγκτα: [see the note before last; and cf. also vi. 8. 2 ἐπαγωγὰ καὶ οὐκ ἀληθῆ. ἐπαγωγά evidently implies untruthfulness, but the Athenians must not be taken as admitting that what they would have said to an assembly would have been *merely* false or misleading: this clause is their interpretation of the meaning of the Melian ὀλίγοι, cf. ὅπως δή at the beginning of it.]

μηδ' ὑμεῖς ἑνὶ λόγῳ, κ.τ.λ.: I agree with Graves, against Classen, that grammatically ἑνὶ λόγῳ is to be taken with ὑπολαμβάνοντες; but for all that μηδ' ὑμεῖς is related to τὸ πλῆθος of the Melians, not to the Athenians: 'do not you, moreover, confine yourselves to a single reply as your assembly would have been obliged to do in answer to us, but take up our arguments one by one as we put them forward. This will give you yet greater security in face of our dangerous eloquence.'

[A ms. note refers to iv. 22. 1, where this method of conference was proposed by the Spartan envoys at Athens in 425, and the same term ξύνεδροι is used as in 86 below. It was presumably common enough in real life, for practical negotiation about concessions in detail from one side or the other. To record a conversation at such length was an isolated Thucydidean experiment (cf. Σ^Msc₂ ἐν πᾶσι μὲν ὁ Θουκυδίδης ἔφυγε τὴν συνήθειαν ⟨τοῦ λόγου⟩, οὐχ ἥκιστα δὲ ἐνταῦθα), and his dialogue is anything but a haggling over detail. This is one element of the general problem of the Dialogue, why Thucydides chose this particular and unusual form.

Gomme promised a discussion of the Dialogue, and of its place in the composition of the *History*, but he did not leave enough material even to show certainly what general line he intended to take, and no attempt can be made here to reconstruct his views. Points about the Dialogue will here be taken up as they arise, and I add a general note at the end of c. 113; for the question of the date of composition, see 91. 1 n.]

86. ξύνεδροι: [this recalls iv. 22. 1; cf. preceding n.]

ἡ μὲν ἐπιείκεια: a notable word here, 'generosity and reasonableness';
see i. 76. 4, iii. 40. 3, iv. 19. 2.

τὰ δὲ τοῦ πολέμου παρόντα ἤδη, κ.τ.λ.: it is worth while again to
compare iv. 88. 1, the Akanthians καὶ περὶ τοῦ καρποῦ φόβῳ ἔγνωσαν
οἱ πλείους, and Brasidas' words, iv. 87. 2, γῆν δὲ τὴν ὑμετέραν δῃῶν
πειράσομαι βιάζεσθαι; and, with τῷ δικαίῳ below and δικαίως - - -
δίκαια in c. 89, his καὶ οὐκ ἀδικεῖν ἔτι νομιῶ (ibid.). But Brasidas was
'imposing' freedom on Akanthos, while Athens, so the Melians say,
brings servitude to Melos; and Athens does not deny it.

δουλείαν: I believe that we should translate this 'subjection' or
'servitude', rather than 'slavery', though we cannot be sure of the
exact feeling evoked. See n. on v. 9. 9 (vol. iii, 646).

87. εἰ μὲν τοίνυν: 'τοίνυν is, then, essentially an Attic, and a collo-
quial, particle . . . conversational and lively'—Denniston, 569 (frequent in Aristophanes and Plato). 'Well, then' is its general meaning;
but here 'of course' seems, at first sight at least, the better translation. (It occurs only five times in Thucydides, in each case in Attic
speech, three times in this dialogue (see 89, 105. 1), at iii. 45. 4 and
at viii. 53. 3—this last a very clear case of 'well, then'.

[The Athenians point to the same present facts, but urge the
Melians to a different response, viz. to draw the proper conclusion
from Athens' overwhelming superiority, the background of the whole
discussion. The Melians are invited to exclude the one inference
which does not flow inevitably from τὰ παρόντα, their ὑπονοίας τῶν
μελλόντων, i.e. 86 πεισθεῖσι δὲ δουλείαν. The possible consequences of
surrender are not in their control: τὰ παρόντα compel them to surrender, whatever the consequences.]

εἰ δ' ἐπὶ τοῦτο: [sc. ξυνήκετε; the reference would be clearer if Thucydides had written ἢ ἐπ' ἄλλο τι above.]

88. δοκοῦντας: [some apology for the ὑπόνοιαι of which the Athenians
had complained in 87.]

καὶ περὶ σωτηρίας: καί does not, surely, only point to the next clause,
καὶ ὁ λόγος, but means 'is indeed about our safety'.[1] The Athenians
in 87 had meant by σωτηρία material security—crops, homes, lives,
all that is endangered by war (without necessarily indicating what
was to be the result of this one—total destruction); the Melians
are thinking of 'our very existence as a Greek πόλις, a member of
the Greek world', that is, of ἐλευθερία.

89. μετ' ὀνομάτων καλῶν, ὡς ἢ, κ.τ.λ.: cf. Euphemos at Kamarina,
vi. 83. 2 καὶ οὐ καλλιεπούμεθα ὡς ἢ τὸν βάρβαρον μόνοι καθελόντες

---

[1] ['Safety' somewhat narrows the meaning of σωτηρία: 'survival' would be
more adequate here.]

εἰκότως ἄρχομεν: and, in a very different context, iii. 82. 8 μετὰ ὀνόματος ἑκάτεροι εὐπρεποῦς.

[The speakers do not renounce in principle the claim arising from Athens' conduct in the Persian Wars; they only exclude it from the present discussion. It would normally be used in such a context, and even Thucydides, impatient as he was with the set themes (cf. H. Strasburger, *Hermes* lxxxvi (1958), 17–40, esp. 23–4), allowed one statement of it by Athenian speakers, though he prefaced it with an apology (i. 73. 2) and followed it with an answer (i. 86. 1). Euphemos (cf. vi. 83. 2 n.) and the present speaker have to sign off it explicitly, because it is an argument that the reader would expect, and it had in the Greek world some rhetorical weight. Similarly, Thucydides is not to be understood as implying that the Spartan origin of the Melians was either bogus or, in the normal treatment of these themes, unimportant. These exclusions fit in with Thucydides' general reluctance to dwell on such themes; we have no means of telling whether they fit as well with what was actually said on this occasion.

It is another and a larger question whether Thucydides thought, or had reason to think, that Athenian political speakers regarded the claim as hollow and were consciously deceiving when they exploited it. The nearest parallel to μετ' ὀνομάτων καλῶν is iii. 82. 8 (above), and there he certainly treats οἱ ἐν ταῖς πόλεσι προστάντες as merely cynical; but that is, indeed, 'a very different context'. The Dialogue goes beyond iii. 82 in that the Athenians here set out to provide a reasoned case for the practices concealed behind the ὀνόματα καλά—not, this time, mere anarchy but a coherent system. The second half of this sentence proposes to start ἐξ ὧν ἑκάτεροι ἀληθῶς φρονοῦμεν, with the implication that the Melians also consciously recognize and accept the principle propounded (cf. ἐπισταμένους πρὸς εἰδότας); but they are not represented as accepting it, though they protestingly conform in 90. Is this a fair description of the conscious thoughts of the Athenian envoys, or of what they actually said? This is not a matter of the naked brutality of language which appears to have been regular in Greek diplomacy (cf. J. R. Grant, *CQ* N.S. xv (1965), 261–6), but of abandoning the normal moral theory of Greek public life: hereafter, as the briefest incursion into Demosthenes (let alone Isokrates) will show, Greek orators continued to prate about justice, often quite unrealistically. Either, Thucydides had reason to think that in the privacy of this conference the Athenian speakers explicitly gave up what they regarded as a hollow pretence; or, he has abandoned reporting and ἃ ἀληθῶς φρονοῦμεν is rather something which he claims to detect as the reality behind Athenian thoughts.]

ἢ ἀδικούμενοι νῦν ἐπεξερχόμεθα: 'seek retribution', as in iii. 38. 1.

[This, and the counter-argument ὡς ἡμᾶς οὐδὲν ἠδικήκατε, are topical questions on a different plane from the matters discussed in

the previous note. On this plane it is not possible for both parties to
be fully justified, though both would claim it: if the Athenians had
a complaint, the Melians would say that they had not committed
the action complained of, or that it did not constitute ἀδικία. The
mere introduction of this topic suggests to me that there was something that might have been discussed; but other critics have found
no difficulty in supposing that what is here excluded is a theoretical
possibility with no foundation in fact. If there was some substantial
complaint (cf. also 84. 2 n.), Thucydides did not wish to report discussion of it. He is, indeed, often and necessarily selective; but we
are entitled to ask why he selected one thing and not another.]

λόγων μῆκος ἄπιστον: [the combination seems to imply that a very
long speech is, as such, less credible or persuasive than a short one;
but, though it was conventional to associate brevity with sincerity,
this seldom stopped Greeks making long speeches. The point may
be rather that the content of the Athenian speech would be ἄπιστον
to the Melians, just as they will not persuade (πείσειν) the Athenians;
if so, the phrase does not imply that the Athenians knew that their
arguments under these heads would be dishonest.]

Λακ. ἄποικοι ὄντες οὐ ξυνεστρατεύσατε: the translation, 'though a
colony from Sparta you did not march with her in the war' (Stahl),
gives perhaps an easier meaning to the verb than 'because you are
a colony from Sparta you did not march with us, i.e. join the confederacy' (Classen and Boehme, followed by Steup): but it only
says in effect what is said in the second clause, ἡμᾶς οὐδὲν ἠδικήκατε.
[Gomme therefore preferred Classen's rendering. But the antithesis
seems to be between Melos' relations with Sparta and her relations
with Athens: the emphatic position of ἡμᾶς suggests that 'we', the
Athenians, have no part in the first clause. For what it is worth,
cf. also Σ^{ABCF} τοῖς Λακεδαιμονίοις οὐ ξυνεστρατεύσατε.]

ἀπὸ τῆς ἴσης ἀνάγκης: cf. Brasidas again, iv. 87. 3, προσεῖναι δέ τί
μοι καὶ κατὰ δύο ἀνάγκας τὸ εὔλογον, where the ἀνάγκαι were not equal.
'In ordinary speech, δίκαια enter the picture when judgement is
made between persons who are subject to the same compelling power'
(moral or material, of course): e.g. between two citizens of a state,
or between a citizen and an alien when there is, within a certain
sphere, explicit law or custom establishing τὸ ἴσον; even between
master and slave if there exists law or custom limiting the master's
power, but, theoretically, δίκαια οὐ κρίνεται between two men one
of whom has the right to command and the other must obey. It is in
every way a sophistry for the Athenians to go on δυνατὰ δὲ οἱ προύχοντες πράσσουσι, κ.τ.λ.; for two states, or at least two states in the
Greek world, were in this like two citizens of one city, ἐν ἴσῃ ἀνάγκῃ
(e.g. each morally bound to respect the ἐλευθερία of the other), even
though one might be richer and more powerful than the other:

therefore δίκαια κρίνεται for them. When Kallikles in *Gorgias* asserts the right of the stronger to take what he can, he is upholding φύσις against νόμος, and within the state as clearly as between two states. That states did not often act then, as they have not acted since, as citizens within a state were expected to act, was true; but this is not the point made by the Athenians.

[There was another version of this note, marked 'alternative' (and perhaps written later, though this is far from clear) :]

'When both sides start from the same basis of necessity'.[1] For ἀνάγκη, a word of conveniently wide meaning, the nearest comparison in Thucydides is perhaps in Brasidas' speech, iv. 87. 3; and it is implied, though not expressed, in ὑπὸ τριῶν τῶν μεγίστων νικηθέντες of the Athenians at Sparta, i. 76. 2.

This is here a sophistic and cynical argument, but we must be clear what it means. 'By human reasoning'[2] (not, by the way, 'in the language of practical men' as opposed to philosophers) justice is only possible where there is ἰσονομία: a τύραννος or a δυναστεία (see iii. 62. 3) in a Greek city, or a king of Persia, might be, the Greeks well knew, wise or benevolent as well as capable, but he does not in the strict sense administer *justice*, but pardons or punishes, taxes or does not tax, according to his will, can be generous but not (properly speaking) just, although of course δίκαιος, like 'just', was often enough used of the righteous ruler. That is why the Greeks regarded the Persian Wars as a defence of νόμος. The same is true of a master towards a slave and of an imperial power towards its subjects or intended subjects; cf. i. 76. 3–4—if only the weak will behave reasonably and give way, the strong will promise not to be harsh (reserving to themselves of course the right to define the meaning of 'harsh').

[A ms. note referred further to de Romilly, *Imp.* 298 n. 1; and to 'Diodotos on πενία and ἀνάγκη', i.e. iii. 45. 4.

This is a passage of central importance, and I print both versions of Gomme's note since it may help to show what sort of conclusions he had begun to entertain about the Dialogue. He had evidently not made up his mind, but I have no doubt myself that the 'alternative' version (the second printed above) is nearer the mark. That is, the Athenians do assimilate the relation between an imperial power and its subjects to the relation between master and slave; they deny that δίκαια κρίνεται between them, or that ἴση ἀνάγκη exists between the powerful and the weak; and I would say, mainly

---

[1] ['Compulsion' (as in the other version) or 'constraint' renders ἀνάγκη better than 'necessity'.]

[2] [So Σ^Msc² ὁ ἀνθρώπινος λογισμός: but it seems more likely that it means 'when we are talking about relations between human beings', i.e. not about standards set by the gods (cf. 105. 2, with n.) or eternal ἄγραφοι νόμοι, or otherwise leaving the straightforwardly human sphere.]

on the strength of 105. 2, that the actual behaviour of states in practice is, if not the whole point, at any rate the main evidence on which the Athenian principle is based. The passage is then sophistic in the sense that Thucydides' speakers, like many of the sophists, show themselves ready to challenge received ideas as being out of line with the facts; but not, as Gomme sometimes seems to mean, sophistic in one of the modern senses, that the reasoning involves some sort of trick.

The Greeks, sometimes bellicose but not worshippers of war as such, talked much of justice in inter-city relations. In the Classical period, as Thucydides' narrative shows, no city could feel comfortable in the role of aggressor; major treaties from the middle of the fifth century tried to provide for peaceful settlement of disputes (18. 4 δικαίῳ χρήσθων καὶ ὅρκοις), and in the *koinai eirenai* of the fourth century at least lip-service was paid to the principle of respecting the autonomy of all cities alike. But it is true, though it was not normally acknowledged so openly, that inter-city arbitration flourished only ἀπὸ τῆς ἴσης ἀνάγκης and was never easy to apply to οἱ προύχοντες, who exercised their power as opportunity offered; they preferred, indeed, to justify themselves, and, as in our time, found no great difficulty in doing so. Generally speaking, there existed between cities no sanction comparable to the rule of law within the city (for the question of divine sanction, see nn. to 105. 1–2), and in a time when that rule and all other restraints on the individual came under question it was inevitable that someone should suggest that justice between cities was not merely flouted in practice but unmanageable in theory.

For all that, the Athenian speakers have not taken up the position of Kallikles in *Gorgias* (Gomme, above), or Thrasymachos in *Rep.* i, that justice actually is the interest of the stronger, or (in the formulation more familiar to us) that might is right. Terms like δίκαιον retained their standard meaning for Thucydides, as is shown most clearly when he denounces their abuse by others, iii. 82–3. The Athenians here allow that justice is a usable concept between cities on the same level of power: only in the case of disproportionate power it does not apply and never has applied, and we all know that this is so. But the open admission is abnormal, for evidence enough remains to show that the ordinary citizen, even of a great power acting arbitrarily, preferred to think that his city's action was morally justified.]

90. ᾗ μὲν δὴ νομίζομέν γε, χρήσιμον: [Bekker adopted ἡμεῖς δή from the margin of a late MS., with no pause after νομίζομέν γε; Krüger and Stahl preferred ἡμεῖς μὲν δή, and Kalliphatides proposed καὶ μὲν δή, which Gomme approved, referring to his note on iii. 113. 4.

But the parallel is not very exact, and Steup and Stuart Jones were surely right to keep the text here, and punctuate it as they do. It presents no difficulty ('it is useful, at any rate in the way we see it') : for the use of μέν see Denniston, 382.]

τὸ κοινὸν ἀγαθόν: [Σ^{ABFc₂} τὴν ἐλευθερίαν, which H₂ has taken into the text; but 'the common good' is wider than this.]

τὰ εἰκότα καὶ δίκαια: Hermann, who was followed by Stahl, was surely wrong in bracketing καὶ δίκαια on the ground that the Melians have just said that, falling in with the Athenian proposal, they will ignore τὸ δίκαιον. [There is no inconsistency: the Melians have accepted, under protest, that they are not to rely on τὸ δίκαιον as such, but they seek to turn the Athenian position by claiming that the observance of conventional justice is in fact a general advantage, ξυμφέρον.

This is an unusual sense of εἰκότα, 'fair', approximating to ἐπιεικῆ ; an extension of the meaning 'reasonable', cf. ii. 74. 2. i. 37. 1 οὐκ εἰκότως, 'unfairly', is not very different.]

καί τι καὶ ἐντὸς τοῦ ἀκριβοῦς, κ.τ.λ.: 'and to get some benefit from them, if he can persuade his judges (or, public opinion), even short of the exact limits'. [τὸ ἀκριβές is, in effect, what a state like Athens might do if it used its disproportionate power as it stood, to the full and ruthlessly (cf. i. 99. 1 with n. ; and vi. 18. 6 is not very different in sense) ; 'short of' this represents a concession which the great power need not have made, cf. i. 76. 3.] Crawley's 'to profit by arguments not strictly valid', in effect followed by Warner, gives a wrong colouring to this. πείσαντά τινα refers rather to the kind of eloquence that we find in the Plataian speech, which (in a better world) would have won complete acquittal. And in that speech what would be useful, advantageous to Sparta is not altogether forgotten, iii. 56. 7, 57. 1–2. [For the concept of 'persuading' the hegemonic power, cf. also ML 52. 27. πείσαντά is the reading of H₂ as well as recc.

Had the Melians left it at that, there would have been a somewhat different case for the Athenians to answer. Having allowed the Melians to stake a claim in equity, Thucydides apparently did not want to have the theory further discussed; and indeed, the κοινὸν ἀγαθόν is not of practical importance to a powerful state while it retains its power. That, no doubt, is why the Melians go on to the case where it would become important to Athens, if her empire should fail; and thus they open the way for the Athenians to make their arrogant answer, and so to give a different turn to the discussion.]

καὶ πρὸς ὑμῶν, κ.τ.λ.: for Athens was running a greater risk for greater ends (ii. 64. 5) than any other city. This *need* not be a prophecy after the event, any more than πάντα γὰρ πέφυκε καὶ ἐλασσοῦσθαι, ii. 64. 3. See next n.

91. 1. οὐ γὰρ οἱ ἄρχοντες ἄλλων, κ.τ.λ.: cf. Nikias' equally sophistic argument, vi. 11. 2–3.

Arnold points out that, according to Xenophon, *HG* ii. 2. 19, it was the generosity of Sparta that saved Athens from utter destruction in 404 when lesser states demanded it; and this section of the dialogue has indeed an air as though it were written after 404—partly because it is not strictly in place; for the Melians had not used the argument of special danger from Sparta (i.e. οὐ γὰρ οἱ ἄρχοντες ἄλλων, κ.τ.λ., is not logical), and the special danger from revolted allies (in the event of ultimate defeat) would clearly not be lessened by an Athenian victory over Melos now, especially if followed by its destruction. Yet the prophecy is by no means accurate: the states which particularly clamoured for the destruction of Athens were (according to the partial Xenophon) Thebes and Corinth, supported by many other Greeks; the one-time subjects of Athens are not mentioned. (For other references to this, not all in accord with Xenophon, see Busolt, iii/2. 1634 n. 2.)

Besides this the statement 'we have little to fear from Sparta' is reasonable enough in the period of the uneasy truce, especially after the events of 421 B.C. and after Mantineia in 418. 'We fear our revolted subjects more' may be conventional rhetoric—the usual danger to which a tyrant is subjected, be he ·individual or city.

[The illogicality of which Gomme complains above is more formal than substantial. At any time after the resumption of war in 413 (and the Dialogue was surely not completed before this) and the disaster in Sicily, the Melians' σφαλέντες ἄν would automatically call up the prospect of a defeat by Sparta, as it does here; the Athenians might reasonably consider that the only defeat they need in fact fear was at the hands of Sparta, and they could dismiss the alternative of a successful spontaneous attack by their subjects—§ 2 περὶ μὲν τούτου ἡμῖν ἀφείσθω κινδυνεύεσθαι. The introduction of Sparta is thus natural enough. (I made too much of the alleged illogicality in *PCPhS* N.S. vi (1960), 3–4, and the parenthesis ἔστι δέ - - - ὁ ἀγών need not be taken as an attempt to retrieve the apparent anachronism by recalling us to the situation as it formally was in 416: the point may simply be that the present argument, ἀγών, is not with Sparta but with the Melians.)

Nevertheless, the arguments for a late date are not decisive. (*a*) It cannot be maintained that it was impossible, before the event in 404, for Athens to expect lenient treatment from Sparta. Already in 425 and 421 the Spartans had shown how ready they were to come to easy terms. Even after Aigospotamoi the Athenians contemplated the possibility that they might gain peace by not very substantial concessions (X. *HG* ii. 2. 11), and if they could (mistakenly) expect such treatment then they were surely capable of forming a similar expectation at the present stage, when feelings were less embittered. (So Steup, though he gave no reasons.) (*b*) Gomme was surely right about the inaccuracy of the prophecy, though attempts have been made to retrieve it. Isokrates' rhetoric (viii. 78, Athens in 404 had found Sparta more merciful than her own subjects or the rest of Greece, cf. 105) cannot be used to undermine the accuracy of Xenophon's narrative, as it is by De Sanctis, *Rend. dei Lincei*, 6. vi (1930), 299 ff., an imperfect answer to Momigliano, *Mem. Acc. Sc. di Torino*, 2. lxvii (1930), 11. Xenophon's own phrase πολλοὶ δὲ καὶ ἄλλοι τῶν Ἑλλήνων may include former allies of Athens among those who pressed for her destruction (so de Romilly, *Imp.*, 275–7), but it certainly does not draw attention to them.

This passage could thus have been written well before 404, indeed quite soon after the Melian affair. It does not follow that it was in fact written earlier than 404, though on balance this seems to me the more probable.

The introduction of this prospect of an attack on Athens by her subjects, αὐτοὶ ἐπιθέμενοι, leads away from the question what Sparta might do and towards the question which occupies 91. 2–99, whether the subjection of Melos will improve Athens' position as against her existing allies. (The further question, whether the execution of the Melians will benefit Athens, is not formally under discussion but cannot have been absent from Thucydides' mind.)]

93. ἡμεῖς δέ - - - κερδαίνοιμεν ἄν: [cf. iii. 39. 8, 46. 3.]

94. ὥστε [δέ]: [Steup argued that ὥστε in the sense of *itaque* is inappropriate here, since the Melian proposal does not flow directly from what the Athenians have just said; and that it would therefore be better to retain δέ.]
ἡσυχίαν ἄγοντεας: a clear case of this meaning 'to be neutral'. It might have meant simply 'if we do not resist you by force'.

95. τὸ δὲ μῖσος, κ.τ.λ.: compare, and contrast, Perikles' words, ii. 64. 5, and Kleon's, iii. 39. 5. The sentiment is not unknown in our own day: 'they' (that is, any people but the speakers) 'respect force only'.

96. τὸ εἰκός: [again, an unusual sense of εἰκός (cf. 90 n.). From the Athenians' reply in 97 it is clear that the meaning is approximately 'reasonable'.]
τούς τε μὴ προσήκοντας, κ.τ.λ.: another artificial argument, and not only in its grammar, for cities that were not 'colonies' from Athens, e.g. Mytilene, had revolted. [But the allies were predominantly Ionian, and so ἀπ' Ἀθηναίων (vii. 57. 4, see n. there); and it

was rhetorically convenient to overlook the non-Ionic elements. Cf. further Hdt. i. 146. 2; Th. i. 12. 4; Meritt and Wade-Gery, *JHS* lxxxii (1962), 69–71, on the offering of cow and panoply at the Panathenaia, and the assimilation of the allies to colonies; J. P. Barron, *JHS* lxxxiv (1964), 46–8.]

97. τοὺς μέν: τοὺς μὴ προσήκοντας, Stahl and edd. generally; but it means any city (within, say, the Aegean area), kin to Athens or not, that maintains its independence; for it is contrasted with ἡμᾶς. Note also the order—κατὰ δύναμιν belongs to both μέν- and δέ-clauses: 'as far as right goes they think neither lacks it; it is, they say, a matter of power—some survive and, as for us, it is fear that makes us refrain from attacking'.

ἔξω καὶ τοῦ πλεόνων ἄρξαι: [it does not make a large difference, but Krüger's conjecture τοῦ καί is confirmed by the reading of Π¹¹, and καί goes more easily with πλεόνων than with the whole phrase.]

νησιῶται: cf. iv. 120. 3, 121. 2, 122. 5, and my note on 121. 2; [and vii. 57. 7.]

εἰ μὴ περιγένοισθε: [Steup's objection to these words rests on his belief that, with the gen., περιγενέσθαι must mean positive victory (*überwinden*) as opposed to mere survival (as περιγίγνεσθαι above, used absolutely). But the Melians have 'got the better of' the Athenians if they merely survive the assault as in 426; while it is true that these three words add nothing that could not be understood without them, that is not a valid reason for deleting them (and consequently ναυκρατόρων).

The notion that the continued independence of Melos might damage Athens in relation to her existing empire is both unattractive and unreal as it is presented here. We must remember, however, that Melos had (a) successfully resisted whatever pressure had been brought on Thera to submit to Athens (ii. 9. 4 n.); (b) contributed (probably) to Alkidas' expenses in 427 (iii. 32. 2 n.); (c) resisted Nikias in 426 (iii. 91. 3); (d) ignored the Athenian assessment of 425; (e) very possibly, done something in the immediate past which could be construed as provocation (v. 84. 2, 89 nn.).

To point these matters out is not to justify Athens; but, since Thucydides' presentation has the effect of weighting the sympathies of most readers in favour of Melos, it is right to bear in mind that there may have been something to be said on the other side. Again, it would help if we had some idea of the feelings of the hoplites from other islands who took part in the operation (84. 2 n.).]

98. ἐν δ' ἐκείνῳ: [a reference back to their alternative proposal in 94, which in a different way might contribute to Athens' ἀσφάλεια.]

τῶν δικαίων λόγων: [the Melians, consistently with the position implied in 89 ὡς ἡμᾶς οὐδὲν ἠδικήκατε, will of course maintain that they have not done anything to provoke the Athenian attack: see 97 n.]

πολεμώσεσθε: [H₂ has the active, πολεμώσετε, which may be right; Thucydides has otherwise only the passive, i. 36. 1, 57. 2 and 3, perhaps iii. 82. 1, but cf. προσπολεμώσασθαι middle in iii. 3. 1. H₂ has also μελλήσαντας below, as probably Σ^Msc₂ (τοὺς μηδὲ διανοηθέντας, κ.τ.λ.) and in the opinion of most edd. rightly.]

99. τῷ ἐλευθέρῳ: [there is some difficulty in taking their existing freedom as a reason why they will be slow to take measures against Athens. Stahl proposed τῶν ἐλευθέρων, 'those of the free who are mainlanders', noting that not all mainlanders were free and citing Σ^Msc₂ τοὺς ἐλευθέρους τῶν ἠπειρωτῶν in support (this is the wrong way round for Stahl, but that is no great matter). Steup objected that we expect Thucydides to state or imply some reason why main-landers should be slower than islanders (Σ^Msc₂ μὴ δεδιότες γὰρ ἡμᾶς ὡς ἂν κατὰ γῆν οὐ μέλλοντας αὐτοῖς ἐπιστρατεύειν provides such a reason, but not all of this can have been explicit in the text), and he suggested that some qualification of τῷ ἐλευθέρῳ had fallen out, e.g. ἀκινδύνῳ or ἀδεεῖ (another possibility would be τῷ (e.g.) ⟨τοῦ δέους⟩ ἐλευθέρῳ, 'their freedom from fear': either would account for the scholiast's paraphrase). As the text stands, we have to read the reason why the mainland cities are less afraid of Athens out of the word ἠπειρῶται itself; and Thucydides might have trusted us to take that point without further explanation (contrast vi. 77. 1, Hermokrates' reference to the islanders' readiness for servitude). But in that case I can find nothing in τῷ ἐλευθέρῳ except a general statement that free men are slow to take precautions against the loss of their freedom, which may be true but hardly helps the argument. If the text needs alteration, supplement on Steup's lines is probably the right answer.]

τῆς ἀρχῆς τῷ ἀναγκαίῳ: see iii. 45. 4 and my note. Poverty and hunger may 'compel' a man to run risks that he otherwise would not run, and to take violent action; so may subjection to the rule of others. [For τῷ ἀλογίστῳ, cf. again iii. 45. 6 ἀλογίστως: the whole chapter, iii. 45, is relevant.]

100. [We here leave the question whether the Athenians are really acting in their own interest (but there is a considerable exchange still to come about the morality of their action, 104–105. 2), and pass to the questions of Melos' honour and her actual prospect of survival.]

101. οὔκ, ἤν γε σωφρόνως βουλεύησθε: it is not for the weak, any more than for the poor and humble, or for subjects, to contend,

like Achilles or Ajax or Hector (cf. vol. iii, 732), for the prize of
valour. They must behave well, σωφρονεῖν, as good children or con-
tented subjects: so will it be well for both ruler and ruled (91. 2).
[A ms. note added the example of Chios, viii. 24. 4–5.] We remember
Odysseus' words to Hekabe, in demanding the surrender of Polyxene
for sacrifice (E. *Hec.* 225–8)—

> μήτ' ἀποσπασθῇς βίᾳ
> μήτ' ἐς χερῶν ἄμιλλαν ἐξέλθῃς ἐμοί·
> γίγνωσκε δ' ἀλκὴν καὶ παρουσίαν κακῶν
> τῶν σῶν. σοφόν τοι κἂν κακοῖς ἃ δεῖ φρονεῖν—

and Lysias' cripple (xxiv. 17): οἱ μὲν γὰρ πλούσιοι τοῖς χρήμασιν
ἐξωνοῦνται τοὺς κινδύνους, οἱ δὲ πένητες ὑπὸ τῆς παρούσης ἀπορίας
σωφρονεῖν ἀναγκάζονται.

[The basic meaning of σώφρων is not so much 'of sound mind'
(LSJ), but 'thinking in the kind of way that keeps you safe', as in
these instances; the moral sense is secondary. See Addenda.]
ἀπὸ τοῦ ἴσου: [cf. 89, ἀπὸ τῆς ἴσης ἀνάγκης. The meaning appears to
be 'the contest of bravery, to avoid shame, cannot be conducted on
equal terms between you and us', i.e. that questions of honour can
no more arise between such unequals than questions of justice: it
might be possible, but with more difficulty, to extract the meaning
that the penalty αἰσχύνην ὀφλεῖν is not comparable with the penalty
of losing σωτηρία, but the former interpretation is the more probable,
cf. Fraenkel on A. *Ag.* 1423. In either case, to ask the Melians to
disregard the claim of honour, μὴ αἰσχύνην ὀφλεῖν, is to put the proposal in terms very hard for Greeks to accept: cf. A. W. H. Adkins,
Merit and Responsibility, 222 ff. and 241 n. 8. For the aspect which
such a proposition would present to the Athenians themselves, see
ii. 63. 2 (where ἀνδραγαθίζεσθαι has acquired a meaning exactly
opposite to that implied by ἀνδραγαθία here and elsewhere, cf.
Adkins, 234–5: is that a Thucydidean twist, or did Perikles himself
use the word in this way?): and the Athenians in 103. 2 allow
that most people (τοῖς πολλοῖς) in this situation would refuse
ἀνθρωπείως σώζεσθαι.]

102. κοινοτέρας: ['more impartial', in the sense that a judge ought to
be κοινός between two parties of unequal power, as iii. 53. 2. Most of
the parallels cited by edd. refer quite generally to the unpredictable
chances of war, but Lys. ii. 10 is very close, the Athenians there
taking up the position here assigned to the Melians, extracting com-
fort from the unpredictability and relying on the justice of their
cause. Cf., again, iii. 45. 6: this is a point which orators will always
turn in the direction that suits their situation.

The reversal by which a weaker may defeat a stronger force is of

course a commonplace (e.g. ii. 11. 4, and the Melians were to have
some unexpected successes, 115. 4, 116. 2 below) ; and Thucydides is
particularly conscious of the incalculable element in war (i. 140. 1
is a notable expression of this). But he saw this throughout as a re-
grettable limitation on the calculation which a prudent man or state
ought to employ (cf. the stress on Perikles' foresight in ii. 65), and
it is most unlikely that Thucydides asks us to applaud the Melians'
attitude to τύχη, however much in other circumstances he might
allow approval of τόλμα or τὸ δραστήριον.]

ἀνέλπιστον - - - ἐλπίς: cf. again Diodotos at iii. 45. 5–6.

103. 1. τοῖς δ' - - - ἀναρριπτοῦσι: [with ἀναρριπτοῦσι understand κίνδυνον, its almost invariable object in this metaphorical sense (e.g.
iv. 85. 4, 95. 2), rather than take τὸ ὑπάρχον as the object and ἐς
ἅπαν adverbially (Krüger).]

ἐν ὅτῳ ἔτι, κ.τ.λ.: [Gomme rejected the suggestion that ἐλλείπει might
be transitive (as E. El. 609, A.R. i. 515), on the ground that this 'seems
inconsistent with ἐν ὅτῳ ἔτι φυλάξεται' ; but found the result 'neither
clear nor satisfactory'. Denniston also, on Eur. loc. cit., noted that
ἐλλείπει was probably intransitive in our passage, though he did not
explain how he would take it. But Arnold was satisfied with Portus'
interpretation, *neque ullum amplius locum relinquit cavendi ab eius
dolis quamvis cognitis*, and Σ^Msc₂ οὐδὲν αὐτοῖς ὑπολείπεται ἐν ᾧ, γνωρί-
σαντες τὸ ἀβέβαιον τῆς ἐλπίδος, ἔτι φυλάξονται is not far off this line.
Most edd. have agreed: this gives a very much stronger sentence
than anything that can be extracted from the intransitive ἐλλείπει,
and gives its full point to ἅμα—the recognition comes precisely at
the point when it can no longer do any good.

The sermon on hope is manifestly relevant to Athens' hopes of the
expedition to Sicily next year; and Cornford, *Thuc. Mythistoricus*,
184–5, made the most of the irony. For the most part, the Dialogue's
argument of empire is not transferable from Melos to Syracuse, the
conditions being radically different ; but if these words were written
after 413 the application is here unavoidable. In particular, δάπανος
γὰρ φύσει is much more appropriate to the Athenian than to the
Melian situation. Gomme (ms.) noted the contrast with vi. 9. 3,
where Nikias charges the Athenians with their readiness περὶ τῶν
ἀφανῶν καὶ μελλόντων κινδυνεύειν.]

2. ἀνθρωπείως: 'by human means', i.e. practically, 'by their own
efforts'; but the efforts, when applied to the case of the Melians,
would mean surrender without a struggle. [This comes near to a
reductio ad absurdum of the common view (e.g. Steup). I believe the
point is rather that to act in such a way that only a miracle will
save you is to exceed the limits imposed by our condition as men
(cf. vi. 78. 2 οὐκ ἀνθρωπίνης δυνάμεως βούλησιν ἐλπίζει), but to respect

these limits is to act 'as befits a man', ἀνθρωπείως. It could almost be rendered 'rationally', i.e. going on what we know about men and taking measures which it is open to men to take; cf. W. Müri, *Mus. Helv.* iv (1947), 254.]

λυμαίνεται: [the unconventional, and here very harshly expressed, contempt for oracles is very much Thucydides' own; cf. ii. 54. 3, v. 26. 3. Whether the real Athenian envoys would have expressed themselves so, is highly doubtful. The Melians are not in fact represented as having cited oracles or claimed encouragement from seers. The point is dragged in unnecessarily: Thucydides' mind was perhaps once more on the Sicilian expedition, cf. viii. 1. 1.]

104. ὅσιοι πρὸς οὐ δικαίους: [for the relation between ὅσιον and δίκαιον, see Plato's *Euthyphron*, esp. 11e–12e, where Sokrates is at trouble to show that the concepts are not simply identifiable; and the ordinary uses of ὅσιος (not always an easy word) bear him out. Here, however, the Melians clearly claim that the Athenians are less likely to enjoy the favour of the gods because they are οὐ δίκαιοι, and (at the very least, by implication) that they themselves, the Melians, are δίκαιοι. The Athenians (*a*) have already argued (89) that τὸ δίκαιον is irrelevant in the present situation, and (*b*) are about to argue (105. 2) that the gods (δόξῃ—so far as man can tell) equally act on the rule that disproportionate force overrides τὸ δίκαιον; but at no point do they contradict the assertion that the Melians are, in ordinary terms, 'in the right' and themselves 'in the wrong'. What Thucydides himself thought about the (in the conventional sense) rights and wrongs of the case is, to me, at least doubtful; but the fact that he has left this highly emotive phrase in this respect unanswered is more damaging to Athens than anything else in the Dialogue. The fact that the Athenian speakers now go off on a different (but, for ordinary people, no less alarming) tack does not show that no answer was possible.]

τὴν Λακ. ἡμῖν ξυμμαχίαν: [either (*a*) the Melians were members of the Peloponnesian League[1] (32. 6 n.), in which case they should be covered by the Peace of Nikias and it is surprising that they do not complain about broken oaths; or (*b*) they had a separate alliance with Sparta; or (*c*) there was no formal alliance, but the Melians expect on other grounds that Sparta, with or without her League, will take action on their behalf in this instance. For the meanings of ξυμμαχία see vi. 6. 2 n.: the mere occurrence of the word here does not prove the existence of a formal alliance; the presence of the article (τὴν - - - ξυμμαχίαν) is justified by the references made already to the Spartan

---

[1] Diod. xii. 65. 1–2, under 424/3 (this should be 426), takes Melos as a member of the League, specially loyal because of her Spartan origin. Ephoros no doubt spoke of this old connection, and this may have confused Diodoros.

connection in 89 and 91. The words εἰ μή του ἄλλου suggest that the compulsion on Sparta consists primarily, or solely, in the two grounds stated, kinship and honour, and the subsequent discussion turns wholly on Sparta's accessibility to moral suasion and contains nothing at all about oaths. Moreover, if there had been a formal alliance, ξύμμαχοι would have been much more effective than ἄποικοι in 89. (106 προδόντας is indeterminate, given the variety of uses to which this favourite verb is put.) We must not expect Thucydides to explain the relations between Sparta and Melos more clearly than he has explained the situation between Melos and Athens.]

105. 1–2. τῆς μὲν τοίνυν πρὸς τὸ θεῖον εὐμενείας, κ.τ.λ.: it is worth comparing Herodotos' picture of Athens in 479 B.C., in her answer to Alexander of Macedon, viii. 143: καὶ αὐτοὶ τοῦτό γε ἐπιστάμεθα ὅτι πολλαπλασίη ἐστὶ τῷ Μήδῳ δύναμις ἤ περ ἡμῖν - - - ἀλλ' ὅμως ἐλευθερίης γλιχόμενοι ἀμυνεύμεθα οὕτως ὅκως ἂν καὶ δυνώμεθα - - - θεοῖσί τε συμμάχοισι πίσυνοί μιν ἐπέξιμεν ἀμυνόμενοι καὶ τοῖσι ἥρωσι. You have the gods on your side whether you are resisting the almost irresistible might of Persia or advising the Melians of the folly of *their* resisting the might of Athens. Herodotos' world is indeed very different from that of Thucydides. [But, however great the difference, we cannot illustrate it from this passage, given the observable tendency of orators in all ages and situations to discover that the gods are on their side.]

For τοίνυν which gives an almost offhand air to this statement, see 87 n.

2. ὑπὸ φύσεως ἀναγκαίας: both gods and men (as we all believe in the one case and can see for ourselves in the other) must obey this law of nature, οὗ ἂν κρατῇ, ἄρχειν. We should remind ourselves of two aspects of Greek belief and doctrine: one, that the gods are not supernatural, only superhuman—that marks a great gulf between them that men must not attempt to cross, but both are born of Earth: ἓν ἀνδρῶν, | ἓν θεῶν γένος· ἐκ μιᾶς δὲ πνέομεν | ματρὸς ἀμφότεροι, κ.τ.λ. (Pindar, *Nem.* vi. 1 ff.);[1] second, that the gods are in consequence subject to the universal laws of nature as are men. This is well put in the last chapter of Kitto's *Sophocles: Dramatist and Philosopher* (1958).

[The question remains, however, whether the gods are in fact subject to the law here alleged or, on the contrary, to the law of justice which the Melians expect them to uphold (104). The gods of Homer and of Greek myth in general were immoral enough, and the emphasis on the mere power of Zeus can be flamboyant enough (e.g. *Il.* viii. 5–27): but the link between morality and religion had long been asserted—it is, for instance, fiercely expressed in E. *El.* 583–4

---

[1] [I believe this interpretation of Pindar to be right (cf. C. M. Bowra, *Pindar* (1964), 96–7); but other views have been taken of this passage.]

ἢ χρὴ μήκεθ' ἡγεῖσθαι θεούς, | εἰ τἄδικ' ἔσται τῆς δίκης ὑπέρτερα—and the belief in the personified Dike as the registrar of Zeus was a not negligible factor for cohesion in Greek society. In ordinary circumstances the belief in the gods as guardians of justice coexisted happily enough with the stories which Xenophanes (fr. 10) and Plato (*Rep.* 377 e ff.) found so shocking; and even if strong temptation would overbear scruples based on religion, perhaps for Greeks more easily than in some other societies, the feeling remained that the restraint ought to operate. To deny it thus, taking the facts as self-evident, goes some way to range Thucydides' Athenians with immoralists like the Kallikles of Plato's *Gorgias* who deny (as, however, these Athenians do not) the ordinary sense of 'justice' altogether; and they were certainly felt to be shocking even in this age of uninhibited questioning.

Thucydides cannot of course use such a phrase as φύσις ἀναγκαία without some reference in his own mind to the contemporary controversy about φύσις and νόμος, for which see F. Heinimann, *Nomos und Physis*, esp. 129–30 and 167 n. 7. In this connection it must be kept in mind that there was not one 'sophistic' doctrine on the question here involved, but many: 'physical necessity' might be the expression of the will of Zeus, or superior to it, etc. For Thucydides, the use of such a phrase need not call up the precise doctrine set out in *Gorgias* 483 eff., as it does for us.

It has been stated in 89, but again without argument and simply as a fact which we all really acknowledge, that human justice does not apply between the strong and the weak; and it has been argued since (91. 2–99) that it is against Athens' interest to leave Melos unsubjected. To complete the case, we need the assertion of something like this φύσις ἀναγκαία, a positive and irresistible drive to use the power one has.]

καὶ ἡμεῖς οὔτε θέντες τὸν νόμον, κ.τ.λ.: it is true that Athens had not established this law, nor was she the first to follow it; but it is arguable that she was the first to introduce it into the Greek political world. From 445 B.C. at least she was consciously doing something new, attempting to create some sort of unity in Greece (see vol. i, 380–5, 388–9), even while leaving a quite genuine 'autonomy' to each state in her league (vol. iii, 557). It is not that her behaviour was harsher or more oppressive than that of Sparta, for instance— nothing she did was as harsh as Spartan treatment of Messenia; but Sparta did not (after the incorporation of Messenia into Lakonia) try to create unity, only domination. It is this fact which gives meaning to the hostility of the Greek world towards Athens at the beginning and during the course of the Peloponnesian War, and to the goodwill which, in spite of all her crimes and her blunders, Sparta enjoyed.

For the 'law' of the rule of the stronger see the similar expression of it in i. 76 by the Athenian delegates at Sparta. It has not un-naturally been concluded by many that both speech and Melian dialogue belong to the same period in the composition of the *History*; on this see the Appendix. [The Appendix, unfortunately, was not written; and this particular conclusion is valid only if it can be shown that this opinion, or at least the expression of it, was confined to one period in Thucydides' life. Other relevant passages are iv. 61. 5, and to some extent vi. 18. 3; vi. 83. 4, emphasizing fear as the dominant motive, is close to i. 76. 2 and to earlier parts of this dialogue, but does not enunciate the 'law'. A ms. note calls attention to Hdt. vii. 8 a 1, which other edd. have cited for the form of the expression.]

κειμένῳ: [κοινῷ Π¹¹ can be disregarded (it could only be understood as 'this law which is in fact common to all', which does not help the sense); καινῷ H₂ʸ ρ· Pl₂ makes more of a point, 'nor is this a new law, which we are the first . . .': but the plain antithesis between θέντες and κειμένῳ is more effective.]

3. ἤν - - - βοηθήσειν ὑμῖν πιστεύετε αὐτούς: [Stahl and others take δόξαν πιστεύειν as an expression comparable to πίστιν πιστεύειν, which is not attractive (see Steup's n.); nor would the deletion of αὐτούς, making ἤν the subject of βοηθήσειν, give a very satisfactory sense. Reiske's ᾗ, adopted by Steup, produces a more straightforward result, but we should perhaps keep ἤν as an acc. of respect, ἤν (sc. δοκοῦντες) πιστεύετε.]

διὰ τὸ αἰσχρὸν δή: see iv. 19. 3, vi. 10. 2 and 11. 6 (especially, ὅσῳ καὶ περὶ πλείστου καὶ διὰ πλείστου δόξαν ἀρετῆς μελετῶσι); and v. 104. It was indeed true that, quite apart from such conduct as that of Alkidas (iii. 31. 2–33. 1), Sparta was ready in 425 to betray the cities she had promised to liberate (see n. on iv. 20. 4), and did betray them in 421 (v. 18. 5–8), and it is not surprising that the Athenians wondered that the Melians could be so 'innocent', so 'inexperienced in evil'. One might have expected them to mention these instances of Spartan ill-faith, but that, nearly everywhere, the discussion is on a sophistic level (especially here, 107).

[Cf. also i. 69. 5, ἐπεὶ αἵ γε ὑμέτεραι ἐλπίδες ἤδη τινάς που καὶ ἀπαρα-σκεύους διὰ τὸ πιστεῦσαι ἔφθειραν. Gomme (ad loc.) notes Thasos, Euboea, Poteidaia as examples, but they were not conspicuously ἀπαράσκευοι, and I am not quite sure which states do qualify.]

4. πλεῖστα ἀρετῇ χρῶνται: [in view of Sparta's reputation for the conscious inculcation and practice of ἀρετή (cf. vi. 11. 6, quoted in the previous n.), any passage which throws light on the nature of that ἀρετή is of special interest. Here, Spartan policy abroad, τὰ μὲν ἡδέα καλὰ νομίζουσι, τὰ δὲ ξυμφέροντα δίκαια, is contrasted with their ἀρετή at home; which by implication involves doing what is honour-able even if it is unpleasant, and what is just even if it is contrary to

175

one's own interest. This is a very 'co-operative' kind of virtue, in Adkins's term, and essentially similar to the non-Greek values from which Adkins (see 101 n.) would have us distinguish Greek values even in the classical period.]

ἀλόγου: [picking up ἀλόγως at the end of 104.]

106. τῷ ξυμφέροντι αὐτῶν: [once more the Melians have been forced to confine themselves to argument about expediency; and, as when discussing Athens' interest (98), they are driven to consideration of remoter general consequences, an easy target for the Athenians' realism.]

107. τὸ ξυμφέρον μὲν μετ' ἀσφαλείας εἶναι, τὸ δὲ δίκαιον καὶ καλὸν μετὰ κινδύνου δρᾶσθαι: in what a different mood the old Athenian boast, that is here recalled, had before been uttered: e.g. Perikles' speech, ii. 63–4.

[δρᾶσθαι is now found in H₂.]

108. βεβαιοτέρους: [with κινδύνους, 'less dangerous risks'; cf. iii. 39. 6 τὸν μετὰ τῶν ὀλίγων κίνδυνον ἡγησάμενοι βεβαιότερον.]

τῆς Πελοποννήσου ἐγγὺς κείμεθα: [Melos is not so very close, indeed it is slightly nearer to Sounion than to any point in Lakonia; but it is the nearest of the Cyclades for a Spartan fleet setting out into the Aegean or across it, and therefore of some tactical importance— cf. viii. 39. 3, 41. 4, and nn. to iii. 29. 1, 32. 2.]

πιστότεροι ἑτέρων ἐσμέν: an argument of no great force in itself and, such as it is, not likely to appease the Athenians. But the latter do not take this point, but continue the argument of words.

109. μετὰ ξυμμάχων πολλῶν: [a point which Perikles makes the most of in ii. 39. 2.]

110. 1. πολὺ δὲ τὸ Κρητικὸν πέλαγος, κ.τ.λ.: [as demonstrated by Alkidas in 427, and by several fleets in the early stages of the Ionian War.]

2. ὅσους μὴ Βρασίδας ἐπῆλθεν: these are the cities of the Thracian region, Maroneia, Abdera, and many others, that Brasidas did not attack (or 'approach', cf. iv. 85. 2; but see n. on iv. 87. 6) after his capture of Amphipolis, though the way was open to him and there were some in each city ready to welcome him; cf. vol. iii, 581. [There was of course no immediate probability that Sparta would try to repeat Brasidas' invasion of the Thraceward area: this is rhetoric, reminding the Athenians of what they had lost and threatening them with more. Argument is nearly at an end, and the parties are taking up their final positions.]

ξυμμαχίδος τε καὶ γῆς: 'both allied territory and your own', corresponding chiastically to ἐς τὴν γῆν ὑμῶν καί - - - τῶν ξυμμάχων above. So edd. take this; but γῆς cannot mean 'your own territory' by contrast with some other. The words are not wanted. Valla did not translate them, and Stahl bracketed them. An easier and better remedy was Duker's, to bracket καί only, when τῆς οἰκειοτέρας becomes 'your own' and the territory of the allies is added.

111. 1. τούτων μὲν καὶ πεπειραμένοις, κ.τ.λ.: the difficulty in this sentence is not removed either by Classen's insertion of ἡμῖν after γένοιτο to provide the necessary contrast with ὑμῖν, or by Stahl's bracketing of καί after ὑμῖν, with comma after γένοιτο, though this is an improvement on the text of Stuart Jones. It is well illustrated by two different English translations—Crawley's: 'some diversion of the kind you speak of you may one day experience, only to learn, as others have done, that the Athenians never once withdrew from a siege for fear of any. But we are struck', etc. This gives the right meaning to μέν, which is answered by δέ in § 2 ('Yes, this might happen, but it is all irrelevant'); but it ignores the tense of πεπειραμένοις, which surely implies or requires ἡμῖν. Warner's translation is: 'it is a possibility, something that has in fact happened before. It may happen in your case, but you are well aware', etc. This translates the perfect participle (and implies ἡμῖν with it), and gives what we naturally expect for the second half of the sentence, '*but* you are well aware', where the Greek has καί.

[We certainly cannot refer πεπειραμένοις to the *future* experience of the Melians (Arnold, Crawley); and I would so far agree with Gomme, that the Athenians had more continuous experience of the fact than anyone else. But Mytilene and others had also 'experience' of the inefficacy of such diversions, and so in a looser sense had the whole Aegean world, Melos included. Gomme concluded: 'καὶ ὑμῖν seems anomalous. Stahl's corrections to the text do however help.' It seems to me that the text may stand: 'it would not be outside your experience either, nor are you unaware . . .']

οὐδ' ἀπὸ μιᾶς πώποτε πολιορκίας: [if we restrict δι' ἄλλων φόβον to fear of invasion, etc. (so Σ^{Msc₂} διὰ τὸ φοβηθῆναι περὶ τῶν συμμάχων ἢ περὶ τῆς γῆς τῆς ἑαυτῶν δῃουμένης), this might be true, and examples would be Aigina (i. 105. 3), Poteidaia, Mytilene (iii. 16. 1). The Athenians were driven off from the Λευκὸν τεῖχος of Memphis by the troops of Megabyzos (i. 104. 2, 109. 4) not by any invasion of Attica. Much more conspicuously, by the time these words were written, Athens had not been deterred by the occupation of Dekeleia from pressing on with the siege of Syracuse (cf. vii. 28. 3: for the date of composition of that passage, see n. there). Here, still more clearly than in 103, Thucydides must have intended a reference, with all the irony which that involves, to the state of mind in which Athens had begun and continued that operation.]

2. ὑμῶν τὰ μὲν ἰσχυρότατα ἐλπιζόμενα μέλλεται: 'your strongest points are in the future and depend on hope' [(so LSJ, taking μέλλεται as middle, μέλλω IV sub fin.: but most edd. take it as passive, comparing X. *An.* iii. 1. 47).] Cf. 87: and (ms.) again, vi. 9. 3. [Gomme was also troubled by the emphatic position of ὑμῶν, when there is no real change of subject. The position is presumably emphatic, since a 3rd pers. anaphoric pronoun immediately after ἀλλά would be exceptional (only Lys. xx. 14?): the emphasis is probably due to the return from the generalization to the Melians and what they have actually said.]

σωφρονέστερον γνώσεσθε: cf. 89, 101.

3. οὐ γὰρ δή - - - γε: see i. 122. 4, with n.

αἰσχροῖς - - - αἰσχύνην - - - τὸ αἰσχρόν - - - αἰσχύνην αἰσχίω: a remarkable sophistic play with this notion. Of the more than fifty instances of αἰσχρός, αἰσχύνη, and αἰσχύνεσθαι in Thucydides (all but five in speeches) the great majority have the normal meaning of disgraceful, shameful action or weakness, or sense of shame at wickedness or weakness; occasionally the weakness is implied rather than expressed, as in i. 84. 3 and v. 9. 9 ('shame at being weaker or more fearful than one's fellows'), most notably here, ἐπὶ τήν - - - αἰσχύνην and τὸ αἰσχρὸν καλούμενον. ἄνοια here is the opposite of σωφροσύνη, which has already been recommended to the Melians (above, and 101, where αἰσχύνη has its normal meaning) and was so remarkably practised by the Chians (viii. 24. 4–5): the folly of resisting obviously superior force. This insistence on τὸ ἀσφαλές (below, § 4 and viii. 24. 5) is as different from the imaginative daring of Perikles (especially ii. 63. 2–3) and Phormion as from that of Brasidas, not to mention that of the Greeks fighting against the overwhelming might of Persia. See *JHS* lxxi (1951), 75–9 (= *More Essays*, 101–11).

Stahl distinguishes the meanings of αἰσχρός and αἰσχύνη here: with αἰσχροῖς κινδύνοις he compares iii. 59. 3, τῷ αἰσχίστῳ ὀλέθρῳ (*miserrima pernicie*) λιμῷ τελευτῆσαι, D. xviii. 178 and X. *Mem.* iii. 8. 6–7; and this difference of meaning between αἰσχροῖς and the first αἰσχύνη he defends by a similar change of meaning of αἰσχύνη here (*pudor*) and below (*contumelia*). But the last is the shame that accompanies the folly of resisting the all-powerful aggressor in defence of one's independence and is the same as the shame of running into foreseeable and foreseen dangers, and the first αἰσχύνη and τὸ αἰσχρὸν καλούμενον are the false sense of shame so close to the sense of honour ('I should be ashamed to be less brave than others') that leads men to such foolish resistance. The whole sentence is very elaborately devised; and its ending, αἰσχίω μετὰ ἀνοίας ἢ τύχῃ προσλαβεῖν, 'the more shameful because combined with folly than had it been brought about by misfortune', seems quite artificial—even these Athenians could hardly have called defeat through misfortune in any sense shameful.

[The notion that defeat due to misfortune is αἰσχρόν is, however, much easier to entertain in Greek than when the adjective is translated 'shameful'. Two points must be borne in mind. (1) Failure, however caused, was αἰσχρόν or κακόν in the Homeric world: this is the burden of Adkins's book (101 n.), and, though he over-estimates the degree to which these Homeric values were carried over into the classical world (cf. 105. 4 n.), this sense of αἰσχρόν certainly survived and is relevant here. Stahl rightly defended the text against commentators who did not see how αἰσχροῖς could be combined with κινδύνοις, and his examples prove his case: the first of his discriminations (above) is surely correct, and probably the second. (2) The language in which the Athenians recommended submission to Melos would, in real life, necessarily be very different from that of Thucydides' Perikles, speaking ἐν ἀρχούσῃ πόλει (ii. 63. 3); and what he thought suitable for a subject city is roughly enough expressed, ἀσφαλῶς δουλεύειν. Of Gomme's comparisons, only that with the Greeks of 480–479 is really apt: there the odds were apparently overwhelming and advice in the style here offered to Melos would not have been evidently inappropriate, but the Greek victory showed that the Persians were not after all quite so dangerous as they had looked. Here, it is fair to ask the Melians to look carefully at their chances before they decide for suicidal heroism. A very near comparison is the reported speech of Phrynichos, viii. 27. 2–3, with its scornful repetition of the word αἰσχρόν and the same slight equivocation on its meaning: he calculated the chances, and decided οὐδέποτε τῷ αἰσχρῷ ὀνείδει εἴξας ἀλόγως διακινδυνεύσειν, since total defeat would be αἴσχιον than timely retreat.]

[ἐπαγωγοῦ: cf. 85 n.]

ἑκόντας: 'intentionally', 'with their eyes open', rather than 'willingly'. Cf. iv. 30. 2.

[τύχῃ: the MSS. reading τύχης is retained by Steup; but τύχῃ was certainly the reading of Σ^Msc₂, and an attractive instance of Thucydidean variation. See Ros, 176 f., though he does not cite this example.]

4. μέτρια προκαλουμένης: cf. again the Athenians at Sparta, i. 76. 3–4. There is almost a sincerity in this appeal to the Melians to 'behave sensibly', to give up an opposition which can do them no good, and surrender. 'You still have a chance.'

[There is, indeed, no reason to question the 'sincerity' of this offer, but we are hampered by not knowing the circumstances (cf. 84. 2, 89, 97 nn.) or the precise terms. To impose on Melos nothing worse than the status of an ordinary tribute-paying member of the League may have been moderation itself; or to impose anything may have been quite unjustified. The contrast between the 'moderate proposal' and the execution remains.]

τοῖς δὲ κρείσσοσι καλῶς προσφέρονται: a curiously vague phrase here—'the right attitude towards the stronger'. It might have been used of the Greeks of 480, when the Melians too gave modest help in the resistance to Persia (Hdt. viii. 46. 4; ML 27. 21). [This is presumably euphemism, to make acceptance less difficult; as also οὐκ ἀπρεπές above.]

5. ἧς μιᾶς πέρι καὶ ἐς μίαν βουλήν: effective rhetoric; but the reminder that they have but one city is not in itself very forceful.

[There is no doubt of the general meaning, 'you have only the one city, and its safety or disaster hangs on this one opportunity for deliberation' (cf. 103. 2 ἐπὶ ῥοπῆς μιᾶς ὄντες); but the syntax is not easy. There is nothing at all obvious to be made of the MSS. ἦν (intended, presumably, to give the participles something to agree with) or ἤν: ΣMsc² ὅτι περὶ πατρίδος ἡ σκέψις μιᾶς οὔσης, περὶ ἧς ἐν μιᾷ βουλῇ ἢ κατορθώσετε ἢ σφαλήσεσθε encourages belief that the scholiast's text had ἧς. For τυχοῦσάν τε καὶ μὴ κατορθώσασαν as a method of putting an alternative, cf. ii. 35. 1 ἐν ἑνὶ ἀνδρὶ πολλῶν ἀρετὰς κινδυνεύεσθαι εὖ τε καὶ χεῖρον εἰπόντι πιστευθῆναι. The ἴστε of some recc. for ἔσται (scitis Valla) looks like a guess made to give a construction for the participles, but, as Stahl says, we need a future, in the participles if not in the verb.

Stahl thought that one could take ἔσται as ἔξεσται and supply βουλεύεσθαι, and thus achieve a sentence no harder than 95; but there, if the overall structure is involved, the individual parts of the sentence are more straightforward. Rauchenstein took ἧς μιᾶς πέρι - - - ἔσται as parallel to Lys. xii. 74 οὐ περὶ πολιτείας ὑμῖν ἔσται: but it is hard to tuck in the whole of καὶ ἐς μίαν - - - κατορθώσασαν under the wing of this construction. It seems more likely that there is something wrong with the clause: either a lacuna, or ἔσται is corrupt.]

112. 2. πόλεως ἑπτακόσια ἔτη ἤδη οἰκουμένης: an indication of the major difficulty which faced Athens in her attempt at ἀρχή. This astonishing political division of Greece into hundreds of small communities had lasted a long time, and successfully by comparison with other peoples.

[Thucydides does not explicitly lend his authority to the comfortable round number (it continued in use for some time: Isokrates vi. 12 makes Archidamos III in the 360s refer to 700 years of Spartan glory; for Ephoros the return of the Herakleidai seems to have been 700 years before Leuktra, see FGrHist 70 T 10, F 223 with

Jacoby's n.). He gives no other hint of the absolute chronology of the heroic period, though it would not be out of character for him to have accepted one of the estimates current in his time (see i. 12. 3, with n.), and he may well have thought the Melian 700 years a fair approximation. Taken precisely, this would give 1116 as a *terminus ante quem* for the Dorian settlement of Sparta. We have no way of guessing what interval he would interpose between the foundation of Sparta and that of Melos; but this rather suggests that Thucydides had a relatively high date for the fall of Troy, something like the date implied in Hdt. ii. 145. 4.]

πειρασόμεθα σῴζεσθαι: [the argument, as presented by Thucydides, has left the Melians no rational ground for hope; and he was justified, in that no rescue appeared from the gods or from Sparta, and their 700 years' tradition of freedom was no help to them. As to the motive which in reality induced them to defy Athens, we can only speculate. It is hard to see any significant factor in the situation which is not, in one way or another, covered in the Dialogue; but no doubt they saw the possibilities in less stark terms. Thus, they will have imagined crises elsewhere that might distract Athens' attention, though perhaps no more concretely than Thucydides' Corinthians, i. 122. 1 ἄλλα τε ὅσα οὐκ ἄν τις νῦν προΐδοι: and they will have rated the hope from Sparta higher, much like the various East Greeks who appealed to Sparta for help against the Persians between Cyrus' conquest and 480, in spite of the fact that no previous appeal had been answered. With the examples of Plataia and Skione before them, they can have had little illusion about the fate they would meet when their city was taken—the usages of their world were harsh enough, even though in their case there was no revolt to punish —but it is likely that some would genuinely feel, at least beforehand, that any fate was preferable to the tame surrender to which they were summoned.]

3. προκαλούμεθα: [answering the Athenian μέτρια προκαλουμένης in 111. 4. The proposition has been advanced, and answered, already in 94–5.]

113. μόνοι γε, κ.τ.λ.: [elsewhere this is by Thucydides' own judgement a fault to which all mankind is liable (iv. 108. 4), including the Athenians (iii. 3. 1); and the fault lies very near the virtue commended in ii. 42. 4, ἐλπίδι μὲν τὸ ἀφανὲς τοῦ κατορθώσειν ἐπιτρέψαντες, ἔργῳ δὲ περὶ τοῦ ἤδη ὁρωμένου σφίσιν αὐτοῖς ἀξιοῦντες πεποιθέναι. Cf. also Kleon on the Mytileneans, iii. 39. 3. The unreal μόνοι here expresses just the exasperation of the Athenian speakers: cf. i. 70. 7 μόνοι γάρ, κ.τ.λ., where again the Athenians are in effect praised for their adventurous initiative.]

πλεῖστον δὴ παραβεβλημένοι: [this closing sentence again can hardly fail to remind the reader how much the Athenians committed to hope (though not so much to chance, in Thucydides' view) next summer in Sicily.

Gomme's discussion of the Dialogue promised, in a marginal note at this point, to deal with 'especially its *sophistic* character—few examples, as noted above—and Thucydides' silence about *Sparta* giving no help or encouragement (as no express *judgement* on Athens, 116)'. By 'sophistic character' he seems to have meant the very general level at which it proceeds (105. 3 n.), a certain artificiality in some of the arguments (96, 108, 111. 3 nn.), and some points of language (e.g. 111. 3 n.); but he made fewer observations on the language, and cited fewer parallels, than was usual with him. He seems also to have thought that the Athenians were being in some sense dishonest (84. 3, 111. 4 nn.); and he was evidently shocked by the contrast between these Athenian sentiments and others expressed elsewhere.

Thucydides' uncompromising Dialogue is of evident importance for any general estimate of his attitude and purposes, and theories of its meaning are at least as various as general theories about the historian himself. There is no catching up with the bibliography, and no more can be done here than to indicate some of the possible approaches, and discuss them briefly.

1. Could the Dialogue have been, to any extent, a record in the terms laid down in i. 22. 1? Failing good argument to the contrary, we must respect the narrative statement in 84. 3, that the Athenians were refused access to the πλῆθος (cf. vol. i, 253, on i. 72. 1). Thucydides had then received some account of these proceedings, so probably he knew something of what was said. Dionysios' assertion (*Th.* 41) that he could not have information from participants is a gross over-simplification; indeed, it has recently been argued (F. E. Adcock, *Thucydides and his History*, 32–3) that we cannot exclude even Melian informants. It could have been known, as well as guessed, that the Athenians dwelt on the futility of resistance and of hoping for help from Sparta, and urged the Melians to be realistic; and known also that there were no set speeches.

2. We have further to ask, what use Thucydides made of any such material. There can be no certain answer, but we can clarify the question. (*a*) Thucydides selects occasions for speeches, and we have to think about his possible reasons. The critic who argues (e.g.) that the Dialogue is about the value of massacres to an imperial power must ask why there are speeches about Melos but not about Skione. (*b*) He also necessarily selects within the chosen occasion, as (e.g.) in the Mytilene debate, where the ἄλλαι γνῶμαι of iii. 36. 6 must include some speeches very unlike the two we are given. Again, we have to ask why Thucydides selected what he did. On this

occasion, it is likely that there was in reality more argument about past relations between Melos and Athens, whether or not there had been a recent quarrel (84. 2 n.); but this was not what interested Thucydides. (c) The most devoted believer in the authenticity of the speeches must allow that Thucydides tidied up his speeches, as well as imposing his own style upon them. Diplomacy in real life could not achieve the logical rigour of the Dialogue: but, so far as this involves distortion, it is unavoidable and probably unimportant. (d) The main controversy has been over the question, how far Thucydides substituted arguments and views of his own for those of the speakers. It has often been maintained (e.g. de Romilly, *Imp.* 274) that the real conference could not have kept up the Dialogue's high level of generalization. We must be careful here not to make false inferences from the practice of our own day (cf. Finley, 64–5, on the different degrees to which different ages tolerate extreme generalization), but the contention has some plausibility. That is, the real Athenians could indeed at some stage have lost patience with the Melians' protestations about justice and told them to attend to the realities of power; but would they have expressed this, at the start (89), in a general proposition of this unconventional kind? Did they in fact claim this proposition as ἃ ἀληθῶς φρονοῦμεν, or is this Thucydides appealing to his readers to be honest with themselves? Similar and related doubts arise about the treatment of the gods in 105. 1–2.

3. It is thus at least possible that Thucydides has imposed some alien thoughts on his Athenian speakers, and we must ask why he did so; and in any case we have to ask what he wished to underline by composing a dialogue here, and concentrating on this line of argument. Since the Dialogue is apt to arouse sympathy for the Melians and abhorrence of Athenian brutality, and since we can never forget or condone the eventual execution of the Melians, it is a common thesis (certainly among English-speaking critics) that Thucydides meant to indict the moral decline of Athens under the stress of war; more specifically, that the argument from expediency in the Mytilene debate, Diodotos as well as Kleon, shows a deterioration from the high level of the Funeral Speech, and the open cynicism of the Dialogue a further decline. Cf. (e.g.) Finley, 208–12. The fact that Athens went straight on next year to her ambitious and disastrous attack on Syracuse has prompted reflections on ὕβρις and ἄτη, most fully worked up by Cornford, *Thuc. Mythistoricus*, ch. x. (We need not doubt that there are forward references in the Dialogue— see 103. 1, 111. 1, 113 nn.—but see the warning in Gomme, *Essays*, 186 n. 2. It is not certain that there is any forward reference to the fall of Athens, see 91. 1 n.) It has also been held that Thucydides here shows hostility to democracy or sympathy with old-fashioned

oligarchic ideals, but I shall not argue this: Thucydides' alleged oligarchic bias may be left till viii. 97. 2 n., and there is no trace of ideological argument in the Dialogue. On these views, Melos is the chosen occasion because it was naked aggression, without the excuse that Athens was punishing revolt, as at Skione.

4. There seem to me to be insuperable objections to the views described in (3). (a) This is a misreading of the Mytilene debate, where the argument from expediency was forced on Diodotos, and simpler feelings were the main basis of the second debate (iii. 36. 4; cf. *Phoenix* xvi (1962), 71–9). Thucydides does indeed detect a decline, but in the quality of leadership (ii. 65. 8–12; Gomme, *JHS* lxxi (1951), 78 = *More Essays* 107–8; cf. M. Pavan, *Hist.* x (1961), 19–29), the decline from Perikles to Kleon and his like. The Dialogue is about principles not persons: we are not told anything about personalities, those responsible either for the expedition or for the massacre, nor are ἴδιαι φιλοτιμίαι καὶ ἴδια κέρδη (ii. 65. 7) involved. There is, however, no detectable decline in principle from i. 76. 2–4 (and, whenever he wrote that, Thucydides thought it appropriate for Perikles' Athens) to the Dialogue, only the removal of ὀνόματα καλά (89). To put it another way, if the Dialogue indicts Athens, it can only be as a general indictment of imperialism as such, and Thucydides cannot be taken as merely hostile to Athenian imperialism: the rhetoric of (e.g.) ii. 64. 3 is too warm, his regret (even exasperation) at Athens' eventual defeat too evident at ii. 65.

(b) The contrast between the 'cynicism' of the Dialogue and the high ideals of the Funeral Speech is rooted in the difference of context (iii. 3 n.). Speaking to his countrymen, Thucydides' Perikles stresses more altruistic aspects, and it would be absurd to deny that the empire conveyed benefits as well as harms, or that the Athenians could feel generous impulses; the stress in the Dialogue on 'prudence', which Gomme contrasted (101, 107, 111. 3 nn.) with the heroic and adventurous utterances of Athenians in other parts of the *History*, is inevitable for speakers counselling submission. (Part of the difficulty is that there are not many such speakers in histories: there are more in tragedy—an example is quoted in 101 n.—and they do not attract sympathy.) But there is little essential contradiction. If we are to deplore the immoral arrogance of the imperialists in the Dialogue, we must in fairness to some degree deplore the empire in other contexts, even when gilded by the rhetoric of the Funeral Speech; the empire may have its benevolent aspect, but we may still ask by what right the Athenians imposed their will on others, even for good. It was not always for good. The critic who detects in the Dialogue a decline from Periklean standards must clear his mind about the nature of those standards, and the kind of treatment which Thucydides' Perikles thought suitable for subjects. The concrete implications of ii. 13. 2 τὰ τῶν ξυμμάχων διὰ χειρὸς ἔχειν are not reassuring.

5. Less trouble awaits those who take Thucydides as backing the Athenian side in the argument. He was not in any ordinary sense making out a case for Athens—had that been his object, he would not have assigned the phrase ὅσιοι πρὸς οὐ δικαίους (104, see n.) to the Melians without allowing the Athenians a direct answer—but no utterance which we can fairly take as the historian's own prevents us from supposing that the basic doctrine of 89 and 105 is one which he might entertain; and we can imagine him thinking the Melians at least guilty of an error of judgement (G. Méautis, *REG* xlviii (1935), 250–78, who regards 103 as the key passage, Thucydides' dislike of the incalculable). A more promising variant on this approach is that of H.-P. Stahl, *Thukydides* (1966: valuable in general for his insistence that we give full consideration to the narrative, not only to the speeches, when speculating about Thucydides' purposes), 158–71: Thucydides does not defend or blame, but describes; in this case, how even in the face of imminent disaster men refuse to face the facts of their situation, an extreme example for Diodotos' thesis in iii. 45. This is surely important, and a large part of the truth, though not perhaps the whole of it. On this view there is clear reason for selecting Melos: unlike Skione, or Mytilene or Plataia, Melos was given an option, peaceful surrender instead of useless resistance.

6. But if the Dialogue is to make the impression proposed in theories of the kind described in (5), we must assume not only that Thucydides believed his Athenians' doctrine to be a correct analysis of inter-state relations, but that he could count on enough readers who would also accept it as a basis to be taken for granted. That might be few enough: his world is full of men and cities who profess quite different principles, but he might be that belligerent kind of writer who is content to utter unpalatable truth in the confidence that he will eventually make his impression on the few who matter. The real question is, whether the doctrine was entirely stable for him. Its use is as a description of the behaviour of οἱ προύχοντες, Sparta or Athens. It is imposing in the abstract, and the abstraction is of a kind to which we may well think Thucydides especially prone, generalization about 'the Spartans' and others. But he knew as well as anyone that it is of no help at the individual level: those who wish to stir Spartans to action do not say 'τὰ ἡδέα and τὰ ξυμφέροντα (105. 4) dictate this policy', they make speeches like those of Sthenelaidas (i. 86) or Brasidas (iv. 126). When Perikles wishes to revive the Athenians' spirits in 430, he talks of glory (ii. 64. 3), and Thucydides does not write as if he himself were insensible to the appeal. The φύσις ἀναγκαία of 105. 2 is not the whole story.

7. Public statements by Thucydides' speakers about the Athenian empire usually make some concession to the human desire for self-justification. Thucydides' Athenians at Sparta in 432 do indeed state a law of human nature and reject the δίκαιος λόγος as a basis for argument (i. 76. 2), but they also recite Athens' performance at Marathon and Salamis, describe how the hegemony fell into her hands, allow something for fear; Perikles (above) concentrates on glory, Euphemos on the need for security (vi. 82–3). Thucydides' own narrative (i. 95–6) underlines the external factors which contributed to Athens' assumption of leadership. Only the Dialogue makes no concessions. It is thus not only the logical end of Diodotos' line of thought, but has its place at one end of a spectrum of opinion about Athenian imperialism. I would, with some modification, maintain the thesis too one-sidedly presented in *PCPhS* N.S. vi (1960), 1–10, that the Dialogue is (among other things) part of Thucydides' examination of the problem of empire. His feeling that the power of Athens was somehow admirable seems to me beyond question: see (4) (*a*) above. His residence among the enemies of Athens gave him special familiarity with the charges that were made against her, and his temperament somehow inclined him to believe that Athens' relations with her subjects were generally bad, probably worse than they were in fact. He could see through attempts to justify Athens on conventional lines, and observation persuaded him that great powers in fact pursue their own interest, whatever their spokesmen may say. For a man who was not a theoretical immoralist like Plato's Kallikles, that presented an alarming problem, and he recurred to it, emphasizing different aspects. The privacy of the Dialogue, and its occasion, gave him the opportunity to discuss the question nakedly, undistracted by the ὀνόματα καλά which inevitably had their place in a set speech. We need not think that this was his last word upon the subject to which he so often returned. (This view will not commend itself to those critics for whom Thucydides is a secure observer with fixed opinions; and between them and those for whom the *History* gives an impression of tension and internal struggle, the difference is perhaps too subjective for fruitful argument. For myself, I continue to think that the question of empire troubled Thucydides.)

8. Though Thucydides chose to write on the question of forcing Melos to join the empire and about the Melians' choice between suicide and surrender, one effect of his Dialogue is to draw attention to the subsequent execution, so that Melos lives in our memories far more vividly than Skione; and we tend to forget Hysiai altogether (83. 2, with n.). We do not have to suppose that Thucydides intended quite this effect; and here the date of composition has some importance for our judgement, since it is not clear how soon Melos

became a standing instance of Athens' crimes. Aristophanes' casual reference to Melian hunger in *Av.* 186 (cf. Gomme's n. to 116. 3) suggests that it did not lie heavy on the Athenians' conscience in spring 414. Xenophon, *HG* ii. 2. 3, describes how the Athenians were kept awake on the night of the news of Aigospotamoi by the thought that they might suffer atrocities such as they had committed, Melos at the head of the list; but Melos' priority there is partly due to the fact that it was a Spartan colony. By the time of Isokrates' *Panegyricus* in 380, Melos with Skione is the regular charge against imperial Athens, Melos slightly in the lead (iv. 100, 109–10). If the Dialogue was written some appreciable time before 404 (see 91. 1 n.), this position may not yet have been established: that is, Melos may not have seemed an important event to Thucydides, at any rate no more remarkable than any other mass execution, but useful for his argument, as a case where (*a*) Athens was not punishing a revolt, (*b*) the victim was given an option, indeed urged to peaceful surrender. For later posterity, the Dialogue has contributed more than anything to the scandal, but that need not have been the author's intention.

9. As to 'Thucydides' silence about Sparta', on which Gomme (above) proposed to comment, it is complete enough. We are not even told that Melos ever made appeal to her; and 115. 2 stresses the fact that Sparta held back from renewing the war even after provocation nearer home. Melos' hopes (104, etc.) were indeed futile; and Thucydides' prolongation of this topic (105. 3–110) is primarily a reinforcement of his observation that powerful states are guided only by their interest, Sparta being a most effective instance precisely because of her reputation for the practice of ἀρετή (105. 4 n.).

Gomme's own final view of the Dialogue is uncertain. He once told me, but briefly and without argument, that he regarded it as intended to show the moral decline of Athens, and certain of his notes (above) suggest that he retained this view; others, notably the 'alternative' version of the n. on 89, suggest that he may have begun to explore other possibilities. Though I believe that the view of the Dialogue as an indictment of Athens is mistaken, Gomme's insistence on the contrast between the sentiments of these Athenians and the idealism of Perikles' speeches is not valueless. If Aristeides and Kimon had spoken and acted on the principles of the Dialogue, there would have been no empire: on one plane it may have been a correct observation that the abstraction called Ἀθηναῖοι attended only to its own interest, on another plane Athens could not have developed her power unless many individuals had been ready to act on the less cool ideals to which Thucydides' Perikles gave expression. In the Dialogue Thucydides pursues only one line of his thought and observation; and in the light of the execution to follow in 116. 4, his concern with the abstractions here may well be felt disagreeable and insensitive.]

114. 1. κατὰ πόλεις: [the allies of 84. 1 came then from quite a number of islands.]

2. φυλακήν - - - καταλιπόντες: in accord with usual practice (vol. i, 18–19).

115. 1–3. *Skirmishing in the Peloponnese*

115. 1. ἐς τὴν Φλειασίαν: [cf. 83. 3.]

2. οἱ ἐκ τῆς Πύλου Ἀθηναῖοι: [in winter 419/18 the Athenians had brought the Messenians back from Kranioi for this express purpose, λῄζεσθαι (56. 3). Krüger therefore wished to delete Ἀθηναῖοι here, but there were no doubt Athenians in charge, at least, and Athens is made responsible not only here but at vi. 105. 2, vii. 18. 3.]

τὰς μὲν σπονδὰς οὐδ' ὣς ἀφέντες: see 25. 3 n. [For the question how far this should have been regarded as a breach of the Peace, see also vi. 105. 1 n. Thucydides here and in vii. 18. 3 makes it clear that these raids could easily have been taken as a *casus foederis* (see the text, v. 18. 4); and Sparta's forbearance is the more remarkable in view of the presumption that Melos had appealed for help on the lines of 110. 2.]

2–3. ἐκήρυξαν δέ - - - ἡσύχαζον: [by land the invitation could most easily have been taken up by the Boeotians, whose relations with Sparta, strained in the early part of 419 (52. 1), had evidently been restored by summer 418 (57. 2, etc., 64. 4). There is no reason to think that they did respond, and § 3 perhaps excludes them. Their δεχήμερος ἐκεχειρία (26. 2, 32. 5–7) was presumably no bar to action of the kind proposed, if the Peace did not inhibit Athens' raids from Pylos; but direct attack across a land border would be very much more like open war, and the Boeotians no doubt preferred to wait till Sparta was ready for that. Inaction on the part of Megara is easily understood.

By sea Corinth was the obvious agent. As Corinth had neither sworn to the Peace nor succeeded in making a separate truce (32. 6), she was still technically at war with Athens. If ἐπολέμησαν means more than that, as it would normally do, we should like to be told how and where they fought; but the reference may be only to casual raids on Athenian shipping.]

3. ἰδίων τινῶν διαφορῶν ἕνεκα: [as the words stand, they suggest some new ground of quarrel which Thucydides thinks too trivial to explain. This is possible: but §§ 2–3 as a whole are very compressed and not at all explicit, and the suspicion arises that this is a note not fully worked out, that the quarrels here referred to are really those which have been fully explained earlier.

For Corinth's current relations with Sparta, see 82. 6 n.]

115. 4. *A Melian Success*

4. τὸ κατὰ τὴν ἀγοράν: [Duker took this to be the market which the Athenians had set up for their own needs, comparing i. 62. 1, iii. 6. 2; and most edd. follow him. But the Melians are the subject, and there is some expectation that the landmark is something permanent: it would be more natural to understand 'that part of the Athenian fortification which was opposite their (the Melians') agora'. ὅσα πλεῖστα ἐδύναντο suggests, though it does not certainly imply, a fairly large haul: if the Athenians kept food and other stores in this area, that may be because this was a convenient place for unloading their ships; we should expect the Melian agora to be close to precisely such a place.]

116. 1. *More Quarrels in Argos*

116. 1. τῶν ἐν τῇ πόλει τινὰς ὑποπτεύσαντες: [cf. 84. 1. μέλλησιν here is not 'delay', as the plural in 82. 4, but the intention conveyed in μελλήσαντες; cf. 66. 2 n.]

116. 2–4. *Surrender and Destruction of Melos*

3. Φιλοκράτης ὁ Δημέου: nothing else is known about him.

[Thucydides does not say whether he replaced Kleomedes and Teisias (84. 3), who might well have been in trouble after their second failure of vigilance, or supplemented them. Kleomedes and Teisias received their first payment for the Melian expedition (84. 1 n.) before the end of the archon-year 417/16, but almost certainly after the election of generals for 416/15. They are described in ML 77 (*IG* i². 302) as στρατηγοί (στρα[is preserved in l. 32, and στρατεγοῖς ἐς Μέλον is a safe restoration here and in l. 29), which presumably means that they were already generals for 417/16. The chances are that they had been re-elected for 416/15, and so were known to be available to continue with the operation if the Melians resisted beyond the end of the year, as they did; though we cannot quite exclude the possibility that they handed over command to other generals at the end of the Athenian year, without Thucydides telling us of it. Philokrates must have held office for 416/15.]

κατὰ κράτος ἤδη πολιορκούμενοι: cf. Aristophanes, *Birds* (produced in the spring of 414) 186 τοὺς δ' αὖ θεοὺς ἀπολεῖτε λιμῷ Μηλίῳ. It would not seem from this that the Athenians felt any remorse for their treatment of Melos, nor that Aristophanes was opposed to it. Cf. the Megarian episode in *Acharnians*, [where the sufferings of Megara are simply material for the comedy to exploit.

Σ Ar. *Av.* 186 (= Suda λιμὸς Μηλιαῖος, cf. Hesych. λιμῷ Μηλίῳ) ends καὶ οἱ Μήλιοι πολιορκούμενοι ὑπὸ Ἀθηναίων λιμῷ ἐπείσθησαν (ἐπιέσθησαν Porson) καὶ παραδεδώκασιν ἑαυτούς, ὡς Θουκυδίδης ἐν τῇ πέμπτῃ. The starvation is implicit in Thucydides' narrative (cf. 115. 4), and there is no need, with Herwerden, to make it explicit by inserting, e.g., σιτοδείας τε before γενομένης.

Another scholion on Av. 186 ascribes the reduction of Melos by hunger to Nikias. Suda ὑπερακοντίζεις, a fuller version of Σ Av. 363 (ὑπερακοντίζεις σύ γ᾽ ἤδη Νικίαν ταῖς μηχαναῖς), has the note Σύμμαχος· πρὸς τὴν Μήλου πολιορκίαν, and for Nikias' ingenuity cites also Phrynichos, Monotropos, fr. 22, produced in the same year 414; and ends confusedly ἢ ὅτι φρονιμώτατα Μηλίους λιμῷ ἀνεῖλεν. A. E. Raubit-schek, Hist. xii (1963), 80–2, ingeniously suggested that Ephoros, consciously correcting Thucydides, had recorded a subjection of Melos at some time after 425, and its revolt during the Peace of Nikias; and that these scholia and Diod. xii. 80. 5 are relics of this alternative account. It is not impossible that Symmachos, a late commentator on Aristophanes, should have preserved for us a stray fragment deriving from Ephoros; and in Diodoros the words Νικίου στρατηγοῦντος might, though they need not, cover the reduction of Melos as well as the other half of the clause. But Diodoros' sentence, which briefly mentions Nikias' capture of Kythera and Nisaia, and the destruction of Melos, immediately after Mantineia will hardly command much confidence in spite of Raubitschek's arguments; and in any case Thucydides could hardly not have heard of an earlier subjection and revolt of Melos, and if he knew of it his account would be so misleading that we could not acquit him of intent to deceive. It is more likely that the ancient commentators on Aristophanes did not know why Nikias' μηχαναί (Ar.) or εὑρήματα (Phryn.) were specially topical in spring 414, and were merely guessing. (Their guesses can be distressingly wild, e.g. Σ. Ar. Nu. 6.) The relevant detail may merely be lost for us; or perhaps this was an aspect of Nikias that was much talked of at the time of his appointment to the Sicilian command in 415.]

γενομένης καὶ προδοσίας τινός: [if there was still, after all this, a party inside Melos that favoured Athens, this lends point to the Melians' refusal to let the Athenians speak to the πλῆθος (84. 3); but the treachery may be only the fruit of hunger and exhaustion, cf. iii. 27. 3.]

4. οἱ δὲ ἀπέκτειναν, κ.τ.λ.: according to Ps.- Andokides iv. 22, that unreliable witness, it was Alkibiades who moved the selling into slavery, and then bought one of the women and made her his mistress and had a son by her. [This is the most indigestible error in the whole speech: Raubitschek in his defence of the speech, TAPhA lxxix (1948), 200, sees all the difficulties, but his explanation of this passage does not do away with them. On And. iv see below, pp. 287–8.]

Plutarch, Alc. 16. 5–6, has the story too, adding that he bore most blame for the execution of the Melians because he supported the motion. If this is true, Thucydides' silence is notable. [Gomme added 'unless he knew nothing of Athenian politics'—but if Thucydides could discover as much as he did about the internal affairs of Athens in 415 and 411, he could surely have discovered what, if anything, Alkibiades had done in regard to Melos—and he referred forward to further comment which he never wrote. It is to be noted that Plutarch has τῷ ψηφίσματι συνειπών, where Ps.-And. 22 has γνώμην ἀποφηνάμενος and in § 23 makes Alkibiades wholly responsible. For the relation between Plutarch and Ps.-And., see A. R. Burn, *CQ* N.S. iv (1954), 138–42. It is not of course impossible that Alkibiades supported the decree; but if he proposed it Thucydides' silence is indeed notable.

Exasperation at Melian resistance and the expense involved (cf. Isoc. xv. 113), and the desire to make an example, were presumably the reasons for this act of inhumanity, which Thucydides reports in the same bare factual way in which he had reported the fact of Skione (32. 1) and Hysiai (83. 2). The effect of the 'example' was soon overlaid by the greater effect of Athens' disaster in Sicily, so that we have no means of telling how effective it would have been in frightening present subjects or future enemies (and so no means of estimating the validity, in their own terms, of the Athenians' arguments in 91. 2–99).]

The destruction of Melos was remembered afterwards, by the Athenians in 405 when news came of Aigospotamoi, along with their treatment of Hestiaia, Skione, Torone, and Aigina (by no means all treated alike), X. *HG* ii. 2. 3; by Isokrates in defending Athens by imputing more and greater crimes to Sparta, xii (*Panath.*) 62–6, καὶ γὰρ ἂν αἰσχυνοίμην - - - εἰ τῶν ἄλλων μηδὲ τοὺς θεοὺς ἀναμαρτήτους εἶναι νομιζόντων ἐγὼ γλιχοίμην καὶ πειρώμην πείθειν, ὡς περὶ οὐδὲν πώποτε τὸ κοινὸν ἡμῶν πεπλημμέληκεν (Melos, Skione, Torone); and an echo of the noise made by the deed sounds not only in Plutarch, but in Strabo, who, in the briefest and driest catalogue of islands in the Cretan Sea, says of Melos that it is more notable than the others, that its position is 700 stades from Skyllaion promontory and much the same from Diktynnaion, Ἀθηναῖοι δέ ποτε πέμψαντες στρατείαν ἡβηδὸν κατέσφαξαν τοὺς πλείους (x. 5. 1, 484).

[The nearest thing to a defence by an Athenian writer is Isokrates in *Panegyricus* iv. 100–2, where he runs the instances of Melos and Skione together, and 101 εἴ τινες τῶν πολεμησάντων ἡμῖν σφόδρα φαίνονται κολασθέντες amounts to a claim that Melos was at war with Athens (cf. 84. 2 above); but his defence of the empire in general is rather that Athens' record was on balance good.]

Such of the Melians as escaped the massacre were restored to the island after Aigospotamoi by Lysandros (X. *HG* ii. 2. 9).

[*IG* xii. 3. 1187, from Melos, reads (in Attic letters) Ἐπόνφες |
Ἀθεναῖος | Πανδιονίδος | φυλὲς | Κυθέρριος. Hiller compared 1181 where
(if it is complete, which is far from certain) the name Κλιό|νφας
appears, and concluded that Epomphes was a Melian traitor (cf.
116. 3) who acquired Athenian citizenship. While it would be rash
to claim either that Kliomphas was a Melian name or that Epomphes
could not be Attic, the threefold assertion of the dedicator's status
is odd (his mention of his tribe in such a context is virtually unparalleled), and allows the inference that he was an abnormal kind of
Athenian; and the dating of this inscription to the period of the
Athenian occupation is epigraphically admissible.

Both Gomme's and my notes have from time to time touched on
the question, how far various sections of book v can be regarded as
finished work. There are surprising omissions: (*a*) the record of
Athens' activities in the north is scrappy throughout, markedly so
at the point where the record of Athenian expenditure for 418–414
(ML 77) gives us some check (cf. 83. 4 nn.); (*b*) remarkably little is
said about the internal politics of Athens, though general probability and such passages as 43–6 suggest that Thucydides, however
early he wrote any of this, could have told us more. It is especially
frustrating that he did not mention in its chronological place the
ostracism of Hyperbolos, alluded to in passing at viii. 73. 3. Besides
the omissions, there are some noticeable loose ends, and some
passages whose wording suggests that they were not finally revised.

This is perhaps the logical place to list and discuss these phenomena.
But there are similar phenomena in book viii to be discussed, and in
order not to swell the present volume further I reserve the discussion of this book's incompleteness till the final volume.]

BOOKS VI AND VII

EDITORIAL NOTE

Gomme left an outline commentary on vi. 6–14 in typescript, but it was clearly an early draft, omitting treatment of some of the most difficult problems in those chapters. For the rest, there were only brief manuscript notes, of which some undoubtedly represented the first stage of his work on a commentary but the majority seemed rather to be lecture-notes. Where I have drawn upon this material or upon his marginal jottings in books and offprints I have indicated my debt by adding 'Gomme, ms.'; but I have not given any such indication when he was simply agreeing or disagreeing with a view already expressed by a predecessor. It would not have been practicable to do what has been done in book v, and I have accordingly written on books vi and vii *ab initio*.

K. J. D.

BOOK VI

1. *Athenian Designs on Sicily*

1.1. τῆς μετὰ Λάχητος καὶ Εὐρυμέδοντος: the force sent under Laches and Charoiades in 427 consisted of twenty ships (iii. 86. 1); Laches was relieved in the winter of 426/5 by Pythodoros (iii. 115. 2 ff.); and in the spring of 425 Eurymedon and Sophokles were sent out with forty ships (iv. 2. 2). The total, sixty ships, is precisely what they propose (8. 2) to send in 415; μείζονι παρασκευῇ must therefore refer to the greater scale of land forces now envisaged.

καταστρέψασθαι: the ambition to reduce the Sicilian cities to the status of subjects, not simply to create a political situation favourable to Athens, is represented by Thucydides as present in the minds of the Athenians in 427. Laches and Charoiades were sent εἰ σφίσι δυνατὰ εἴη τὰ ἐν τῇ Σικελίᾳ πράγματα ὑποχείρια γενέσθαι, and the generals recalled in 424 were punished for making peace ἐξὸν αὐτοῖς τὰ ἐν Σικελίᾳ καταστρέψασθαι (iv. 65. 3).

ἄπειροι οἱ πολλοὶ ὄντες: Plutarch's story (*Nic.* 12. 1) of the animated discussions of Sicilian topography which took place all over Athens at this time is not wholly irreconcilable with Thucydides; men who had been in Sicily in 427–424 would have found willing audiences, but the picture which they painted was not necessarily more accurate, or more conducive to cool thinking, than the reminiscences of uneducated observers usually are. Less easy to reconcile is Th. ii. 65. 11, where the error of judgement implied here is, though not denied, subordinated in importance to the political disunity of 415 (cf. H. D. Westlake, *CQ* n.s. viii [1958], 102 ff.). vi. 1. 1 and ii. 65. 11 were 'thought at different times' (Gomme, *JHS* lxxi [1951], 72 = *More Essays*, 95–7), and the latter was 'thought' at a time when the theme of political disunity was uppermost in Thucydides' mind (cf. 15. 3 n.). A further element in the situation, incitement to the enterprise by seers and oracle-mongers, is mentioned only in retrospect (viii. 1. 1; cf. Plu. *Nic.* 13. 1 f.), and for anecdotes about prophecies of doom we must go to later writers, e.g. [Pl.] *Thg.* 129 c, Plu. *Nic.* 13. 3 ff., *Alc.* 17. 5, and Paus. viii. 11. 2.

2. ὁλκάδι οὐ πολλῷ τινι ἔλασσον ἢ ὀκτὼ ἡμερῶν: the distance is c. 500 nautical miles (= c. 930 km.). Since (*a*) Ephoros F 135 says that five days and nights were needed for the circumnavigation, (*b*) this yields an average speed of 4·2 knots (= c. 7·1 km.p.h.), (*c*) ancient data as a whole suggest that a sailing ship could expect to maintain 4–4·5 knots under reasonable wind conditions, and (*d*) in

ii. 97. 1 Thucydides specifies, in giving a distance in terms of sailing time, both days and nights, it seems that he is referring here to sailing by day only. Cf. L. Casson, *TAPhA* lxxxii (1951), 136 ff., 143 f., n. 34, and R. van Compernolle, *BIBR* xxx (1957), 1 ff. It is, however, possible that either Thucydides or Ephoros (or both of them) is offering an estimate which his contemporaries might have disputed.

ἐν εἰκοσισταδίῳ μάλιστα μέτρῳ - - - διείργεται: the strait at its narrowest is 2·8 km. wide; ancient estimates other than Thucydides' vary between 6 and 12 'stades' (cf. Holm, i. 328). The point selected is seldom indicated, but Thucydides' argument here necessitates his thinking of the narrowest point. On the problem of the 'stade' and the margin of error in measuring distances across water, cf. vii. 59. 3 n. and p. 468.

2–5. *The Colonization of Sicily*

We might have expected Thucydides to amplify his judgement (1. 1), that the Athenians did not realize the magnitude of their task, by giving us an account of the population and resources of Sicily as they were in 415. Instead, he tells us the origin of each element in its population, both foreign (2. 2 ff.) and Greek (3–5), with a brief mention (2. 1) of its mythical populations (cf. Münch, 42 ff., 49 ff., on the structure of the excursus and its relation to 1. 2).

Elsewhere Thucydides digresses in order to correct inaccuracies in published works (cf. i. 97. 2 on the Pentekontaetia) and tradition (cf. vi. 54. 1) or in order to give his readers interesting material which they are unlikely to find elsewhere (e.g. ii. 97, on Thrace; 96 is in substance, though not in form, a part of this digression). It is therefore unlikely that he is repeating in these chapters information available at the time in well-known books; it is to be presumed that he is either giving the results of personal research in Sicily or reproducing material from a little-known written source. Whether he ever went to Sicily is a question to which there is no agreed answer, and my own answer (p. 467) is that he probably did not; but whatever answer is given, these chapters provide internal evidence that they are drawn at least in part from a written source and that the dialect of the source was probably Ionic.

(*a*) In these chapters alone Thucydides qualifies numerals by ἐγγύς (or ἐγγύτατα) instead of his usual μάλιστα, περί, ὅσον, ὡς, or ἐς. There is, I think, only one plausible explanation of this fact: that he found the expression ἐγγύς in a literary source and retained it, instead of substituting μάλιστα, because he was not sure whether the writer meant by it quite what he himself would have meant by μάλιστα. It follows that his source used ἐγγύς with those data which it

accompanies in Thucydides' own work, and not with the data which
it does not accompany.

(b) Specifically Ionic influence is suggested by 3. 1 βωμὸν ὅστις νῦν
- - - ἐστὶν ἰδρύσαντο, which has no parallel in Attic prose and few
elsewhere (Page, *Sappho and Alcaeus*, 20 f.) ; but cf. J. E. Powell,
Lexicon to Herodotus, s.v. ὅστις 2e, and especially Antiochus of Syracuse, *FGrHist* 555 F 2 τὴν γῆν ταύτην, ἥτις νῦν Ἰταλία (*sic* codd.)
καλεῖται - - - εἶχον Οἴνωτροι (Hellanikos, *FGrHist* 4 F 42b, to which
a manuscript note in Weir Smyth's copy of Stahl drew my attention,
would be another instance if we could be at all sure that we are
reading Hellanikos' own words). Herbst–Müller suggest (ii. 18) that
Thucydides means 'they built an altar, and there is one there now',
with which one might compare D.L. i. 75 ὁ δὲ ἱερὰν ἀνέθηκε, ἥτις νῦν
(sc. but not at first) Πιττάκειος καλεῖται. But this does not diminish
the significance of the Ionic parallels, and Appian, *BC* v. 109 (cf.
3. 1 n. below) tells against it on the question of fact.

(c) 3. 2 τοῦ ἐχομένου ἔτους, where ἐχόμενος is used as an attributive
adjective, 'following', has parallels in Hdt. ii. 12. 1 τῆς ἐχομένης γῆς,
'the adjacent land', and X. *Cyr.* vii. 2. 5 πρὸς τὴν ἐχομένην ἄκραν ;
the nearest parallels in Attic prose to the temporal use of the word,
Isoc. x. 38 περὶ τῶν ἐχομένων διελθεῖν, and Pl. *Lg.* 958 b ὁ τῶν δικασίμων
μηνῶν ἐχόμενος - - - μήν are syntactically a little different.

(d) It is possible that 2. 2 ὡς ἡ ἀλήθεια εὑρίσκεται and the allusive
obscurity of 4. 1 Ὕβλωνος - - - προδόντος (codd.) τὴν χώραν also point
to the use of a written source (though Jacoby, IIIb. 610, denies this
for 2. 2). Cf. Ἀθ. π. 15. 2 on Peisistratos and Megakles' daughter,
which would be puzzling (διὰ τὸ μὴ βούλεσθαι τῇ τοῦ Μεγακλέους
θυγατρὶ συγγίγνεσθαι) if we did not have Hdt. i. 61. 1 f.

Three known authors must be considered for identification as this
source, but the first of them is wholly enigmatic: Hippys of Rhegion
(*FGrHist* 554), to whom were attributed a history of Sicily, κτίσις
Ἰταλίας, and χρονικά or περὶ χρόνων. The Suda notice dates him to
the fifth century ; he was certainly mentioned by Phainias of Eresos
(fr. 12 Wehrli) at the end of the fourth ; but one of our nearest
approximations to a verbatim quotation from his works (F 3) incorporates a dating by Olympiads. Whether he was pre-Thucydidean
or not—and the absence of all mention of him in what is said about
early Italy and its colonies by Strabo and, above all, by Dionysios
(who had a penchant for early historians) tells against the Suda—
we know nothing of his opinion on any part of the material which
Thucydides presents, and he can be no more than a shadow in the
background (cf. Jacoby, IIIb. 482, who, however, is not accurate in
saying that 'the *Vita*', i.e. the Suda notice, 'knows only the epitome
of his Σικελικαὶ πράξεις by Myes', for the notice simply says that
Hippys wrote Σικελικαὶ πράξεις, 'of which Myes later made an

epitome'). The fact that Thucydides, apparently well supplied with foundation-dates for the oldest cities in Sicily and Syracusan colonies, offers no dates for the foundations of Zankle and Himera, whose history was so intimately bound up with that of Rhegion, makes it virtually certain that a Rhegine writer was not his chief or only source, and may be thought to indicate that if he used two or more sources they did not include a Rhegine.

With Hellanikos' (*FGrHist* 4) *Priestesses of Hera* we are on firmer ground. We know from F 82, which concerns the foundation of Sicilian Naxos by Theokles, that this work must have dated the Sicilian colonies in terms of the Argive priestesses, i.e. in terms which could be translated into other chronological systems. We do not know whether it was published before Thucydides vi–vii; but we find that almost every opinion which Hellanikos is known to have expressed on the early history of Sicily is in conflict with the statements made by Thucydides (cf. van Compernolle, 450 ff., 479 ff., and Münch, 45 ff.). He dated the arrival of the Sikels to the third generation before the Trojan war (F 79b); Thucydides implies (2. 2–4 'the Sikanoi were the first . . . when Troy was taken Trojan fugitives arrived . . . the Sikels crossed from Italy about 300 years before the Greeks arrived') that the Sikels came after the Trojan War. Hellanikos, though he believed (F 84) that a Trojan called Elymos escaped to Sicily, regarded the Elymoi (F 79b) as an Italian people expelled from their homeland by the Oinotroi; Thucydides (2. 3) says that they came from Troy. Hellanikos (F 111) derived the name Ἰταλία from Italic *uitulus*, Thucydides (2. 4) derives it from the Sikel king Italos; and Hellanikos derived the name Γέλα from a mythical Gelon (F 199), Thucydides (4. 3) from the river Gelas. It is therefore certain that *Priestesses of Hera* was not the sole source of these chapters of Thucydides, and improbable that Thucydides used it at all (on Jacoby's argument [Ia. 456] that Thucydides found in Hellanikos a statement on the Iberian origin of the Sikans, see below). We must remember that Thucydides distrusted Hellanikos' history of Athens as 'chronologically inaccurate' (i. 97. 2), and we may suspect that *Priestesses of Hera* was too well known a work for Thucydides to think reproduction of its contents necessary. A further argument against the use of Hellanikos is the fact that whereas Hellanikos presumably gave each colony a precise date Thucydides qualifies some of his intervals of time by ἐγγύς, describes other events as 'afterwards' or 'about the same time', and gives no indication of date at all for some events. Especially noticeable is 2. 5, where the Sikels are dated 'ἐγγύς 300 years before the arrival of the Greeks'; Hellanikos gave exact dates for the Sikel migration (F 79b. 3) and for Naxos (F 82), so that an exact interval could have been extracted from him.

Antiochos of Syracuse (*FGrHist* 555) is the most likely of all the candidates (the suggestion was first made by Niebuhr and elaborated by E. Wölfflin, *Antiochos von Syrakus und Coelius Antipater* [Winterthur, 1872]; the criticisms of this thesis by O. Böhm, *Fontes rerum Sicularum quibus Thucydides usus sit* [Ludwigslust, 1875], are still salutary, though hypersceptical). Antiochos' Sicilian history ended with the events of 424 (Diod. xii. 71. 2) and was presumably written in Ionic, as his other work περὶ 'Ιταλίας certainly was (F 2). Like Thucydides, he believed (F 2 and F 5) that the name 'Ιταλία was derived from the Sikel king Italos and that the Sikels migrated from Italy under pressure from the Oscans (Οἴνωτροι καὶ 'Οπικοί, F 4). No disagreements between him and Thucydides can be demonstrated, but three apparent disagreements merit discussion:

(i) Dion. Hal. *AR* i. 22. 5 says that Antiochos failed to give a date for the Sikel migration, whereas Thucydides dates it; but Dionysios is no doubt referring to the περὶ 'Ιταλίας, from which he quotes explicitly in *AR* i. 12. 3; he takes no account of the Σικελικά, in which Antiochos may very well have dated in Sicilian terms an event which he had not dated in Italian terms (L. Pareti, *Studi siciliani ed italioti* [Firenze, 1920], draws this important distinction, which Jacoby, *Atthis*, 352 n. 2, overlooks).

(ii) Jacoby argued (Ia. 456) that since Antiochos began his Sicilian history (T 3) with the Sikan king Kokalos, he accepted the Sikans' tradition that they were αὐτόχθονες, and that when Thucydides (2. 2) rejects this tradition and affirms, ὡς ἡ ἀλήθεια εὑρίσκεται, that they came from Iberia he is following Hellanikos. Yet Antiochos can have given alternative traditions, as Herodotos often does. Also, Dion. Hal. *AR* i. 22. 2 suggests that Hellanikos expressed no opinion on the Sikans. Dionysios there (22. 3 ff.) cites Hellanikos, Philistos, Antiochos, and Thucydides on the origin of the Sikels, but for the Sikans he simply reproduces Thucydides, as is demonstrable from the relation between his text and that of Thucydides (cf. 2. 5 n.); this is most easily explained if he found nothing relevant in Hellanikos and (see above) was using Antiochos' work on Italy, not his work on Sicily. Jacoby subsequently (IIIb. 610 f.) expressed misgivings about the argument which he had used in Ia.

(iii) Antiochos F 10 represents Kroton as founded after Sybaris and before Syracuse; Eusebios dates Kroton and Sybaris to 709 or 708 and agrees approximately with Thucydides in dating Syracuse *c.* 735. But since Thucydides and Eusebios sometimes disagree, e.g. on Selinus (see below) it is illegitimate to argue that Eusebios' dates for Kroton and Sybaris must come ultimately from the same source as his and Thucydides' date for Syracuse, and that therefore the source of the Thucydidean date for Syracuse cannot be Antiochos. Many streams run together in Eusebios. In general, it never follows, if one author says '$a-b = 5$' and another '$b-c = 6$', that either author believed that $a-c = 11$.

Three further considerations point to Antiochos as a source of Thucydides:

(i) The possibility that iii. 88. 2 f. are also derived from him; the substance of the passage is given by Paus. x. 11. 3, with considerable differences from Thucydides in wording and detail, and the first item, the foundation of Lipara, is there cited as from Antiochos ἐν τῇ Σικελιώτιδι συγγραφῇ (cf. van Compernolle, 473 ff.).

(ii) Thucydides' source seems best informed on events belonging to, or associated with, the history of Syracuse.

(iii) If Thucydides first saw a copy of Antiochos' work during the years when he was 'with the Peloponnesians' (cf. v. 26. 5), e.g. in Corinth, and knew that it was not widely circulated, we have a motive for his digression (Dover, *Maia* N.S. vi [1953], 15 f.).

The majority of Thucydides' foundation-dates are expressed with reference to Syracuse; and since Selinus is dated by reference to Megara, and Megara was destroyed by Gelon, these two cities may have earned their place in the list of dates through their relationship with Syracuse. Thucydides anchors his dates to later times at one point only, by the statement (4. 2) that Megara was 245 years old when it was destroyed by Gelon. As Gelon died in 478/7 (Diod. xi. 38), had ruled in Syracuse for seven years (Arist. *Pol.* 1315^{b}36), and had already destroyed Megara when envoys from Greece approached him in 481/0 (Hdt. vii. 156. 2–157. 1), Megara was destroyed in 483 ±1, and the foundation date implied by Thucydides is 728 ±1. The relation between Megara and Syracuse is unsatisfactorily vague. Naxos founded Leontinoi four years after the foundation of Syracuse, and 'after Leontinoi' Katane (3. 3). 'About the same time' the Megarians arrived in Sicily (4. 1). They occupied Trotilon, 'afterwards' shared in Leontinoi 'for a short time', and then occupied Thapsos, where the man who had brought them to Sicily died (4. 1). They then—how long afterwards, Thucydides does not say—founded Megara Hyblaia. Thucydides clearly did not know either the interval of time between Leontinoi and Katane or whether the arrival of the Megarians preceded Leontinoi or followed Katane; had he known, he would not have said 'after it' and 'about the same time' in a context containing precise expressions such as 'in the next year' and 'four years later'. He was satisfied only that Leontinoi existed before Megara. If we call the interval between Leontinoi and Megara x and the interval between Leontinoi and Katane y (cf. Beloch, i. 2². 221 f.), and are content with the probable inference, from the tenor of 3. 3–4. 1, that Thucydides believed x to be small, we arrive at the following table of Thucydidean dates (all dates ± 1; '*c.*' = Thucydides' ἐγγύς):

Sikel migration	$c.$ 1033+x
Naxos	733+x
Syracuse	732+x
Leontinoi	728+x
Katane	728+x—y
Megara	728
Gela	688+x
Akrai	662+x
Kasmenai	$c.$ 642+x
Selinus	628
Kamarina	$c.$ 597+x
Akragas	$c.$ 580+x

Upon what evidence did such figures rest?

(i) The hypothesis that the colonies maintained from the beginning lists of annual magistrates or priests is anachronistic in attributing to the eighth and seventh centuries a historical curiosity which even in the fifth century was only imperfectly developed (cf. Dover, loc. cit. 13 ff.; *contra*, Dunbabin, 450 ff.) or the adoption of an isolated element from the complex administrative systems of the Near East. More important objections are:

(*a*) Greek historians disagreed often and seriously about foundation-dates. How was disagreement possible if the foundation-date of each colony could be discovered by counting up a list?

(*b*) Hellanikos (F 79) concluded that two prehistoric events, the arrival of the Elymoi and the arrival of the second wave of Sikels, were separated by four years. This, at least, cannot have been discovered from Greek eponymous lists; therefore other grounds for the establishment of dates existed. (Gomme [ms. note] suggested that Hellanikos' 'four years', like the ten years of the Trojan War, may have been enshrined in a narrative poem.)

(*c*) Some of Thucydides' figures can be explained as the product of calculation from generations (see below). If in fact they were discovered from lists, the apparently simple explanation is illusory and we have to accept a remarkable series of arithmetical coincidences.

(ii) Two of Thucydides' explicitly stated figures, 70 (5. 2) and 245 (4. 2), are multiples of 35. His other figures are not; they can be accounted for, after a fashion, by calculations (e.g. those of G. Vallet and P. Villard in *BCH* lxxvi [1952], 295 ff. and 350 ff.) which allow a certain elasticity. For example, 100 (4. 2) could have been treated as three generations by someone who regarded 35 as one generation (van Compernolle, 456 and *BIBR* xxviii [1953], 198); hence 135 (5. 3) is one possible equivalent of four generations, 'about 20' (5. 2) could be half a generation, and even 108 (4. 4) and 44 (4. 3), neither of which is immediately explicable in terms of a 35-year generation, have been forced into a 35-year scheme by the observation that their sum, 152—the interval, that is, between Syracuse and Akragas—is three generations (100 years) plus one generation (35) plus a half-generation (17). Calculations of this kind are, however, antiquated by the coherent scheme which van Compernolle (411 ff.) has constructed upon the basis of some early fifth-century dates, using a strict 35-year generation throughout and assuming that Antiochos gave a value of one year to x and that he could not deny, but could only reduce to a minimum, a traditional priority of Naxos over Syracuse. Van Compernolle's scheme is this:—

Sikel migration	1034/3	= Battle of Kyme (474/3)+(16×35)
Naxos	734/3	= Syracuse+1
Syracuse	733/2	= Gelon's Olympic victory (488/7)+ (7×35)
Leontinoi	729/8	= Megara+1
Megara	728/7	= Gelon's destruction of Megara (483/2) +(7×35)
Gela	689/8	= Gelon's last year (479/8)+(6×35)
Akrai	663/2	= Syracuse−(2×35)
Kasmenai	643/2	= Gelon's occupation of Kasmenai (485/4) +(4½×35)
Selinus	628/7	= Syracuse−(3×35)
Kamarina	598/7	= Hippokrates' re-foundation of Kamarina (493/2)+(3×35)
Akragas	581/0	= Theron's Olympic victory (476/5)+ (3×35)

In this scheme the most impressive single item—impressive because of the complete certainty of its terminal point—is the relation between the foundation of Akragas and Theron's Olympic victory. The terminal dates adopted for Kasmenai and Kamarina admit of a slight margin of uncertainty, but so slight that they can be regarded as positively supported by the arithmetical relationship which results from their adoption. The terminals for Syracuse and Gela are the least satisfactory; one may wonder why the foundation of Syracuse should be dated by reference to an Olympic victory which Gelon won before he became ruler of Syracuse, and why this victory was not adopted as the terminal for calculation of the foundation of Gela. One must also ask why, if Antiochos worked entirely on a generation of 35 years and if (as seems to me inescapable, see above) ἐγγύς is his term, he attached it to some of the dates but not to others. The kind of thing which ἐγγύς might mean may be seen from Thucydides' own use of μάλιστα (om. Bψ) in vii. 42. 1, where Demosthenes and Eurymedon arrive with '73 ships μάλιστα'; I have suggested (loc. cit. 14) that this implies 'if all the figures (vii. 16. 2, 20. 2, 31. 3, 31. 5, and 33. 5) from which this total is calculated are correct'. If Antiochos established all his foundation-dates (i) by adding $35n$ to fifth-century dates and (ii) by subtracting $35n'$ from the dates arrived at in process (i), we should expect either that every date would be qualified by ἐγγύς or that category (ii) only would be qualified, or that none would be. As it is, the qualification is attached to some of the former category and to none of the latter. The possibility must therefore be considered that we have not yet identified all the data which were among the ingredients from which Antiochos constructed his scheme. Such data could be: (i) Genealogies of families other than the Emmenidai and Deinomenidai, and at some point even in conflict with those two genealogies; in some cases, the appearance of names in eponymous lists maintained from the early or middle sixth century might provide fixed points. (ii) Oral tradition of the same nature as the tradition which made Naxos earlier than Syracuse, but relating to later periods and possibly incorporating precise figures. (iii) Oral tradition, in each colony, about the age of the colony. It is hard to believe that λόγιοι ἄνδρες in Syracuse or Selinus in the third quarter of the fifth century could not offer an opinion, however ill-founded, on the age of their own city in years (cf. Th. v. 112. 2, where Melians describe their city as '700 years old').

If F 2 of Antiochos is a trustworthy guide, the character of his work was more like that of Herodotos than that of Hellanikos (cf. Jacoby, *Atthis*, 352 n. 2). We would therefore expect that he indicated some chronological relations in terms simply of generations (cf. Hdt. vi. 86. 2) and that it might be no easier to discover from his work the foundation-dates of colonies than to discover from Herodotos the salient dates of the Eastern Greeks and the oriental kingdoms in the sixth century. Nevertheless, our sample of Antiochos is so small that no one could be justified in rejecting, on historiographical grounds, his identification as the calculator whose work underlies these chapters of Thucydides. Herodotos, after all, was acquainted with the principle of calculating dates on the basis of a fixed value for a generation (ii. 142. 2; cf. van Compernolle, 136 f.), and he repeats one story (iv. 144. 2) in which the significant figure of 17 years appears.

The only approach to confirmation of any Antiochean–Thucydidean dates is provided by Pindar, who in *O.* 2. 93 says that 'the city (sc. Akragas) has not produced in a hundred years a greater benefactor ... than Theron'. The poem was composed in 476 (*POxy.* 222 = *FGrHist* 415. 1. 18; $Σ^A$ is defective and $Σ^B$ wrong); it is clear that in such a context we cannot take 'a hundred years' too literally, but its relation to Thucydides' date for Akragas is none the less interesting.

Some of the Thucydidean dates occur in later writers. In the various versions of Eusebios' *Chronikon* Naxos, Syracuse, and Katane are founded within the period 741–734 (the interval between Naxos and Syracuse is not the same in all versions and no interval is left between Syracuse and Katane); there too Gela is dated 690; [Skymnos] 296 ff. and Σ Pi. *O.* 5. 16 date Kamarina to Ol. 45, i.e. 600–596; and Σ Pi. *O.* 2. 93 (see above) dates Akragas to Ol. 50, i.e. 580–576. These passages support the *text* of Thucydides, and are interesting as showing that subsequent writers, as has been posited for Antiochos, assign a very low value to *x* (so low, indeed, that one suspects that *x* was sometimes disregarded altogether), but must on no account be regarded as 'corroborating' or 'confirming' Thucydides' statements, for we do not know on what evidence, other than Thucydides himself, they rest. Polyainos v. 5 gives the Megarians six months in Leontinoi—which, in his story, is ruled, or at least dominated, by Thukles, who has brought 'Chalkideans from Euboea' with him—and a further winter at Trotilon (cj. Maaswijk; Τρώϊλον and Τρωγίλιον codd.). Even if we allow him Thapsos for Trotilon–Trogilos and overlook his ignorance of Naxos, his chronology is more likely to be an inference from Thucydides (and his whole story an attractive piece of fiction built upon Thucydides) than a valuable independent tradition (Bérard, 83 f., takes it very seriously). The element of subjectivity in the evaluation of *x* would permit some writers to give higher dates than others for Leontinoi, Syracuse, and Naxos, and some of the differences between later writers may be attributable to this subjectivity. The main differences are:

(i) *Syracuse*. (*a*) The *Marmor Parium* almost certainly dated Syracuse in the first half of the eighth century. The figure is lost, and interpretation of 'in the 21st year of the reign of Aischylos at Athens' depends on *MP*'s date for Aischylos. Kastor of Rhodes (*FGrHist* 250 F 4) dated him 778/7–756/5, but *MP*'s dates for Athenian kings, where legible, are demonstrably higher than Kastor's by thirty years or more; we do not know the view which its source took of Alkmeon and the ten-year archons who in Kastor come between Aischylos and the start of the annual archonship in 683 (Jacoby, IId 669). Philistos (*FGrHist* 556 F 2) referred to the Olympiad 756/5–753/2 in some connection; A. W. Byvanck (*Mnemosyne* 1936/7, 197) suggested that this was his date for Syracuse, but it is equally possible that he was referring to Naxos (Vallet and Villard, *BCH* lxxvi [1952], 323) or indeed to Kyme. Cf. also van Compernolle, *BIBR* xxviii (1953), 182 ff.

(*b*) If the source of Eusebios' date (706) for Kerkyra believed, as a source of Strabo 269 did (cf. Jacoby on Timaios F 80), that Kerkyra and Syracuse were contemporary, or if the source of Eusebios' date (709) for Kroton believed, as Antiochos (F 10) did, that Kroton and

Syracuse were contemporary, it follows that someone must have believed that Syracuse was founded in the last decade of the eighth century (van Compernolle, loc. cit. 188 ff. and xxix [1955], 221 ff.); but perhaps neither condition was satisfied (Vallet and Villard, *BIBR* xxix [1955], 205 f.).

(ii) *Megara*. Ephoros dated Megara before Syracuse (F 137, from Strabo 267 and [Skymnos] 264 ff.); in so doing, he may also have differed from Thucydides not only in chronology but also on the salient facts of the story, as the Megarians in Thucydides' narrative 'play the part of late-comers' (Pace, 169).

(iii) *Selinus*. Either Ephoros or Timaios (whichever is the source of Diod. xiii. 59. 4) believed that Selinus was founded 242 years before its destruction in 409, i.e. in 651. It is this early date, not the Thucydidean date (628), which was adopted by later chronographic tradition and emerges, with downward variations of a few years, in the versions of Eusebios. Its ultimate source is obscure; van Compernolle (*BIBR* xxvii [1952], 341 ff.) appears to argue that because Diodoros had no access to Philistos except through the medium of Timaios, therefore his date for Selinus goes back to Philistos; *non sequitur*. H. Wentker (*MDAI[R]* lxii [1956], 137 ff.) argues from ξυγκατῴκισε in vi. 4. 2 that the Megarian settlement at Selinus under Pammilos was a second settlement, since (he says) Thucydides uses κατοικίζειν only of *re*-establishing a population; he therefore accepts both 651 and 628, assigning the short-lived 'first megaron' of Demeter Malophoros (Dunbabin, 280 ff.) to 651 and Pammilos to 628. But in ii. 17. 2 τὸ μαντεῖον προῄδει μὴ ἐπ᾽ ἀγαθῷ ποτε αὐτὸ κατοικισθησόμενον the reference cannot be to resettlement, and it can be so in i. 38. 2 only if we credit Thucydides with a conscious belief, which we meet for the first time in Plu. *QG* 11, that Eretrians preceded Corinthians at Kerkyra.

(iv) *Akragas*. The Eusebian tradition gives one date for the tyranny of Phalaris (571/566–) which is consistent with Thucydides' date for the foundation of Akragas, and another (652/649–625/4) which is not.

The existence of widely differing alternatives for some of the most important dates in Thucydides' list (cf. the difference between Diod. v. 9 and Eusebios on Lipara, which Thucydides does not date) is most easily explained as the consequence of different evaluations of the unit 'generation' (cf. van Compernolle, 63 ff., 219 ff., and 237 ff., on the tracing of different evaluations beneath the chronological traditions relating to Gyges, Carthage, and Sybaris) and, to a lesser extent, of the need, or at least the desire, to harmonize genealogies which interposed different numbers of generations between the same two events. It is unlikely that the correct sequence and absolute dates of the early colonies in Sicily will ever be settled, or the account given by Thucydides vindicated or refuted, by the finding of any kind of historical records dating from the eighth and seventh centuries, because the measure of disagreement among the Greek writers themselves suggests that there are no such records to find. We have, however, the inarticulate record (lucidly summarized by Bérard, 278 ff.—but no summary can remain up to date for very long) of the great quantity of Corinthian pottery which was imported over a long period by the colonies.

In the many discussions of the archaeological evidence since K. F. Johansen, *Les Vases sicyoniens* (Paris, 1923), and Humfry Payne, *Necrocorinthia* (Oxford, 1931) and *Protokorinthische Vasenmalerei* (Berlin, 1933), we have often been reminded that archaeological chronology depends ultimately on literary evidence and citation of the former as 'corroboration' of the latter is circular argument. These reminders do not always do justice to the conviction which internal coherence in archaeological chronology can (rightly) carry. In some respects the archaeologist, deprived of literary evidence and compelled to rely solely on stratification, associations, and his own judgement of the direction and pace of changes in painting and manufacture, is in a stronger position than the literary historian who is required (e.g.) to put the works of Plato in chronological order. Whereas the literary historian is bound to reckon with periods of intense literary productivity alternating with barren periods, the archaeologist, in assigning durations to stages in the development of a given type of pottery, can take account of the relative abundance of the graves, and the relative depths of the deposits, which yield each stage (cf. Vallet and Villard, *BIBR* xxix [1955], 200 n. 2). Moreover, Corinthian pottery is found on many sites associated with other fabrics, so that the coherence of any theory of its history must be reconcilable with equally coherent theories of the development of these other fabrics (cf. R. M. Cook, *Greek Painted Pottery* [London, 1960], 261 ff.).

The essential literary evidence to which Johansen and Payne attached importance was (i) the tradition (Strabo 243) that Kyme was the earliest Greek colony in the Central or Western Mediterranean, and (ii) the sequence in which Thucydides places Syracuse, Megara, Gela, and Selinus, and the intervals between them which he states or implies. On the evidence available it was apparent that no other sequence would be satisfactory, but the archaeological evidence established a certain claim to independence by failing to accord exactly with the intervals. For example, the round aryballos was found in abundance at Kyme, rarely at Syracuse, hardly at all at Megara, and not at all at Gela, which produced instead a few aryballoi in transition between the round and the ovoid types and an abundance of the ovoid (Johansen, 18 and 181 ff.; Payne, *Necrocorinthia*,

7). Selinus was believed (see below) to have yielded very little Late Protocorinthian or Transitional pottery but a greater amount of Early Ripe Corinthian (Payne, ibid. 22; for the terminology cf. Dunbabin, *JHS* lxviii [1948], 68). Yet, taking the material as a whole, it appeared that the interval between Syracuse and Selinus might have been rather greater than Thucydides suggests (Payne, loc. cit.; R. J. Hopper, *ABSA* xliv [1949], 177 ff.) and the interval between Megara and Gela rather smaller (Johansen, 182). Reconciliation of archaeological with literary evidence was partially achieved by adjusting the chronological relationship between Late Protocorinthian, Transitional, and Early Ripe Corinthian (Hopper, 180) and it is significant that this adjustment was defensible on archaeological grounds (Dunbabin, *Gnomon* xxv [1953], 245; K. Kübler, *Kerameikos*, vi/1 [Berlin, 1959], 110 and 120) without reference to the literary problem of Selinus. Recent excavation of Megara, Leontinoi, and Naxos has produced Late Geometric material, including (from Megara) a cup of a type comparable with that of *Perachora*, i. 55 f., pl. 12. 1–2; this is regarded by Vallet and Villard (*BCH* lxxvi [1952], 335 f., 340 and fig. 9b; cf. *Megara Hyblaea*, ii. 1 ff., pls. 1–3) as earlier than the earliest from Syracuse and thus as supporting Ephoros' date for Megara. That claim has been accepted firmly by A. W. Byvanck (*BVAB* xxxiv [1959], 70 f.). But the relative dating of the Megara cup, the Cycladic amphora from Syracuse illustrated in *BCH* lxxvi (1952), 330 fig. 7, and the fragments from Leontinoi (*NSA* 1955, 365 fig. 65. 14) and Naxos (*BA* 1964, 164, fig. 41) is clearly a delicate matter upon which more than one opinion may be held and abstention from opinion can be respected.[1] At Syracuse fresh deep excavation of Ortygia might produce helpful evidence; argument *ex silentio* is at least as perilous in archaeology as in any other historical study (cf. Pace, i. 169), especially when the silence, however impracticable it may be to try to break it at the moment, is not in principle unbreakable.

Selinus has set a problem of a different kind. Investigation of material from there stored at Palermo (J. Bovio-Marconi, *Ampurias* xii [1950], 79 ff., and M. T. Piraino, *Kokalos* iii [1957], 127 n. 16) has brought to light some notable Protocorinthian and Transitional pieces which, without invalidating any chronology based on Payne's equation of the Thucydidean date for Selinus with the beginning of Early Ripe Corinthian, cast doubt on 628 itself as the foundation-date and give a new plausibility to the non-Thucydidean date 651 (Vallet and Villard, *BCH* lxxxii [1958], 16 ff., and Cook, op. cit. 265).

It is important to recognize that from a purely historiographical point of view Thucydides' and Ephoros' dates for Megara are, and

---

[1] I have profited from discussion of this subject with Dr. J. N. Coldstream; the responsibility for any mis-statement is mine.

have always been, of equal validity. The fact that Thucydides was
a better historian than Ephoros (so that we like him better and
respect him more) is irrelevant, for on a question of foundation-
dates in the eighth and seventh centuries neither of them was necessarily following his own line of reasoning or fully apprised of the
reasoning which had been followed by others; and the first person
who took the essential step leading to the conclusion that Megara
was founded after Syracuse was not necessarily earlier or more
learned, intelligent, or fortunate than the first person who took the
essential step leading to the opposite conclusion. Priority in colonization being a matter of honour, it would be best simply to recognize
the existence of rival versions, one first known to us from Thucydides,
the other first known to us from Ephoros. It would be irrational
'loyalty' to Thucydides to pretend that his chronology of the Sicilian
colonies can command today the respect which it seemed to deserve
twenty years ago; it would be equally irrational to believe that in
twenty years time the case against his chronology will necessarily
be stronger. It may well be that archaeological evidence, as it
accumulates year by year from different sites (cf. Vallet and Villard, loc. cit. 24, on the relevance of the material from Marseilles,
and we may expect in due course the publication of the material
found on Pithekussai) will not, at any given moment, favour either
the Thucydidean or the Ephoran chronology with absolute con-
sistency.

2. 1. ᾠκίσθη δὲ ὧδε τὸ ἀρχαῖον: the archetype evidently had ἥδε
(*sic*). ἥδε (AEcfg) is objectionable in that (i) we need a forward-
looking demonstrative (cf. τοσάδε ἔθνη and vii. 57. 1 τοσοίδε), and
(ii) if τὸ ἀρχαῖον means 'in early times' it is vague. ὧδε (ψ) gives
perfect sense: 'its original colonization was as follows', i.e. 'I will
now describe . . .'. Cf. 4. 6 and X. *An.* i. 1. 6 ἦσαν - - - Τισσαφέρνους
τὸ ἀρχαῖον ('originally') ἐκ βασιλέως δεδομέναι. The *ratio corruptelae*
is θηδεωδε > θηδεηδε. Haacke's ἤδη and Classen's τῇδε need not be
considered seriously; the former because it is open to the same objections as ἥδε, the latter because τῇδε is not used by Thucydides
except in a locative sense.

καὶ τοσάδε ἔθνη ἔσχε τὰ ξύμπαντα: ἔθνη is probably the subject, sc.
'Sicily' as object; cf. i. 12. 3 Δωριῆς Πελοπόννησον ἔσχον and Antiochos
F 1 τὰς νήσους δὲ ἔσχον; but Stahl draws attention to S. *Ph.* 1147
ἔθνη θηρῶν οὓς ὅδ᾽ ἔχει χῶρος.

Κύκλωπες καὶ Λαιστρυγόνες: by Thucydides' time the peoples and
places of *Od.* ix–x were assumed to have existed in the West (cf.
Bérard, 312 ff.). The earliest indication of such a belief is Hes. fr. 150
(Merkelbach and West). 25 f. Αἴτν]ην παιπαλόεσσαν/[- - - Ὀ]ρτυγίην
Λαιστ[, and in *Th.* 1014 ff. Agrios and Latinos, descendants of Odysseus

and Kirke, rule over the Etruscans. Euripides placed the scene of *Kyklops* (date unknown) by Mt. Etna. Hekataios may possibly have located Skylla and Charybdis on the Straits of Messina, but Bérard is not justified in inferring (p. 312) from F 82 that he did.

2. ὡς δὲ ἡ ἀλήθεια εὑρίσκεται: cf. p. 199.

ἀπὸ τοῦ Σικανοῦ ποταμοῦ τοῦ ἐν Ἰβηρίᾳ ὑπὸ Λιγύων ἀναστάντες: Hekataios F 45 mentioned a town Sikane in Spain. Avienus iv. 379 ff. (Holder) *Sitana* (sic) *civitas propinquo ab amni sic vocata Hibericis*, placing it between Hemeroskopion and Tyris, evidently identified it with the Roman Sucro, the modern Jucar, of which the mouth lies some 40 km. south of Valencia. On the other hand, Servius on Verg. *A*. viii. 328 identified it with the Roman Sicoris, the modern Segre, a tributary of the Ebro. Thucydides' mention of Ligurians suggests that he himself thought of it as no further south than the Ebro. In Aischylos fr. 199 Λίγυς στρατός is used (if the interpretation of the pasage in Strabo 183 is correct) of a people which Herakles would encounter between Massalia and the Rhone. Hdt. v. 9. 3 speaks of Λίγυες οἱ ἄνω ὑπὲρ Μασσαλίης οἰκέοντες, and [Skylax] 2 f. (cf. [Skymnos] 200 ff.) describes the population from the Rhone to Ampurias as 'mixed Iberians and Ligurians', but nowhere is there any mention of Ligurians further south and west than that.

Σικανία: in *Od*. xxiv. 307 Σικανίη is mentioned without further explanation; Hdt. vii. 170. 1 accepts it as the name of Sicily in the time of 'Minos'.

πρότερον Τρινακρία καλουμένη: Θρινακίη νῆσος is where Odysseus' men ate the cattle of the Sun (*Od*. xi. 107). Thucydides is our first evidence for the name Τρινακρία; it would seem that when Θρινακίη had been identified with Sicily and the general shape of Sicily, with its three 'corners', had become known, Θρινακίη was believed to be a corruption or modification (cf. Strabo 265) of Τρινακρία, and the allegedly 'correct' name prevailed. Τρινακία in Η^γρ· ψ represents somebody's attempt at an intermediate stage (there is a comparable etymology in *An. Par*. iv. 183 Θριαί· ἐπεὶ τρίαι εἰσίν, οἷον τρισσαὶ κατὰ τὸν ἀριθμόν). The popular view did not, however, pass unchallenged; cf. Σ *A.R*. iv. 965 and Steph. Byz. s.v., who offers a derivation from θρῖναξ, an object which Sicily does not actually resemble. Cf. Freeman, i. 462 ff., Jacoby on Timaios F 37, and K. Ziegler in *RE* xiA. 601 ff.

3. Ἰλίου δὲ ἁλισκομένου - - - ἀφικνοῦνται: since the *Tabula Iliaca* (U. Mancuso, *MAL* xiv [1911], 662 ff.; cf. *PMG* 205) carries the subscription Ἰλίου πέρσις κατὰ Στησίχορον and labels one figure Αἰνείας ἀπαίρων εἰς Ἑσπερίαν, it is arguable that Stesichoros described Aineias not only as escaping from Troy (cf. *Il*. xx. 307 f.) but also as sailing to the West; but there is room for doubt on the fidelity of the *tabula*'s interpretation of Stesichoros (J. Vürtheim, *Stesichoros'*

Fragmente und Biographie [Leyden, 1919], 34 f.), and, as Mancuso says (720 f.), the fact that one of Aineias' companions in the *tabula* is 'Misenos' suggests a flight to Campania rather than to Sicily. With the exception of 'Stesichoros' it is not until Thucydides' own time that we encounter the legend of Trojan fugitives in the West. Whereas Antiochos F 6 speaks of Rome as existing before the Trojan War—and it is a fair inference, from the manner in which Dionysios refers to him on this question, that he was silent on any 're-foundation' by Trojans—Hellanikos F 84 recognizes Aineias as founder of Rome. Hellanikos F 31, a passage of Dionysios which tells the story of the foundation of Rome and ends with the words ὁ μὲν οὖν πιστότατος τῶν λόγων, ᾧ κέχρηται τῶν παλαιῶν ξυγγραφέων Ἑλλάνικος ἐν τοῖς Τρωϊκοῖς, περὶ τὴν Αἰνείου φυγὴν τοιόσδε ἐστί, mentions, as distinct from Aineias' party, ὅσοι σὺν Ἐλύμῳ καὶ Αἰγέστῳ (*sic*) ναυτικόν τι συνεσκευασμένοι ἔτυχον προεξεληλυθότες τῆς πόλεως.

Despite νικῶ = 'I have won', etc., and i. 23. 2 εἰσὶ δ᾽ αἳ καὶ οἰκήτορας μετέβαλον ἁλισκόμεναι, the translation '*during* the capture of Troy' is strongly supported by Hellanikos F 31. So too Hdt. i. 85. 3 ἁλισκομένου τοῦ τείχεος (taken as perfective in sense by Goodwin, *MT* § 27) may be translated 'during the capture of the citadel'.

πλοίοις goes with ἀφικνοῦνται, not with διαφυγόντες; there is a contrast between the sea-voyage of the Trojans and the landlubberly procedure of the Sikels.

ξύμπαντες μὲν Ἔλυμοι ἐκλήθησαν: cf. van Compernolle, *Phoibos* v (1950/1), 183 ff., for a full survey of ancient and modern opinion on the origin of the Elymians.

Φωκέων τινὲς τῶν ἀπὸ Τροίας: according to Strabo 254 Apollodoros (F 167) said that 'some say' that Philoktetes founded Chone, near Kroton, and that men from Chone 'with Aigestos the Trojan' founded Segesta. Philoktetes, Thessalian in *Il.* ii. 716 ff. and Malian in Sophokles, is nowhere in extant literature a Phokian, but Phokian participation in Western colonies of the heroic age is mentioned from the fourth century onwards. Metapontion is attributed by Ephoros F 141 to Daulios, tyrant of Krisa; Antiochos (F 12) at any rate believed that the Achaians who founded Metapontion in historical times were not the first to occupy the site; cf. Lykophron 930 ff., 1067 ff., on Lagaria and Temessa (F. Zucker, *WJA* iv [1949/50], 335 ff.). There is no reason to think the mention of a Phokian element in Sicily by Paus. v. 25. 6 independent of Thucydides. Kahrstedt, *WJA* ii (1947), 17, seems to think that Thucydides wrote Φωκαιῶν, which is impossible unless Thucydides held very unorthodox views on the date of the Ionian migration. Holm, i. 87, suggests that Thucydides erroneously gave the Phokians credit for the long voyages to the West which were the peculiar achievement of the

Phokaians later, but that does not explain why Thucydides should bring them to Sicily and to Segesta in particular. Incidentally, the detail ἐς Λιβύην πρῶτον cannot be the product of inference, as Segesta is on the north coast of Sicily; Segesta not being Greek, a poem of the Νόστοι genre is more likely as the ultimate source of Thucydides' statement than local tradition of the type exemplified in iv. 120. 1.

4. Σικελοὶ δ' ἐξ Ἰταλίας - - - φεύγοντες Ὀπικούς: the theory that the Sikels migrated from Italy was universally accepted in antiquity, e.g. by Hellanikos F 79a, Antiochos F 4, and Philistos F 46; Hellanikos and Philistos even offered dates, respectively 'in the third generation before the Trojan War, in the 26th year of Alkyone's office at Argos' and 'eighty years before the Trojan War'. Present archaeological evidence confirms that there was a disturbance in eastern Sicily, involving the obliteration of some earlier sites, at a period which on the basis of Mycenaean imports and artistic influences may be identified as the early thirteenth century B.C., though it was not accompanied by the extension to Sicily of any specifically Italic cultural features; cf. L. Bernabò Brea, *Sicily before the Greeks* (London, 1958), 135 f., 146 ff., 153, and 169. On Ὀπικούς cf. p. 201.

ὡς μὲν εἰκός: 'as was natural' or 'as one would expect' (sc. of a people which is not seafaring and of an occasion which, given favourable weather conditions, did not need real ships); cf. H. D. Westlake, *Hermes* lxxxvi (1958), 450 ff., on the use of this expression in Thucydides.

τηρήσαντες τὸν πορθμὸν κατιόντος τοῦ ἀνέμου: south, south-east, and east winds, such as would be needed for a safe crossing (north or north-east winds, which are common, might have driven the Sikel rafts on a route increasingly divergent from the coast of Sicily), are rare in the Straits of Messina, whereas the alternating north and south currents are complicated but predictable (*Sailing Directions for the Mediterranean* [U.S. Hydrographic Office, Washington, 1952], iii. 403 f.). Dion. Hal. *AR* i. 22. 1 φυλάξαντες κατιόντα τὸν ῥοῦν makes better sense than Thucydides, but that is not to say (as Vollgraff, *Mnemosyne* 1905, 422 f., says) that Thucydides must have written κατιόντος τοῦ ῥοῦ. Σ^recc· λήγοντος seems to be simply a misinterpretation of κατιόντος (the meaning of which is shown by ii. 84. 3), not a pointer to a different reading.

εἰσὶ δὲ καὶ νῦν ἔτι ἐν τῇ Ἰταλίᾳ Σικελοί: it would be interesting to know where.

Σικελῶν: the remarkable v.l. Ἀρκάδων (H₂ ψ) may be a slip of the mind, or it may represent the importation into Thucydides of an otherwise unattested theory.

5. τούς τε Σικανοὺς κρατοῦντες μάχῃ ἀνέστειλαν πρὸς τὰ μεσημβρινὰ καὶ ἑσπέρια αὐτῆς: cf. § 2. The boundary between the western (Sikan) and eastern (Sikel) cultures seems to have been well within the

eastern half of the island at the end of the eighth century, and to have retreated westwards during the seventh (Bernabò Brea, op. cit. 174 ff.; cf. Kahrstedt, loc. cit. 18 f.). Unless the material criteria are misleading as to political and linguistic divisions (as they may well be), the Sikan withdrawal before Sikel pressure was both a later and a slower process than Thucydides' words suggest.

ἀπέστειλαν (codd.) = 'pushed away' (ἀνέστειλαν Bekker; cf. Isoc. xii. 44) is curious, but seems at least to have stood in Dionysios' text of Thucydides, for his statement (AR i. 22. 2) that the Sikels settled in the west of Sicily is explicable only if he misinterpreted this passage of Thucydides, taking τοὺς Σικανούς as the object of κρατοῦντες alone and ἀπέστειλαν as intransitive, 'departed', as in (possibly) iii. 89. 5 and (certainly) D. xxxii. 5 (Dover, *Maia* N.S. vi [1953], 12 f.).

ἔτη ἐγγὺς τριακόσια πρὶν Ἕλληνας - - - ἐλθεῖν: cf. § 4 n. and pp. 201 and 203.

6. ἄκρας τε ἐπὶ τῇ θαλάσσῃ ἀπολαβόντες καὶ τὰ ἐπικείμενα νησίδια: if this is true, it is very surprising that no trace of Phoenician occupation has been revealed by excavation of Ortygia and Thapsos, for no sites would have suited the Phoenicians better (Dunbabin, 20 ff. and 326 f.). Thucydides has perhaps inferred from the situation as he knew it that Phoenician settlements of the same type as Motya must have existed throughout Sicily before the arrival of the Greeks; on the factors contributing to this (no doubt widely shared) belief cf. Pareti, *Archivio storico per la Sicilia orientale* x (1934), 14 ff. Possible Phoenician etymologies have been sought for place-names all over Sicily (Holm, i. 80 ff.), but must be treated with caution in view of our inability to exclude Sicilian aboriginal etymologies (Freeman, i. 244 ff. and 559 ff.), and for names which have a superficial resemblance to Semitic words.

Σολόεντα: the Phoenician site is actually at Cannito, not Solunto (*Archaeological Reports* 1963/4, 39); on Motya cf. ibid. 40 f.

3. 1. Χαλκιδῆς ἐξ Εὐβοίας πλεύσαντες μετὰ Θουκλέους οἰκιστοῦ Νάξον ᾤκισαν: from Chalkis and also from Aegean Naxos, according to Hellanikos F 82; Ephoros F 137 makes Thukles an Athenian (cf. the similar fate of Tyrtaios in the fourth century [Dover, *Entretiens Hardt* x (1963) 192 f.] and Homer in the second) and describes the colonists as 'Ionians'. Cf. van Compernolle, *BIBR* xxvi (1950/1) 163 ff., who points out the links between Aegean and Sicilian Naxos, notably the prominence which both gave on their coins to the cult of Dionysos.

καὶ Ἀπόλλωνος Ἀρχηγέτου βωμόν - - - ἱδρύσαντο: Apollo was called Archegetes (e.g. by Pindar, in connection with the dispatch of Battos to Cyrenaica, *P*. 5. 50) in so far as he enjoined or sanctioned colonizing enterprises through his oracle (perhaps not always the oracle at Delphi; cf. W. G. Forrest, *Historia* vi [1957], 173 n. 6). Accordingly, the cult of Apollo Archegetes was conspicuous in colonies; cf. Wernicke in *RE* ii. 44 and Jessen, ibid. 441 ff.

On ὅστις cf. p. 199. Since Naxos was obliterated by Dionysios I in the course of a campaign summarized by Diod. xiv. 15. 2 under the Attic year 403/2, the words 'outside the city' might be held relevant to the date of composition; but the location of the altar is the only point in which Thucydides is interested here, and 'the city' can just as well mean '⟨the site on which⟩ the city ⟨stood from its foundation until recently⟩' as 'the city ⟨which has been there since its foundation⟩'. Appian, *BC* v. 109 refers to Ἀρχηγέτης, Ἀπόλλωνος ἀγαλμάτιον which existed in Roman times and was believed to have been erected by the original colonists.

2. Ἀρχίας τῶν Ἡρακλειδῶν ἐκ Κορίνθου ᾤκισε: the aristocracy of Corinth, like other Dorian aristocracies, claimed descent from Herakles (cf. i. 24. 3, where Phalios, founder of Epidamnos, is γένος τῶν ἀφ' Ἡρακλέους) through Aletas (Ephoros F 18b; cf. Dunbabin, *JHS* lxviii [1948], 63); *MP* A 31 is eccentric in calling Archias 'tenth from Temenos' (cf. Jacoby ad loc.). In Plu. *Mor.* 772 c (cf. Diod. viii, fr. 10) the dispatch of Archias is the subject of a melodramatic story of uncertain age; cf. Andrewes, *CQ* xliii (1949), 70 ff.

ἐκ τῆς νήσου: i.e. Ortygia. Settlement on the mainland (ἡ ἔξω πόλις) was very early (cf. Dunbabin, 50 ff.); the connecting mole was certainly in existence by the last quarter of the sixth century, as Ibykos (*PMG* 321) refers to it (cf. Bowra, *Greek Lyric Poetry*, ed. 2 [Oxford, 1961], 243 f.).

4. 1. Λάμις: a curious name, for which Hγρ· offers Λαμπίας; emendation (e.g. Δᾶμις, suggested by Cobet, *Mnemosyne* 1886, 12) is unjustified, considering how many Greek names are 'un-Greek'. The one early Greek grave on Thapsos may be that of Lamis (Dunbabin, 19).

καὶ ὑπὲρ Παντακύου τε ποταμοῦ Τρώτιλόν τι ὄνομα χωρίον οἰκίσας: Vergil, *A*. iii. 688 ff. *uiuo praeteruehor ostia saxo / Pantagiae Megarosque sinus Thapsumque iacentem / ... iacet insula contra / Plemyrium undosum* implies that the 'Pantagias' lay north of Megara. Trotilon may be La Bruca, an inlet on the south shore of the bay of Catania (Dunbabin, 18).

τοῖς Χαλκιδεῦσιν - - - ξυμπολιτεύσας καὶ ὑπ' αὐτῶν ἐκπεσών: Blakeway, *ABSA* xxxiii (1932/3), 206, saw in this event an effect of hostility between Corinth and Megara and co-operation between Corinth and Chalkis. This reconstruction (cf. Forrest, loc. cit. [3. 1 n.], 160 ff.) rests on (i) friendly relations, attested by the importation of Corinthian pottery, between Corinth and the Chalkidean colonies in the West; (ii) the story that before Corinth colonized Kerkyra she expelled Eretrians from it (Plu. *QG* 11); the fact that when Kerkyra began to strike coins she used Euboic types on the Chalkidic standard is of less relevance now that the beginnings of coinage have been down-dated (P. Jacobsthal, *JHS* lxxi [1951], 85 ff., and E. S. G. Robinson, ibid. 156 ff.); (iii) the friendly relations between Corinth and Samos which Th. i. 13. 3 implies for the late eighth century; (iv) help given by Samos to Chalkis in 'the war against Eretria' (Hdt. v. 99. 1) and the exceedingly probable identification of this war with the ancient war between Chalkis and Eretria, in which 'the rest of the Greek world took sides', mentioned in Th. i. 15. 3, v. n. (I am not sure that the Hellenistic statement [Plu. *Mor*. 153 f and Σ Hes. *OD* 654] that Amphidamas of Chalkis, at whose funeral games Hesiod won a tripod, was killed in *this* war, is more than a combination of inferences); (v) identification of the border war in which Orsippos, a Megarian Olympic victor in 720, was killed (Paus. i. 44. 1) as a war against Corinth. The connection between the two great Euboean states and the West is now illuminated by identification of 'Cycladic' and 'Boeotian' pottery from the West as Euboean (J. Boardman, *ABSA* lii [1957], 1 ff. and 25). The 'Lelantine War' (cf. Strabo 448) and the alignment of states which took part in it are not a necessary hypothesis to account for a quarrel between two sets of Greeks living in the same city in Sicily (on Polyainos' story cf. p. 206), but there were, after all, many joint enterprises which did not break up; the chronological convergence of the evidence on the last quarter of the eighth century is impressive, and there is no need (cf. Jacoby, *CQ* xxxv [1941], 108 f.) to complicate the issue by citing Archilochos frr. 3 and 56.

καὶ Θάψον οἰκίσας: Thapsos is the very low-lying peninsula in the centre of the bay of Megara.

προδόντος τὴν χώραν: this seems to need fuller explanation (παραδόντος cj. Classen) and perhaps Thucydides forgot that the details of the story known to him (a ms. note of Gomme asks 'from Antiochos?') would not be known to his readers; cf. p. 199.

2. ὑπὸ Γέλωνος τυράννου Συρακοσίων ἀνέστησαν: Hdt. vii. 156. 2 gives more details; the παχεῖς became citizens of Syracuse, the δῆμος was sold into slavery.

ἔτεσιν ὕστερον ἑκατὸν ἢ αὐτοὺς οἰκίσαι: if the meaning is 'after they themselves had founded (sc. Megara)', the accusative αὐτούς is abnormal. Translate, therefore, 'after they had founded Megara itself' (M. Platnauer, *CR* xxxv [1921], 149), the ethnic Μεγαρεῖς being used, as well as Μέγαρα, for the name of the place, as in § 1; cf. 94. 1 n.

Πάμιλλον πέμψαντες Σελινοῦντα κτίζουσι, κ.τ.λ.: lit., 'sending Pammilos' (not 'Pamillos'; cf. Hdn. i. 162) 'they founded Selinus;

and coming from Megara, their mother-city, he founded it with them'. αὐτοῖς may go in sense with οὔσης or with ἐπελθών or with ξυγ-. But if the Sicilian Megarians 'sent' Pammilos, he was the οἰκιστής, even if he had previously come from their mother-city, and the οἰκιστής is not spoken of as 'helping' (ξυγ-) the nation which 'sends' him to found a colony; also, the expected connection would be ὅς or γάρ, not καί, though Krüger compares X. HG i. 7. 4 ἐπιστολὴν ἐπεδείκνυε μαρτύριον· καὶ (codd.: ἦν cj. Stephanus) ἔπεμψαν οἱ στρατηγοὶ κ.τ.λ. It is therefore probable, as ξυγ- suggests (cf. what happened at Zankle, § 5), that Pammilos came from Megara Hyblaia and that the name of a co-founder from the mother-city (who 'helped' Pammilos) has been lost (Stein); on the significance of κατ- cf. p. 207. J. Weidgen, RM lxxvi (1927), 368, attempts to solve the problem and at the same time remove the predicative article (which, however, does not need to be removed; cf. K–G i. 592) by substituting τις for τῆς.

3. Ἀντίφημος ἐκ Ῥόδου: Pace, 198, illustrates a cup dedicated to him in later times.

ἐποίκους ἀγαγόντες: in all but one of the twenty-three passages in which Thucydides uses the word ἄποικοι he is speaking of the origin of a community or of its relation to its mother-city; all six of his instances of ἔποικοι involve 'send', 'lead', etc., and are essentially about the place occupied rather than the mother-city; five of the six, too, concern colonization which replaced (ii. 27. 1, 70. 2, v. 5. 1, viii. 69. 3) a Greek population or renewed (iv. 102. 2) an earlier Greek attempt at settlement. It is argued by Wentker, MDAI(R) lxiii (1956), 130 f., that Thucydides' language here implies that there had been an earlier Rhodian settlement on the site of Gela; unfortunately v. 116. 4 τὸ δὲ χωρίον (sc. Melos) αὐτοὶ (sc. the Athenians) ᾤκισαν ἀποίκους ὕστερον πεντακοσίους πέμψαντες makes argument from terminology obviously precarious. The same people may be ἄποικοι or ἔποικοι according to the aspect under which they are regarded, as in English 'emigrant' and 'immigrant' (ATL iii. 285). Cf. Hdt. vii. 182 φεύγουσα ἐξοκέλλει - - - ὡς γὰρ δὴ τάχιστα ἐπώκειλαν τὴν νέα Ἀθηναῖοι - - - ἐκομίσθησαν ἐς Ἀθήνας.

ἀπὸ τοῦ Γέλα ποταμοῦ τοὔνομα ἐγένετο: Steph. Byz. s.v. says that γέλας (cf. Latin gelu) was the local word for πάχνη. Σᴱ (i.e. Tzetzes) has Stephanus's discussion in abbreviated form and attributes the etymology (wrongly, as we see from Stephanus) to Hellanikos.

νόμιμα δὲ Δωρικὰ ἐτέθη αὐτοῖς: Wentker, loc. cit. 131 ff., suggests that this remark has a particular point in that the Cretans, despite their dialect and some of their institutions, were not regarded as unambiguously Dorian (cf. Konon, FGrHist 26 F 1. 36, on the foundation of Gortyn). He adds that 'Gela' is a 'neutral' name (see above) lacking associations with any Aegean traditions, and compares

vii. 57. 9, where nothing is said of the 'race' of the Cretans in the Athenian force; that passage, however, proves nothing, since the point 'Dorians versus Dorians' is suppressed when the point 'mother-city versus colony' is made, as in the case of Megara in the preceding section.

5. Ζάγκλη δέ - - - ἀπὸ Κύμης - - - λῃστῶν ἀφικομένων ᾠκίσθη: on the foundation of Zankle cf. G. Vallet, *Rhégion et Zancle* (Paris, 1958), 59 ff. Ephoros, if he is the source of [Skymnos] 238 ff. and of Strabo 268, eliminated the raiders from Kyme and made Zankle a colony of Naxos; Paus. iv. 23. 7, where Krataimenes is called a Samian and the Messenians play the part which Thucydides and Herodotos give to the Samians, represents a conflation of this section with § 6 (see note).

Περιήρης καὶ Κραταιμένης: cf. Callim. fr. 43. 58 ff., who relates that the inhabitants invoke a founder without naming him, on the instructions of the Delphic oracle, since they could not agree on whether Perieres or Krataimenes should be honoured the more.

ὄνομα δέ - - - Ζάγκλη ἦν - - - κληθεῖσα: the name is δανκλε on the city's coins, Ζάγκλη in literature. Callim. loc. cit. 70 f. connects the name with the sickle which, after being used by Kronos to castrate Uranos, fell to earth and lay hidden; Timaios F 79 tells the same story of 'Drepane' = Kerkyra.

ὕστερον δ' αὐτοὶ μὲν ὑπὸ Σαμίων καὶ ἄλλων Ἰώνων ἐκπίπτουσιν: according to Hdt. vi. 22–4 the Samians sailed westwards, on the invitation of Zankle, to take part in the foundation of a colony at Kale Akte, but were persuaded by Anaxilas, tyrant of Rhegion, to seize Zankle itself (cf. van Compernolle, 281 ff.).

6. Ἀναξίλας Ῥηγίνων τύραννος - - - Μεσσήνην - - - ἀντωνόμασεν: Herodotos says nothing of this, but mentions the change of name in another connection, vii. 164. 1. The coins are instructive. We can distinguish (i) the first issues of Rhegion, on the Euboic–Chalkidic standard, with a human-headed bull type and the legend ρεγινον, (ii) the first issues of Zankle, on the same standard, with a dolphin type and the legend δανκλε, (iii) the issues of the Samians at Zankle, still on the Euboic–Chalkidic standard, with a lion's head obverse and a calf's head reverse, the legend being sometimes ρεγινον and sometimes μεσσενιον, (iv) the second issues of Anaxilas, now on the Euboic–Attic standard, with mule-car obverse and hare reverse, again stamped either ρεγινον or μεσσενιον (-σα-). Cf. E. S. G. Robinson, *JHS* lxvi (1946), 13 ff., and Vallet, op. cit. (§ 5 n.) 337 ff.

Strabo 268 and Paus. iv. 23. 6 ff. both associate the change of name with the importation of Messenians from the Peloponnese. Strabo gives no indication of date; Pausanias represents the Messenians as invited by Anaxilas, but dates the event absurdly to Ol. 29. 1, i.e. 664/3. This reflects a conflation, in his source, of one tradition associating the Messenian leader Aristomenes with a Messenian War in the seventh century and a second tradition (elaborated by Rhianos) associating him with the Messenian War which according to Plato (*Lg.* 698 d–e) restricted Sparta's freedom of action at the time of Marathon (Jacoby, IIIa. 131 ff.). Whatever the measure of truth in Plato's story (cf. L. H. Jeffery, *JHS* lxix [1949], 26 ff., for discussion of some archaeological evidence which tells somewhat against the scepticism of Jacoby, loc. cit. 109 ff. and 169 ff.) it is important that Thucydides gives a different reason for the change of Zankle's name (Jacoby, 172). Anaxilas' sentiment was shared by his henchman Mikythos (Hdt. vii. 170. 4), who later, in exile at Tegea, described himself in his dedications at Olympia as both Rhegine and Messenian (Paus. v. 26. 5, cf. *DGE³* 794).

αὐτοῖς (codd.: αὐτός Dobree) may be right, as an unemphatic possessive, the dative being used instead of the genitive because of the adjacent genitive ξυμμείκτων ἀνθρώπων; cf. 18. 6, vii. 71. 5, and (gen. for acc.) v. 33. 1.

5. 1. καὶ Ἱμέρα ἀπὸ Ζάγκλης ᾠκίσθη: cf. Vallet, op. cit. 85 ff.

οἱ Μυλητίδαι καλούμενοι: either a family group (cf. Πεισιστρατίδαι, etc.; Μύλης, stem Μυλητ-, is found as the name of a mythical Lakonian in Paus. iii. 1. 1) or a class name or gentile name (cf. εὐπατρίδαι and Πραξιεργίδαι) of unknown etymology. Strabo 272 seems to have misunderstood the situation in saying that Himera was colonized by men from Mylai, another Zanklean colony; cf. Freeman, i. 411 n. 3.

καὶ φωνὴ μέν - - - ἐκράθη: the inscriptions of Himera, so far as they go (*SGDI* 3247–51) preserve ᾱ.

3. ἀναστάτων δὲ Καμαριναίων γενομένων πολέμῳ ὑπὸ Συρακοσίων δι᾽ ἀπόστασιν: Thucydides implies (cf. τὴν γῆν below) that Kamarina was totally destroyed on this occasion (which Σ Pi. *O.* 5 dates to 552–49), but excavation of the site shows that it was not (Dunbabin, 106 f.). Hdt. vii. 154–6 relates that Kamarina (he does not say 'the land' or 'the site' of Kamarina) was awarded to Hippokrates of Gela by Corinthian and Kerkyrean arbitrators in the war between Hippokrates and Syracuse (493 or 492), and that it was depopulated by Gelon (cf. van Compernolle, 303 ff.). He does not mention the early depopulation by Syracuse or the rejection of 'colonial' status implied by the word ἀπόστασις.

ὑπὸ Γελῴων: stylistically and historically a necessary correction (by Dodwell) of ὑπὸ Γέλωνος (codd.). Diod. xi. 76. 5 places the refounding of Kamarina by 'the Geloans' under 461/60, long after Gelon's death. Pi. *O.* 5. 9, written in 452 (or, if not genuine, as if for a victory which was won in 452), calls Kamarina τὰν νέοικον ἕδραν.

6. The Segestan Embassy at Athens

6. 1. τῇ ἀληθεστάτῃ προφάσει: on this expression cf. i. 23. 6 n.,
L. Pearson, *TAPhA* lxxxiii (1952), 205 ff., and G. M. Kirkwood,
AJPh lxxiii (1952), 37 ff.

τοῖς ἑαυτῶν ξυγγενέσι: in view of 8. 2, where the εὐπρέπεια (cf. viii.
66. 1) of the Athenian plan is expressed in the decision actually
taken, it seems that 'their own kin' means Leontinoi and 'their
allies' primarily Segesta. No other 'kinsmen' or 'allies' were ostensibly in need of help at this time. Leontinoi was Ionian (3. 3). The
sentiments attached to community of ancestry and dialect were
normally taken into account in the language of diplomacy, as were
traditional enmities between Ionians and Dorians (80. 3, 82. 2, vii.
5. 4). They were naturally vulnerable to attack as merely formal
and specious (e.g. 76. 2), but they were not without influence, cf.
vii. 57 f. n. Leontinoi had been depopulated by Syracuse in 422,
but some of its former inhabitants maintained resistance from bases
within its old territory (v. 4. 2 ff.).

καὶ τοῖς προσγεγενημένοις ξυμμάχοις: προ- (EGM) and προσ- (cett.)
exemplify a universal uncertainty in the transmission of these prefixes in prose texts; cf. 18. 5, 31. 5, 40. 1, 90. 3. If προ- is right here,
the reference is to the fact that, unlike some states who might become allies of Athens after the present issue had arisen, Segesta
entered into alliance in the middle of the fifth century (*IG* i². 19
= ML 37, *SEG* x. 7, xiv. 1). If προσ- is right, the meaning is either
(i) 'those who had *also* become her allies', sc. in addition to those
whose claim rested on kinship, or (ii) 'those who had accrued to her as
allies', i.e. whose strength was added to her own, cf. 90. 3. The latter
interpretation is tautological, since allies necessarily 'accrue'; the
former is possible, but it is προ-, not προσ-, which gives most point
to εὐπρεπῶς and to the contrast between overt propriety and covert
aggression. Diod. xii. 83. 3 τῶν Λεοντίνων τὴν συγγένειαν προφερομένων
καὶ τὴν προϋπάρχουσαν συμμαχίαν *may* give additional support to προ-.

2. Ἐγεσταίων [τε] πρέσβεις: the only defence of τε (om. Cantabrigiensis 2629) is the supposition (Müller) that Thucydides had it in
mind to continue (e.g.) καὶ οἱ ξυναγορεύοντες but embarked on a vast
parenthesis (ὅμοροι γὰρ ὄντες, κ.τ.λ.), eventually abandoned the
sentence which he had begun, and betrayed his conception only by
the words τῶν τε Ἐγεσταίων πολλάκις λεγόντων καὶ τῶν ξυναγορευόντων
αὐτοῖς in § 3. Rather than suppose this degree of incoherence, we
may prefer to omit τε, emend it to τότε (Stein), or transpose it to
follow παρόντες (Steup); v. 10. 9, cited by Herbst, 12 f. in defence of
τε, is not comparable.

περί τε γαμικῶν τινων: ἐπιγαμία, the choosing of a wife from another
state without thereby depriving one's children of citizen rights, was

a subject of interstate agreement (Arist. *Pol.* 1280^b15, cf. Busolt–Swoboda, i. 223 n. 2 and Thalheim, *RE* s.v.) and therefore, on occasion, of inter-state disputes; but we know no more of this aspect of the quarrel between Segesta and Selinus.

καὶ περὶ γῆς ἀμφισβητήτου: Diod. xii. 82. 3 ff. offers a few more details, and adds surprisingly (82. 7) that Segesta looked for help first to Akragas and Syracuse, then to Carthage.

τὴν γενομένην ἐπὶ Λάχητος καὶ τοῦ προτέρου πολέμου Λεοντίνων οἱ Ἐγεσταῖοι ξυμμαχίαν ἀναμιμνήσκοντες τοὺς Ἀθηναίους: πόλεμος *c. gen.* means 'war against' or 'war conducted by' (e.g. i. 32. 4);[1] from the standpoint of Segesta or Athens, the Sicilian war of 427 was a war about Leontinoi, but not πόλεμος Λεοντίνων. ξυμμαχία Λεοντίνων, however, is straightforward Greek for 'alliance with Leontinoi', cf. 2. 6, 33. 2, and Bétant s.v. (not LSJ). The Segestans therefore reminded Athens not of the alliance which Athens had made with Segesta, but of the alliance which she had made with Leontinoi. Thucydides comments implicitly on the unusualness of this procedure by disrupting the complex τὴν γενομένην - - - ξυμμαχίαν in order to juxtapose Λεοντίνων and οἱ Ἐγεσταῖοι; 24. 3 τῆς ἀπούσης πόθῳ ὄψεως has a certain similarity, but is less remarkable. Thucydides has told us nothing of an Athenian alliance with Leontinoi made during Laches' period of command in Sicily, and the extant renewal (*IG* i². 52 = ML 64, *SEG* x. 48, cf. iii. 86. 3 n.) of the original treaty is securely dated to 433/2. This does not, however, create serious difficulty, for (i) frequent renewal of Greek treaties was common (e.g. D. xxiii. 172); (ii) if the treaty was renewed by Laches, it could be described as γενομένην, just as the renewal of 433/2 is described on the stone in the words τὲγ χσυμμαχίαν ἐποέσαντο (observed by Gomme, ms. note), since γενέσθαι serves as the passive of ποιήσασθαι; (iii) alternatively, τὴν γενομένην Λεοντίνων ξυμμαχίαν might mean not 'the act of alliance which was made' but 'the fighting-on-the-same-side which occurred'; ξυμμαχία in 80. 1 probably means something like this (see note), and it may do so in 34. 1. Schwartz, 288 f., comes close to this second interpretation in suggesting that Λεοντίνων ξυμμαχία means the combination of states of which Leontinoi was, as it were, the focus, comparing iii. 86. 3 οἱ τῶν Λεοντίνων ξύμμαχοι, which obviously includes Leontinoi herself (as οἱ ἀμφὶ Περικλέα includes Perikles) but is not equivalent to Λεοντῖνοι καὶ οἱ ξύμμαχοι = 'the alliance headed by Leontinoi'.

καὶ τοὺς λοιποὺς ἔτι ξυμμάχους αὐτῶν διαφθείροντες: αὐτῶν cannot refer to Segesta, since we should expect σφῶν, and even in the mouth of a Segestan the suggestion that destruction of the allies of Segesta would give Syracuse the mastery of Sicily would be curious.

---

[1] I was wrong to add (*PCPhS* clxxxiii [1953/4], 4) 'from the standpoint of the opposing party'; cf. E. Roos, *Opusc. Ath.* iv (1961), 14.

The nearest reference for αὐτῶν is Leontinoi, but αὐτ- takes its reference from the sense of the context, and does not always refer to the nearest noun; cf. 73. 2, vii. 25. 9, And. iii. 26. Since in the final recommendation given by the envoys, σῶφρον δ' εἶναι μετὰ τῶν ὑπολοίπων ἔτι ξυμμάχων ἀντέχειν τοῖς Συρακοσίοις, it is action by Athens which is recommended, 'the allies still remaining' must there mean allies of Athens; and this creates a presumption that τοὺς λοιποὺς ἔτι ξυμμάχους αὐτῶν has the same reference, so that αὐτῶν will be the Athenians. (The fact that the Athenians are ἐκείνων in καὶ τὴν ἐκείνων δύναμιν is no obstacle; cf. v. 30. 3, Pl. *Euthyphro* 14 d.)

3. πέμψαι: so H₂; πέμψαντες (cett.) would be acceptable only if we supposed that an infinitive is lost from the text.

7. *Operations in Greece and Macedonia*

7. 1. πλὴν Κορινθίων: although the Corinthians were represented in Agis' army in the Mantineia campaign (v. 57. 2), they took no part in his attack on Argos in the following year (v. 83. 1 n.). These abstentions may possibly reflect their dissatisfaction with Spartan leadership.

καὶ σῖτον ἀνεκομίσαντό τινα ζεύγη κομίσαντες: the word-order and the absence of the neuter plural τινα elsewhere in Thucydides show that τινα goes with σῖτον: 'they brought in wagons and brought home some corn'. The repetition of (-)κομισ- arouses suspicion, but cf. Pl. *Prt.* 328 e ὅ - - - ῥᾳδίως ἐπεκδιδάξει, ἐπειδὴ καὶ τὰ πολλὰ ταῦτα ἐξεδίδαξε. As it is winter, the Peloponnesians are carrying off stored grain, and their 'ravaging of the land' is destruction of buildings, vineyards, and trees (Gomme, ms. note).

ἐς Ὀρνεάς: Orneai was an ally of Argos in 418 (v. 67. 2 n.); presumably Sparta retained control of it after the democratic revolution in Argos had dislodged Spartan control of Argos itself in 417.

2. οὐ πολλῷ ὕστερον: Thucydides does not indicate whether this was after the expiry of the period for which the truce was made or a violation of the truce.

πανστρατιᾷ ἐξελθόντες: H₂ ψ (cj. F. Portus cl. *egressi* Valla). πανστρατιᾷ ἐξελθόντων (cett.) could only refer to the Athenians, and the sense forbids that. Although Thucydides sometimes (e.g. v. 33. 1) uses a genitive absolute where he might have made the participle agree with an expressed noun or pronoun, there is no parallel for Ἀργεῖοι - - - ἐξελθόντων (sc. Ἀργείων) - - - ἐπολιόρκουν; on v. 33. 1 cf. 4. 6 n. The reference to 'being killed at Orneai' in Ar. *Av.* 399 merely confirms that Athenian troops had been involved in fighting there before 414; it tells us nothing else.

3. ἐς Μεθώνην τὴν ὅμορον Μακεδονίᾳ: Methone, which lay just north of Pydna and *c.* 10 km. south of the mouth of the Haliakmon (the other Methone is distinguished as τῆς Λακωνικῆς in ii. 25. 1), had become a tributary ally of Athens by 432/1 (*ATL* list 23. II. 67 ~ 26. II. 53; cf. iii. 136), was treated indulgently and protected against the tentative aggressions of Perdikkas (*IG* i². 57 = *ATL* D3–6), and was loyal in 423 (iv. 129. 4).

ἱππέας - - - σφῶν τε αὐτῶν καὶ Μακεδόνων τοὺς παρὰ σφίσι φυγάδας: it is possible that the Macedonian exiles were all cavalry, in which case the analysis of the sentence is: 'cavalry, (*a*) Athenian, and (*b*) Macedonian, viz. the exiles'. But in co-ordinations of the type (A B) + (C D) the first of the co-ordinating particles may accompany B, not A, when there is an important antithesis between B and some part of the (C D) clause; cf. 14, 15. 2, 18. 1, 24. 1, 63. 2, 94. 2, *IG* ii². 1264. 4 ff. ἐπεμελήθησαν - - - ὅπως ἂν οἱ ἱππεῖς τόν τε σῖτον κομίσωνται - - - καὶ τἆλλα πάντα διατελοῦσι πράττοντες, and Lüdtke, 7 f., 11, 33.

ἐκακούργουν τὴν Περδίκκου: in 421 Perdikkas had been in alliance with Athens (v. 6. 2); in 417 he had been persuaded by the Spartans to abandon this alliance (v. 80. 2), and an Athenian fleet blockaded Macedonia in the winter of 417/16 (v. 83. 4).

4. παρὰ Χαλκιδέας - - - ἄγοντας πρὸς Ἀθηναίους δεχημέρους σπονδάς: Chalkidike, seduced from its allegiance to Athens by Perdikkas and Brasidas, never returned to it, despite the provisions of the peace treaty (v. 21. 2, 26. 2, 35. 3 ff.). On 'ten-day truce' cf. v. 23. 1, 26. 2 nn.

YEAR 17: 415–414 B.C. (CC. 8–93)

8. 1–2. *First Assembly and Appointment of Generals*

The decision to send a fleet to Sicily and to put Alkibiades, Nikias, and Lamachos in command of it was taken at an assembly (8. 2) which we will call '*A*'. Four days later (8. 3) assembly '*B*' was held for the purpose of making more detailed provisions. At that assembly the original issue, whether to go to Sicily or not, was thrashed out afresh (9–24). The outcome (25–26. 1) was a decision to empower the generals to raise what forces and material they thought necessary. We know from And. i. 11 that there was at least one further assembly τοῖς στρατηγοῖς 'when Lamachos' flagship was already anchored outside the harbour', and we should expect that there was more than one opportunity for the generals to report progress; the series of assemblies required for this purpose we shall call collectively '*C*'.

Additional information about the assemblies may be gathered from literary and epigraphic sources. Ar. *Lys.* 387 ff. show that the

Adonia coincided with one assembly, but does not tell us with which, since

$$\ἔλεγε\ δ'\ - - - Δημόστρατος$$
$$πλεῖν\ ἐς\ Σικελίαν\ - - -$$
$$- - - ὁ\ δὲ\ Δημόστρατος$$
$$ἔλεγεν\ ὁπλίτας\ καταλέγειν\ Ζακυνθίους$$

would be a natural way of saying in verse what might be more precisely expressed in prose: 'Demostratos proposed, in the course of a debate about the implementation of the decision to sail to Sicily, the enrolment of hoplites from Zakynthos.' πλεῖν ἐς Σικελίαν is, as it were, the μέν-clause which re-states what is taken for granted. Plu. *Alc.* 18. 3 and *Nic.* 12. 6 add nothing except the identification of Thucydides' τις τῶν Ἀθηναίων (25. 1) as Demostratos, whom Plutarch also treats as the author of the decree summarized in 26. 1; this information may be only an inference from Aristophanes (Eupolis frr. 96–7 give a comic poet's characteristic view of Demostratos' forensic eminence a few years later).

Plutarch's treatment of Nikias as 'first' general, Alkibiades as 'second', and Lamachos as 'third' (*Nic.* 12. 4, 15. 1, 3, *Alc.* 18. 1 f.) reflects the Hellenistic writers' tendency to translate collegiate command into terms of subordination (cf. Dover, *JHS* lxxx [1960], 73) and in any case contradicts his treatment of Alkibiades as 'first' general in *Nic.* 14. 4. Nothing in Thucydides' narrative suggests that any one of the three generals was superior in status to the others, and there is much (e.g. 47 ff., 50. 1) irreconcilable with such a supposition. Both Thucydides and the composer of *IG* i². 302 (= ML 77). 49 ff.[1] name Alkibiades first—naturally enough, since he was the chief proponent of the expedition—but they differ in the order of the other two.

The fragmentary inscriptions collected in *IG* i². 98/99 (= ML 78) must refer to the Sicilian expedition. They mention 'the departure of sixty ships' and 'sixty ships' again, one of them contains detailed provisions for the recruitment and payment of different categories of troops, and another requires the assembly to decide whether one general or more than one should be appointed. The script and spelling of these fragments are consistent with the date 416/15.

An interior join between fragments *d* and *g* is physically possible and is positively indicated by the sense resulting from the join. There are no grounds of configuration or sense to justify the joining of *a* and *f* (as is done by Kirchner in *IG* i²) or of any other fragments. Part of the top of *a*, the right margins of *b*, *f*, and *g*, and the left margin of *c* are preserved. *c* and *d* + *g* must belong to different stelae ('stele

---

[1] Meritt's numeration, in all references to this inscription.

I' and 'stele II' below), since *c*, which has a small portion of a smooth back preserved, is 130 mm. thick, whereas *g*, with no trace of a smooth back, is 138 mm. thick. No other fragment exceeds 130 mm. in thickness, and in none can any trace of a smooth back be discerned. If Kirchhoff's supplementation of line 1 of fragment *a* is correct (and alternative possibilities imply a line of extraordinary length), *a* can hardly have had less than 60 letters a line. It must be remembered that the document is of unfamiliar type, and supplementation by reference to formulas does not take us very far.

The text given below is what I read on the fragments when I examined them in Athens in 1963. In the apparatus criticus Kh = Kirchhoff (in *IG* i); Kn = Kirchner (in *IG* i²); L = information given to me by D. M. Lewis after he had examined the fragments in 1953 (he was the first to observe the relative thickness of *c* and *g*); P = his readings of the squeezes at Princeton in 1965; O = my readings from the squeezes in the Ashmolean Museum, Oxford:

Assembly A. Fragment *b* (stele unidentified) requires the assembly to decide whether to appoint one general or more. The context of its mention of sixty ships is not clear, and the mention is therefore compatible with the hypothesis that the original proposal to send a force of this size was contained in the lost text above *b*. The decree presumably ended by recording the assembly's decision on the generals and the names of those appointed; so *IG* ii². 43 (= *GHI* 123), of 377, includes the provision (72 ff.) 'elect ambassadors' and ends (75 ff.) with 'the following were elected . . .'.

[- - - - - - - - - - -]ναν[..4..]ν[.....10.....]νι[..4..]οιο[..5...]
[- διαχεροτονεͅσαι τὸν δεͅμ]ον αὐτίͅκα μάλα εἴτε δοκεῖ ἑνα στρατ[εͅγ]
[ὸν - - - - - - - - - - - h]ελέσθαι τύχεͅι ἀγαθεͅι νυνὶ hοίτινε[ς] α̣
[- - - - - - - - - - - - -]τͅο[.] τὸς πολεμίος hōς ἂν δύνōνται πλει
[στ - - - - - - - - - - -]ὀͅσθὸν δὲ καὶ τὸν χσυμμάχο̄ν hοποͅσ̣   5
[- - - - - - - - - - - - π]όλες ἐς τεͅμ βολεͅν τεͅν Ἀθēναίο̄[ν]
[- - - - - - - - - - - - h]εͅχσέκοντα νεō̄ν hόταμπερ[...]
[- - - - - - - - - - -]αις ᾀμ βόλō̄ντ[αι....9.....]
[- - - - - - - - - - -]λλο[........16........]

1 fort.]νͅτ[. . . .]οͅτο[·2–3 suppl. Kh   3 fort. [ὸν εἴτε πλείος supplendum]hελέσθαι LO   5 suppl. Kh   ]ὀͅσθὸν O   6]πόλες Köhler ap. Kh   7 hόταμ[LO   8 suppl. Kh

The fact that a proposal to entrust an expedition of such magnitude and importance to a single general was seriously entertained is the most interesting contribution to our knowledge offered by any of these fragments. The individual envisaged was presumably Alkibiades; cf. 15 n. and Wentker, 136 ff., 183 n. 510.

Assembly A or B. Fragment *c* (stele I) makes provision for finance, the holding of assemblies in the future, and the 'correction' of some provision made now or earlier. *B* is the most likely occasion, but neither *A* nor even an early stage of *C* can be ruled out.

[. . .] βολὲν καθότι ἄριστα ϙ[- - - - - - ἐά]
ν τε ἀπὸ τô τιμέματος δοκêι [- - - - - - ἐάν]
τε τὲμ πόλιν ἀναλôν hόσον a[- - - - - - τὰ]
ϛ hεϙσέκοντα ναῦς ἐὰμ προσ[- - - - - -]
μενον êι ἐσφέρεν hόταν δεε[- - - - - - ἐκκ]   5
λεσίαν ποιεσάντōν δέκα hε[μερôν - - - - π]
ερὶ ἄλλο μεδενὸς πρότερον [- - - - - -]
ε ἐκκλεσίαν ποιêν τὸς πρυτ[άνες - - - - - -]
αι τοῖς στρατεγοῖς τὸν νεôν [- - - - - -]
οις· περὶ δὲ τô ἔκπλο τôν νεôν [- - - - - - ἐ̂]   10
πανορθôσθαι ἐν τôι δέμōι ho[- - - - - - ἐ̂]
κκλεσίαν ποιόντōν hόταν κε[- - - - - -]
ον καὶ τês ἄλλēς hυπēρεσίας [- - - - - -]
καὶ ἀργυρίο ἐς καλλιέρεσιν [- - - - - -]
[.] hεϙϲακοϙίōν [καὶ] χιλίōν [- - - - - -]   15

1–3 suppl. Kh   1 καθοτι P et ϙ[OP   5–6, 8, 10–11 suppl. Kh
15 χιλίōν h[L: χιλίōν hο[πλιτôν Kh

Assembly C (i) Fragment *a* (stele unidentified) makes detailed provisions which cannot have been made until the generals had delivered some report on their progress and their needs.

[ἔδοχϲεν τêι βολêι καὶ τôι δ]έμōι [- - - - - -
[- - - - - - 20 - - - - - - - εἰ̂]πε. τύχε̄[ι ἀγαθêι - - - - - -
[- - - - - - 22 - - - - - - - -]μένας μισ[θ - - - - - -
[- - - - - - 21 - - - - - - - τ]ετταράκον[τα - - - - - -
[- - - - - - 19 - - - - - - πελ]τάσταις χρ[- - - - - -   5
[- - - - - - 22 - - - - - - - τ]οχϲότας π[- - - - - -
[- - - - - - 23 - - - - - - - -]δεει ἐκ το[- - - - - -
[- - - - - - 21 - - - - - - τ]έτταρας ὀβο[λὸς - - - - - -
[- - - - - - 17 - - - - -κυβε]ρνέτας δὲ καὶ [- - - - - -
[- - - - - - 19 - - - - - - τ]αμίαν δὲ χϲυμπ[- - - - - -
[- - - - - - 20 - - - - - -] hē̄ βολὲ hόταμ με[- - - - - -   10
[- - - - - - 16 - - - τοῖ]ς τριεράρχοις κα[- - - - - -
[- - - - - - 21 - - - - - - - -]τομ πολεμιον λ[- - - - - -
[- - - - - - 21 - - - - - - - - -]λον hότι αν[- - - - - -

1–6 suppl. Kh   7 τοϙ[O   8 suppl. Kh   11 με[O   12 suppl. Kh
13]τομ L   λ[P   14]λλον O

(ii) Fragments *d* + *g* (stele II) repeal an earlier decree, and for that reason are unlikely to belong to *A* or *B*.

226

[-]το[. . 5 . . .
[-]σοτοντ[.]
[- - - - - -]αι ἒ φρορο̂σι τὲ[μ πόλιν ἒ τὲ]ν χόραν τ
[- - - - - -]ν hὸς ἂν μὲ περιπο[λε̂ι μεδὲ μ]ισθοφορε̄̂
[ι - - - - - -]το πλὲν hοπόσοις [. . . 7 . . . .h]ε̄̂ βολὲ καὶ   5
[- - - - - - - ἔ]νοχον ἒναι ζεμία[ι . . . 6 . . .]αι μέτε τον
[- - - - - - - πρ]υτάνες· λῦσαι δὲ [. . . 7 . . . .]αι τὸ φσέφι
[σμα - - - - - τ]ο̂ ἔκπλο τὸν ἐχσέ[κοντα νεὂ]ν hέὸς ἂν h
[- - - - - - - ἐ]π’ ἄλλο ἔργον με̄̂[δ’ ἐπ’ ἄλλε̄ν σ]τρατιὰν
[- - - - - - - τ]ρισχιλίο̄ν. ἐ[ὰν δέ τις εἴπε̄ι] ἒ ἐπιφσ   10
[ε̄φίσε̄ι - - -]ς ἐχσαιρ[. . . . . . .14. . . . . . .]ον μ[.]
[- - - - - - - λ]ογιϛ[. . . . . .20. . . . .]

1]ιο[fort. recte Kh   3 τ]ὲν O   3–4 suppl. Kh   5]στο LO:
]ετο Kh   ἂν[Kh: ἂ[ν Kn   6]ένοχον Kh suppl. Kh   7 π]ρυτάνες LO
7–8 suppl. Kn   9]στρατιαν L   9–11 suppl. Kn   11]ς Kh:]ε ?
στό]λον Kh   12 suppl. tent. Meritt (per epist.):]ογιτ[L: equidem cum
sigma desiderem, tau potius vestigiis congruere confiteor

Occasion unknown. The remaining fragments (the stele is in each
case unidentifiable) cannot be assigned to one assembly or another:

Fragment *e*.   ]μο[
                                      ]τε̄ι Ἀθε̄̂νᾶι κ[
                                   στρα]τιόταις διανε[μ
                                      ]εναι τὸν νεὸν [
                                      ]ρχσοσι[5

1]μο[Kh:]ιο[P   2 τε̄ι Ἀθε̄ναίαι perperam Kh   3 suppl. Kh
5]ά̣ρχσὸσι[Kh: sed (e.g.) (-)φ]ά̣ρχσοσι[suppleri potest

Fragment *f*.   ]τεγϙ[. . . 7 . . . .]
                                   hεκ]ατὸν τριέρε̣[ς.]
                                   ] πολεμιοι hότι
                                   ]α̣στέσασθαι το
                                   ἐπιτ]έδειον ἒναι h   5
                                   ]αμ ποι χρεσ
                                   ]ς ναυσὶν
                                   πρυ]τανε
                                   ]ντ

1 κ[P   2 suppl. Kn   5]τε̄̂δειον LO   8 suppl. Kn

Fragment *h*.   ]αν[
                                      ]ιτοι̣[
                                   ]ος χσυμμάχος α[
                                   ]ς κ[αὶ] τομ φορον [
                                   ]σθαι τ[5
                                   ]ο̣ε̣[

4]ις κ[αὶ] Kn   5]σθαι P   6 fort.]θε̣[: fort.]ο̣τ[L:]οι[Kn

8. 1. ἀσήμου ἀργυρίου: uncoined bullion, as opposed to ἀργύριον ἐπίσημον.

ὡς ἐς ἑξήκοντα ναῦς μηνὸς μισθόν: since the crew of a trireme numbered nearly 200 (Hdt. vii. 184. 1, viii. 17), the rate of pay envisaged was one drachma per sailor per day; cf. 31. 3 n.

2. τά τε ἄλλα ἐπαγωγὰ καὶ οὐκ ἀληθῆ: cf. 46.

τῷ κοινῷ: so H₂ψ: τοῖς κοινοῖς (cett.) is inappropriate, since the reference is to Segesta alone, and the treasury of a single state is τὸ κοινόν (cf. 6. 3).

αὐτοκράτορας: cf. i. 126. 8 n. As a rule, the respect in which an official is made αὐτοκράτωρ is specified (e.g. 26. 1, IG i². 91. 9) or obvious from the context (e.g. v. 45. 2, And. i. 15). If we are to be guided by the context here, the generals were empowered to decide, without reference back to Athens, when the objects detailed in βοηθοὺς μὲν κ.τ.λ. had been effected, and to decide on the military and diplomatic means to be used. It is noteworthy that their terms of reference contain no mention of the primary purpose of the expedition, the conquest of Syracuse; this is because Alkibiades, and no doubt many others, hoped that much could be achieved by diplomacy alone (17. 4, 48), and for this the consistent maintenance of εὐπρέπεια was desirable. To send generals αὐτοκράτορες to 'help Segesta, re-establish Leontinoi . . . and take such other measures as they should judge to be in the best interests of Athens' was to preserve appearances without sacrificing real aims.

Ἀλκιβιάδην τε τὸν Κλεινίου, κ.τ.λ.: on the order of names cf. p. 224.

ξυγκατοικίσαι δὲ καὶ Λεοντίνους: 'to co-operate ⟨with the survivors of Leontinoi⟩ in ⟨re-⟩establishing ⟨the city of⟩ Leontinoi'. For the importance of this in Athenian eyes cf. Pl. *Mnx.* 243 a.

ἤν τι περιγίγνηται αὐτοῖς τοῦ πολέμου: περιγίγνεσθαι and περιεῖναι are normally used (i) of persons, *c. gen.*, 'gain the upper hand', (ii) 'be left over', especially of a financial surplus. Sense (i) here would be tortuous, lit. 'if anything of the war is victorious for them', and sense (ii) ambiguous: either (*a*) 'if anything survives the war ⟨between Syracuse and the survivors of Leontinoi⟩ for them (sc. Leontinoi)', i.e. 'if any people of Leontinoi are left', or (*b*) 'if the war ⟨between Syracuse and the survivors of Leontinoi⟩ is still going on', or (*c*) 'if any campaigning season is left', or (*d*), more generally (Arnold, Krüger), 'if the war makes good progress'. Interpretation (*a*) is unlikely, as the Athenians obviously do not envisage that no one at all will be available for resettlement (cf. also 50. 4 and E. Roos, *Eranos* lix [1961], 22 f.). Interpretation (*b*) cannot be ruled out, as it is possible that lip-service was paid to the idea that Syracuse might cease to prohibit the re-establishment of Leontinoi (cf. 48). In the context, however, we should rather expect αὐτοῖς to refer to the Athenian generals as the beneficiaries of περιγίγνηται, and what vagueness remains in Thucydides' words no doubt reflects a quite deliberate vagueness in the original decree. Hude's ἦν ⟨τέ⟩ τι, supported by Roos (8 ff.), relates the conditional clause to the third stated purpose of the expedition and rests on the assumption that the Athenians must have declared their hand pretty fully.

8. 3–26. *Second Assembly*

There is no debate in which Thucydides has given us so striking a representation of rhetorical technique at work. Both the speakers are men whom he must have seen and heard before his exile; and though he casts their arguments into his own peculiar language, the reader requires in at least two passages to visualize their gestures and facial expressions and to hear their tone of voice in his mind's ear (9. 2 n., 23. 1 n.). No statement or prediction or factual implication in these speeches can be taken at its face value; everything is coloured; everything is exaggeration, insinuation, or half-truth. This does not mean that Nikias and Alkibiades were more dishonest than modern politicians or barristers, or that the Athenian assembly was any less responsible than a modern jury; it serves only to remind us that persuasion is a serious art and that all the vital decisions in the history of the Athenian democracy were taken by a sovereign assembly under the impact of rhetoric, not by a small body of professional representatives who can decide first and explain their decisions afterwards. Much has been said about the 'real motives' of the Sicilian expedition—it has been suggested, for example (F. M. Cornford, *Thucydides Mythistoricus* [London, 1907]), that the project was hatched in the minds of Athenian merchants who wanted to increase their sales in the western Mediterranean—but the mechanism of 'real motives' does not always receive the scrutiny which it deserves. No project, however economically desirable to one class or another, could be put into effect until the assembly had been presented with what seemed to it an adequate reason; but any reason which was accepted by the assembly can be the real and only reason, and there is no justification for looking behind or beyond it without positive evidence. Generalized beliefs about human society are dogma, not evidence. Thucydides tells us in intelligible terms why Alkibiades wanted the expedition (15. 2) and why a majority of the Athenians wanted it (24. 3; cf. Hatzfeld, 143 ff., and de Romilly, *Imp.*, 71 ff.). If we are to reject what he says as inadequate, we ought at least to show that his concepts of political motivation are at variance with our other evidence for Greek society, and in particular with what can be learnt by reading between the lines in the orators. Since we cannot show that, we could only fall back on the hypothesis that Greek conceptions of political motivation as a whole were dominated by conventions which concealed realities; and such a hypothesis could be sustained only by ruling out *a priori* the premiss that the structure and conditions of one society may differ from those of another. It is better sense to believe that they do differ and that Thucydides has given us an essentially truthful picture of Athenian society; that Alkibiades' ambition was to gain at least a Periklean status by establishing a claim on the gratitude and attention of the people superior to the claims of actual and possible rivals; and that the people, accustomed, like all ancient peoples, to an essentially predatory economy, took for granted the desirability of foreign conquest and could easily be stimulated to an enterprise of which the gain appeared to outweigh the risk.

8. 4. ἀκούσιος μὲν ᾑρημένος ἄρχειν: Nikias was not necessarily unwilling to hold the office of general, but to be appointed to command this particular expedition; cf. 23. 3 n. Thucydides says nothing of any attempt by Nikias to speak against the expedition at the previous debate; possibly the prevailing mood would have made the attempt hopeless, and Nikias thought that a few days' reflection would make the assembly more amenable (Gomme, ms. note; cf. iii. 36. 4, vi. 31. 1). It does not follow (as is suggested by A. Momigliano, *RF* n.s. vii [1929], 374 ff., and G. De Sanctis, ibid., 444 ff.) that Nikias really thought the expedition strategically sound and that Thucydides has misled us on this point. According to 34. 6, Nikias' pessimistic attitude to the expedition was known at Syracuse; and Lys. xviii. 2 f. must be referring to the expedition when he says ὅσα οὐ βουλόμενος (sc. ὁ Νικίας) ἀλλ᾽ ἄκων ἠναγκάσθη ποιῆσαι.

προφάσει βραχείᾳ καὶ εὐπρεπεῖ: πρόφασις here is the reason actually given; contrast 6. 1 (see note).

9–14. *Speech of Nikias*

9. 1. ἄμεινον: 'advisable', as in the terminology of oracular responses, cf. i. 118. 3, ii. 17. 1. Words meaning 'better' or 'worse' do not always require to be treated as comparatives; hence the construction ἄμεινόν ἐστιν ἐκπέμπειν - - - καὶ μή - - - ἄρασθαι; cf. Pl. *Phd.* 105 a οὐ γὰρ χεῖρον πολλάκις ἀκούειν and Kühner–Gerth, ii. 306 f.

οὕτω βραχείᾳ βουλῇ - - - ἄρασθαι: the most striking alliteration in Thucydides; cf. i. 78. 1 βουλεύεσθε βραδέως ὡς οὐ περὶ βραχέων and Schmid, 197, n. 3. Yet alliteration can be accidental; cf. X. *Cyr.* vii. 5. 41 ἀνθρώπων δὲ πολὺ πλέον πλῆθος περιειστήκει βουλομένων προσιέναι, καὶ πολὺ πρότερον ἢ οἱ φίλοι παρῆσαν, where it is not possible to discern any rhetorical reason for the accumulation of initial labials.

2. νομίζων ὁμοίως ἀγαθὸν πολίτην εἶναι ὃς ἄν - - - προνοῆται:
despite the frequency of νομίζων, οἰόμενος, ἐπιστάμενος, ἐλπίσας, etc.
in a causal sense, νομίζων here must be concessive (Haacke), 'while
at the same time believing that a man who takes some thought both
for his personal safety and his property is just as good a citizen'
(sc. as I, who take risks). i. 69. 5 'you are prepared to risk a conflict
against a much more powerful enemy, ἐπιστάμενοι καὶ τὸν βάρβαρον
αὐτὸν περὶ αὐτῷ τὰ πλείω σφαλέντα' is probably comparable, though
the continuation, 'and that many of our successes against the
Athenians have resulted from their mistakes' suggests that (in
spite of καί) ἐπιστάμενοι might mean 'simply because you know . . .'
It is essential to visualize Nikias' gestures and imagine his tone of
voice, as Thucydides obviously would have done; cf. 23. 1 n. προῆται,
'sacrifices' (Stob. iv. 1. 61), deprives ὁμοίως of any point and makes
nonsense of what follows: 'for such a man is more likely than anyone
else to want his country's enterprises to succeed, for his own sake.'
οὔτε νῦν, ἀλλὰ ᾗ ἂν γιγνώσκω βέλτιστα, ἐρῶ: νῦν sc. παρὰ γνώμην
ἐρῶ. The ellipse is less striking than that of ii. 62. 1 δηλώσω δὲ καὶ τόδε,
ὅ μοι δοκεῖτε οὔτ' αὐτοὶ πώποτε ἐνθυμηθῆναι οὔτ' ἐγὼ ἐν τοῖς πρὶν
λόγοις (sc. δοκῶ δηλῶσαι), and for the layout of the sentence cf. D.
lvii. 3 οὐ μὴν ἀλλὰ - - -, ἃ νομίζω - - -, ἐρῶ πρὸς ὑμᾶς. Valla's translation
ita nunc quae optima esse sentio dicam suggests that he read ἄλλα ἢ
ἄν (cj. Stahl, auct. Reiske). Whatever Thucydides himself intended,
for a period in the history of his text ἀλλὰ ᾗ ἄν and ἄλλα ἢ ἄν would
both have been represented by the sequence of letters αλλαηαν. The
reading ἀλλα ῆι αν (*sic*) in the newly discovered tenth-century fragments at Modena (A. Pertusi, *Aevum* xxxiii [1959], 1 ff.) shows that
more than one accentuation was known to the copyist.
3. καὶ πρὸς μὲν τοὺς τρόπους τοὺς ὑμετέρους: on πολυπραγμοσύνη and
ἀπραγμοσύνη cf. 18. 7 n., 87. 2 n. We shall hear more from Nikias
(11. 5, vii. 14. 2, 4, 48. 3 f.) about the Athenian character; cf. de
Romilly, *Imp.*, 312. A more spirited speaker, such as Demosthenes or
Thucydides' Kleon (iii. 37. 1 f.) could lash his audience with uninhibited vigour, but Nikias' words in the same vein sound curiously
plaintive and academic; cf. Hp. *de Arte*, 6 εἰ μέν - - -, ἀσθενὴς ἦν
ἂν ὁ ἐμὸς λόγος.

10. 1. δεῦρο ἐπαγαγέσθαι: so far as our evidence goes (cf. 34. 8),
no part of the demands for ships or money which Sparta made on
some Western Greek states in 431 (ii. 7. 2) was ever met, and even
in 411–407 Sikeliot help to the Peloponnesians in the Aegean was
on a modest scale. The picture which Nikias draws of significant
Sikeliot intervention in the Aegean (10. 4, vii. 64. 1) is of the same
character as the picture of Athenian recruitment in the western
Mediterranean with which Alkibiades later seeks to frighten Sparta

(90. 3 f.). It is, however, true to say that in the Archidamian War the situation might have been different if Syracuse had been able to establish herself firmly in control of the whole of Sicily; cf. H. D. Westlake, *Historia* ix (1960), 394 ff. Hermokrates adopts for argument's sake (36. 4) a similar view to Nikias'; cf. de Romilly, *Imp.*, 211 n. 1.

2. ὀνόματι: the parenthesis shows that he means '*even* if you are inactive, it will be a peace *only* in name', not '*so long as* you are inactive, it will be a peace *at any rate* in name'.

οὕτω γάρ - - - ἐναντίων: primarily Alkibiades at Athens (v. 43. 2 f.), Kleobulos and Xenares at Sparta (v. 36. 1).

αὐτά: this refers not to the peace treaty itself but to actions in relation to it; cf. § 5 ὥστε χρὴ σκοπεῖν τινα αὐτά, referring to the whole situation of which Nikias has described some possible consequences, and ii. 43. 1 καὶ ὅταν ὑμῖν μεγάλη δόξῃ εἶναι (sc. ἡ πόλις), ἐνθυμουμένους ὅτι τολμῶντες - - - ἄνδρες αὐτὰ ἐκτήσαντο.

ταχεῖαν τὴν ἐπιχείρησιν: the article implies that an attack is ultimately inevitable; only its time and nature are subjects for discussion.

διὰ ξυμφορῶν: above all, the capture of the Spartiates at Sphakteria (v. 15. 1 f.); the death of Brasidas and the consequent absence of advocates for energetic action in the Thracian area (v. 13, 16. 1) were also important factors.

ἐκ τοῦ αἰσχίονος ἢ ἡμῖν: Athens had some cause for αἰσχύνη in 421, but the comparative does not in itself imply that Nikias admits this. τοῦτο χεῖρον ἐκείνου = 'this is not as good as that', and does not mean that either is bad; cf. iii. 37. 4 ἀμαθέστεροι τῶν νόμων ἀξιοῦσιν εἶναι ('do not claim to be as wise as the law'), i. 84. 3, X. *Cyr.* viii. 8. 27 *passim*, Hp. *Vict.* 17, And. ii. 1 ἕτερος - - - ἐμοῦ κακίων.

πολλὰ τὰ ἀμφισβητούμενα ἔχομεν: the continued refusal of Chalkidike to accept Athenian rule, and the Athenian raids from Pylos (v. 56. 2 f., cf. 115. 2), were contrary to the provisions of the peace treaty.

3. εἰσὶ δ' οἵ - - - ἐδέξαντο: within the Peloponnesian League, Corinth, Elis, Megara, and Boeotia resisted the Spartan proposals for a peace treaty and were not parties to it (v. 17. 2).

οἱ μὲν ἄντικρυς πολεμοῦσιν: on the data given by Thucydides, this reference can only be to Corinth. Since Corinth was a member of the Peloponnesian League at the time of the peace treaty, the Athenians regarded her as bound by it, despite her rejection of it. Hence the later Corinthian request for a 'ten-day truce' was refused by Athens, and the relation between the two states at that time was ἄσπονδος ἀνοκωχή (v. 32. 5 ff.). But in the summer of 416 there was fighting between Corinthians and Athenians ἰδίων τινῶν διαφορῶν ἕνεκα (v. 115. 3, see note).

οἱ δέ - - - δεχημέροις σπονδαῖς - - - κατέχονται: Boeotia made a ten-day truce with Athens shortly after the peace treaty (v. 26. 2).

4. οὕς - - - χρόνῳ: cf. § 1 n.

5. μετεώρῳ τε ⟨τῇ⟩ πόλει - - - κινδυνεύειν: probably 'in a delicate position' (cf. D. xix. 122), adequately explained by §§ 2 f.—cf. Hp. *VM* 19, where μετέωρα καὶ ἄπεπτα καὶ ἄκρητα is said of elements in the body not in the location and condition in which they should be for good health—but Spratt suggests that the word is proleptic and deliberately chosen with an eye to one of its meanings, 'out at sea'. In that case Krüger's substitution of τῇ for τε would be preferable to Stuart Jones's addition of ⟨τῇ⟩; one or other of these emendations is necessary, but palaeographically there is nothing to choose between them.

Χαλκιδῆς: cf. § 2 n., and 7. 4.

κατὰ τὰς ἠπείρους: so far as the empire is concerned, the ἤπειροι are Thrace, Macedonia, and Asia Minor (in i. 7, where there is no reference to the empire, the word is simply opposed to 'islands'). Independent evidence for 'hesitant obedience' in these areas in 415 is lacking; Nikias' rhetorical statement is of a type which cannot be effectively challenged.

Ἐγεσταίοις δὴ οὖσι ξυμμάχοις: so F₂GH₂MᵖᶜψΣᴹᶜᶠ; ξύμμαχοι (CABEFMᵃᶜ) is ruled out by οὖσι. It might appear that the sceptical force of δή extends only to ξυμμάχοις, or at the most to ἀδικουμένοις also. Since, however, there seems to be no other passage in which δή precedes all the words to which it refers, unless it is itself preceded by ἵνα, ὅτι, ὡς, etc., or by a word meaning 'say' or 'think' (Pl. *Lg.* 963 b ὧν δὴ διαφέρων can hardly be cited in support of δὴ οὖσι ξυμμάχοις), it is likely that δή here colours Ἐγεσταίοις, and that Nikias is expressing scepticism about the primary ostensible purpose of the expedition (8. 2).

αὐτοί: so H₂ (cj. Reiske); αὐτῶν cett. αὐτοί is essential for the contrast between *our* wrongs and the supposed wrongs of our supposed allies; αὐτῶν would make no such point.

11. 1. διὰ πολλοῦ γε - - - χαλεπῶς ἂν ἄρχειν δυναίμεθα: 'the argument needs more emphasis than Nikias gives it' (Gomme, ms. note).

2. Σικελιῶται δ' ἄν μοι δοκοῦσι - - - Συρακόσιοι: 'it seems to me that the Greeks of Sicily, to judge from their present condition, would be even ⟨καί⟩ less formidable (sc. than they are now) if they were ruled by Syracuse.' That must be the meaning if the text is sound. Editors have naturally been impressed by the partial similarity of this sentence to § 3 νῦν μὲν γὰρ | κἂν ἔλθοιεν - - - | ἐκείνως δ' | οὐκ εἰκὸς κ.τ.λ., and have therefore favoured either the insertion of some such words as ⟨οὐδένα κίνδυνον παρέχειν⟩ after ἔχουσι (cf. Stephanus's 'Valla': *Siceliotae, ut nunc saltem se habent, mihi uidentur*

233

parum formidabiles, multoque minus nobis formidabiles fore, etc.; Valla actually wrote *Sicilienses mihi uidentur, ut nunc se res habent, etiam si imperio potiantur Syracusani, minus infesti in nos fore*) or the hypothesis that words to that effect are actually understood from ὥς γε νῦν ἔχουσι (Herbst, 81 ff.; Schwartz, 330 f.). There is nothing to be said for the latter alternative, and the former is unnecessary. The existence of the first ἄν suggests that the text is sound; one would expect Nikias, if he were making an explicit antithesis of the kind envisaged, to distinguish unambiguously between the actual and the hypothetical. Cf. also Pl. *Smp.* 183 b ὃ δὲ δεινότατον, ὥς γε λέγουσιν οἱ πολλοί, ὅτι κ.τ.λ. The position of the second ἄν unfortunately throws no light on whether καί is conjunction or adverb; cf. 10. 4 καί (adverb) πάνυ ἄν - - -, 11. 3 κἄν (adverb).

3. **οὐκ εἰκὸς ἀρχὴν ἐπὶ ἀρχὴν στρατεῦσαι**: the argument is not impressive, and might not have seemed to the Athenian audience consonant either with their proverbial beliefs (τίκτει γὰρ κόρος ὕβριν) or with the facts of history, but it has much in common with the Athenian argument in v. 91. 1.

4. **δείξαντες τὴν δύναμιν δι' ὀλίγου ἀπέλθοιμεν**: 'display our power and soon depart' (cf. v. 14. 1 πληγέντες ἐπί τε τῷ Δηλίῳ καὶ δι' ὀλίγου αὖθις ἐν Ἀμφιπόλει), 'depart after displaying our power for a short time' (cf. i. 77. 6 πρὸς τὸν Μῆδον δι' ὀλίγου ἡγησάμενοι), or 'depart after displaying our power at close quarters' (cf. ii. 89. 9 δι' ὀλίγου τῆς ἐφορμήσεως οὔσης)? Σ^Mcf paraphrases as ταχέως ἀπέλθοιμεν, rightly; for since Nikias goes on to say that τὰ διὰ πλείστου ('what is furthest away') πάντες ἴσμεν θαυμαζόμενα he cannot be advising the Athenians to do something 'at close quarters'.

τὰ γὰρ διὰ πλείστου - - - θαυμαζόμενα καὶ τὰ πεῖραν ἥκιστα τῆς δόξης δόντα: in the MSS. these words come after ἐπιθοῖντο, and Rauchenstein's transposition of them to stand after ἀπέλθοιμεν (*Ph.* xxxvi [1877], 242), though adopted by all recent editors, is both unjustified by the sense and contrary to Thucydidean rhetorical technique. The three possibilities envisaged are: (i) not to go, (ii) to go briefly and safely, (iii) the danger of defeat; and Nikias' view of the consequences of defeat in the particular case of the proposed expedition is supported by his generalization about the contrary situation, in which θαυμαζόμενα is contrasted with ὑπεριδόντες and πεῖραν takes up σφαλείημεν. The next statement, ὅπερ - - - πεπόνθατε κ.τ.λ. is related to the generalization just as in 33. 6 ὅπερ καὶ Ἀθηναῖοι - - - ηὐξήθησαν is related to the preceding generalization (33. 5) 'few overseas expeditions succeed, and when they fail they bring renown to their adversaries', a generalization which follows from the particularization (33. 4) 'if we defeat Athens, we shall win great renown' (cf. ii. 43. 4, iii. 43. 1, v. 103. 2, and Meister, 28 f.). Rauchenstein's transposition has the further disadvantage that it brings into the closest proximity, linking them by γάρ, δι' ὀλίγου and διὰ πλείστου, which at first glance appear to be opposites (cf. Müller) but in fact are not (cf. above); this creates a serious ambiguity.

Evidently (Gomme, ms.) Thucydides did not feel that he could attribute to Nikias in 415 the proud boast of 431/30 μόνη γὰρ τῶν νῦν ἀκοῆς κρείσσων ἐς πεῖραν ἔρχεται (ii. 41. 3).

5. ἐφίεσθε: so ψ, cf. Σ^Mcf: ἐφίεσθαι cett. In amplification of ὅπερ - - - πεπόνθατε we require not an infinitive but another indicative; cf. 91. 4. The insertion of καὶ before καταφρονήσαντες in G¹ is an attempt to make sense of the infinitive by making the whole complex διὰ τὸ παρὰ γνώμην - - - ἐφίεσθαι a single causal expression.

6. τὰς διανοίας κρατήσαντας θαρσεῖν: since elsewhere in Thucydides κρατεῖν has an accusative object only when it means 'defeat in battle', accompanied by μάχη or μαχόμενοι, and a genitive object in the sense 'get the better of', either τάς should be emended to τῆς (Schwartz, 331, cl. 38. 4) or the phrase should be interpreted as 'get the better of them in planning' (cf. perhaps D. xxi. 18 κρατούσῃ τὸν ἀγῶνα). To take τὰς διανοίας with θαρσεῖν, 'plan confidently when one is victorious', lessens the force of the antithesis τύχας | ἐπαίρεσθαι || διανοίας | θαρσεῖν. Cf. the distinction between διάνοιαι and τύχαι in Archidamos' speech, i. 84. 3.

δόξαν ἀρετῆς μελετῶσιν: ἀρετή here is primarily the courage which brings victory, the quality of the ἀνὴρ ἀγαθός in the usual Greek sense of the term. Contrast v. 105. 4 (see note).

7. ἀνδρῶν βαρβάρων: cf. 9. 1 and 12. 1 n. on this rhetorical point, and Freeman, 95.

δι' ὀλιγαρχίας ἐπιβουλεύουσαν: in the context of Nikias' argument it is surprising to find oligarchy treated as a weapon brought to bear upon Athens by Sparta. Does he mean that Sparta is trying to foment an oligarchic conspiracy in Athens ('by promulgating the principles of oligarchy', Bloomfield), or that Sparta is hostile because she is an oligarchy, or that her hostility is particularly important and dangerous because she is an oligarchy? διά c. gen. with εἶναι, γίγνεσθαι, ποιεῖσθαι, etc. is common enough (cf. 10. 2) and Thucydides is extending normal usage here a little further than D. xv. 19 οὐκ ἔστιν ὅπως, εἰ δι' ὀλιγαρχίας ἅπαντα συστήσεται, τὸν παρ' ὑμῖν δῆμον ἐάσουσιν. Hence 'a city, under oligarchic government, which has designs upon us' (cf. A. H. Wratislaw, JPh. ii/2 [1868], 151). The words lose nothing in rhetorical effect by their lack of precision, cf. p. 229; 'a charge suddenly introduced and immediately dropped' (Gomme, ms. note).

12. 1. νεωστί: it was fifteen years since the major attack of the plague and six since the peace treaty. Thucydides himself (26. 2) omits any such qualification as βραχύ τι. Thucydides is perhaps too sanguine on the plague, for nothing could replace the thousands of citizens who died in it (cf. iii. 87 n.), and his Nikias is too cautious on the subject of money. We do not know how large a reserve had been accumulated by 415, since the statement of And. iii. 8 'because of the Peace of Nikias we put 7,000 talents on to the Akropolis' represents as an achievement what was no doubt a plan only partly fulfilled (cf. *ATL* iii, 346); but it was, after all, enough to sustain the Sicilian expedition and its reinforcements.

δίκαιον ἐνθάδε εἶναι ἀναλοῦν: if C is wrong in omitting εἶναι, there is either a variation of construction after μεμνῆσθαι, δίκαιον εἶναι being co-ordinated with ὅτι - - -, or εἶναι is governed by ὥστε and co-ordinated with ηὐξῆσθαι. Neither interpretation is impossible, but both obscure to some extent the sequence of thought, since we expect καὶ ταῦτα to be a reflection upon the fact just stated, not part of what they should remember; cf. 17. 1, 23. 3, 38. 1, 39. 1, Rauchenstein, *Ph.* xxxvi (1877), 242. Of other possibilities suggested, εἶναι = ἐξεῖναι (Σᴹ; δίκαιον sc. ἐστι, as normally) is pleonastic and a little off the point; and ἐνθάδε εἶναι = ἐνθάδε (Steup, cl. Pl. *Prt.* 317 a and τὸ νῦν εἶναι in documentary inscriptions) is also off the point, since εἶναι with adverbs of time and place has a limiting sense, 'at any rate' (cf. 14 ἑκὼν εἶναι). C's text is thus preferable.

φυγάδων: the Segestans were not exiles; their fault, as Nikias represents it, is not to be Greek (9. 1, 11. 7), and in those references he ignores Leontinoi. Now he ignores Segesta and derides Leontinoi (λόγους μόνον παρασχομένους, whereas the Segestans had brought cash), whose cause had been pleaded earlier by the Segestan envoys (6. 2) and was now pleaded (19. 1) by themselves. It is the general practice of rhetoric to predicate of a whole the good or ill that belongs to one of its parts; Platt's ingenious suggestion (*JPh.* xxxiii [1914], 272) ἀνδρῶν (sc. τῶν μὲν φυγάδων, τῶν δὲ ἐπικουρίας δεομένων implies too charitable a view of ancient orators.

ξυναπολέσαι: so a corrector in Ottobonianus gr. 211 (cj. Reiske, cl. Valla's *in perniciem trahere*). ξυναπολέσθαι (cett.) is untranslatable, since neither ξυναπολέσθαι nor πταίσαντας could have a causative sense, and τοὺς φίλους would thus have no construction.

2. εἴ τέ τις - - - παραινεῖ: Nikias does not name Alkibiades, but makes his reference immediately clear by closer specification of Alkibiades' characteristics.

νεώτερος: since Alkibiades took part in the Poteidaia campaign as a hoplite (Pl. *Smp.* 219 e, cf. Plu. *Alc.* 6. 3; for the problems involved in the evidence, see Hatzfeld, 27 f., 62 ff.; his 64 n. 2 and 65 n. 1 are the essential clues to their solution) he cannot have been born later than 452, and was therefore at least 36 on the occasion of this debate. Thucydides comments on his youth in connection with the events of 420, but suggests at the same time that Athens was less mistrustful

of youth than other cities were (v. 43. 2). We do not know whether
30 was the statutory minimum age for generals, as it was for councillors and jurymen; whether it was or not, it is always rhetorically
possible to suggest that a man younger than oneself is too young.
For the sentiment of the whole section cf. E. *Su.* 231 ff. :

> ἀπώλεσας πόλιν
>
> νέοις παραχθείς, οἵτινες τιμώμενοι
> χαίρουσι πολέμους τ' αὐξάνουσ' ἄνευ δίκης,
> φθείροντες ἀστούς, ὁ μὲν ὅπως στρατηλατῇ,
> ὁ δ' ὡς ὑβρίζῃ δύναμιν ἐς χεῖρας λαβών,
> ἄλλος δὲ κέρδους οὕνεκα.

Laches in Pl. *La.* 189 a 7 is credited with a more enlightened attitude:
'Provided that my teacher is a good man himself, I don't care if
he's rather young, or not yet well known, or under any disadvantage
of that kind.'

ἀπὸ τῆς ἱπποτροφίας: on horse-breeding as a manifestation of
wealth cf. Ar. *Nu.* 12–18, al., Isoc. xvi. 33, D. xviii. 320.

διὰ δὲ πολυτέλειαν - - - ἐκ τῆς ἀρχῆς: either (i) 'as his expenditure
necessitates, gain (sc. in money)', or (ii) 'by means of expenditure
(sc. in command) gain (sc. in political prestige)'. Cf. Lys. xix. 56 f.,
where it is assumed that the φιλοτιμία manifested in choregiai and
other liturgies is designed to secure election to offices and thereby
to make twice what one spent. Interpretation (ii) would by no
means be far-fetched, but in this context it is likely that Nikias is
making the more damaging accusation. Cf. the criticism of Athenian
demagogues in *Hell. Oxy.* 7 Bart. (2 G–H) 2: ἐπιθυμοῦντες ἀπαλλάξαι
τοὺς Ἀθηναίους τῆς ἡσυχίας καὶ τῆς εἰρήνης καὶ προαγαγεῖν ἐπὶ τὸ
πολεμεῖν καὶ πολυπραγμονεῖν, ἵν' αὐτοῖς ἐκ τῶν κοινῶν ᾖ χρηματίζεσθαι
and the similar but less concrete charge against the successors of
Perikles in Th. ii. 65. 7.

μηδὲ τούτῳ ἐμπαράσχητε τῷ τῆς πόλεως κινδύνῳ - - - ἐλλαμπρύνεσθαι:
D. M. Lewis, in his unpublished Princeton dissertation, 'Towards
a Historian's Text of Thucydides', points out that the quotation of
this passage by Σ Ar. *Pax* 450, though in other respects garbled, has
ἀπολαμπρύνεσθαι, a Herodotean word ('become famous', 'emerge
with credit') which is more attractive than the repeated ἐν-; but it is
significant that Dio, Josephus, and Appian, all fond of Thucydidean
words, use ἐλλαμπρύνεσθαι in the sense of the simple verb ('show off').

μὴ οἷον νεωτέρῳ βουλεύσασθαι: for the construction cf. A. *Th.* 731 f.
χθόνα ναίειν - - - ὁπόσαν καὶ φθιμένοισιν κατέχειν; we might have expected νεωτέρου or νεωτέρων (cf. 22 οὐ πάσης ἔσται πόλεως ὑποδέξασθαι)
or νεώτερον or νεωτέρους (cf. X. *An.* iv. 1. 5 ἐλείπετο τῆς νυκτὸς ὅσον
σκοταίους διελθεῖν τὸ πεδίον). Hence Pluygers's emendation νεωτέρους
(*Mnemosyne* 1862, 92), giving an easier reference to οὕς in the next

sentence; but οὕς does not demand a plural antecedent, cf. Kühner–
Gerth, i. 55 f., 86.

13. 1. παρακελευστούς: neither the form of the word nor its context
justifies its interpretation as active. Nikias suggests that Alkibiades
has called on the younger men for support; hence τοῖς πρεσβυτέροις
ἀντιπαρακελεύομαι. We cannot know whether Thucydides intended
-λεύσ- or -τούς; *Lex Patm.* gives -λεύσ- in its lemma and yet explains
the word as οἱ ἐκ παρακελεύσεως τι λέγοντες (cf. Photios s.v.). The
passive interpretation is supported by X. *An.* i. 3. 13 οἱ μὲν ἐκ τοῦ
αὐτομάτου - - - οἱ δ᾽ ὑπ᾽ ἐκείνου ἐγκέλευστοι. In Dio lii. 15. 4 τά τε
πραττόμενα ὀρθῶς διοικηθείη - - - μήτε τοῖς παρακελευστοῖς ἐπιτρεπόμενα,
κ.τ.λ., π. means simply 'supporters' and we cannot tell exactly how
Dio analysed the word in Thucydides.

εἴ τῳ τις παρακάθηται τῶνδε: the whole clause is appositional to τοῖς
πρεσβυτέροις; εἴ τῳ = ᾧτινι (sc. τῶν πρεσβυτέρων), and τις and τῶνδε are
the younger men. The sentence shows that it was not customary for
the supporters of a particular speaker to sit all together; R. Sealey,
Hermes lxxxiv (1956), 241, draws the opposite conclusion, as if
καθημένους were συγκαθημένους and the εἴ τῳ τις clause were not there.
ὅπερ ἂν αὐτοὶ πάθοιεν: these words refer to δυσ-, and (as ἄν shows)
are a warning, not an imprecation such as we find in D. xviii. 89
ὧν διαμάρτοιεν: 'and not to conceive an ill-starred desire—as it may
prove to be for the young men themselves—for distant gain'.

τῶν ἀπόντων: the word has more emotional associations for the
Greeks than for us. Cf. (Gomme, ms.) Pi. *P.* 3. 19 ff. ἀλλά τοι
ἤρατο τῶν ἀπεόντων· οἷα καὶ πολλοὶ πάθον. ἔστι δὲ φῦλον ἐν ἀνθρώποισι
ματαιότατον, ὅστις αἰσχύνων ἐπιχώρια παπταίνει τὰ πόρσω.

ἐλάχιστα κατορθοῦνται: Thucydides predicates the intransitive active
κατορθοῦν of persons, the passive of enterprises. Hence ἐλάχιστα and
πλεῖστα are the only possible subjects of κατορθοῦνται, and the plural
verb is questionable and easily corrigible. It is, however, supported
by many passages in which the neuter plural subject is qualified by
a numeral (e.g. 62. 4) or by 'many' and refers to events on different
occasions (cf. Kühner–Gerth, i. 65 f.); there are, moreover, passages
in which no special reason for abnormality is discernible, e.g. Hp.
Fract. 11 διίστανται μὲν τὰ ὀστέα, φλέβια δὲ ἐκχυμοῦνται.

οἷσπερ νῦν ὅροις: Nikias clearly envisages possible boundaries other
than those existing, and is thus not merely reminding his audience
that Sicily is separated from Greece by natural barriers. Nor, on
the other hand, need he be referring to any explicit provision, e.g.
in the treaty of Gela (iv. 65. 1 f.). His point is that no Sikeliot warships or troops have intervened in Greece. οὐ μεμπτοῖς may be a
more positive commendation than it looks; cf. X. *Cyr.* ii. 1. 11 σώματα
μὲν ἔχοντες ἀνδρῶν ἥκετε οὐ μεμπτά.

τῷ τε 'Ιονίῳ κόλπῳ: Hdt. vi. 127. 2 so names the sea off Epidamnos; from there to Brindisi is the only stretch of open sea which is unavoidable in travelling between Italy and Greece. A. *Pr.* 840 appears to use the term more vaguely, of the Adriatic.

τῷ Σικελικῷ: sc. κόλπῳ, which is freely applied to expanses of water wide enough to be called πόντος or πέλαγος, cf. 62. 2 Τυρσηνικὸς κόλπος, vii. 58. 2 Τυρσηνικὸς πόντος. In iv. 53. 3 τὸ Σικελικὸν πέλαγος is the sea between the Peloponnese and Sicily.

2. τοῖς δ' 'Εγεσταίοις ἰδίᾳ εἰπεῖν: τοὺς μὲν Σικελιώτας - - - ξυμφέρεσθαι is something for which the older men must vote; ξυμμάχους μὴ ποιεῖσθαι is something which they must do in the future; whether εἰπεῖν is conceived as something for which they must vote (grammatically subordinate to ψηφίζεσθαι and co-ordinated with ξυμφέρεσθαι) or as something which by virtue of their decision they must do (co-ordinated with ψηφίζεσθαι) is left obscure.

τὸ πρῶτον πόλεμον: so ψ; τὸν πρ. π. cett. There is no question of a contrast between 'the first war' and any later war, nor can τὸν πρῶτον πόλεμον mean 'the beginning of the war'. Hence τὸ is necessary; Hude's additional τὸν, to give 'the war' instead of '(a) war', is not.

μετὰ σφῶν αὐτῶν: not normal Greek for 'by themselves', but it is prompted by the symmetrical antitheses ἄνευ / μετά and Ἀθηναίων / σφῶν αὐτῶν.

14. ὦ πρύτανι: the ἐπιστάτης τῶν πρυτανέων; cf. Busolt–Swoboda, 1029 f.

ἀναψηφίσαι: a procedural term, cf. *SEG* x. 38B. 11 ff. τὰ χσυνγεγραμμένα μὲ ἔναι ἀναφσεφίσα[ι] ἐὰμ μὲ ἑκατὸν παρôσιν τὸν δêμοτôν.

τὸ μὲν λύειν τοὺς νόμους: 'in the realization that with so many witnesses you cannot be charged with (*or* blamed for) λύειν τοὺς νόμους'. αἰτίαν σχεῖν, as normally, has a personal subject and a dependent infinitive; the article here is due to the antithesis between λύειν and τῆς πόλεως, as in 17. 8 τὸ μέν - - - ἐσβάλλειν - - - ἱκανοί (G. Behrendt, *Ueber den Gebrauch des Infinitivs mit Artikel bei Thukydides* [Berlin, 1886], 8). To rescind an enactment could be described as λύειν τοὺς νόμους in so far as (i) a precise distinction between νόμος and ψήφισμα is not always observed, e.g. i. 139. 1 f., 140. 3 f. ~ Ar. *Ach.* 532, And. i. 86 ~ [Lys.] vi. 52, cf. iii. 37. 3 n., (ii) whoever proposes the rescinding of an enactment or takes steps which imply or lead to its rescinding can be said to λύειν that enactment, e.g. D. xx. 26, 96 (cf. Dover, *JHS* lxxx [1960], 73 f.), (iii) a single enactment or legal provision can be called οἱ νόμοι, as in English 'the law' can be collective or individual, e.g. Isoc. xviii. 3 ~ 2, [D.] liii. 11. So [Lys.] vi. 29, referring to the decree of Isotimides (ψήφισμα in And. i. 8, 86), says ὑμεῖς δ' αὐτὸν ἐξηλάσατε ἐκ τῆς πόλεως τοῖς θεοῖς βεβαιοῦντες τοὺς νόμους οὓς ἐψηφίσασθε. Yet since Nikias is asking the *epistates* to put the issue of the expedition to the vote again, and hopes that the earlier decision will be rescinded (15. 1 τὰ ἐψηφισμένα - - - λύειν), he cannot mean 'with so many witnesses you will not be accused of rescinding enactments', for the more witnesses there are, the more clearly will the *epistates* be seen to do what Nikias wants him to do. Is it then that the action for which Nikias asks could in some circumstances be illegal, but is not in the present circumstances? It does not seem that *ἀναψήφισις was in itself illegal. Certain decrees include sanctions against their own reconsideration, but there is no evidence for a general law, and in the debate on Mytilene the issue of legality is not raised; Duker saw (and Marchant did not) the importance of Mytilene for this passage. Moreover, it is very doubtful whether an individual who contravenes a law of the community to which he belongs can be said (in Classical Greek) to λύειν that law. One automatically λύει a contract or treaty by failure to carry out one's obligations; λύειν τὸν νόμον is used of the Persian royal judges (Hdt. iii. 31. 5), the ultimate authority on Persian law and custom, and of a nation breaking its own custom (Hdt. vi. 106. 3, Isoc. ix. 63); but E. *IA* 1268 θέσφατ' εἰ λύσω θεᾶς is the only putative Classical instance of λύειν = 'disobey', and its authenticity is suspect in the light of ibid. 1486 θέσφατ' ἐξαλείψω and S. *OT* 407 μαντεῖα - - - λύσομεν, where ἐξαλείφειν and λύειν refer to fulfilment of divine commands by obedience. It therefore seems likely that Nikias means 'with so many witnesses, you will not be accused of abolishing (sc. by setting a precedent) our established procedure'. The witnesses would testify that the assembly was genuinely divided and that the *epistates* was not acting frivolously or maliciously (cf. Arnold). It was possible to bring a man to trial not for contravention of an explicit law but for any action which might be regarded as contrary to public interest; the charge against Socrates said ἀδικεῖ (not ἀσεβεῖ) Σωκράτης, and the decree of Kannonos mentioned in X. *HG* i. 7. 20 provided for the situation ἐάν τις τὸν Ἀθηναίων δῆμον ἀδικῇ (cf. Dover, *JHS* lxxv [1955], 17 ff.).

⟨κακῶς⟩ βουλευσαμένης: κακῶς is in H₂ψ and the paraphrase of Σ^GMcf; aesthetic considerations recommend it.

ἰατρὸς ἂν γενέσθαι: *SEG* x. 98. 14 τὲν βλαβὲ]ν ἰᾶσθαι δ[ιπλὲν (c. 420) shows that the application of medical metaphors to law and politics (e.g. E. *Ph.* 893) is not confined to literature; cf., in a legal context, Pl. *Lg.* 862 b 6 τὸ μὲν βλαβὲν ὑγιὲς τοῖς νόμοις εἰς τὸ δυνατὸν ποιητέον, and, on the antithesis ὠφελεῖν / βλάπτειν in medical writers, Weidauer, 72 f.

15. Alkibiades

15. 2. βουλόμενος τῷ τε Νικίᾳ ἐναντιοῦσθαι: for the co-ordination βουλόμενος Α τε Β τε ἐπιθυμῶν cf. 61. 5, viii. 44. 1. Alkibiades' motives in replying are (i) the desire to oppose the argument which Nikias has just sustained, because (*a*) as a political rival, he is bound to try to discredit Nikias, and (*b*) Nikias has by allusion attacked him, and he must defend himself (cf. 16. 1); (ii) (*a*) the desire to enhance his political standing by advocating and helping to execute a course of action which may be a spectacular success, and (*b*) the confidence that it will in fact be a success.

τὰ πολιτικά: τὰ πολεμικά CG; but ὧν καὶ ἐς τἆλλα - - - καὶ ὅτι - - -, suggesting that διαβόλως ἐμνήσθη is a particular instance of the 'difference' between the two men, points to τὰ πολιτικά, which is in any case preferable as a word of wider application. (In X. *Cyr.* i. 5. 12 πολιτικώτατον and πολεμικώτατον are variants, and there the latter is correct.) The personal terms in which Thucydides sometimes describes political motivation (cf. especially 28. 2, viii. 89. 3 f.) may be taken by those who choose to do so as signifying that he failed to see the 'real' causes of political decisions and preferred to describe them as if he were staging a drama or recounting a myth. They may, on the other hand, be taken as a reminder that Thucydides knew more about the nature of Greek political life than we do; after all, it is not as if he were unwilling to generalize about nations or classes when he did not think that an event ought to be explained in terms of individuals. Cf. v. 43. 2 and de Romilly, *Imp.*, 226.

καὶ Καρχηδόνα λήψεσθαι: Alkibiades exploits this remarkable ambition in his speech at Sparta, 90. 2; he says nothing of it in this debate, nor does Nikias attack it. We see from this passage that at least in Thucydides' judgement it was more than simply a rhetorical bogy; cf. the suggestion which he attributes to Hermokrates in 34. 2. Ar. *Eq.* 1303 f., where Hyperbolos is credited with αἰτεῖσθαι ἑκατὸν (sc. τριήρεις) εἰς Καρχηδόνα, is not (to us) unambiguous. It may be that in the extravagant mood of 425/4, described in iv. 65. 4, some Athenians seriously believed that Athens could attack Carthage as well as the Sikeliots, but there is another possibility, that at some time during the latter part of the Athenian operations in Sicily (425–4) the advantages of co-operation with Carthage against Syracuse had been discussed. Certainly this was the policy of the Athenian generals when 415 passed without a decisive victory (88. 6), and of the city in the last years of the war (*IG* i². 47, Meritt, *HSt.* Suppl. i [1940], 247 ff.). On these conflicting strands in Athenian strategy cf. Treu, *Historia* iii (1954/5), 45 f. Ar. *Eq.* 173 f. treats Karia and Carthage as termini of the Athenian sphere (assonance influences the choice), and *V.* 700 describes the empire as extending from 'the Black Sea to Sardinia', implying that Athens considered herself mistress of the Sicilian and Tyrrhenian seas. But much is left out; it is important that even in comic rhetoric the poet says 'Sardinia', not 'Cadiz'.

3 f. ὅπερ καὶ καθεῖλεν - - - ἔσφηλαν τὴν πόλιν: § 4 explains in detail the judgement delivered in § 3. καθελεῖν is a strong word, which Thucydides uses elsewhere of physical destruction (e.g. 100. 3), of the repeal of a decree or the abolition of a practice (i. 13. 5 τὸ λῃστικὸν καθῄρουν), and often of final and decisive victory (e.g. v. 103. 1 κἂν βλάψῃ, οὐ καθεῖλεν, vi. 11. 3), especially with reference to Spartan hopes of winning the Peloponnesian War (e.g. i. 77. 6, iii. 13. 7, iv. 85. 2, viii. 2. 4; cf. Schadewaldt, 13, 100, and A. Rehm, Ph. lxxxix [1935], 138). Either, then, Thucydides wrote these words immediately after the Athenian defeat in Sicily, in the mistaken belief that final defeat was imminent and certain (Schwartz, 332 f.; H. Strasburger, Ph. xci [1936], 137 ff.), or he wrote them after Aigospotamoi and is referring to the actual final defeat. We may rule out any intermediate date of writing, for mistaken certainty, as opposed to a rational estimate of probability, is hardly conceivable between the summer of 412 and Aigospotamoi. Equally, we may rule out (Wilamowitz, Hermes lxiv [1929], 476 and Strasburger, loc. cit. 144) any interpretation which refers οὐ διὰ μακροῦ to the interval between 415 and 405; in terms of cause and effect within the framework of the Peloponnesian War, an interval of ten years is διὰ μακροῦ, and it is noteworthy that when he wrote ii. 65. 12 Thucydides was impressed by the protraction of Athenian resistance after the Sicilian disaster, not by its brevity. Since the words φοβηθέντες γάρ - - - ἀχθεσθέντες accord so closely with Thucydides' description (28. 2) of the feeling against Alkibiades in 415, the hypothesis that the whole passage refers exclusively to the events of 415–413 deserves prior consideration.

καὶ ἄλλοις ἐπιτρέψαντες will refer not to the transfer to others of any specific powers granted to Alkibiades (*pace* Wilamowitz ap. Schadewaldt, 100, and Hatzfeld, 151), but simply to the fact that when a democracy drives one of its leading men into exile it necessarily 'hands over to' or 'follows the lead of' his rivals (ἐπιτρέπειν, like 'hand over', can be used absolutely). κράτιστα διαθέντι τὰ τοῦ πολέμου will refer to Alkibiades' strategy from 420 to 415, and this is a surprising judgement (cf. de Romilly, Imp., 227). If we are to trust Thucydides' own narrative in book v, Alkibiades' interventions in the Peloponnese from 420 to 416 failed in their general design, and the words which Thucydides gives to Alkibiades in vi. 16. 6 are a thin rhetorical disguise of failure; it is also arguable that if Athens had refrained from all provocation in the Peloponnese it would have been much harder to rouse the Spartans into giving any kind of help to Syracuse, though such an argument might be thought insensitive to the predicament of some of Sparta's Peloponnesian neighbours. As for Alkibiades' strategy in Sicily, one has the impression from the narrative in book vi that the Athenian defeat was rooted ultimately in the adoption, and the failure (50. 1, 52. 1; the success at Katane, 51. 1 f., was accidental), of the plan which Alkibiades pressed on his colleagues at Rhegion (48); Lamachos' plan (49) might have succeeded, if Thucydides' account of the political and military situation in Syracuse (32. 3, 63. 2, cf. 69. 1) is correct, and the last part of vii. 42. 3 (see note) indicates that Thucydides himself believed Lamachos' plan the right one. Granted that if Alkibiades had not been exiled his energy and perceptiveness would not have been put at the disposal of Sparta (Schadewaldt, 16); but in καὶ ἄλλοις ἐπιτρέψαντες and again, more plainly, in ii. 65. 11, all the emphasis is laid on the change for the worse in political and strategic leadership among the Athenians, without any reference to the positive harm done by Alkibiades from the enemy's camp. Granted also that if Alkibiades had remained in command with Nikias in 415–14 the Athenian campaign might have been rescued, despite the inadequacy of the initial plan (vii. 42. 3 n.); but what grounds had Thucydides for thinking that in 413–12? The possibility that at that date Thucydides was actually mistaken about salient aspects of the campaign, and that the bulk of the narrative of books vi–vii (and v also?) was written when he had a more accurate picture, some time after the writing of vi. 15, cannot be entertained; for in ii. 65. 11, which was patently written after the end of the war (to which 65. 12 explicitly refers), he reaffirms the crucial importance of the political decisions taken after the departure of the Sicilian expedition, i.e. the exile of Alkibiades (cf. H. D. Westlake, *CQ* N.S. viii [1958], 106 ff.). The alternative possibility (still on the hypothesis that vi. 15 was written soon after 413) is that Thucydides' judgement on Alkibiades was independent of the story which he had to tell, was based on some degree of personal acquaintance, and was coloured by bias (cf. P. A. Brunt, *RÉG* lxv [1952], 59 ff.). There is, however, one major objection to any hypothesis which entails the reference of καθεῖλεν to 413. Few historians are less likely than Thucydides to judge a state defeated when it was not. He shows himself consistently aware of the part played in war by the accidental and the unexpected, and he had every reason to know how easily the enemies of Athens could let a decisive chance pass through vacillation or delay or tensions within the Peloponnesian League. If he really committed himself soon after 413 to the judgement that defeat in Sicily καθεῖλεν Athens, he was not then the man we know.

We are thus bound to consider the alternative hypothesis, that καθεῖλεν refers to the final defeat; and this hypothesis may take two forms.

(i) First, we may refer ἔσφηλαν τὴν πόλιν also to the final defeat, and take φοβηθέντες γάρ - - - καὶ ἄλλοις ἐπιτρέψαντες as referring to the time of Alkibiades' second exile in 407/6 (X. *HG* i. 5. 16 f.). κράτιστα

διαθέντι τὰ τοῦ πολέμου will then understandably refer to the energy
and determination which he displayed, with a good measure of
success, from his acceptance by the fleet at Samos in 411 (viii. 81)
down to his second exile (cf. Lys. xix. 52, and Gomme, *JHS* lxxi
[1951], 72 ff. = *More Essays*, 99 f.) ; and Thucydides is affirming that
the essential cause of the second exile was the same kind of suspicion
as caused the first. We understand from X. loc. cit. that the pretext
was the defeat of Alkibiades' subordinate at Notion ; but Xenophon
speaks also of the popular belief (shared by the fleet) that this defeat
was due to Alkibiades' ἀμέλειάν τε καὶ ἀκράτειαν, and Plu. *Alc.*
36. 1 explains ἀκράτεια: Thrasybulos, son of Thrason, alleged that
Alkibiades gave subordinate commands to unworthy drinking-
companions and was interested only in a life of dissolute luxury (cf.
Diod. xiii. 73. 6). If these allegations are what Thucydides had in
mind, he is not necessarily open to a charge of obscurity; for if
Athens, at the time of his writing vi. 15, had finally been defeated,
and if he assumed knowledge of this fact on the part of his readers,
the possibility that a later age, interested in the stratification of his
work, might find an ambiguity in καθεῖλεν would hardly enter his
head. The importance which he attached to the second exile of
Alkibiades is clear from ii. 65. 12 : 'they did not give in until they had
come to grief (ἐσφάλησαν) through an internal collapse caused by the
dissensions of individuals'. These words cannot refer to the political
disturbances which came *after* they 'gave in', and must therefore
refer (as obliquely as 65. 11 does to 415) to the absence of Alkibiades
from the scene and the rejection of his advice to the generals at
Aigospotamoi (X. *HG* ii. 1. 25 f., Plu. *Alc.* 36. 6–37. 2, Diod. xiii.
105. 3 f.). I assume that Thucydides did not countenance the allegation of Lys. xiv. 38 (cf. ii. 58) that Alkibiades conspired with Adeimantos to bring about the Athenian defeat at Aigospotamoi, and
I suspect that Pl. *Mnx.* 243 d is a rhetorical adaptation of Th. ii.
65. 12.

  (ii) We may, alternatively, refer ἔσφηλαν τὴν πόλιν to the defeat in
Sicily. φοβηθέντες γάρ - - - καὶ ἄλλοις ἐπιτρέψαντες will then refer to
415. The conflict between the narrative and κράτιστα διαθέντι τὰ τοῦ
πολέμου is still a conflict, but much more easily explicable; having
the evidence for Alkibiades' conduct in 411–406, Thucydides could
hardly fail to conclude that if only he had been retained in Sicily the
Athenians would not have been defeated (cf. Plu. *Alc.* 32. 4), and
from this conclusion it would not be too long a step to a favourable
reassessment of his strategic conceptions in 420–415 as a whole.
On this interpretation the judgement, if it is to be called biased, is
at least given its bias by knowledge of later events (cf. de Romilly,
Imp., 227 f.), and was ' "thought" at a different time from the general
narrative of the Sicilian expedition' (Gomme, loc. cit. 74). But here

it is not possible to absolve Thucydides of obscurity, for the suppressed premiss in the argument is that the failure of the Sicilian expedition (ἔσφηλαν τὴν πόλιν) was the turning-point of the war and led to ultimate defeat. This is made more explicit in ii. 65. 11, where the Sicilian expedition is singled out for mention among all the enterprises undertaken by Athens after the death of Perikles and is treated as initiating the last long stage of the war: 'after their defeat in Sicily . . . they nevertheless held out. . . .' Furthermore, although καθεῖλεν might appear entirely unambiguous to Thucydides, it is surprising that he should go on to speak of the earlier exile of Alkibiades in the knowledge that there was also a second exile, and that he should refer in ἔσφηλαν τὴν πόλιν (words which in themselves are by no means unambiguous, cf. Strasburger, 145) to an event other than καθεῖλε τὴν πόλιν.

It appears from these considerations that the most satisfactory interpretation of the passage is that which refers both καθεῖλεν and ἔσφηλαν to the same event, the final defeat, φοβηθέντες γάρ - - - ἐπιτρέψαντες to the second exile of Alkibiades, and οὐ διὰ μακροῦ accordingly to the interval between the second exile and the end of the war (cf. Andrewes, *Historia* x [1961], 9 f). Rehm, loc. cit., follows a counsel of despair in suggesting that 15. 4 is the work of someone who amplified a marginal note of Thucydides by using the language of 28. 2.

τῆς - - - παρανομίας ἐς τὴν δίαιταν: cf. Plu. *Alc.* 16, And. iv. 10 ff., for anecdotal material.

διαθέντι: so H₂: διαθέντα cannot be retained unless some such words as ⟨καταπαύσαντες τῆς ἀρχῆς⟩ (Gertz), ⟨ἔπαυσαν τῆς ἡγεμονίας⟩ (Wilamowitz, *Hermes* lxiv [1929], 477), or ⟨ἀφελόμενοι⟩ (Herbst, 83 ff.) are inserted in the neighbourhood of ἀχθεσθέντες; the exact words will naturally be related to the critic's historical interpretation of the passage as a whole. διαθέντι is not easy linguistically: 'became his enemies, in the belief that he wanted to become tyrant, even though in strategy he was superior to everyone, because as individuals they resented his behaviour, and, by handing over to others, . . .' or 'and, individually resenting him because of his behaviour, although in his public capacity his strategy was superior to everyone's, and so handing over to others . . .'. The former interpretation diminishes the force of the antithesis between δημοσίᾳ and ἰδίᾳ, and in the latter ἀχθεσθέντες, of which the indirect object is (sc. αὐτῷ) διαθέντι, is immediately preceded by another dative which must be given a causal sense. All the difficulties are removed by adopting διαθέντος from the second correction-stratum in Paris. gr. 1638 (cj. Herwerden, cf. W. Vollgraff, *Mnemosyne* 1905, 427). For διατιθέναι = 'handle' 'treat', cf. 57. 4 and Pl. *Chrm.* 162 d ὀργισθῆναι αὐτῷ ὥσπερ ποιητῇς ὑποκριτῇ κακῶς διατιθέντι τὰ ἑαυτοῦ ποιήματα.

16–18. *Speech of Alkibiades*

According to D. xxi. 145 Alkibiades λέγειν ἐδόκει πάντων, ὥς φασιν, εἶναι δεινότατος; an interesting tradition presented by Theophrastos (fr. 134 Wimmer) is that Alkibiades excelled in εὑρεῖν τὰ δέοντα καὶ νοῆσαι but spoke hesitantly, searching all the time for the right words. Here in Thucydides he is capable of elaborate sophistry (e.g. 16. 4 f., 18. 6 f., cf. 92. 3 f.) and even perhaps of adapting contemporary scientific doctrines (18. 6 n.), but the persuasive power of his speech lies in his unhesitating generalizations on matters of historical fact (17. 7, 18. 1 f., 6, cf. 89. 4 ff.) and on the dogmatic confidence with which he interprets the present (16. 2, 6, 17. 2 ff., 8, 18. 3, cf. 91. 1 ff.) or predicts the future (17. 6, 18. 4 f., cf. 91. 6 f., 92. 5). Periklean reminiscences, both verbal and substantial, are conspicuous: 17. 7, 18. 1, 2, 3, 6, see nn. (cf. de Romilly, *Imp.*, 210, and Gomme, *JHS* lxxi [1951], 78 f. = *More Essays*, 108–9).

16. 1. ἀνάγκη γὰρ ἐντεῦθεν ἄρξασθαι: speakers in Thucydides commonly begin by defending themselves against actual or potential accusations; cf. 82. 1, 89. 1, i. 37. 1, and (less obviously) ii. 60.

ἐπιβόητος: picked up by τὰ ἴδια ἐπιβοώμενος in § 6. περιβόητος (M^{yp.}c^{yp.}f^{yp.}) is inappropriate; in 31. 6, the only passage in which Thucydides uses it, it implies admiration.

τοῖς μὲν προγόνοις μου: he may mean that men felicitate (or ought to felicitate) his dead ancestors for what he himself does (cf. ii. 11. 9 and Isoc. vii. 56), or that the credit for what he does belongs to his ancestors in so far as they enabled him, by accumulating wealth and establishing a tradition of political and military ambition, to do it, or (sc. ἔφερεν) that horse-racing brought renown to his ancestors and brings it to him.

2. ὅσα οὐδεὶς πω ἰδιώτης πρότερον: the implied contrast is not simply with the tyrants of an earlier age but with states (cf. v. 50. 4).

ἐνίκησα δὲ καὶ δεύτερος καὶ τέταρτος ἐγενόμην: in 420 the chariot race at Olympia was won by Lichas (v. 50. 4), and ἐλπίζοντες αὐτὴν καταπεπολεμῆσθαι can hardly refer to 424, however much allowance we make for rhetoric; the year of Alkibiades' victory was therefore 416. It is of no importance that Isoc. xvi. 34 speaks of Alkibiades' chariots as coming first, second, and third; the fact 'first, second, and fourth' would naturally become 'first, second, and third' in a law-court eighteen years later, to say nothing of the extreme ease of textual corruption of the former to the latter. The real difficulty is created by the epinikion composed by Euripides, from which Plu. *Alc.* 11. 2 f. quotes ἅρματι πρῶτα δραμεῖν καὶ δεύτερα καὶ τρίτα βῆναι. Plutarch is aware that this poem is irreconcilable with

246

Thucydides, but offers no solution; but in *Dem.* 1. 1, where he quotes another passage of the epinikion, he reveals incidentally that its authenticity could be disputed—on what grounds, he does not say, but it is possible that irreconcilability with Thucydides was the sole ground. It is tempting to suppose that the epinikion was neither by Euripides nor even contemporary, but a poetic counterpart of the 'speech of Nikias to the Syracusans' attributed to Lysias (fr. xcix Thalheim), and composed long enough after the event to adopt the version of the facts which is found in Isokrates. Yet Bowra, *Historia* ix (1960), 68 ff., points out some peculiarly Euripidean features in the language of the quotations; his solution is that Alkibiades exaggerated his achievement, Euripides accepted the exaggerated version, and Thucydides is correcting it. The suggestion that the third place in the race was disputed (i.e. that Alkibiades thought that one of his chariots 'really' came third, while the judges thought otherwise) has a disquieting flavour of editorial ingenuity, but may be right none the less. There are modern parallels in popular disagreement with the judges' award of third-place medals, e.g. the 1960 Olympics and the 1963 Monza *grand prix*. On the credit which athletic victory conferred on the victor's city cf. Pi. *O.* 4. 10 ff., 8. 20, Lys. xix. 63.

ἐκ δὲ τοῦ δρωμένου καὶ δύναμις ἅμα ὑπονοεῖται: the distinction between the actual (δρώμενον) and the potential (δύναμις) would be lost by the superficially attractive emendation ὁρωμένου (suggested by Vollgraff, *Mnemosyne* 1905, 427 f., and Platt, *JPh.* xxxiii [1914], 272 f.); Platt's interpretation 'Though such things are *only* conventionally a distinction, *yet* . . . from a visible display, etc.' overlooks the relation between ἐνόμισαν and νόμῳ and makes the wrong point.

3. ἥδ᾽ ἡ ἄνοια: so Gᵞᵖ· Mᵞᵖ·c, and Σᴹᶜᶠ includes the words οὐκ ἄχρηστός ἐστί μου ἡ ἄνοια in his paraphrase; ἡ διάνοια cett. If the more vigorous ἥδ᾽ ἡ ἄνοια is right, here and in 17. 1 ἡ - - - ἄνοια - - - δοκοῦσα εἶναι Alkibiades seems to be harping on a particular accusation made by Nikias; yet Nikias has not accused him of 'folly' (cf. H. Richards, *CQ* viii [1914], 77) and has used the word ἀνόητος, without any personal reference, only in a generalization about extension of empire (11. 1). No doubt there was sometimes a slight discrepancy between what Thucydides had actually written and his mental picture of what he had written.

4. οὐδέ γε ἄδικον - - - ἀνταξιούτω: the argument is: 'an unfortunate man recognizes that he is inferior; therefore, it is reasonable that a prosperous man should behave as superior', cf. X. *Smp.* 4. 51 ἐμοὶ γὰρ αὖ τῶν φίλων οἱ μὲν εὖ πράττοντες ἐκποδὼν ἀπέρχονται, κ.τ.λ.; 'as the unfortunate man is to the ordinary man, so is the ordinary man to the prosperous man; if ordinary men expect the prosperous to treat them as equals, let them themselves first treat the unfortunate as equals.' Since most Greeks believed that the gods

intervened in human life and that misfortune might be a punishment for one's own sins or the sins of one's ancestors, pity had less scope in Greek ethics than in ours, and people hesitated to associate with those whom the gods were apparently punishing. No doubt practice was less callous than theory, but in rhetoric and gnomic (e.g. E. *El.* 605 ff., 1131) it is taken for granted that in misfortune one loses one's friends.

5. προσποίησίν τε ξυγγενείας τισὶ καὶ μὴ οὖσαν καταλιπόντας: the generalization is nicely borne out by Duris of Samos, who claimed to be a descendant of Alkibiades (Plu. *Alc.* 32. 2), but a Hellenistic historian's claim of kinship with a great figure of Classical times is a special case. Possibly Thucydides has in mind people who claimed descent from Odysseus (e.g. Andokides [Hellanikos F 170]), Palamedes, or Ajax (cf. Pherekydes F 2). οὐκ οὖσαν is 'untrue'; cf. Aeschin. iii. 100 ἐλπίδων οὐκ ἐσομένων.

6. Πελοποννήσου γὰρ τὰ δυνατώτατα ξυστήσας: Alkibiades could fairly claim to have been the architect of the Athenian alliance with Argos, Elis, and Mantineia, and it was his persuasiveness, on an embassy to Argos (where he had great influence, cf. 61. 3, 88. 9 n., Plu. *Alc.* 11. 3) in the summer of 418 (v. 61. 2 f.), which set in motion the campaign which was ended by the Spartan victory at Mantineia. The Argives, Eleans, and Mantineans would no doubt have been pleased to be described as Πελοποννήσου τὰ δυνατώτατα—Lykomedes of Mantineia inspired and gratified the Arkadians by similar compliments in 369 (X. *HG* vii. 1. 23)—but the description has little bearing on the political realities of 415. Cf. the absurd exaggeration of Isoc. xvi. 15 διακοσίους ὁπλίτας ἔχων τὰς μεγίστας πόλεις τῶν ἐν Πελοποννήσῳ Λακεδαιμονίων μὲν ἀπέστησεν, ὑμῖν δὲ συμμάχους ἐποίησεν. Λακεδαιμονίους ἐς μίαν ἡμέραν κατέστησα - - - ἀγωνίσασθαι: the Argives and their allies, blithely confident, had courted an annihilating defeat in the Argolid in 418, and were only saved by two of their number who negotiated with Agis. Sparta's allies were aggrieved at this, but Alkibiades' policy had come very close to assuring Sparta lasting domination of the Peloponnese (v. 58–60). Not long after, at the battle of Mantineia, few of Sparta's allies were present (v. 63. 4).

οὐδέπω καὶ νῦν βεβαίως θαρσοῦσιν: in consequence of the battle of Mantineia Spartan prestige was enhanced (v. 75. 3), the Argive alliance fell to pieces (v. 81. 1, cf. vii. 31. 1), an oligarchy was temporarily established in Argos (v. 81. 2), and Sparta intervened to her own advantage in Sikyon (ibid.). On this aspect of the matter, the only possible justification of Alkibiades' confident statement (and it is not much of a justification) is that Sparta lost control of Argos later (v. 82, cf. *IG* i². 96 + *SEG* x. 104); but the claim ἄνευ μεγάλου ὑμῖν κινδύνου καὶ δαπάνης is true.

17. 1. ἡ ἐμὴ νεότης καὶ ἄνοια παρὰ φύσιν δοκοῦσα εἶναι: as reckless ἄνοια is not, in Greek eyes, contrary to the nature of youth, παρὰ φύσιν here means 'contrary to the nature of the sane and healthy man' (cf. Hp. *Aer.* 38 ὁκόταν θερμανθῇ μᾶλλον τῆς φύσιος), i.e. 'insane': 'what is regarded (sc. by Nikias and others) as my "youth" and "insane folly"'. ταῦτα - - - ὡμίλησε = 'such were the dealings...'; the extent to which ταῦτα must be recalled when the hearer comes to ἔπεισεν is uncertain.

ἐς τὴν Πελοποννησίων δύναμιν: whereas Πελοπόννησος in Thucydides is a geographical term, Πελοποννήσιοι means not 'the inhabitants of the Peloponnese' but 'Sparta and her allies'. Ignoring the fact that Argos, the major power concerned, had not been an ally of Sparta, Alkibiades represents himself as negotiating successfully with 'the area controlled by Sparta and her allies'; for δύναμιν cf. ii. 7. 1 πόλεις τε ξυμμαχίδας ποιούμενοι ὅσαι ἦσαν ἐκτὸς τῆς ἑαυτῶν δυνάμεως. The alternative interpretation, equating τὴν Πελοποννησίων δύναμιν with Πελοποννήσου τὰ δυνατώτατα (16. 6) gives a unique sense to Πελοποννήσιοι.

ὀργῇ πίστιν παρασχομένη: probably 'inspiring confidence in them by its spirit' (cf. Pl. *Grg.* 454 e δύο εἴδη θῶμεν πειθοῦς, τὸ μὲν πίστιν παρεχόμενον ἄνευ τοῦ εἰδέναι, τὸ δ' ἐπιστήμην and D. xxii. 22 ὅταν τις ψιλῷ χρησάμενος λόγῳ μὴ παράσχηται πίστιν ὧν λέγει) but possibly 'offering (providing) in (by) its spirit, a pledge (guarantee, sc. of good faith)', cf. 12. 1 and 83. 1. While the arguments, in content and form, were all that the occasion required, it was the sincerity underlying them which achieved conviction. If parallelism with λόγοις τε πρέπουσιν is desired, it is better to read παρασχομένη, as ABEF do (the difference in meaning is not significant), but against parallelism must be set Thucydidean variation.

ὁ Νικίας εὐτυχὴς δοκεῖ εἶναι: Nikias, who after the last battle in the harbour recalls his reputation for good luck (vii. 77. 2), had not so far been associated with any failures or setbacks; cf. v. 16. 1 and Bender, 38 and 45. According to Plu. *Nic.* 6. 2 he attributed his successes to luck in order not to offend the gods by presumption, just as a man today says 'it was a fluke' in order not to be thought self-satisfied. Plutarch may be guilty of anachronism here; to the Greeks of the fifth century good luck seemed to be a proof of the gods' favour (cf. 103. 3 n.), as wealth certainly did (cf. 16. 4 n.), and Nikias was outstandingly wealthy. Alkibiades' argument only makes sense if εὐτυχία is treated as an abiding characteristic, and that is logically irreconcilable with its treatment as pure chance.

2. ὄχλοις τε γὰρ ξυμμείκτοις πολυανδροῦσιν αἱ πόλεις: the Sikeliot tyrants at the beginning of the fifth century carried out many transplantations of population (Hdt. vii. 156. 2 f., Diod. xi. 49), and their settlements were upset after they and their power had gone, by a fresh set of transplantations in 461/60 (Diod. xi. 76. 3 f.). Between then and 415 the only transplantation of which we know is the Syracusan incorporation of the δυνατοί of Leontinoi, with the expulsion of its remaining population, in 423 (Th. v. 4. 2 ff.). This recent case would naturally be prominent in the minds of Alkibiades' audience, since it was one of the pretexts of the expedition; but the basis of his generalization is a conception of Sicilian affairs formed early in the fifth century and no doubt deeply rooted in Athens and elsewhere.

καὶ ῥᾳδίας ἔχουσι τῶν πολιτῶν τὰς μεταβολὰς καὶ ἐπιδοχάς: E alone has πολιτῶν, which gives admirable sense; cf. i. 2. 3 τῆς γῆς ἡ ἀρίστη αἰεὶ τὰς μεταβολὰς τῶν οἰκητόρων εἶχεν and Hdt. viii. 75. 1 ὡς ἐπεδέκοντο οἱ Θεσπιέες πολιήτας. πολιτειῶν (cett.) would demand a sense of πολιτεία, 'body (list) of citizens', which is normal in Hellenistic Greek but is not Classical (cf. ΣMcf ad loc. and Dover, CQ N.S. iv [1954], 82); the acceptable Classical sense 'constitution' (cf. Isoc. iv. 114 πολιτειῶν μεταβολάς = 'revolutions') would be irrelevant to Alkibiades' argument unless we interpreted ἐπιδοχάς elaborately as 'additions to the citizen body resulting therefrom'.

3. νομίμοις κατασκευαῖς: for νόμιμος = 'the usual kind(s) of' cf. D. ix. 48, and for κατασκευαί = 'buildings', i.e. in the present context 'farms' or 'farm buildings', or even 'fittings' (cf. X. Cyr. vii. 5. 72 ἔχομεν δὲ καὶ οἰκίας καὶ ἐν ταύταις κατασκευάς), cf. ii. 16. 1, 65. 2, Hell. Oxy. 17 Bart. (12 G–H). 4 f. The corruption ὡς περὶ > ὥσπερ occurs also in some manuscripts of X. Cyr. viii. 7. 6.

ὅτι δὲ ἕκαστος - - - ταῦτα ἑτοιμάζεται: instead of spending his money, the Sikeliot 'accumulates it in readiness'; whether ἑτοιμάζεται is middle, as in vii. 31. 5 (ταῦτα being its object, sc. ἕκαστος as subject), or passive, as in vii. 62. 1 (ταῦτα being its subject) makes no significant difference to the sense; for ἕτοιμος used of money, cf. 22 ad fin. In either case the reference, as the context of the argument shows, is to action by individuals, not states. The Sikeliot does not invest his money in land and buildings, but accumulates it (cf. Herwerden, Mnemosyne 1880, 149) in the expectation that in circumstances described as μὴ κατορθώσας he will leave his present domicile and live elsewhere. Whether μὴ κατορθώσας has a highly general reference, 'if his career is unsuccessful' (cf. Isoc. xix. 4 διὰ τοῦτ' οἴονται καλὸν εἶναι τὸν κίνδυνον, ὅτι μὴ κατορθώσαντες οὐδὲν μέλλουσιν ἀποτείσειν) or refers specifically to failure in the alternative processes ἢ ἐκ τοῦ λέγων πείθειν - - - ἢ στασιάζων (cf. vii. 70. 4 ἢ διὰ τὸ φεύγειν ἢ ἄλλῃ ἐπιπλέουσα) it is clear that a man μὴ κατορθώσας is not in a position to get land or money ἀπὸ τοῦ κοινοῦ (Herbst, 88 ff.). Three conclusions follow: (i) 'taking' precedes accumulation, as we should expect. (ii) ὅτι does not = 'because'—for if it did, ἄλλην γῆν would have to be the object of λαβών as well as of οἰκήσειν, and ταῦτα would have the rather obscure meaning 'money for this purpose'—but = 'that which', being the object of λαβών and describing a category of money directly referred to by ταῦτα ('money . . . wherewith he thinks to settle . . .', Arnold); cf. X. *Cyr.* i. 6. 11 ὅτι δ' ἂν - - - λαμβάνῃ τις, ταῦτα καὶ τιμὴν νομιοῦσι and D. lvii. 12 ὅτι γνοίησαν - - -, τούτοις ἤθελον ἐμμένειν. So far, then, literally: 'that having received which from the common treasury each man thinks that, if he is unsuccessful, he will dwell on other land, this he accumulates'. Cf. v. 89 οὔθ' ὑμᾶς ἀξιοῦμεν - - - ὡς ἡμᾶς οὐδὲν ἠδικήκατε λέγοντας οἴεσθαι πείσειν and D. xxiii. 190 τὸ μὲν οἷς ἔμελλεν ἐκεῖνος λαβὼν μηδέν - - - βλάψειν ἀντιλέγειν. (iii) ἢ ἐκ τοῦ λέγων πείθειν - - - ἢ στασιάζων, 'either through persuasive oratory' (cf. 60. 3) 'or (sc. the threat of) faction', must refer to the means of acquiring money. Alkibiades is here casting a double slur upon the Sikeliots, affirming not only that they keep their money ready in the expectation of expulsion, but that the money itself is acquired by doubtful means. It is taken for granted by the Greeks, as we see from the comedians' and orators' references to men whom they dislike, that a dishonest man may make money out of public office and a prominent position in public life (cf. 12. 2 n.). 'Persuasion by speaking, or faction' is essentially the common antithesis between argument and force; Sikeliot propensities to both are indicated in § 4. The meaning of the whole sentence is thus: 'He holds in readiness the money which he has taken from public funds, by persuasive oratory or the threat of faction, in the expectation that if his career (sc. of making money at public expense) is checked he will go and live elsewhere' (cf. Dover, *PCPhS* clxxxiii [1954–5], 5 f.).

4. ὡς ἕκαστοι: in view of ὄχλοις ξυμμείκτοις πολυανδροῦσιν αἱ πόλεις we are probably meant to understand neither 'different states' nor 'different factions', but more generally 'different groups' between which the boundaries are not those of state or party.

εἴ τι καθ' ἡδονὴν λέγοιτο: this foreshadows the strategy which Alkibiades later advocates (48). It is possible that there is also an allusion to development of rhetoric in fifth-century Sicily (cf. L. Radermacher, *Artium Scriptores* [*SAWW* 227. 3], 11 ff., 28 ff.); but Thucydides makes no clear or direct reference to that in his narrative or in any of the speeches.

εἰ στασιάζουσιν: it is possible that this might refer to inter-state warfare rather than to factions within states, but if it did Alkibiades would be assuming a natural unity of Sicily contrary to the general tenor of his argument. Lys. ii. 21 ἔτι στασιαζούσης τῆς Ἑλλάδος ᾧ τινι χρὴ τρόπῳ τοὺς ἐπιόντας ἀμύνασθαι and Theognis 780 f. ἀφραδίην ἐσορῶν καὶ στάσιν Ἑλλήνων λαοφθόρον both refer to Greek disunity in the face of the Persian threat, and choose their words deliberately to emphasize the unnaturalness of such disunity.

5. ὅσους ἕκαστοι σφᾶς αὐτοὺς ἠρίθμουν: ὅσους (recc.) is essential;

ὅσοι (codd.) could only mean 'as numerous as those who, each state separately, counted themselves'.

ἀλλὰ μέγιστον δή - - - ὡπλίσθη: statements of this kind are as much used by a Greek as by a modern speaker; they can be denied by his opponent (20. 4) but they cannot be refuted except after laborious research, by which time it is too late to counteract their effect on the audience.

ἐν τῷδε τῷ πολέμῳ: in v. 26. 2 ff. Thucydides defends his view that the Archidamian War, the period of the Peace of Nikias, the Sicilian expedition, and the subsequent fighting constituted a single war, and accordingly he describes each year in his narrative as 'the *n*th year of this war'. The need to argue for such a view is apparent from, e.g., And. iii. 8 f., where the Peloponnesian War is clearly not seen as a unity (cf. Ullrich, 7 ff., for ancient names for the war and its components). Unless the words here attributed to Alkibiades are an anachronism (as Ullrich argues, 57 f., n. 70), Alkibiades in 415 not only held the view which the historian adopted later but took it for granted in arguing before the Assembly. It is not altogether easy to decide from Alkibiades' speech as a whole whether he, like Nikias (10. 2 f.), is representing the peace as unreal or whether, as his words in 18. 2 f., 6, might suggest, he thinks of peace as established but undesirable. The most important consideration is his own conduct from 421 to 415, which showed what he thought of the peace treaty; the present situation he regards not as peace, but as perilous inactivity (18. 2 ἡσυχάζοιεν, 3 τὸ ἥσυχον, 6 ἡσυχάζῃ) in the constant presence of malignant enemies (17. 7 f.). It may well be that Thucydides has correctly reproduced an outlook of the time (cf. Andrewes, *Historia* x [1961], 8), and that in v. 26 he is arguing against the historically incorrect outlook of the later years. To admit this is not to deny that for a year or two after the peace treaty of 421 Thucydides may himself have thought the peace real, nor does it throw any light on the extent to which he spent that year or two in preparing for circulation a history of the years 431–421 (cf. v. 26. 6 n.; N. G. L. Hammond, *CQ* xxxiv [1940], 146 ff.). Classen deleted the whole of § 5 as an interpolation based upon v. 68. 1. The possibility of interpolation cannot be rejected, in view of the interests revealed, and the style achieved, by the composer of iii. 17 and iii. 84, but Classen's fundamental reason was a bad one: that 'no one in 415 could have assumed a continuation of the war against the Peloponnesians'.

7. οἱ γὰρ πατέρες - - - ἰσχύοντες: Alkibiades is not arguing that because the Athenians in the past had survived desperate situations they should now deliberately create another one, but, as his continuation shows, that they had in the past deliberately taken risks as the only way of acquiring their pemire. He ignores the fact that the

Delian League was created, at a time when Athens and Sparta were allies, on the initiative of the Ionian states, and that essential steps towards the conversion of the League into an empire (i. 98. 4–99) had been taken while the Spartan alliance was still in force.

8. οὔτε ἀνέλπιστοί πω μᾶλλον - - - ἐγένοντο: 'the Peloponnesians have never had so little hope of success against us.'

ὑπόλοιπον γὰρ ἡμῖν ἐστιν ἀντίπαλον ναυτικόν: this is true, since Alkibiades could not reasonably have envisaged in 415 that it would be necessary, two years later, to send to Sicily a force almost as substantial as the original expedition; it was only this reinforcement which denuded Athens.

18. 1. ὥστε τί ἂν λέγοντες εἰκός - - - μὴ βοηθοῖμεν; it is not quite clear whether Thucydides intends λέγοντες and σκηπτόμενοι to be parallel and of equal weight ('with what rational argument should we ourselves shrink from the enterprise, or with what excuse to our allies in Sicily should we refrain from helping them?') or σκηπτόμενοι to be subordinate in sense to λέγοντες ('with what rational argument should we either ourselves shrink . . ., or, making it an excuse to our allies . . ., refrain from helping them?'). The former gives a more symmetrical structure ('argument / decision not to act // excuse / failure to help') and for the position of ἤ cf. 7. 3 n. and viii. 46. 1 μηδὲ βουληθῆναι κομίσαντα ἢ ναῦς Φοινίσσας - - - ἢ ῞Ελλησι πλέοσι μισθὸν πορίζοντα τοῖς αὐτοῖς - - - τὸ κράτος δοῦναι.

ὅτι οὐδὲ ἐκεῖνοι ἡμῖν: 'that *they* did not ⟨help⟩ *us*'; cf. Hdt. i. 3. 1 ἐπιστάμενον πάντως ὅτι οὐ δώσει δίκην· οὐδὲ γὰρ ἐκείνους διδόναι and Denniston, 195.

οὐ γὰρ ἵνα δεῦρο ἀντιβοηθῶσι προσεθέμεθα αὐτούς: Alkibiades is speaking of the Athenian intention, not of the formal terms of the alliances; we know of no Greek alliance in which *A* promises to help *B* but *B* does not promise to help *A*; since, however, neither party would be expected to help the other until called upon to do so, alliances which were formally reciprocal could be unilateral in practice.

δεῦρο κωλύωσιν αὐτοὺς ἐπιέναι: cf. 10. 1 n.

2. παραγιγνόμενοι προθύμως τοῖς αἰεί - - - ἐπικαλουμένοις: cf. 87. 5 and Isoc. iv. 52 διετέλεσαν κοινὴν τὴν πόλιν παρέχοντες καὶ τοῖς ἀδικουμένοις ἀεὶ τῶν ῾Ελλήνων ἐπαμύνουσαν. The theme is common in laudations of Athens; Alkibiades extends it here, as the occasion demands, to alliance with βάρβαροι (such as Segesta, Inaros in 460, and Amorges [viii. 5. 5, al., And. iii. 29], whose activities were known to Thucydides by the time book vi was written). Perikles in ii. 40. 4 elevates the theme on to a higher plane of generalization by saying οὐ γὰρ πάσχοντες εὖ ἀλλὰ δρῶντες κτώμεθα τοὺς φίλους; cf. (and contrast) Isoc. iv. 80 τῷ ποιεῖν εὖ προσαγόμενοι τὰς πόλεις, ἀλλ᾽ οὐ βίᾳ καταστρεφόμενοι.

εἴ γε ἡσυχάζοιεν πάντες ἢ φυλοκρινοῖεν - - - μᾶλλον κινδυνεύοιμεν: after the previous reference to 'all those who have ruled an empire' any hearer would take ἡσυχάζοιεν πάντες to refer similarly to all imperial powers (Preuss, 18), but the continuation shows that it refers to all Athenians; hence Hude's ἡσυχάζοιμεν πάντως ἢ φυλοκρινοῖμεν. If we are willing to understand 'as Nikias would do' and so to defend the MSS.' text, we must admit that Thucydides has expressed himself badly.

τὸν γὰρ προύχοντα - - - προκαταλαμβάνει: to us, surveying Greek history as a whole, this generalization does not seem conspicuously true; Athenian and Spartan reactions to the growth of Persian power constitute the only obvious case in which τὸν προύχοντά τις προκατελάμβανεν; Sparta's reactions to the growth of Athenian power during the Pentekontaetia were of the opposite character, as her allies increasingly complained.

3. διὰ τὸ ἀρχθῆναι ἂν ὑφ' ἑτέρων αὐτοῖς κίνδυνον εἶναι: cf. Perikles in ii. 62. 3 and 63. 2 f. on the dangers of inactivity in an imperial city, and especially his comparison of Athens' position in the world to that of a tyrant within a state (ii. 63. 3); de Romilly, *Imp.*, 56 f., 210 ff., 243, 313, and 315 n. 3. ἄρχειν is used, here and below, straightforwardly; cf. the formula ἐν τῶν πόλεων ὧν Ἀθηναῖοι ἄρχουσιν in *IG* i². 56. 14 f. (R. Meiggs, *CR* lxiii [1949], 9 f.).

4. στορέσωμεν τὸ φρόνημα: for the colourful metaphor, which is found nowhere else in Classical prose, cf. A. *PV* 190. Σ^{Mcf} infers that Thucydides is speaking here not in his own manner but κατὰ Ἀλκιβιάδην; cf. 41. 3 f. n.

ἄρξομεν, ἢ κακώσομέν γε Συρακοσίους: although these words are co-ordinated by τε / καί with the final clause ἵνα στορέσωμεν, the mood (in both senses of the word) is changed; the use of εἰ δόξομεν instead of ἢν δόξωμεν helps the change, for many instances of εἰ with the future resemble the English 'going to' and imply that a future contingency can already be seen to be probable. Emendation of ἄρξομεν and κακώσομεν to subjunctives diminishes the rhetorical effect. Cf. E. *El.* 58 f. ἀλλ' ὡς ὕβριν δείξωμεν Αἰγίσθου θεοῖς—γόους τ' ἀφίημ' αἰθέρ' ἐς μέγαν πατρί. The ambition to 'lead' or 'rule' (ἄρχειν) the whole Greek world existed at Sparta as well as at Athens, but under the different name ἡγεῖσθαι; cf. 92. 5, viii. 2. 4.

5. τὸ δὲ ἀσφαλές, καὶ μένειν - - - καὶ ἀπελθεῖν: literally 'safety, both for staying . . . and for departing'; the infinitives amplify τὸ ἀσφαλές, and ἀσφαλές is not to be regarded as an attributive adjective qualifying the substantive τὸ μένειν. Cf. X. *An.* i. 3. 13 οἷα εἴη ἡ ἀπορία ἄνευ τῆς Κύρου γνώμης καὶ μένειν καὶ ἀπιέναι.

ἤν τι προχωρῇ: cf. 6. 1 n. προ- H^{γρ.}: προσ- (cett.) would mean 'if we receive any addition', i.e. 'if any states come over to us as allies', which is far too specific.

ναυκράτορες γὰρ ἐσόμεθα καὶ ξυμπάντων Σικελιωτῶν: *ναυκράτορες* (Valckenaer) is inescapable, cf. Hdt. v. 36. 2 *ναυκρατέες τῆς θαλάσσης*. *αὐτοκράτορες* (codd.), 'we shall be able to do what we like with even the combined strength of the Sikeliots' has no parallel.

6. διάστασις τοῖς νέοις ἐς τοὺς πρεσβυτέρους: the point of the dative *τοῖς νέοις* is avoidance of the ambiguity inherent in an accumulation of genitives; cf. S. *OT* 266 ff. *τὸν αὐτόχειρα τοῦ φόνου τῷ Λαβδακείῳ παιδὶ Πολυδώρου τε καὶ τοῦ πρόσθε Κάδμου*, and 4. 6 n.

ἐς τάδε ἦραν αὐτά: the sentiment is Periklean, cf. i. 144. 4 *οἱ γοῦν πατέρες ἡμῶν - - - ἐς τάδε προήγαγον αὐτά· ὧν οὐ χρὴ λείπεσθαι κ.τ.λ.* Immediately below we find another Periklean echo in *ὥσπερ καὶ ἄλλο τι*; cf. i. 142. 9 *τὸ δὲ ναυτικὸν τέχνης ἐστί, ὥσπερ καὶ ἄλλο τι, καὶ οὐκ ἐνδέχεται, ὅταν τύχῃ, ἐκ παρέργου μελετᾶσθαι.* Cf. also § 3 n.

τό τε φαῦλον καὶ τὸ μέσον καὶ τὸ πάνυ ἀκριβὲς ἂν ξυγκραθὲν μάλιστ' ἂν ἰσχύειν: Alkibiades is adapting to the 'body politic' a common medical doctrine that health depends on the correct blending of unlike elements (Hp. *VM* 18); cf. ibid. 14 on the mixture of extremes in a healthy diet and the harm done by *ἀπόκρισις*, and *Aer.* 12 on the beneficial effects of a moderate climate (*κρῆσις τῶν ὡρέων*) on temperament. The doctrine that right action is a mean between extremes is, of course, related to this; cf. H. Kahlreuter, *Die Μεσότης bei und vor Aristoteles* (Diss. Tübingen, 1911) and G. Grossmann, *Politische Schlagwörter aus der Zeit des Peloponnesischen Krieges* (Zürich, 1950), 12 ff., 82.

τρίψεσθαί τε αὐτὴν περὶ αὐτήν: cf. viii. 46. 2 *αὐτοὺς περὶ ἑαυτοὺς τοὺς Ἕλληνας κατατρῖψαι.*

καὶ πάντων τὴν ἐπιστήμην ἐγγηράσεσθαι: the subject of *ἐγγηράσεσθαι* is *ἐπιστήμην* (military and naval skill; cf. Schwartz, 335), the point of *ἐγ-* being 'in the city'; cf. vii. 56. 3 *τὴν σφετέραν πόλιν ἐμπαρασχόντες προκινδυνεῦσαι*, where *ἐμ-* means 'in the combination of forces constituted by themselves and their allies'. With *ἀγωνιζομένην* we return to the city as subject; for the succession of subjects A—B—A cf. 86. 2, vii. 18. 3.

7. γιγνώσκω - - - μοι δοκεῖν: there is at first sight tautology here, but Alkibiades is delivering his *γνώμη*, of which the rest of his speech is the supporting argument, and he signals this formally by the word *γιγνώσκω.* Cf. X. *Cyr.* viii. 4. 7 *θεοὺς ὄμνυμι ἦ μὴν ἐμοὶ δοκεῖν πλέον σε διαφέρειν, κ.τ.λ.*

πόλιν μὴ ἀπράγμονα: on the 'philosophy' of *πολυπραγμοσύνη* cf. § 3 n. (the Periklean tradition), 87. 2 n., and de Romilly, *Imp.*, 77 f.

οἳ ἂν - - - ἥκιστα διαφόρως πολιτεύωσιν: appeal to traditional practice and character is rhetorically cogent; Kleon similarly exploits it in the debate on Mytilene, iii. 37. 3 f.

255

19–23. *Second Speech of Nikias*

19. 2. παρασκευῆς δὲ πλήθει - - - τάχ' ἂν μεταστήσειεν αὐτούς: this was a mistake; cf. 24. 2. If a smaller force had been sent, it might not have secured in the first year success enough to justify prolonging its efforts, and if it had been destroyed its loss would not have been so deadly (cf. Grote, v. 555).

20. 1. ξυνενέγκοι μὲν ταῦτα ὡς βουλόμεθα: cf. the vow prescribed in some fourth-century decrees, e.g. *IG* ii². 112 (= *GHI* 144). 6 ff. εὔξασθαι - - - ἐὰν συνενείγκηι Ἀ[θη]ναίων τῶι δήμωι τὰ δόξαντα - - - [θυσί]αν καὶ πρόσοδον ποιήσεσθα[ι] (362/1), al. In the fifth century the words τύχῃ ἀγαθῇ sometimes open a proposal recorded in a document (e.g. iv. 118. 11). D. ix. 76 uses a similar formula: ὅτι δ' ὑμῖν δόξει, τοῦτ', ὦ πάντες θεοί, συνενέγκοι.

2. ἐπὶ γὰρ πόλεις - - - μέλλομεν ἰέναι μεγάλας: one thinks simply of Syracuse and Selinus; but τό τε πλῆθος - - - πολλάς shows that Nikias has in mind the real intention of the Athenians, the subjugation of all Sicily.

ὡς ἐγὼ ἀκοῇ αἰσθάνομαι: Nikias, so far from ignoring (Pohlenz, *NGG* 1919, 123) the argument which Alkibiades expounded in 17. 2 ff. and summed up with the words ἐξ ὧν ἐγὼ ἀκοῇ αἰσθάνομαι in 17. 6, is denying its truth. If the words here are to be adequately translated, they cannot be spoken with exactly the same inflection as in 17. 6; cf. 9. 2 n. on the 'mind's ear'.

οὔτε δεομένας μεταβολῆς: Thucydides returns to this theme in vii. 55. 2, and note.

ἐς ῥᾴω μετάστασιν: 'a change to a less oppressive regime'; cf. ῥᾷον - - - ὑπακούσονται in 69. 3.

πολλὰς τὰς Ἑλληνίδας: there is no need to suspect τὰς Ἑλληνίδας as interpolated; 'and as to their number', lit. 'for one island many, the Greek ones', i.e. 'the Greek cities among them are numerous, for a single island'. Here again it is advisable to imagine Nikias' tone of voice; cf. 9. 2 n.

3. κατὰ τὸ Λεοντίνων ξυγγενές: cf. 3. 1, 3, 6. 1 n.

4. χρήματά τ' ἔχουσι, κ.τ.λ.: τὰ μέν sc. ἔχουσι, but with τὰ δέ we pass to a fresh finite clause of which τὰ δέ is subject, specifying the exceptional source of wealth in each of the two cities ἐπὶ ἃς μᾶλλον πλέομεν.

καὶ ἐν τοῖς ἱεροῖς ἐστι Σελινουντίοις: the archaic and classical temples of Selinus constituted at this date as splendid a group as could be found anywhere in the Greek world; no doubt they contained rich dedications, but we do not know whether they enjoyed any exceptional revenue which would justify Nikias' statement.

καὶ ἀπὸ βαρβάρων τινῶν ἀπαρχὴ ἐσφέρεται: ἀπαρχῆς φέρεται (ABCEFM) is hardly translatable: 'tribute is paid' (φέρεται impersonal) 'from a tithe of' (i.e. offered by) 'some native peoples'. The division ἀπ' ἀρχῆς (Gψ)—accepted by Haacke in the sense 'from time immemorial', but cf. 2. 1 n.—is even less attractive linguistically. The sense we need is: 'a tithe is paid by some native peoples', and this is given by ἀπαρχὴ φέρεται. ἀπαρχή in the Classical period is usually (though not invariably, cf. Pl. *Lg.* 806 d) used of a tithe or proportion of produce, or its equivalent in money, paid to a god, i.e. to a fund kept in a temple and regarded as a god's; so the sixtieth part of the tribute of the Athenian empire, paid in coin to Athena, is called ἀπαρχή (e.g. *ATL*, lists 33. 7, 34. 7). Duker saw that φέρειν, φόρος, and φορά are used of the payment of tribute by subject to ruler (so is ἀποφέρειν, e.g. X. *Cyr.* viii. 6. 8), εἰσφέρειν and εἰσφορά of payment by individuals into public funds or by members of an association into a common treasury (e.g. viii. 45. 5 and X. *Cyr.* vii. 1. 12 πολλὰ κἀγαθὰ ἀλλήλοις εἰσενεγκεῖν); hence ἀπαρχὴ ἐσφέρεται (S²) is not appropriate. More complex emendations, e.g. ἀπὸ βαρβάρων τινῶν ἀρχῆς or [ἀπὸ] βαρβάρων τινῶν ἀπ' ἀρχῆς, need not be considered.

ἵππους τε πολλοὺς κέκτηνται: cf. 21. 1 n.

σίτῳ οἰκείῳ καὶ οὐκ ἐπακτῷ χρῶνται: the contrast with Athens is pointed, but the special relevance of the remark is that states which do not rely on imported corn are less vulnerable to naval blockade.

21. 1. εἰ ξυστῶσιν: the grammar is eccentric, for Attic prose (less so for poetry; cf. Jebb on S. *OT* 198), and ἤν (H⁸, cj. Herwerden) is tempting; cf. the vv. ll. ἤν - - - φαίνηται and εἰ - - - φαίνηται in X. *Cyr.* viii. 7. 23. To the parallels for εἰ assembled (and emended) by Stahl, *SV*, 297 f., add *IG* i². 16 (= ML 31). 18 f., where the sense, 'if (sc. that magistrate) gives judgement against him, the judgement shall be invalid', requires ε]ὶ μὲν καταδικάσ[ηι rather than the ε]ὶ μὲν καταδικάσ[ει (which would suggest 'if, as seems likely, he is going to give judgement against him . . .') adopted by (e.g.) Wade-Gery, 181.

καὶ μὴ ἀντιπαράσχωσιν - - - ἱππικόν: it is noteworthy (cf. Freeman, 102) that Nikias does not think in terms of transporting cavalry from Athens; cf. 22, 'archers and slingers, so that we may hold our own against the enemy cavalry'. Presumably it was simply not practicable to transport enough cavalry with their horses to make much difference (cf. 43 fin., 74. 2 ~ 94. 4).

2. καὶ οὐκ ἐν τῷ ὁμοίῳ στρατευσόμενοι καὶ ὅτε - - - ἤλθετε - - - ἀλλά - - - ἀπαρτήσοντες: the essential framework is πλεῖν {πολύ τε | καὶ στρατευσόμενοι}. If the correct analysis thereafter is οὐ στρατευσόμενοι | ἀλλ' ἀπαρτ-, we require ἀπαρτήσοντες (AᵃᶜCEFᵃᶜGM); if it is στρατευσόμενοι {οὐκ ἐν τῷ ὁμοίῳ | ἀλλ' ἀπαρτ-}, ἀπαρτήσαντες (aBf, cf. Σᴹᶜ) is possible. Since 'going to the help of an ally in the Aegean' is a recurrent process at the time of speaking (cf. Preuss, 20) the aorist ἤλθετε represents the imagined point of view of the troops who will be in Sicily. The intransitive ἀπαρτᾶν, though imitated from Thucydides by Dio li. 4. 2, al., does not occur elsewhere in extant Attic literature; but its meaning, 'be separate', 'be detached' (not, as one might have thought, 'be dependent'), is clear enough from the instances of the passive and the transitive active. The MSS.' text καὶ οὐκ ἐν τοῖς τῇδε ὑπηκόοις deprives ὁμοίῳ of any reference and offers us a meaningless parenthesis. Emendation is required on the lines of καὶ ὅτε ἐν τοῖς (F. Portus), καὶ οὗ ἐν τοῖς (Herbst, 93 ff. and *Ph.* xvi [1860], 337 ff., stressing the desirability of a locative rather than a temporal word), or καὶ ὅτε τοῖς (Badham, *Mnemosyne* 1875, 20 f., and Steup; καιοτε > καιονε through the common confusion of τ and υ, and ονε then 'corrected' to οὐκ ἐν). Hence: 'with the prospect of a campaign on quite different conditions from those in which you took the field against some other state as an ally of your subjects in this part of the world'. ὅθεν = 'where', its form being influenced by ἐκ τῆς φιλίας: 'where the supply of your additional requirements' (i.e. requirements in addition to what you took with you) 'from friendly territory was easy'. Despite the absence of the article in ἐν φιλίᾳ (X. *Cyr.* i. 6. 9), διὰ φιλίας (id., *An.* v. 5. 3), etc., H. Richards's emendation (*CQ* viii [1914], 77) of τῆς to γῆς, claimed and adopted by Bodin, is unnecessary; the article is antithetical in type, pointing the contrast between φιλίας and ἀλλοτρίαν, cf. *Od.* xx. 310 ἐσθλά τε καὶ τὰ χέρεια.

ἐξ ἧς μηνῶν οὐδὲ τεσσάρων τῶν χειμερινῶν ἄγγελον ῥᾴδιον ἐλθεῖν: οὐδέ cannot be divorced in sense from the word which follows it (S. *El.* 630 f. and 1304 are possible exceptions, but fall far short of taking οὐδέ with ἄγγελον here); hence: 'from which it is not easy for a messenger to come (sc. to Athens) even within four months during the winter' (Heitland, *JPh.* xxiv [1896], 4 f., and Marchant). More literally, '. . . not even within four months during (*or* among) the wintry (sc. months)'; Hdt. ii. 68. 1 τοὺς χειμεριωτάτους μῆνας τέσσερας, referring to the habits of crocodiles in Egypt, does not justify the analysis 'not even within four months, I mean the four winter months'. Nikias exaggerates (cf., inter alia, 74. 2, where a trireme is sent to Athens during the winter to ask for reinforcements, 88. 7, where envoys travel from Syracuse to Corinth during the same winter, and vii. 16. 2, where Eurymedon sets out for Sicily with ten ships at the winter solstice), but he is true to Greek sentiment; cf. And. i. 137 τίς γὰρ κίνδυνος μείζων ἀνθρώποις ἢ χειμῶνος ὥρᾳ πλεῖν τὴν θάλατταν;

22. καὶ ἤν τινα ἐκ Πελοποννήσου δυνώμεθα ἢ πεῖσαι ἢ μισθῷ προσαγαγέσθαι: i.e. allies (notably Argos, cf. 29. 3 and vii. 57. 9) and Arkadian mercenaries (cf. 43 n. and vii. 57. 9).

τὸν δὲ καὶ αὐτόθεν σῖτον - - - ἄγειν: although Nikias has emphasized in 21 the importance of taking enough men and equipment from their own resources at the start, the first part of 22 speaks of raising troops also from allies; hence καὶ with αὐτόθεν is climactic, 'actually from Attica itself'. For the separation of τὸν δέ from σῖτον cf. τὸν μέν - - - Δημοσθένη vii. 86. 3; we may analyse the words either as 'the grain (sc. which is necessarily part of the supplies of any army)' or as 'and this further thing, namely grain' (cf. 41. 4 n.; on this interpretation, the gender of σῖτον is anticipated, as commonly happens with demonstratives, and Weidgen's τὸ δέ [RhM lxxvi (1927), 370] is unnecessary. Cf. A. Ag. 988 ff. πεύθομαι δ᾽ ἀπ᾽ ὀμμάτων νόστον - - -· τὸν δ᾽ - - - ὑμνῳδεῖ θρῆνον - - - θυμός).

καὶ σιτοποιοὺς ἐκ τῶν μυλώνων πρὸς μέρος ἠναγκασμένους ἐμμίσθους: for the scale of 'requisitioning' or 'conscription' of labour and material, cf. 44. 1; of the machinery of its operation and its legal and constitutional basis we know nothing. In D. xxxvi. 32 πρὸς μέρος νείμασθαι = 'divide fairly'; but this does not show us whether Nikias wishes the σιτοποιοί to be assigned proportionately to the various units of the force or to be so conscripted that the burden is fairly distributed over the Attic mills ('ὡς καὶ ἐν τοῖς μυλῶσιν ἀπολείπεσθαι', Doukas). So far as our evidence goes, σιτοποιοί were normally slaves, and female slaves at that (L. A. Moritz, Grain-mills and Flour in Classical Antiquity [Oxford, 1958], 34 ff.), but here we are to think of 'master-bakers' who are free men—people like Thearion (Ar. fr. 1), but no doubt less distinguished—each accompanied by a number of slaves. The army will not be left to improvise its own milling (ctr. X. Cyr. vi. 2. 31 χειρομύλας χρὴ αὐτόθεν παρασκευάσασθαι αἷς σιτοποιησόμεθα.)

καὶ λόγῳ ἂν μάλιστα ἕτοιμα εἶναι: Nikias' vindication comes in 46.

23. 1. ἣν γὰρ αὐτοὶ ἔλθωμεν ἐνθένδε - - - καὶ διασῶσαι: after αὐτόθεν (21. 2, 22 bis) and καὶ μὴ ἐπὶ ἑτέροις γίγνεσθαι, there is naturally emphasis on αὐτοί and perhaps also on ἐνθένδε, which should be taken with παρασκευασάμενοι: 'for if we go ourselves (i.e. not relying on our supposed allies in Sicily) . . . superior in all arms, even so it will be difficult for us to conquer our enemies and bring our own force home safe.' ὑπερβάλλοντες τοῖς πᾶσι appears to be rhetorically expanded into 'with a force raised at Athens, not merely a match for the enemy but actually superior . . .', the implication being that it will be hard enough with a superior force and with a merely equal force it will be impossible; cf. ii. 45. 1 καὶ μόλις ἂν καθ᾽ ὑπερβολὴν ἀρετῆς οὐχ ὅμοιοι ἀλλ᾽ ὀλίγῳ χείρους κριθεῖτε. The rejected alternative, however, is qualified by a group of words which in a v.l. recorded by H₂ (cf. ψ) begins with πλεῖν (which Σᴴ absurdly explains as = πλέον) but in all other MSS., and in the main text of H, with πλήν.

(i) If πλήν is correct, and (a) τὸ ὁπλιτικόν is in apposition to τὸ μάχιμον, the meaning is: 'not just equally matched—but not, of course ⟨ a "match" ⟩ for their fighting force, their hoplites—but superior in all arms'. The qualification πλήν γε κ.τ.λ. may be taken as applying either (1) to both alternatives, or (2) to the former alternative only.

1. (A) Nikias may be taking it for granted that *any* force sent would *have* to be a match for the Syracusan hoplites; therefore the alternatives 'a match / superior in all arms' refer to arms other than the hoplites. But the tone of what he has said already shows that he does not take any such thing for granted; note especially 21. 1 οὐ ναυτικῆς καὶ φαύλου στρατιᾶς μόνον δεῖ, ἀλλὰ καὶ πεζὸν πολὺν ξυμπλεῖν, 22 init. ὁπλίτας τε οὖν πολλούς μοι δοκεῖ χρῆναι ἡμᾶς ἄγειν, and his emphasis on the strength of the Sikeliot cities in hoplites (20. 4), contradicting what Alkibiades says (17. 3 ff.) on the subject and especially combating the implications of 18. 5. Nikias' most conspicuous fear is that the Athenians will not send enough hoplites; how then can he take it for granted that any force sent would contain enough?

(B) It was suggested by Gomme (*CR* xxxiv [1920], 81 ff.), following Dobree, that Nikias means 'but of course you need not be a match in numbers for the Syracusan hoplites ⟨sc. because Athenian hoplites are so greatly superior in quality⟩'. As it turned out, the Sikeliot hoplites did prove inferior in the early battles; but Thucydides' Nikias is not the man to foresee or assume this, when all his efforts are bent on avoiding the dangers of inadequate strength and overconfidence (cf. H. A. Murray, *BICS* viii [1961], 36 ff.).

2. If the qualification applies to the words μὴ ἀντίπαλον μόνον only, the contrast is between 'a match, except in hoplites' and 'superior in all arms, including hoplites'. If that is so, the former cannot be purely hypothetical—for it would then prompt the question 'What about a match including hoplites?', and could not be simply a rhetorical preparation for 'superior in all arms'—but refers to the actual force proposed at the previous debate and taken for granted so far in the present debate. This force consisted of sixty ships (8. 2), the ναυτικὴ καὶ φαῦλος στρατιά of 21. 1; if Thucydides means Nikias to be referring in the latter passage not to a hypothetical force, but to the actual one proposed, there is no difficulty in supposing that he is referring to this actual force also in the words 'a match for them—except, mind you, not for those forces which really do the *fighting*, their hoplites'. This seems to me the correct interpretation. It is important here to hear in the mind's ear Nikias' tones of voice, first contemptuous and then minatory, and to visualize his gestures (cf. Dover, *PCPhS* clxxxiii [1954–5], 6 ff.).

If (b) τὸ ὁπλιτικόν were not in apposition to τὸ μάχιμον, the meaning

would be: '. . . not with simply our hoplite force a match for them—
except that it isn't a match for that element in their forces which
does the fighting' (i.e. their cavalry?)—'but superior in all arms . . .'.
The objection to this is the allusiveness of τὸ μάχιμον and the fact that
no one had proposed or contemplated a force of which the strength
would lie in its hoplites; the whole danger, to Nikias' way of thinking,
lay in the essentially *naval* character of the force.

(ii) De Romilly adopts πλεῖν, comparing (for the infinitive) Pl. *R.*
405 c παρασκευάζειν τὸν βίον αὐτῷ μηδὲν δεῖσθαι νυστάζοντος δικαστοῦ
and (for γε) 37. 1 ἐπὶ νεῶν γε ἐλθόντας = 'remember, they will have
come by ship' (cf. also 11. 1 τῶν δ' - - - διὰ πολλοῦ γε - - - χαλεπῶς
ἂν ἄρχειν δυναίμεθα = 'it would be hard for us to rule them, considering the distance'). With this reading, the meaning will be:
'. . . with a force not simply a *match* for them—for going by sea,
remember, to meet their fighting force, their hoplites—but superior
in all arms . . .' The reservation can legitimately apply to both
alternatives, because it is a reminder of a difficulty which must
affect both. It may, however, be felt that the relationship between
παρασκευάζειν and δεῖσθαι in *R.* 405 c, essentially a οὕτως / ὥστε relationship, is not at all like the expression ἀντίπαλον παρασκευασάμενοι
πλεῖν, and that πλευσόμενόν γε, not πλεῖν γε, would be the true parallel
to 11. 1 and 37. 1. Cf. 33. 1 πείθων γε ἐμαυτὸν κ.τ.λ. and X. *Smp.*
3. 6 καὶ πῶς ἄν, ἔφη, λεληθοῖ ἀκροώμενόν γε αὐτῶν ὀλίγου ἀν' ἑκάστην
ἡμέραν; πλεῖν is therefore to be rejected.

For ἀντίπαλον παρασκευασάμενοι cf. X. *Cyr.* vi. 1. 26 συστήσων, εἴ τι
δύναιτο, ἀντίπαλον ἑαυτῷ.

τῶν μὲν κρατεῖν τὰ δὲ καὶ διασῶσαι: Nikias, in contrast to the easy
confidence which prevails in his audience (24. 3), reminds them that
a safe return cannot be taken for granted. Thucydides represents
him as doing so in an allusive form of words of which the meaning
is in many contexts quite clear (e.g. 30. 2) but in this case no more
certain and indisputable to its original hearers than to us. Gomme
(*CR* xxxiv [1920], 82) refers τὰ δέ to the friends and allies of Athens,
but this hardly does justice to the pessimistic tone of the sentences
which follow; essentially τῶν μέν = 'what we want to conquer'
and τὰ δέ = 'what we want to save'. Cf. Pl. *Smp.* 193 b ἵνα τὰ
μὲν ('further punishment') ἐκφύγωμεν, τῶν δὲ ('what we desire')
τύχωμεν.

2. τῇ πρώτῃ ἡμέρᾳ ᾗ ἂν κατάσχωσιν εὐθὺς κρατεῖν τῆς γῆς: since
κατασχεῖν in the sense 'land' normally has εἰς or the relative οἷ (cf.
iv. 62. 3), ᾗ should agree with ἡμέρᾳ. 'They must gain control of the
land *or* know that if they are defeated everything will be hostile to
them' = 'they must gain control of the land, for if they are defeated
—and this they must understand— . . .'; cf. 68. 3.

3. παρίημι αὐτῷ τὴν ἀρχήν: on another famous occasion (iv. 28. 3)

Nikias' bluff was called, if it is fair to call it bluff. In any case, παρίημι must be interpreted 'I *offer* to resign'; neither an Athenian nor a modern general can divest himself of office merely by his own declaration.

24–26. *Conclusion of the Debate*

24. 1. ἢ - - - μάλιστα ⟨ἂν⟩ οὕτως ἀσφαλῶς ἐκπλεῦσαι: when the context precludes misunderstanding, an aorist or imperfective infinitive dependent on νομίζειν may have a future or potential sense, as when it depends on ἐλπίζειν or εἰκός; ἄν is therefore not needed here. The phenomenon, denied, and therefore removed by emendation, by Stahl (*Quaestiones Grammaticae ad Thucydidem Pertinentes*, 8 ff.), is explained and defended by Classen in his excursus on ii. 3. 2.

3. καὶ ἔρως ἐνέπεσε τοῖς πᾶσιν ὁμοίως ἐκπλεῦσαι: cf. Plu. *Alc.* 17. 2 on Alkibiades' encouragement of the long-standing Athenian appetite for the conquest of Sicily: ὁ δὲ παντάπασι τὸν ἔρωτα τοῦτον ἀναφλέξας - - - Ἀλκιβιάδης ἦν, and Isoc. x. 52 on the Trojan War: τοσοῦτος δ' ἔρως ἐνέπεσεν τῶν πόνων καὶ τῆς στρατείας ἐκείνης.

τοῖς μὲν γὰρ πρεσβυτέροις, κ.τ.λ.: Thucydides divides 'everyone alike' into (*a*) the older men, (*b*) the men of military age, and (*c*) ὁ πολὺς ὅμιλος καὶ στρατιώτης; and this involves a cross-division. For γάρ introducing the amplification of 'everyone alike' cf. Lys. ii. 70 ἐτελεύτησαν τὸν βίον ὥσπερ χρὴ τοὺς ἀγαθοὺς ἀποθνῄσκειν, τῇ μὲν γὰρ πατρίδι τὰ τροφεῖα ἀποδόντες, τοῖς δὲ θρέψασι λύπας καταλιπόντες, and Denniston, 67 f. ὡς = 'in the belief that . . .'. On the associations of τῆς ἀπούσης πόθῳ ὄψεως cf. 13. 1 n., and for θεωρίας cf. Isoc. iv. 182 πόλεμος - - - θεωρίᾳ μᾶλλον ἢ στρατείᾳ προσεοικώς. After θεωρίας the construction changes to the nominative *ad sensum*; cf. ii. 53. 4 ἀνθρώπων νόμος οὐδεὶς ἀπεῖργε, τὸ μὲν κρίνοντες - - - τῶν δὲ ἁμαρτημάτων οὐδεὶς ἐλπίζων, κ.τ.λ., Hdt. viii. 74. 2, and Lüdtke, 60 ff.; and with ὁ δὲ πολὺς ὅμιλος, κ.τ.λ. we must understand 'thought', upon which the future infinitives depend. στρατιῶται are not 'soldiers' as opposed to sailors, but simply members of a στρατιά; in ii. 88. 1, 89. 1, the word is used of men who are nearly all sailors. The analysis of ὁ δὲ πολὺς ὅμιλος καὶ στρατιώτης is disputable: (i) 'The mass of the people (sc. who were staying at home) and also the members of the expedition'; for the absence of the article with στρατιώτης cf. Pl. *Prt.* 314 a παρὰ τοῦ καπήλου καὶ ἐμπόρου, and for the collective singular cf. 84. 2, iv. 10. 3, and Kühner–Gerth, i. 13 f. (ii) 'The mass of the people, including . . .', cf. Denniston, 291, W. J. Verdenius, *Mnemosyne* 1953, 179 f. (iii) Taking στρατιώτης as an adjective (cf. 58. 1 n. and Kühner–Gerth, i. 271 ff.) and καί as linking it with πολύς; cf. A. *Ag.* 63 πολλὰ παλαίσματα καὶ γυιοβαρῆ and Fraenkel on *Ag.* 403. As any one of these three interpretations is possible, it is not necessary to consider Dobree's deletion of καί or τε and re-grouping of the words to mean : 'thought that they would both earn money at the present time by serving on the expedition and would also . . .'

ἔν τε τῷ παρόντι - - - ὑπάρξειν: this passage, like Ar. V. 684 f., indicates that money received from imperial sources by the hellenotamiai, whether as tribute or in other categories, was not spent exclusively on armaments, but was available for general purposes of state ; the more money the state had to spend, the closer came the ideal of ἔμμισθος πόλις (Plu. Per. 12. 4, cf. [X.] Resp. Ath. 1. 3, Gomme, CR xxxiv [1920], 82 f.). Thucydides does not say explicitly (for the malcontents of § 4 are not identified) that the rich were less enthusiastic than the poor ; Plu. Nic. 12. 3—we should like to know his source for this—says that 'contrary to expectation' the rich did not back up Nikias in decrying the expedition, 'in the fear that it should be thought that they were trying to escape trierarchies and other liturgies'.

25. 1. παρελθών τις τῶν Ἀθηναίων: Demostratos, according to Plu. Nic. 12. 6, but that may be only an inference from Ar. Lys. 387 ff. For Thucydides' suppression of names cf. 60. 2 ; but more often (e.g. i. 139. 3 and iv. 78. 1) he names men whom he has no occasion to mention again.

2. ὁ δὲ ἄκων μὲν εἶπεν: δέ refers back, contrasting Nikias with τις, and μέν refers forward, contrasting him with οἱ Ἀθηναῖοι (26. 1) ; the meaning is something which cannot be said directly in Attic Greek, *ὁ μὲν δέ (ctr. SEG x. 3. 30 αἱ μὲν δέ κα, κ.τ.λ. [Kyrene]). Krüger's ὁ δὲ ἄκων μέν, εἶπε ⟨δέ⟩, though it has a parallel in Lys. xiii. 85 μὴ ἐπ' αὐτοφώρῳ μέν, ἀπέκτεινε δέ, is unnecessary.

αὐτῶν δ' Ἀθηναίων ἔσεσθαι ὁπλιταγωγούς: this text is plainly unsatisfactory, for it is the Athenian proportion of the whole fleet which matters, not their proportion of troop-transports. The right reading is provided by H₂, αὐτῶν Ἀθηναίων, ὧν ἔσεσθαι (cj. Krüger): '. . . with not less than a hundred triremes from Athens itself—of which as many as they thought fit would be troop-transports—and they must send for others from their allies' (a double parenthesis, as ὁπλίταις δέ resumes the construction of τριήρεσι μέν). We see from 31. 3 and 43 that the expedition did in fact comprise one hundred Athenian triremes, of which forty were troop-transports, and thirty-four allied triremes ; on the nature of troop-transports, cf. 43 n.

ὁπλίταις δέ - - - πεντακισχιλίων μὲν οὐκ ἔλασσον, κ.τ.λ.: the total in fact was 5,100 (43).

καὶ ἐκ Κρήτης: except for a small-scale Athenian intervention in 429 (ii. 85. 5 f.), the Peloponnesian War did not involve Crete; the Cretans who served in the Athenian expedition were mercenaries (vii. 57. 9). At a later date Aristotle commented (Pol. 1269ᵃ39 ff.,

1273ᵇ18 ff.) on the fact that Cretan cities, each dependent economically on a subjected population of περίοικοι, could not afford to become involved with external enemies.

26. 1. αὐτοκράτορας εἶναι - - - πράσσειν ᾗ ἂν αὐτοῖς δοκῇ ἄριστα εἶναι [Ἀθηναίοις]: cf. 8. 2 n. In such a formula, it is inept to delete Ἀθηναίοις.

2. καταλόγους ἐποιοῦντο: the expression ἐκ καταλόγου (e.g. vii. 16. 1) and the antithesis in 43 between hoplites ἐκ καταλόγου and hoplites who are θῆτες, together with ὑπὲρ τὸν κατάλογον = 'past military age' in D. xiii. 4, show that there was a single κατάλογος which contained the names of all those required by virtue of their capital and age to serve as hoplites; the κατάλογοι now mentioned (cf. 31. 3), in which, apparently (43), 1,500 men were entered, represent a selection from the comprehensive κατάλογος (Jones, 163).

ἄρτι δ' ἀνειλήφει ἡ πόλις ἑαυτήν: cf. 12. 1 n.

καὶ τοῦ ξυνεχοῦς πολέμου: i.e. the Archidamian War.

27–29. *Mutilation of the Herms*

EXCURSUS: THE HERMS AND THE MYSTERIES

Discussion of chapters 27–9 necessarily embraces also 60–1. The relation of the events described in these chapters to (i) the operations of war and (ii) the account given in Andokides, *De Mysteriis*, is fundamental to the chronology of 415 and relevant to the chronology of the following two years.

(i) *Calendar Equations*

It does not seem easy at the present time to make any statement about the Athenian calendar which is both significant and undisputed. It is certainly not possible to offer an equation between an Athenian date and a Julian date in the neighbourhood of 415 without making certain assumptions; what is important is that the assumptions made should be defensible by citation of evidence drawn from years as close to 415 as possible, and it appears to me possible to defend a certain set of equations entirely by evidence drawn from the quarter-century within which the year 415 falls.

Since the moon takes a fraction more than 29½ days to go round the earth, moon and month can be kept in step for some time by an alternation of 29-day and 30-day months; but they cannot be kept in step indefinitely by this simple alternation, and, moreover, it is evident that the Athenians could on occasion decide to intercalate a day or a series of days.

At least at one point during the years 424/3–417/16 the moon and the month were out of step at Athens, *either* because many more than half of a succession of months had 30 days each, *or* because many more than half had 29 each, *or* because some days had been intercalated (as is demonstrable at a later period), or omitted, at irregular and unpredictable intervals. The evidence for this lack of coincidence between moon and months is Ar. *Nu.* 607 ff., where the poet felicitously represents the gods as complaining that festivals had not been held on the days on which they were expecting them by calculation κατὰ σελήνην.[1] We see from Th. iv. 118. 12, 119. 1 that in 424/3 14 Elaphebolion at Athens = 12 Geraistios at Sparta, and from v. 19. 1 that in 422/1 25 Elaphebolion at Athens = 27 Artemisios at Sparta. These passages of Thucydides show that on each of the two occasions *either* the Athenian *or* the Spartan calendar was out of step with the moon, and they leave open the possibility that *both* were out of step. We do not know whether *Nu.* 607–26 belongs to the original version of the play, performed in Elaphebolion 423, or to some stage of its revision. The play was never completely revised, and was never performed again; the latest datable stratum of revision (553 ff. [cf. *Σ*]) belongs to the period 419–417.

Precisely the same passage of Aristophanes is evidence that moon and month were normally expected to be in step; otherwise the passage has no humorous point (as it would have none in a community which used a calendar like ours). Elsewhere in the play coincidence of moon and month is taken for granted, notably in 16 ff.,

> ἐγὼ δ᾽ ἀπόλλυμαι
> ὁρῶν ἄγουσαν τὴν σελήνην εἰκάδας·
> οἱ γὰρ τόκοι χωροῦσιν,

taken in conjunction with 1131 ff.,

> πέμπτη, τετράς, τρίτη, μετὰ ταύτην δευτέρα,
> εἶθ᾽ ἣν ἐγὼ μάλιστα πασῶν ἡμερῶν
> δέδοικα καὶ πέφρικα καὶ βδελύττομαι,
> εὐθὺς μετὰ ταύτην ἔσθ᾽ ἕνη τε καὶ νέα,

and with 749 ff., where Strepsiades says that if he could lock up the moon in a box, so that it could rise no more, he would not have to pay any interest,

> ὁτιὴ κατὰ μῆνα τἀργύριον δανείζεται.

---

[1] In ii. 28 Thucydides adds κατὰ σελήνην to νουμηνίᾳ in referring to the solar eclipse of 3 Aug. 431. He thereby indicates his awareness of the possibility that moon and month could on occasion be out of step, and as he goes on to make a general comment on solar eclipses exactitude is appropriate to the context. I do not see how any more can, or why it should, be made of that passage.

We see from *IG* i². 302 (*AFD* 160 ff.; ML 77) that in 415/14:

(*a*) 66 ff. : on Prytany II. 20 the Treasurers of Athena lent the helleno-tamiai 9 talents, which the hellenotamiai gave to the athlothetai for the Panathenaia.

(*b*) 73 f. : on Prytany VIII. 3 they gave 300 talents to the helleno-tamiai, who gave the sum [τêι ἐν Σικελίαι (?) σ]τρατιâι.

(*c*) 75 f. : on Prytany VIII. 20 they gave 4 talents 2,000 drachmai to the hellenotamiai ἐς τὰ(ς) ναῦς τὰς ἐς Σι[κελίαν . . . .]ς τὰ χρέματα.

The sum mentioned in (*b*) was waiting for the Athenian force when it returned to Katane after its attack on Kentoripa (vi. 94. 4). 'At the beginning of spring' (vi. 94. 1) the force had sailed from Katane to damage Syracusan cultivation around the site of Megara and in the plain of the Terias; from this foray it returned to Katane before departing for Kentoripa. It does not sound as if the departure for Kentoripa should be dated before 1 April; the arrival of the money from Athens should therefore be dated after 1 April.

We should expect Athens to do her best to send the money off before the end of March. What we restore in (*c*), ἐσκομισάσα]ς or διακομιόσα]ς, depends on whether we believe (i) that the sum of 300 talents was given to the hellenotamiai in readiness for the earliest prac-ticable sailing, that they kept it while the reinforcements due to sail with it (250 cavalrymen and 30 mounted archers) were assembled, and that they received the smaller payment on Prytany VIII. 20 immedi-ately before the sailing, or (ii) that the ships sailed immediately after Prytany VIII. 3 and had returned, in need of reimbursement for the expenses of the voyage, by Prytany VIII. 20. The second alternative implies a quick turn-round and a surprisingly large reimbursement. I therefore prefer the former alternative, assuming that the greater part of the sum paid out on Prytany VIII. 20 was intended for the generals in Sicily, as advance payment of subsistence for the re-inforcements.

On this hypothesis, Prytany VIII. 3 would fall in the third week of March, Prytany VIII. 20. in the first week of April, and the arrival of the ships at Katane in the middle of April.

This would date the payment for the Panathenaia, on Prytany II. 20 of 415/14, precisely six prytanies before the first week of April 414. The Panathenaia were celebrated on 28 Hekatombaion. We should expect the payment to be made immediately before the festival, when the amount of money required was known.[1]

---

[1] The argument of J. A. Davison, *JHS* lxxviii (1958), 31 f., who believed that the payment was made into an 'imprest account' from which provision would eventually be made for the Great Panathenaia of 414/13, seems to me invalidated by (i) Dem. xxiv. 26–9, where it is represented as plausible that

We see from *IG* i². 304B (cf. Meritt, *TAPhA* xcv [1964], 204 ff.) that in 407/6 the sequence of ten prytanies which constituted a conciliar year equalled a sequence of twelve lunar months. But it is demonstrable from the preserved figures of capital and interest in *SEG* x. 227 (= ML 72) that in 426/5–423/2 the average length of a conciliar year was 366 days, an approximation to a solar year (cf., most recently, Mabel Lang in *Hesperia* xxxiii [1964], 146 ff.). The equations which we shall consider below show that in the period 422/1–412/11 the conciliar year cannot have equalled either a sequence of 12 lunar months or a sequence of 13. In default of positive evidence, we should not be justified in assuming that it had a total of days completely devoid of astronomical significance. I therefore assume that it continued, in that period, to be an approximation to the solar year; but since 366 days exceed a solar year by three-quarters of a day, we must be prepared for the possibility of a sequence of conciliar years of 365 days apiece.

On these assumptions, Prytany II. 20 of 415/14 would fall $\frac{6}{10} \times 366$ (or 365) days earlier than 4 April ± 3, i.e. 28/9 Aug. ± 3 of 415.

On the further assumption that the payment to the athlothetai was made immediately before the festival, the Panathenaia of 415/14 are to be dated 30 Aug. ±3 of 415.

There is only one precise equation by which this provisional conclusion can be controlled. That is 13 Skirophorion 433/2 = 27 June 432 (Diod. xii. 36. 2; *SPAW* 1904, 95 f.; Meritt, *The Athenian Calendar*, 88).

The interval from 13 Skirophorion 433/2 to 28 Hekatombaion 415/14 is:

Remaining days of Skirophorion 433/2	=	16 or 17
17 years (432/1–416/15) @ 354 days	= 6,018	
n intercalated months @ 30 days	=	30*n*
First 28 days of 415/14	=	28
Total	= 6,062 (or 6,063) + 30*n*	

The interval from 27 June 432 to 30 August ± 3 415 is:

Remaining days of 432	=	187
16 years (431–416) @ 365¼ days	= 5,844	
1 Jan. to 30 Aug. ± 3 415	=	242 ± 3
Total	= 6,273 ± 3	

The value of 30*n* therefore lies within the limits 207 to 214. An allocation of 7 intercalated months (= 210 days) falls within these

the νομοθέται should be convened on 12 Hekatombaion to make provision for 'the Panathenaia', i.e. the ordinary Panathenaia, of 353/2 (Dion. Hal. *Ad Amm.* 4), and (ii) the fact that payment for goods is not uncommonly made after delivery.

limits, and suggests that 28 Hekatombaion 415/14 can in fact be equated with 30 August 415.

There is no other precise Athenian–Julian equation to serve as a control, but there are three other lunar–conciliar equations, two precise and one approximate, to control the conclusion that Prytany II. 20 of 415/14 fell just before 28 Hekatombaion and to indicate whether or not the allocation of seven intercalated months between Skirophorion 433/2 and Hekatombaion 415/14 is plausible.

(a) *SEG* x. 227 (= ML 72). 79: 23 Skirophorion 423/2 = Prytany X. 20 423/2.[1]

Remaining days of Skirophorion 423/2 =		6 or 7
7 years (422/1–416/15) @ 354 days	=	2,478
n intercalated months @ 30 days	=	$30n$
27 days of Hekatombaion 415/14	=	27
Total	=	2,511 (or 2,512) $+30n$

Remaining days of Prytany X 423/2	=	17
7 conciliar years (422/1–416/15) @ 366 days	=	2,562
Reduction in conciliar years for closer approximation to solar year	=	—0 to —7
Prytany I 415/14	=	36 or 37
20 days of Prytany II 415/14	=	20
Total	=	between 2,628 and 2,636

The value of $30n$ therefore lies within the limits 116 and 125. An allocation of 4 intercalated months (= 120 days) falls midway between these limits, and indicates that some of the conciliar years 422/1–416/15 had only 365 days apiece. (Cf. Meritt, *The Athenian Year*, 205.)

(b) *SEG* xiii. 21 records the sale of property of men condemned for impiety in 415. Erechtheis holds Prytany VII. The year cannot be 415/14, because in that year Erechtheis held Prytany II (*IG* i². 302 [= ML 77]. 67). It should therefore be 414/13, and *SEG* x. 229 shows that Erechtheis held Prytany VII in a year in which money was

---

[1] Pritchett in *AJP* lxxxv (1964), 40 f., denies the reading]δοει φ[, asserting that the first letter is not visible at all and that the fifth cannot be φ. The photograph which he publishes does not seem to me consonant with his argument (cf. Meritt, ibid. 412 ff.). In any case, in such a context it is hard to see what ΟΕΙ followed by part of a circular shape could be except ὀγδόῃ φθίνοντος. As for Σκιροφοριῶνος, no other restoration is possible without assuming *either* an abnormal spelling (and for such an assumption cogent positive grounds must be adduced) *or* a degree of divergence between festival and conciliar equations much greater than is revealed by examination of the equations (a), (b), and (c).

paid 'for Sicily' (10 f.) and 'to Demosthenes Aphidnaios' (12 f.). In *SEG* xiii. 21 we find that 7 Gamelion and 25 Gamelion both fall within Prytany VII.

(c) According to Arist. Ἀθ. π. 32. 1 Prytany I. 1 411/10 was due to fall on 14 Skirophorion 412/11.

Let us see how these data cohere with the hypothesis that 27 Hekatombaion 415/14 = Prytany II. 20 415/14.

Total of days

27 Hekatombaion 415/14	0	0	Prytany II. 20 415/14
		308 to 310	End of conciliar year 415/14
Remaining days of 415/14	327		
1 intercalated month @ 30 days	357		
		529 to 533	Prytany VII. 1 414/13
1 Gamelion 414/13	535		
7 Gamelion 414/13	541		
25 Gamelion 414/13	559		
		565 to 570	Prytany VIII. 1 414/13
		673 to 676	End of conciliar year 414/13
End of festival year 414/13	711	1,038 to 1,042	End of conciliar year 413/12
End of festival year 413/12	1,065		
1 Skirophorion 412/11	1,390 or 1,391		
		1,403 to 1,408	End of conciliar year 412/11
14 Skirophorion 412/11	1,403 or 1,404	1,404 to 1,409	Prytany I. 1 411/10

Perhaps the most important item in this table is the relation between Gamelion and Prytany VII in 414/13. In relation to the proposition that the Athenians in the late fifth century intercalated miscellaneous days on such a scale that attempts to correlate festival, conciliar, and Julian dates are not a profitable use of the historian's time, *SEG* xiii. 21 is a random sample, and a particularly good sample in that it shows the situation as it was approximately halfway through a year. It tends to support the view that intercalation of miscellaneous days did not occur on a scale sufficient to deter us from the attempt to derive further equations from the few that survive. It must be remembered that whereas in the study of the early sixth century we have every reason for satisfaction if we can date an event within ten years, and in the Pentekontaetia if we can date an event within a year, in the study of the Peloponnesian War time is well spent if the margin of error in the dating of an event can be reduced to ten days. It appears to me that the margin of error in dating the Panathenaia of 415/14, the dispatch of 300 talents in the spring of 414, and the Athenian expedition to Kentoripa is less than that.[1]

One complication remains to be mentioned. *IG* i². 76 (= ML 73), a decree relating to the offerings at Eleusis, provides (line 53) for the intercalation of a second Hekatombaion in the following year. It is held by Dinsmoor (*The Archons of Athens*, 335 ff.) and Meritt (*AFD* 173) that this decree was passed in 416/15; and if that is correct it follows that there were two Hekatombaions in 415/14. In that case, then:

either the Panathenaia of 415/14 were celebrated in Hekatombaion I, Hekatombaion II is the intercalated month posited above in the discussion of *SEG* xiii. 21 and Arist. *Ἀθ. π.* 32. 1, and the four intercalated months posited in discussion of *SEG* x. 227. 79 all fell in the years 422/1–416/15,

or the Panathenaia of 415/14 were celebrated in Hekatombaion II, Hekatombaion I must be reckoned as one of the four inter- calated months posited in discussion of *SEG* x. 227, and a month was intercalated in the first half of 414/13.

If the second of these alternatives is correct, every reference to 'Hekatombaion 415/14' on pp. 266–9 is to be understood as a reference to Hekatombaion II.

I do not find the immediate grounds for dating *IG* i². 76 to 416/15 at all impressive, and there are even, in my view, counter-indications; but the strength of the case for this dating rests on the pattern of intercalation in which it must be a coherent element, and in par- ticular on the fact that Antiphon vi, delivered in a year in which 16 Hekatombaion = Prytany I. 1 and Erechtheis held the first prytany (§§ 11–12 ~ 44 f.), must be given a date earlier than 411 and later than the time at which the circulation of written versions of forensic speeches began. But no decision on *IG* i². 76 or Antiphon vi can affect the equations:

Panathenaia 415/14 = 30 August 415 (with the margin of error indicated above)

Dispatch of 300T = first week of April 414

[1] I am aware that in equating Prytany II. 20 of 415/14 with 29 August 415 I differ by 2 days from Meritt's table in *AFD* (176) and by 4 days from his revised table in *The Athenian Year*, 218. In view of the approximations in- volved in my calculations, and the uncertainty introduced into many such calculations by the possibility that some festival years may have exceeded 354 (or 384) days—through a planned excess of 30-day months and/or the intercalation of individual days—the difference does not seem to me im- portant for the purposes with which my excursus is concerned.

270

(ii) *The Sequence of Events in 415*

Certain relations between events are not as precise as has some-times been assumed. The herms were mutilated during the period of preparation; whether early in the period or very shortly before the expedition was due to sail, neither Thucydides nor any other ancient source tells us. The fleet sailed θέρους μεσοῦντος ἤδη (vi. 30. 1), which means not 'at the time of the summer solstice' but 'after the middle period of the summer had begun', an expression which could be used of any date between early May and late July. Isaios vi. 14 speaks of a certain Pistoxenos who went on the expedition (fifty-two years earlier) 'in the archonship of Arimnestos', i.e., strictly speak-ing, before 1 Hekatombaion 415; but even if we could be sure that Isaios knew the date of departure so precisely, his evidence would not be disturbing or surprising, and, in any case, if he knew that the expedition was voted and prepared during the archonship of Arimnestos he would not be pedantic about the date of departure.

A further complication has been introduced by the celebration of the Adonia, which occurred at some stage during the preparations (Freeman, ii. 114, has no justification for saying 'the day of their sailing'). The relevant passage of Aristophanes is quoted and ex-plained on p. 224. The date of the Adonia is disputed. 4 Munichion, suggested by Meritt (*Hesperia* iv [1935], 574 f., cf. F. R. Walton, *HThR* xxxi [1938], 69 ff.), is acceptable only if Adonis is identified with the Eros associated with Aphrodite in the sanctuary on the north slope of the Akropolis. 19 or 20 July, on which the Adonia were celebrated by Syrians and in the eastern part of the Roman empire generally (F. Cumont, *Syria* viii [1927], 330 ff., xvi [1935], 46 ff.), implies a surprisingly late date for the departure of the expedition; and, what is more important, if the Athenians really assigned the Adonia not to a numbered day in their own festival calendar but to an event (the rising of Sirius) in the solar year, it was unusual, even unique, among Athenian festivals (cf. Cumont ap. Hatzfeld, *RÉG* l [1937], 302 ff.). Early autumn, suggested by Deubner, *Attische Feste*, 221, is obviously irreconcilable with Aristophanes, and Deubner in fact, by some slip of the mind, treats Aristophanes' evidence as if it had been invented by Plutarch. If the vase-painting reproduced in his plate 25. 2 represents the Adonia, either the bunch of grapes which the woman therein is carrying is an artist's symbol for fruit in general (cf. ὥρια - - - ὅσα δρυὸς ἄκρα φέρονται offered to the dead Adonis in Theocr. 15. 112) or grapes were kept throughout the winter (cf. the criticism of Deubner by A. D. Nock, *Gnomon* x [1934], 290 ff., who puts the case for a date in the spring).

We can now turn to the sequence of events presented by Thucydides and by Andokides i (*De Mysteriis*). In Thucydides the sequence is:

1. Mutilation of 'most' of the herms in one night (27. 1).
2. Rewards offered for information, and a guarantee of immunity for anyone who might incriminate himself in informing (27. 2).
3. Information from some 'metics and slaves' about (*a*) earlier mutilations of statues and (*b*) profane performances of the mysteries in private houses. Alkibiades is implicated in the latter (28. 1).
4. Decision that Alkibiades should none the less set sail with the expedition, to be recalled for trial when necessary (29. 3).
5. Departure of the expedition (30. 1).
6. Information is laid and many arrests are made (53. 2, 60. 2).
7. Some of those denounced go into exile (implied by 60. 4).
8. Confession by one of the accused, implicating others (60. 2 f.).
9. Release of this man and of those not implicated. Execution of those who have not already fled (60. 4).
10. Recall of Alkibiades to answer the accusation of profanation (53. 1, 61. 4 f.).
11. Escape of Alkibiades at Thurioi on his way home (61. 7).
12. Condemnation of Alkibiades in his absence (ibid.).

There are two events which cannot be fitted precisely into this sequence:

13. κατὰ τὸν καιρὸν τοῦτον ἐν ᾧ περὶ ταῦτα ἐθορυβοῦντο a Spartan force came as far as the Isthmos, causing a fear in Athens that there was a plot to betray the city (61. 2). If the reference of τούτον and ταῦτα is strict, it is to the period after the case of the herms was regarded as settled and Athenian energies were turned on to clearing up the matter of the mysteries (61. 1). Cf. MacDowell, 184.
14. κατὰ τὸν αὐτὸν χρόνον Alkibiades' associates in Argos were suspected of an oligarchic plot, and hostages held by Athens on behalf of the Argive democracy were sent back to Argos for execution (61. 3).

Taken by itself, the account is straightforward and unobjectionable. It gives us a clear impression that no information was laid about the herms until after the expedition had left. The recall of Alkibiades came after the expedition had secured the allegiance of Naxos and Katane, failed to get that of Messene and Kamarina, and made a brief demonstration against Syracuse (50–2). It was followed by an operation against Hykkara, dealings with Segesta, a march across country from Hykkara to Katane, dealings with the Sikels, and an unsuccessful attack on Hybla Geleatis (62), after which τὸ θέρος ἐτελεύτα. The end of the Thucydidean θέρος is the end of October (cf. vol. iii, 706 ff.). It would be possible to estimate the minimum time required for the voyage from Athens to Rhegion and the operations of cc. 50–2, and for those of c. 62, but quite impossible to estimate maxima; we have no basis for determining, for example, how long the fleet rested at Rhegion (44. 3), we do not know whether a period of inactivity intervened between the attack on Hybla and the end of the campaigning season, and the brevity of the narrative in 62 may well be deceptive. We must wait and see what periods are suggested by the other data, and decide then on their coherence.

Evidence independent of Thucydides is provided by Andokides i (*De Mysteriis*), and to a lesser extent by Plutarch's *Alcibiades*. One must remember that Andokides is pleading for his life (and incidentally for his reputation) sixteen years after the events which he describes. His attitude to the facts of the case is far removed from that of an objective historian; nevertheless, we are not entitled to reject his evidence unless we can show in what respects it is to his advantage to conceal or misrepresent facts, and there is an encouraging degree of coincidence between the documents incorporated in his speech, listing men denounced by various informers, and the inscriptions which record the sale of the effects of the men condemned (*SEG* xiii. 12 ff., xix. 23 ff.).

Andokides deals with the herms and the mysteries separately (11 ff. and 34 ff. respectively) and gives little explicit indication of the chronological relation between the two sequences. The essentials of his account are:

1. The expedition is ready to leave; an assembly is being held τοῖς στρατηγοῖς; Alkibiades is denounced for profaning the mysteries, and the prytaneis receive information from a slave called Andromachos (11 f.).

2. Information is given by Teukros, a metic, on the herms and the mysteries (15, 34 f., both passages with documents).

3*a*. Information on the mysteries from Agariste (16).

3*b*. Information on the herms from Diokleides (37 ff.).

4*a*. Information on the mysteries from a slave called Lydos (17).

4*b*. General alarm; the city under arms; Andokides and others arrested (45 ff.).

5*a*. Rewards given at the Panathenaia to Androma hos and Teukros (28).

5*b*. Andokides confesses. Release of those not implicated. Execution of Diokleides for false information. End of general alarm (65 f.).

Presumably Teukros gave his information on the herms and on the mysteries at the same time. It would not have been easy for him to justify withholding part of his information until a later date (Diokleides, as we shall see, gave a cogent reason for his own delay);

and if he did withhold it, I see no way in which it could have helped Andokides' case to conceal this fact. If, therefore, the expedition left before Teukros informed, Thucydides' μετοίκων (28. 1) is misleading; if it left after, his περὶ μὲν τῶν Ἑρμῶν οὐδέν is false. The former alternative is more easily explicable. Thucydides says in 53. 1 that the Athenian people in this matter accepted evidence from unworthy sources, arresting good men on the testimony of bad; his apparent irony in 60. 4 (ὁ δὲ δῆμος ὁ τῶν Ἀθηναίων ἄσμενος λαβών, ὡς ᾤετο, τὸ σαφὲς κ.τ.λ.) is an indication of his feelings. In 28. 1 he has sacrificed accuracy to indignant rhetoric (cf. p. 328 and vii. 42. 3 n.).

Thucydides' statement in 61. 1, 'now that they thought they had the truth about the herms, they were all the more convinced that the profanation of the mysteries was Alkibiades' doing' must not be taken to mean that no serious inquiry was pursued into the profanation until after Andokides' confession. I see no good reason why the information of Agariste and Lydos (items 3a and 4a in Andokides' sequence) should not have preceded that of Diokleides (MacDowell, 183 f., places them much later), and no reason why the *Salaminia* should not have been sent off to bring Alkibiades home very soon after Andokides' confession.

The following indications of time may be extracted from Andokides:

1. The first information about the mysteries was given *immediately* before the expedition was due to sail.

2. Andromachos and Teukros received their rewards at the Panathenaia. One would not expect any rewards to be paid until the guilt of the men denounced was established by trial or 'confessed' by flight. I therefore assume that the *Salaminia* returned to Athens before the Panathenaia. (Note that Alkibiades was not the only person recalled from Sicily; there were others with him, some accused of profaning the mysteries and others of mutilating the herms [53. 1].)

3. Diokleides alleged that he recognized the mutilators by the light of a full moon (And. i. 38). According to Plu. *Alc*. 20. 8 the mutilation actually occurred on the last night of a lunar period (ἕνης καὶ νέας). If both Andokides and Plutarch are right, Diokleides in fabricating his story made a fundamental mistake about the state of the moon on the night of the mutilation. Is this credible? No one, in designing a story about the recognition of people at night—a story which, if disbelieved, may cost him his life—can fail to satisfy himself of the plausibility of the narrative on the issue which is crucial, the means of recognition. Diokleides did not, after all, make up his story on the spur of the moment; when it was eventually questioned, he revealed that he had been put up to it by Alkibiades Phegusios and Amiantos of Aigina (65). Now the mention of the full moon in Andokides' account of Diokleides' information (38) has a simple

purpose: it explains why he was up and about at that hour of the night. He had to go to Laureion; ἀναστὰς δὲ πρῷ ψευσθεὶς τῆς ὥρας βαδίζειν· εἶναι δὲ πανσέληνον. Although Andokides discredits Diokleides and endorses the confession of fraud which brought the informer to execution (65 f.), he nowhere mentions or implies any fatal flaw or inconsistency in the story itself or any consideration, other than his own more circumstantial story, which led to the discovery of its falsehood.

According to Plu. *Alc.* 20. 6 'Thucydides did not name the informers, but others name Diokleides and Teukros' (there follow two quotations from the comic poet Phrynichos). 'Yet those who laid information made no certain or reliable revelation. One of them (εἷς δ' αὐτῶν), on being asked how he recognized the faces of the mutilators, answered "by the light of the moon". He was totally discredited, ἕνης καὶ νέας οὔσης ὅτε ταῦτ' ἐδρᾶτο.' It looks as if Plutarch's source did not name Diokleides as the man caught out. We may wonder whether the story of the blunder originally referred to the mutilation of the herms at all, and suspicion is strengthened by Diod. xiii. 2. 3 f.: 'It came about that the herms were mutilated. . . . A private citizen came to the Council and said that τῇ νουμηνίᾳ, in the middle of the night, he had seen some men going into the house of a metic, and Alkibiades among them. Being asked by the Council how, since it was night, he recognized their faces, he said he had seen them by the light of the moon. So this man convicted himself of false accusation' (sc. because he had himself spoken of νουμηνία) 'and was disbelieved.' Neither Plutarch nor Diodoros suggests that the informer who blundered was taken seriously for long or did any harm. In Diodoros' account there is no significant point of contact with Diokleides at all. The presence of Alkibiades and the importance of his going into a house show that the anecdote originally referred not to the herms but to the mysteries, and as such it is consistent and acceptable. Its source, I suggest, was a fourth-century orator illustrating by examples from the past (cf. Antiphon v. 59 f., D. xxi. 58 ff., 182 f.) an argument about the unreliability of informers. The mistake of Diodoros' source, perhaps under the influence of the mention of the moon in Andokides, was to detach the anecdote from the less spectacular impiety and attach it to the one which assumed a more conspicuous role in tradition (cf. p. 280), and Plutarch perpetuated the mistake. Once the mistake had been made, the statement that the herms were mutilated on a night when there was no moon followed from it.[1]

I therefore conclude (cf. *CR* N.S. xv [1965], 247 ff.) that the herms were mutilated under a full moon—useful, in any case, for an operation

---

[1] Grote, vi. 35 n. 1, rejected the testimony of Plutarch and Diodoros on the moon but still insisted that they were speaking of Diokleides.

on such a scale in an unlit ancient city. Assuming, as above, a high degree of coincidence between moon and month, the possible dates for the mutilation are (± 2 in each case) 25 April, 25 May, 23 June, and 23 July.

4. Diokleides affirmed that shortly after he had witnessed the mutilation he was approached by Euphemos, one of the men concerned, and he asked Euphemos for money. Euphemos and some associates promised to give him two talents εἰς τὸν εἰσιόντα (ἐπιόντα cj. Emperius) μῆνα, but they failed to do so; therefore he was now informing against them (And. i. 38 ff.). It is possible that ὁ εἰσιὼν μήν might mean 'the month now beginning' or 'the month which has just begun' (cf. Hdt. vi. 59: 'when a king dies and another comes to the throne, οὗτος ὁ εἰσιών [i.e. the *next* king] releases any Spartiate who is a public debtor') but to Andokides' Athenian hearers the words εἰς τὸν εἰσιόντα μῆνα would most naturally mean 'in the next month'; cf. IG i². 94 (of 418/17), where ἐπὶ τῆς βολῆς τῆς ἐσιόσης (31 f.) is distinguished from ἐπὶ τῆσδε τῆς βολῆς (21), and Ἀθ. π. 31. 2 τοὺς δὲ αἱρεθέντας ἄρχειν τὸν εἰσιόντα ἐνιαυτόν (~ 32. 1). Since it was necessary for Diokleides' story that the period in which he was promised payment should have elapsed, and the mutilation occurred on the night of a full moon, we must posit an interval of one and a half months between the mutilation and his information.

Now, if Diokleides informed at the beginning of Hekatombaion, the time left for the arrest of Andokides and his friends, the confession of Andokides, the dispatch of the *Salaminia* to Sicily and its return with the news that Alkibiades had escaped at Thurioi, all before the Panathenaia (28 Hekatombaion), is very short, though not impossibly short. If we are to make sure of allowing enough time for these events, we must put Diokleides' information at the beginning of Skirophorion, and construct this scheme:

c. 16 Munichion	c. 25 May	Mutilation of the herms.
Beginning of Thargelion	Early June	Departure of the expedition.
1 Skirophorion	6 July	Information of Diokleides.
End of Skirophorion	Early August	Alkibiades leaves Katane.
28 Hekatombaion	2 September	Rewards given to informers.

This allows two months for the voyage from Athens to Sicily, the pause at Rhegion and the operations of cc. 50–2, and two and a half months, from mid-August to the end of October, for the operations of c. 62.

(iii) *Politics and Prosopography*

The following list includes all those known to have been denounced for complicity in the impieties of 415. H = denounced for mutilation of herms; M= denounced for profanation of mysteries; A = Andokides i; $S_1 = SEG$ xiii; $S_2 = SEG$ xix.

		Charge and Informer	*Result*
Adeimantos, son of Leukolophides, Skambonides	M	Agariste A 16	Fled[1] A 16; S_1 17. 17, 53, 116, 131, 174, 178; 21. 10, 24
Akumenos	M	Lydos A 18	Fled[1] A 18
Alkibiades, son of Kleinias, Skambonides	M[2]	Andromachos A 11 ff. (cf. Th.)	Fled[1] A 13, 16 (+Th.)
	M[2]	Agariste A 16	
Alkibiades Phegusios[3]		False information A 65	Fled[1] A 65; S_1 19. 3 f.
Alkisthenes	H	Teukros A 35	Fled or executed[4] A 35, 52, 67
Amiantos of Aigina		False information A 65	Fled[1] A 65
Andokides, son of Leogoras, Kydathenaieus	H[5]	Diokleides; himself A 40, 48, 61 (cf. Th.)	Pardoned Th.; cf. A. 48 ff.
Antidoros	H	Teukros A 35, 52	Fled or executed[4] A 35, 52, 67
Antiphon	M	Teukros A 15	Fled[1] A 15
Apsephion	H	Diokleides A 43	Fled but returned A 44, 66
Archebiades	M	Andromachos A 13	Fled[1] A 13
Archidamos	H	Teukros A 35	Fled or executed[4] A 35, 52, 67
Archippos[6]	M	Andromachos A 13	Fled[1] A 13
Aristomenes[6]	M	Andromachos A 13	Fled[1] A 13
Autokrator	M	Lydos A 18	Fled[1] A 18
Axiochos, son of Alkibiades,[7] Skambonides	M	Agariste A 16	Fled[1] A 16; S_2 24. 11; 25. 13
Chairedemos, son of Elpias (-os ?), Ach[	H	Andokides A 52, 67	Fled[1] A 59, 68; S_1 19. 7 f.
Charippos	H	Teukros A 35	Fled or executed[4] A 35, 52, 67
Charmides[8]	M	Agariste A 16	Fled[1] A 16

	Charge and Informer	Result
Charmides, son of Aristoteles	H Diokleides A 47 f.	Released A 66
Diakritos	H Andokides A 52, 67	Fled[1] A 59, 68
Diogenes	M Andromachos A 13	Fled[1] A 13
Diognetos	M Teukros A 15	Fled[1] A 15
Eryximachos[9]	H Teukros A 35	Fled or executed[4] A 35, 52, 67
Eukrates, son of Nikeratos, Kydantides	H Diokleides A 47	Released A 66
Euktemon	H Teukros A 35	Fled or executed[4] A 35, 52
Euphemos, son of Telokles[10]	H Diokleides A 40, 47	Released A 66
Euphiletos, son of Timotheos, Kydathenaieus	H Teukros A 35 H Andokides A 56, 61 ff. M[11] ? S₁ locc. citt.	Fled or executed[4] A 35, 52, 67; S₁ 17. 88; 21. 14
Eurydamas[12]	H Teukros A 35	Fled or executed[4] A 35, 52, 67
Eurymachos, son of Eu[	H Teukros A 35	Fled or executed[4] A 35, 52, 67; S₁ 13. 183
Glaukippos	H Teukros A 35	Fled or executed[4] A 35, 52, 67
Gniphonides	M Teukros A 15	Fled[1] A 15
Hephaistodoros	M Teukros A 15	Fled[1] A 15; S₁ 12. 10
Isonomos	M Teukros A 15	Fled[1] A 15
Kallias, son of Alkmeon	H Diokleides A 47	Released A 66
Kallias, son of Telokles[10]	H Diokleides A 42, cf. 47	Released A 66
Kephisodoros, metoikos in Peiraieus[6]	M Teukros A 15	Fled[1] A 15; S₁ 12. 33
Kritias	H Diokleides A 47	Released A 66
Leogoras	M Lydos A 17, 19 H Diokleides A 47	Escaped prosecution[13] A 17 Released A 66, cf. And. ii. 7 f.

	Charge and Informer		*Result*
Lysistratos	H	Andokides A 52, 67	Fled[1] A 59, 68
Mantitheos	H	Diokleides A 43	Fled, but returned A 44, 66
Meletos[14]	M	Andromachos A 12 f.	Fled[1] A 13, cf. 35, 52, 67
	H	Teukros A 35	
Menestratos	H	Teukros A 35	Fled or executed[4] A 35, 52, 67
Nikides,[15] son of Phoinikides, Meliteus	M	Andromachos A 13	Fled[1] A 13; S_1 13. 172, 176; 15. 17 f.; 17. 85 f., 167
Nisaios, son of Taureas	H	Diokleides A 47	Released A 66
Oionias,[16] son of Oionochares, Ateneus	M	Andromachos A 13	Fled[1] A 13; S_1 13. 177, 179; 14. 311; 19. 8 f.; 21. 33
Panaitios (1)	M	Andromachos A 13	Fled[1] A 13
Panaitios (2)[17]	H	Andokides A 52, 67	Fled[1] A 59, 68; S_1 13. 170 f.[18]
Pantakles	M	Teukros A 15	Fled[1] A 15
Phaidros, son of Pythokles, Myrrhinusios	M	Teukros A 15	Fled[1] A 15; S_1 13. 188 f.; 15. 2(?); 17. 112
Pherekles,[19] son of Pherenikaios, Themakeus	M	Lydos A 17; S_1 17. 93 f.	Fled or executed[4] A 35, 52; S_1 loc. cit.
	H	Teukros A 35; S_1 loc. cit.	
Philokrates	M	Teukros A 15	Fled[1] A 15
Phrynichos, son of Orchesamenos[20]	H	Diokleides A 47	Released A 66
Platon	H	Teukros A 35	Fled or executed[4] A 35, 52, 67
Polyeuktos	H	Teukros A 35	Fled or executed[4] A 35, 52, 67
Polystratos, son of Diodoros, Ankylethen	M	Andromachos A 13	Executed A 13; S_1 12. 26 f.; 13. 180 f.; 15. 5 f.; 17. 75
Pulytion	M[21]	Andromachos A 12, 14	Fled[1] A 13
	M	(Thessalos)[22] Plu. *Alc.* 19. 2 f., 22. 4	

		Charge and Informer	Result
Smindyrides	M	Teukros	Fled[1]
		A 15	A 15
Taureas	H	Diokleides	Released
		A 47	A 66
Teisarchos	M	Teukros	Fled[1]
		A 15	A 15
Telenikos	H	Teukros	Fled or executed[4]
		A 35	A 35, 52, 67
Teukros, metoikos	M	Teukros	Pardoned
		A 15	A 15
Theodoros Phegaieus	M	(Thessalos)[23]	Fled or executed[4]
		Plu. *Alc.* 19.	A 35, 52, 67
		2 f., 22. 4	
	H	Teukros	
		A 35	
Timaios	H	Diokleides?	Released?
		Plu. *Alc.* 21.	(cf. A 66)
		4[24]	
Timanthes	H	Teukros	Fled or executed[4]
		A 35	A 35, 52, 67
- - -, son of Diodoros,			Fled or executed[4]
Eiteiaios			S_1 17. 12 f.
- - -, Anagyrasios			Fled or executed[4]
			S_1 19. 1 f.
- - -, Phegusios[25]			Fled or executed[4]
			S_1 19. 3 f.
Various others[26]	M	Lydos	Fled or executed[4]
		A 17	
Twenty-eight others[27]	H	Diokleides	Released
		A 43	A 66

Notes

1. Since Alkibiades did not flee immediately after his denunciation, but only when recalled from Sicily, the same may be true of many others whom Andokides describes as fleeing in consequence of denunciation; cf. Th. vi. 53. 1.

2. Andokides' narrative, separating the mutilation from the profanation, makes it clear that Alkibiades was not accused of mutilating herms, and Thucydides was plainly aware of this; cf. vi. 53. 1 n., 61. 1. The only link betweeen Alkibiades and the herms in Thucydides is vi. 28. 2 ἐβόων ὡς - - - οὐδὲν εἴη αὐτῶν ὅτι οὐ μετ' ἐκείνου ἐπράχθη, i.e. Alkibiades was suspected vaguely of being 'behind' or in sympathy with the mutilation. Plutarch preserves the distinction in *Alc.* 19. 1 and even emphasizes it in saying (20. 5) τοῖς περὶ τοὺς Ἑρμᾶς ὑβρίσμασι καὶ τὰ μυστικὰ συμπλεκόντων. This nicety was foreign to popular tradition, which associated the spectacular person with the spectacular act (cf. D. lviii. 67, where the fortification of Eetioneia in 411 is attributed to

Kritias). Lys. xiv. 41 οἱ μὲν πολλοὶ αὐτῶν ἡταιρήκασιν - - - οἱ δὲ μυστήρια πεποιήκασι καὶ τοὺς Ἑρμᾶς περικεκόφασι refers to the class of people to which, he says, Alkibiades and his family belonged, rather than to Alkibiades individually; but in the middle of the fourth century we find in D. xxi. 147 the bald statement (sc. Ἀλκιβιάδης) τοὺς Ἑρμᾶς περιέκοπτεν. This confusion is fully established in Diod. xiii. 2. 3 f., 5. 1, and is a major cause of chronological difficulties (cf. p. 275). Pausanias Atticista, fr. 72 Erbse, s.v. Ἑρμοκοπίδαι, may speak for the grammarians: 'They say that Alkibiades did this in collaboration with the Corinthians.'

3. See n. 25.

4. The inscriptions do not reveal which of the men whose property was sold were dead and which were in exile.

5. Lys. vi. 51 explicitly accuses him also of profaning the mysteries, but this is not easily reconcilable with And. and with Th. vi. 60. 2 f.

6. Archippos, Aristomenes, and Kephisodoros may be the comic poets of those names (MacDowell, 211); naturally men of comic talent would be in demand for mock-celebrations of the mysteries. Archippos' first victory fell 'in the 91st Olympiad' (Suda, s.v.), i.e. 416/15. Aristomenes was active in 439/8 and 389/8, but none of the known titles can be dated during the period 425/4–395/4. Kephisodoros produced a play in 403/2 (Lys. xxi. 4, where the MS. has 'Kephisodotos', not known as the name of a comic poet). The man denounced in 415 was a metic, but many metics were made citizens after the democratic restoration.

7. This Alkibiades was the grandfather of 'our' Alkibiades; cf. 50. 1 n., v. 43. 2 n.

8. We are not given the patronymic of the Charmides involved in Agariste's denunciation, and, whoever he was, it is not absolutely certain that he was denounced; Agariste only said that a profanation took place at his house. If she did denounce him, and if he was the son of Aristoteles, he fled about the same time as Alkibiades and after being released from the prison to which Diokleides' false allegation had brought him.

9. Εὐρυξίμαχον cod. And.; corr. Stephanus; cf. PA 5186–8 and below (p. 284) on Akumenos and Eryximachos.

10. Τηλεκλέους cod. And., cf. Τηλεκλείδης: Τηλο- Kirchner; cf. PA 13580–4.

11. S₁ 17. 19, 21. 13, say that Euphiletos was condemned 'on both charges'.

12. Εὐρυμάδαντα cod. And., a name nowhere attested; corr. apographa.

13. Lydos alleged that Leogoras had been present, but asleep, at a profanation in the house of Pherekles. Speusippos, a member of the council, proposed that all those denounced by Lydos should be tried at once. Leogoras brought and won an action παρανόμων against Speusippos.

14. On the men called Meletos, cf. MacDowell, 208 ff. It is not necessary to posit more than one of them in the denunciations. Denounced by Andromachos, Meletos may have remained in Athens (just as Alkibiades remained with the fleet) and fled only when denounced by Teukros for complicity in the mutilation.

15. Νικιάδην cod. And.; but the inscriptions record a Νικίδης, and this is probably the same person.

16. 'Ιωνίαν cod. And.; probably an error for the Οἰωνίας of the inscriptions.

17. There must be two Panaitioi, for it is essential to Andokides' argument that he should reduce to a minimum the number of men for whose exile his own information was responsible; if the Panaitios whom he denounced had already been denounced by Andromachos and so almost inevitably doomed to execution or exile, Andokides would not have failed to mention the fact.

18. We do not know to which Panaitios the inscription refers.

19. We are concerned with only one Pherekles; S₁ 17. 94 classifies him as guilty 'on both charges'—which shows, incidentally, that his slave, Lydos, did denounce his own master, though A 17 does not make that clear.

20. Φρύνιχος ὁ ὀρχησάμενος cod. And.; -μενοῦ Wilhelm.

21. Although Andromachos said that the profanation had taken place in Pulytion's house, the name of Pulytion is absent from the list in A 13. See, however, n. 22.

22. Plutarch quotes the εἰσαγγελία of Alkibiades, Pulytion, and Theodoros—i.e. the charge on which they were actually tried in absence—as standing in the name of Thessalos, not in the name of Andromachos' master Pythonikos.

23. Cf. n. 22.

24. Plutarch gives Timaios, whom Andokides does not mention, the role which A 48 gives to Charmides.

25. This may be the man who put Diokleides up to his story; cf. n. 3.

26. ἀπογράφει τούς τε ἄλλους καὶ τὸν πατέρα κ.τ.λ., says A 17, and no complete list of those denounced by Lydos is given.

27. Diokleides denounced forty-two men, according to A 43; 'forty' in A 47 presumably implies 'apart from myself and my father'.

Despite Thucydides' discouraging statement (60. 2, cf. 60. 4 f., 61. 1) that 'no one from that day to this has been able to say who really committed the mutilation', which shows that he was not satisfied by Andokides' confession, a fresh attempt to discover who committed the impieties of 415, and why, is profitable. Three essential points are:

(i) Diokleides' information was false, as he confessed; upon this point, it is not easily conceivable that Andokides, even sixteen years after the event, could have hoped to deceive a jury. The question here is to discover whether any political bond unites the men whom Diokleides denounced.

(ii) We have no reason to believe that any of the other denunciations described by Andokides were false. No doubt the prevailing feeling in 415 encouraged people to pay off old scores by incriminating personal enemies; no doubt Andokides, in peril of death, may not have told the whole truth either in 415 or in 399. Nevertheless, we have no grounds for saying of any of the individuals denounced 'this man was innocent'.

(iii) Only a small proportion of the men denounced can be identified with individuals known to us from other sources. Some of them bear quite common names; of the rest, plausible identifications do not necessarily tell us anything about political associations.[1]

Mysteries. Athenian society in the late fifth century embraced a wide variety of opinions on the existence and nature of the gods, on the value and efficacy of ritual, and on the extent to which supernatural beings could take a joke. Alkibiades and his friends are not likely to have cherished simple piety; parody of the mysteries at a private entertainment could no doubt be exceedingly funny; and no more need be said on the question whether, or why, the mysteries were parodied. A good parallel from our own history is provided by George Selwyn's parody of the communion service at Oxford in 1745 (S. P. Kerr, *George Selwyn and his Times* [London, 1909], pp. 37 ff.).

The identifiable participants in the profanations are connected, directly or through intermediaries, with Alkibiades: his relation Axiochos, his friend Adeimantos (whose fortunes were so closely linked with his in later years), a certain Archebiades who may be the lover of Alkibiades' son (Lys. xiv. 27), and others who were at least on the periphery, and in some cases near the centre, of the 'Socratic circle', namely Phaidros (cf. Pl. *Phdr.* 224 a, *Smp.* 176 d, *Prt.* 315 c, and Lys. xix. 15) and Akumenos. Akumenos (the name is very rare) appears in Plato as father of the doctor Eryximachos, who plays a prominent part in the *Symposium* and was also a friend of Phaidros (*Phdr.* 268 a). Charmides, if he is not the same man as Charmides the son of Aristoteles, could be the son of Glaukon, cousin of Kritias and uncle of Plato.

The prosecution represented a curious alliance of forces which illuminates the nature of the enmities which Alkibiades provoked (cf. viii. 53. 2). The moving spirit among the demagogues, 'those who thought that Alkibiades stood in the way of their secure leadership of the Assembly' (28. 2), was Androkles (viii. 65. 2), a member of the council (And. i. 27) in 416/15 and in 411 τοῦ δήμου μάλιστα προεστῶτα (Th. ibid.), whom Plu. *Alc.* 19. 1 represents as 'producing' (προήγαγε) the 'metics and slaves' of Th. vi. 28. 1. The εἰσαγγελία, however, stood in the name of Thessalos, son of Kimon (Plu. *Alc.* 19. 3, 22. 4), whose standpoint one would expect to be profoundly different from that of Androkles. Peisandros, who raised to 10,000

---

[1] I am grateful to the University of Cincinnati for permission to read an unpublished doctoral dissertation by Ruth Allen, 'The Mutilation of the Herms'. I have made use of some of Miss Allen's prosopographical researches, but have ignored probable or possible identifications of individuals whose political alignment is unknown.

drachmai the reward offered for information (And. i. 27), is presumably the opportunist whom we know from book viii.

Herms. Hardly any of the men denounced by Teukros and Andokides are identifiable, but their most interesting aspect is their overlap with the profaners of the mysteries. Euphiletos and Pherekles were guilty of both offences, and so were 'Meletos' and 'Theodoros', assuming that each of them is one person. Teukros, who confessed to profanation, was evidently close enough to the mutilators to denounce many of them. Eryximachos may be the son of Akumenos, though mutilating statues seems an unlikely prank for a man who is represented in the *Symposium* (of which the 'dramatic date', for what it is worth, is 416; cf. *Smp.* 173 a ~ Ath. 217 a) as a doctor of some standing, and I suspect that Eryximachos the mutilator was in fact a nephew or cousin of Akumenos. Andokides' father was alleged to have been present in a house during a profanation, but successfully denied his presence (And. i. 22).

To this extent the Athenians were right in believing that the same people, or at least the same section of society, were concerned with both impieties. Peisandros again appears as a zealous ζητητής, together with Charikles (possibly the man who later became one of the thirty tyrants), and it is to these two that Andokides (i. 36) attributes the portentous judgement that the mutilation was part of a wide conspiracy to subvert the democracy.

It is not at first easy to see why such impieties should have been taken as evidence of a political conspiracy. Thucydides' statement that they were so taken is supported by a detail in Diokleides' story: Euphemos, in trying to buy Diokleides' silence (And. i. 42), assures him 'If we secure what we wish, you will be one of us.' The following considerations are relevant:

(i) Since it was believed by many (cf. *Oedipus Tyrannus*) that when the gods were offended by the action of one member of a community they might punish the whole community if it failed to discover the guilty man, a group which wanted the Sicilian expedition to fail or to be cancelled might commit an impiety in the hope that popular morale would be affected by fear of divine punishment (and with the confidence of agnostics that no gods would punish *them*). This popular attitude would be particularly important on the eve of an overseas expedition because of the belief that it was perilous to sail on the same ship as a man who had offended gods (cf. A. *Th.* 602 ff., E. *El.* 1354 f., X. *Cyr.* viii. 1. 25, [Lys.] vi. 19, And. i. 137 ff., and— on the mechanism of 'infection'—Ant. ii. *a.* 10). Such an interpretation of the mutilation is implied by the story which attributed it to Corinthians (Philochoros F 133, Kratippos F 3), a story of which there is no hint in Thucydides or Andokides. Inside Athens there may have been some men who would have welcomed the failure of an enterprise which seemed likely to increase the revenues at the disposal of the democracy and its power and ideological influence in the Greek world; such were the men who in 411 were prepared to negotiate for peace at the cost of Athens' walls and fleet. There were certainly men—Nikias was one of them—who would have welcomed the cancellation of the enterprise on strategic grounds and the employment of Athenian resources and energies nearer home. Yet 27. 3 τοῦ ἔκπλου οἰωνὸς ἐδόκει εἶναι καὶ ξυνωμοσίᾳ ἅμα - - - γεγενῆσθαι does not say that it was thought that the mutilation was deliberately designed to affect the expedition; and if such an idea was entertained it is remarkable that a different crime committed by the most ambitious and persuasive proponent of the expedition should so easily be represented as done μετὰ τοῦ αὐτοῦ λόγου. It should also be noted that fear of divine displeasure did not in fact make the Athenians postpone the departure of the expedition until they should discover who had mutilated the herms.

(ii) It was not entirely a strange idea that a revolutionary conspiracy should advertise itself by mutilating statues. The more spectacular the crime, the stronger the impression of the numbers, power, and ubiquity of the conspirators; and when their chosen moment comes, the uncommitted individual may hesitate to act against them for fear that they have a majority on their side (cf. viii. 66. 2).

(iii) νόμος covers both the 'constitution' and traditional religious observances, and παρανομία can describe the contravention of either. This fact forges the essential link between impiety and political conspiracy (cf. Grote, vi. 7 f.). Alkibiades was a notorious example of those who conduct themselves as if they were above the law (for the anecdotage accumulated from his own time onwards cf. And. iv. 10 ff. and Plu. Alc. passim, and for the kind of conduct which could be stigmatized as παρανομία cf. Lys. iii. 10. 5 ff.). The impieties prompted in the Athenians the thought that a whole section of their society had demonstrated the will to do as it pleased and, if not resisted, would have demonstrated also the power to do so. The terms in which Androkles and others attacked Alkibiades will not have been very different from those in which D. xxi. 208 ff. attacks the class with which Meidias is identified, and the popular association of treason with contempt for custom (the linking idea is the pursuit of self-interest) is illustrated by Isoc. xx. 10: 'we have twice been deprived of our liberty' (sc. in 411 and 404) 'not by men tainted with other vices, but διὰ τοὺς καταφρονοῦντας τῶν νόμων καὶ βουλομένους τοῖς μὲν πολεμίοις δουλεύειν τοὺς δὲ πολίτας ὑβρίζειν'.

Evidently statues could be mutilated 'by young men in drunken sport' (28. 1); superstition was not strong enough to protect gods from the ordinary vandalism by which young people are sometimes impelled to assert anonymous power. The mutilation of all the herms in Athens may have been no more than an unusually grandiose and spectacular piece of vandalism of a kind which appeals to some people at a certain stage of drunkenness. Andokides is silent on the question of motive (i. 61): 'Euphiletos put the proposal to us while we were drinking.' A little more detail is provided by his statement (i. 67) εἰσηγησαμένῳ Εὐφιλήτῳ πίστιν τῶν ἐν ἀνθρώποις ἀπιστοτάτην, κ.τ.λ., which suggests that he was a member of a club whose members guaranteed their loyalty to each other by concerting a crime for which each could (in theory) be denounced by the others if he were subsequently disloyal. Such a club might have purposes which we could call 'political'; that is, in addition to drinking too much, enjoying each other's company, and congratulating themselves on their own importance, the members might support each other by money and advocacy in political life.[1] Some such clubs—not all— could become important centres of conspiracy once a genuinely revolutionary situation had arisen, as they did in 411 (viii. 54. 4 and 65. 2), but it does not follow that any of them in normal times, or all of them even in abnormal times, would seriously initiate or even welcome an oligarchic revolution. It is noteworthy that even in 415, according to Plu. *Alc.* 18. 8 (though Plutarch may be drawing an inference from Thucydides' 'other mutilations'; cf. Hatzfeld, 168 n. 2), some people dismissed the mutilation of the herms as the vandalism of ἀκόλαστοι young men.

Diokleides' Denunciations. If the profaners were Alkibiades and his friends and did what they did for fun, and if the mutilators were a club of silly young men whose desire for public notice landed them in more trouble than they had bargained for, we might expect the false allegations of Diokleides to be something much more serious, the deliberate political exploitation of the situation which had been created. It is possible to argue that their purpose was to hit back at the enemies of Alkibiades (cf. Hatzfeld, 193 f.), among whom we may classify, for reasons of varying cogency, several of the identifiable victims.

First, one of the two instigators of the denunciation was named by Diokleides as Alkibiades Phegusios; unless he is the 'nephew and fellow exile' of the great Alkibiades, captured and executed for treason in 408 (X. *HG* i. 2. 13), he is not otherwise known, but his name is significant in so far as (according to Th. viii. 6. 3) it was a Spartan name which entered the family of Kleinias at an early date through friendship with a Spartan family.

---

[1] If the lost work πρὸς τοὺς ἑταίρους (Plu. *Them.* 32. 4) is genuine, Andokides was oligarchic in sympathy, and if fr. 5 (Blass) comes from this work it was composed before the summer of 415; but it does not seem to have been known to the author of *Vit. X Or.* ([Plu.] *Mor.* 835 a), whose usual fault is to lump too much together.

Secondly, among the victims, Eukrates was a brother of Nikias (no doubt an allegation that Nikias himself mutilated statues at night would have strained the credulity of the Athenians even in their most suspicious mood); Taureas (whose son Nisaios was also denounced) was probably the man of that rare name whom Alkibiades had insulted publicly (And. iv. 20 f., D. xxi. 147, Plu. *Alc.* 16. 5); while Charmides was a son of Aristoteles, and the Aristoteles who was later one of the thirty tyrants belonged (X. *HG* ii. 3. 46) to that section of the oligarchs of 411 which was opposed to the return of Alkibiades (cf. the attribution of Ἀλκιβιάδου λοιδορίαι to Antiphon, who shared with Aristoteles a willingness to sacrifice the empire rather than recall Alkibiades [Th. viii. 68. 3, 90. 1 f., 91. 3, and 97. 3]).

If Kritias was the notorious son of Kallaischros we encounter a very different alignment, for that Kritias in a later year (fr. 3) was the proposer of the decree recalling Alkibiades.

The position of Andokides and his family is obscure. Andokides belonged to the same club as Eryximachos, and his father Leogoras could at least be accused of presence in the house of Pulytion when the mysteries were parodied. On the other side stands the evidence of the speech against Alkibiades (And. iv) attributed to Andokides. No one believes that Andokides delivered this speech on the occasion to which it refers—the speaker envisages, at the beginning of 415, an ostracism which must result in the departure of himself or Nikias or Alkibiades—and the historical obstacles to the supposition that anyone actually composed it in 415 seem to me insuperable (cf. A. R. Burn, *CQ* N.S. iv [1954], 138 ff.; A. E. Raubitschek, *TAPhA* lxxix [1948], 191 ff., attempts to explain away the difficulties one by one, but their cumulative force is too much for any such attempt). The speech is therefore a piece of historical fiction, and as such may well belong to the fourth century and even to Andokides himself; a parallel is provided by the 'Speech of Nikias to his Syracusan captors', which Theophrastos, to the disgust of Dionysios (*Lys.* 14), attributed to Lysias. It is by no means improbable that an early fourth-century author should distort the nature of ostracism; the famous story of the last ostracism, at which, after it had been taken for granted that either Nikias or Alkibiades would be ostracized, Hyperbolos fell victim because the adherents of the two protagonists combined against him (Plu. *Alc.* 13. 4 f.), will have provided the idea for the speech. But who is the imagined speaker? Someone in antiquity thought it was Phaiax (Plu. *Alc.* 13. 3; is this the origin of the statement in *Vit. X Or.* 835 a that Andokides composed a 'Defence against Phaiax'?), presumably because the speaker says that he has been on an embassy to Sicily and Italy (41), and Phaiax's mission to the West was well known from Th. v. 4 f.; this identification produced in turn a variant version of the story of the ostracism of Hyperbolos (Plu. *Alc.* 13. 8). An equally plausible identification is Leogoras, who, like the speaker (ibid.), had been on an embassy to Macedonia (*IG* i². 57 [= ML 65]. 51, cf. And. ii. 11). The possibility that Andokides wrote the fictitious speech early in the fourth century and cast his distinguished father in the role of an opponent of Alkibiades has interesting implications for the political alignments of 415.

Since political prosopography is a type of study which requires a higher degree of caution than any other historical field, it is right to emphasize the extent to which the hypothesis that Diokleides' allegations were intended as a blow against the enemies of Alkibiades rests upon assumptions. To reduce even further the temptation to believe that kinsmen and acquaintances consistently support each other's policies, it should be noted that in Pl. *Prt.* 315 c–316 a we find Alkibiades, Adeimantos, and Eryximachos in the house of Kallias, son of Hipponikos, a member of the Κήρυκες and a man who strenuously opposed the recall of Alkibiades in 411 (Th. viii. 53. 2) and was a prosecutor of Andokides in 399 (And. i. 112 ff.); that Peisandros, politically close to Aristoteles in 411 (Th. viii. 98. 1), wanted drastic and immediate action against the men denounced by Diokleides (And. i. 43) and in 411 tried to dispose of Andokides (And. ii. 14); and that Phaidros, together with Sokrates and members of Plato's family, was a friend of Kephalos and his intransigently democratic sons Polemarchos and Lysias (Pl. *Phdr.* 227 c, *R.* 327 b, 328 b), as was also Nikias' son Nikeratos (*R.* 327 c).

27. 1. εἰσὶ δὲ κατὰ τὸ ἐπιχώριον, ἡ τετράγωνος ἐργασία, πολλοί, κ.τ.λ.: 'they are numerous, according to the custom of the country—the (sc. well-known) four-cornered pattern . . .' The Athenians were credited with the invention of that form of herm which consisted of a pillar, square in section, topped by a head and ornamented by an erect phallos (Hdt. ii. 51. 1 f., Paus. iv. 33. 4). For the whole history of this art-form, cf. R. Lullies, *Die Typen der griechischen Herme* (Königsberg, 1931), and Nilsson, *Geschichte der griechischen Religion*, i². 190 ff.; *CVA* Denmark iii. pl. 139. 2 is an excellent illustration of a sculptor making a herm. The fact that the compiler of the Patmos Scholia explained Ἑρμαῖ λίθινοι as τετράγωνος ἐργασία does not mean that the latter words (del. Bauer) were absent from his text of Thucydides; cf. Steup (p. 263) and Dover, *CR* N.S. v (1955), 134 ff. For ἐργασία = 'style' or 'type' cf. *IG* ii². 244. 55, 1666. 39 ff.

περιεκόπησαν τὰ πρόσωπα: the obvious way to mutilate a herm is to knock off its phallos, and Ar. *Lys.* 1094, where men who enter ἐστυκότες are warned 'Mind the Hermokopidai don't see you!', shows (as Hudson saw) that this in fact was done. If πρόσωπα means, as it normally means, 'faces', it might seem that Thucydides in an anxiety to avoid αἰσχρολογία (cf. the coy periphrasis for αἰδοῖα in X. *Hier.* 1. 4) is falsifying the facts, and falsifying them unnecessarily, as he need not have specified the exact nature of the mutilation. πρόσωπον = 'façade' in Pi. *P.* 6. 14 and E. *Ion* 189 does not help, for Thucydides could hardly have used the ordinary word for 'face' to mean a part of a statue other than its face. The natural explanation is that the mutilators damaged the face of every herm and the phallos where there was one to damage (cf. Σ^M ~ Paus. Att. fr. 72 Erbse: τοὺς τραχήλους καὶ τὰ αἰδοῖα); there is some reason to think (Lullies, op. cit. 46; cf. Herter, *RE* xix. 1690) that by the end of the fifth century herms without erect phalloi were coming into fashion, and it may be that the mutilation of the god's face was felt to be a more serious sacrilege than knocking off a feature of old-fashioned crudity.

2. μηνύειν ἀδεῶς τὸν βουλόμενον: the language is documentary; ἀδεῶς = 'with ἄδεια', a guarantee of immunity from prosecution (e.g. *IG* i². 92. 16), and for τὸν βουλόμενον cf. doc. ap. And. i. 84.

3. ἐπὶ ξυνωμοσίᾳ - - - δήμου καταλύσεως γεγενῆσθαι: ἐπί c. *dat.*, as often, has the sense 'in furtherance of . . .', 'with . . . in mind', almost 'as an expression of . . .', and the genitives are objective, cf. A. *Ch.* 978 ξυνώμοσαν θάνατον, Ar. *Lys.* 1007 τὸ πρᾶγμα - - - ξυνομώμοται.

28. 2. ἐμποδὼν ὄντι σφίσι μὴ αὐτοῖς τοῦ δήμου βεβαίως προεστάναι: Thucydides consistently represents Athenian political life as a competition for προστασία; cf. ii. 65. 11, where (silent on the competition of the 440s from which Perikles emerged as victor) he refers to the 'decisions taken after the departure of the expedition' as made κατὰ τὰς ἰδίας διαβολὰς περὶ τῆς τοῦ δήμου προστασίας, and viii. 89. 3, where the weakness of the Four Hundred is seen to be the ἴδιαι φιλοτιμίαι characteristic of oligarchies, in which all the participants ἀξιοῦσιν - - - πολὺ πρῶτος αὐτὸς ἕκαστος εἶναι. Here there is an important difference, in that Thucydides treats Alkibiades' enemies as a group ('preventing *them* from leading the people *themselves*'); Alkibiades was a giant, and men who were potentially rivals of one another combined to overthrow him.

οὐ δημοτικὴν παρανομίαν: δημοτικός describes not only the political allegiance of a man (e.g. And. ii. 26) but also, on occasion, his treatment of his fellow citizens as equals; so X. *Mem.* i. 2. 60 describes Sokrates as δημοτικὸς καὶ φιλάνθρωπος.

29. 1. ἕτοῖμος ἦν - - - κρίνεσθαι εἴ τι τούτων εἰργασμένος ἦν - - - εἰ μὲν τούτων τι εἴργαστο, - - - ἄρχειν: if it is permissible to transpose these words into *oratio recta*, they will be: ἑτοῖμός εἰμι κρίνεσθαι εἴ τι τούτων εἴργασμαι ('to be tried, to discover whether I have committed any of these acts'), καὶ εἰ μὲν τούτων τι εἴργασμαι ('and if I have'), (sc. ἐτοῖμός εἰμι) δίκην δοῦναι, ἐὰν δ' ἀπολυθῶ, (sc. ἀξιῶ) ἄρχειν; but a man writing *obliqua* in his own language does not perform this grammatical exercise. ἐτοῖμος ἦν - - - κρίνεσθαι εἴ τι - - - ἦν can be defended by vii. 33. 6 βουλόμενοι - - - εἴ τις ὑπελέλειπτο ἐξετάσαι - - - περιέμενον, and εἴργαστο by iii. 32. 2 ἔλεγον οὐ καλῶς τὴν Ἑλλάδα ἐλευθεροῦν αὐτόν, εἰ ἄνδρας διέφθειρεν (cf. Goodwin, *MT* § 691). The ensemble is, however, suspiciously clumsy, and it is possible that εἴ τι τούτων εἰργασμένος ἦν is an interpolation, occasioned by the fact that κρίνειν commonly means 'condemn' in later Greek.

3. δεδιότες τό τε στράτευμα μὴ εὔνουν ἔχῃ: this text, which is presented by all our MSS., is recorded as a variant by Σ^{Mcf}, whose paraphrase, φοβούμενοι τὸ στράτευμα ὡς οὐκ εὔνουν αὐτοῖς, clearly points to a reading μὴ εὔνουν οὐκ ᾖ; this is a less attractive alternative, since in the context we should expect εὔνουν to mean εὔνουν τῷ ἀγωνιζομένῳ, i.e. to Alkibiades. The nature of the Greek state normally precluded a difference of allegiance between 'civilians' and 'the army'; the present case is a striking exception, but in the years 410–407 the different loyalties of the fleet in the Hellespont and the assembly at Athens became of practical significance (cf. Andrewes, *JHS* lxxiii [1953], 4 f.).

θεραπεύων ὅτι, κ.τ.λ.: 'protecting him, because . . .', for θεραπεύειν ὅτι does not occur elsewhere in the sense 'cherishing the fact that . . .'; for θεραπεύειν = 'look after the interests of' cf. Isoc. iv. 152 τῶν μὲν συμμάχων καταφρονοῦντες, τοὺς δὲ πολεμίους θεραπεύοντες.

καὶ τῶν Μαντινέων τινές: Mantineia, when we last heard of her (v. 81. 1), had unwillingly come to terms with Sparta. The Mantineans who went to Sicily with the Athenians are classified as mercenaries in 43 and vii. 57. 9, but no doubt there were also some (τινες here) who came as volunteers with the connivance of their government—in terms of c. 22, 'persuaded', not 'hired'. It appears that Alkibiades' estimation (16. 6–17. 1) of his own importance in relation to Argos and Mantineia was widely accepted (cf. 61. 5)—but not, perhaps, by Thucydides (cf. 69. 3, vii. 57. 9, and de Romilly, *Imp.*, 197 n. 5).

ἄλλους ῥήτορας ἐνιέντες: Spratt observes the striking associations of ἐνιέναι with fire (iv. 115. 2, Hdt. viii. 32. 2, etc.), to which we may add fighting spirit, madness, and poison; cf. LSJ s.v.

ἐν ἡμέραις ῥηταῖς: '*within* a prescribed period' (sc. from receipt of the summons) gives satisfactory sense, cf. D. xxiii. 72 ὁ νόμος κελεύει τὸν ἁλόντα - - - ἔν τισιν εἰρημένοις χρόνοις ἀπελθεῖν, Aeschin. ii. 109 βουλεύσασθαι τὸν δῆμον ὑπὲρ εἰρήνης ἐν τάκταις ἡμέραις; but cf. 65. 1 n.

μετάπεμπτον κομισθέντα: neither word is superfluous, since κομισθῆναι can be used either of voluntary action or as a true passive: 'they wanted him to return and stand trial when he was summoned home'. Cf. Hp. *Flat.* 8 τὰ δένδρα ἀνασπαστὰ πρόρριζα γίνεται, D. xviii. 68 ὥστε τῆς ἐλευθερίας αὐτεπαγγέλτους ἐθελοντὰς παραχωρῆσαι Φιλίππῳ.

30–32. 2. *Departure of the Expedition*

30. 1. θέρους μεσοῦντος ἤδη: cf. p. 271 and v. 57. 1 n.
ἐς Κέρκυραν ξυλλέγεσθαι: we are reminded (not for the first time; cf. iv. 2. 3) of the words of the Kerkyrean envoys in 433, i. 36. 2 τῆς τε γὰρ Ἰταλίας καὶ Σικελίας καλῶς παράπλου κεῖται : and cf. X. *HG* vi. 2. 9. ἐπὶ ἄκραν Ἰαπυγίαν: cf. 34. 4, 44. 2, vii. 33. 3; Strabo 281 σκοπελὸς ὃν καλοῦσιν ἄκραν Ἰαπυγίαν shows that the expression is a name, not a description.

2. τὰ μὲν ὡς κτήσοιντο, τοὺς δ' εἴ ποτε ὄψοιντο: these words explain μετ' ἐλπίδος τε - - - καὶ ὀλοφυρμῶν: '(for they expected) that they would conquer Sicily, but (lamented because they wondered) if they would ever see their men (again)'. For ὡς = 'thinking that' or 'saying that' cf. 35. 1; for εἰ = 'wondering if' cf. E. *HF* 791 φόβος γὰρ εἴ μοι ζῶσιν οὓς ἐγὼ θέλω; and for ὁρᾶν = 'see again' cf. S. *OT* 824 εἰ - - - μοι φυγόντι μή 'στι τοὺς ἐμοὺς ἰδεῖν.

31. 1. ὅμως δὲ τῇ παρούσῃ ῥώμῃ - - - ἀνεθάρσουν: literally, 'nevertheless, because of the strength which was present, through the quantity of each item which they saw, they took courage in the seeing'. ῥώμη cannot here mean 'confidence' or 'energy' (as it sometimes does, e.g. vii. 18. 2, cf. vi. 17. 8 ἔρρωνται) ; as Thucydides, speaking of the spectators as a whole, not of a handful of doubters, has just described them as struck with apprehension, there was no 'prevailing confidence' in them which could cause them to take heart. If he means the confidence of the participants in the expedition, 'the prevailing confidence' and 'because of the quantity . . .' are two distinct causes of the spectators' taking heart; but they are not grammatically co-ordinated. On the other hand, if ῥώμη means material strength, διὰ τὸ πλῆθος ἑκάστων is tautologous. Whatever ῥώμη means, the accumulation of two datives of different point with ἀνεθάρσουν is stylistically objectionable. This last objection is removed by punctuating not after ἑώρων but after ὄψει: 'which they saw with their own eyes', distinguishing between what they saw and what they felt, as in 49. 2 τῇ γνώμῃ ἀναθαρσοῦντας - - - καὶ τῇ ὄψει καταφρονεῖν μᾶλλον, Hp. *De Arte* 2 καὶ ὀφθαλμοῖσιν ἰδεῖν καὶ γνώμῃ νοῆσαι; for the pleonasm ἑώρων τῇ ὄψει cf. iii. 112. 4 οὐ καθορωμένους τῇ ὄψει, iv. 34. 3, Hp. *De Arte* 13 ἰδεῖν ὄψει ᾗ - - - πάντες - - - ὁρῶσι, Aeschin. iii. 119 ὁρᾶτε τοῖς ὀφθαλμοῖς, [Lys.] vi. 51 εἶπε τῇ φωνῇ τὰ ἀπόρρητα. The tautology remains. It cannot be removed by deleting διὰ τὸ πλῆθος - - - ὄψει as an intrusive gloss, for no commentator is likely to have added τῇ ὄψει to ἑώρων, or by deleting simply διά - - - ἑώρων, for that leaves the two datives uncomfortably juxtaposed, and in any case a glossator is unlikely to have used the characteristically Thucydidean ἑκάστων. Perhaps, however, we may allow Thucydides sometimes to expand a phrase by repeating its sense in other words, though the nearest apparent parallel, ii. 35. 3 μία κλίνη - - - τῶν ἀφανῶν, οἳ ἂν μὴ εὑρεθῶσιν ἐς ἀναίρεσιν, involves an explanation of a local term. Herbst, 96 f., suggests that τῇ παρούσῃ ῥώμῃ represents the psychological aspect of the armament, while διὰ τὸ πλῆθος κ.τ.λ. looks forward to the details which follow; cf. Pl. *Smp.* 190 b ἰσχύν - - - καὶ τὴν ῥώμην and Kratinos fr. 411 ἐρρῶσθαι, interpreted by *A B* 8. 3 as προθυμεῖσθαι. (For emendations cf. Badham, *Mnemosyne* 1875, 22, and Stahl ad loc.)

παρασκευὴ γὰρ αὕτη πρώτη ἐκπλεύσασα μιᾶς πόλεως - - - πολυτελεστάτη δή - - - ἐγένετο: the opening words, lit. 'This (force), being a force sailing out of a single city with Greek power, was the first (of such forces) which . . .', create the expectation of a continuation 'was so vast and expensive', but the sentence actually continues, 'was more expensive and splendid than any up to that time'. If the text is right, Thucydides has tried to say one thing in two ways at once (cf. Linwood), and the result is, lit., 'was the first which was more expensive than any before'. This sense is acceptable to Marchant and Bodin, but the point, that this force was a greater step beyond its predecessors than any one of them had been before *its* predecessors, is a curious (one might say, absurd) point for Thucydides to make. There surely can be no doubt what Thucydides meant, that this was the greatest expedition ever mounted by one Greek city (cf. iii. 39. 1 Μυτιληναίους μάλιστα δὴ μίαν πόλιν ἠδικηκότας ὑμᾶς); the limitation here, 'Greek', may glance at Carthage, cf. Schwartz, 336. The only problem is the reconciliation of the obvious meaning with the manuscript text; simply to translate as if the text bore that meaning (so Herbst–Müller, ii. 18) will not do. The combination of alternative expressions can perhaps be compared with E. *Ba.* 842 πᾶν κρεῖσσον ὥστε μὴ 'γγελᾶν βάκχας ἐμοί, which may combine 'anything is better than that the bacchanals should laugh at me' with 'anything is acceptable which ensures that the bacchanals do not laugh at me', but even there the interpretation 'any (suggestion of yours) is preferable (to possible alternatives) provided that . . .' must be considered. The simplest emendation is the insertion of ⟨ἥ⟩ before πρώτη; cf. 44. 1, where ἡ πρώτη παρασκευή means this force as opposed to the reinforcements of 413 (and in viii. 17. 4 ἡ ξυμμαχία - - - ἡ πρώτη looks forward to 37). Or again, πρώτη may be deleted as the relic of a gloss ἡ πρώτη by a glossator who had 44. 1 in mind. I doubt whether any conflation of αὕτη with a corruption αυτη > α'τη > πρώτη should be considered; in 55. 2, where πρώτη is a corruption of αὐτῇ, the cause was the immediate proximity of πρῶτος, not αὐτῇ < α'τη. (Krüger's emendation of the superlatives to datives, agreeing with δυνάμει and having an absolute sense, is lame in itself and irreconcilable with what Thucydides goes on to say.)

2. καὶ ἡ ἐς Ἐπίδαυρον - - - μετὰ Ἁγνωνος: Perikles took this force out in the summer of 430 (ii. 56), ravaging places in the NE. Peloponnese; Hagnon and Kleopompos relieved him and took it to Poteidaia later in the summer (ii. 58). The details of its composition given there agree with those given here except that nothing is said there of the 'numerous allies who sailed with them', presumably as troops, since by 431 no allied states except Chios and Lesbos had warships of their own. With ἡ we must understand παρασκευή in the sense 'force', from § 1, but in § 3 παρασκευῇ φαύλῃ refers to the structure and equipment of the force, not to the force itself, Thucydides writes as if he had used, e.g., στρατιά in § 2. Bodin makes the thought tidier—perhaps too tidy—by inserting ⟨στρατιά⟩ after μετὰ Περικλέους.

ξυνέπλευσαν: ξυν- is justified by καὶ Λεσβίων - - - πολλοί.

3. οὗτος δὲ ὁ στόλος: understand ἐξέπλευσε from ἐπὶ βραχεῖ πλῷ ὡρμήθησαν.

δραχμὴν τῆς ἡμέρας: the fact that Thucydides specifies the rate of pay suggests that it was unusually high. So it was, in retrospect, but not necessarily higher than had been customary for a generation. It is the rate which Tissaphernes promises the Peloponnesians in 412 (viii. 29. 1). The Segestan envoys brought 60 talents 'as a month's pay for 60 ships', which implies a drachma per day per man; cf. 8. 1 n. It is the Athenian rate given in iii. 17. 4 (a chapter of doubtful authenticity), and there is some reason to think it antedated the war; it makes good sense of *IG* i². 295 (= ML 61). Boeckh, i³. 344, while accepting the authenticity of iii. 17, nevertheless asserted that 3 obols a day was the normal rate, and his view has been generally adopted, e.g. by Gomme on iii. 17, though not by Jones, 7 n. 27, 32 n. 54. viii. 45. 2, where Alkibiades tells Tissaphernes that the Athenians ἐκ πλέονος χρόνου have paid their sailors 3 obols a day, should not be set against the evidence given above. Obviously the Athenians would be compelled to economize after 413; and given the circumstances and purpose of Alkibiades' talk with Tissaphernes we should not take ἐκ πλέονος χρόνου any more seriously than the explanation which Alkibiades gives for this low rate. (Ar. *V.* 684 f. σοὶ δ' ἤν τις δῷ τοὺς τρεῖς ὀβολούς, ἀγαπᾷς· οὓς αὐτὸς ἐλαύνων καὶ πεζομαχῶν καὶ πολιορκῶν ἐκτήσω πολλὰ πονήσας does not refer, as Kolbe thought [*Ph.* lviii (1899), 550 n. 272], to rates of pay, but means that the revenue from which juries were paid was available because of the victories won by Philokleon's generation on land and sea.)

καὶ ναῦς παρασχόντος κενάς: elsewhere in Thucydides κεναὶ νῆες are ships without men, e.g. i. 27. 2, ii. 90. 6, viii. 19. 3. Since the state paid the sailors their basic wage (the extra wages paid by the trierarchs going only to certain categories) the point of κενάς must be that whereas the state provided the ships and conscripted and assigned the petty officers (see below), the crews were not, strictly speaking, 'provided', but recruited from volunteers (cf. vii. 13. 2 n., 60. 5 n.), the trierarchs themselves being responsible for organizing recruitment. Cf. Busolt–Swoboda, i. 573 f., and Kolbe, loc. cit. 536, 539 ff. An alternative is to interpret κενάς, contrary to Thucydides' usage, as 'without equipment'. Our evidence on trierarchic responsibilities, abundant from fourth-century sources, is meagre in the fifth, and we do not know for certain whether a trierarch was responsible, as he was not in the fourth, for the initial conversion of a hull into a ship, as distinct from repairs and replacements of losses. A further alternative is to adopt καινάς, the reading of H₂ ψ (cj. Naber).

καὶ ὑπηρεσίας ταύταις τὰς κρατίστας: in addition to the rowers (ἐρέται), a trireme's crew comprised certain 'specialists' or 'petty officers', e.g. κυβερνήτης (vii. 62. 1), κελευστής (vii. 70. 6), πρῳράτης ([X.] Resp. Ath. 1. 2), ναυπηγοί, and πεντηκόνταρχοι (ibid.). IG ii². 1951 (s. iv. in.) mentions all these, plus an αὐλητής (94 ff. and 328 ff.) and two or three τοξόται who are Athenian citizens (106 ff., 339 f.). Cf. Amit, 29 f., and Buck, no. 7 (Delphi, s. v) A. 10 ff. Ar. Eq. 541 ff. implies that the πρῳράτης came between the rower and the helmsman in skill and responsibility. We have no reason to think that any list which we could compile from the extant evidence would be complete. These specialists are called ὑπηρεσίαι (viii. 1. 2, IG ii². 212. 59 ff.) or collectively ὑπηρεσία, whether of many ships (Th. i. 143. 1) or a single ship (e.g. Lys. xxi. 10, and especially D. l. 25, al., where they are distinguished throughout from the ναῦται of the ship; LSJ is badly wrong here). The usage is at first sight curious, since ὑπηρέτης means 'servant' or 'subordinate', but it probably originated in sailing-ships, the helmsman, carpenter, etc. being regarded as ὑπηρέται of the master and so later of the trierarch. Cf. L. J. D. Richardson, CQ xxxvii (1943), 55 ff., for an etymological discussion which does not, however, reach any firm conclusion on ὑπηρεσία. Other collectives in -ια are ἑταιρεία, γυμνητεία (vii. 37. 2), μνοία (PMG 909. 5), cf. E. Ba. 803 δουλεύοντα δουλείαις ἐμαῖς, and parallels for the oscillation between the plural and the 'super-collective' singular are provided by some modern usages of 'trade', 'staff', 'aircrew', and 'faculty'. τοξεύματα in vii. 43. 2 is similar.

τοῖς θρανίταις τῶν ναυτῶν: the θρανῖται sat outside the ζύγιοι (or whatever these were called in Thucydides' day) and, by virtue of the θρᾶνοι after which they were named, half above them, while the θαλαμιοί sat three-quarters below the ζύγιοι (Ar. Ra. 1074; Σ ad loc., which satisfies Amit [99 ff.], does nothing to explain the joke). J. S. Morrison, The Mariner's Mirror xxvii (1941), 14 ff. (cf. id., CQ xli [1947], 122 ff.) seems to me to have given a definitive interpretation of the relevant works of art. The superior status and (on this occasion) extra pay of the θρανῖται were justified by an estimation of their work as harder and more skilled and by their exposure to greater risk of injury from collision and missiles (cf. vii. 34. 5 n.). In Ar. *Ach.* 162 ὁ θρανίτης λεὼς ὁ σωσίπολις are the sailors *par excellence*. **καὶ ταῖς ὑπηρεσίαις**: the common editorial statement that Σ^{GMcf} did not have these words in his text originated in the mistaken belief (not shared by Σ) that the ὑπηρεσίαι of a ship included all the rowers. **σημείοις**: we are inadequately informed (and so was Σ^{GMcf}) on the nature of Greek naval standards, but they were used in an elementary signalling system ('raising the σημεῖον' is the signal to attack in i. 49. 1) and such a system requires a general's σημεῖον to be distinctive; cf. Diod. xiii. 46. 3, 77. 4, where the general's σημεῖον is red. **καὶ τῷ ταχυναυτεῖν**: the word is probably not a Thucydidean invention, for it recurs in the fourth century as a technical term, *IG* ii². 1623. 284 (333/2 B.C.), Aeschin. iii. 97, cf. ταχ[υδρ]αμοῦσι *GHI* 149. 11 (Kios, *c.* 360 B.C.). **καταλόγοις τε χρηστοῖς ἐκκριθέν**: cf. 26. 2 n. A good register is one which excludes men who are dead, crippled, in prison, or fictitious, and includes all those capable of service; 'honest' registers, one might say (H. A. Murray, *BICS* viii [1961], 37; cf. F. W. Mitchel, *GRBS* v [1964], 103).

4. ἔριν: essentially 'rivalry', 'competition', the ἔρις ἔργοιο of *Od.* xviii. 366, the beneficial ἔρις of Hes. *Op.* 11 ff., cf. the competitive blessings of A. *Eu.* 974 f. (J. I. Beare, *CR* xii [1898], 115). Elsewhere in Thucydides ἔρις means 'disagreement', and Marchant accordingly insists here that it means 'quarrelling' (about who was best equipped); but since rivalry, among people as uninhibited as the Athenians, necessarily involves resentment, boasting, and ridicule, the distinction between different senses of ἔρις cannot be drawn as sharply as Marchant would wish. Cf. Ar. *Nu.* 312, where χορῶν ἐρεθίσματα refers to the City Dionysia.

καὶ ἐς τοὺς ἄλλους Ἕλληνας ἐπίδειξιν μᾶλλον εἰκασθῆναι, κ.τ.λ.: except in iv. 36. 3 ('compare'), εἰκάζειν in Thucydides means 'infer', 'conjecture', and the nearest parallel to the present passage is i. 10. 2 διπλασίαν ἂν τὴν δύναμιν εἰκάζεσθαι ἀπὸ τῆς φανερᾶς ὄψεως τῆς πόλεως ἢ ἔστιν. Yet no one is likely to have conjectured that the Athenians were not mounting a military expedition but merely making a display; the sense we need is 'it was *as if* they were making a display . . .' (cf. Arnold), and this requires εἰκάζειν = 'represent', 'portray'. Hence lit., 'the result was . . . that a display to the rest of the Greek world was-as-if-made . . . rather than an armament against an enemy'. For ἐς τοὺς Ἕλληνας cf. Pl. *Smp.* 179 b ἱκανὴν μαρτυρίαν παρέχεται ὑπὲρ τοῦδε τοῦ λόγου εἰς τοὺς Ἕλληνας.

5. τήν τε τῆς πόλεως ἀνάλωσιν δημοσίαν: the word-order is suspect, cf. Kühner–Gerth, i. 614, 624, and δημοσίαν should probably be deleted; cf. viii. 23. 5 τὸν ἑαυτοῦ στρατὸν ἀναλαβών, where B alone (and not Π²⁴) has πεζὸν after στρατόν. In Ar. *Ach.* 1210 τῆς ἐν μάχῃ συμβολῆς βαρείας (cited as a parallel by Chambry, *RPh.* xxi [1897], 105), A. *Ch.* 496 φίλτατον τὸ σὸν κάρα, E. *El.* 1006 μακαρίας τῆς σῆς χερός, the fact that the adjective is emotionally charged makes the hyperbaton intelligible. Th. i. 51. 3 ἡ ἀπαλλαγὴ ἐγένετο ἀλλήλων and iv. 43. 4 τῷ εὐωνύμῳ κέρᾳ ἑαυτῶν, cited by Classen–Steup, should probably be treated as a related but different phenomenon, trajection of the genitive.

πολλὰ ἂν τάλαντα ηὑρέθη - - - ἐξαγόμενα: to us this is anticlimactic, but πολλὰ τάλαντα ('a vast sum of money') can bear a lot of emphasis; cf. Ar. *Nu.* 1065 f. Ὑπέρβολος δ' - - - πλεῖν ἢ τάλαντα πολλὰ εἴληφεν.

6. στρατιᾶς πρὸς οὓς ἐπῇσαν ὑπερβολῇ: 'the scale of the expedition, considering (*or* in relation to, in comparison with) its objective'; i.e. the forces used were regarded as capable of overwhelming their enemies in Sicily. It was Alkibiades' view of the Sikeliots, not Nikias' view, which predominated; cf. Athenian hopes of 'subjugating Sicily' (iv. 65. 3) with a far less imposing force ten years earlier.

32. 1. ὑπὸ κήρυκος: i.e. one herald spoke for all of them; cf. Hdt. ix. 98. 2 ὑπὸ κήρυκος = 'through a herald'.

οἵ τε ἐπιβάται καὶ οἱ ἄρχοντες: in 43 ἑπτακόσιοι θῆτες ἐπιβάται τῶν νεῶν, i.e. travelling on triremes, a few on each (see note), are distinguished from the hoplites who travelled in troop-transports; elsewhere ἐπιβάτης, 'on board', is used of whatever categories of troops on board ships are spoken of in the context (cf. the relation between vii. 60. 4, 62. 3, 67. 2, 70. 3 and 5). As it is improbable that the 700 thetes poured libations from golden and silver cups while the hoplites poured none, the meaning is: '⟨sc. representatives of⟩ the troops on board and the commanders ⟨sc. of ships, detachments, forces, etc.⟩'.

2. ἐπὶ κέρως: 'in column' or (when also κατὰ μίαν, as in ii. 90. 4) 'in line astern'; ἤδη, contrasted with τὸ πρῶτον, = 'from then on', 'thereafter'.

32. 3–41. *Debate at Syracuse*

On the political structure of Syracuse at this date cf. 41. 1 n., 96. 3 n., and especially vii. 55. 2 n. The political standpoint of the second speaker, Athenagoras, is made plain by Thucydides' explicit statement (35. 2) and by the theoretical defence of democracy which forms part of his speech. The political standpoint of Hermokrates is less clear. Athenagoras treats him by implication as an oligarchic conspirator, and has won supporters in modern times; so Freeman, to whom Athenagoras' speech was the speech of 'an honest, thoughtful and patriotic man' (ii. 121), says that Hermokrates 'might well be pleased to see the cause of oligarchy flourish in any city' (ii. 69), and more recently H. J. Diesner, *Wirtschaft und Gesellschaft bei Thukydides* (Halle, 1956), 155 f., has treated Hermokrates as an oligarch. The evidence, however, does not warrant the supposition that Hermokrates was any more committed to an anti-democratic faction than Nikias, or, indeed, Perikles, or any other prominent political figure whose motives were from time to time impugned by eloquent and ambitious rivals. Xenophon represents Hermokrates (*HG* i. 1. 28) as ostentatiously correct in his relations with his sovereign, the people of Syracuse, when the blow of exile fell upon him; later, he was less scrupulous in his attempts to return from exile (Diod. xiii. 63, 75), but that tells us nothing of his politics in 415. Athenagoras is wrong on so many questions of fact on which we can form an independent opinion that he is hardly a reliable guide to Syracusan politics.

The debate has many points of contact with the debate at Athens; note especially 33. 4 f. ~ 21. 1, 33. 5 ~ 21. 2, 22, 36. 4 ~10. 2, 37. 1 f. ~ 21. 1, and de Romilly, *Imp.*, 206 f., 243 f.

Neither of the two main speakers nor the general who speaks last makes any mention of the earlier Athenian intervention in Sicily or of the defeat of Athenian designs by the conference at Gela in 424; cf. the omissions discussed in 72. 2 n.

32. 3. ἐλέχθησαν τοιοίδε λόγοι: if τοιοίδε refers forwards, 'speeches of the kind which I will illustrate', it is unique in Thucydides in being so far separated from the content to which it refers (contrast τοιάδε at the end of the sentence). Probably, therefore, it refers back, 'to that effect', i.e. some speeches in which the news ἠγγέλλετο and others in which οὐκ ἐπιστεύετο; cf. A. *Ch.* 480 κἀγώ - - - τοιάδε, 'I too make a similar prayer', Pi. *P.* 4. 156 ἔσομαι τοῖος, 'I will do what you ask', and [Lys.] xx. 31 χρὴ δὲ ὑμᾶς - - - τοιούτους εἶναι, implying 'showing the gratitude which we expect'. Schwartz (336) thought it necessary for this sense to delete ἀπό τε ἄλλων and punctuate strongly after λεγόντων, but Thucydides' point is 'speeches to this effect were made; among them was that of Hermokrates', and τῶν μέν - - - λεγόντων serves to amplify and remind us of the reference of τοιοίδε (J. Weidgen, *RhM* lxxvi [1927], 370 f., suggests παντοῖοι δή). Ἑρμοκράτης ὁ Ἕρμωνος: we last encountered him at Gela in 424, iv. 58 ff. Thucydides nowhere 'introduces' him in detail, but cf. 72. 2 n. We are reasonably well informed on his career in later years, but ignorant of his antecedents and rise to eminence (cf. H. D. Westlake, *BRL* xli [1958/9], 239 ff.). In X. *HG* ii. 2. 24 and Diod. xiii. 91. 3 the father of the tyrant Dionysios is named Hermokrates, but that may be an error for Hermokritos, a name borne by one of Dionysios' sons (*IG* ii². 103 [= *GHI* 133]. 21).

33–34. *Speech of Hermokrates*

33. 1. ὥσπερ καὶ ἄλλοι τινές: sc. ἔδοξαν or δόξουσι, according to how early in the debate Thucydides imagines Hermokrates as speaking; the reference is not to political speakers in general, but to those who support Hermokrates' views on this occasion.

ἢ λέγοντες ἢ ἀπαγγέλλοντες: λέγειν here seems to imply origination; mere repetition of what is first formulated by another is ἀπαγγέλλειν. πείθων γε ἐμαυτόν: the expression is a rhetorical commonplace; cf. And. i. 70 and D. xxiii. 19 ὥς γ' ἐμαυτὸν πείθω, D. v. 3 πεπεικὼς ἐμαυτὸν ἀνέστηκα.

3. μήτε ἀπιστήσαντες τοῦ ξύμπαντος ἀμελήσετε: if they despise the Athenians, they will take inadequate precautions; if they disbelieve the news, they will take none; hence τοῦ ξύμπαντος may (like τοῦ παντός in 40. 1) mean 'everything'.

6. τοῦ Μήδου παρὰ λόγον πολλὰ σφαλέντος: sc. περὶ ἑαυτῷ; the disastrous expedition of Xerxes illustrates the generalization of § 5, 'even if most of their failures are of their own making'; cf. i. 69. 5, where the Corinthians at Sparta speak of τὸν βάρβαρον αὐτὸν περὶ αὑτῷ τὰ πλείω σφαλέντα.

34. 1. ἐς τοὺς Σικελοὺς πέμποντες: this advice at least was taken (45), but the other embassies advocated here and by the general at the end of the debate (41. 4) were not undertaken until the end of the campaigning season (73. 2, 75. 3), when Athenian superiority in the field had been demonstrated. There is no evidence that any approach was made to Carthage. Reading between the lines of Hermokrates' speeches here, at Kamarina (78. 1 ff.), and at Gela in 424 (iv. 64), one senses the hostility to Syracuse which existed in the West; the Syracusans may now have thought that to ask for help as soon as there was a threat from Athens might only give heart to their enemies.

ξυμμαχίαν ποιώμεθα ἡμῖν: as there can be no question of importing an idiom from the Romance languages and translating ποιώμεθα ἡμῖν as 'make for ourselves', ἡμῖν must go with ξυμμαχίαν (cf. E. El. 1229 φονέας ἔτικτες ἆρά σοι) and is made easier by ξυμ- (cf. 57. 2 τῶν ξυνωμοτῶν σφίσι); Duker's paraphrase ἵνα ξυμμάχους αὐτοὺς ποιῶμεν ἡμῖν hits the mark. It is also possible that ἡμῖν is emphatically antithetical to Ἀθηναίους, i.e. 'make them allies of *ours* and persuade them *not* to receive the *Athenians*'; cf. ii. 71. 2 οὐ δίκαια ποιεῖτε οὐδ' ἄξια οὔθ' ὑμῶν οὔτε πατέρων, where, if he had made no distinction between 'you' and 'your fathers', Thucydides would presumably have written ὑμῶν αὐτῶν.

2. ἐς Καρχηδόνα - - - πέμψαι: cf. 15. 2 n.

οὐ γὰρ ἀνέλπιστον αὐτοῖς: 'for envoys from Sicily will not come as a surprise to them' may be indicated by the grammatical form of the sentence, but 'an Athenian attack is not a possibility which they discount—indeed, they are afraid of it all the time' is surely the sense of the argument.

ἤτοι κρύφα γε ἢ φανερῶς ἢ ἐξ ἑνός γέ του τρόπου: Σ^{Mcf} remarks that the last ἤ is περιττός, since 'secretly' and 'openly' are exhaustive alternatives, and many editors have agreed with him. Contrast Ar. *Th.* 429 f. ὄλεθρόν τιν' ἡμᾶς κυρκανᾶν ἀμωσγέπως, ἢ φαρμάκοισιν ἢ μιᾷ γέ τῳ τέχνῃ. But though 'secretly, perhaps, or even openly—or somehow or other, I don't mind how' may be bad logic, it is acceptable rhetoric; cf. E. *IT* 895 ff. τίς - - - ἢ θεὸς ἢ βροτὸς ἢ τί τῶν ἀδοκήτων - - -; (E. *Hel.* 1137 and A. *Th.* 197 are not parallels; the reference in the former is to heroes, in the latter to adolescents.)

4. ὅμως εἰρήσεται: cf. D. xiv. 24 παράδοξον μὲν οἶδα λόγον ὃν μέλλω λέγειν, ὅμως δ' εἰρήσεται.

ἀπαντῆσαι Ἀθηναίοις ἐς Τάραντα: if Hermokrates' proposal had been adopted, and if there had been time (as there was not) to put it into effect, the probable outcome was the annihilation of the Sikeliot fleets and the rapid imposition of Athenian rule on Sicily and South Italy; which has important implications for the problem of the essential authenticity of this speech (cf. Gomme, *Essays*, 168 f.). Bender, 82 f., underestimates the qualitative difference between Sikeliot and Athenian sailors at this time. Westlake, *BRL* xli (1958/9), 246 f., suggests that Hermokrates deliberately put forward an impossibly daring plan (as people sometimes do) in order to jolt his audience into an awareness of the issue.

ὅτι οὐ περὶ τῆς Σικελίας πρότερον ἔσται ὁ ἀγὼν ἢ τοῦ ἐκείνους περαιωθῆναι τὸν Ἰόνιον: the MSS.' dative περὶ τῇ Σικελίᾳ is appropriate with ἀγών, as in Pl. *Prt.* 313 e μὴ περὶ τοῖς φιλτάτοις κυβεύῃς τε καὶ κινδυνεύῃς (cf. G. H. Thomas, *ABAW* vi [1852], 671 ff.), and τοῦ - - - περαιωθῆναι is simply a variation of construction, cf. S. *Aj.* 1239 f. πικρούς - - - τῶν Ἀχιλλείων ὅπλων ἀγῶνας ('contest *for* the arms . . .'). Hence, lit., 'the contest will not be about Sicily' (i.e. will not endanger Sicily) 'before it is about their crossing of the Ionian sea'. Cf. Doukas's paraphrase: οὐ φοβητέον ἡμῖν περὶ τῇ Σικελίᾳ ἢ αὐτοῖς ἀγωνιστέον περὶ τοῦ περαιωθῆναι τὸν Ἰόνιον. Classen–Steup's 'an den Küsten Siziliens' involves deletion of τοῦ.

ὑποδέχεται γὰρ ἡμᾶς Τάρας: Hermokrates' confidence in the sympathy of Taras seems to have been justified; cf. 44. 2.

5. εἰ δὲ μὴ δοκοίη: since the logic of antithesis here points to an Athenian decision, the alternatives open to the Athenians appear to be: (*a*) not to move from Kerkyra at all, (*b*) to leave their supply ships at Kerkyra and cross the Ionian sea with their triremes alone, either (i) by oars, in which case they can be attacked when tired, or (ii) by sail, in which case the Sikeliot fleet can retire into Taras, leaving the Athenians to starve on the (apparently) inhospitable western shores of Iapygia. But it may be that μέν / δέ contrast not the two protases but the two complexes, so that εἰ δὲ μὴ δοκοίη will mean 'but if we decided not to (sc. for any reason)'. I feel that everything from ἐπιθοίμεθ' ἄν to ἐς Τάραντα is about 'us', not 'them'; ἡμῖν is in an entirely unemphatic position, καί before ὑποχωρῆσαι poses an alternative to 'attack', and Hermokrates naturally wants to stress Sikeliot freedom of action.

6. τούτῳ τῷ λογισμῷ: with ἀποκληομένους, as ἐς λογισμὸν καταστήσαιμεν in § 4 shows, not with ἡγοῦμαι.

ὡς ἐγὼ ἀκούω: the volume of maritime traffic throughout the eastern Mediterranean must have ensured that the gossip of any port was soon known in another.

7. τῶν δ' ἀνθρώπων πρὸς τὰ λεγόμενα καὶ αἱ γνῶμαι ἵστανται: the generalization occurs in similar form in i. 140. 1 εἰδὼς τοὺς ἀνθρώπους - - - πρὸς τὰς ξυμφορὰς καὶ τὰς γνώμας τρεπομένους, and cf. D. xxiii. 96.

ἰσοκινδύνους ἡγούμενοι: 'equal to the danger', in the sense 'capable of dealing with the danger', would be an anglicism; the meaning is 'being in no more danger than the attackers' (ἤτοι ἐν ὁμοίῳ κινδύνῳ καταστήσοντας αὐτούς, ἢ ἰσοπαλεῖς, Σ^{Mf}; *in pari discrimine futuros*, Portus); cf. ὁμοίως 64. 1 n., and Gomme, *CR* xxxiv (1920), 83 f., xliii (1929), 15.

9 πείθεσθε οὖν, κ.τ.λ.: 'do as I bid you, best of all by making this venture (sc. which I have suggested), or, failing that, (sc. let me persuade you to) make every other preparation for war with all speed.' After εἰ δὲ μή the construction of πείθεσθε changes. καὶ παραστῆναι παντί is then either an infinitive in imperatival sense (cf. the MSS.' text at 17. 1 and i. 35. 5), facilitated by πείθεσθε, or requires us to understand χρή (⟨δεῖ⟩ add. Portus) from πείθεσθε.

οἱ δὲ ἄνδρες: 'they', i.e. 'the enemy' or 'our men' according to context, in the urgent language of the battlefield; cf. v. 10. 5, Ar. *Eq.* 244.

35. *Reaction to Hermokrates' Speech*

35. 1. τοῖς δέ - - - τί ἂν δράσειαν, κ.τ.λ.: we expect οἱ δέ in antithesis to οἱ μέν, and if τοῖς δέ is right we must, with Abresch, understand ἔρις ἦν (cf. ii. 54. 3 ἐγένετο - - - ἔρις τοῖς ἀνθρώποις μὴ λοιμὸν ὠνομάσθαι - - - ἀλλὰ λιμόν). Twice elsewhere in this book, 76. 3 and 77. 2, Thucydides involves his readers in grammatical difficulties by writing τοὺς μέν - - - τοὺς δέ - - - τοῖς δέ instead of τοὺς μέν - - - τοὺς δέ - - - τοὺς δέ; here presumably he wishes to avoid οἱ μέν - - - οἱ δέ - - - ἄλλοι δέ. There is little to be gained by reading οἱ δ' (A^{ac}BCGM) ⟨ὅτι⟩ ἀληθῆ, since the force of ὀλίγον δ' ἦν, κ.τ.λ. would be greatly diminished by mentioning the believers between two categories of unbelievers. Madvig's λέγεται, οἱ δέ, εἰ καὶ κ.τ.λ. destroys the liveliness of λέγει.

36-40. *Speech of Athenagoras*

We know nothing of Athenagoras. The speech which Thucydides attributes to him is valuable in that it contains an explicit theoretical defence of democracy and illustrates, with a clarity which owes something to caricature, the technique and language of political attack. Comparison with modern parliaments is not wholly to the disadvantage of Syracuse, but comparison with other men whom we meet in the pages of Thucydides is very much to the disadvantage of Athenagoras, whom Stein (*RhM* lv [1900], 547 f.) compares with Thersites. His statements of fact and estimates of probability are uniformly wrong; he plays the part of προστάτης τοῦ δήμου (cf. 28. 2 n., and above all Thucydides' description of Kleon in iii. 36. 6; the verbal resemblances between that passage and the description of Athenagoras are noteworthy) by telling his audience what it wishes to hear (a combination of 'they won't attack' with 'if they do, you'll beat them') and by making much of his own role as watchdog and protector of the people against their internal enemies.

36. 2. ὅπως τῷ κοινῷ φόβῳ τὸν σφέτερον ἐπηλυγάζωνται: the MSS. have τό, not τόν, and this may be interpreted as (i) 'their own *fear*', understanding δέος from δεδιότες, despite the intervening masculine φόβῳ and the antithesis between κοινῷ and σφέτερον, or (ii) 'their own *policy*', 'their own *purpose*', which is improbable (*pace* Herbst, 97 ff.) since τὰ σφέτερα would be both more normal and in the present case specially desirable for the avoidance of ambiguity. As Dexippos in his imitation (*FGrHist* 100 F 6. 14 ὅπως ἂν τὸ σφέτερον δέος ἐπηλυγάζησθε), Σ^Mcf in his paraphrase, and Valla in his translation all adopted (i), it may be that they actually had τὸν σφέτερον in their texts, and that that is what Thucydides wrote. If we could ask Athenagoras exactly what it was that Hermokrates and his friends feared—and he certainly supposes them to be afraid, as οἱ δεδιότες ἰδίᾳ τι shows—he might reply, 'They are afraid of being *unmasked*'; at which point, familiar with 'unmask' = 'vilify' in the language of modern open diplomacy, we might not pursue the matter any further.

τοῦτο δύνανται· οὐκ ἀπὸ ταὐτομάτου, κ.τ.λ.: δύνασθαι in Thucydides = 'signify', 'mean', 'amount to' (cf. Hp. *Aer.* 1, D. xviii. 26), and a demonstrative almost at once followed by a sentence in asyndeton can hardly fail to refer forward, so that the MSS.' text means 'This is what these reports amount to: they do not arise of their own accord . . .' But a statement of the *origin* of the reports does not suit δύνανται, which therefore requires (*pace* Herbst, loc. cit.) τοῦτο to refer back, not forward: '*that* is what these reports amount to', i.e. 'they mean that the rumour-mongers are trying to conceal their own fears'. This in turn requires the connecting relative αἵ (ψ: cj. Classen) before οὐκ ἀπὸ ταὐτομάτου. Cf. Isoc. xiv. 16: 'What will they think when they hear that the Thebans have persuaded you to spare no state which was under Spartan control?' ὁ γὰρ τούτων λόγος οὐδὲν ἀλλ' ἢ τοῦτο (referring back) φανήσεται δυνάμενος· οὐ γὰρ κ.τ.λ. (explaining *why* the Theban argument 'amounts to this').

3. ὥσπερ ἐγὼ Ἀθηναίους ἀξιῶ: 'for that is how I regard the Athenians', ἀξιῶ almost meaning 'rate highly'. Krüger's emendation to οἵουσπερ gives the sense 'and I consider the Athenians to be men of that quality'; but iii. 14. 2 γίγνεσθε δὲ ἄνδρες οἵουσπερ ὑμᾶς οἱ Ἕλληνες ἀξιοῦσι (sc. γίγνεσθαι or εἶναι) is no closer to his proposal than E. *El.* 70 ἰατρὸν εὑρεῖν, ὡς ἐγώ σε λαμβάνω, D. xviii. 255 οὑτωσὶ περὶ τῆς τύχης ἀξιῶ, and Aeschin. iii. 232 φατὲ μὲν εὐτυχεῖς εἶναι, ὡς καί ἐστε are to the MSS.' text.

4. τὸν ἐκεῖ πόλεμον μήπω βεβαίως καταλελυμένους: Athenagoras adopts the same mistrustful view of the peace treaty of 421 as Nikias (10. 2 ff.) and Alkibiades (17. 5).

37. 1. οἷς γ' ἐπίσταμαι, κ.τ.λ.: 'since, I presume . . .' Thucydides does not mean us to infer that Athenagoras, for all his scorn, really knows that the invasion is coming and betrays his knowledge inadvertently.

τήν τε ἄλλην παρασκευήν - - - οὐκ ὀλίγην οὖσαν: τε co-ordinates this generalization with the particular statement οὔθ' ἵππους ἀκολουθήσοντας; the punctuation of Stuart Jones, a comma after πορισθῆναι but none after παρασκευήν, is not intelligible.

2. παρὰ τοσοῦτον γιγνώσκω: 'I would go so far as to declare my opinion that . . .'; the expression is obscure, but clearly related to ii. 89. 4 παρὰ πολὺ ἡσσηθέντες 'decisively beaten', vii. 71. 3 παρ' ὀλίγον ἢ διέφευγον ἢ ἀπώλλυντο 'there was no margin to spare between escape and destruction', and the other expressions listed by LSJ, s.v. παρά III 5 a, and influenced by the many passages in which παρά with a quantitative word is associated with risk and danger. It is unlikely that there is any implicit comparison with Hermokrates, 'this is the extent to which my opinion differs from his', since there is no emphatic pronoun (contrast X. *Cyr.* vi. 1. 9 ἐγὼ δ' - - - τοσοῦτον διαφέρομαι τοῖς πρόσθεν λέγουσιν· οὗτοι μὲν γὰρ κ.τ.λ.) and Hermokrates has in any case professed confidence in Syracusan victory.

εἰ πόλιν ἑτέραν τοσαύτην - - - ἔλθοιεν ἔχοντες καὶ ὅμορον οἰκίσαντες τὸν πόλεμον ποιοῖντο: ἔχων with a verb of motion is so common in the sense 'with', i.e. 'bringing', that 'if they brought with them a city as large as Syracuse' is far preferable to 'if they possessed a city as large as Syracuse and came against us', and ὅμορον (ὅμοροι recc., cf. 2. 3 ὅμοροι τοῖς Σικανοῖς οἰκήσαντες) οἰκίσαντες means 'when they had established it upon our borders'. In so rhetorical a context the extravagance of the conception (mitigated by our recollection of Nikias' words in 23. 2, 'you must think of us as going to found a city in an alien land') is no argument against the soundness of the text (cf. Herbst, 101 ff.).

ξυστήσεται γάρ: Athenagoras expresses himself a little more confidently than Hermokrates (33. 4 f., cf. 34. 4).

38. 1. λογοποιοῦσιν: an orators' word in the sense 'fabricate'; Plato uses it of composing speeches or other works in prose, and λογοποιός is first given a derogatory sense by Demosthenes.

2. ἤτοι λόγοις γε τοιοῖσδε καὶ ἔτι τούτων κακουργοτέροις ἢ ἔργοις: to preserve the balance of the sentence (cf. 34. 2, 40. 1, ii. 40. 2) τοιοῖσδε - - - κακουργοτέροις should be taken as a virtual parenthesis, with slight pauses after γε and before ἤ. Vollgraff (*Mnemosyne* 1905, 421 ff.) felt the awkwardness of making the only pause before ἤ, but his remedy, emendation of καὶ ἔτι to ἢ ἔτι and deletion of ἢ ἔργοις, would need also transposition of λόγοις and τοιοῖσδε.

αὐτοὺς τῆς πόλεως ἄρχειν: the procedure which Athenagoras has in mind here and in 40. 2 is (i) establishing a reputation for sagacity and a claim on the gratitude of the people by giving timely warning of an impending danger, (ii) being elected to office with special powers to deal with the danger, (iii) using such office to establish one's own rule. The circumstances in which Dionysios attained power (Diod. xiii. 91 f.) had some elements in common with this process.

3. τυραννίδας δὲ ἔστιν ὅτε καὶ δυναστείας ἀδίκους: there is an affinity (Gomme, ms.) between Athenagoras' charges and the Athenians' fears of a 'conspiracy to establish a tyranny' when the herms were mutilated; but there is also a difference. Since the Deinomenid tyranny at Syracuse ended in 466 (Diod. xi. 67 f., especially 68. 6) the statement 'and sometimes tyrannies' is of the same character as Alkibiades' allegation (17. 2) ὄχλοις γὰρ ξυμμείκτοις πολυανδροῦσιν αἱ πόλεις, but even more reckless in its abuse of history. One wonders at first whether Thucydides thought that a Syracusan politician speaking to his own countrymen in 415 could really make such a statement, and this may provoke a suspicion that Thucydides composed the details of the speech after Dionysios had established himself as tyrant at Syracuse in 406. Probably, however, he classifies among τυραννίδες the attempts of Tyndaridas in 454 (Diod. xi. 86 f.; note πλεονάκις, 86. 5).

4. ὑμᾶς μὲν τοὺς πολλοὺς πείθων, τοὺς δὲ τὰ τοιαῦτα μηχανωμένους κολάζων - - - τοὺς δ' αὖ ὀλίγους - - - διδάσκων: 'the many' and 'the few' are exhaustive alternatives, and 'those who design plots like these' are naturally among 'the few'. If we take τοὺς δ' αὖ ὀλίγους as

'the upper class (sc. in general)', or treat the antithesis between
πείθων and κολάζων as more important than considerations of logic,
allow Athenagoras to speak of himself as 'punishing' malefactors
in so far as he can persuade the people to punish them (cf. κρίνειν =
'prosecute', Antiphon iv. a. 1, al.), and attach no importance to the
fact that δ' αὖ in Thucydides is normally used with the second of two
items (e.g. 34. 5, 80. 4, ii. 44. 4, 45. 1, v. 14. 2, viii. 78, 92. 11, 94. 2,
104. 2), once with the second of three (viii. 2. 1), and not at all with
the third of three—if we accept these conditions, we can leave the
MSS.' text alone. Otherwise we must follow Weil in deleting δέ and
emending κολάζων to κολάζειν: 'persuading you, the people, to
punish the plotters . . . and exposing the upper class . . .' Cf. D. xix.
267 ὑμᾶς εὖ φρονεῖν δεῖ τοὺς πολλοὺς καὶ μὴ ἐπιτρέπειν τὰ τοιαῦτα, ἀλλὰ
κολάζειν δημοσίᾳ.

5. τί καὶ βούλεσθε: 'what do you *want*?', with a rhetorical affectation
of bewilderment. Cf. D. xviii. 24.

ὦ νεώτεροι: Hermokrates himself can hardly be young; he is 'experienced in war' (72. 2) and represented his city as an ambassador
nine years earlier. In 39. 2 Athenagoras distinguishes between οἱ
δυνάμενοι and οἱ νέοι, but here he concentrates his hostility on the
latter, treating Hermokrates as supported by the young (cf. H. D.
Westlake, *BRL* xli [1958/9], 250); the Greeks conventionally attributed irresponsible ambition and violence to youth (cf. 12. 2 n.),
and in addition the sinister associations of νεώτερος were rhetorically
useful.

μᾶλλον ἢ δυναμένους ἐτέθη ἀτιμάζειν: ΣMcf says οὐκ ἀτιμαζόμενοι,
ἀλλὰ κωλυόμενοι διὰ τὴν ἡλικίαν; here, as often in Thucydides, μᾶλλον
ἤ virtually = 'and not'.

μὴ μετὰ πολλῶν ἰσονομεῖσθαι: ἰσονομία, the situation in which all have
the same rights, is one face of democracy; δημοκρατία, 'power in the
hands of the majority', is another. Belief in the rightness of ἰσονομία
is justified here by the assumption that men are 'the same'; so Maian-
drios in Hdt. iii. 142. 3 defends ἰσονομία and attacks tyranny on the
ground that a tyrant is δεσπόζων ἀνδρῶν ὁμοίων ἑωυτῷ.

39. 1. καὶ ἄρχειν ἄριστα βελτίστους: 'best at ruling best' is a strange
expression, though vii. 42. 3 τῇ πρώτῃ ἡμέρᾳ μάλιστα δεινότατός ἐστι
has some affinity with it, and 'better at ruling best' (C) is stranger.
Schwartz (337) suggested ἄριστα ⟨καὶ βουλεύειν ξυνετώτατα καὶ
κρίνειν τῶν πολλῶν εἶναι⟩ βελτίους. This, however, is unsatisfactory,
since Athenagoras' reply loses much of its force if its *distinguo* is
anticipated. The best remedy is the deletion of either ἄριστα or
βελτίστους, preferably the former; Cobet (*Mnemosyne* 1886, 15) deleted the latter.

φύλακας μὲν ἀρίστους εἶναι χρημάτων τοὺς πλουσίους: Athenagoras is thinking not of the competence of the rich to look after their own property, but of the part which they can play in the administration of the state. The Athenian practice of restricting offices such as that of the Treasurers of Athena to the highest property-class was in accord with this theory.

κρῖναι δ' ἂν ἀκούσαντας ἄριστα τοὺς πολλούς: the theory that the mass of the people are the best *fitted* to decide issues of state is not easily defended, and Athenagoras does not attempt to defend it; the traditional defence (Arist. *Pol.* 1281ᵃ40 ff.) that the larger the sovereign body the more completely the deficiencies of some individuals will be offset by the capacities of others, takes no account of the power of rhetoric to deceive and to arouse collective prejudices. There is more in D. xxiv. 37, where, after stating the dogma that γνῶναι καὶ δοκιμάσαι τὸ βέλτιστον resides in the majority, the speaker goes on to say that no one can induce a majority by bribery (δια-φθείρας) to abandon its course. The argument that whether fitted or not the mass of the people *ought* to decide issues of state rests in part on the observation that decisions taken on their behalf by autocratic or oligarchic governments are rarely in their interest, on the faith that a habit of decision makes a better man than a habit of ignorant obedience (cf. ii. 40. 2), and on the moral principle that those who stand to lose everything have a right to decide whether they shall risk losing it. This last principle underlies the characteristically Greek argument of § 2, that 'the upper class in power allows the masses a share in the risks but takes all the gains for itself'; cf. Hp. *Aer.* 23, 'those who are independent are braver than those ruled by kings, for the latter fight to increase another's power while the former take the prizes of victory for themselves'.

καὶ ταῦτα ὁμοίως καὶ κατὰ μέρη καὶ ξύμπαντα ἐν δημοκρατίᾳ ἰσομοι-ρεῖν: since Athenagoras has allocated three functions or capacities— administration, deliberation, and decision—each to a different category of the population, viz. the rich, the intelligent, and the majority, it does not matter much whether we interpret ταῦτα as 'these categories' or 'these capacities'. By ἰσομοιρεῖν he may mean that in a democracy (*a*) each of the three categories is allowed to play the part which, in his view, it is right that it should play, (*b*) each individual has the same privileges and opportunities as every other member of the same category, and (*c*) each individual, irrespective of his category, has the same protection under the law as everyone else. κατὰ μέρη can express the first of these propositions, lit. 'taken a part at a time'; it could also cover the second proposition; in which case ξύμπαντα, 'taken all together', expresses the third. One might have expected him to put the matter more clearly by saying τούτους ὁμοίως καὶ κατὰ μέρη καὶ καθ' ἕκαστον, and it may be that Thucydides is deliberately putting into his mouth the kind of 'both . . . and . . .' which is very common in the language of politics but does not always bear logical scrutiny. Cf. a speech made by Mr. John Vorster on becoming Prime Minister of South Africa in September 1966, to the effect that the policy of 'separate development' is designed 'to do justice to every population group as well as every member thereof'. It is difficult to see how a policy of separate development *per se* could do justice or injustice to a group but not to a member of the group, or vice versa.

2. ἀλλ' ἔτι καὶ νῦν - - - εἰ εἰδότες τολμᾶτε: the MSS.' text means: 'Yet even now, most stupid of all men, if you do not realize that your aims are wrong, you are either the most unintelligent of all Greeks known to me, or the most immoral, if your attempts are made with full knowledge.' The point of ἔτι καὶ νῦν will be: 'although your aim is impossible of fulfilment (ἀδύνατα - - - κατασχεῖν) you still go on with your foolish or wicked behaviour.' The structure of εἰ μή - - -, ἤ - - - ἤ - - -, εἰ - - - is strange, but it has an affinity with 18. 1 (see note). The real difficulty lies in the sequence: 'Most foolish men, you are either foolish or immoral'; but this difficulty is removed by the insertion of ⟨γάρ⟩ after the first εἰ (Gomme, *CR* xxxiv [1920], 84; H. Richards, *CQ* vi [1912], 224, had made a similar proposal, but with a substantial transposition), thus converting εἰ ⟨γὰρ⟩ μή - - - τολμᾶτε into a parenthesis, making ἀλλ' before ἤτοι a resumption of the initial ἀλλ', and associating ἔτι καὶ νῦν with the imperative αὔξετε, 'even at this late hour'; cf. Pl. *Cri.* 44 b ἀλλ' ὦ δαιμόνιε Σώκρατες, ἔτι καὶ νῦν ἐμοὶ πιθοῦ καὶ σώθητι. Similar repetition of ἀλλά is found in Herodas 1. 20 f. ἀλλ'—οὐ τοῦτο μή σε θερμήνῃ—ἀλλ' ὦ τέκνον, κ.τ.λ.; cf. S. *El.* 783 ff. νῦν δ'—ἡμέρα γὰρ τῇδ' - - - νῦν δ' κ.τ.λ. and X. *An.* iii. 2. 25 δέδοικα μή, ἂν ἅπαξ - - -, μὴ κ.τ.λ. 'Adverbial' ἀλλά, reinforcing a plea, is, of course, common; cf. Pl. *Phd.* 104 e ὃ τοίνυν ἔλεγον ὁρίσασθαι - - -, ἀλλ' ὅρα δὴ εἰ οὕτως ὁρίζῃ, κ.τ.λ. If Gomme's ⟨γάρ⟩ is rejected, Madvig's deletion of ἢ ἀμαθέστατοί ἐστε as the product of an intrusive gloss on ἀξυνετώτατοι leaves the resumptive ἀλλά intact but removes the logical and structural difficulty, giving us something more like And. ii. 2: 'They must be the most foolish of mankind or the most unpatriotic; for if (εἰ μέν γε - - -) . . ., they are most foolish . . ., but if . . ., they can only be unpatriotic.'

40. 1. ἡγησάμενοι τοῦτο μὲν ἂν καὶ ἴσον καὶ πλέον οἱ ἀγαθοὶ ὑμῶν [ἤπερ τὸ τῆς πόλεως πλῆθος] μετασχεῖν: given the antithesis between τοῦτο μέν and εἰ δ' ἄλλα βουλήσεσθε, τοῦτο must mean 'in this way', 'if you do this', which is not difficult when we compare 33. 6 ὅπερ (= 'and in precisely this way') καὶ Ἀθηναῖοι - - - ηὐξήθησαν, ii. 40. 3 ὃ (= 'whereas') τοῖς ἄλλοις ἀμαθία θράσος - - - φέρει, iv. 125. 1 φοβηθέντες, ὅπερ φιλεῖ μεγάλα στρατόπεδα ἀσαφῶς ἐκπλήγνυσθαι, Pl.

Smp. 204 a αὐτὸ τοῦτό ἐστι χαλεπὸν ἀμαθία 'it is precisely in this respect that stupidity is objectionable'. To take τοῦτο with μετασχεῖν, 'this share of yours would be equal . . .', or to emend it to τούτου (Badham, *Mnemosyne* 1875, 25) and refer it to τὸ κοινόν, spoils a most obvious antithesis. οἱ ἀγαθοὶ ὑμῶν is probably not an after-thought but is to be taken closely with πλέον (cf. Marchant), the point being 'those of you who play the game will get a fair share, and those who play it well will get an extra share'; cf. vii. 75. 5 ἀπηυτομολήκεσαν γὰρ πάλαι τε καὶ οἱ πλεῖστοι παραχρῆμα and D. xviii. 204 Κυρσίλον καταλιθώσαντες οὐ μόνον αὐτὸν ἀλλὰ αἱ γυναῖκες αἱ ὑμέτεραι τὴν γυναῖκα αὐτοῦ. Athenagoras recognizes the principle of rewarding merit. ἥπερ is unique in Attic prose, though used by Hdt. and Hippokrates (v.l. in Isoc. v. 115); since Thucydides uses ὅτιπερ in iv. 14. 2 and nowhere else, ἥπερ cannot be rejected out of hand, but it must be observed that ὅτιπερ, unlike ἥπερ, is found in Comedy and fourth-century prose. Σ^Mcf offers the paraphrase: 'the good among you must realize that this is just and even more than just, that you should share in the same things in which the whole city shares'. It would appear that he read ὧνπερ, not ἥπερ, in his text, and the validity of this inference is not impaired by the fact that he misinterpreted τοῦτο and thereafter went astray in his understanding of the sentence as a whole (cf. Dover, *PCPhS* clxxxiii [1954/5], 8 f.). ὧνπερ gives us entirely satisfactory Greek; for the omission of the verb in a ὅσπερ-clause cf. 13. 1, [Lys.] vi. 12, and (after 'the same') Isoc. iv. 106, xviii. 38. The *ratio corruptelae* is simple: the comparative πλέον produced by association a word for 'than', which is often ἥπερ in late Greek (cf. the scholia on i. 32. 1, v. 90, etc.; ἥπερ is a gloss on ἤ in v. 87 and iii. 3). For the interpolation of ἤ cf. viii. 94. 3 (after μείζονος) and Diod. xiii. 15. 1 (after πρότερον). Cf. also X. *Cyr.* i. 6. 18, where some MSS. have corrupted ὥσπερ to ὅτιπερ under the influence of a preceding λέγεις.

εἰ δ' ἄλλα βουλήσεσθε: on the political sense of βούλεσθαι cf. 82. 4 n.

41. *Speech of the General*

41. 1. οὐδένα ἔτι εἴασε: not 'forbade', as a matter of constitutional right, but (as Bloomfield saw) 'he said that no one else ought to come forward, and this prevailed'; cf. 72. 2, vii. 48. 2. The inference that the general was 'presiding' over the assembly (Freeman, ii. 129, Hüttl, 74, 80, 86 n. 144) is unjustified.

2. διαβολὰς μὲν οὐ σῶφρον κ.τ.λ.: without naming anyone, the general makes it fairly clear where his sympathies lie.

3 f. τοῦ τε τὸ κοινὸν κοσμηθῆναι - - - τὴν δ' ἐπιμέλειαν - - - ἕξομεν - - - τὰ δὲ καὶ ἐπιμεμελήμεθα ἤδη κ.τ.λ.: if τε is right, τοῦ - - - ἀγάλλεται is co-ordinated with καὶ τῶν - - - ἐπιτήδειον and τὴν δ' - - -

ἔξομεν is (as Doukas saw) a parenthesis; τὰ δέ will then mean not 'the latter' (i.e. the sending of embassies) but 'and there are other matters which . . .', cf. iii. 11. 7 τὸ δὲ ναυτικὸν ἡμῶν παρεῖχέ τινα φόβον - - - τὰ δὲ καὶ ἀπὸ θεραπείας - - - περιεγιγνόμεθα, Hp. VM 16 τὰ δὲ δὴ καὶ πολὺ μέζω, 'and the following evidence is even more important'. I see no objection to this interpretation; Abresch's γε, which requires strong punctuation after ἀγάλλεται, was founded on the supposition that τὰ δέ must refer to the sending of embassies, and on the conclusion that if this was within the province of the generals καὶ τῶν - - - διαπομπῶν (the definite article looks back to 34. 1) must not be excluded from their ἐπιμέλεια but must be co-ordinated with αὐτῶν. Schwartz (337), adopting γε, punctuated after ἔξομεν and deleted τὰ δὲ καί, making τῶν - - - διαπομπῶν the object of ἐπιμεμελήμεθα.

For the magnificent metaphor ἀγάλλεται, with which κοσμηθῆναι accords well in its common sense 'adorned' (cf. X. An. i. 9. 23), cf. the personification of war in i. 122. 1 and Radford, 32. The credit may be due to the Syracusan general, not to Thucydides; his words seem to belong with the memorable metaphors listed by Arist. Rhet. 1411ᵃ. Plu. Cic. 2. 4 μεταφορᾶς ὀνομάτων καὶ ἁρμονίας καὶ τῶν ἄλλων οἷς ὁ λόγος ἀγάλλεται is a frigid imitation.

42–46. 4. The Athenians Arrive at Rhegion

42. 1. ἐν ἑκάστῳ ἐκλήρωσαν: for the use of the lot in dividing a command between colleagues, cf. 62. 1, viii. 30. 1. X. Cyr. vi. 3. 34 represents the commanders of Kyros' chariot regiments as deciding by lot what position each regiment should occupy in the battle-line. ἅμα πλέοντες: thus H₂ (cf. Valla: si pariter navigarent): ἀναπλέοντες (cett.) is certainly wrong; in the only passage in Thucydides in which ἀναπλεῖν appears (i. 104. 2) it describes sailing up a river from the sea. On the general problem of moving fleets cf. Gomme, Essays, 190 ff.

2. καὶ εἴρητο αὐταῖς προαπαντᾶν: cf. 44. 4 n.

43. ἐς τὴν Σικελίαν: but not by the direct route across the open sea, as becomes plain in 44. 2 ff.; ἐς therefore = 'on their way to . . .', and ἐπεραιοῦντο = 'they started to make the crossing ⟨sc. of the Adriatic⟩'. τριήρεσι μὲν κ.τ.λ.: the figures given by Diod. xiii. 2. 5 are, as often, slightly different: 140 ships and over 7,000 troops (of all arms). τούτων Ἀττικαὶ μὲν ἦσαν ἑκατόν: in omitting any connecting particle with τούτων Thucydides is following the style of fifth-century inventories and traditiones of all kinds; cf. IG i². 314. 99. αἱ δ' ἄλλαι στρατιώτιδες: Thucydides does not tell us how many (if any) of the 34 allied triremes were troop-carriers (στρατιώτιδες, ὁπλιταγωγοί), how many soldiers a troop-carrier held, or how it differed from a fighting trireme. One conclusion can be drawn with certainty: if troop-carriers could not be used for fighting, some of the allied triremes were fighting ships and not troop-carriers. This conclusion follows from vii. 37. 3, where the Athenians fight with 75 ships after receiving only 9 as reinforcements (vii. 16. 2 ~ 31. 3) and losing 6 (vii. 23. 4, 24. 2). It is also arguable *a priori* that a troop-carrier cannot have been a normal trireme with a normal crew plus a large number of soldiers crammed on board; for had there been room for the soldiers, it would mean that the trireme normally was much bigger and heavier, and therefore much slower, than it need have been. The same argument applies against the hypothesis that the troop-carrier was an abnormally large trireme with an augmented crew. There remain three possibilities:

(i) It could not be used as a fighting trireme at all. In that case, it is strange that on two occasions (viii. 30. 2, 62. 2) Thucydides mentions that troop-carriers were included in a fleet but does not trouble to mention their numbers, and strange above all that he says nothing about troop-carriers in describing the arrival of the reinforcements brought by Demosthenes and Eurymedon in 413 (vii. 42. 1). Since they brought as many troops as the original expedition, their 73 ships must have included troop-carrying space equivalent *at least* to 40 troop-carriers. Of the 110 ships which the Athenians manned for the final battle in the harbour (vii. 60. 4), which represented the total available to them at that time, including those in poor condition (60. 2), a proportion must have come to Sicily as troop-carriers, but Thucydides there draws no distinction.

(ii) It was a normal trireme with a skeleton crew of sailors and a full complement of soldiers, who manned the oars, as soldiers on occasion could (cf. 91. 4). This hypothesis would account for the passages mentioned under (i), and it would mean that once they had landed their troops the troop-carriers constituted a reserve of fighting ships which could be manned for battle by the crews of triremes which had been damaged. But it does not account for the term στρατιῶτις (one would expect, e.g., 'the troops themselves rowed 40 of the ships' rather than '40 of the ships were στρατιώτιδες') and it does not explain the transfer of the entire crew of the *Paralos* to a στρατιῶτις in 411 (viii. 74. 2, cf. 86. 9).

(iii) It had a skeleton crew of sailors, was rowed by soldiers, and differed structurally from the normal trireme, but was (given some time) reconvertible into a fighting ship. This hypothesis—and, I think, only this—accounts for all the passages in which the term is used as well as those in which we are surprised to find that it is not; the πλοῖα μεγάλα of vii. 4. 5 may be στρατιώτιδες. Horse-transports (cf. ii. 56. 2) are obviously a different matter, as horses cannot row

309

and the space-requirement for one horse is less elastic than the space for its weight in men.

Χίων καὶ τῶν ἄλλων ξυμμάχων: 85. 2 and vii. 57. 4 explain why the Chians are specially mentioned here, but not why Methymna is subsumed under 'the others' nor who else contributed triremes. There is no mention anywhere of ships from Kerkyra or Kephallenia as crossing with the Athenians in 415, but Thucydides' belief that they were present may be inferred from his postponement of this catalogue until the fleet is leaving Kerkyra for Italy.

ἐκ καταλόγου: cf. 26. 2 n.

ἑπτακόσιοι δὲ θῆτες ἐπιβάται τῶν νεῶν: it appears from iii. 91. 1 ~ 95. 2 and iv. 76. 1 ~ 101. 3 that there were normally ten men equipped as hoplites on each trireme, and approximately the same conclusion follows from ii. 80. 4, 90. 5, 92. 2, 7 ~ 102. 1 (cf. n.); *IG* i². 97 (*SEG* xii. 26). 9 ff., 15 ff., needs too much restoration to be of much use, but *IG* ii². 1951 (s. iv in.) lists eleven ἐπιβάται on one ship (83–93) and ten on another (316–25). The reading of H₂, ἑξακόσιοι, gives us precisely ten ἐπιβάται to each Athenian 'fast' trireme, and may be right. θῆτες (for the continued use of this term as an economic rating cf. *IG* i². 45 [= ML 49]. 39 ff.) would require to be armed at public expense to play the part of ἐπιβάται. The specification ἐπιβάτας τῶν ὁπλιτῶν ἐκ καταλόγου ἀναγκαστούς in viii. 24. 2 implies that ἐπιβάται were normally θῆτες; much later, Arist. *Pol.* 1327ᵇ9 τὸ μὲν γὰρ ἐπιβατικὸν ἐλεύθερον καὶ τῶν πεζευόντων ἐστί makes the opposite assumption. Possibly the chief function of ἐπιβάται was to defend any palisade that might be erected for the protection of triremes pulled up for the night on a beach in hostile or treacherous territory.

καὶ Μαντινέων καὶ μισθοφόρων: vii. 57. 9 (cf. n.) indicates that the Mantineans, in spite of their political friendship with Athens, were regarded as mercenaries; hence καί = 'and other' (cf. W. J. Verdenius, *Mnemosyne* 1954, 38).

Κρῆτες: cf. 25. 2 n.; these Cretans were mercenaries (vii. 57. 9).

καὶ σφενδονήταις Ῥοδίων ἑπτακοσίοις: the Rhodians had a reputation for great skill with the sling; cf. X. *An.* iii. 3. 16. 700 is a remarkably large number, especially for an arm which achieved practically nothing (cf. 69. 2), and Beloch, ii/2². 290, not unreasonably questioned the text.

καὶ Μεγαρεῦσι ψιλοῖς φυγάσιν: the pro-Athenians in Megara had taken refuge with the Athenians in 424, iv. 74. 2. φυγάσιν to some extent explains ψιλοῖς; exile had impoverished them.

τριάκοντα ἀγούσῃ ἱππέας: we hear no more of these cavalry; in 64. 1 the Athenians have none.

44. 1. τοσαύτη ἡ πρώτη παρασκευὴ πρὸς τὸν πόλεμον διέπλει - - - τὸν Ἰόνιον κόλπον: the punctuation of this complex is disputed; the simplest procedure is to print a comma after διέπλει and a stop or colon after ξυνέπλει, so that διέπλει has two subjects, παρασκευή and ὁλκάδες μέν + πλοῖα δέ. 'There sailed across (A) the first force, to do the fighting' (for πρός cf. ii. 77. 1, iii. 69. 2), 'of the size which I have described, and (B) carrying its supplies, (a) thirty transports, viz. (i) carriers of grain and (ii) carrying the bakers, etc., and (b) a hundred ships which sailed, requisitioned, with the transports.' Removal (om. Cantabrigiensis 2629) of ἅ would require us to understand ξυνέπλεον in τούτοις δέ - - - ἐργαλεῖα from ξυνέπλει later; to remove the stop after ξυνέπλει similarly requires us to understand ἠκολούθουν with ὁλκάδες μέν + πλοῖα δέ from ξυνηκολούθουν τῇ στρατιᾷ ἐμπορίας ἕνεκα later; and to introduce another finite verb by emending ἄγουσαι to ἄγουσι gives us a narrative present in a context to which it is entirely inappropriate.

2. πρός τε ἄκραν 'Ιαπυγίαν: cf. 30. 1 n.

οὐ δεχομένων αὐτοὺς ἀγορᾷ οὐδὲ ἄστει: according to Diod. xiii. 3. 4, Kroton allowed them to buy provisions.

Τάραντος δὲ καὶ Λοκρῶν οὐδὲ τούτοις: on Taras cf. 34. 4 n. and on Lokroi v. 5. 2 n.

3. καὶ πρός [τε] τοὺς 'Ρηγίνους λόγους ἐποιήσαντο: on καί - - - τε cf. Denniston, 535. τε here can hardly be co-ordinated with καὶ τὰς πρόπλους ναῦς προσέμενον; οἱ δὲ οὐδέ - - - προσοίσονται is not parenthetic, as Linwood thought, but καὶ πρός - - - οἱ δέ - - - οἱ δέ - - - καί - - - constitute a sequence of four stages of equal weight. Arnold supposes a 'change of plan' in the layout of the sentence; cf. 6. 2 n. On Rhegion cf. 46. 2 n.

ἀλλ' ὅτι ἂν καὶ τοῖς ἄλλοις 'Ιταλιώταις ξυνδοκῇ, τοῦτο ποιήσειν: there is no explicit indication that representatives of the Italiot cities met, either regularly or in emergency, to discuss questions of common interest.

4. καὶ τὰς πρόπλους ναῦς ἐκ τῆς 'Εγέστης ἅμα προσέμενον: three in number (46. 1). In 42. 2 we were told that three ships were sent ahead from Kerkyra 'to Italy and Sicily' to discover the attitude of the Western cities and to rejoin the main fleet with this information. It does not appear (43. 1) that they rejoined it before it left Kerkyra; presumably they went as far as Rhegion, came back while the fleet was sailing along the Italian coast, and were then sent off again to Segesta. Thucydides' choice and order of words show that he knows he has told us of the existence of these ships but not of their going to Segesta: 'they waited for the ships which had sailed ahead to return from Segesta', not 'they waited for the ships which had sailed ahead and were coming from Segesta'.

45. καὶ ἔς τε τοὺς Σικελοὺς περιέπεμπον: in 88. 4 Thucydides gives us a rough indication of which Sikel areas were under Syracusan control, but is nowhere precise. Cf. also vii. 1. 4, 32. 2.

ἐπὶ ταχεῖ πολέμῳ: not, of course, a war which would be short, but a war which would soon be upon them.

46. 2. οὓς πρῶτον ἤρξαντο πείθειν: *οὓς πρώτους κ.τ.λ.* (H_2 [cj. Herwerden]) gives the sense 'the first state which they had attempted to win over', and may be right; cf. 3. 1. *πρῶτον* gives a sense which could be analysed as 'the attempt to win over this state was their first step in the campaign', which is not very different from saying that *πρῶτον* simply reinforces *ἤρξαντο*, as it does in i. 103. 4 and Ar. *Nu.* 1351.

Λεοντίνων τε ξυγγενεῖς ὄντας καὶ σφίσιν αἰεὶ ἐπιτηδείους: the kinship of Rhegion with Leontinoi (cf. 44. 3) rested on her foundation from Euboean Chalkis (Antiochos [*FGrHist* 555] F 9), with an admixture of Messenians (cf. 4. 6 n.). Her friendliness to Athens had been demonstrated in the war of 427–424 (iii. 86. 5, cf. iv. 25. 1 ff.). Neither here nor in 44. 3 does Thucydides say a word about the alliance which Athens had made and renewed *ἐς ἀΐδιον* with Rhegion (*IG* i^2. 51, ML 63) at the same time as her 'old alliance' with Leontinoi. Presumably the attitude of consistent friendliness seemed to Thucydides so much more important than the formal obligation of an alliance that he thought it unnecessary, if he stated the former, to mention the latter. Now Rhegion was obviously waiting to see how the situation would develop before committing herself; and (unlike the Sikels) she appears to have taken no active measures to help either side at any stage of the campaign. The Athenians did, however, raise money from her; cf. *SEG* xvii. 7. 11 f. *'Ρεγῖ[νοι - - -]|* 𐅈XX𐅃[.

καὶ τῷ μὲν Νικίᾳ προσδεχομένῳ ἦν - - - τοῖν δὲ ἑτέροιν καὶ ἀλογώτερα: the comparative has been variously interpreted: (*a*) with reference to the previous sentence, 'even more unexpected (sc. than the refusal of Rhegion)'; (*b*) with reference to *προσδεχομένῳ*, 'even more inexplicable (sc. than it was unexpected)' (Marchant), which draws too subtle a distinction between the unexpected and the inexplicable; and (*c*) 'exceptionally hard to explain' or 'harder to explain than it ought to have seemed' (cf. 65. 1 *πολλῷ ἀσκεπτότερον*, 'with far less caution than they should have used'). Probably, however, the comparative is merely antithetical, of the type *εὖ τε καὶ χεῖρον* (ii. 35. 1), *καί* being used as in X. *HG* iii. 2. 17 *οἱ μέν τινες - - - ἀπεδίδρασκον - - - ὅσοι δὲ καὶ ἔμενον, κ.τ.λ.* ('but those who *stayed* . . .'; cf. Denniston, 321 ff.); hence 'to Nikias the news was *expected*, but to the other two it was *inexplicable*'. For the sense of *ἄλογος* here cf. Isoc. iv. 150 *καὶ τούτων οὐδὲν ἀλόγως γέγονεν ἀλλὰ πάντ' εἰκότως ἀποβέβηκεν*, D. xxiii. 158 *τῆς ἀλόγου καὶ ἀπροσδοκήτου σωτηρίας*.

3. ἃ ὄντα ἀργυρᾶ πολλῷ πλείω τὴν ὄψιν - - - παρείχετο: the point must be that the expensive dedications in the temple at Eryx did not reveal the comparative poverty of the state which controlled the sanctuary. Thucydides cannot mean that silver looks expensive but is not; the Athenian envoys, accustomed to live in a city which possessed both splendid dedications *and* a big financial reserve, wrongly assumed that one implied the other. Emendation of ἀργυρᾶ to ἐπάργυρα (Meineke, *Hermes* iii [1869], 372), 'of silver plate over base metal', or to ὑπάργυρα (Naber, *Mnemosyne*, 1886, 327 f.), 'of gold plate over silver' (cf. Grote, v. 542), entails the unlikely hypothesis that the majority of dedications in a famous sanctuary were of a peculiar kind.

ἐκπώματα καὶ χρυσᾶ καὶ ἀργυρᾶ: a traditional manifestation of wealth; cf. X. *Cyr.* viii. 4. 15 πολὺ μᾶλλόν με τῆς θυγατρὸς μνηστῆρα λήψεται ἢ ἐὰν ἐκπώματα πολλά μοι ἐπιδεικνύῃ.

καὶ τὰ ἐκ τῶν ἐγγὺς πόλεων καὶ Φοινικικῶν καὶ Ἑλληνίδων αἰτησάμενοι: what Greek cities? The only Greek city 'near' was Selinus, with which Segesta was at war; and the only Greek city on the north coast of Sicily was Himera (62. 2), which was unlikely (ibid.) to co-operate enthusiastically in a scheme designed to provoke Athenian intervention. It seems that the story exaggerated 'from everywhere round about' into 'from all the neighbouring cities, Greek and Phoenician alike', and that Thucydides accepted the story in this form without realizing that it was nonsense. In extenuation we must remember that, unlike a modern historian, he did not form a mental picture of a map whenever he heard a place-name; diagrammatic maps of the known world existed (cf. Ar. *Nu.* 206 ff.), but X. *Hipparch.* 4. 6 seems to imply the absence of maps which would be of any practical value. For αἰτεῖσθαι = 'borrow' (not recognized by LSJ, s.v. αἰτεῖν II) cf. Lys. xix. 27.

4. παρεῖχε: sc. 'this procedure'; cf. 60. 2.

46. 5–50. 1. *Conference of the Athenian Generals*

46. 5. οἱ δὲ στρατηγοὶ πρὸς τὰ παρόντα ἐβουλεύοντο: as Lamachos was killed in 414 and Nikias in 413, how did Thucydides find out what was said at this conference? Certainly if he had had the opportunity to learn anything from Alkibiades (cf. P. A. Brunt, *RÉG* lxv [1952], 65 ff.), he would not have let it slip; but that is not to say that he had such an opportunity before he wrote this narrative. Allegations about what each general had proposed would have been obtainable after the event, perhaps to excess, from their apologists (De Sanctis, *RF* N.s. vii [1929], 449 ff.). Other people may have been present at the conference (Thucydides does not say that it was secret); but the most likely source would be those to whom the generals talked, complacently or complainingly, at the time, for the Greeks had only a rudimentary conception of military discretion, let alone security. Cf., however, 62. 1 n. It is noteworthy that on this occasion, as on others, nothing could be done by a collegiate command until a majority agreed; cf. 50. 1, vii. 48. 1.

47. ἐφ' ὅπερ μάλιστα ἐπέμφθησαν: Nikias is adhering to part of the terms of reference, but only to a part of them, for he ignores καὶ τἄλλα πρᾶξαι, κ.τ.λ. (8. 2 n.); contrast his letter to Athens, vii. 11. 2. His confidence in proposing an extremely restricted plan was no doubt strengthened by the fact that he alone had been right about Rhegion.

ὅσασπερ ᾐτήσαντο: 8. 1.

αὐτοῖς: αὐτούς (ABEFGM) would mean 'themselves', the Athenians, as the subject of διαλλάξαι; but the unemphatic position suggests that αὐτοῖς, the Segestans, is right.

ἐπιδείξαντας μὲν τὴν δύναμιν - - - ἀποπλεῖν οἴκαδε: cf. Nikias' argument in 11. 4.

καὶ τῇ πόλει δαπανῶντας τὰ οἰκεῖα μὴ κινδυνεύειν: these words exactly sum up the attitude which Nikias took during the debate at Athens; cf. 10. 5, 12. 1, 22 f.

48. ἀλλ' ἔς τε τὰς πόλεις ἐπικηρυκεύεσθαι: Alkibiades is prepared to put to the test the hopes which he expressed in 17. 4; cf. viii. 12. 1 for his confidence in his own powers of persuasion.

πρῶτον δὲ πείθειν Μεσσηνίους: on the importance of the location of Messene cf. iv. 1. 2, 24. 4, Treu, *Historia* iii (1954/5), 43.

ἢν μὴ οἱ μὲν Ἐγεσταίοις ξυμβαίνωσιν, κ.τ.λ.: it is interesting that Alkibiades, who was represented in 15. 2 as entertaining the ambition to conquer at least the whole of Sicily, is here represented as making the attack upon Syracuse and Selinus conditional on their refusal to fulfil certain demands; it is Lamachos, whose voice we have not heard before, who goes directly to the point and does not think that conditions are worth mentioning. Thucydides, however, is not composing a tragedy but describing a historical situation; and there is no occasion for surprise if Alkibiades, faced with a necessity of making his colleagues agree, with a minimum of friction, on a workable initial plan, did not say exactly what we might have expected. In any case, ἢν μὴ κ.τ.λ. is something of an afterthought, and the demand which it incorporates, the re-establishment of Leontinoi, is far from trivial; in view of Perikles' argument about the Peloponnesian demand for the rescinding of the Megarian Decree (i. 140. 4–141. 1), Alkibiades may not seriously have expected that Syracuse would pay so high a price for peace. Cf. also 50. 1 n.

49. 1. Λάμαχος δὲ ἄντικρυς ἔφη χρῆναι πλεῖν, κ.τ.λ.: although ἄντικρυς with 'say' can mean 'plainly', 'outright', the context here suggests that it should be taken with πλεῖν, 'sail direct', not with

ἔφη; cf. Plutarch's clarification, *Nic.* 14. 3 Λαμάχου μὲν ἄντικρυς
ἀξιοῦντος πλεῖν ἐπὶ Συρακούσας - - - Ἀλκιβιάδου δὲ τὰς πόλεις ἀφιστάναι
Συρακοσίων, εἶθ' οὕτως ἐπ' αὐτοὺς βαδίζειν, κ.τ.λ.

3. ἀποληφθῆναι: 'cut off' by the arrival of the Athenians, before they
could be brought into the city; ἀπολειφθῆναι (ABMˢ) could be made
to fit (Herbst–Müller, ii. 23) the picture which Lamachos is painting
if we took it to mean 'stay behind' διὰ τὸ ἀπιστεῖν σφᾶς μὴ ἥξειν.

καὶ ἐσκομιζομένων αὐτῶν τὴν στρατιὰν οὐκ ἀπορήσειν χρημάτων: i.e.
when the Athenians had landed, the Syracusans would attempt
a belated evacuation of the countryside, but their attempt to get
themselves and their property (χρήματα) into the city would be
intercepted by the Athenians; cf. the Peloponnesians' thwarted expectation in 431 (ii. 18. 4). Steup's proposal to insert, e.g., ⟨ἐσβαλοῦσαν
ἔτι⟩ before ἐσκομιζομένων, giving the latter a purely temporal sense,
with no causal flavour, is not necessary.

**4. ναύσταθμον δὲ ἐπαναχωρήσαντας καὶ ἐφορμηθέντας Μέγαρα - - -
ποιεῖσθαι**: ἐφορμηθέντας obviously cannot here be a form of ἐφορμᾶν
'impel', and the passive of ἐφορμεῖν means 'be blockaded' (e.g. i.
142. 7, viii. 20. 1). The simplest emendation is ἐφορμισθέντας (Schae-
fer): 'then they should bring their ships to Megara, anchor them
there, and make that the station for their fleet'; Thucydides uses
the aorist middle of this verb in iv. 8. 5 (ἐφορμίσασθαι), but X. *HG*
i. 4. 8 has the passive, Ἀλκιβιάδης πρὸς τὴν γῆν ὁρμισθείς. An alternative is Böhme's ἐφόρμησιν τά, '. . . make Megara the station for their
fleet and a base for the blockade of Syracuse', cf. iii. 33. 3 φυλακὴν
σφίσι καὶ ἐφόρμησιν παρασχεῖν, i. 90. 2 τήν τε Πελοπόννησον πᾶσιν
ἔφασαν ἀναχώρησίν τε καὶ ἀφορμὴν ἱκανὴν εἶναι. Yet the definite article
with Μέγαρα in this context does not sound quite right; 75. 1 is different, for there we have a succession of new proper names each with
the article, giving the effect 'here, and there, and there'. It is re-
grettable that the reading of H here is not fully legible, but at least
it does not have ἐφορμηθέντας.

50. 1. ὅμως προσέθετο καὶ αὐτὸς τῇ Ἀλκιβιάδου γνώμῃ: most readers
of Thucydides feel that Lamachos' plan was right (cf. Grote, vi.
28 f.), and it is a fair inference from vii. 42. 3 (q.v.) that Thucydides
himself thought so. Yet it was reasonable at this early stage in the
campaign to expect to find allies in Sicily who would welcome the
humiliation of Syracuse; and to begin by a direct attack on Syracuse,
as if the attitude of other cities were immaterial, might have aroused
fears and scruples like those felt by the Akarnanians when Ambrakia
was at their mercy and the Athenians urged its capture (iii. 113. 6).
Lamachos may therefore have voted in the end for Alkibiades' plan
simply because Alkibiades persuaded him. On the other hand, if
Lamachos was not convinced, he may have compromised because

Alkibiades' plan was at any rate more enterprising than Nikias' and because Alkibiades enjoyed a political prestige superior to his own; if Alkibiades' plan were rejected, when its rejection became known (as it would) morale might suffer, and if the campaign then failed Lamachos and Nikias might both be in political peril.

50. 1–53. *Diplomatic Overtures; the Athenians at Katane*

50. 1. τῇ αὐτοῦ νηΐ: literally his own (cf. 61. 6), not simply the ship in which he sailed as general. According to Hdt. viii. 17, his great-grandfather Kleinias (E. Vanderpool, *Hesperia* xxi [1952], 1 ff.) had paid for and owned the ship in which he fought at Artemision. A. E. Raubitschek, *RhM* xcviii (1955), 260 n. 4, regards this Kleinias as Alkibiades' father, assuming that Plu. *Alc.* 1. 1 rests on something more than an inference from Herodotos combined with the datum that Alkibiades' father was named Kleinias.

2. ἐκ πασῶν: i.e. without regard for the three divisions into which the fleet had been organized during the voyage to Rhegion. Cf. *IG* i². 24 (= ML 44). 3 ff. *hιέρειαν --- ἐχs Ἀθēναίōν hαπα[σōν καθίστα]σθαι*, implying 'without regard to tribe'.

καὶ ἕνα σφῶν αὐτῶν: it is remarkable if Thucydides did not know whom; possibly he felt that this was the proper way in which to refer to a command in which nothing happened.

3. Ναξίων δὲ δεξαμένων τῇ πόλει: cf. 20. 3; and for the money raised from Naxos cf. *SEG* xvii. 7. 1 f.

ἐπὶ τὸν Τηρίαν ποταμόν: identifiable from Diod. xiv. 14. 3 and Plin. *NH* iii. 89 as the Fiume di San Leonardo (Ziegler, *RE* ixA. 724 f.).

4. τὰς ἄλλας ναῦς: i.e. the sixty minus the ten mentioned in the next sentence.

51. 1. ἐσελθόντες ἠγόραζον ἐς τὴν πόλιν: the words ἐς τὴν πόλιν were deleted by Herwerden on the grounds that they were both superfluous and oddly separated from ἐσελθόντες, but the stylistic objections could be met much better—and a more easily explicable corruption posited—if ἐσελθόντες, not ἐς τὴν πόλιν, were deleted. For the 'pregnant' use of ἐς with φαίνεσθαι, παρεῖναι, etc., cf. 62. 4 and Kühner–Gerth, i. 543 f.

2. ἐψηφίσαντό τε ξυμμαχίαν τοῖς Ἀθηναίοις: for Katane's monetary contribution cf. *SEG* xvii. 7. 7 f. Κα[ταναῖοι ---]|ϟ𐅄𐅄[.

3. ἐς τὴν Κατάνην: although Thucydides does not elsewhere use ἆραι with ἐς, cf. vii. 49. 2 ἐς τὴν Θάψον ἀναστάντας and Kühner–Gerth, i. 543 f. The alternative is to take ἐς τὴν Κατάνην with κατεσκευάζοντο.

52. 1. τὰ ὅρκια εἶναι --- μεταπέμπωσιν: Kamarina cannot have sworn at Gela in 424 'I will not receive more than one Athenian ship unless I want to'; that would have been a poor contribution to the peace of Sicily. The same objection applies to interpretation of this passage as a reference to the undertaking which Sparta in 431 requested from her friends in the West (ii. 7. 2), τά τε ἄλλα ἡσυχάζοντας καὶ Ἀθηναίους δεχομένους μιᾷ νηΐ; furthermore, we are not told that there was any question of oaths or a formal treaty at that time. Kamarina could have sworn at Gela 'I will not receive more than one Athenian ship except with the agreement of the other states which are parties to this peace treaty', but that is different from what Thucydides implies here. The reference must therefore be, as Doukas and Haacke saw, to the treaty which Laches had made with Kamarina in 427–425, first mentioned in 75. 3 below. Kamarina must have sworn on that occasion that she would always receive a single Athenian ship, while the Athenians for their part swore that they would not attempt to bring in more than one ship except at Kamarina's own request.

53. 1. τὴν Σαλαμινίαν ναῦν: cf. iii. 33. 1 n.

καὶ ἐπ' ἄλλους τινὰς τῶν στρατιωτῶν - - - καὶ περὶ τῶν Ἑρμῶν: as the text stands, two separate partitive genitives are attached to ἐπ' ἄλλους τινάς: 'for certain others, among the members of the expedition, (a) of those who, with Alkibiades, had been informed against for impiety towards the mysteries, and (b) of those (sc. who had been informed against for impiety) towards the herms'. Hude's insertion of ⟨μέν⟩ before μετ' αὐτοῦ does nothing to clarify the sentence (cf. Preuss, 28 ff.), which could be expressed accurately only in the form ἐπ' ἄλλους τινὰς τῶν στρατιωτῶν, τοὺς μὲν τῶν μετ' αὐτοῦ μεμηνυμένων περὶ τῶν μυστηρίων ὡς ἀσεβούντων γενομένους, τοὺς δὲ τῶν καὶ περὶ τῶν Ἑρμῶν μεμηνυμένων. Thucydides is using the idiom A οἱ δὲ B = οἱ μὲν A οἱ δὲ B (cf. Denniston, 165 ff.) and has also fallen into a certain degree of obscurity in a desire to avoid being cumbersome. Emendation is not justified.

54–59. *The End of the Tyranny at Athens*

(i) *Thucydides' Contentions*

The digression is marked by a strongly polemical tone (54. 1 f., 55, cf. 59. 1), and its four chief contentions are:

(A) When Hipparchos was killed by Harmodios and Aristogeiton not he, but Hippias, was the reigning tyrant.
(B) The murder did not originate in any determination on the part of the Athenians to rid themselves of tyranny, but was the accidental product of a personal relationship between

Hipparchos, Harmodios, and Aristogeiton (54, 56, 59. 1). The implication is that, given a difference of behaviour or temperament on the part of any one of those three men, the murder might not have been committed.

(C) The murder did not end the tyranny, for Hippias reigned for a further three years and was eventually expelled by a combination of Sparta with the Alkmeonidai, who were in exile (59. 2 ff.).

(D) Until the murder, the tyranny had not been oppressive (54. 5 f., 59. 2).

(ii) *Internal Consistency*

On (C) and (D) there is no sign of inconsistency within the limits of the digression.

On (B) there are parts of Thucydides' account which do not entirely justify the tone of 54. 1 and 59. 1. Whatever the reason for Aristogeiton's emotion, he and Harmodios did after all plan the overthrow of the tyranny (54. 3), not mere personal revenge on Hipparchos; it was Hippias, not his offending brother, whom they planned to kill (57. 1 f.), and it was presumably in this plan that their fellow conspirators (56. 2 f.) were interested. In ensuring that we understand the seed from which the conspiracy grew Thucydides does nothing to make us understand the fact that it did grow (cf. S. Brunnsåker, *The Tyrant-Slayers of Kritios and Nesiotes* [Lund, 1955], and H. J. Diesner, *Historia* viii [1959], 12 ff.).

On (A) Thucydides presents a more serious problem of inconsistency. It is not important that he refers in 53. 3 to the tyranny τῶν παίδων (not τοῦ παιδός), for it goes without saying that a tyrant's brothers, so long as they are on good terms with him, enjoy great power, and Thucydides' quarrel is not with a tradition which recognized this reality by speaking of the Peisistratidai collectively but with one which misrepresented the 'constitutional' position (F. Cornelius, *Die Tyrannis in Athen* [Munich, 1929], remarks that it is misleading to ask whether Hippias or Hipparchos was 'in power', since power resided constitutionally with the magistrates and the control exercised by the Peisistratidai was 'unofficial'. This is true, but it is not we who raise the question; it is Thucydides). Nor is it important, on the other hand, that the composer of Archedike's epitaph (59. 3) does not fit any mention of her uncle into his elegiacs. Nor again does 56. 1 ἐπαγγείλαντες - - - ἀπήλασαν reveal any uncertainty in Thucydides' mind; it would, if Hippias were the subject of the preceding verbs διενοεῖτο and προυπηλάκισεν, but Hipparchos is the subject, and the plural verbs represent a natural way of describing action taken by Hippias on the instigation of Hipparchos. The real difficulty lies in 54. 5. Hipparchos did not, says Thucydides, resort to force, but devised a way of insulting Harmodios; οὐδὲ γὰρ τὴν ἄλλην ἀρχὴν ἐπαχθὴς ἦν ἐς τοὺς πολλούς, ἀλλ᾽ ἀνεπιφθόνως κατεστήσατο. As the text stands, if the subject of ἦν and κατεστήσατο ('established', sc. τὴν ἀρχήν, cf. 55. 3) is Hipparchos, Thucydides, when he wrote those words, does not appear to have held the belief for which he has just argued and will argue again, that Hipparchos was never the reigning tyrant. If the subject is Hippias, Thucydides has fallen into extreme obscurity by forgetting or ignoring the nature of the preceding sentence. The former alternative is incredible, and cannot be upheld by the suggestion (Mabel Lang, *Historia* iii [1954/5], 397 n. 6, cf. Marga Hirsch, *Klio* xx [1926], 141) that there is some reservation or doubt in Thucydides' mind. In the context of the argument 'Hippias, not Hipparchos, was tyrant' the words 'Hipparchos established his rule without provoking resentment' go far beyond any possible indication of hesitancy or doubt. Three alternatives remain:

(*a*) The subject of the verbs is Hippias. This is hardly credible if 54. 4 and 54. 5 ff. were composed as a continuous whole ('he, sc. Hipparchos, designed a means of insulting Harmodios . . . for he, sc. Hippias, was not an oppressive ruler in other ways either . . .'). Thucydides may have composed the two parts of 54 on different occasions and put them together when the general point of his argument occupied his mind to the exclusion of the connection between 54. 4 and 54. 5; he does not always take enough trouble to put himself in the reader's place (cf. 4. 1 n., 15. 3 f. n.) and our difficulty in identifying the subjects of verbs is one consequence of his negligence (cf. 18. 6 n., 73. 2, vii. 18. 3). Yet in writing οὐδὲ γάρ he commits himself to a sequence of thought of so precise a kind that he must have had a clear idea (right or wrong) of what his own words in 54. 5 meant.

(*b*) τὴν ἀρχήν means not the position occupied by the ruling tyrant but the 'unofficial' power wielded by his brother. This is hardly possible in view of 55. 3, where ἡ ἀρχή is synonymous with ἡ τυραννίς, referring to the rule of *the* tyrant, and καθίστασθαι is used of *the* tyrant establishing himself in supreme power.

(*c*) The text is corrupt. Hude proposed ἐπαχθεῖς ἦσαν - - - κατεστήσαντο, referring, as οὗτοι in the next sentence does in any case, to Peisistratos and Hippias. Schwartz (337 f.), removing the punctuation after κατεστήσαντο, suggested τὰ ἄλλα ἡ ἀρχὴ ἐπαχθὴς ἦν - - - κατεστήσαντο. The *ratio* of the corruption implied by Hude is -εῖς > -ής through itacism, followed by correction of the verbs to conform (cf. vii. 13. 2 n.); Schwartz implies a more complicated process.

Solution (*a*) is not, I think, wholly impossible, but there is no really plausible alternative to emendation.

(iii) *Relation to Other Accounts*

Of extant writers before Thucydides only Herodotos (v. 55 f., 62 ff.) gives us an account of the end of the tyranny; of later writers, the fullest is Aristotle, *Ἀθ. π.* 17 ff. Aristotle's account presupposes that of Thucydides, for he denies (18. 4) the truth of a detail in vi. 56. 3; he draws heavily on Herodotos, and cites him by name on a detail in the earlier history of the tyranny (14. 4). There is much in *Ἀθ. π.* which is drawn neither from Herodotos nor from Thucydides, and here, as in other parts of *Ἀθ. π.*, Androtion's *Atthis* is the most likely source (Jacoby, *Atthis*, 156).

On the question who was tyrant Herodotos supports Thucydides, for he describes Hipparchos at the time of his death as Ἱππιέω τοῦ τυράννου ἀδελφεόν (55. 1), of which 'brother of Hippias who was afterwards tyrant' would, in the context, be a somewhat perverse translation. He uses the term Πεισιστρατίδαι once (vi. 39. 1) in describing action during Hippias' reign (cf. Th. vi. 56. 1), and elsewhere, with reference to the period after the murder of Hipparchos, in the sense 'Hippias and his sons and remaining kin'. The irrelevance of the use of the collective term to the problem of Hipparchos' status before his murder is shown by the use of the plural in Hdt. vi. 123. 2 ἐξηγρίωσαν τοὺς ὑπολοίπους Πεισιστρατιδέων - - - οὐδέ τι μᾶλλον ἔπαυσαν τυραννεύοντας, with reference to the period *after* the murder. Aristotle modifies the Thucydidean picture by representing the four sons of Peisistratos as inheriting their father's power (17. 3, cf. 16. 7). Hipparchos and Hippias were κύριοι τῶν πραγμάτων διὰ τὰ ἀξιώματα (they were sons ἐκ γαμετῆς) καὶ διὰ τὰς ἡλικίας and Hippias ἐπεστάτει τῆς ἀρχῆς because he was the elder of the two, πολιτικός by nature, and sensible (18. 1). This view that power was essentially shared, *auctoritas* residing in the eldest and wisest, is neither the view of Herodotos and Thucydides nor the view which Thucydides denies, but a compromise, perhaps a deliberate compromise, to reconcile Thucydides with the view which Thucydides attacks (Jacoby, *Atthis*, 158, n. 43).

On the cause of the murder Herodotos expresses no opinion. Aristotle agrees with Thucydides to the extent of making a lover's bid for Harmodios the ultimate cause of the conspiracy, though the rejected lover is now Thessalos, not Hipparchos (18. 2). Hipparchos in *Ἀθ. π.* is a patron of the arts, as in [Pl.] *Hipparchus*, 228 b–c, and possibly it was this 'rehabilitation' of his memory which helped to shift the blame for the hybristic treatment of Harmodios and his sister on to Thessalos, νεώτερος πολὺ καὶ τῷ βίῳ θρασὺς καὶ ὑβριστής (cf. Lang, 402 and Brunnsåker, 14). In Diod. x. 17. 1, on the other hand, Thessalos is the virtuous brother.

Herodotos and Aristotle are firmly and consistently with Thucydides in denying that the murder ended the tyranny.

On the character of the tyranny in general, Hdt. v. 62. 2 ἐμπι-κραινομένου Ἀθηναίοισι διὰ τὸν Ἱππάρχου θάνατον implies agreement at least that the tyranny was *more* oppressive after the murder, though Herodotos' political standpoint would hardly have allowed him to share Thucydides' predilection (54. 5) for the tyrants (cf. W. Pere-mans, *MKVAW* xvi/4 [1954] 13 f., 20 f.). Aristotle echoes the judge-ment that Hippias was more oppressive after the murder (19. 1), and has a further approximation to Thucydides in presenting a tradition favourable to the reign of Peisistratos as a 'golden age' (16), but (perhaps in accordance with the *a priori* reconstruction of archaic tyrannies characteristic of the fourth century) makes the death of Peisistratos the first stage in the increase of severity (16. 7).

Thus the set of beliefs which Thucydides attacks does not appear in either of the other two extant historical accounts, and we must seek it elsewhere.

(A) Thucydides tells us here (54. 2) and in i. 20. 2 that 'the majority' of the Athenians believed that Hipparchos succeeded Peisistratos. The skolia which begin ἐν μύρτου κλαδὶ τὸ ξίφος φορήσω (*PMG* 893, 895) must have existed in some form in the fifth century (cf. ibid. 894 ~ Ar. *Ach.* 1902), since the opening line is adapted in Ar. *Lys.* 632. We cannot be quite certain that this form included either of the continuations which we know, τὸν τύραννον κτανέτην ἰσονόμους τ' Ἀθήνας ἐποιησάτην (893, cf. 896) or ἄνδρα τύραννον Ἵππαρχον ἐκαι-νέτην (895), but doubt on that point might be thought hypercritical, and it is reasonable to accept as fact the existence, before Thucydides, of a skolion which could give rise to the belief that Hipparchos was the reigning tyrant when he was murdered. This was not necessarily the intention of the composer; cf. (C) below, E. von Stern, *Hermes* lii (1917), 365 ff., and Brunnsåker, 23 f. Less equivocal testimony is to be found in [Pl.] *Hipparchus*, 228 b, where Hipparchos is the eldest son of Peisistratos, and in *Marmor Parium* A 45, where he is Πεισιστράτου δ[ιά]δ[οχ]ον. The compiler of *MP* is hardly likely to have chosen a tradition known to him only through its rejection by historians. There must be a historian behind *MP*, and the most probable candidate is Hellanikos (Jacoby, *Atthis*, 1 n. 5, 156). Hel-lanikos must have said something about the end of the tyranny; as his *Atthis* was known to Thucydides when Thucydides wrote i. 97. 2, it can have been in circulation by the time Thucydides wrote vi. 54–9; and no other historian known to us, except Herodotos, wrote before the end of the fifth century a work in which we can plausibly find a place for an account of the end of the Peisistratid tyranny (on Charon of Lampsakos cf. p. 324). This prompts the inference that in 54. 1 (τοὺς ἄλλους) Thucydides is deploring the acceptance of a belief promoted by Hellanikos, just as in i. 20. 3 the beliefs which he deplores were promoted by Herodotos, and that the purpose of the digression is to disprove not simply a vulgar error but an error disseminated by a historian of repute.

(B) The tradition which treated Harmodios and Aristogeiton as heroes who had sacrificed their lives in the cause of liberty, and which found expression not only in laudatory skolia but in the privilege of meals in the prytaneion granted to their kin (*IG* i². 77. 5 ff., cf. *SEG* x. 40) is at odds with the general tone of Thucydides' digression, but there is nothing alien to Greek sentiment either in an erotic relationship between a man and a youth bound together to a dangerous enterprise (cf. Aeschin. i. 132 ff., Arist. *Rhet.* 1401ᵇ10 ff.) or in the idea that the roving eye of a tyrant could be the cause of his downfall; one of the conventional arguments against tyranny was that it enabled tyrants to indulge their appetites in despite of their subjects (cf. Hdt. iii. 80. 5, X. *Hier.* i. 26). Where Attic tradition laid emphasis on the heroism of the tyrannicides and saw their act not as an example of fearful jealousy and pride but as an example of a freedom-loving people's reaction against tyranny, Thucydides diminishes the stature of the tyrannicides by emphasizing the element of chance and individual emotion.

(C) Pseudo-Plato and *MP*, united in presenting Hipparchos as the successor of Peisistratos, do not agree on the consequences of the murder. Whereas *Hipp.* 229 b refers to the three years of Hippias' rule which followed it, *MP* dates both the murder and the expulsion of the Peisistratidai ἐκ τ[οῦ Π]ελαργικοῦ τείχους to the same year, the archonship of Harpaktides, 511/10 (cf. 59. 4 n.), and makes no mention of Hippias. The extent to which we can give a positive content to 'Attic tradition' on this point is obscure. The skolia must not be pressed too hard, for it is possible to say that the tyrannicides 'killed the tyrant and made Athens ἰσόνομοι' and at the same time believe that after the death of Hipparchos his brother maintained for a month or two, or a year or two, a length of time about which no one troubles to be precise, a precarious rule of which the end had become inevitable (cf. Arist. *Pol.* 1315ᵇ20 ff. on Psammetichos at Corinth and Thrasybulos at Syracuse, and Diod. xi. 53 on Thrasydaios at Akragas). Again—and this consideration is of fundamental importance—if we translated 54. 1 'everything that the Athenians say about the end of the tyranny is untrue' it would follow that Thucydides is attributing to Athenian tradition *all* the beliefs against which he argues, including necessarily the belief that the tyranny did not outlast the murder of Hipparchos. Such a translation, however, is not compulsory. 'The Athenians give an account which is completely inaccurate' might be nearer the mark; cf. οὐδὲν ὑγιές in, e.g., Ar. *Ach.* 955 οἴσεις οὐδὲν ὑγιές = 'what you'll be taking is completely worthless', *Ec.* 325 ὑγιὲς οὐδέν - - - δράσουσα = 'up to no good', Pl. *Smp.* 172 b παντάπασιν ἔοικέ σοι οὐδὲν διηγεῖσθαι σαφές. Such inaccuracy can be manifested not in a completely consistent set of falsehoods but in a set of stories which are not reconcilable with each other. For example, a story or song which implied that Hipparchos was reigning tyrant would be irreconcilable, on the grounds given by Thucydides in 55. 3, with a story which allowed Hippias three years of power after the murder; but popular traditions, even as told by one and the same individual, easily digest much more serious contradictions than that (cf. Schadewaldt, 86 ff.). It would therefore be dangerous to assume that *MP*, whether or not derived from Hellanikos, gives us the consensus of Athenian popular tradition in the fifth century.

(D) Our evidence for popular attitudes towards the tyranny in Thucydides' day suggests that they were strongly hostile. The use of 'tyrant' and 'tyranny' in the language of abuse is vividly portrayed by Ar. *V.* 488 ff., cf. *Lys.* 616 ff.; in *Eq.* 447 ff. the Sausage-man declares that he will prove that Kleon's grandfather was one of the bodyguard of Βυρσίνη (i.e. Myrrhine), daughter of Hippias; Antiphon's accusers cast against him the reproach (fr. 1) that his grandfather was a δορυφόρος of the tyrants; and the younger Alkibiades was defended and attacked in court through the relations of his ancestors with the tyrants (Isoc. xvi. 25 ff., Lys. xiv. 39). This being the feeling, Thucydides' contention that the tyrants were careful and intelligent and their exactions were light is not likely to have commended itself to a majority.

(iv) *Sources*

Herodotos and Hellanikos must be included among Thucydides' 'sources' in so far as the former's work was certainly, the latter's probably (cf. i. 97–2), available to him. Thucydides, however, speaks of himself (55. 1) as 'having a more accurate knowledge than others, through what I have heard (ἀκοῇ)'. These words do not imply that Thucydides was actually related to the Peisistratidai; a distant relationship is possible (cf. Hermippos ap. *Vit.* i. 18, [Pl.] *Hipparch.* 228 b, Wilamowitz, *Hermes* xxxiv [1899], 225 f.), but only a distant one (cf. Wade-Gery, 164 n. 1); what Thucydides himself says merely shows us that he had information from a source which he regarded, for reasons unknown to us, as peculiarly reliable (cf. Jacoby, *Atthis*, 164 and 342 n. 69). This ἀκοή is mentioned explicitly only in connection with the seniority of Hippias; Thucydides gives no indication of the extent of his dependence upon it for the rest of his account, and we are left to infer that he is following it in so far as he is denying other views. It is not always easy to decide whether a given element in his narrative was part of the tradition available to him or was his own conclusion (justified or not) from other data; the accessibility of Hippias (57. 2) is a case in point.

Thucydides quotes or mentions inscriptions:

(a) In 54. 7, to show that Peisistratos son of Hippias held the archonship, and thus to support his contention (54. 6) that the tyrants 'always took care that one of themselves should hold office'.

(b) In 59. 3 (the result of autopsy at Lampsakos?) to prove that Archedike, whose 'father and husband and brothers and sons were tyrants' was a daughter of Hippias and wife of Hippoklos and that Hippias even before his expulsion was seeking alliances with friends of the Persian king. The inscription itself does not tell us that Hippias arranged his daughter's marriage *before* his expulsion, but it is possible that Charon's *Annals of Lampsakos* was available to Thucydides and threw light on this (Jacoby, *Abhandlungen zur griechischen Geschichtsschreibung* [Leiden, 1956], 178 ff., emphasizes, however, the importance of Th. i. 97. 2 for the date of Charon).

(c) In 55. 1 f., the 'stele about the wrongdoing of the tyrants', to prove that Hippias was the eldest son of Peisistratos. The nature of this stele is obscure. It cannot have been simply a declaration of outlawry against Hippias and his sons; since Hippias was 'written first after his father' (55. 2), it named the long-dead Peisistratos, and it must also have named the dead Hipparchos, or Thucydides would not have been able to draw any inference from the position of Hippias' name. On the other hand, the archaic and classical periods provide no parallel for a purely narrative inscription. Presumably, then, the purpose of the stele was to outlaw for ever the surviving Peisistratidai and their issue and everyone who might be found to be a descendant (even an illegitimate descendant) of those members of the family who were already dead. Possibly also the preamble gave the reason for this act in a general form (e.g. 'These men inflicted great wrongs upon the Athenian people'), enough to justify Thucydides' description of the stele as 'about the wrongdoing of the tyrants'. *SIG*³ 58 (Miletos, *c.* 450), which condemns certain named men, with all their issue, to perpetual exile and offers a reward to anyone who kills them, exemplifies decrees of this type.

According to Lycurg. *Leocr.* 117 the Athenians melted down a bronze statue of Hipparchos son of Charmos (Τιμάρχου cod., Χάρμου Harpokration) which was on the Akropolis, and made from it a bronze stele on which they decided to inscribe τοὺς ἀλιτηρίους καὶ τοὺς προδότας, including Hipparchos himself; accused of treason (προδοσία), he had not stood trial and so had been condemned to death in absence. But he was ostracized in 488/7 (Androtion F 6, Ἀθ. π. 22. 4), among the 'friends of the tyrants', so that the stele described by Lykurgos cannot have been erected until at least three years after the Persian attempt to restore the tyrant, and this would be surprisingly late for Thucydides' stele, for which one would have expected the immediate aftermath of Marathon to be the latest possible date and 510/9 not impossibly early. I take Lykurgos in fact to be saying that the Athenians decided to use the stele made from Hipparchos' statue as a public list of traitors and ἀλιτήριοι in the future, not simply to record on it a particular group held guilty at the time of Hipparchos' condemnation.

Ἀθ. π. 16. 10 refers to a general Attic law against tyranny—an early law, as it uses ἄτιμος in the sense 'outlaw', misunderstood by Aristotle's generation—and it is possible that this formed part of Thucydides' stele, but there are no positive links (cf. 55. 1 n.). Thucydides' stele may have been of bronze, as some others on the Akropolis outlawing traitors and their descendants are known to have been (D. ix. 45, Σ Ar. Lys. 273, [Plu.] Vit. X Or. 834 b, Melanthios FGrHist 326 F 3, Krateros FGrHist 342 F 17).

In connection with the date of composition of book vi it is important to remember that Thucydides could not personally inspect any inscription at Athens between 424 and 404.

(v) *Political Relevance*

The issue between Thucydides and Herodotos on the one side and the beliefs which Thucydides denies on the other was more than an academic difference of opinion and more than the correction of vulgar error by research. It involved the relationship between the Alkmeonidai and the tyrants, and the Alkmeonidai were the maternal family of Perikles and Alkibiades. The curse which they inherited from their alleged sacrilege in suppressing the conspiracy of Kylon was politically exploited in the fifth century (cf. i. 127. 1 f. and Dover, *JHS* lxxvii [1957], 236). The charge of treacherous communication with the Persians at Marathon was thought by Herodotos to deserve an earnest refutation (vi. 121 ff.), in which he declares them μισοτύραννοι (123. 1) who ἔφευγον πάντα χρόνον τοὺς τυράννους (this statement seems to be false, cf. 54. 6 n.) and reaffirms that the credit for freeing Athens from tyranny belongs to them, not to the murderers of Hipparchos. Given the importance of tradition about the ancestors of men who were active in politics in the late fifth century, it was not possible to express an opinion about the end of the tyranny without augmenting or diminishing the political stature of Perikles and Alkibiades. The opinions which Thucydides denies, and which we have seen reason to attribute to Hellanikos, diminished it; Thucydides' digression was in fact, whatever his own intention, a contribution to the political controversy of his own generation (cf. Jacoby, *Atthis*, 153, 160 f., 186 ff.).

(vi) *Relation of the Digression to its Context*

In 53. 3 Thucydides tells us that the Athenian people's fear of the tyranny in 415 was accentuated by their belief, which they derived from tradition, that the tyranny of the Peisistratidai had in its last stages been oppressive (sc. however mild it might have been before) and that it had not been ended by the murder of Hipparchos or by any effort of their own but by Sparta in co-operation with the exiled Alkmeonidai. The digression, which opens with γάρ, gives in detail the vindication of this belief, and the narrative is resumed in 60. 1 with the words 'reflecting on these events, and recalling all that they knew about them by tradition, the Athenian people . . .'. Yet in the latter part of the first sentence of the digression he appears to contradict his own purpose, saying (apparently) that the Athenians did not know what he has just told us that they did know: 'In describing these circumstances in some detail I shall show that even the Athenians themselves, not to mention others, give a completely inaccurate account' (cf. p. 322) 'of the tyrants, their own tyrants, and of what actually happened.' The problem created by this contradiction may be treated in three ways:

(a) By the hypothesis that the prevalent opinion in Athens changed, so that Thucydides is telling the literal truth in saying that in 415 they were motivated by one opinion while at the time of writing they hold another. The past ἐφοβεῖτο (53. 3) does not contradict the present οἴονται (54. 2), but the hypothesis raises some awkward questions:

1. If Thucydides' belief about the successive states of Athenian opinion is correct, why did that opinion change? The mechanism of such changes in popular tradition is not easy to envisage. The suggestion of T. R. Fitzgerald, *Historia* vi (1957), 279 f., that opinion in 415 was a consequence of Herodotos, opinion in later years a consequence of Hellanikos, vastly overestimates the influence of historians; there was clearly no such influence on the fourth-century orators, and presumably none on audiences which were subjected to (e.g.) And. iii. 3 ff., Aeschin. ii. 172 ff.

2. If Thucydides' belief was incorrect, why did he hold it? This question at least is answerable. Thucydides was not back in Athens until eleven years after 415, and if he knew that the argument about the ineffectiveness of the tyrannicides had been used by some powerful orator among the enemies of Alkibiades as a means of stimulating fear of tyranny he might have drawn from that fact a general conclusion which he found inapplicable at the end of the war.

3. In either case, why did he not make the fact of change clearer by more effective means than a past tense in one sentence and a present tense in another? Tempting though it may be to fall back on the familiar theory of incomplete revision, we must attach importance to the fact that 60. 1 could not be written in its present form until a digression intervened between it and 53. 3, and could

certainly not be written in forgetfulness of 53. 3. The hypothesis that Athenian opinion changed thus involves attributing to Thucydides the extraordinary exposition: 'The Athenians believed p; p is the truth, and in proving it I will show that the Athenians are wrong to believe the opposite. . . . Now, because they believed p . . .'

(b) By the hypothesis that Thucydides did not believe that Athenian opinion had changed but changed his own belief about that opinion. It would follow that some parts of 53. 3–60. 1 were written when he held one belief, other parts when he held another, and that the two different elements were combined either by Thucydides himself or by a later editor.

1. Marga Hirsch, 136 ff., suggested that the later stratum was 53. 3 and 59. 2–60. 1, while Jacoby *Atthis*, 158 n. 47, suggested, with considerable hesitation, that it was 54–60. 1. The most serious obstacle to any theory of this kind is that Thucydides could not choose the point at which to insert his digression without full awareness of 53. 3, and could not write 60. 1 without awareness that by recapitulating 53. 3 it restated what his digression (on this theory) was designed to deny.

2. Schwartz, 180 ff., drew from this consideration the logical conclusion that the combination of the different elements was the work of an editor. Thucydides, Schwartz suggested, wrote 54–59 as an independent essay and used it, as much as he intended to use it, in i. 20. 2. After his death the editor found the full original, was encouraged to insert it here by the words ἐπὶ ξυνωμοσίᾳ ὀλιγαρχικῇ κα τυραννικῇ in 60. 1, and wrote 53. 3 and 60. 1 ὧν ἐνθυμούμενος - - - τὴν αἰτίαν λαβόντας to link it to the narrative. This theory too strains credibility on more than one point. An editor *might* fail to see the polemical point of 54. 1, despite its being the first sentence of the essay; but could an editor fail to see the polemical tone of the whole essay, and would an editor want to create a contradiction, where none existed before, by writing link-passages which say the opposite of what the polemical tone would suggest ought to be said? Again, Schwartz does not explain why the editor inserted the essay in what must have been, on Schwartz's hypothesis, the middle of a sentence rather than after πεπρᾶχθαι; or why he inserted it in this part of Thucydides' work at all, on the very slender pretext of the word τυραννικῇ, when there was a much more inviting place for it at viii. 68. 4.

(c) By the hypothesis that the contradiction is illusory. It is not possible to contend that Thucydides is arguing merely against some section of the Athenians; τὸ πλῆθος in i. 20. 2, ὁ δῆμος in vi. 53. 3, οἱ πολλοί in 54. 2, combine to dispose of that argument. The solution lies, I think, on different lines. We have seen (p. 322) that there are no adequate grounds for thinking that the Athenians in general

327

believed that the tyrannicides brought the tyranny to an end immediately. Thucydides does not accuse them of this error in i. 20.
2; he could be held to accuse them of it in vi. 54–59 only if we
translated ἀκριβὲς οὐδὲν λέγοντας as 'saying *nothing* that is true',
took the skolion *PMG* 893 with absolute literalness, assumed that
when so taken it reflected majority opinion, and assumed also that
Hellanikos, or whoever was the source of *MP* 45, also followed
majority opinion. But we are entitled to put the problem another
way round and approach 53. 3–60. 1, without any preconceptions
about the combination of different strata, from the direction from
which anyone reading the work for the first time approaches it, i.e.
from 53. 2. We encounter the plain statement that the Athenian
people in 415 believed that the tyrannicides had not ended the
tyranny. When in the next sentence we encounter severe criticism
of Athenian belief for its inaccuracy, we naturally assume that
Thucydides is going to assert that the tyrannicides *did* end the
tyranny. We read further in the digression, and before we come to
the end of it we discover that he is not asserting that, but is agreeing
with Athenian opinion on this point. At that stage we realize that
Thucydides, not for the first time, has misled us in a way in which an
author most commonly misleads his readers: by forgetting that we
do not know what he knows. When he wrote the words ἀκριβὲς
οὐδὲν λέγοντας, he knew what he was going to say in the rest of the
digression; we cannot know until we have read it. Precisely because
of what he had written in 53. 3, it did not occur to him that anyone
would take ἀκριβὲς οὐδέν to include an opinion that the tyrannicides
ended the tyranny; authors, however obscurely they express themselves, do not commonly entertain the possibility that the reader
will take them to be implicitly denying what they have just explicitly
asserted. What Thucydides meant by ἀκριβὲς οὐδὲν λέγοντας was that
some elements in Athenian opinion on the Peisistratidai were false—
notably the opinion that Hipparchos succeeded Peisistratos—and
that these and other elements were irreconcilable with the one
important true element, the opinion that the tyrannicides did not
end the tyranny.

This hypothesis has the advantage that elsewhere Thucydides
demonstrably creates obscurity by insufficient explicitness (cf. p. 199)
and the rhetorical strain in him demonstrably betrays him into
exaggeration (cf. p. 274).

One question remains: why did Thucydides *want* to correct so
carefully misconceptions about the end of the tyranny? Not, I think,
in order to make people think kindly of Perikles and Alkibiades,
for his references to the role of the Alkmeonidai are subservient to
his essentially destructive purpose. Nor again to suggest similarities
between the situations of 514 and 415; to discover such similarities

(Münch, 68; Schadewaldt, 91 ff.) we have to adopt a standpoint far removed from that of the candid reader. The most plausible explanation is that he succumbed here to the temptation before which all historians and commentators are by their very nature weak, the temptation to correct historical error wherever they find it, regardless of its relevance to their immediate purpose. The seed from which the digression grew must have been the use in 415 of the argument: 'Beware, men of Athens, of the would-be tyrant; for nothing is easier than to give yourselves into the hands of a tyrant, *but nothing harder than to escape him again. Why, not even the tyrannicides . . .*'

54. 1. ἐπὶ πλέον διηγησάμενος: 'amplifying', 'explaining in detail'; the comparative in the sense 'more than might be expected or thought appropriate' is common enough, and it is not necessary to understand here 'than in i. 20. 2'.

οὔτε τοὺς ἄλλους: cf. p. 321.

ἀκριβὲς οὐδὲν λέγοντας: cf. p. 322.

2. ὥσπερ οἱ πολλοὶ οἴονται: cf. p. 327.

3. ὡς ἀπὸ τῆς ὑπαρχούσης ἀξιώσεως: i.e. so far as his influence as a μέσος πολίτης allowed.

4. ἐν τρόπῳ δέ τινι ἀφανεῖ: τρόπῳ cj. Levesque; τόπῳ (codd.), with which the paraphrase of Σ^Mcf, *pace* Bodin–de Romilly, seems to be reconcilable, is unlikely, since (i) τόπος is not used metaphorically until Isokrates, and not = 'occasion' until much later, and (ii) an insult depends for its effect on its publicity, and this fact and the event related in 56. 1 show that τόπος could not be literal. Cf. the vv. ll. τρόπον / τόπον in Isoc. x. 4. Herbst–Müller, ii. 26, regard τόπῳ as guaranteed by ἐν, but cf. vii. 67. 2.

5. οὐδὲ γὰρ τὴν ἄλλην ἀρχὴν ἐπαχθὴς ἦν: cf. p. 319.

καὶ ἐπετήδευσαν ἐπὶ πλεῖστον δὴ τύραννοι οὗτοι ἀρετὴν καὶ ξύνεσιν: on οὗτοι cf. p. 319, and on ἀρετήν v. 105. 4 n. The unobtrusive and lenient exercise of power was 'good' in so far as refraining from forcing the will of others is good, and 'intelligent' because it provoked least opposition; cf. W. Müri, *MH* iv (1947), 259 f.

εἰκοστὴν μόνον πρασσόμενοι τῶν γιγνομένων: δεκάτην, according to Ἀθ. π. 16. 4; lexicographers and paroemiographers (e.g. Zenob. iv. 76) took their information on this point from Aristotle, and Meursius's *Pisistratus* (Leiden, 1623) took it from them, apparently forgetting Thucydides, so that Peisistratos' alleged δεκάτη was accepted as a fact by editors long before the discovery of Ἀθ. π. No doubt the specific term εἰκοστή may be subsumed under the generic δεκάτη, just as in English an exaction of 5 per cent could be called a 'tithe', and in principle the more precise evidence is preferable to the more general. The point of Thucydides' argument is that despite

the modesty of their exactions the tyrants nevertheless executed
the tasks for which exactions are required, 'beautifying the city
and carrying their wars to a conclusion' (cf. viii. 75. 2 ὤρκωσαν - - -
ὅρκους - - - τὸν πρὸς Πελοποννησίους πόλεμον προθύμως διοίσειν and
i. 11. 2) 'and sacrificing in the temples'.

6. αὐτὴ ἡ πόλις: αὐτή belongs to the predicate: 'in other respects the
city observed *without interference*' (cf. the meanings 'by itself', 'of its
own accord', 'on its own initiative') 'the laws previously in force'.
αἰεί τινα ἐπεμέλοντο σφῶν αὐτῶν ἐν ταῖς ἀρχαῖς εἶναι: *SEG* x. 352 (ML
6), a fragment of an archon-list erected in the last quarter of the fifth
century, illustrates this generalization in a remarkable manner:

> *ON]ETO[P*
> *H]ΙΠΠΙΑ[Σ*
> *Κ]ΛΕΙΣΘΕΝ[ΕΣ*
> *Μ]ΙΛΤΙΑΔΕΣ*
> *ΚΑ]ΛΛΙΑΔΕΣ*
> *. . . . .]ΣΤΡΑΤ[ΟΣ*

(The scepticism of J. W. Alexander, *CJ* liv [1958/9], 307 ff., about the
nature of this inscription is shown to be unjustifiable by C. W. J.
Eliot and M. F. McGregor, *Phoenix* xv [1960], 27 ff.). Since Miltiades
was archon in 524/3 (Dion. Hal. *AR* vii. 3. 1), the fragment refers to
the early years of the reign of Hippias (T. J. Cadoux, *JHS* lxviii
[1948], 104 ff., 109 ff.); the sons of Peisistratos murdered Miltiades'
father Kimon, but concealed their guilt from him and 'treated him
well', eventually sending him as their viceroy to the Chersonese
(Hdt. vi. 39. 1; cf. Wade-Gery, 155 ff.). That Kleisthenes—the
Alkmeonid, unless we posit another Athenian bearer of this rare
name, or supplement the even rarer *Π]ΛΕΙΣΘΕΝ[ΕΣ* (M. Guarducci,
ASAA N.S. iii–v [1941/3], 122)—held the archonship between Hippias
himself and Miltiades is a discovery of the first importance. Hdt.
i. 64. 3 says that the Alkmeonidai went into exile after Peisistratos'
victory at Pallenis, and (vi. 123. 1) that they were in exile from the
tyrants 'at every period'. It now appears that Hippias not only
recalled them but was reconciled with them; their later exile, which
ended with their triumphant expulsion of Hippias and his family,
must have begun after the murder of Hipparchos, when 'the tyranny
became harsher . . . and Hippias killed many citizens' (59. 2). The
list does not show us what Thucydides means by σφῶν αὐτῶν: re-
latives or political associates? The text itself permits no certain
inference. τὴν ἐνιαύσιον ἀρχήν refers to the eponymous archonship
only—cf. i. 93. 3 ἐπὶ τῆς ἐκείνου ἀρχῆς, ἧς κατ' ἐνιαυτὸν Ἀθηναίοις
ἦρξε—but in the years when this was not held by a relative of
the tyrant there may still have been a relative ἐν ταῖς ἀρχαῖς, as

polemarch or archon basileus. The mechanism by which the tyrants ensured this is not known; the simplest means to power is influence over a loyal electorate, but πλὴν κ.τ.λ. indicates a breach of the existing constitution, possibly by the substitution of nomination for election.

καὶ Πεισίστρατος ὁ Ἱππίου τοῦ τυραννεύσαντος υἱός: ΠΕΙΣΙ]-ΣΤΡΑΤ[ΟΣ is the most attractive supplement in SEG x. 352. 6, which would date the archonship to 522/1; cf. below on the altar of the Twelve Gods. The elder Peisistratos 'died old' (54. 2); Hippias was ἤδη γέρων (59. 4), πρεσβύτερος (Hdt. vi. 107. 3), when he landed at Marathon and lost a tooth in a fit of coughing, and appears to have died before Xerxes began to prepare his invasion (Hdt. vii. 6. 2, cf. viii. 52. 2; a story in Suda s.v. makes him die on Lemnos, returning from Marathon). It is perfectly possible that the younger Peisistratos by 522/1 was already thirty (cf. 55. 1 n. on Hippias' marriage, and Cadoux, 107 f.), which in the fifth-century democracy was probably the minimum age for the archonship; the democratic age-limits cannot be strictly applied to the son of a reigning tyrant, but investment of a mere boy with the archonship is hardly consistent with 'allowing the city to be governed by the law already in existence'. Cf. § 7 n. for the epigraphic complication.

τῶν δώδεκα θεῶν βωμὸν τὸν ἐν τῇ ἀγορᾷ: for an account of the excavated remains of the sanctuary and altar cf. Margaret Crosby, Hesperia Suppl. viii (1949), 82 ff., Homer Thompson, ibid. xxi (1952), 47 ff., and xxii (1953), 46 f. The original altar is assignable on archaeological grounds, without reference to Thucydides' data, to 'the second half of the sixth century' (Crosby, 97; cf. Thompson, Hesperia xvi [1947], 198 f.), its enlargement to the period 430–420 (Crosby, 98 f.). If iii. 68. 5 (see note) and Hdt. vi. 108. 4 are both true, an altar of the Twelve Gods existed at Athens in 519 B.C.

καὶ τὸν τοῦ Ἀπόλλωνος ἐν Πυθίου: the sanctuary was in the southeast part of the city, between the Olympieion and the Ilissos; cf. Judeich, 386.

7. ἀμυδροῖς γράμμασι: the inscription survives (IG i². 761 = ML 11 = Kirchner, Imagines Inscriptionum Atticarum, no. 11), and its letters are by no means 'faint' to us, as Greek inscriptions go; but no doubt the letters of any inscription a hundred years old were faint to Thucydides by contrast with the great number of much more recent inscriptions to be seen in Athens. Possibly, too, they had once been painted and the paint had largely worn off. Allowance must perhaps be made for rhetorical exaggeration of the difference between old and recent inscriptions, for Thucydides is not above pride in the trouble he has taken. Architecturally speaking, a date c. 520 is acceptable for the fragments of the altar (W. B. Dinsmoor in Studies in the History of Culture [Menasha, Wis., 1942], 197). The

script is identical with that of the dedication *hίππαρχος ἀνέθε̄[κεν
ho Πεισισ]τράτο* in the Ptoion in Boeotia (L. Bizard, *BCH* xliv [1920],
237 ff.), and has stronger affinities with Attic documents of the 480s
or even later (e.g. the Hekatompedon inscription of 485/4, *IG* i².
3 = Kirchner, no. 19) than with any of the Akropolis dedications
of the late sixth century; the classical forms of *A* and *E* are especially
notable. Presumably the Peisistratidai employed a craftsman, not
necessarily an Athenian, independent of the workshops which produced the inscriptions on the Akropolis dedications; it should be
observed that his *A* and *E*, however rare on stone before the 480s,
occur sporadically in the signatures of vase-painters in the sixth
century (cf. Jeffery, 74 f.), thus introducing into the history of the
alphabet an irregularity comparable with the irregularities introduced into the history of language by *μηθενί* in *IG* ii². 43 (*GHI* 123).
37 (378/7), *οὐθέν* ibid. 1607. 24 and 1608. 54 (373/2), and, above all,
καθελόντωσαν ibid. 204. 47 f. (352/1). E. Löwy (*SAWW* ccxvi/4
[1937], 12 ff.) suggested that the original had become hard to read
and was re-cut by an archaizing craftsman (cf. Dinsmoor, 198), but
he does not take account of the Ptoion dedication. Cf. A. E. Raubitschek, *Dedications from the Athenian Akropolis*, 447 f., on the use of
Ionic script at Athens after 480.

A different possibility was suggested by the discovery of a sherd
bearing the name P(e)isistratos in retrograde lettering (E. Vanderpool, *Hesperia* Suppl. viii [1949], 407), for, if this was an ostrakon
cast in an ostracism, it shows the presence and political prominence
in Athens of a man named Peisistratos after 489/8 (*Ἀθ. π.* 22. 3 f.).
For the three years 499/8–497/6 we have no archons' names, and the
archon of 496/5 was named Hipparchos (Dion. Hal. *AR* v. 77. 6), no
doubt the man ostracized in 488/7 (cf. 55. 1 n.). The problem of the
script on the altar might therefore be solved (cf. Meritt, *Hesperia*
viii [1939], 59 ff.) by the hypothesis that Peisistratos son of Hippias
was archon in 497/6, an election reflecting Athenian anxiety for good
relations with Persia (Hdt. v. 103. 1), and that the dedicator at the
Ptoion was a son of his, not his uncle. This hypothesis, however,
is not wholly reconcilable with the political history of the period (cf.
Gomme, *AJPh* lxv [1944], 327 ff.). It implies that Thucydides, in
selecting his one piece of evidence to prove his generalization about
the constitutional situation under the tyrants, ignored or forgot the
archonship of 497/6; and acceptance of this implication is a high
price to pay for a sherd of uncertain purpose. It also runs counter
to the architectural indications, and the script of the altar is no
more obviously at home among Attic dedications of 500–495 than
among those of 525–520. Moreover, the script of the sherd may well
be as early as the first half of the seventh century (Vanderpool,
loc. cit.; Jeffery, 70).

The aorist participle τοῦ τυραννεύσαντος does not mean that Hippias *had been* tyrant at the time of his son's archonship, but is of the common 'identifying' type, cf. Hdt. ix. 106. 1 κατέλιπε δὲ ἄνδρα τοιόνδε Μασκάμην γενόμενον (sc. ὕστερον), D. xxi. 178 ὁ τοῦ βελτίστου πατὴρ Χαρικλείδου τοῦ ἄρξαντος, and is past only from the standpoint of writer and reader (cf. L. Campbell, *CR* iv [1890], 425 f.).

55. 1. εἰδὼς μὲν καὶ ἀκοῇ ἀκριβέστερον ἄλλων: cf. p. 323.

ὡς ὅ τε βωμὸς σημαίνει: the altar by itself does not in the least tell us whether any of Hippias' brothers had sons, but only that Hippias had one; the stele is the essential evidence.

περὶ τῆς τῶν τυράννων ἀδικίας: Herwerden (*Mnemosyne* 1880, 156) suggested ἀτιμίας, which would make admirable sense in the light of Ἀθ. π. 16. 10, but cf. p. 324; I do not think that anything is amiss with ἀδικίας.

Θεσσαλοῦ μὲν οὐδ' Ἱππάρχου οὐδεὶς παῖς γέγραπται: Ἀθ. π. 17. 4 adds a fourth son, Iophon, describes 'Thessalos' as a παρωνύμιον of Hegesistratos, and represents Iophon and Hegesistratos as sons of Peisistratos by his Argive wife. Iophon plays no part in the narrative of Ἀθ. π. 18 f., and is mentioned elsewhere only in Plu. *Cat. Mai.* 24. 8, which need not be supposed independent of the source of Ἀθ. π. In Herodotos there is no Thessalos, but Hegesistratos is the son of Peisistratos by an Argive wife and is sent by his father to rule Sigeion (v. 94. 1). In this confused situation Thucydides' use of a documentary inscription is the firmest point, but it is not a certain inference from what he says that Hegesistratos and Iophon were not mentioned in the document. His reference to γνήσιοι ἀδελφοί implies that there were νόθοι: and he knew, or thought he knew, which were which, either because the stele made this plain or on other grounds, good or bad. Thessalos was evidently a person in his own right and not someone else's παρωνύμιον (on this curious word, which is not attested in the sense 'additional name' until long after Aristotle—Pherekydes F 25 a is not a verbatim quotation—cf. D. Loenen, *Mnemosyne* 1948, 85 f., who posits interpolation in Ἀθ. π. 17. 3; but if Aristotle meant 'a [sc. additional] name derived [sc. from Thessaly]' there is no linguistic objection).

ἐκ Μυρρίνης τῆς Καλλίου τοῦ Ὑπεροχίδου: nothing is known of Kallias son of Hyperochides (-οχ- [C], not -εχ-, is the correct form, cf. *IG* xii Suppl. 2. 125). According to Kleidemos F 15 the daughter of one Charmos became the wife of Hippias after the return of Peisistratos from his first exile, and this datum accords with the existence of a Hipparchos son of Charmos (who can hardly be Hippias' father-in-law) in the early years of the fifth century (cf. 54. 7 n. and p. 324). Textual corruption Χάρμου > Καλλίου is always possible; I do not see how Thucydides can have misread the name on the stele (Jacoby IIIb Suppl. i. 71)—surely his own knowledge of tradition would make him expect to find the name of Charmos—or why we should not suppose that Hippias' marriage to the daughter of Charmos was cut short by her early death and so childless.

2. ἐν τῇ αὐτῇ στήλῃ: αὐτῇ H₂^γρ· (cj. Poppo cl. Valla); πρώτῃ (cett.) makes no sense in a context where only one stele has been mentioned, and Herbst–Müller's defence of it (ii. 25 f.) rests on the idea, neither historically plausible nor in full conformity with Thucydides' own words, that one stele listed the men, another their crimes.

56. 1. κανοῦν οἴσουσαν: i.e. to go in procession as κανηφόρος, a normal function for girls; cf. Ar. *Lys.* 646 f. κἀκανηφόρουν ποτ᾽ οὖσα παῖς καλή.

ἐν πομπῇ τινί: Ἀθ. π. makes this the Panathenaia, which is obviously not what Thucydides has in mind, cf. § 2.

διὰ τὸ μὴ ἀξίαν εἶναι: if they alleged that she was not ἐν ἀξιώματι (Philochoros F 8) the insult necessarily touched her brother's status.

2. οὐχ ὕποπτον ἐγίγνετο ἐν ὅπλοις - - - γενέσθαι: cf. 58. 2 n.

57. 1. ἔξω ἐν τῷ Κεραμεικῷ καλουμένῳ: the Kerameikos, in the north-west of the city, was divided in half by the city wall, as the location of its extant boundary stones shows (Judeich, 167 f., 175, 329; *Hesperia* ix [1940], 267; cf. Kallikrates–Menekles *FGrHist* 370 F 4). Pl. *Prm.* 127 b ἐκτὸς τείχους ἐν Κεραμεικῷ shows that Classen's emendation ἐν τῷ ἔξω Κεραμεικῷ καλουμένῳ is not necessary.

3. παρὰ τὸ Λεωκόρειον καλούμενον: the Leokor(e)ion is located by Phanodemos F 8 ἐν μέσῳ τῷ Κεραμεικῷ (cf. Judeich, 338 ff.). D. liv. 7, 'as I was taking a walk ἐν ἀγορᾷ ... Ktesias passed me κατὰ τὸ Λεωκόριον', adds nothing useful. The name of the sanctuary is explained by Aelian *VH* xii. 28 by an aetiological myth of familiar type; the daughters of an Attic hero Leos were sacrificed with their father's consent when an oracle made their sacrifice a condition of their city's preservation (cf. D. lx. 29). It is perhaps surprising that in Thucydides' account Hippias dispatches the procession, Hipparchos marshals it (or another part of it) near its starting-point, and no one of comparable importance is on the Akropolis to receive it. In Ἀθ. π. 18. 3 this is not so; Hipparchos dispatches and marshals the procession, while Hippias waits for it on the Akropolis. Lang (404 ff.) accepts this εἰκὼς λόγος and points out that the conspirators would naturally want to seize the Akropolis as soon as they had slain the tyrant. However, the tyrannicides, whether or not they wanted to seize the Akropolis, could only kill the tyrant by going to where the tyrant was, and Thucydides evidently had some reason to believe that neither Hippias nor Hipparchos was on the Akropolis.

4. ξυνδραμόντος τοῦ ὄχλου: not to facilitate Aristogeiton's escape, but to pick up Hipparchos and see what was happening, in the normal manner of crowds.

οὐ ῥᾳδίως διετέθη: Ἀθ. π. 18. 4 ff. relates how Aristogeiton was long tortured until he provoked Hippias into killing him. In a later source (Polyainos viii. 45, al.) we hear of the fortitude of his mistress Leaina under torture.

58. 1. ἐπὶ τοὺς πομπέας τοὺς ὁπλίτας: the text is sound, as ὁπλίτας is adjectival (cf. X. *Cyr.* vii. 5. 62 οἱ ὑβρισταὶ ἵπποι) or participial (cf. 57. 2 τῶν ξυνωμοτῶν σφίσι) in character. In any case, a specification of the category of πομπεῖς is required if Hipparchos was marshalling another of the many categories which made up the procession. **ἐκέλευσεν αὐτούς - - - ἀπελθεῖν ἐς αὐτὸ ἄνευ τῶν ὅπλων**: a similar story is told of Peisistratos in Ἀθ. π. 15. 4 f., Polyainos i. 21. 2.

2. μετὰ γὰρ ἀσπίδος καὶ δόρατος εἰώθεσαν τὰς πομπὰς ποιεῖν: it appears from an inscription of Thasos in the early fourth century (J. Pouilloux, *Recherches sur l'histoire et les cultes de Thasos* [Paris, 1954], 371, no. 141. 18 ff.) that an ἐγχειρίδιον was a normal item of hoplite equipment at that place and date (the other items being listed as greaves, breastplate, helmet, shield, and spear). Thucydides' point is that the hoplites in the Panathenaic procession carried *only* shield and spear, so that possession of any other weapon was suspicious. The tyrannicides had expected help from shields and spears, but Hippias was not in a position at the moment to know what they expected; no doubt it occurred to him afterwards that the arrest of the men carrying ἐγχειρίδια (under the armpit, presumably; cf. Pl. *Grg.* 469 d) gave him something less than complete security, and that the category οὓς ἐπῃτιᾶτο might not be complete. Ἀθ. π. 18. 4 denies the story given here and asserts that procession μεθ' ὅπλων was an innovation of the democracy (Herwerden's deletion of μετὰ γάρ - - - ποιεῖν as an interpolation was antiquated by the discovery of Ἀθ. π.). We have no means of knowing who is right, for the portrayal of men with shields and helmets in the Parthenon frieze is reconcilable with both—though not, I think, by Mommsen's hypothesis (*Feste der Stadt Athen*, 144 f.), based on the absence of *Angriffswaffen* from the frieze, that the custom was *twice* changed between Hippias and Aristotle. Even if Aristotle had available the text of a decree which provided for the carrying of arms in the procession (Mommsen, 101 f., n. 5), it is not a safe inference that every item in a series of provisions in a decree is an innovation; 'let *a, b, c* be done' may = 'let *a* and *c* continue to be done and *b* now begin to be done'. Brunnsåker's suggestion (31 f.) that Hippias prohibited the carrying of arms after 514/13 is unlikely, for Hippias was not in a position to regulate the next Great Panathenaia, and one cannot see the Kleisthenic democracy upholding a prohibition of such obvious tyrannical purpose. The credit of the Athenian people is deeply involved in this issue—as Thucydides was well aware in forming his own view of the tyranny—for if they carried no arms they could not be blamed for cowardice in failing to attack the body-guard or for stupidity in being deprived of their arms by a trick, and this is more than enough reason for the establishment of a popular fiction (cf. E. Pfuhl, *De Atheniensium pompis sacris* [Berlin, 1900], 18 f., n. 115). The skolion (*PMG* 893. 1, 895. 1) ἐν μύρτου κλαδὶ τὸ ξίφος φορήσω ὥσπερ Ἁρμόδιος καὶ Ἀριστογείτων, if it reflected a belief that the tyrannicides concealed their daggers under myrtle foliage—and if such a belief made sense, which is questionable (cf. J. A. Davison, *CR* N.S. x [1960], 2)—would be consistent with both accounts; but Ar. *Lys.* 631 f. does not justify such an inference, and there are simpler explanations of ἐν μύρτου κλαδί (Bowra, *Greek Lyric Poetry²* [Oxford, 1961], 392 n. 1, cf. V. Ehrenberg, *WSt.* lxix [1956], 57 ff.).

59. 3. Ἱπποκλου γοῦν τοῦ Λαμψακηνοῦ τυράννου: Hippoklos of Lampsakos was one of the Greek tyrants who enjoyed Persian support, and may have been a Persian imposition from the first. He accompanied Dareios on the expedition across the Danube, and was among those who opposed Miltiades' proposal to destroy the Danube bridge (Hdt. iv. 138. 1).

Ἀθηναῖος ὢν Λαμψακηνῷ: Thucydides is not speaking of Lampsakos with the contempt of Solon (fr. 2. 3 f.) for Pholegandros and Sikinos, or of Themistokles, in one version of a famous anecdote (Pl. *R.* 330 a), for Seriphos, but reminding us of the previous enmity between Lampsakos and Chersonese and the Peisistratidai (Hdt. vi. 37 ff., cf. Wade-Gery, 160 f.). For the rhetorical juxtaposition cf. 6. 2 n. and Hdt. vii. 161. 3 εἰ Συρηκοσίοισι ἐόντες Ἀθηναῖοι συγχωρήσομεν τῆς ἡγεμονίης.

ἐπίγραμμα ἔχον τόδε: Aristotle's attribution (*Rhet.* 1367ᵇ19) of this epigram (*GVI* i. 539) to Simonides could by chance be right, but since sepulchral epigrams of that period did not include any reference to their authors Simonides was credited with much more than he actually composed; cf. M. Boas, *De epigrammatis Simonideis* (Groningen, 1905).

4. καὶ Ἀλκμεωνιδῶν τῶν φευγόντων: not 'those of the Alkmeonidai who were in exile', but 'among the exiles, the Alkmeonidai'; cf. Hdt. v. 62. 2 and Ἀθ. π. 19. 3, where the Alkmeonidai appear only as the most active and prominent of the exiles. For the detailed story of the part played by the Alkmeonidai and the Spartans in the expulsion cf. Hdt. v. 55 f., 62 ff.

ἐχώρει ὑπόσπονδος ἔς τε Σίγειον: on the Athenian capture of Sigeion cf. Hdt. v. 94 f.; the chronology of the war between Athens and Mytilene is full of problems, but at least it is not disputed that Sigeion was firmly in Athenian hands by the time of which Thucydides is speaking.

ὕστερον ἔτει εἰκοστῷ: Hippias was expelled in 511/10 (*Ἀθ. π.* 19. 6 ~ 21. 1 ~ Dion. Hal. *AR* i. 74. 6, v. 1. 1, cf. Cadoux, 112 ff.) and Marathon was fought in the autumn of 490 (*pace* Munro, *CAH* iv. 232 f., whose proposal to date it a year earlier is dealt with by Cadoux, 117), i.e. by inclusive reckoning in the twenty-second archon-year or the twenty-first natural year after the expulsion. Either, then, Thucydides is dating from Hippias' arrival in Persia—an event of which neither he nor anyone else is likely to have known the precise date, though it is clear from Hdt. v. 91. 1, 94. 1, 96 that Hippias spent some time at Sigeion—or he is rounding the number; cf. i. 18. 2, where Xerxes' invasion is dated 'in the tenth year' after Marathon. N. G. L. Hammond's attempt (*Historia* iv [1955], 384 f.) to date the expulsion in the first month of the archon-year 510/9, the Persian expedition against Athens setting out before the corresponding month of 490/89, requires the discarding of too much of our evidence for the succession and dates of the archons in the last decade of the sixth century.

60–61. *The Recall of Alkibiades*

The major problems in these two chapters have been discussed in the note on cc. 27 ff.

60. 1. ἐπὶ ξυνωμοσίᾳ ὀλιγαρχικῇ καὶ τυραννικῇ: a modern historian of the archaic period would not speak of oligarchy and tyranny in the same breath; but after a century of democracy the conception of the tyrant as popular champion had faded (the example of Dionysios renewed it in the minds of fourth-century philosophers), and the Athenians regarded oligarchy and tyranny indifferently as the antithesis of democracy. Cf. p. 284 ff.

2. εἷς τῶν δεδεμένων: Andokides, in fact; cf. And. i. 48 ff., p. 273.

οὔτε τότε οὔτε ὕστερον: evidently Thucydides was not satisfied that Andokides' confession was the whole truth of the matter. Why he was not satisfied, we do not know. ὕστερον naturally implies 'down to the time of writing', but the expression does not betray how long a period that was—whether, for example, Thucydides wrote these words after he had returned from exile and had had the opportunity to talk to Andokides and others implicated.

3. εἰ μὴ καὶ δέδρακεν: probably '(sc. even) if he had not actually *done* it' (Denniston, 304; cf. ii. 11. 6). But 'even if he had *not* done it' also makes sense, and in Antiphon ii. *β.* 6 ἔστι δέ - - - εἰκός - - - ἐπὶ τοῖς ἱματίοις διαφθαρῆναι - - - εἰ δὲ μὴ καὶ ἐπὶ τοῖς ἱματίοις διεφθάρη ἀλλ' ἑτέρους ἰδὼν ἄλλο τι κακὸν ποιοῦντας - - - ἀπέθανεν ὑπ' αὐτῶν, τίς οἶδε; either 'but if he was *not* killed for his clothes' or 'but if he was not killed for his *clothes*' is acceptable sense. Given the parallels, neither the fact that we would expect εἰ μὴ καὶ δέδρακεν to mean 'unless he had actually done it' nor the corruption ὅπως μή > μὴ ὅπως in 18. 2 need tempt us to join Arnold in emending to εἰ καὶ μὴ δέδρακεν.

4. ἐπανεῖπον ἀργύριον τῷ ἀποκτείναντι: the principle was not new; we find it in the Milesian decree against tyrants, *SIG*³ 58. It is also implied by Ar. *Av.* 1071 ff.

61. 1. μετὰ τοῦ αὐτοῦ λόγου καὶ τῆς ξυνωμοσίας ἐπὶ τῷ δήμῳ: 'with the same plan, the conspiracy against the democracy'; λόγος corresponds to more than one sense of the English 'calculation'. For καί (deleted by Badham, *Mnemosyne* 1875, 236) cf. Denniston, 291.

2. μέχρι 'Ισθμοῦ παρελθοῦσα πρὸς Βοιωτούς τι πράσσοντες: lit., 'coming into their presence as far as the Isthmos'; the nominative πράσσοντες (Cf) accords better with Βοιωτῶν ἕνεκα - - - ἥκειν in the next sentence than the accusative πράσσοντας (cett.) agreeing with Βοιωτούς. And. i. 45 says 'the Boeotians were out in force on our frontier', cf. p. 272.

ἐν Θησείῳ τῷ ἐν πόλει: it is clear from Paus. i. 17. 2 that the Theseion lay south-east of the Agora (Judeich, 351 f.). ἐν πόλει here is 'in the city', not, as commonly, 'on the Akropolis', and the point of the distinction is that there were four sanctuaries of Theseus (Philochoros F 18), including at least one in Peraieus (Judeich, 456).

3. τοὺς ὁμήρους τῶν Ἀργείων τοὺς ἐν ταῖς νήσοις κειμένους: cf. v. 84. 1.

5. θεραπεύοντες τό τε πρὸς τοὺς ἐν τῇ Σικελίᾳ στρατιώτας τε σφετέρους καὶ πολεμίους μὴ θορυβεῖν: τε is slightly deferred, and co-ordinates θεραπεύοντες with καί - - - βουλόμενοι; cf. 7. 3 n. There is no semantic difference between τό - - - μὴ θορυβεῖν and μὴ θορυβεῖν; cf. 1. 2, 14 n. For θεραπεύειν = 'take care' cf. vii. 70. 3 ἐθεράπευον - - - μὴ λείπεσθαι τὰ ἀπὸ τοῦ καταστρώματος, i. 19. 1; θορυβεῖν is used both transitively and intransitively. Hence, in the words of Σ^Mcf: θεραπεύοντές τε τὸ πρὸς τοὺς ἐν Σικελίᾳ στρατιώτας τε σφετέρους καὶ πολεμίους μὴ θορυβεῖν, ὥστε μηδένα θόρυβον συλληφθέντος τοῦ Ἀλκιβιάδου μήτε ἀπὸ τῶν Ἀττικῶν στρατιωτῶν ἀγανακτούντων γενέσθαι μήτε ἀπὸ τῶν πολεμίων καταφρονησάντων.

δι' ἐκείνου νομίζοντες πεισθῆναι σφίσι ξυστρατεύειν: cf. 29. 3 n.

6. τὴν ἑαυτοῦ ναῦν: literally his own; cf. 50. 1 n.

καὶ ἐπειδὴ ἐγένοντο ἐν Θουρίοις: Tod in *Geras Antoniou Keramopoullou* (Athens, 1953), 197 ff., establishes that Θούριοι is the name of the state (Steph. Byz. s.v. Ἀμφίδολοι cites it together with Λεοντίνοι and Δελφοί), Θουρία the name of its territory. Cf. 104. 2 n.

7. ἐπεραιώθη ἐς Πελοπόννησον: cf. 88. 9 n.

62. *Operations on the North Coast*

Thucydides does not help us to understand the nature and purpose of these operations. Both the generals in command were dead by the end of 413, and he may have preferred not to guess at what he could not discover of their intentions (contrast 47 ff., but cf. 46. 5 n. Thucydides' silence on strategic intentions does not necessarily imply ignorance on his part: cf., e.g., ii. 56). Since the Athenian destination is described as 'Selinus and Segesta' (§ 1), it might appear that now that Alkibiades has gone Nikias and Lamachos are putting Nikias' plan (47) into effect (Schwartz, 338 ff.; Preuss, 31 ff.). In fact, however—and this is highly relevant to our interpretation of 15. 3 and vii. 42. 3—the operation is in much closer accord with the plan put forward by Alkibiades and accepted (48, 50. 1): 'communicate with all the Greek cities except Selinus and Syracuse . . . win over the Sikels . . . *and then* attack Selinus and Syracuse' (Treu, *Historia* iii [1954/5], 44 f.). They make overtures to Himera—in reminding us that this was the only Greek city on that coast Thucydides implies that they could go no further in 'communicating with all the Greek cities'—refrain from an actual demonstration against Selinus (though Nikias advocated this in 47), oblige Segesta by capturing her Sikan enemy Hykkara, and 'show the flag' to the Sikels. The unsuccessful attack on Hybla Geleatis is probably an attempt to do for Archonides (vii. 1. 4) or other Sikel friends what the capture of Hykkara did for Segesta. Thus by the end of the summer they have done their best to execute the first stage of Alkibiades' plan; whether they completed it by approaching Gela and Akragas, or whether they judged from what they learnt that such approaches were bound to fail, Thucydides does not say. They then (63. 1) embark on the second stage of Alkibiades' plan, the attack on Syracuse.

62. 1. καὶ λαχὼν ἑκάτερος: cf. 42. 1 n.

ξύμπαντι: cf. iii. 95. 1 ἄρας οὖν ξύμπαντι τῷ στρατεύματι; the absence of τῷ στρατεύματι here is facilitated by the presence of τοῦ στρατεύματος in the preceding clause.

ἐπὶ Σελινοῦντος καὶ Ἐγέστης: as they did not go to Selinus, and only Nikias went as far as Segesta, the words describe simply the part of Sicily towards which they set out. The remoter place is named first, as in viii. 88.

2. ἥπερ μόνη ἐν τούτῳ τῷ μέρει τῆς Σικελίας Ἑλλὰς πόλις ἐστίν: Himera was totally destroyed by the Carthaginians in 409 (Diod. xiii. 62, cf. xi. 49. 4). If Thucydides were merely telling us the geographical location of Himera, ἐστίν would present no more serious a problem than οἰκοῦσιν in i. 56. 2 Ποτειδεάτας, οἳ οἰκοῦσιν ἐπὶ τῷ ἰσθμῷ τῆς Παλλήνης, Κορινθίων ἄποικοι = 'Poteidaia, a city situated on the isthmus of Pallene, a Corinthian colony'. But his present

339

statement, repeated in vii. 58. 2 ἐν ᾧ καὶ μόνοι Ἕλληνες οἰκοῦσι, is of a different type (pace Patzer, 31, 67, de Romilly, Imp. 214 n. 3) because it is a statement of race (contrast vii. 57. 2 τότε and 57. 8 νῦν) and thus appears to afford evidence for date of composition. However, Diod. xiv. 47. 6 and 56. 2 speaks of 'Ἱμεραῖοι as a people independent of Carthaginian rule, and in the north of Sicily, in 397-6, and Cic. Verr. ii. ii. 86 speaks of them as re-establishing themselves near their original city in the territory of the Carthaginian foundation, Thermai. Thucydides may have thought of the city of Himera and these survivors as a continuous entity; this is not a very natural explanation of what he says, but cf. vii. 57-8 n.

3. αἱροῦσιν Ὑκκαρα - - - πολέμιον: located by Itin. Ant. 91 sixteen Roman miles west of Palermo, and therefore the modern Carini (Ziegler, RE ix. 97 f.). When there was hostility between Segesta and Greek Selinus, a Sikan town might have been expected (by Nikias, or by Thucydides) to be on the side of Segesta; hence there is a strong force of contrast in μέν / δέ here.

διὰ τῶν Σικελῶν: the desirability of getting the enslaved population of Hykkara back to the east coast in marketable condition, and therefore in the troop-carriers, was one reason for taking the troops back overland. Presumably Archonides, ruler of the Sikels inland from Himera and a good friend of Athens (vii. 1. 4) was still alive, and the long march was not made more arduous by fighting.

4. Νικίας δὲ εὐθὺς ἐξ Ὑκκάρων ἐπὶ Ἐγέστης παραπλεύσας: 'direct' (cf. iv. 118. 4) 'from Hykkara to Segesta', i.e. without any further diversions such as the attack on Hykkara.

καὶ τἀνδράποδα ἀπέδοσαν: the words appear to mean 'gave back' (or 'rendered') 'the slaves', but to whom? In E. Cy. 236 ff. ἔφασκον - - - κἄπειτα συνδήσαντες ἐς θἀδώλια τῆς νηὸς ἐμβαλόντες ἀποδώσειν τινὶ πέτρους μοχλεύειν it would be strange if the active ἀποδώσειν did not mean 'sell' (Ar. Ra. 1235, sometimes cited in this connection, is open to varied interpretations), and we should therefore accept ἀποδιδόναι = 'sell' as a fifth-century usage, obsolete in the fourth, like (e.g.) διαβάλλειν = 'cross' (intransitive).

5. καὶ ἐς τοὺς τῶν Σικελῶν ξυμμάχους περιέπλευσαν: 'they sailed round to the allies of the Sikels' is unsatisfactory sense; who could the 'allies of the Sikels' be? The genitive must be partitive, meaning 'those of the Sikels who were their allies', and it is probable that Thucydides wrote τῶν Σικελῶν either before ἐς or after ξυμμάχους. 'Sailed round' is also unsatisfactory, as the Sikels were essentially an inland people, and better sense is given by περιέπεμψαν (Hˢ, cj. Stahl); for the repetition περιέπεμψαν - - - πέμπειν cf. 88. 6.

ἐπὶ Ὕβλαν τὴν Γελεᾶτιν: κώμη Καταναίων in Pausanias' time (v. 23. 6) and probably to be identified with Paternò, some 14 km. WNW. of Katane (Ziegler, RE ix. 25 ff. and Dunbabin, 129 ff., 144 f.).

R. Battaglia's identification of it as a site in the territory of Gela (*Archivio storico siciliano* ix [1957/8], 13 ff.) seems to me groundless.

63–71. *Athenian Landing at Syracuse*

63. 2. οἷον δὴ ὄχλος φιλεῖ θαρσήσας ποιεῖν: one of Thucydides' characteristic asides on the behaviour of men in the mass; cf. de Romilly, *Imp.*, 323, 329 f., W. Müri, *MH* iv (1947), 269 ff., and Meister, 75 ff., 80 ff.

3. εἰ ξυνοικήσοντες σφίσιν αὐτοὶ μᾶλλον ἥκοιεν: 'whether they themselves (sc. the Athenians) had come to live with them (sc. the Syracusans)'; there is antithesis between αὐτοί (cj. Bekker) and Λεοντίνους, as well as between ξυνοικήσοντες and κατοικιοῦντες and between ἀλλοτρίᾳ and οἰκείαν, but the MSS.' αὐτοῖς reduces the antithesis as well as giving us an unwanted 'full' reflexive. αὐτοῖς is probably an intrusive v.l. on σφίσιν; Plu. *Nic.* 16. 1 ἠρώτων εἰ Καταναίοις συνοικήσοντες ἢ Λεοντίνους κατοικιοῦντες ἥκουσιν suggests that Plutarch read *either* σφίσιν (which he took as = αὐτοῖς) *or* αὐτοῖς, but not both. For a similar corruption cf. Hp. *Aer.* 22, where the MSS. have ἐπειδὰν ἀφίκωνται παρὰ γυναῖκας καὶ μὴ οἷοί τ' ἔωσι χρῆσθαι σφίσιν αὐτοῖς, and vii. 48. 3, where the MSS.' addition of αὐτῶν to σφῶν gives the wrong sense.

64. 1. εἰδότες οὐκ ἂν ὁμοίως δυνηθέντες καὶ εἰ ἐκ τῶν νεῶν πρὸς παρεσκευασμένους ἐκβιβάζοιεν: 'realizing that (sc. if they landed unopposed) they would not be able (sc. to occupy a position) in the same way as if they were to disembark from their ships' (ἐκβιβάζοιεν [CGH₂ ψ] is no doubt right as against ἐκβιάζοιεν [cett.]—for the 'absolute' use cf. X. *HG* ii. 1. 24—since Thucydides elsewhere uses the middle, never the active, of βιάζεσθαι and its compounds) 'against prepared opposition or were to be detected in moving by land', i.e. they would be able to occupy a position much *better* than by disembarking against prepared opposition. This interpretation is defended by Herbst–Müller ii. 27, Rose, *CR* xlii (1928), 169, and Gomme, *CR* xliii (1929), 15, and is certainly right if the text is right. In i. 124. 2, ii. 20. 4, and iii. 66. 2 οὐχ ὁμοίως means 'less', not 'more'; in vii. 28. 4 οὐχ ὁμοίως καὶ πρίν is clarified at once by ἀλλὰ πολλῷ μείζους. It is noteworthy that Σᴹᶜᶠ in his paraphrase (οὐχ ὁμοίως - - - οὔτ' εἰ κατὰ θάλασσαν - - - ἐπιπλέοιεν) and Valla in his translation (*non perinde se valituros si . . . descenderent*) take no account of καί, and possible that it was (rightly) absent from their texts; but Valla ignores a necessary καί at viii. 19. 2.

τοὺς γὰρ ἂν ψιλοὺς τοὺς σφῶν: this is oddly archaic Greek. For the insertion of ἄν between article and noun *DGE³* 412. 3 (Olympia, s. vi a.C.) seems the only parallel, and for τοὺς σφῶν (we would expect τοὺς σφετέρους) [X.] *Resp. Ath.* 2. 14.

τῶν Συρακοσίων: with τοὺς ἱππέας, not with τὸν ὄχλον.

ὅθεν - - - οὐ βλάψονται: 'by a route on which . . .' or 'in circumstances in which . . .' rather than simply 'where . . .'; they are thinking for the moment not of operations from the base which they will establish but of how to establish the base itself.

περὶ τοῦ πρὸς τῷ Ὀλυμπιείῳ χωρίου: cf. p. 480.

Συρακοσίων φυγάδες: there were always exiles. The 'fifth column' of vii. 48. 2 is a related but not identical phenomenon.

2. ἔτι ὑπολοίπους ὄντας τῶν σφίσιν εὔνων: the rest had fled when the Athenians entered Katane, cf. 51. 2.

3. καὶ τὰς ναῦς ἐμπρήσειν: the triremes would be drawn up on shore.

τῷ σταυρώματι: the article reflects the assumption that the temporary camp of a force would naturally be protected by a stockade.

65. 1. καὶ εἶναι ἐν διανοίᾳ καὶ ἄνευ τούτων ἰέναι παρεσκευάσθαι ἐπὶ Κατάνην: εἶναι ἐν διανοίᾳ = 'to be in process of planning' is supported by vii. 25. 9 ἐν ἐλπίσιν εἶναι = 'be hopeful' and viii. 14. 1 ἐν θαύματι ἦσαν καὶ ἐκπλήξει, and may take the same construction as διανοεῖσθαι, just as in Pl. R. 578 e ἐν φόβῳ γενέσθαι takes the same construction as φοβεῖσθαι. Since καί with ἄνευ τούτων cries out for interpretation as an adverb (cf. Pl. Smp. 202 a), and 'to be making plans for being prepared to go' is pleonastic (the aorist παρασκευάσασθαι [cj. Didot] would be hardly less so), it appears that ἰέναι is the infinitive dependent on εἶναι ἐν διανοίᾳ and παρεσκευάσθαι is an interpolated gloss on εἶναι ἐν διανοίᾳ (Acacius). Furthermore, they were not yet 'prepared'—cf. below ἐπεὶ δὲ ἕτοιμα αὐτοῖς καὶ τὰ τῆς παρασκευῆς ἦν—which is another reason for not taking καί as a conjunction.

ἤδη γὰρ καὶ τῶν ξυμμάχων Σελινούντιοι καὶ ἄλλοι τινὲς παρῆσαν: the parenthesis explains why it was possible for the Syracusans to take the field πανδημεί; the allied forces were entrusted with the defence of the city, as an Argive force was entrusted with the defence of Mantineia in 421 (v. 33. 2).

καὶ αἱ ἡμέραι ἐν αἷς ξυνέθεντο ἥξειν ἐγγὺς ἦσαν: we might have expected 'when the end of the period within which they had promised to come was at hand' or 'when the day on which they had promised to come was at hand', but we have 'when the days on which they had promised to come were at hand', since they could not arrive at Katane until the day after their departure from Syracuse. Cf. Aeschin. iii. 62 ἧκον οἱ τῆς κρίσεως χρόνοι. ἐγγύς is 'upon them', not simply 'near'; when Tyrtaios (8. 29) exhorts the Spartan soldier to fight his enemy hand-to-hand ἐγγὺς ἰών he does not mean 'going *near*', and in E. Hp. 1001 ἐγγὺς ὤν = παρών. The translation of Classen–Steup, 'when the days on which they had promised to approach (ἥξειν ἐγγύς) had arrived (ἦσαν)', treats ἦσαν very oddly.

ἐπὶ τῷ Συμαίθῳ ποταμῷ: the modern Giarretta (Ettonigmann, *RE* viiA. 1072 f., cf. Str. 272).

2. ἐπὶ τὰς ναῦς καὶ τὰ πλοῖα: ὁλκάδες, distinguished from πλοῖα in 30. 1 and 44. 1, must here be subsumed under πλοῖα.

3. ἐς τὸ κατὰ τὸ Ὀλυμπιεῖον: ABCFGM have τόν for the first τό, and ἐς τὸν κατὰ τὸ Ὀλυμπιεῖον μέγαν λιμένα (H₂), though not, as it stands, acceptable sense (cf. Powell, *CR* lii [1938], 3), points to ἐς τὸν μέγαν λιμένα κατὰ τὸ Ὀλυμπιεῖον (cf. 96. 3) as the right answer. Valla's *in magnum portum ante Olympium* (*sic*) is no doubt simply his translation of the text of H.

προσελάσαντες ἐς τὴν Κατάνην: 'riding into (sc. the territory of) Katane to make contact', cf. 105. 1 ἐς τὸ Ἄργος and 63. 3 προσελάσαντες - - - πρὸς τὸ στράτευμα.

66. 1. τῇ μὲν γάρ - - - κρημνοί: cf. p. 483.

2. παρά τε τὰς ναῦς σταύρωμα ἔπηξαν: both Athenians and Syracusans later (vii. 25. 5, 38. 2) planted posts in the sea to protect their own ships in harbour, but nothing of that kind is suggested by Thucydides here; the Athenians have no cause yet to fear Syracusan ships. This stockade, like the Athenian ἔρυμα in viii. 55. 3, is on the beach, and is designed to allow the troops to re-embark under the protection of a small defensive force if they are defeated.

καὶ ἐπὶ τῷ Δάσκωνι ἔρυμά τι - - - καὶ τὴν τοῦ Ἀνάπου γέφυραν ἔλυσαν: cf. p. 481, and on ἔρυμα cf. 94. 2 n.

3. τὴν Ἐλωρινὴν ὁδόν: cf. p. 479.

67. 1. τεταγμένον ἐπὶ ὀκτώ: cf. iv. 94. 1 n.

ἐν πλαισίῳ: the purpose of bringing the carriers ashore must have been to supply the forward half of the hoplite force with food and drink quickly if it succeeded in pushing the enemy right away from the battlefield and found it necessary to keep in close contact overnight. At the same time, as the line of communication between the beachhead and the furthest forward position of the hoplites would be vulnerable to enemy cavalry, the carriers needed protection, which was afforded by the rear half of the hoplite force. The formation called πλαίσιον was normally used on the move, as in X. *An.* i. 8. 9, iii. 2. 36, *Cyr.* vi. 3. 3, and *HG* iv. 3. 4 (cf. Th. vii. 78. 2 n.). It had a 'mouth' and a 'tail' (X. *An.* iii. 4. 42 f.), which suggests similarity to a snake rather than to a square, and Arrian *Tact.* 29. 7 f. treats the square as a special case, the normal πλαίσιον being ἑτερόμηκες. In the present instance approximation to a square is probable, in order to create the maximum space in the centre for the carriers and baggage. Such a formation cannot charge, carriers and all, to save the situation when the fighting force is yielding, but it can move slowly forward and hold up the enemy while the line that has yielded retreats and re-forms.

2. Σελινούντιοι μὲν μάλιστα, ἔπειτα δὲ Γελῷων ἱππῆς, τὸ ξύμπαν ἐς διακοσίους: either (*a*) 'up to 200 in all' refers to both Selinuntians and Geloans, in which case the nature of the troops from Selinus is not specified, or (*b*) it refers only to Geloan cavalry, in which case neither the nature nor the number of the troops from Selinus is specified. Since it is Thucydides' custom to specify both nature and number (cf. 43 and vii. 33. 1), neither interpretation is wholly satisfactory; a further argument against (*a*) is that there were enough allied troops to take over the defence of the city when the Syracusans marched out to Katane (cf. 65. 1 n.). It is difficult, however, to suppose that a number is lost, since μάλιστα, ἔπειτα δέ - - - is clearly a substitute for an exact number. Since τὸ ξύμπαν, if it refers only to Geloans, adds nothing to the sense (unless we are to infer, with Classen–Steup, that they came in several small detachments; perhaps they did), we must draw the conclusion that Thucydides knew roughly the total of Selinuntians plus Geloan cavalry but did not know the numbers or nature of the Selinuntian contingent separately.

68. 1. οἳ πάρεσμεν ἐπὶ τὸν αὐτὸν ἀγῶνα: not 'it is unnecessary for me to address a long exhortation to you when you and I have come to fight the same battle', for he goes on to speak (αὐτὴ γάρ, κ.τ.λ.) not of their common interest in victory but of their superiority to the Syracusans as fighters and of the disastrous consequences of defeat. ὦ ἄνδρες - - - οἳ πάρεσμεν, κ.τ.λ. (cf. iii. 30. 1 Ἀλκίδα καί - - - ὅσοι πάρεσμεν, κ.τ.λ.) is a single vocative expression, of which the point is the same as in iv. 10. 1 ἄνδρες οἱ ξυναράμενοι τοῦδε τοῦ κινδύνου. Nikias is acutely aware of the mixed composition of his force, as he shows in vii. 61. 1 and 63, and therefore chooses a form of address which emphasizes their unity; cf. Luschnat, 74 f.

2. καὶ νησιωτῶν οἱ πρῶτοι: there is nothing derogatory in the term 'islanders' here; contrast 77. 1 and vii. 5. 4.

3. ἐξ ἧς κρατεῖν δεῖ ἢ μὴ ῥᾳδίως ἀποχωρεῖν: lit. 'from which you must conquer or not easily withdraw', i.e. (since ἤ = εἰ δὲ μή: cf. [X.] *Resp. Ath.* 2. 12) 'from which, if you do not conquer, as you must, you will not easily withdraw'. It is remarkable, but perhaps characteristic of Thucydides' Nikias (cf. his forebodings in 11. 1, 21. 2, and 23. 1 f.; Luschnat, 76 ff.), that in this first encounter with an anxious and unpractised enemy he should talk to his troops as if they were in a desperate situation. Contrast Phormion at Naupaktos (ii. 89); but Thucydides to some extent underwrites Nikias' attitude by using the words ἀνελπίστου σωτηρίας in 69. 3.

69. 1. οἱ δὲ καὶ διὰ σπουδῆς προσβοηθοῦντες: if these are different from the men who had gone off into the city, then (*a*) we are not told any more about those who had gone away, and are left to infer that they did not return; (b) we are not told whence the people who 'come running' came or why they were late. It is thus better to interpret οἱ δέ as 'these men' not as 'and there were others who . . .'; cf. ὁ δέ in i. 87. 2 and S. *El.* 711 χαλκῆς ὑπαὶ σάλπιγγος ᾖξαν· οἱ δ' ἅμα - - - ἔσεισαν.

2. οἵ τε λιθοβόλοι: these threw stones by hand; cf. Pl. *Lg.* 834 a λίθῳ ἐκ χειρός τε καὶ σφενδόναις ἁμιλλωμένων.

μάντεις τε σφάγια προύφερον τὰ νομιζόμενα: Marchant comments (71. 1) on the detail in which Thucydides reports this first battle between Syracusans and Athenians, including elements common to all battles. The dates in ii. 2. 1 and the title of Archidamos in ii. 10. 3 are similar examples of the dramatic sense with which Thucydides 'sets the stage' before our eyes.

3. οἱ αὐτόνομοι - - - τὸ δ' ὑπήκοον: cf. vii. 57. 3 n.

καὶ εἴ τι ἄλλο - - - ὑπακούσεται: H₂ has ὑπακούσονται (so too the explicit reference to the word in Σ^cf) and the nominative participle ξυγκαταστρεψάμενοι (so too Σ^Mcf; cf. -όμενοι in E). This is obviously right (cj. Haacke) and gives the sense: 'in the hope that their subjection to Athens' (αὐτοῖς, not σφίσι) 'would weigh less heavily upon them when they had helped Athens to make a further conquest'; the greater the number of tributary states, the smaller the burden borne by each state. The alternative text -αμένοις - - - ὑπακούσεται is unsatisfactory; it would mean, literally, either (a) 'in the hope that it would be obeyed by them more easily when they had helped (sc. Athens) to make a further conquest', ὑπακούσεται being impersonal, or (b) 'in the hope that it (sc. τὸ ὑπήκοον) would obey them (sc. the Athenians) more easily when they (sc. the Athenians) had made a further conquest with it'. (a) is doubtful, because ὑπακούσεσθαι, like ἀκούσεσθαι, has an active sense (cf. 71. 2), so that ὑπακούσεται is a most unlikely passive (Preuss, 38; ὑπακουσθήσεται cj. Schütz) and it is difficult to see any reason for the adoption of impersonal expression here. (b) is doubtful because the subject-allies have already been referred to in the plural (εἶχον), and even if this difficulty were removed by emendation to εἶχεν (κρατῶσι could be left intact, as referring to the whole army) ξυγ- is more appropriate to subordinates helping to realize the intentions of a superior than to a superior taking his subordinates with him.

Thucydides seldom refers to any respect in which the ὑπήκοοι had an interest in promoting the extension of the Athenian empire, but cf. vii. 63. 3 n.

70. 1. καὶ τοῦτο ξυνεπιλαβέσθαι τοῦ φόβου: not only because fighting in heavy rain is miserable, but because thunder and rain could be unfavourable omens, as the antithesis shows; the more experienced men knew that the time of year, not divine displeasure, was the cause. Cf. vii. 79. 3. D. l. 23 evidently speaks for (and to) experienced men of a later period: ἔτι δὲ συνέβη τῆς νυκτὸς ὥρᾳ ἔτους ὕδωρ καὶ βροντὰς καὶ ἄνεμον μέγαν γενέσθαι (ὑπ' αὐτὰς γὰρ Πλειάδων δύσεις οἱ χρόνοι οὗτοι ἦσαν), ἐξ ὧν τίνα οὐκ οἴεσθε, ὦ ἄνδρες δικασταί, τοῖς στρατιώταις ἀθυμίαν ἐμπεσεῖν;

3. οἱ γὰρ ἱππῆς τῶν Συρακοσίων πολλοὶ ὄντες καὶ ἀήσσητοι εἶργον: the story of Polyainos i. 39. 2 that the Athenians used caltrops, effectively, to protect themselves against the Syracusan cavalry in this battle is worth mentioning. It is probably not true, for Thucydides attaches such importance (64. 1) to the threat of the cavalry that he could not easily have passed over in silence an effective countermeasure; but it gives the name of the Syracusan cavalry commander, Ekphantos, and may go back, via Philistos, to a contemporary rumour of a type which people at war readily believe, excusing their own failure (and the battle as a whole was a Syracusan failure) by attributing to the enemy the use of an unexpected weapon. In retrospect it seems fair to say that the achievement of the Syracusan cavalry in preventing the Athenian hoplites from following up their victory and in thus inducing Nikias and Lamachos to put off any further assault of Syracuse until the following spring (71. 2) was one of the decisive moments of the whole campaign. What were the Athenian archers and slingers (43) doing, whose function it was to prevent this fatal domination of the battlefield by cavalry (22)? Presumably it had been thought, when they were recruited, that they were numerous enough and good enough; and now they proved not to be so. The successful cavalry attack described in vii. 6. 3 shows that even if the normal role of cavalry in a hoplite battle was limited, it was capable, if well used at the right moment, of decisive intervention; hence the fears of Nikias and Lamachos at this point in the campaign must not necessarily be dismissed as unreasonable. Thucydides does not pause here for any comment or reflection of his own; but his view that the decision taken by the Athenian generals was wrong can be inferred from vii. 42. 3 (see note).

71. 1. πρὸς μὲν τὸ ἱερὸν οὐκ ἦλθον: Paus. x. 28. 6 has a story that the Athenians at no time disturbed the sanctuary, its treasure, or its priest. It is not clear, however, that they had any opportunity to do so; the Syracusans established a φρούριον there during the winter (75. 1). There is an anecdote in Diod. x. 28 about the way in which Hippokrates of Gela prevented the Syracusans from removing the treasure of the sanctuary, kept his own hands off it, and made political use of this scrupulousness.

72–75. 2. *Aftermath of the Battle; Preparations for the Winter*

72. 1. ἀπέπλευσαν ἐς τὴν Νάξον καὶ Κατάνην διαχειμάσοντες: they actually go first to Katane (71. 1), whence they make an attempt on Messene (74. 1), then to Naxos, apparently with the intention of making that their winter camp (74. 2), and finally back to Katane at an advanced stage of the winter (88. 5).

2. ἀνὴρ καὶ ἐς τἆλλα ξύνεσιν οὐδενὸς λειπόμενος - - - ἐπιφανής: this is an 'introduction' of a type commonly used when a character is presented to the reader for the first time: cf. i. 79. 2 (Archidamos), 126. 3 (Kylon), v. 43. 2 (Alkibiades), vi. 54. 2 (Aristogeiton), viii. 68. 1 (Antiphon), 68. 4 (Theramenes), 90. 1 (Aristarchos). Four times, however, this ἀνήρ-formula is used of a character already presented: here (for we have met Hermokrates in the debate at Syracuse, 32. 3, and at Gela, iv. 58); i. 139. 4, of Perikles, mentioned several times before and once (i. 127. 1, ὢν γάρ - - -) in connection with the diplomatic preliminaries to the war; iv. 21. 3, of Kleon, already introduced (ὤν - - -) in iii. 36. 6; and iv. 81. 1, of Brasidas. It might be thought that these cases provide valuable evidence on the stages of composition; but if Thucydides wrote both iv. 58 and vi. 32 ff. after vi. 72. 2, then either he forgot that Hermokrates was 'introduced' at 72. 2—in which case why did he not 'introduce' him at iv. 58 or vi. 32. 3?—or he remembered and did not mind, in which case the grounds for thinking that he wrote iv. 58 and vi. 32 ff. after 72. 2 dissolve. Again, it is hard to imagine that i. 139. 4 was written at a stage when Thucydides had not mentioned Perikles, or thought that he had not mentioned him, in any earlier connection. And since Kleon is introduced twice, either (*a*) whichever of iii. 36. 6 and iv. 21. 3 Thucydides wrote second, he forgot that he had written the other, or (*b*) he was willing to introduce the same character twice in different connections, or (*c*) most probably, he had not decided, at the time of his death, which of the two introductions to delete. In the present case, mention of Hermokrates' qualities as a participant in war is more relevant here than on the other occasions, where he is presented as a political speaker. The trouble largely stems from the word ἀνήρ; in English, 'Hermokrates, a man who . . .' suggests the introduction of a new character, whereas in Greek it may do this (as in v. 43. 2) or it may signal merely the giving of information about the quality of a character, whether or not some of his acts are already known to us. (This, however, does not cover the case of Kleon, whose two introductions have so much in common.) On the whole question of Thucydides' method of introducing persons cf. G. T. Griffith, *PCPhS* clxxxvii (1961), 21 ff., especially 30 f.

κατὰ τὸν πόλεμον: since ὁ πόλεμος, with the article, is used for 'war' in general (cf. ii. 100. 2, vi. 41. 3, and Isoc. xviii. 31 πολλῶν καὶ καλῶν τοῖς προγόνοις ἐν τῷ πολέμῳ πεπραγμένων), evidence of Hermokrates' 'experience' and 'courage' may have been of much longer standing than the fighting with Athens.

3. ἰδιώτας ὡς εἰπεῖν χειροτέχναις: the dative (F¹Hˢ) is essential; the accusative (cett.), giving the sense 'they had fought against the most experienced nation in Greece as unskilled craftsmen, as it were' (Classen thought that χειροτέχνης was derogatory) is obviously inferior to 'their battle against the most experienced nation in Greece had been, as it were, a battle of unskilled men against craftsmen'. The metaphor may be Hermokrates' own (cf. 41. 3 n. on the oral preservation of memorable phrases, and H. Stein, *RhM* lv [1900], 548—who, however, believes that a written biography of Hermokrates was one of Thucydides' sources) but it is not unparalleled; cf. X. *Cyr.* i. 5. 11 οὕς - - - ἐπίσταμαι ἰδιώτας ὄντας ὡς πρὸς ἡμᾶς ἀγωνίζεσθαι, *Hipparch.* 8. 1 αὐτοὺς μὲν ἀσκητὰς φαίνεσθαι τῶν πολεμικῶν - - - τοὺς δὲ πολεμίους ἰδιώτας. For the sense of ἰδιώτης cf. ii. 48. 3 καὶ ἰατρὸς καὶ ἰδιώτης, Hp. *Aff.* 1, Pl. *Sph.* 221 c πότερον ἰδιώτην ἤ τινα τέχνην ἔχοντα.

4. καὶ τὸ πλῆθος τῶν στρατηγῶν καὶ τὴν πολυαρχίαν: the remedy proposed by Hermokrates is twofold (§ 5): the generals should be (*a*) few in number, and (*b*) empowered to act on their own discretion (αὐτοκράτορας), their right to this discretion being guaranteed by an oath of the assembly. Yet πολυαρχία can hardly describe a state of affairs in which the generals have to refer too often to the sovereign assembly; in X. *An.* vi. 1. 18 πολυαρχίας οὔσης is contrasted with εἰ ἕνα ἕλοιντο ἄρχοντα, and cf. the Homeric οὐκ ἀγαθὸν πολυκοιρανίη· εἷς κοίρανος ἔστω. The second remedy of Hermokrates is therefore a remedy for τῶν πολλῶν τὴν ἀξύντακτον ἀναρχίαν and πολυαρχία is the state of affairs, 'multiplication of authority', necessarily resulting from an excessive number of generals and from conflicting orders; this is one aspect of the πολυψηφία which, according to the Mytilenean speaker in iii. 10. 5, impeded collective action against Athens within the Delian League. The parenthesis ἦσαν γὰρ κ.τ.λ. explains primarily πλῆθος, and πολυαρχία needs no separate explanation. Neither before nor after the reform is there any indication that there was any provision for rotation of authority among the generals.

5. ἅ τε κρύπτεσθαι δεῖ μᾶλλον ἂν στέγεσθαι: the Ten Thousand conferred command on Xenophon (*An.*, loc. cit.) for this among other reasons; cf. 46. 5 n.

73. 1. ἐψηφίσαντό τε πάντα ὡς ἐκέλευε: evidently Athenagoras was no longer influential. He cannot have relished swearing an oath which gave such wide discretion to Hermokrates. Athenagoras in fact drops out of the narrative altogether after 41. 1.

τούτους τρεῖς: '(sc. only) these three'; cf. Ar. *Nu.* 424 τὸ Χάος τουτὶ καὶ τὰς Νεφέλας καὶ τὴν γλῶτταν, τρία ταυτί. Presumably three represent one per tribe; on the number of tribes at Syracuse cf. 100. 1, Holm, ii. 418, and Hüttl, 32 ff.

2. καὶ τόν - - - πόλεμον βεβαιότερον πείθωσι ποιεῖσθαι ἐκ τοῦ προφανοῦς ὑπὲρ σφῶν τοὺς Λακεδαιμονίους: cf. 17. 5 n., 34. 3. The words chosen here suggest that Thucydides' own view of the unreality of the peace at this period was that which he attributes to Nikias in 10. 2 ff.

74. 1. οἱ δὲ τούς τε ἄνδρας διέφθειραν πρότερον - - - - οἱ ταῦτα βουλόμενοι: 'they' (sc. the friends of Syracuse, informed by Alkibiades) 'had already killed the conspirators; and now those who were opposed to receiving the Athenians, organizing themselves as an armed faction, prevailed on the city not to receive them.' The text is in order, and Herwerden's deletion of οἱ ταῦτα βουλόμενοι is unjustified; the anti-Athenian faction is not identical in extent with the friends of Syracuse. For the characteristically Thucydidean expression ταῦτα βούλεσθαι cf. ii. 79. 2 ἐδόκει δὲ καὶ προσχωρήσειν ἡ πόλις ὑπό τινων ἔνδοθεν πρασσόντων· προσπεμψάντων δὲ ἐς Ὄλυνθον τῶν οὐ ταῦτα βουλομένων ὁπλῖταί τε ἦλθον καὶ στρατιὰ ἐς φυλακήν, viii. 92. 5, and for the negative reference of ταῦτα cf. v. 46. 4 τὴν μὲν ξυμμαχίαν οἱ Λακεδαιμόνιοι Βοιωτοῖς οὐκ ἔφασαν ἀνήσειν, ἐπικρατούντων τῶν περὶ τὸν Ξενάρη τὸν ἔφορον ταῦτα (= τὸ μὴ φάναι τὴν ξυμμαχίαν ἀνήσειν) γίγνεσθαι.

2. ὅρια καὶ σταυρώματα: ὅρια, normally 'boundaries', must have a technical military sense here; cf. Hesych. ὅριον· τείχισμα, φραγμόν. ὅρα (Σ Patm.) is a vox nihili, but explains the uncial corruption by which ὅρια καί (which we owe to Mʸᵖ·Cʸᵖ·) became θρᾶκας in the archetype.

75. 1. ἐτείχιζον - - - τὸν Τεμενίτην ἐντὸς ποιησάμενοι, τεῖχος παρὰ πᾶν τὸ πρὸς τὰς Ἐπιπολὰς ὁρῶν: cf. pp. 471 ff.

2. καὶ τὰς τῶν Ἀθηναίων σκηνὰς καὶ τὸ στρατόπεδον ἐμπρήσαντες: these σκηναί were obviously not tents, which the Athenians would have taken with them, but wooden structures which it was not worth their while to dismantle and re-erect elsewhere.

75. 3–88. 2. Negotiations with Kamarina

75. 3. κατὰ τὴν ἐπὶ Λάχητος γενομένην ξυμμαχίαν: cf. 52. 1 n. and iii. 86. 2. Marchant's strange idea (derived from G. Meyer, Progr. Ilfeld 1889) that Kamarina had only a truce, not an alliance, with Syracuse perverts his comments on many passages in these chapters; it is incompatible with the plain statement of 88. 2, where Marchant compromises on an ἐπιμαχία.

μὴ προθύμως - - - πέμψαι ἃ ἔπεμψαν: cf. 67. 2.

4. Εὐφήμου: nothing else is known of this man; for us, he is more like the unnamed Athenians of i. 72 than Diodotos (iii. 41), of whom we are told the patronymic and a fragment of information.

76–80. *Speech of Hermokrates*

76. 2. οὐ Λεοντίνους βούλεσθαι κατοικίσαι, ἀλλ᾽ ἡμᾶς μᾶλλον ἐξοι-κίσαι: *paronomasia*, exemplified here and in § 4 οὐκ ἀξυνετωτέρου κακοξυνετωτέρου δέ, may actually have characterized the oratory of Hermokrates (cf. his striking *parison* in iv. 61. 7, and Schmid, v. 197 n. 2), but it is a Gorgianic trick which occurs in other Thucydidean speeches also (e.g. i. 33. 4, iii. 39. 2).

οὐ γὰρ δὴ εὔλογον: the antithesis εὔλογος/ἄλογος recurs in 79. 2 and is picked up by Euphemos in 84. 2–85. 1. εὔλογος, 'admitting of a rational explanation which may convince the hearer', is almost 'consistent' here; if the reasons alleged for two actions are inconsistent, the suspicion that one of them is not a true reason is aroused. Cf. A. *Th.* 508 Ἑρμῆς δ᾽ εὐλόγως ξυνήγαγεν: it is by chance that Hyperbios faces Hippomedon, but it is as if it had been decided rationally. Cf. also Meister, 24.

τὰς μὲν ἐκεῖ πόλεις ἀναστάτους ποιεῖν: the obvious reference is to Hestiaia (i. 114. 3), Aigina (ii. 27. 1), Poteidaia (ii. 70. 3), Skione (v. 32. 1), and Melos (v. 115. 4).

Χαλκιδέας δὲ τοὺς ἐν Εὐβοίᾳ: the example is especially appropriate since Chalkis had revolted during the Pentekontaetia (i. 114) and was thereafter among the states subject to a degree of judiciary control by Athens (*IG* i². 39 [= ML 52]. 70 ff.). On δουλωσαμένους cf. *ATL*, iii. 155 ff.

3. ἑκόντων - - - ὡς ἐπὶ τοῦ Μήδου τιμωρίᾳ: for the enthusiasm with which ἡγεμονία was offered to Athens in 478, and the anti-Persian intentions of the League thus formed, cf. i. 95. 1, 96. 1, and *ATL* iii. 225 ff. As it appears from vii. 57. 4 that Thucydides accepted the view that all the Ionians without exception were of Athenian origin (E. *Ion* 1581 ff., Hdt. i. 147. 2) ὅσοι ἀπὸ σφῶν ἦσαν ξύμμαχοι cannot refer to Ionians, or it would be tautologous with τῶν τε Ἰώνων. It must therefore refer to later strata of Athenian colonization (cf. vii. 57. 2). Not all Athenian subjects in the Aegean were Ionic or Attic—Lesbos and Rhodes are notable exceptions—but to take account of that would have weakened both the point Hermokrates has just made and part of his later argument (77. 1).

τοὺς μὲν λιποστρατίαν - - - κατεστρέψαντο: if the text is right, the analysis of the sentence is: '(sc. they subjected) some (sc. having accused them of) failure to provide troops, (sc. they subjected) others (sc. having accused them of) attacking one another, and

350

having brought (sc. a charge) against others, as they were able (sc. to bring) some specious charge against them separately, they subjected (sc. them)'. For Thucydides' dislike of τοὺς μέν / τοὺς δέ / τοὺς δέ or τοῖς μέν / τοῖς δέ / τοῖς δέ cf. 35. 1 and (a more difficult case) 77. 2 (and contrast the lucidity of D. xviii. 61). For λιποστρατία cf. i. 99; the war between Samos and Miletos, which led to the revolt of Samos from Athens (i. 115. 2 ff.) provides an example of ἐπ' ἀλλήλους στρατεύειν, which is not mentioned in the generalizations of i. 99.

77. 1. ἔχοντες παραδείγματα τῶν τ' ἐκεῖ Ἑλλήνων - - - καὶ νῦν ἐφ' ἡμᾶς ταὐτὰ παρόντα σοφίσματα: 'having (sc. available for our consideration) the examples furnished by the Greeks of the Aegean' (contrast iv. 92. 4 παράδειγμα δὲ ἔχομεν τούς - - - Εὐβοέας and D. xxiii. 107 ἦν ἰδεῖν παράδειγμα 'Ολυνθίους, which exemplify the normal construction) 'and the same tricks being directed on us now in Sicily'. Cf. viii. 92. 7 ᾤοντο - - - τοὺς ἐκ τοῦ ἄστεως ὅσον οὔπω ἐπὶ σφᾶς παρεῖναι, and for the construction of ἔχειν, i. 144. 3 ἧσσον ἐγκεισομένους τοὺς ἐναντίους ἕξομεν.

οὐκ Ἴωνες τάδε εἰσίν: cf. E. Andr. 168 οὐ γάρ ἐσθ' Ἕκτωρ τάδε. At Gela, ten years earlier, Hermokrates had decried racial divisions and stressed the unity of Sicily (iv. 61. 2 and 64. 3); now, with Leontinoi obliterated and Naxos and Katane irretrievably committed to Athens, he exploits the racial pride of the Dorian states in the maintenance of freedom by valour. The racial issue is raised also in 82. 2, v. 9. 1 (Brasidas at Amphipolis), vii. 5. 4, viii. 25. 3, 5, and, in a humorous context, by Theokritos' Syracusan women at Alexandria (15. 90). Cf. p. 433, de Romilly, Imp., 83, and Luschnat, 81 ff.

2. ἢ μένομεν ἕως ἂν ἕκαστοι κατὰ πόλεις ληφθῶμεν: cf. the argument of iv. 61. 1, 64. 4, and D. xviii. 45.

ἐπὶ τοῦτο τὸ εἶδος τρεπομένους ὥστε τοὺς μέν - - - κακουργεῖν: viii. 56. 2 τρέπεται ἐπὶ τοιόνδε εἶδος ὥστε τὸν Τισσαφέρνην - - - μὴ ξυμβῆναι (for εἶδος cf. X. Cyn. 9. 7 τῷ αὐτῷ εἴδει πρὸς αὐτοὺς χρῆσθαι τῆς θήρας) suggests that ὥστε here governs the infinitives, not the indicative δύνανται: 'a policy of dividing some of us by argument, making others among us fight against each other with the prospect of (help from) allies, and damaging others according as they are able (to do so) by making some specious proposal to them individually'. A dative after κακουργεῖν is abnormal; in Pl. R. 416 a ἐπιχειρῆσαι τοῖς προβάτοις κακουργεῖν it is tempting to explain κακουργεῖν as epexegetic or even as an intrusive gloss on ἐπιχειρῆσαι, and there is no other parallel. On the other hand, Thucydides pays the price of linguistic abnormality to achieve variety (35. 1, 76. 3); anyone who is not willing to pay that price here must (like Herwerden, following Bauer) change λέγοντες to λέγοντας, take the dative τοῖς δέ with λέγοντας, understand αὐτούς (as in 76. 3) with κακουργεῖν, and then either (a) delete δύνανται and interpret ὡς ἑκάστοις as = ἑκάστοις (cf. 17. 4, vii. 65. 1) or (b) interpret as τοῖς δέ τι προσηνὲς λέγοντας, ὡς ἑκάστοις δύνανται ⟨sc. λέγειν⟩, κακουργεῖν.

καὶ οἰόμεθα - - - δυστυχεῖν: lit., 'and do we think that when a distant neighbour is being destroyed first this fate will not come to oneself, but that the man who undergoes it before one is alone in his misfortune?' For the word-order cf. Lys. iv. 4 ἡμεῖς ἦμεν αὐτὸν οἱ κριτὴν ἐμβαλόντες, and for the idea D. xxi. 220 ἕκαστον αὐτὸν χρὴ προσδοκᾶν τὸν πρῶτον μετὰ ταῦτ' ἀδικησόμενον γενήσεσθαι and X. Cyr. ii. 1. 8.

78. 1. ἐνθυμηθήτω οὐ περὶ τῆς ἐμῆς - - - μαχούμενος: although Hermokrates is represented at Gela as urging that neutrality was only a postponement of disaster, he did not there draw attention to any possible divergence of interest between Syracuse and other Sikeliot states, much less (as he does here, § 2) suggest that any states would actually welcome the downfall of Syracuse.

ἔχων δὲ ξύμμαχον ἐμὲ καὶ οὐκ ἐρῆμος: ἐρῆμος (H[s]: -ον cett.) is essential, for 'bereft' is the opposite of having an ally, not of being an ally.

τὴν ἐκείνου φιλίαν οὐχ ἧσσον βεβαιώσασθαι: this is not exactly sarcastic, nor need we suspect βεβαιώσασθαι, for φιλία is here a diplomatic relationship and not an attitude of mind; cf. φιλί[ας] γενομένας = 'when peace has been concluded', SIG³ 1122. 7 (ML 38; Selinus, s. v) and viii 37. 1 σπονδὰς εἶναι καὶ φιλίαν κατὰ τάδε. The undertone is sinister rather than sarcastic; those whose φιλία with Athens is 'ensured' lose their freedom of action.

2. οὐκ ἀνθρωπίνης δυνάμεως βούλησιν ἐλπίζει: cf. iii. 39. 3 ἐλπίσαντες μακρότερα μὲν τῆς δυνάμεως, ἐλάσσω δὲ τῆς βουλήσεως. οὐ γὰρ οἷόν τε - - - ταμίαν γενέσθαι: i.e. a man cannot regulate fortune so that only what he desires occurs. For the metaphor cf. 18. 3.

3. τοῖς αὑτοῦ κακοῖς ὀλοφυρθείς: Lys. ii. 37 σφᾶς αὐτοὺς ὠλοφύραντο— the aorist middle governing the accusative—strongly suggests that we should here translate 'lamented' (passive) 'for the evil fate which he has suffered'. That is language appropriate to one dead and gone (cf. ii. 51. 5 τὰς ὀλοφύρσεις τῶν ἀπογιγνομένων) and the continuation βουληθείη αὖθις φθονῆσαι is grimly humorous.

79. 2. καὶ δεινὸν εἰ ἐκεῖνοι μέν - - - σωφρονοῦσιν: cf. 76. 2 n. Rhegion acted ἀλόγως because she acted on suspicion and it would have been hard for her to make a persuasive case, especially as she was an ally of Athens (cf. 46. 2 n.); Kamarina acts εὐλόγῳ προφάσει because her action can be plausibly defended.

τοὺς μὲν φύσει πολεμίους - - - τοὺς δὲ ἔτι μᾶλλον φύσει ξυγγενεῖς:

'those who are by nature your enemies' (cf. D. xxi. 49 φύσει τῆς πρὸς ὑμᾶς ἔχθρας αὐτοῖς ὑπαρχούσης πατρικῆς) reflects the racial antagonism already exploited by Hermokrates and accepted (82. 2) by Euphemos; the expression 'those who are even more by nature your kinsmen' is curious, but implies that whereas natural enmity can be abjured nothing can change or undo the fact of kinship. Contrast D. xxiii. 56 οὐ γένος ἐστὶν φιλίων καὶ πολεμίων, ἀλλὰ τὰ πραττόμεν' ἐξεργάζεται τούτων ἑκάτερον.

3. πρὸς ἡμᾶς μόνους: for rhetorical purposes the help already received from Selinus and elsewhere (65. 1, 67. 2) is ignored.

80. 1. ἰέναι δὲ ἐς τὴν ξυμμαχίαν προθυμότερον: in v. 30. 5 ἰέναι ἐς τὴν ξυμμαχίαν means 'enter into the alliance' in the sense 'become a party to the alliance which was being offered'. It cannot have that sense here, since Kamarina is already an ally of Syracuse, as Thucydides makes clear (ἀμφοτέρων ὄντας ξυμμάχους and 88. 2); ξυμμαχία must therefore be not a formal agreement, but a state of affairs in which two or more nations fight on the same side (cf. 6. 2 n.). It is unlikely that Classen–Steup's interpretation 'send your troops into the territory of your ally' would have occurred to a Greek hearer.

2. τοῖς μὲν οὐκ ἠμύνατε σωθῆναι: 'you did not protect the victims so that they survived'; the syntax is daring, but cf. A. *Th.* 14 f. πόλει τ' ἀρήγειν καὶ θεῶν ἐγχωρίων βωμοῖσι, τιμὰς μὴ 'ξαλειφθῆναί ποτε.

3. οὐδὲν ἔργον εἶναι: explained by Σ^Mcf as οὐ χαλεπὸν εἶναι, which Classen–Steup accept; but περὶ ὧν, κ.τ.λ. prompts comparison with (e.g.) ii. 36. 4 μακρηγορεῖν ἐν εἰδόσιν οὐ βουλόμενος ἐάσω and indicates 'there is no point . . .'.

καὶ μαρτυρόμεθα ἅμα, εἰ μὴ πείσομεν, ὅτι, κ.τ.λ.: εἰ μὴ πείσομεν belongs in sense after ὅτι, and the force of ὅτι probably extends down to ὑφέξετε.

81–87. *Speech of Euphemos*

This speech invites comparison (de Romilly, *Imp.*, 242 ff., 250, and H. Strasburger, *Hermes* lxxxvi [1958], 29 ff.) with the speech of the Athenians in i. 72 ff. The Athenians at Sparta were essentially apologetic; they reminded their audience at length of the pre-eminent role of Athens in the Persian Wars (73. 2–75. 1), of the readiness with which the allies had asked Athens to assume leadership (75. 2), of the *fear* of Sparta which made it necessary for them to maintain and strengthen their empire (75. 3–76. 2), and of the moderation which they exercised in the rule of the empire (76. 3–77. 6); and having thus implanted the idea that it would be unfair and unreasonable of the Peloponnesians to fight Athens, they ended with warnings about the unforeseeable outcome of such a war (78).

Euphemos, on the other hand, is not concerned to prevent action, but to stimulate it. He declares that he will not expatiate on the services which Athens gave to Greece in the Persian Wars (83. 2; contrast i. 73. 2 'we *must* speak about what happened in the Persian Wars, even if the familiarity of the theme makes this tedious to you'). His argument is realistic: 'we built up our empire to protect ourselves against our hereditary enemies, the Peloponnesians; we had a right to subdue the Ionians, because they had sailed with Xerxes against us; we have come to Sicily because Syracuse is a threat to our security; and as she is a threat to yours also, you will be wise to make use of us while we are here.' One sentiment occurs in similar form in both speeches: i. 75. 5 πᾶσι δὲ ἀνεπίφθονον τὰ ξυμφέροντα τῶν μεγίστων πέρι κινδύνων εὖ τίθεσθαι as part of the argument 'we could not let the empire go, because that would strengthen Sparta' and vi. 83. 2 πᾶσι δὲ ἀνεπίφθονον τὴν προσήκουσαν σωτηρίαν ἐκπορίζεσθαι in the same connection (cf. de Romilly, *Imp.*, 250 n. 2).

82. 2. τὸ μὲν οὖν μέγιστον μαρτύριον αὐτὸς εἶπεν, ὅτι, κ.τ.λ.: 'now, the most important evidence' (sc. for my claim that our empire is justifiable) 'was given by my opponent himself, when he said that ...'. ΣMcf read μαρτυρίαν, which gives a slightly different sense: 'my opponent himself made the most important point when he bore witness that ...', lit. 'as for the biggest thing' (cf. viii. 92. 5) 'he himself said evidence that ...'. μαρτυρία, however, is not elsewhere used by Thucydides.

ἔχει δὲ καὶ οὕτως: 'and that is indeed the case; for we ...'; cf. E. *El.* 1102 f. πέφυκας πατέρα σὸν στέργειν ἀεί· ἔστιν δὲ καὶ τόδ'· οἱ μέν εἰσιν ἀρσένων, κ.τ.λ. and Denniston ad loc. The translation 'The position is this: we ...' (cf. Aeschin. iii. 51 ἔχει δ' οὕτως· ἐγὼ μὲν κ.τ.λ.) would be appropriate if the details which follow were a *correction* of the view to which the speaker has just referred; but they are an amplification. There is a certain similarity of exposition in Hp. *Reg.* 7 δοκεῖ δέ μοι ἄξια γραφῆς εἶναι, ὁπόσα τε ἀκαταμάθητά ἐστιν - - - ἀκαταμάθητα οὖν καὶ τάδ' ἐστίν, διὰ τί ἄρα, κ.τ.λ.

ἡμεῖς γάρ - - - ἐσκεψάμεθα ὅτῳ τρόπῳ ἥκιστα αὐτῶν ὑπακουσόμεθα: with the MSS.' text, lit. 'for we, being Ionians for Peloponnesians, who are Dorians and more numerous and our neighbours, considered in what way we might least be subject to them'. The datives in this interpretation have no point; 'in the eyes of the Peloponnesians' is inappropriate, as there was no room for doubt on whether or not the Athenians were Ionians, and the situation is not saved by Marchant's interpretation of Ἴωνες as virtually equivalent, in this context, to πολέμιοι. Nor can both Πελοποννησίοις and αὐτῶν, with the same reference, be objects of ὑπακουσόμεθα; in iv. 93. 2 τῷ δὲ Ἱπποκράτει ὄντι περὶ τὸ Δήλιον ὡς αὐτῷ ἠγγέλθη - - - πέμπει, κ.τ.λ., where αὐτῷ is strictly superfluous, there is no change of case. Herwerden's deletion of αὐτῶν is the simplest remedy: 'we, who are Ionians, considered by what means we might be least subject to the power of the Peloponnesians, who are Dorians, more numerous than we, and our neighbours'. Classen's remedy is more elaborate: "Ιωνες ὄντες ⟨καὶ⟩ Πελοποννησίοις Δωριεῦσι καὶ πλείοσιν οὖσι [καὶ] παροικοῦντες ἐσκεψάμεθα ὅτῳ τρόπῳ ἥκιστα αὐτῶν ὑπακουσόμεθα. On the issue of 'race' cf. 77. 1 n.

3. ἡγεμόνες καταστάντες οἰκοῦμεν: = ἡγεμὼν ἡ πόλις ἡμῶν καθέστηκε. Cf. ii. 37. 1 τό - - - ἐς πλέονας οἰκεῖν and i. 124. 3 ἀκινδύνως - - - οἰκοῦμεν. **ἐς τὸ ἀκριβὲς εἰπεῖν:** the implication is that the explanation already given suffices for all practical purposes; the rights and wrongs of the issue are for the finicky. The point of ἐντὸς τοῦ ἀκριβοῦς in v. 90 is rather different.

4. ἦλθον γὰρ ἐπὶ τὴν μητρόπολιν ἐφ' ἡμᾶς μετὰ τοῦ Μήδου: the fact that the Athenians had voluntarily sacrificed their city and country in 480 was (rightly) a focus of Athenian pride ever afterwards; cf. Lys. ii. 33 ff., where formal rhetoric for once expresses emotion with great effect. Contemptuous animosity against the Ionians for their failure to make a similar sacrifice must have played a part in rhetorical justifications of the empire from the time when it first needed justification; whether or not it played any significant part in the immediate aftermath of the Persian War depends on whether the Ionians' unlucky fight for freedom in the 490s or their reluctance to desert at Salamis (Hdt. viii. 85. 1) was uppermost in Athenian minds. Euphemos' attitude to the Ionians is very different from fourth-century nostalgia as exemplified in Isoc. iv. 122 τῆς ἡμετέρας πόλεως τοὺς "Ιωνας ἀπέστησαν, ἐξ ἧς ἀπῴκησαν καὶ δι' ἣν πολλάκις ἐσώθησαν: cf. Isoc. xii. 69 on the economic recovery and prosperity of Ionia under Athenian leadership.

δουλείαν δὲ αὐτοί τε ἐβούλοντο καὶ ἡμῖν τὸ αὐτὸ ἐπενεγκεῖν: δουλείαν βούλεσθαι is doubtful Attic usage, with no closer parallel than Arist. *Pol.* 1309ᵇ17 τὸ βουλόμενον τὴν πολιτείαν πλῆθος and 1310ᵃ21 οἱ δημοκρατίαν βουλόμενοι. It is, however, defensible in two ways: (i) τὴν αὐτίκα ἀκινδύνως δουλείαν in 80. 5 shows that δουλεία, though formally a noun, may be treated syntactically as an infinitive (cf. Hp. *VM* 5 τὴν ὁμολογεομένως ἰητρικήν, A. *Ch.* 177 'Ορέστου κρύβδα δῶρον ἦν τάδε, and *Th.* 908 f. διαλλακτῆρι δ' οὐκ ἀμέμφεια φίλοις), and (ii) expressions such as τὰ Συρακοσίων βουλόμενοι, 'supporting the Syracusan cause' (50. 3), are not very far removed from the combination of βούλεσθαι with an abstract noun as object. The former explanation is facilitated by the co-ordination of δουλείαν with the infinitive ἐπενεγκεῖν (Herbst, *JbClPh* Supplbd. iii [1857/60], 31 ff.). There is also the possibility of understanding φέρειν from the following ἐπενεγκεῖν, with δουλείαν; cf. 79. 1 ὅταν ὑπ' ἄλλων (sc. ἀδικῶνται) καὶ μὴ αὐτοί - - - ἀδικῶσιν and

355

A. *Ag.* 864 f. καὶ τὸν μὲν ἥκειν, τὸν δ' ἐπεισφέρειν κακοῦ κάκιον ἄλλο πῆμα λάσκοντας δόμοις. δουλεύειν (H₂) would remove all difficulties, but leaves the corruption inexplicable.

83.2. τὸν βάρβαρον μόνοι καθελόντες : while dismissing this and other boasts as καλλιεπεῖσθαι, Euphemos is careful to mention them. πᾶσι δὲ ἀνεπίφθονον : cf. p. 354.

3. λόγου μὲν ἡδονῇ τὸ παραυτίκα τερπομένους : i.e. they accept, in their present suspicious mood, whatever arguments accord with that mood; the language is a little forced in order to make the familiar contrast between specious oratory and practical wisdom (cf. especially iii. 37. 2 f., 38. 4 ff., and 40. 3), but Euphemos is trying to use Hermokrates' own weapons against him.

4. καὶ τὰ ἐνθάδε διὰ τὸ αὐτὸ ἥκειν - - - καταστησόμενοι : this Euphemos has not yet said; he is going on to say it. Either, therefore, φαμέν must be understood from the preceding εἰρήκαμεν (cf. 9. 2 n.) or it must be restored (Marchant) to the text.

84. 1. ἧσσον ἂν τούτων πεμψάντων τινὰ δύναμιν Πελοποννησίοις : cf. 10. 1 n. The argument implies that Athens does not intend to destroy Syracuse (cf. vii. 64. 1 n.), but only to restore Leontinoi and ensure her protection for the future by stimulating resistance to Syracusan imperialism.

2. εὔλογον : cf. 76. 2 n.

85. 1. ἀνδρὶ δὲ τυράννῳ ἢ πόλει ἀρχὴν ἐχούσῃ : Euphemos draws a fresh conclusion from the comparison made by Perikles (ii. 63. 2, and note) which Kleon (iii. 37. 2) converted into an equation. Cf. de Romilly, *Imp.*, 126.

οὐδὲν ἄλογον ὅτι ξυμφέρον οὐδ' οἰκεῖον ὅτι μὴ ˈπιστόν : cf. 76. 2 n. The point of οἰκεῖον is no doubt the frequent reference to the claims of kinship (76. 2, 77. 1, 79. 2, 80. 2).

2. νεῶν παροκωχῇ αὐτονόμους : cf. vii. 57. 4 n., p. 434. The distinction of status between contributors of ships and contributors of money is drawn much more sharply here than in i. 96. 1 and 99.

3. ὥστε καὶ τἀνθάδε εἰκὸς πρὸς τὸ λυσιτελοῦν - - - ἐς Συρακοσίους δέος καθίστασθαι : both the infinitive καθίστασθαι (E: -ανται F : -αται cett.) and τἀνθάδε (CGM : ἐνθάδε cett.) are necessary : 'it is therefore to be expected that we should try to establish the situation here in Sicily . . .'. (πρὸς τό - - -) ἐς Συρακοσίους δέος is ambiguous : '(as is required by) our fear of Syracuse' or '(as is required by the need to inspire) fear in Syracuse'. The latter has a parallel in X. *An.* i. 2. 18 τὸν ἐκ τῶν Ἑλλήνων εἰς τοὺς βαρβάρους φόβον, but the former has better parallels in Th. iii. 37. 2 ἐς τοὺς ξυμμάχους τὸ αὐτό (sc. τὸ ἀδεές) ἔχετε, 'you are similarly unafraid of your allies' and iii. 14. 1

τὰς τῶν Ἑλλήνων ἐς ὑμᾶς ἐλπίδας, and it accords with Euphemos' references (83. 4, 84. 1) to Athenian fears of Syracusan attack. The distorted paraphrase of Σ^Mcf, ὃ λέγομεν δέος ἡμῖν εἶναι διὰ Συρακοσίους, πρὸς τὸ ἡμῖν λυσιτελοῦν καθίσταται, must arise from his reading ἐνθάδε (or taking τἀνθάδε as an adverb), taking καί before ὃ λέγομεν as an adverb, and making δέος object of καθίστασθαι.

βίᾳ ἢ καὶ κατ' ἐρημίαν: these words most naturally go with ἄρξαι (Σ^GMcf), and ἀπράκτων ἡμῶν ἀπελθόντων explain them: 'they intend, when they have united you in suspicion of us, themselves to rule Sicily, either by force' (i.e. by attacking and subduing those who resist) 'or' (sc. without the need to use force) 'when you have no one to help you' (sc. as will be the case) 'when we have failed and gone away'. The alternative interpretations are to take the words (i) with ξυστήσαντες—but 'unite you in suspicion of us by force' is self-contradictory—or (ii) with ἀπράκτων ἡμῶν ἀπελθόντων—but although one may 'fail and depart' κατ' ἐρημίαν, i.e. through lack of support, I doubt whether one can be said to ἀπελθεῖν βίᾳ, i.e. be driven away by force; 86. 5 ἀπελθεῖν - - - σφαλεῖσαν is a much more natural expression.

86. 1. οὐκ ἄλλον τινὰ προσείοντες φόβον: Kamarina was in fact among the allies of Leontinoi who asked Athens for help in 427 (iii. 86. 2 f.).
2. ᾧπερ καὶ ἡμᾶς ἠξιοῦτε λόγῳ πείθειν, τῷ αὐτῷ ἀπιστεῖν: we owe ᾧπερ to fG: 'It is not right to mistrust that same argument by which you thought it justifiable to persuade us'; cf. Hp. *Flat.* 14 οἷσι δὲ λόγοισι ἐμαυτὸν ἔπεισα, τοῖς αὐτοῖσι τούτοισι καὶ τοὺς ἀκούοντας πείθειν πειρήσομαι. ὅπερ (cett.) would mean: '. . . to mistrust that same consideration of which you thought it justifiable to persuade us by argument', in which λόγῳ would be pleonastic (in 17. 3, λέγων πείθειν, λέγων is antithetical to στασιάζων).
ὅτι δυνάμει μείζονι πρὸς τὴν τῶνδε ἰσχὺν πάρεσμεν: prima facie 'a force greater than is required to meet their strength'; cf. 31. 6 στρατιᾶς πρὸς οὓς ἐπῆσαν ὑπερβολῇ. But how would Euphemos answer the question: 'If your force is bigger than the war against Syracuse requires, for what purpose is it bigger?' As Jowett points out, the speaker would naturally want to stress Athenian conformity with *necessity*. There is some incompatibility between the 'natural' sense of the words and the requirements of the argument, and the latter deserve priority; we must therefore translate: 'with a larger force' (sc. than in 427), 'as the strength of our enemy requires'.
πολὺ δὲ μᾶλλον τοῖσδε ἀπιστεῖν: for the sequence (sc. ὑμᾶς) ἀπιστεῖν - - - (sc. ἡμᾶς) ὑποπτεύεσθαι - - - (sc. ὑμᾶς) ἀπιστεῖν cf. 18. 6 n.; ὑποπτεύεσθαι elsewhere in Thucydides (e.g. 87. 1, 92. 2) is always passive, and nowhere middle in Attic. The sentence is so clumsy as to be textually suspect; cf. Herwerden, *Mnemosyne* 1880, 162.

3. οὔτε ἐμμεῖναι δυνατοὶ μὴ μεθ' ὑμῶν: Euphemos is perilously frank, as suits his argument 'make the most of us while we are here' (84. 5); and to allay his listeners' fears he adopts precisely the argument used (11. 1) by Athenian opponents of the expedition.

οὐ στρατοπέδῳ, πόλει δὲ μείζονι τῆς ἡμετέρας παρουσίας: 'our presence' here = 'we who are present'; cf. S. *El.* 948 f. παρουσίαν μὲν οἶσθα καὶ σύ που φίλων ὡς οὔτις ἡμῖν ἐστιν and 1103 f. τίς οὖν ἂν ὑμῶν τοῖς ἔσω φράσειεν ἂν ἡμῶν - - - παρουσίαν; Herwerden's dictum 'recte comparatur urbs cum urbe, non exercitu', being untrue, affords no ground for suspecting the text.

4. ἔδειξαν δὲ καὶ ἄλλα ἤδη καὶ τὰ ἐς Λεοντίνους: 'their treatment of Leontinoi, among much else' is the subject of the plural verb; cf. viii. 96. 5 ἔδειξαν δὲ οἱ Συρακόσιοι = 'and Syracuse was the proof of this', Aeschin. iii. 62 ὡς αὐτὸ ἔδειξε τὸ ἔργον. For the grammatical abnormality cf. Kühner–Gerth, i. 65 f. Alternatively, (ἀπο)δεικνύναι can mean 'be seen to do' (cf. Hp. *Fract.* 19 βραχύτερον τὸν μηρὸν ἀποδεῖξαι = 'have the thigh visibly shorter', Isyllos E 1 καὶ τόδε σῆς ἀρετῆς - - - τοὖργον ἔδειξας, and *GVI* i. 1912 [Cyrenaica, s. iv a.C.] δαίμων - - - σοί τιν' ἔδειξεν ἀράν), in which case καὶ ἄλλα, κ.τ.λ. might be the object of ἔδειξαν; but the parallel from book viii is of greater weight.

87. 2. πολλὰ δ' ἀναγκάζεσθαι πράσσειν: cf. § 3 and the famous reproach which the Theban herald addresses to Theseus in E. *Su.* 576, πράσσειν σὺ πόλλ' εἴωθας ἥ τε σὴ πόλις. Cf. V. Ehrenberg, *JHS* lxvii (1947), 46 ff.

3. τῶν ἡμῖν ποιουμένων: the position of ἡμῖν suggests that it is emphatic, although nothing else in the context does.

τούτῳ ἀπολαβόντες χρήσασθε: cf. Pl. *Grg.* 405 e περὶ ὅτου βούλει τοῦ σώματος ἀπολαβὼν σκόπει.

4. διὰ τὸ ἑτοίμην ὑπεῖναι ἐλπίδα τῷ μὲν ἀντιτυχεῖν - - - τῷ δέ - - - μὴ ἀδεεῖ εἶναι κινδυνεύειν: 'because the expectation is always in the mind of the victim that he will obtain from us help with which to match his opponent' (ἀντι-; in ψ the words are divided differently, ἄν τι τυχεῖν, and H₂ records ἂν τυχεῖν as a v.l.—cf. the vv.ll. ἀντιλαβεῖν and ἄν τινα λαβεῖν at X. *Cyr.* viii. 1. 17—but 21. 1 ἀντιπαράσχωσιν - - -, ᾧ ἀμυνούμεθα, ἱππικόν should be recalled) 'and of the aggressor, that, if we are going to come . . .'. ἀδεεῖς (codd.) is grammatically impossible; ἀδεεῖ (Krüger) means 'that he will not be unafraid to take a risk' and is hardly to be preferred to the equally simple emendation ἀδεές (Reiske) 'that making the venture' (sc. of attacking his intended victim) 'will not be without danger'; for ἀδεής in the sense 'not frightening', cf. i. 36. 1 τὸ δὲ θαρσοῦν - - - ἀσθενὲς ὂν πρὸς ἰσχύοντας τοὺς ἐχθροὺς ἀδεέστερον ἐσόμενον.

ἀναγκάζονται ὁ μὲν ἄκων σωφρονεῖν. ὁ δ' ἀπραγμόνως σῴζεσθαι:

= ὁ μὲν ἀναγκάζεται ἄκων σωφρονεῖν, τὸν δ᾽ ἀπραγμόνως σῴζεσθαι ἀνάγκη; a grammatical brachylogy rather than a zeugma.

5. τὴν κοινὴν τῷ τε δεομένῳ καὶ ὑμῖν νῦν παροῦσαν ἀσφάλειαν: on this characteristic Athenian claim cf. 18. 2 n.; and for the structure of the sentence cf. 7. 3 n.

ἀλλ᾽ ἐξισώσαντες τοῖς ἄλλοις μεθ᾽ ἡμῶν τοῖς Συρακοσίοις - - - καὶ ἀντεπιβουλεῦσαι - - - μεταλάβετε: lit. 'having made equal to the others with us change your policy to one of attacking Syracuse'. 'Behaving like other states' (sc. which gladly accept our help) is a very doubtful interpretation (*pace* Σ^Mcf). Setting aside S. *El.* 1194 μητρὶ δ᾽ οὐδὲν ἐξισοῖ, where the presence of οὐδέν makes a difference, the only certain example of intransitive ἐξισοῦν is v. 71. 3 Σκιρίταις - - - ἐσήμηνεν ἐπεξαγαγόντας ἀπὸ σφῶν ἐξισῶσαι τοῖς Μαντινεῦσιν, where it means 'extend the line so as to be equal to the opposing line' and may be a military technical term (Schwartz, 341). If Euphemos is using this technical term, as would be appropriate, we must delete τοῖς ἄλλοις as an intrusive gloss: 'becoming, with the addition of our forces, a match for Syracuse' (the idea, though not the grammar, is that of X. *Cyr.* vii. 5. 65 ὁ σίδηρος ἀνισοῖ τοὺς ἀσθενεῖς τοῖς ἰσχυροῖς). Alternatively, emend τοῖς Συρακοσίοις to the accusative (W. A. Camps, *CR* N.S. v [1955], 17), translating: 'by joining forces with us, make Syracuse equal' (sc. and no longer superior) 'to the other states' (sc. of Sicily); cf. Hdt. viii. 13 ὅκως ἂν ἐξισωθείη τῷ Ἑλληνικῷ τὸ Περσικὸν μηδὲ πολλῷ πλέον εἴη, Isoc. iv. 91 ζητοῦντες αὐτοὺς ἐξισῶσαι (sc. ἡμῖν). Marchant's 'accepting, as others do, the security which we offer', as if ταύτην τὴν ἀσφάλειαν ἐξισώσαντες τῇ τῶν ἄλλων, is very obscure.

88. 1–2. *Result of the Negotiations*

88. 1. πλὴν καθ᾽ ὅσον˝[εἰ] - - - ᾤοντο: εἰ (del. Reiske) is not defensible on the analogy of καθάπερ εἰ, ὡς εἰ, etc., which are semantically quite different.

τοὺς ὀλίγους ἱππέας ἔπεμψαν: 67. 2.

ἔλασσον δοκῶσι νεῖμαι: ἔλασσον δοκῶσιν εἶναι codd.; Valckenaer's conjecture (cf. Valla, *ne minoris facere viderentur Athenienses*) is preferable to Duker's ἔλασσον δοκῶσιν εὖνοι, since Thucydidean usage requires an infinitive with δοκεῖν + adjective.

88. 3–8. *Further Operations and Negotiations in the Winter*

88. 4. οἱ πολλοὶ ἀφειστήκεσαν: since ἀφειστήκεσαν must mean 'had revolted from Syracuse' (vii. 58. 3), not 'stood aloof from Athens', and there is a contrast between the Sikels of the plains and those of the hills, the MSS.' text is untenable unless we understand (as we cannot) an emphatic 'already' with ἀφειστήκεσαν in antithesis to εὐθύς in the second member. Canter's οὐ (*Nov. Lect.* viii. 16) is therefore necessary: 'the Sikels of the plains . . . had not revolted in great numbers, but the inland settlements . . . at once, with few exceptions, joined the Athenians.' Later in the summer 'many of the Sikel tribes' (sc. of the plains) 'which had previously been spectators (περιεωρῶντο) came to join the Athenians' (103. 2). For οἰκήσεις cf. X. *Cyr.* vii. 4. 1, on the Carians: τὰς οἰκήσεις ἔχοντες ἐν ἐχυροῖς χωρίοις.

5. τόν τε χειμῶνα μεθορμισάμενοι ἐκ τῆς Νάξου ἐς τὴν Κατάνην - - - διεχείμαζον: they had sailed off 'to Naxos and Katane to pass the winter' (72. 1) before their attempt on Messene and the debate at Kamarina. Now, therefore, 'they settled down to see the winter through'.

6. ἐς Καρχήδονα: cf. 15. 2 n.

καὶ ἐς Τυρσηνίαν: cf. vii. 57. 11 n.

πλινθία καὶ σίδηρον: 'iron', distinguished from 'tools' in vii. 18. 4, was for the clamps and dowels which would bind the blocks together. If πλινθία, 'bricks' or 'small blocks', is the right reading, these must have been manufactured at Katane by the Athenians on the assumption that the material would not be available to them at Syracuse, transported to Syracuse in the spring, and used for some parts of the circumvallation. Σ Patm. read πλινθεῖα, which he explains as τὰ ἐν τύποις ξύλα, οἷς τὰς πλίνθους κατεσκεύαζον (cf. *IG* ii². 1672. 203 [327 B.C.] 'four πλινθεῖα for the towers at Eleusis'). This is surely right, despite the different sense 'brick-works' which the word has in Ar. fr. 283 (Poll. x. 185). Transport of enough bricks to matter would have been a tall order for the Athenians; transport of equipment for making bricks would not.

7. οἱ δ᾽ - - - τῶν Συρακοσίων ἀποσταλέντες πρέσβεις: cf. 73. 2.

κατὰ τὸ ξυγγενές: cf. 6. 1 n.

88. 9–93. *Alkibiades at Sparta*

88. 9–10. *Arrival of Alkibiades*

88. 9. ἐς Κυλλήνην τῆς Ἠλείας πρῶτον: since a Corinthian fleet anchored at Pheia on the coast of Elis in the spring of 413 (vii. 31. 1), it is possible that Elis had been brought back under Spartan control after the collapse of her alliance with Argos and Mantineia. If so, Alkibiades went direct to enemy territory; contrast the apologia of Isoc. xvi. 9 (followed by Plu. *Alc.* 23. 1), contending that Alkibiades had gone first to Argos but 'was compelled to take refuge in Sparta' when Athens demanded that Argos should surrender him. It is not to be taken for granted, however, that Elis was back in the League;

the language of X. *HG* iii. 2. 21 (describing the start of hostilities between Sparta and Elis in 402) suggests the opposite (cf. Wade-Gery, 276 f.), and her absence from the catalogue of Th. viii. 3. 2 is noteworthy.

διὰ τὴν περὶ τῶν Μαντινικῶν πρᾶξιν: cf. 16. 6 n. Sparta was willing to treat him as a friend because of his desertion, but he himself insisted on a guarantee of safety; the purpose of γάρ is to explain ὑπόσπονδος.

10. τῶν τε ἐφόρων καὶ τῶν ἐν τέλει ὄντων: in iii. 36. 5 οἱ ἐν τέλει at Athens, who are persuaded to put the issue of Mytilene afresh to the assembly, are plainly the prytaneis (not, as Gomme suggested ad loc., the generals). The reference of the expression in any given passage depends on the state concerned and on the level of authority required for the issue concerned; thus it would not necessarily have the same reference in 'οἱ ἐν τέλει declared war on Athens' and 'οἱ ἐν τέλει fined a butcher for giving short weight'. In the present passage we are not told (yet) of a *decision* to send envoys to Syracuse, but of the *consideration* given to the sending of envoys, and οἱ ἐν τέλει here may be either a little more or a little less than the kings, elders, and ephors; 'A τε καὶ B' = 'both A by themselves and subsequently B, of which A were a part'. These facts do not preclude interpretation of τὰ τέλη τῶν Λακεδαιμονίων in some passages (e.g. i. 58. 1, iv. 86. 1, 88) as including the Spartiate assembly; cf. X. *HG* iii. 2. 23 ἔδοξε τοῖς ἐφόροις καὶ τῇ ἐκκλησίᾳ σωφρονίσαι αὐτούς. πέμψαντες οὖν πρέσβεις - - - εἶπον ὅτι τοῖς τέλεσι τῶν Λακεδαιμονίων δίκαιον δοκοίη εἶναι, κ.τ.λ. and v. 3. 23 ἐπιτρέπειν τοῖς τέλεσι τῶν Λακεδαιμονίων (= ἐπιτρέπειν Λακεδαιμονίοις ἀλλ' οὐκ αὐτῷ τῷ Ἀγησιλάῳ) χρήσασθαι τῇ πόλει ὅτι βούλοιντο. Kahrstedt, *Griechisches Staatsrecht*, i (Göttingen, 1922), 205 ff., collects and discusses the material but is too rigid in the definition which he gives to this group of expressions. Cf. v. 27. 2, 77. 1 nn.

89–92. *Speech of Alkibiades*

89. 2. τὴν προξενίαν ὑμῶν κατά τι ἔγκλημα ἀπειπόντων: cf. v. 43. 2 n. Since it was his grandfather who renounced the proxeny, the renunciation cannot belong to the time of Kleisthenes and Kleomenes, and the obvious time for it is the late 460s, when the pro-Lakonian sentiment championed by Kimon received its decisive setback.

τοῖς μὲν ἐμοῖς ἐχθροῖς δύναμιν - - - περιέθετε: cf. v. 43. 2, and for the highly personal conception of politics—which recedes later in this chapter—cf. 15. 2 n. and *Hell. Oxy.* 7 Bart. (2 G–H). 3 on Timolaos.

3. δικαίως: the conception of justice which is assumed in this argument is characteristic of Greek political and international relations.

τῷ δήμῳ προσεκείμην μᾶλλον: Alkibiades is contrasting himself not with Nikias and those who sometimes advocated policies at variance with the popular mood, but with other men of his own class, some of whom we meet in the pages of Plato.

4. τοῖς γὰρ τυράννοις αἰεί ποτε διάφοροί ἐσμεν: this theme is developed by Isoc. xvi. 25 f. with reference to Alkibiades' maternal ancestors, the Alkmeonidai; his paternal ancestor and homonym appears there as an associate of Kleisthenes in the expulsion of the tyrants. His opponents, however, could point to the fact that his grandfather was ostracized: Lys. xiv. 39, [And.]. iv. 34; cf. Raubitschek, *TAPhA* lxxix (1948), 203 ff. and Vanderpool, *Hesperia* xxi (1952), 5 ff.; and cf. 54. 6 n. on the archonship of Kleisthenes under Hippias.

πᾶν δὲ τὸ ἐναντιούμενον τῷ δυναστεύοντι δῆμος ὠνόμασται: the definition is the converse of the prevailing Athenian assumption (cf. 60. 1 n.) that oligarchy and tyranny amount to much the same thing. It is not, however, an arbitrary definition; δυναστεύειν is the exercise of power unrestricted by a constitution or code of laws (cf. iii. 62. 3), and in such conditions those who are outside the δυναστεία necessarily acquire a community of interest.

ἡ προστασία - - - τοῦ πλήθους: cf. 28. 2 n. and § 6 below, n.

τὰ πολλὰ ἀνάγκη ἦν τοῖς παροῦσιν ἕπεσθαι: in view of § 5, which states an exception to τοῖς παροῦσιν ἕπεσθαι, it seems that τὰ πολλά goes with the words which follow it: 'as the city was a democracy, it was necessary that *in most ways* we should adapt ourselves to the situation; but . . .'.

5. τῆς δὲ ὑπαρχούσης ἀκολασίας: ἀκολασία (the opposite of σωφροσύνη in iii. 37. 3) becomes familiar to us in Plato (cf. Isoc. vii. 20) as the characteristic of democracy in the eyes of its critics.

καὶ ἐπὶ τῶν πάλαι: the chronological reference is extremely vague; given the situation in which Alkibiades finds himself, Thucydides may intend a reference to the anti-Spartan forces which prevailed at Athens *c.* 460.

6. τοῦ ξύμπαντος προέστημεν: cf. Athenagoras' equation δῆμος = ξύμπαν (39. 1) and the modern usage 'putting party before country' (= 'opposing the policy of my party') and 'non-political' (= 'excluding all political views but mine'). It is important to remember that Alkibiades is not speaking to an Athenian audience; 'we were leaders of the whole nation' ∼ § 4 'the leadership of the common people' implies the possibility of 'leadership of "the few" ', but would not have been an entirely meaningful concept to the Athenians of the period during which Alkibiades became prominent.

ἐλευθερωτάτη: i.e. least subject to domination or pressure by other states.

καὶ αὐτὸς οὐδενὸς ἂν χεῖρον, ὅσῳ καὶ λοιδορήσαιμι: the MSS.' text means 'and I would' (sc. know it) 'as well as anyone, by the extent to which I abused it'. The grammar is sound, for a ὅσῳ-clause may be treated (e.g. X. *An.* i. 5. 9) like any other conditional relative clause, but the sense is not. Marchant's translation 'and the superiority of my insight' (he understands φρονοίην, not γιγνώσκοιμι) 'would be measured by the amount of abuse I might pour on it', which he explains as 'I might exhibit the extent of my insight by the amount of knowledge I might show of the nature of democracy by abusing it', suffers from the defect that there is nothing in the Greek about the Spartans' understanding what Alkibiades might show them; and similar criticism may be brought against Herbst's '. . . wie ich auch (sc. noch mehr als ein andrer) *das Recht hätte*, auf sie zu schelten'. Bloomfield's (and Hude's) ὅσῳ κἄν, 'by the extent to which I have grounds for abusing it', does not explain ἄν; Spratt, adopting ὅσῳ κἄν, deletes ἄν, and gives the best text of this passage so far attained by conjectural emendation. Conjecture, however, is not required, for the paraphrase of Σ^Mcf καὶ αὐτὸς ἂν ἐγὼ οὐδενὸς ἧττον λοιδορήσαιμι αὐτήν, ὅσῳ καὶ μέγιστα ὑπ' αὐτῆς ἠδίκημαι and Valla's *tum uero ipse, quo maiore iniuria affectus sum, eo magis uitupero* point to a text (as Stephanus and Hudson saw) καὶ αὐτὸς οὐδενὸς ἂν χεῖρον, ὅσῳ καὶ μέγιστα ἠδίκημαι, λοιδορήσαιμι: cf. (Herwerden, *Mnemosyne* 1880, 163) i. 68. 2 προσήκει ἡμᾶς οὐχ ἥκιστα εἰπεῖν, ὅσῳ καὶ μέγιστα ἐγκλήματα ἔχομεν. Hude's further emendation δημοκρατίας γε καταγιγνώσκομεν, adopted by Bodin with a change to κατε-, is not called for.

90. 1. εἴ τι πλέον οἶδα: 'whatever confidential information I' (sc. having been one of the Athenian generals) 'possess'; cf. vii. 49. 4.

2. ἔπειτα καὶ τῆς Καρχηδονίων ἀρχῆς - - - ἀποπειράσοντες: cf. 15. 2 n.

3. ἐχούσης τῆς 'Ιταλίας ξύλα ἄφθονα: this fact was known to Sparta, and may account for her request to her friends in the West in 431 for a great number of ships (ii. 7. 2); cf. vii. 25. 2.

αἷς τὴν Πελοπόννησον πέριξ πολιορκοῦντες - - - καταπολεμήσειν: πολιορκοῦντες is metaphorical; the Athenian navy corresponds to a circumvallation which seals off the enemy from communications with allies and external sources of supply, while operations on land (ἐκ γῆς ἐφορμαῖς) correspond to the assaults on a besieged city; but Argos provided a base for land operations inside the Peloponnese, so that the metaphor must not be pressed too closely, nor must the role of 'blockade' be exaggerated. Abresch's defence of the MSS.' οἷς, referring it to all the items listed from κομίσαντες onwards, is unsatisfactory, and Duker's αἷς, referring to the triremes alone, is necessary, as καὶ τῷ πεζῷ ἅμα shows. Though the scheme is more grandiose than anything which the Athenians seriously contemplated (Greek fears of the consequences of their success in Sicily are described in highly general terms in viii. 2. 1, 4), the principle is that of 431, when they realized that if Kerkyra and the Ionian Islands were

friendly they were in a position πέριξ τὴν Πελοπόννησον καταπολεμή-
σοντες (ii. 7. 3).
τῶν πόλεων τὰς μὲν βίᾳ λαβόντες, τὰς δ' ἐντειχισάμενοι: iii. 85. 3
ἀναβάντες ἐς τὸ ὄρος - - - τεῖχος ἐνοικοδομησάμενοι, X. Cyr. iii. 1. 27
φρούρια ἐντειχίζειν καὶ τὰ ἐχυρὰ κατέχειν, Isoc. iv. 137 τὰς μὲν αὐτῶν
κατασκάπτειν, ἐν δὲ ταῖς ἀκροπόλεις ἐντειχίζειν suggest that ἐντειχισάμενοι, 'building forts in their territory' for the purpose of attrition,
is a method of capture (τὰς δ' sc. λαβόντες) alternative to βίᾳ = 'by
assault', not an alternative to βίᾳ λαβόντες as a whole. (In Plu. Pomp.
28. 2 and Dio xlii. 38. 2 ἐντειχίζεσθαι is 'fortify by an encircling
wall'.)
καὶ τοῦ ξύμπαντος Ἑλληνικοῦ ἄρξειν: cf. 18. 4, and X. Cyr. i. 5. 3
on the ambitions of the king of Assyria.

91. 1. καὶ ὅσοι ὑπόλοιποι στρατηγοί: the reference may not be only
to the two generals left in Sicily, but to the whole board of generals;
we can hardly expect Alkibiades to tell the Spartans that Nikias
would certainly not attempt to realize the aims which have been
described to them. If E's ὡς οἱ is right, ὡς = 'I assure you'; cf. Ar.
Nu. 209 and E. Md. 609, an idiom of the spoken language which
strikes a slightly false note in Thucydides.
3. καὶ εἰ αὕτη ἡ πόλις ληφθήσεται, ἔχεται καὶ ἡ πᾶσα Σικελία: cf.
Lamachos' prediction in 49. 4. In Ar. Pax 250 f., when War says
ἰὼ Σικελία, καὶ σὺ δ' ὡς ἀπόλλυσαι Trygaios exclaims οἷα πόλις τάλαινα
διακναισθήσεται. This may be paratragic, an example of πόλις = 'land
containing cities', as in E. Ion 294 and elsewhere in Euripides and
archaic poetry (cf. Owen ad loc. and Wade-Gery, 232), but it may
alternatively show that 'Sicily' makes Trygaios think simply of
Syracuse.
4. αὐτερέται: cf. vii. 1. 3 n. and, for an earlier example of this practice,
iii. 18. 4.
ἄνδρα Σπαρτιάτην ἄρχοντα: Alkibiades regards this as 'more useful
than the (sc. proposed) expeditionary force', and the purpose of
sending a Spartiate commander is (lit.) 'that he may dispose those
who are present and apply compulsion to those who are not willing',
i.e. that he may be responsible for the tactical disposition and discipline of the troops mustered for action and for ensuring that those
who are liable for service (under the Syracusan constitution) present
themselves for action and training (cf. προσαναγκάζειν in 72. 3 and
vii. 18. 4). That is to say, he will not be simply a technical adviser,
nor will he be a member of a college of generals, possessing only the
same authority as each of his Syracusan colleagues; he is to command the forces of the Syracusans and their allies in the field, just
as a Spartan king commands a Peloponnesian army in the field.
See further 93. 2 n. and vii. 2. 1 n. It could not, of course, be taken

for granted that a Spartan commander would be a success with troops of other nationalities—Alkidas in 428/7 was a disaster (iii. 27. 2, 30 ff.)—but Gylippos' father Kleandridas was an example of what might be achieved (cf. 104. 2 n.), and Brasidas had won great respect from the rebellious subjects of Athens in the north (cf. iv. 108. 2).

6. τειχίζειν τε χρὴ Δεκέλειαν τῆς Ἀττικῆς: cf. 93. 2 n.

ἐν τῷ πολέμῳ: as in 72. 2, it is hard to decide whether the article is generic or demonstrative.

εἰ - - - ταῦτα σαφῶς πυνθανόμενος ἐπιφέροι: the implied distinction between 'perceiving' and 'being informed' (or 'discovering') is curious; the Spartans are in the position of σαφῶς πυνθανόμενοι the facts from Alkibiades, but not of αἰσθανόμενοι already. πυνθανόμενος also suggests a continued rather than a completed process; cf. Antiphon ii. δ. 4 f., where the distinction between σαφῶς πυθόμενον and πυνθανόμενον is important. It is possible that πυνθανόμενος is an intrusive gloss prompted by an unusual sense of σαφῶς, which with ἐπιφέρειν would mean 'outright' or 'without hesitation' or even 'on a proper scale', as it does in 88. 8; cf. § 5 φανερώτερον, vii. 57. 7, and perhaps also E. *El.* 617 φοβεῖται γάρ σε κοὐχ εὕδει σαφῶς = 'does not sleep *properly*' (but Denniston ad loc. hesitates about this). Thus: 'if he brought to bear on them, without reserve, that which he perceived' (sc. by being told, as I have told you) 'they feared more than anything'.

7. τὰ δ' αὐτόματα ἥξει: contrasted with 'captured', this must refer to the desertion of slaves; cf. vii. 27. 5.

καὶ ὅσα ἀπὸ γῆς καὶ δικαστηρίων νῦν ὠφελοῦνται: loss of the products of the land is obvious enough; loss of revenue 'from the law-courts' can only mean that if a high proportion of the citizens are continually under arms (which was the case when Dekeleia was occupied, vii. 28. 2) it is difficult to find juries for the hearing of lawsuits; in consequence there is less paid jury-service available to the ordinary citizen. Since this *saves* the state money, Thucydides must be speaking, in everything from οἷς τε γάρ to ἀποστερήσονται, not simply of state revenue but also of the citizens' sources of income as individuals. προσόδους is quite acceptable in this sense; cf. D. xxvii. 18 al. The idea that jury-pay is a significant part of the Athenian national income is ludicrous (cf. Jones, 50), but highly acceptable to a Spartan audience, just as there are many misconceptions about the British and American economies which are acceptable and encouraging to the Russian public. δικαστηρίων has been variously emended, e.g. to δεκατευτηρίων (Madvig, *Adversaria*, i. 328, and Meineke, *Hermes* iii [1869], 359); ἐργαστηρίων (Badham, *Mnemosyne* 1875, 243, following a tentative suggestion of Krüger) was strongly supported by Gomme (ms. notes), but on the assumption that 'πρόσοδοι of the mines' referred to state revenue (so too S. A. Naber, *Mnemosyne* 1886, 331 ff.). The hearing of private lawsuits was in fact suspended during the last years of the war, as we learn from Lys. xvii. 3; for similar suspensions in the fourth century cf. D. xxxix. 17 and xlv. 4. There are no grounds for supposing a suspension of public prosecutions, so that Boeckh and Dobree were wide of the mark in thinking that the loss envisaged by Alkibiades is loss of fines, and court-fees were a trivial matter in any case. In this passage (cf. 38. 3 n.), Thucydides is attributing to a speaker a brief allusion which becomes fully intelligible to us only in the light of our extant evidence for later events; if, however, private lawsuits had been suspended during the earlier Peloponnesian invasions, the allusion would not seem to him obscure.

92. 3. φυγάς τε γάρ εἰμι τῆς τῶν ἐξελασάντων πονηρίας, καὶ οὐ τῆς ὑμετέρας - - - ὠφελίας: Alkibiades has to contend with the criticism that his zeal is only the habitual (note τήν) anxiety of exiles to take revenge on their own country by helping its enemies. He meets it with a sophistry which is obscure and lame, saying that in coming to Sparta he is not deserting to the enemy, for it is those who have exiled him who are his true enemies. τῆς ὑμετέρας - - - ὠφελίας would be more clearly expressed as ὧνπερ ὑμᾶς ἂν ὠφελοίην.

4. τό τε φιλόπολι οὐκ ἐν ᾧ ἀδικοῦμαι ἔχω, ἀλλ' ἐν ᾧ ἀσφαλῶς ἐπολιτεύθην: as he goes on to define the true patriot (φιλόπολις) in terms which are meant to apply to himself (cf. Jowett ad loc.), he cannot mean 'I was once patriotic, but am so no longer.' The substantival relative clauses must be treated as if they were nouns governed by ἐς: 'I am patriotic not towards conditions in which I am wronged but towards those in which I exercised my rights as a citizen in security', a mixture between the historical (as shown by the tenses) and the hypothetical (cf. ἐν ᾧ used of a rejected hypothetical event in 55. 3).

5. ἐς ταλαιπωρίαν πᾶσαν: cf. Plu. *Alc.* 23. 3 ff. on the way in which Alkibiades adapted himself to life at Sparta; vii. 19. 1 n.

τοῦτον δὴ τὸν ὑφ' ἁπάντων προβαλλόμενον λόγον: at this point the sophistry of §§ 2 ff. and Alkibiades' attempt to dissociate himself from the common run of exiles seem to break down; but it is possible that he is referring to an adage of wider application, cf. the English 'set a thief to catch a thief'.

οὐ βίᾳ, κατ' εὔνοιαν δὲ ἡγῆσθε: empires and leagues are in fact normally held together βίᾳ: an empire held together by goodwill is a superior achievement, and therefore an ideal; cf. de Romilly, *JHS* lxxviii (1958), 92 ff. Alkibiades' attempt to excite Spartan ambitions may be compared with the efforts of the Theban embassy at Athens in 395 (X. *HG* iii. 5. 14).

93. *Consequences of Alkibiades' Speech*

93. 2. ὥστε τῇ ἐπιτειχίσει τῆς Δεκελείας προσεῖχον ἤδη τὸν νοῦν καὶ τὸ παραυτίκα καὶ τοῖς ἐν τῇ Σικελίᾳ πέμπειν τινὰ τιμωρίαν: 'they now began to turn their attention to the fortification of Dekeleia and, as an immediate measure, to the sending of some help to their friends in Sicily.' τὸ παραυτίκα is used as in 83. 3, the infinitive after προσεῖχον τὸν νοῦν is analogous to the infinitive after διανοεῖσθαι, and there is no need for Herwerden's emendation τῷ. Thucydides draws a clear distinction here between long-term and short-term plans. A full year passed before the plan for fortifying Dekeleia was put into effect, and it has been suggested (Wilamowitz, *Hermes* lx [1925], 297 ff.; cf. Schwartz, 198 f.) that Thucydides may have incorporated in Alkibiades' speech advice which was not in fact given until later. If Thucydides did that, he accepted the logical consequences here and in vii. 18. 1 καὶ ὁ Ἀλκιβιάδης προσκείμενος ἐδίδασκε τὴν Δεκέλειαν τειχίζειν. In fact, there is no good reason for rejecting the explanation of Spartan delay which he gives in vii. 18. 2 f.; cf. Andrewes, *Historia* x (1961), 8. E. T. Salmon (*CR* lx [1946], 13 f.) points out that Sparta had special relations with the demesmen of Dekeleia, for which there was a mythological reason, and that in their early invasions during the Archidamian War they spared Dekeleia (Hdt. ix. 73); but this would not necessarily have made them reluctant to use Dekeleia as a base from which they could damage the rest of Attica, and it may well be that the olive-trees and buildings of Dekeleia itself were spared during the occupation.

Γύλιππον τὸν Κλεανδρίδου: his father's name is confirmed by the unanimous MSS. tradition in vii. 2. 2 and Plu. *Per.* 22. 3; C's Κλεαρίδου here (cf. Κλέαρχον in Diod. xiii. 106. 10) is probably an unconscious reminiscence of the Spartan who plays a prominent part in book v.

προστάξαντες ἄρχοντα τοῖς Συρακοσίοις: προστάσσειν can be used of appointing the commander of a force (cf. vii. 19. 4). In isolation, therefore, the sentence could mean: '(. . . to send help to Sicily) and, having appointed Gylippos to the command (sc. of this force)', (lit.) 'for the Syracusans' (the Syracusan envoys, mentioned in 88. 10) 'they told him to consult with them (sc. the envoys) . . .'. But in the light of 91. 4 we should probably take the words to mean: 'and, having assigned Gylippos to the Syracusans as a commander (sc. on the conditions adumbrated in 91. 4), they told him to consult with them (sc. the Syracusan envoys) . . .'. We shall meet a similar ambiguity in vii. 2. 1, cf. n.

3. ἐς Ἀσίνην: probably the Asine which lies at the SW. corner of the Messenian Gulf, not its namesake in the Lakonian Gulf (cf. iv. 54. 4 n., and Oberhummer, *RE* ii. 1582); for a voyage to the West the more westerly assembly-point is desirable.

4. ἢν ἀπέστειλαν οἱ στρατηγοί: early in the winter, according to 74. 2; if it was really dispatched before the negotiations with Kamarina, the interval of time accords—exceptionally—with the pessimistic estimate of Nikias in 21. 2, by contrast with the comparatively prompt arrival of the Syracusan envoys at Sparta (73. 2 ~ 88. 7 ff.); but it is possible that there is some violation of strict chronological sequence in 73–5.

YEAR 18: 414–413 B.C. (CC. 94–vii. 18)

94. *Operations in Sicily in the Spring*

94. 1. ἐπὶ Μεγάρων τῶν ἐν τῇ Σικελίᾳ, οὕς, κ.τ.λ.: B has the ethnic Μεγαρέων, which is superficially easier as the antecedent of οὕς and is supported by 4. 1 Μεγαρέας ᾤκισαν, as well as by words such as Λεοντῖνοι, which are both ethnic and place-name. Since, however, the site of Megara was uninhabited at this time, 'sailed to ⟨sc. the site formerly occupied by⟩ the Megarians, whom the Syracusans expelled in the time of Gelon' is not in fact easier than 'sailed to Megara, whom (= the population of which) the Syracusans expelled . . .', and it is in favour of the latter that Thucydides elsewhere uses the place-name Μέγαρα when referring to the site as it was in 415/14, viz. 49. 4, 75. 1, and 97. 5.

ὥσπερ καὶ πρότερόν μοι εἴρηται: 4. 2.

2. τούς [τε] ἀγρούς: τε om. B; cf. 7. 3 n.

ἐπὶ ἔρυμά τι τῶν Συρακοσίων: we were told in 75. 1 that the Syracusans made the site of Megara a φρούριον early in the previous winter. If the ἔρυμά τι and the φρούριον are identical, τι betrays absent-mindedness in Thucydides; but ἔρυμα is probably a defensive work which falls short of being τεῖχος (cf. E. Watson-Williams, *Eranos* lx [1962], 102 f.). Possibly, on the other hand, a system of ἐρύματα can be called φρούριον.

ἐπὶ τὸν Τηρίαν ποταμόν: cf. 50. 3 n.

τὸν σῖτον ἐνεπίμπρασαν: if we read ii. 19. 1 in conjunction with ii. 2. 1 it is clear that in Attica the growing grain was ripe two and a half months after 'the beginning of spring'. Conditions being much the same in Sicily as in Attica, Thucydides cannot have imagined that the Athenians easily or effectively burned a growing crop in the course of this operation; it follows that he is referring to the burning of stored grain.[1] It certainly does not follow that he has dated to the beginning of spring an operation actually mounted in the summer; cf. p. 266 and vol. iii, p. 711.

---

[1] My note on this passage in my abridged commentary was, I fear, inept.

3. ἐπὶ Κεντόριπα, Σικελῶν πόλισμα: the name survives in the modern Centorbi, which lies some 40 km. NW. of Katane and is separated from Inessa by the valley of the Symaithos. Cf. vii. 32. 1 for one consequence of the ὁμολογία.

πιμπράντες ἅμα τὸν σῖτον: cf. § 2 n.

τῶν τε Ἰνησσαίων καὶ τῶν Ὑβλαίων: after the death of Hieron the colonists whom he had established at Katane (renaming it Aitna) were expelled, and occupied Inessa, which they called Aitna, Katane reverting to its original name (Diod. xi. 76. 3, Strabo 268). Evidently by Thucydides' time the town had come into the possession of Sikels who were under the control of Syracuse; cf. iii. 103. 1. On Hybla cf. 62. 5 n.

4. τούς τε ἱππέας ἥκοντας: in response to their request at the beginning of the winter, 74. 2.

τάλαντα ἀργυρίου τριακόσια: the record of this payment survives in the accounts of the Treasurers of Athena for 417/16–415/14, IG i². 302 (ML 77). 73 ff. ἐπὶ τῆς Ἀντιοχίδος ὀγδόες πρυτανευόσες τρίτε̄[ι ἡμέραι τῆς πρυ]τανείας ἑλλενοταμίαις καὶ παρέδροις Ἀριστοκρ[άτ]ει Εὐōνυμεῖ καὶ χσυνάρχοσι ⊢ ⊢⊢ ⊢⊢ hοῦτοι δ' ἔδοσαν [τε̄ι ἐν Σικελίαι σ]τρατιᾶι. On the date of this payment cf. p. 266.

95. Events in the Peloponnese and Boeotia

95. 1. μέχρι μὲν Κλεωνῶν ἦλθον: Kleonai was an ally of Argos in the battle of Mantineia (v. 67. 2) and presumably remained under Argive control after the democratic counter-revolution in Argos. As it lay c. 23 km. NNE. of Argos, and yet the Spartan invasion was interrupted by the earthquake, it seems that the Spartans began by going northwards through Arkadia to Phleius (their ally, cf. 105. 3 and v. 83. 3) to join with troops from Phleius and then began their operations with an attack on the territory of Kleonai, NE. of Phleius, intending to work southwards.

σεισμοῦ δὲ γενομένου ἀπεχώρησαν: in 426 the Spartan force invading Attica turned back at the Isthmus because of earthquakes (iii. 89. 1), and similar action in the fourth century is often recorded by Xenophon. (De Guingand, Operation Victory, 69, describes how the news of the Thessalian earthquake in February 1941 was suppressed because it would be taken as an unfavourable omen at a time when the threat of German invasion was growing.) On Spartan religiosity cf. vii. 18. 2 n.

ἐς τὴν Θυρεᾶτιν: in Spartan possession, but terra irredenta in Argive eyes; cf. v. 41. 2. Cf. Fouilles de Delphes, iii. 1, p. 386, for an inscription which may relate to this Argive success.

2. ὁ Θεσπιῶν δῆμος: Thespiai, like Plataia, always tended to look towards Athens and away from the Boeotian confederation. Evidently there had been some doubt of its loyalty to Thebes during the

Athenian invasion of Boeotia in 424, despite the presence of hoplites from Thespiai at Delion (iv. 93. 4, 96. 3), for in the following year Thebes compelled it to demolish its walls, ἐπικαλέσαντες ἀττικισμόν (iv. 133. 1).

οὐ κατέσχεν: cf. Lys. iii. 42 εἰ δὲ μὴ κατέσχον ('if they failed to achieve their aim'), οὐδὲν ἧττον τό γ' ἐπ' ἐκείνοις πεποιῆσθαι.

βοηθησάντων Θηβαίων: βοηθησάντων Ἀθηναίων ABγρ·CEFGM, but this makes little sense; it would be necessary to take the participle as concessive, and would leave unexplained who, if the Athenians arrived on the scene of the revolt, suppressed it. Ἀθηναίων may be just a slip, or it may be a correction by someone who interpreted βοηθησάντων wrongly as 'came to help them' instead of (cf. viii. 92. 6) 'took a hand'.

οἱ δ' ἐξέπεσον Ἀθήναζε: ἐκπίπτειν is used both of being forced away from where one wants to be and of being expelled in civil war; in both senses it may be used with an expression of direction, e.g. viii. 34 ἐκπίπτουσι πρὸς τὴν πόλιν τῶν Χίων. B's ἐξέφυγον (ἐκφεύγειν is used of escaping from one's enemies, e.g. ii. 4. 2) is a banalization.

96–103. *Operations at Syracuse in the Summer*

96. 1. τούς [τε] ἱππέας ἥκοντας: τε om. BE, probably wrongly; the Syracusans learn (*a*) that the Athenian cavalry has arrived, and (*b*) that the Athenians are planning an attack; the position of τε actually clarifies the sense.

χωρίου ἀποκρήμνου τε, κ.τ.λ.: cf. 75. 1 and pp. 469 f.

2. ἐξήρτηται γὰρ τὸ ἄλλο χωρίον the sense of this verb, which in other passages of Classical authors means 'hang down (from . . .)', 'be attached (to . . .)', 'depend (on . . .)' and is not used in any topographical sense, is in doubt. In Plu. *Ant.* 46. 6 τὰ γὰρ μεγάλα πεδία τῶν λόφων τούτων ἐξήρτηται the meaning may be 'lie below', 'slope down from', or 'rise towards', and Strabo 290 'the rivers in Germany flow from south to north', ἐξήρτηται γὰρ ἡ χώρα πρὸς νότον καὶ συνεχῆ ταῖς Ἄλπεσι ποιεῖ ῥάχιν τινά (lit. 'is hung up towards the south'), eliminates the alternative 'lie below'. τὸ ἄλλο χωρίον, as the rest of the sentence shows, means 'the rest of Epipolai' (i.e. other than the προσβάσεις), not 'the locality other than Epipolai'. If Thucydides is saying simply 'Epipolai slopes upwards from the city', then in μέχρι τῆς πόλεως ἐπικλινές ἐστι he is repeating himself; if he means 'Epipolai is a tract of elevated ground' he can hardly have said ἐξήρτηται; and in any case 'the rest of the tract, other than the approaches, is high ground' or '. . . slopes upwards' is a meaningless distinction, since the approaches are approaches *to* the high ground. The sense we need is 'the rest of the tract has steep edges'; I believe that Thucydides expressed this sense by ἐξήρτηται and that Strabo, borrowing from him, is using the word with only a very slight change of sense to mean 'is high and steep', whereas Plutarch has in mind the more general sense of ἐξηρτῆσθαι 'hang upon'. Σ^Mcf introduces a complication by saying μὴ ἐπὶ τοῦ ἐξηρτῆσθαι (Σ^Μ: ἐξῆρθαι Σ^c: ἐξῆρται Σ^f) καὶ μεμετεωρίσθαι ἀκουέσθω, οὔσης τῆς διανοίας τοιᾶσδε· τὸ γὰρ ἄλλο χωρίον πλὴν τῶν προσβάσεων ἅπαν ὑψηλόν ἐστι καὶ κρημνῶδες; but I take ἐξῆρθαι and ἐξῆρται to be corruptions in the transmission of the scholia themselves, not putative variants in Thucydides' text. καὶ ἐπιφανὲς πᾶν ἔσω: cf. p. 473.

3. ἐς τὸν λειμῶνα παρὰ τὸν Ἄναπον: λιμένα BM (λιμῶνα C^ac) makes no sense, since (a) no harbour 'along the Anapos' is mentioned again, nor is one likely, (b) a harbour would be a curious place for a muster of troops, and (c) in 97. 3 the λογάδες who are mentioned here run ἐκ τοῦ λειμῶνος. Krüger's insertion of ⟨τόν⟩ before παρά is unnecessary provided that we interpret Thucydides' words not as 'that meadow-land' (as distinct from others) 'which lies along the Anapos' but 'the (sc. Syracusan) meadowland, along the Anapos'.

ἄρτι παρειληφότες τὴν ἀρχήν: they were elected at the beginning of the winter (73. 1) but Thucydides' point in this context is that they did not take office until the spring, so that this was their first muster (cf. Hüttl, 78).

ἑξακοσίους λογάδας τῶν ὁπλιτῶν ἐξέκριναν πρότερον: only H^s (cf. Valla) has '600', the other MSS. '700'; but this body of troops numbers 600 in 97. 3. Cf. Holm, ii. 418, Hüttl, 33, and Wentker, 16, on the number 600 as a unit of organization at Syracuse.

ὅπως - - - εἶεν φύλακες καί - - - παραγίγνωνται: it is very doubtful whether the optative and subjunctive differ here in 'vividness'; cf. vii. 17. 4 and Ros, 379 ff.

97. 1. ταύτης τῆς νυκτὸς τῇ ἐπιγιγνομένῃ ἡμέρᾳ ἐξητάζοντο καὶ ἔλαθον αὐτούς - - - σχόντες: the MSS.' text says 'the Athenians, on the day which followed this night, were mustered for review and landed . . . unperceived by the Syracusans'. 'This night' must then be the night at the end of which (ἅμα τῇ ἡμέρᾳ, 96. 3) the Syracusans mustered by the Anapos, and 'the day following this night' is the same day to which Thucydides has just explicitly referred. Since the Syracusan muster was still in progress (§§ 2 f.) when the Athenians, marching from Leon, appeared on Epipolai, the Athenians apparently completed their muster at Katane, sailed to Leon, disembarked, and marched on to Epipolai, before the Syracusans had completed the muster which they had begun at dawn. This is pure nonsense; moreover, the sequence of verbal aspect in ἐξητάζοντο καὶ ἔλαθον cannot mean 'mustered their forces and then escaped notice . . .', and 'the following day of this night' is doubtful Greek, though the genitive might be defended as comparative, cf. Pl. Smp. 173 a

τῇ ὑστεραίᾳ ἦ (om. B) ἦ - - - ἔθνεν. ἐξητάζοντο must refer to the Syracusans, and there are two textual remedies: one is, with Krüger, to delete τῇ ἐπιγιγνομένῃ ἡμέρᾳ ἐξητάζοντο as a gloss on ταύτης τῆς νυκτός and καί as syntactical padding inserted after the establishment of the gloss in the text (cf. Herwerden, *Mnemosyne* 1880, 165, and cf. also οὖ in ii. 96. 3); the other is Madvig's insertion of ἦ before τῇ, giving 'on the day following which the Syracusans were being mustered' and consequent deletion of καί as syntactical padding inserted after the loss of ἦ (Classen modified this by conjecturing ἐκεῖνοι for καί). Madvig's text is, however, clumsy and verbose.

κατὰ τὸν Λέοντα καλούμενον: cf. p. 468.
ἐς τὴν Θάψον: cf. 4. 1 n.
2. κατὰ τὸν Εὐρύηλον: cf. p. 470.
3. οἱ περὶ τὸν Διόμιλον ἑξακόσιοι: cf. 96. 3.
5. ἐπὶ τῷ Λαβδάλῳ: cf. p. 474.

98. 1. καὶ ξύμπαντες πεντήκοντα καὶ ἑξακόσιοι ἱππῆς ξυνελέγησαν: Diod. xiii. 7. 4 raises the total to 800 by reckoning 250 from the Sikels. ἔλαβον is, of course, 'were given', not 'requisitioned'.
2. πρὸς τὴν Συκῆν: cf. p. 474.
ἐτείχισαν τὸν κύκλον: cf. p. 473.
4. φυλὴ μία τῶν ὁπλιτῶν: it is natural enough that when the whole hoplite force of Athens was in the field it should have operated in ten tribal 'regiments'; but there is much that we do not know about the use of tribal contingents in a comparatively small force. The Athenian hoplites at Syracuse (excluding ἐπιβάται) numbered 1,500, and if they were drawn, as they presumably were, from all the tribes in roughly equal proportion, one φυλή was 150 hoplites. The allied hoplites totalled 3,600, drawn unequally from a variety of states, not all of which divided the population into the same number of tribes. If φυλή here and in 101. 5 is a term applicable only to the Athenian hoplites, the besieging army consisted of ten units of 150 men each and other units which were numerous and of unequal size, if the internal tribal divisions of each state were maintained, or comparatively few and of equal size, if these divisions were ignored. Rational organization might have suggested distribution of the allies among the ten Athenian tribal units so as to create ten, and no more, large equal units; but 67. 1 and 101. 6 show that, as was usual in Greek composite armies (e.g. the Syracusan, vii. 43. 4, 7), the division into nationalities was fundamental. Apparently men of different tribes could mess together in camp, as Socrates and Alkibiades did at Poteidaia (Pl. *Smp.* 219 e).

99. 1. τὸ πρὸς βορέαν τοῦ κύκλου τεῖχος: cf. p. 473.
ἐπὶ τὸν Τρωγίλον καλούμενον: cf. p. 474.

2. ὑποτειχίζειν δὲ ἄμεινον ἐδόκει εἶναι - - - ἐκείνους δὲ ἂν παυομένους τοῦ ἔργου πάντας ἂν πρὸς σφᾶς τρέπεσθαι: ἐκείνους in the last member of the sentence shows that Thucydides subsumes under a single ἐδόκει both what the Syracusans decided to do and what they thought the Athenians would do. ἂν is eliminated in B, which has ἀναπαυομένους and πάντας πρὸς σφᾶς. The presence of ἄν, however, is necessary, since ἐκείνους, the subject of τρέπεσθαι, refers to the Athenians (distinguished from σφᾶς = the Syracusans) and the Syracusans could not determine what their enemies would do; furthermore ἀναπαύεσθαι, ἀνάπαυλα, ἀνάπαυσις, are used by Thucydides (iv. 11. 3, 20. 2, vii. 73. 2, 79. 2, 4, 6) of halting or resting deliberately rather than of being interrupted. Since ἐκείνους δέ is strongly antithetical, the whole sentence down to τὰς ἐφόδους should describe the course of action decided upon by the Syracusans, not their speculation about the Athenians. This action is, first, 'to build counter-walls where the Athenians were intending to lead their (siege-)wall', and, lit. 'if they did it before they could be prevented, that debarments should be effected'. γίγνεσθαι here, as usual (e.g. 90. 4, 92. 1), simply serves as the passive of ποιεῖν, and ἀποκλῄειν, ἀπόκλῃσις, are used of preventing someone, by putting something in his way, from going where he wants to go (e.g. 64. 3, 101. 4, vii. 60. 1, and cf. ἀποτειχίζειν, ἀποσταυροῦν). This interpretation, which adheres to the usual meaning of ἀπόκλῃσις and gives point to the plural—for wherever the Athenians tried to extend their wall, the Syracusans would build counter-walls to stop them—is preferable to the alternative, in which ἀποκλῄσεις (sc. ἔμελλον, cf. 66. 1) would refer to the Athenian encirclement of Syracuse. The supplementary decision is: 'and at the same time, in case the Athenians should try to intervene' (εἰ ἐπιβοηθοῖεν is used in precisely this sense in 100. 1), 'to send out part of their army as a counter-measure (ἀντι-) against them (αὐτοῖς Bekker: αὐτούς codd.) and themselves occupy beforehand, with their (τοῖς, s.v.l.) stakes, the approaches (sc. to the counter-wall) before the Athenians could stop them'. Clearly the Syracusans could not expect to defeat with only a part of their army the whole of the Athenian army if it chose to intervene. The function of the part referred to (the other part would be busy building the counter-wall) must be to protect the work by erecting a stockade wherever the work was not protected from attack by the nature of the ground; a single night would suffice for the erection (cf. X. HG vii. 4. 32), and a comparatively small force, if alert, could defend it (cf. 100. 1). καὶ φθάνειν, κ.τ.λ. therefore needs no ἄν, as it describes a plan, not a prediction; B offers αὐτοί instead of ἄν, and that is acceptable. The article with σταυροῖς is highly suspect (cf. p. 467), and ἂν τοῖς may be a product of the corruption of αὐτοί. αὐτοί and προκαταλαμβάνοντες rule out ἀντιπέμπειν αὐτοὺς τῆς στρατιᾶς in the

previous member, on syntactical grounds, and Arnold's ἀντιπέμπειν αὐτοὶ τ. στ., on stylistic grounds.

3. κάτωθεν τοῦ κύκλου τῶν Ἀθηναίων ἐγκάρσιον τεῖχος ἄγοντες: cf. pp. 475 f.

100. 1. φυλὴν μίαν καταλιπόντες φύλακα τοῦ οἰκοδομήματος: on the Syracusan tribes cf. 73. 1 n. It would be surprising, however, if one-third of the entire Syracusan force were left to guard the counter-wall, and φυλή here probably denotes a tribal contingent of one age-group.

τούς τε ὀχετοὺς αὐτῶν - - - διέφθειραν: thanks to Arethusa, this de-privation could never be fatal. For the position of the adjectival phrase ποτοῦ ὕδατος cf. Theocr. 3. 21 f. τὸν στέφανον - - - τόν τοι ἐγών - - - κισσοῖο φυλάσσω.

θεῖν δρόμῳ ἐξαπιναίως πρὸς τὸ ὑποτείχισμα: speed was decisive in an assault of this kind. If forewarned, the defenders could concentrate at any point of the stockade which was threatened and would, it seems, be immune from attack; cf. the defensive tactics of the Thebans against the Spartans in 378 (X. HG v. 4. 38). Light-armed troops were chosen and equipped for the attack on the stockade because faster runners were naturally to be found among them than among the hoplites.

μετὰ τοῦ ἑτέρου: cf. 50. 2 n.

πρὸς τὸ σταύρωμα τὸ παρὰ τὴν πυλίδα: cf. p. 467.

2. ἐς τὸ προτείχισμα τὸ περὶ τὸν Τεμενίτην: cf. 75. 1 and p. 472.

101. 1. ἐτείχιζον οἱ Ἀθηναῖοι τὸν κρημνὸν τὸν ὑπὲρ τοῦ ἕλους: cf. p. 473.

τὸ περιτείχισμα: ἀποτείχισμα (99. 1, cf. vii. 4. 1, 6. 4) is a more exact term for what the Athenians were doing, but περι- (cf. vii. 11. 3) can be used of any course in which direction is changed.

2. καὶ τάφρον ἅμα παρώρυσσον: cf. X. HG v. 2. 4 and 4. 38.

4. πρὸς τὴν πόλιν - - - παρὰ τὸν ποταμόν: cf. pp. 481 f.

οἱ τῶν Ἀθηναίων τριακόσιοι λογάδες: cf. 100. 1.

5. καὶ ἡ πρώτη φυλὴ τοῦ κέρως: cf. 98. 4 n. φυλή here is Duker's con-jecture (cl. Valla) for the MSS.' φυλακή; the same corruption has occurred in viii. 92. 4 and X. HG iv. 2. 19.

6. μονωθεὶς μετ' ὀλίγων τῶν ξυνδιαβάντων ἀποθνῄσκει: Plu. Nic. 18. 3 has a story that Lamachos and a Syracusan cavalryman named Kallikrates killed each other in single combat. Σ Ar. Th. 841 dates Lamachos' death 'in the fourth year before' that play, i.e. in the archon-year 415/14, before 1 Hekatombaion 414. But Thucydides' imprecise chronology of this summer neither corroborates nor in-validates that date. See v. 25. 3 n.

102. 2. τὸ μὲν δεκάπλεθρον προτείχισμα: cf. map.

δι' ἀσθένειαν: the first mention of Nikias' illness; cf. vii. 15. 1. He was evidently fit during the battle described in 100. 1 fin.

τὰς γὰρ μηχανὰς καὶ ξύλα ὅσα - - - ἦν καταβεβλημένα: building-tackle, presumably; the Athenians had no occasion yet for siege-engines.

3. ἀποδιωξάντων τοὺς ἐκεῖ: so Bψ; the word explains why it was possible for help to arrive. ἀποδιωξόντων (cett.) would give a more awkward sense: 'help was coming up from the Athenians below, who were intending to drive away the Syracusans there (= on the plateau)'.

103. 1. ἀπετείχιζον μέχρι τῆς θαλάσσης τείχει διπλῷ τοὺς Συρακοσίους: cf. pp. 473, 484.

2. τὰ δ' ἐπιτήδεια τῇ στρατιᾷ ἐσήγετο ἐκ τῆς Ἰταλίας πανταχόθεν: with the exception of the timber collected at Kaulonia in the following year (vii. 25. 2) we are told nothing precise about help and supplies from Italy, which is again mentioned in general terms in vii. 14. 3, 25. 1.

ἦλθον δὲ καὶ τῶν Σικελῶν πολλοὶ ξύμμαχοι τοῖς Ἀθηναίοις: cf. 88. 4 n.

καὶ ἐκ τῆς Τυρσηνίας νῆες πεντηκόντοροι τρεῖς: cf. 88. 6 and vii. 57. 11 n.

3. τοὺς δὲ λόγους - - - ἐποιοῦντο ξυμβατικούς: the tentative approach to Nikias may have been one cause of his fatal complacency next year (vii. 48. 2, 5).

4. ἀνθρώπων ἀπορούντων καὶ μᾶλλον ἢ πρὶν πολιορκουμένων: ἀνθρώπων ἀπορούντων appears at first to be a highly general reference, 'when men are in despair', but with 'and besieged more closely than before' it turns into a specific reference to the Syracusan predicament; 'before' means 'before they had built the counter-walls which were intended to end the siege'.

ὡς ἢ δυστυχίᾳ ἢ προδοσίᾳ τῇ ἐκείνων βλαπτόμενοι: bad luck and betrayal are not, to our way of thinking, indifferent alternatives. Accusations of venality were freely made in Greek states, and accusations of treachery on ideological grounds were common; the nearest modern parallels are to be found in the history of the Republican army during the Spanish Civil War and in the cruel and groundless rumour current in the Eighth Army in 1942 that the surrender of Tobruk was attributable to Nazi sympathies on the part of its South African commander. προδοσία, however, may cover 'giving up' through lack of enthusiasm as well as calculated treachery; that at least is the implication of X. *Cyr.* vi. 3. 27 ἢν δέ τις στρέφηται προδιδόναι θέλων, θανάτῳ ζημιοῦν. On the question of luck, cf. 17. 1 n. To this day, bad luck undoubtedly damages a commander's reputation, for it depresses the morale of those under him and it raises a suspicion that what appears to be a matter of luck may really be determined by some defect in him not yet discovered and defined.

Ἡρακλείδην καὶ Εὐκλέα καὶ Τελλίαν: this Herakleides is not the son of Lysimachos (73. 1), for that man is one of the generals now dismissed; probably he is H. son of Aristogenes, who commanded a Syracusan contingent in the Aegean in 409 (X. *HG* i. 2. 8). It is remarkable that Thucydides does not make the distinction, and Classen–Steup see in that a sign of incomplete revision. Eukles is 'Eurykles' in B, but a Eukles son of Hippon was also in the Aegean in 409 (ibid.). Nothing is known of Tellias.

104. *The Approach of Gylippos*

104. 1. καὶ αἱ ἀπὸ τῆς Κορίνθου νῆες: cf. 93. 3.

Πυθὴν ὁ Κορίνθιος: 'Pythes' in Diod. xiii. 7. 2, but cf. Th. vii. 1. 1 and 70. 1.

πρὸς ταῖς σφετέραις δέκα: since Gylippos and Pythen went to Himera and left their four ships there (vii. 1. 3), and the Corinthian and allied ships which arrived at Syracuse numbered thirteen (vii. 2.1 + 7.1), 'their own ten' here must *include* the two taken by Gylippos and Pythen.

2. ἐς τὴν Θουρίαν πρῶτον πρεσβευσάμενος: πρεσβεύεσθαι is 'send an envoy', and is not used of the envoy himself (*pace* LSJ, s.v. II 3 b, where v. 39. 2 οἱ Λακεδαιμόνιοι [= 'Sparta'] - - - ἦλθον ἐς τοὺς Βοιωτοὺς πρεσβευόμενοι is misunderstood). On the term Θουρία cf. 61. 6 n. (it might be argued that in saying ἐς τὴν Θουρίαν, not ἐς Θουρίους, Thucydides is describing Gylippos' action as the sending of a ship to a place rather than as negotiating with a state, but this passage seems to be the vanishing-point of the distinction [cf. S. Benton, *JHS* lxxxi (1961), 47]). On the politics of Thurioi cf. vii. 33. 5, 57. 11 n.

καὶ τὴν τοῦ πατρὸς ἀνανεωσάμενος πολιτείαν: the text of B is for once inferior to that of ACEFGHM, which have κατὰ τὴν τοῦ πατρός ποτε πολιτείαν. 'Citizenship', let alone one's father's citizenship, is not something which can be 'renewed', and though ἀνανεοῦσθαι does not always involve formality (cf. *SEG* xii. 378. 4 and D. xxiii. 121 τὴν πατρικὴν φιλίαν ἀνανεοῦσθαι) it can hardly mean 'attempt to produce a new manifestation of the relationship implicit in . . .', especially when it is used in the aorist aspect and the context shows that the attempt must have been unsuccessful. But κατά (cf. κατὰ τὸ ξυγγενές) and ποτε (cf. 80. 5 τὴν αὐτίκα - - - δουλείαν) are perfectly intelligible; cf. 75. 3 κατὰ τὴν ἐπὶ Λάχητος γενομένην ξυμμαχίαν πρεσβεύεσθαι. Presumably ἀνανεωσάμενος was interpolated after κατά had been corrupted to καί (cf. Bloomfield ad loc. and Badham, *Mnemosyne* 1875, 244). Wade-Gery, 267, n. 5 argues that Gylippos 'revived in his own person' his father's citizenship, and that that is the force of the middle voice; but since ἀνανεοῦσθαι is never used in Classical Greek in the active, no such conclusion can be drawn (cf. on πρεσβευσάμενος above). Kleandridas, exiled from Sparta in 446/5 (Plu. *Per.* 22. 3), commanded the Thurians successfully in their local wars (Antiochos F 11, Polyainos ii. 10).

κατὰ τὸν Τεριναῖον κόλπον: as Thucydides believes it was a north wind which blew Gylippos out to the open sea, he must have thought that the Bay of Terina was on the coast which runs roughly NE.–SW. from Kroton towards Rhegion. In that area NE. and offshore winds prevail; cf. *Sailing Directions for the Mediterranean* (Washington, D.C., 1952), iii. 46, 53. However, Terina lay on the west coast of Bruttium (Strabo 256; cf. Dunbabin, 161 f.) and the *sinus ingens Terinaeus* (Plin. *NH* iii. 72) was the Bay of Santa Eufemia, where the prevailing winds are WSW. (*Sailing Directions etc.*, ii. 332 f.). Gylippos is unlikely to have gone there, bypassing Sicily, nor would he have gone all the way back from there to Taras. Many unconvincing attempts to absolve Thucydides of geographical error have been made, e.g. interpreting κατά as 'on that part of the east coast which is on the same latitude as . . .' (W. E. Heitland, *JPh.* xxiv [1896], 19 f., wrongly comparing Livy xxiv. 13. 5), or emending to Τεριναῖον ἰσθμόν (Bergk, *Philologus* xxxii [1873], 565; the term is nowhere attested) or Ταραντῖνον κόλπον. The simplest explanation is that Thucydides had Skylletion in mind but mistakenly thought of it under the name Terina.

105. *Fighting in the Peloponnese*

105. 1. ἐς τὸ Ἄργος ἐσέβαλον: cf. 95. 1.

αἵπερ τὰς σπονδὰς φανερώτατα - - - ἔλυσαν: the peace treaty bound 'Athens and her allies' and 'Sparta and her allies' in the following terms (v. 18. 4): ὅπλα δὲ μὴ ἐξέστω ἐπιφέρειν ἐπὶ πημονῇ - - - μήτε τέχνῃ μήτε μηχανῇ μηδεμιᾷ. Now Thucydides suggests that raids based on Pylos, hostile landings in parts of the Peloponnese other than Lakonia, and participation in the Mantineia campaign did not constitute a significant breach of the treaty, whereas an attack on Lakonian territory did (and, as § 2 shows, would have done even if the Athenians had only contributed a contingent to an Argive force carrying out such an attack). Certainly the raids from Pylos could be regarded as the work of Helots in revolt (v. 56. 2 f.), an Athenian attack on Corinthian territory could be excused on the ground that Corinth had refused to be a party to the peace treaty, and even Athenian assistance to Argos could be overlooked—provided that one really wanted to overlook it—on the ground that Argos was not an ally of Athens at the time of the treaty. Elsewhere, however,

Thucydides implies that the Spartans were forbearing in not treating the activity at Pylos as a breach of the treaty (v. 115. 2, where the Athenians at Pylos in 416/15 take πολλὴν λείαν), and in vii. 18. 3 he gives Pylos equal weight with the present attack on Lakonia as a cause of the Spartan decision to renew open hostilities. On the chronological problem raised by this chapter cf. v. 25. 3 n. and Pohlenz, *NGG* 1920, 64 ff.

2. καὶ περὶ τὴν ἄλλην Πελοπόννησον: the territory of Epidauros, cf. v. 55. 4.

Πυθοδώρου καὶ Λαισποδίου καὶ Δημαράτου ἀρχόντων: Pythodoros is probably P. son of Epizelos, Halaieus (cf. Andrewes and Lewis, *JHS* lxxvii [1957], 178); Laispodias (mocked in Ar. *Av.* 1569 as an example of lack of elegance in dress) was one of the ill-fated envoys sent off to Sparta by the Four Hundred (viii. 86. 9); Demaratos is unknown to us.

ἀποβάντες ἐς Ἐπίδαυρον τὴν Λιμηρὰν καὶ Πρασιάς: on Epidauros Limera cf. iv. 56. 2 n.; on Prasiai, ii. 56. 6 n.

ὅσα ἄλλα: B's reading ἄλλα ἄττα gives much easier sense, and for that very reason incurs suspicion. ὅσα ἄλλα is not untranslatable: lit., 'having landed at Epidauros . . . and ⟨at⟩ all the other places ⟨at which they landed⟩, they ravaged . . .', i.e. 'they ravaged the country at Epidauros . . . when they landed there, and likewise at all the other places at which they landed'.

εὐπροφάσιστον μᾶλλον τὴν αἰτίαν - - - ἐποίησαν: i.e. made it easier for them to make their grievance public in a form which could not be rebutted on technical grounds. Cf. 6. 1 n.

3. οἱ Ἀργεῖοι ἐσβαλόντες ἐς τὴν Φλειασίαν: Phleius remained obstinately loyal to Sparta (or, more properly, hostile to Argos) and was therefore a constant object of Argive attack; cf. 95. 1 n.

BOOK VII

1–7. *Arrival of Gylippos; Athenian Fortification of Plemmyrion*

1. 1. ἐς Λοκροὺς τοὺς Ἐπιζεφυρίους: Lokroi, like Taras, had been consistently hostile to the Athenians; cf. vi. 44. 2.

σαφέστερον: by contrast with vi. 104. 1.

ἐς Ἱμέραν: Himera too had rebuffed the Athenians; cf. vi. 62. 2.

2. ὅμως: either (i) 'the ships were not yet at Rhegion, which Nikias had nevertheless dispatched', i.e. 'although Nikias had dispatched them', or (ii) '. . . which Nikias, despite his original neglect' (vi. 104. 3), 'had nevertheless dispatched'. The former interpretation has no parallel in Thucydides; for the allusiveness of ὅμως in the latter, cf. 77. 3 ἡ μὲν ἐλπὶς ὅμως θρασεῖα τοῦ μέλλοντος, 'despite our predicament, I am full of confidence for the future'. In the absence of any grounds for supposing that the existing book-division answers to anything in Thucydides' own conception of his work, there is no objection to interpreting words early in vii in the light of other words at the end of vi. B has ὅμως after αὐτούς, which makes no sense: 'which Nikias, although he learned that Gylippos was at Lokroi, nevertheless dispatched'.

σχόντες Ῥηγίῳ καὶ Μεσσήνῃ: since Rhegion is on the east side of the strait, either περαιοῦνται is an inceptive historic present or mention of Rhegion and Messene is prompted by 'they arrived at Himera', so that all their ports of call are enumerated.

3. τούς τε Ἱμεραίους: co-ordinated with καὶ τοὺς Σελινουντίους.

ὅσοι μὴ εἶχον ὅπλα: (ὅσα κ.τ.λ. B). Since Gylippos and Pythen had four ships, with a total crew of some 800, and in § 5 infr. we find 700 of these serving as infantry (this number includes the epibatai), it seems that Alkibiades' recommendation (vi. 91. 4) to send 'men who would row themselves and serve as hoplites immediately on arrival' had been carried out; Thucydides does not tell us what proportion needed to be supplied with arms from Himera.

τὰς γὰρ ναῦς ἀνείλκυσαν ἐν Ἱμέρᾳ: these ships do not appear later in the campaign, but they must be included in the 'sixteen ships which had fought with Gylippos in Sicily' of viii. 13.

πανστρατιᾷ: στρατιᾷ ACEFGHM. Since the contribution of Selinus was in fact confined (§ 5) to 'some light-armed troops and cavalry', πανστρατιᾷ is to be rejected here; in § 1 also M has it in error for στρατιᾷ.

4. καὶ οἱ Γελῷοι: for the fulfilment of this promise cf. § 5 and 33. 1.

Ἀρχωνίδου: no doubt the Archonides who collaborated with Duketios, the Sikel champion against Syracuse, in the foundation of a colony at Kale Akte (Diod. xii. 8. 2). He was ruler of Herbita, and was succeeded by another Archonides, who was in power in 403/2 (Diod. xiv. 16). *IG* ii². 32 (385/4), a decree honouring a certain Demon, the sons of Demon and Archonides, and probably Archonides, must be a re-publication of a decree originally passed during the Peloponnesian War, for it says (10 f.) ἐν τῶμ πόλε[ων ὅσων Ἀ]θην[αῖο|ι κρατ]ōσ[ι]ν. Herbita is probably to be located near the modern Nicosia, *c.* 70 km. ESE. of Himera (Ziegler, *RE* viii. 531 f.); ταύτῃ therefore refers (not very clearly) to the region inland from Himera. Gylippos' best chance of recruiting Sikels was naturally among the rivals and enemies of a powerful pro-Athenian king who had just died. Cf. vi. 62. 3 and 5 n.

5. καὶ ὁ μὲν Γύλιππος ἀναλαβών, κ.τ.λ.: Diod. xiii. 7. 7 gives a precise figure for the total, 3,000 infantry and 200 cavalry, which is reconcilable with these data.

τῶν τε σφετέρων ναυτῶν: co-ordinated with καὶ Σελινουντίων κ.τ.λ., Ἱμεραίους δὲ κ.τ.λ. being parenthetic; the essential distinction is between troops available on the spot and those who arrived from further afield.

Σικελῶν τε ἐς χιλίους τοὺς πάντας: this was perhaps the only contribution of the Sikels to the Syracusan cause; cf. 57. 11, 58. 3.

2. 1. οἱ δ' ἐκ τῆς Λευκάδος Κορίνθιοι: cf. vi. 104. 1.

Γογγύλος: according to Plu. *Nic.* 19. 7, he was killed in the first battle with the Athenians; this detail, like others in Plutarch's *Nicias*, probably comes from Philistos (*FGrHist* 556 F 56).

ἀφικνεῖται ἐς τὰς Συρακούσας: Thucydides thought that an attempt by Gylippos and Pythen to enter Syracuse via the east coast of Sicily would have entailed a serious risk (1. 1); it was risky for Gongylos too, but he had the advantage of sailing in a single fast ship.

περὶ ἀπαλλαγῆς τοῦ πολέμου μέλλοντας ἐκκλησιάσειν: this is the turning-point of the campaign. Since the loss of their second counter-wall the Syracusans had turned their minds to making peace (vi. 103. 3 f.), but from the moment of the arrival of Gongylos with his heartening news all goes ill for the Athenians. Cf. p. 420.

καὶ Γύλιππος - - - Λακεδαιμονίων ἀποστειλάντων ἄρχων: in the light of 20. 1 οἱ Ἀθηναῖοι - - - ναῦς τριάκοντα ἔστειλαν καὶ Χαρικλέα τὸν Ἀπολλοδώρου ἄρχοντα, we should be inclined to interpret ἄρχων, if this sentence were known to us only as an isolated citation, as 'commander of the ships'. But, as we have seen (vi. 91. 4 n.), the proposal made by Alkibiades to the Spartans was that they should send Gylippos not simply in command of a Spartan contingent but as commander-designate of the Syracusan forces, and the ambiguity of vi. 93. 2 (see note) is resolved in the light of that passage. Thucydides never tells us when the Syracusan envoys who were at Sparta in the winter of 415/14, at the time of Gylippos' appointment (vi. 88. 10, 93. 2), returned to Syracuse; nor does he tell us how the Syracusans received the news of the appointment or what decision they took about the status of Gylippos and his relations with their own generals, should he ever arrive. But the Syracusan envoys left Sparta after Gylippos had consulted them and had demanded ships from Corinth (vi. 93. 3), and it is reasonable to assume that they got back to Syracuse some time in the first half of 414, ahead of the Corinthian ships. The Syracusans did not behave as if they expected Peloponnesian help to materialize in time (cf. vi. 103. 3); nevertheless, they were able to contemplate the form which it was intended to take, so that although the arrival of Gylippos was a surprise to them, his role was not. Once they have joined forces with him (§ 3), he straightway acts as supreme commander (3. 1, 4, 4. 2, 5. 1–6. 2). He soon absented himself from Syracuse in order to raise forces elsewhere in Sicily (7. 2–21. 1), but on his return he seems to have resumed supreme command at least of the land forces (22. 1, 23. 1, 37. 2). He cannot order the Syracusans to fight a naval battle; that is a strategic decision which only the Syracusan assembly can take, and it is taken in consequence of 'persuasion' by both Gylippos and Hermokrates (21. 2–5). Whether or not Gylippos was in charge of the preparations for the first naval battle hangs upon the choice between variant readings (παρεσκευάσατο and παρεσκεύαστο) in 22. 1 (see note) which are codicologically and linguistically of comparable weight. As the Syracusans gained confidence in their fleet, and the combination of military and naval operations became increasingly important, the authority of Gylippos was diminished; Thucydides speaks of 'the Syracusans', without mention of Gylippos, as deciding when to attack and when not to (e.g. 33. 3, 52. 1). Before the final battle in the harbour it is 'the generals and Gylippos' (65. 3) who address the Syracusan and allied soldiers and sailors (cf. 69. 1). When Hermokrates wishes to block the Athenian lines of retreat immediately after the great battle in the harbour, he addresses his persuasive arguments to τοῖς ἐν τέλει οὖσιν: Gylippos is not mentioned in that chapter at all. The retreating Athenians are harried by 'the Syracusans and Gylippos' (74. 2, 82. 1, 83. 2), and throughout the retreat we have the impression that Gylippos has become little more than a member of a collegiate command; it is only when the Syracusans seek a scapegoat for their failure to trap the Athenians at Akraion Lepas that they treat Gylippos as supreme commander (81. 1). Nothing can be inferred from 85. 2 ὁ Γύλιππος - - - ζωγρεῖν ἤδη ἐκέλευεν, since κελεύειν can mean 'urge', or 'recommend'. To sum up: the Syracusans were prepared, by the time that Gylippos arrived, to accept a Spartan supreme commander of their land forces, and they did not at that time envisage naval operations. As their confidence and competence increased, although they never reached by debate a formal decision which went back on what they had previously accepted, it became less practicable every day for Gylippos to insist on exercising the authority which he had at first possessed. The situation is characteristically Greek; and that we have to reconstruct it by a series of inferences from widely separated passages, helped out on occasion by arguments *ex silentio*, is characteristic of Thucydidean studies. Cf. also 58. 3 n.

3. Ἰέτας τότε τι τεῖχος ἐν τῇ παρόδῳ τῶν Σικελῶν: the name is restored (the nearest approach to it in the MSS. is Ἰγέτας H⁸) from Philistos F 25, ap. Steph. Byz., who, however, gives neither a precise historical context nor a location; cf. the *Ietini* of Cic. *Verr.* II. iii. 103 and *Ιαιτινων* on coins (*HN²*, 148). Plu. *Timol.* 30. 6 describes 'the place called Hierai' (*sic* codd.; Ἰέται Dacier) as being 'in the ἐπικράτεια of the Carthaginians', which suggests a location further west than one would expect of a place passed en route from Himera to Syracuse, but there are too many unknown factors to justify the hypothesis of two places called Ietai: what Plutarch actually wrote, the validity of what may be only an inference on his part, the strictness of his terminology, and our ignorance of the location of Gylippos' rendezvous with the troops from Selinus.

ᾗπερ καὶ οἱ Ἀθηναῖοι τὸ πρῶτον: vi. 97. 2.

ἐχώρει μετὰ τῶν Συρακοσίων: cf. p. 473.

4. ἐν ᾧ - - - διπλοῦν τεῖχος: cf. p. 473.

τῷ δὲ ἄλλῳ τοῦ κύκλου: cf. p. 473.

3. 1. θέμενος τὰ ὅπλα ἐγγὺς κήρυκα προσπέμπει: ἐγγύς goes with the preceding words rather than with the following. AEFGHM have προπέμπει, but cf. vi. 6. 1 n.; in Ar. *Eq.* 473 προσπέμπων φίλους is metrically guaranteed.

3. οὐ ῥᾳδίως ξυντασσομένους: cf. vi. 98. 3.

ἐς τὴν εὐρυχωρίαν μᾶλλον: cf. p. 477.

ἐπὶ τὴν ἄκραν τὴν Τεμενῖτιν καλουμένην: cf. vi. 75. 1 and p. 472.

4. τὸ Λάβδαλον: cf. vi. 97. 5, 98. 2, and p. 474.

5. τῷ λιμένι: τῷ μεγάλῳ λιμένι BHψ. In vi. 50. 5 Thucydides refers to 'the harbours' of Syracuse; in vii. 22. 1 f. and 23. 2 he distinguishes between 'the great harbour'—the whole bay of which the mouth is the gap between Ortygia and Plemmyrion—and 'the lesser harbour', the location of τὸ νεώριον (cf. Diod. xiii. 8. 2, xiv. 7. 2), which must be the modern Porto Piccolo, lying between Ortygia and Santa Lucia and facing east. He refers to 'the great harbour' explicitly in vi. 50. 4, 65. 3 (cf. n.), 99. 4, 101. 1, 3, 102. 3, vii. 2. 4, 4. 4, 36. 3, 59. 3. 'The harbour' in 4. 4 (ἐκ μυχοῦ τοῦ λιμένος), 23. 3, 25. 5, 52. 2, 56. 1, 62. 1, 69. 4, 70. 1 f. is shown by the context in each case to mean the great harbour. If, therefore, Thucydides wrote simply τῷ λιμένι here, linguistic considerations would lead us to expect that he meant the great harbour, and that the Athenian ship lay outside its mouth; but 4. 4 (cf. n.) shows that it was the little harbour which the ship was far more likely to be watching.

4. 1. πρὸς τὸ * ἐγκάρσιον τεῖχος ἁπλοῦν: cf. p. 476.

3. ἔτυχον γὰρ ἔξω αὐλιζόμενοι: presumably not with their whole force, for that would be an eccentric way to defend fortifications against a night attack, but with pickets far enough advanced to give the main force time to come out of the fortifications and form up.

αὐτοὶ μὲν ταύτῃ ἐφύλασσον: they did not necessarily doubt the essential loyalty of their allies, but it does not need many traitors to betray a fortification at night.

4. πρὸς τῷ λιμένι τῷ τῶν Συρακοσίων: on the terms used by Thucydides to describe each of the two harbours at Syracuse cf. 3. 5 n. 'The harbour of the Syracusans' is a unique expression, and must mean the little harbour, for (a) that was entirely under Syracusan control, while the great harbour was dominated and in part occupied by the Athenians, and (b) Plemmyrion is a much better station than the Athenians' other fortified area for watching movement into and out of the little harbour, but less convenient for watching the Syracusan portion of the great harbour.

ἤν τι ναυτικῷ κινῶνται: either (i) 'if they (sc. the Athenians) were attacked by sea', or (ii) 'if they (sc. the Syracusans) made any move by sea'. Classen–Steup favour (i) in consequence of their deletion of τῷ τῶν Συρακοσίων, since the reference of the verb is then most naturally to the Athenians; but the deletion is not necessary, and κινεῖσθαι = 'move' (intr.) accords better with Thucydides' usage (and Classical prose usage in general) than κινεῖν = 'provoke'. Cf. viii. 100. 2 εἰ ἄρα ποι κινοῖντο αἱ νῆες and X. Cyr. i. 4. 20 ἢν ἐπὶ σὲ κινῶνται.

6. οὐχ ἥκιστα τότε πρῶτον: i.e. this was the beginning of the deterioration of the crews, and it was also a major cause of their deterioration.

καὶ ἐπὶ φρυγανισμὸν ἅμα ὁπότε ἐξέλθοιεν οἱ ναῦται: soldiers, too, need firewood; but the bulk of the army was on Epipolai, where good warning could be given of the approach of enemy cavalry and intervention was less profitable to the cavalry themselves.

διεφθείροντο: οἱ πολλοὶ διεφθείροντο B. It would make sense to say that the majority of any party which looked for firewood became casualties, but τῷ τε γὰρ ὕδατι σπανίῳ χρώμενοι, co-ordinated with καὶ ἐπί - - - ναῦται, also belongs with διεφθείροντο, and this makes οἱ πολλοί extravagant.

ἐπὶ τῇ ἐν τῷ Ὀλυμπιείῳ πολίχνῃ: cf. p. 480.

7. καὶ τὰς λοιπὰς τῶν Κορινθίων ναῦς: the 'other ships' of 2. 1, which had sailed from Leukas (vi. 104. 1).

5. 1. τὸ διὰ τῶν Ἐπιπολῶν τεῖχος: the wall begun in 4. 1.

2. μεταξὺ τῶν τειχισμάτων: cf. p. 477.

3. οὐκ ἔφη τὸ ἁμάρτημα ἐκείνων, ἀλλ' ἑαυτοῦ γενέσθαι: not all Spartan commanders were diplomats, but the best of them— Brasidas, Gylippos, and (on occasion, cf. X. *HG* ii. 1. 6) Lysander— were eminently successful in dealing with allies. Cf., however, 81. 1 n.

4. Πελοποννήσιοί τε ὄντες καὶ Δωριῆς Ἰώνων καὶ νησιωτῶν καὶ ξυγκλύδων ἀνθρώπων κρατήσαντες: cf. vi. 77. 1 n. on rhetorical use of the Dorian/Ionian antithesis. There, as here, 'islanders' is used contemptuously—not because it is contemptible to live on an island anywhere, but because the states of the Aegean islands ('the islands' and 'the islanders' *par excellence* in ordinary usage; cf. 20. 2 n., vi. 68. 2, v. 84. 1 n.) were conventionally despised by the Dorians of the Peloponnese and Dorian colonists. In ξυγκλύδων Gylippos turns against the Athenian forces the reproach which Alkibiades (vi. 17. 2) used against the Sikeliots.

6. 1. ἐπειδὴ καιρὸς ἦν: we see from 11. 2, as Plu. (*Nic.* 19. 7) also saw, that this was on the following day.

καὶ μηδὲ μάχεσθαι: 'and not to fight at all', cf. [Lys.] xx. 7 'they punish alike those who made a proposal and those who did not'; οὗτος δὲ οὐδὲ γνώμην οὐδεμίαν εἶπε. Denniston, 197 ff., is doubtful about this usage, and the reading of B, καὶ μηδὲ ἀμύνεσθαι, may be worth considering: 'it was going to be the same whether they won all their battles or did not even defend themselves against attack', but this is perhaps too rhetorical for the context—Nikias contemplated failure, but not destruction—and gives an abnormally restricted sense to ἀμύνεσθαι.

2. ἔξω τῶν τειχῶν μᾶλλον ἢ πρότερον - - - κατὰ τὴν εὐρυχωρίαν: cf. p. 477.

4. ἔφθασαν παροικοδομήσαντες καὶ παρελθόντες τὴν τῶν Ἀθηναίων οἰκοδομίαν: lit. 'building past and going past the building of the Athenians'. Steup's deletion of παροικοδομήσαντες as a gloss on παρελθόντες is most attractive, and καί must go with it as syntactical padding; cf. vi. 97. 1.

7. 1. αἱ ὑπόλοιποι δώδεκα: cf. vi. 104. 1 n.

Ἐρασινίδης: Θρασωνίδης B. Both are real names; neither is very common (though Θράσων is); there are no grounds for deciding between them.

μέχρι * τοῦ ἐγκαρσίου τείχους: cf. p. 476.

3. τρόπῳ ᾧ ἂν ἐν ὁλκάσιν ἢ πλοίοις ἢ ἄλλως ὅπως ἂν προχωρῇ: this text cannot stand. Either (a) read ὁπωσοῦν (Hude), or (b) delete ὅπως ἄν as an intrusive variant on τρόπῳ ᾧ ἄν (for which cf. IG xii (7). 67. 62 τρόπωι ὧι ἂν ἐπίστηται [Arkesine] and ii². 204. 22 f. τρόπωι ὅτωι ἂν [ἐπ]ίστω[ν]ται [Athens, 352/1]) and (preferably) move τρόπῳ ᾧ ἄν into its place, giving a layout of familiar type (e.g. vi. 34. 2, viii. 24. 6), emending ἄλλως to ἄλλῳ (H. Richards CQ vi [1912], 227). Thus: ἐν ὁλκάσιν ἢ πλοίοις ἢ ἄλλῳ τρόπῳ ᾧ ἂν προχωρῇ.

8. Nikias Writes a Letter

8. 2. ἢ καὶ μνήμης ἐλλιπεῖς γιγνόμενοι: ACEFGHM have γνώμης. These messengers were not required to express any 'judgement' of their own, and although it is a trivial matter to memorize in the tranquillity of a study all the points made in Nikias' letter, Nikias no doubt was aware that nothing is easier than to forget important points when faced with a critical audience. Moreover, although I see no adequate reason to doubt that Nikias really did write a letter, he certainly did not write what is presented to us here in characteristic Thucydidean idiom, and the real letter may have contained many more detailed facts and figures; cf. C. O. Zuretti, RF l (1922), 1 ff. It may seem surprising that Nikias could find no one in his force whom he could trust to put his views to the assembly with complete conviction, but perhaps he could; the whole point of his writing a letter was to disarm any suspicion on the part of the assembly that the messengers were misrepresenting him.

ἔγραψεν ἐπιστολήν: Thucydides makes it sound as if it were unusual for a general to write home, but there are certainly later examples (e.g. X. HG i. 7. 4, after Arginusai; i. 1. 23, Mindaros' second-in-command after Kyzikos) and one earlier (Kleon's letter from Pylos, if Eup. 308 was correctly interpreted in Hellenistic times [Luc. Laps. 3, etc.]), and Nikias' letter opens with the words (11. 1) 'you have been informed in many other ἐπιστολαί of what we have done so far'. It follows necessarily that by ἐπιστολή Thucydides means 'message' (cf. Hdt. iv. 10. 1, where it is used of verbal instructions, and possibly Cratin. 285, where the fact that it does not mean 'letter' is the reason for the inclusion of the citation in the lexicon of 'Zonaras'); it also follows that ἔγραψεν is emphatic: 'he composed a message in writing'. We would be justified in inferring that this was still a comparatively unusual procedure in 414.

οὕτως ἂν μάλιστα, κ.τ.λ.: BH₂ᵞᵖ have μόλις, not μάλιστα, giving the sense: 'even so' (cf. vi. 23. 1) 'it would be hard for the Athenians to learn his opinion'; but that does not sit happily with μηδὲν ἐν τῷ ἀγγέλῳ ἀφανισθεῖσαν.

3. καὶ ὅσα ἔδει αὐτοὺς εἰπεῖν: not necessarily additional data (cf.

§ 2 n.) but answers to possible questions. There is an element of zeugma in φέροντες, as in ἔχοντες in vi. 77. 1.

τὰ κατὰ τὸ στρατόπεδον διὰ φυλακῆς μᾶλλον ἤδη ἔχων ἢ δι' ἐκουσίων κινδύνων ἐπεμέλετο: since ἐπιμέλεσθαι takes a genitive, either (i) τὰ κατὰ τὸ στρατόπεδον is internal accusative, cf. X. HG v. 4. 4 τά τε ἄλλα ἐπεμελεῖτο τοῖς πολεμάρχοις, ἔχων being intransitive as in ii. 81. 4 τεταγμένοι - - - καὶ διὰ φυλακῆς ἔχοντες, or (ii) τὰ κατὰ τὸ στρατόπεδον is the object of ἔχων, cf. ii. 37. 2 οὐ δι' ὀργῆς τὸν πέλας - - - ἔχοντες and Dio's imitation (xlvii. 36. 2) of our present passage, διὰ φυλακῆς μᾶλλον ἢ διὰ κινδύνων τὸ στρατόπεδον ἐποιοῦντο, or (iii) τά should be omitted, as in BM, sc. αὐτοῦ with ἐπεμέλετο.

9. Operations in Thrace

9. Εὐετίων: otherwise unknown in literature, but Meritt (AFD 86 ff.) suggests in the accounts of the Treasurers of Athena for 414/13, IG i². 297 (cf. SEG x. 229). 2 f. the restoration ho[ῖς Πο|λυμέδēς Ἀτενεὺς ἐγραμμάτευε παρέδομεν στρατēγοῖς ἐς τὰ ἐπὶ Θράικēς Εὐετίōνι Μελ]ēσ[ά]-νδρ[ο . .]||, the number of letters in the line being calculable from the inscription on the reverse side of the stele and the name and demotic of the secretary to the Treasurers being known from IG i². 248. A general Melesandros was killed in Lykia in 430/29 (ii. 69. 1 f.).

μετὰ Περδίκκου: when we last heard of Perdikkas (early in 415, vi. 7. 3 f.) his territory was under Athenian attack; it is never a surprise to find that he has changed sides, but slightly surprising that Thucydides does not in this case tell us when or why he did so.

ἐπ' Ἀμφίπολιν: cf. vi. 7. 4 n.

Θρᾳξὶ πολλοῖς: this has little bearing on the foreign policy of the Odrysian king or any other Thracian potentate, for these Thracians, like others who fought for Athens (27. 1, v. 6. 2 ff.), were presumably mercenaries.

ἐξ Ἱμεραίου: this place never appears in the tribute lists, and its location is unknown.

10–15. The Letter of Nikias

Not even Gylippos' victory and the decisive progress of the counter-wall (6. 3 f.), the sufferings of the crews based on Plemmyrion (4. 6), or the description (8. 1) of Nikias' apprehensions prepare the reader fully for the tone of hopelessness which pervades this letter. Nikias apparently envisages no action of his own by which he might recover the initiative or even arrest the deterioration of his own position; he can only wait for reinforcement, recall, or retreat (14. 3; he does not at this stage envisage disaster). In Greek wars, as in Greek battles, the tide often turns with overwhelming suddenness;

2. 1–6. 4 relate the sequence of events through which the Syracusans were rapidly raised from despair to victory, without adequate explanation of the Athenians' deterioration. Possibly there was widespread illness among them (on which Thucydides remarks in 47. 2), but the fundamental cause was that when Gylippos was added to the one side Lamachos had been subtracted from the other. Nikias, left alone in command, had too little confidence in the practicability of defeating Syracuse (though his faith revived [48] when it seemed desirable to prevent positive action on the part of others), he had a chronic illness (15. 1, cf. vi. 102. 2), and he was temperamentally inclined to blame anyone and anything except himself (13. 2, 14. 2, 4, 15. 1 f.). Nothing can destroy an army's initiative more rapidly than the knowledge that its experienced and trusted commander accepts failure as inevitable.

10. ὁ δὲ γραμματεὺς ὁ τῆς πόλεως: in the fourth century there was a secretary whose sole business was to read documents aloud (Ἀθ. π. 54. 5); this official is presumably the man called γραμματεὺς τῷ δήμῳ in IG ii². 223A. 10 (343/2), al.; the office of the secretary who reads out Nikias' letter must be the same, since the secretary to the prytaneis is always called γραμματεὺς τῇ βουλῇ or γραμματεὺς τῆς βουλῆς in fifth-century documents and γραμματεὺς κατὰ πρυτάνειαν in the fourth century. Cf. Busolt–Swoboda, ii. 1043 f.

11. 1. ἐν ἄλλαις πολλαῖς ἐπιστολαῖς: cf. 8. 2 n.
2. Συρακοσίους ἐφ᾽ οὓς ἐπέμφθημεν: contrast vi. 47, where Nikias' view was that Selinus, not Syracuse, was the primary objective; in conferring with his fellow generals Nikias found it safe to ignore half the formal instructions given to the expedition and the whole of its real purpose, but he could not do that in a letter to the assembly.
3. τοῦ περιτειχισμοῦ: cf. vi. 101. 1 n.
οὐδὲ γὰρ ξυμπάσῃ τῇ στρατιᾷ δυναίμεθ᾽ ἂν χρήσασθαι: οὐδέ appears to rebut the imagined objection, 'why can't you use your force concentrated?'; hence 'for it is not as if . . .'. Cf. [Lys.] vi. 6 'what will people think when they come to Eleusis and see who the king-archon is and remember his crimes?' οὐδὲ γὰρ ἀγνὼς ὁ Ἀνδοκίδης, κ.τ.λ.
4. οὐδὲ γὰρ τῆς χώρας ἐπὶ πολύ - - - ἐξερχόμεθα: the point of οὐδέ here is: 'our offensive fortifications have come to nothing, and we do not have control of the open country *either.*'

12. 2. ὡς ἐγὼ πυνθάνομαι: not only by inference from their training (§ 5); even later in the summer Nikias is in communication with treacherous elements inside Syracuse (48. 2).
3. ὅπερ κἀκεῖνοι πυνθάνονται: the Syracusans too were not confined to observation and deductions from experience; the rate of desertion

described in 13. 2 would have kept them well informed on conditions in the Athenian force.

αἴ τε νῆες διάβροχοι: 'saturated', and so heavier in the water (cf. Hp. *Aer*. 10, where the earth is διάβροχος with rain); triremes were normally hauled on to the shore and 'aired' when the situation permitted (§§ 4 f.); cf. Hdt. vii. 59. 3 (Xerxes at Doriskos) and X. *HG* i. 5. 10 (Lysander at Ephesos).

4. ἀντιπάλους τῷ πλήθει: there was no good reason yet for Nikias to say that the Syracusan navy was the equal of the Athenian in quality. τῷ τε in B (τῷ Hψ: καὶ τῷ cett.) may point to τῷ γε (Bodin).

13. 2. τῶν ναυτῶν [τῶν] μέν - - - ἀπολλυμένων: with the MSS.' text, θεράποντες are a subdivision of ναῦται, as they are in *IG* ii². 1951 (s. iv in.), which distinguishes them from ναῦται ἀστοί and lists at least 59 of them on one ship (lines 117–84). The Kerkyreans used slaves as rowers in 433 (i. 55. 1), but their use at Athens is not attested before 406/5 (X. *HG* i. 6. 24), and the enfranchisement of the slaves who fought in that year suggests that the measure was new and exceptional (Ar. *Ra*. 693 f., Hellanikos 4 F 171 = 323 a F 25). When the Athenians needed extra crews in 428 they found them from the hoplite class and the metics (iii. 16. 1), not by enrolling slaves; cf. Amit, 31 ff., especially 34, on the inaccurate rhetoric of Isoc. viii. 48. The fact that Thucydides specially mentions that the crew of the *Paralos* were free men (viii. 73. 5) is explicable partly on the grounds that he is writing for a panhellenic audience—and states differed in the extent to which they used slaves as rowers (cf. i. 55. 1, viii. 15. 2, 84. 2)—but principally because he wants to emphasize that they were citizens, with strong democratic sentiments; Ἀθηναίους τε καὶ ἐλευθέρους is virtually a single epithet. [X.] *Resp. Ath*. i. 11 ὅπου γὰρ ναυτικὴ δύναμίς ἐστιν, ἀπὸ χρημάτων ἀνάγκη τοῖς ἀνδραπόδοις δουλεύειν, ἵνα λαμβάνωμεν ὧν πράττῃ τὰς ἀποφοράς, καὶ ἐλευθέρους ἀφεῖναι refers to manual work on the building and repair of ships (K. I. Gelzer, *Hermes Einzelschriften* iii [1937], 117 f.). Poppo's deletion of the second τῶν is therefore inescapable on historical grounds, and desirable also linguistically; for if ναῦται = πλήρωμα, the emphatic position of τῶν ναυτῶν is curious, whereas if the casualties to the ναῦται and the defection of the θεράποντες are two different aspects of the deterioration of the πληρώματα the position of τῶν ναυτῶν is intelligible. We should then punctuate strongly after αὐτομολοῦσι, so that καὶ οἱ ξένοι, κ.τ.λ. makes a fresh point. Naturally ξένοι among the crews would suffer from Syracusan cavalry attacks just as much as the Athenian sailors, and so would slaves, but Thucydides is concerned with the special causes of loss in each category.

ἀναγκαστοί: not 'press-ganged' as individuals, but supplied as contingents by subject-allies on demand from Athens; cf. 58. 3 n.

εὐθὺς κατὰ τὰς πόλεις ἀποχωροῦσιν: εὐθύς = 'as soon as they can', 'without more ado', contrasted with the more leisurely defection of the volunteers. Cf. X. *Hiero* 2. 8 εὐθὺς γὰρ ('whenever they like') τοῖς μὲν ἰδιώταις - - - ἔξεστιν ὅποι ἂν βούλωνται πορεύεσθαι - - - οἱ δὲ τύραννοι πάντες πανταχῇ ὡς διὰ πολεμίας πορεύονται. ἀπεχώρουν in H is a correction designed to give εὐθύς a banal meaning, 'at once' (sc. when we arrived in Sicily).

καὶ οἰόμενοι χρηματιεῖσθαι μᾶλλον ἢ μαχεῖσθαι: cf. vi. 31. 5.

οἱ μὲν ἐπ' αὐτομολίας προφάσει ἀπέρχονται: no wholly satisfactory explanation of these words has yet been offered. Their prima facie meaning is 'giving desertion as a pretext'; cf. iv. 80. 2, iii. 86. 4, vi. 78. 1, and D. xxiv. 26, examples which cumulatively outweigh Weidauer's argument (16 f.) that the πρόφασις is the objective reason given by Nikias, not the excuse offered by the deserters. The antithesis is ὡς ἕκαστοι δύνανται, to which Thucydides adds 'and Sicily is large', implying (as we would expect from the usage of the word elsewhere) that αὐτομολία is desertion to Syracuse, while the other categories of defection are not necessarily to Syracuse. If the text is sound, it must be equivalent to οἱ μὲν ἐπ' αὐτομολίᾳ ἀπέρχονται, οἱ δὲ ἐφ' ᾗτινι ἂν προφάσει ἕκαστοι δύνωνται = 'some deserting to the enemy and others on a variety of pretexts'. This interpretation is essentially that of L. Pearson, *TAPhA* lxxxiii (1952), 215, and although it is obscure I do not think it impossible. 'Claiming to be deserters (sc. when they arrive at Syracuse)', suggested by Grote, vi. 111 n. 1, does not quite suit the context, where interest is naturally focused on means of escaping from the Athenian force and not on means of making one's way through Sicily. 'On pretence of being deserting slaves' (Gomme, ms.) will not do, for a man who has declared himself a slave and cannot assert that he is a free man without revealing that he is also an enemy is in an unenviable plight; and 'on the pretext of looking for slaves who have deserted' (H. Richards, *CQ* viii [1914], 79) overlooks the fact that a proposal to seek a slave in enemy territory is an unconvincing excuse for leaving camp. 'With a *pretext* for desertion', as opposed to having no pretexts at all (Haacke and Arnold), makes its antithetical point inadequately and really renders the word αὐτομολίας unnecessary. Numerous emendations have been proposed, of the type which presupposes the kind of corruption exemplified by ναυμαχία > ξυμμαχία (34. 8); the two most respectable are αὐτονομίας (Passow), 'giving as their reason the fact that they are not subjects of ours' (sc. and therefore cannot be kept against their will), in which case the other categories who disappear ὡς ἕκαστοι δύνανται must be supposed to be mainly subjects, and αὐτουργίας (Schwartz, 344). A different type of emendation is represented by ἐπ' αὐτομολίᾳ προφανεῖ (J. A. FitzHerbert, *Mnemosyne* 1924, 412), a somewhat inappropriate oxymoron.

ἀνδράποδα 'Υκκαρικά: cf. vi. 62. 4.

τὴν ἀκρίβειαν τοῦ ναυτικοῦ: almost 'the high quality of the fleet'; cf. vi. 18. 6 τό τε φαῦλον - - - καὶ τὸ πάνυ ἀκριβές.

14.1. βραχεῖα ἀκμὴ πληρώματος: most naturally taken in a temporal sense: 'a crew's period of maximum efficiency is short'; cf. 12. 3 and 63. 4. In viii. 46. 5 καὶ ναυμαχεῖν οὐκ εἴα, ἀλλὰ καὶ τὰς Φοινίσσας φάσκων ναῦς ἥξειν καὶ ἐκ περιόντος ἀγωνιεῖσθαι ἔφθειρε τὰ πράγματα καὶ τὴν ἀκμὴν τοῦ ναυτικοῦ αὐτῶν ἀφείλετο γενομένην καὶ πάνυ ἰσχυράν and in Plutarch's imitation (Caes. 40. 2) ἠξίου τρίβειν καὶ μαραίνειν τὴν τῶν πολεμίων ἀκμὴν βραχεῖαν οὖσαν the point is the effect of delay. Nikias' sequence of thought is (i) at first our fleet was highly efficient (ἤκμαζε 12. 3), (ii) but our ships are saturated and cannot be dried out (12. 3–13. 1), (iii) and we have lost many sailors (13. 2), (iv) therefore we have lost ἡ ἀκρίβεια τοῦ ναυτικοῦ (this consequence of the loss of men in general is attached to the type of loss last specified), (v) and you know that (a) (sc. in any case) a crew is not at its highest efficiency for long, and we have been at Syracuse a long time, and (b) few sailors are really skilful (sc. therefore all the factors in the situation have aggravated and accelerated a process which it is necessarily hard to avoid). If we complain of logical incoherence between (v) (a) and the rest of the argument, and so translate 'the efficient element in a crew is small' (Haacke, cf. βραχύ in iv. 106. 1 and viii. 83. 3), we attribute to Thucydides a degree of tautology of which, even in the speeches, he is elsewhere innocent, and we set too high a logical standard (cf. § 2 below).

ξυνέχοντες τὴν εἰρεσίαν: 'rowing *together*', the one thing upon which the efficient movement of any oared vessel depends.

2. χαλεπαὶ γὰρ αἱ ὑμέτεραι φύσεις ἄρξαι: this appears to have no bearing on the difficulties of the situation as Nikias has described them: the exacting blockade of a naval power, enemy superiority in cavalry, and the desertion of foreigners. It is, however, a theme prominent in Nikias' mind (cf. § 4 below, 48. 4, Bender, 46, and Weidauer, 33), and it was perhaps his habit to suggest that he could have dealt with all difficulties if only he could have relied more on his troops. Greek troops were by modern standards temperamental and recalcitrant, but the Athenians were not necessarily worse than others (cf. 73. 2 and vi. 69. 1).

ἀλλ' ἀνάγκη ἀφ' ὧν ἔχοντες ἤλθομεν τά τε ὄντα καὶ ἀπαναλισκόμενα γίγνεσθαι: lit., 'what we have and what we expend must all come from what we brought with us', i.e. 'what we expend is expended from what we brought with us, and what we have is simply what is left of that.' Given ἐπιπληρωσόμεθα τὰς ναῦς and the fact (§ 3) that supplies are replenished locally, the reference must be to crews, despite the neuter gender; probably Thucydides has the neuter πληρώματα in mind.

3. τὰ τρέφοντα ἡμᾶς χωρία τῆς 'Ιταλίας: we hear nothing of this apart from the ships and timber mentioned in 25. 1 f.

4. βουλομένων μὲν τὰ ἥδιστα ἀκούειν, αἰτιωμένων δὲ ὕστερον: the commonplace contrast between telling an audience the unwelcome truth and telling it what it wishes to hear; cf. ii. 65. 8, vi. 83. 3, and Aeschin. iii. 127 τἀληθὲς ἐρῶ· τὸ γὰρ ἀεὶ πρὸς ἡδονὴν λεγόμενον οὑτωσὶ τὴν πόλιν διατέθηκεν.

ἀπ' αὐτῶν: 'after that' (sc. τῶν ἡδίστων), with the nuance of causal connection which 'after' sometimes has.

15. 1. οὕτω τὴν γνώμην ἔχετε: the implication is: 'don't waste time on criticism; take it for granted that all that could be done has been done, and what must now be done is something fresh.' μὴ μεμπτῶν is a high compliment; cf. X. Cyr. ii. 1. 11 σώματα μὲν ἔχοντες ἀνδρῶν ἥκετε οὐ μεμπτά.

μηδὲ τοῖς παροῦσιν ἀνταρκούντων: the mention of ἄλλη στρατιά and the analogy of the expressions τοῖς παροῦσι βοηθοῦντας (i. 123. 1), τοῖς παροῦσιν ἔπεσθαι (vi. 89. 4) and πρὸς τὰ παρόντα ἐβουλεύοντο (vi. 46. 5) suggest that the meaning is not 'unable to hold out against' (sc. the enemy, cf. Ar. Eq. 540) 'even with our existing resources (sc. let alone after further losses)' but 'unable to cope even with the existing situation (sc. let alone with a reinforced enemy)', ἀνταρκεῖν being used c. dat. like ἀντέχειν and ἀνθίστασθαι.

2. ὡς τῶν πολεμίων, κ.τ.λ.: with σχολαίτερον μέν understand ποριοῦνται, and with λήσουσιν and φθήσονται understand ποριζόμενοι. For the co-ordination of a participial μέν-clause with a finite δέ-clause cf. vi. 69. 1 (τῇ μὲν ἀνδρείᾳ, κ.τ.λ.). Nikias' reproach, referring to the Athenian failure to prevent the assembly of Gylippos' little fleet at Leukas, is singularly unfair in view of his own delay which allowed Gylippos to cross from Rhegion to Messene (1. 2 and vi. 104. 3) and his inability to stop the Corinthian ships which followed (7. 1).

16–18. *Preparations in Greece*

16. 1. τὸν μὲν Νικίαν οὐ παρέλυσαν τῆς ἀρχῆς: cf. vi. 17. 1 n.

Μένανδρον καὶ Εὐθύδημον: if the annual election of generals was held in the fifth century, as it was in the fourth, after Prytany VI (Ἀθ. π. 44. 4), the appointment of Menandros and Euthydemos cannot have been made at an ordinary election, for we are not yet at the winter solstice (16. 2) and a conciliar year beginning before the end of May is irreconcilable with any possible reconstruction of the calendar; but this creates no real difficulty. The Athenians could give temporary and local military command to anybody; Kleon's appointment to command at Pylos in 425 (iv. 28 ff.) did not mean that Nikias or any other of the ten generals resigned his office (cf. iv. 42. 1) or that the board of generals in 425/4 was regarded as having eleven members. X. *HG* ii. 1. 16, where we are told that the Athenians in 405/4 elected three generals 'in addition' (προσ-) but are not told that they relieved anyone else of his command, is obscure; ibid. i. 7. 1 implies that only three appointments had been made to replace the eight generals deposed after Arginusai. Apollodoros of Kyzikos, Phanosthenes of Andros, and Herakleides of Klazomenai, mentioned in Pl. *Ion* 541 c–d as examples of foreigners appointed to command Athenians, were no doubt στρατηγοί in the generic, not the specific, sense. After the arrival of Demosthenes and Eurymedon in Sicily, there were three 'full' generals at Syracuse and the association of Menandros and Euthydemos with them in command seems to have been a matter for their discretion. In the night attack on Epipolai Menandros commanded the attacking force with Demosthenes and Eurymedon (43. 2), but there is no mention of Euthydemos. Neither seems to have been asked for his opinion in the debate which followed the failure on Epipolai (47 ff., esp. 49. 3 f.). In the last battle in the harbour, Eurymedon being by then dead, Demosthenes and Menandros and Euthydemos ἐπὶ τὰς ναῦς τῶν Ἀθηναίων στρατηγοὶ ἐπέβησαν (69. 4).

Euthydemos is likely to be the man of that name who was among the takers of the oath of peace in 421 (v. 19. 2)—probably a general then (Andrewes and Lewis, *JHS* lxxvii [1957], 180)—and also the Euthydemos, son of Eudemos, who was a general in 418/17 (*IG* i². 302 [= ML 77]. 9); we hear nothing of him on the retreat from Syracuse or afterwards, and he may have been killed in the last battle in the harbour. Menandros is probably the general of 405/4 (X. *HG* ii. 1. 16); it is not known whether he escaped at Aigospotamoi, died in the battle, or was executed by Lysander (ibid. ii. 1. 30 f.).

ἐκ καταλόγου: cf. vi. 26. 2 n.

2. Δημοσθένη τε τὸν Ἀλκισθένους καὶ Εὐρυμέδοντα τὸν Θουκλέους: the choice seems a wise one. Demosthenes is last known to have held command in 418/17 (v. 80. 3). He appears in Thucydides' narrative as a quick and energetic general (iv. 8. 3, 9, 29. 2), aggressive, ingenious, and original (iii. 95. 1, 112. 3 f.)—and inevitably rash on occasion (iii. 97. 2)—with a good tactical eye (iv. 3. 2 f.) and capable of learning from experience (iv. 30. 1). It is uncertain how far we should assign to him the credit for the conception of the Athenian attack on Boeotia in 424 (iv. 76 f.) or the blame for its failure (iv. 89). He had won the good opinion of Athens' allies in the north-west (vii. 57. 10) and, rather strikingly, of both Kleon (iv. 29. 1) and Aristophanes (*Eq.* 54 ff.). On his arrival in Sicily he is brisk and forceful and his solutions are drastic (vii. 42. 3 ff.); but once the situation has become desperate he has little positive contribution to make, and on the final retreat he acquits himself less well than Nikias.

Eurymedon had experience of Sicily, though he was fined on his return thence in 424 (iv. 65. 3) and may have been out of favour since. This last point has some bearing on the question whether Demosthenes and Eurymedon were generals for 414/13, and appointed now to Sicily on the assumption that only some flagrant inadequacy on their part could prevent their re-election for 413/12, or pre-elected for 413/12 and given immediate authority to assemble the forces voted; and it tells in favour of the latter alternative. In that case the generals at the winter solstice of 414/13 comprised (i) nine generals—including Nikias—elected for 414/13, (ii) possibly a tenth, a general-suffect, elected after the death of Lamachos, (iii) Menandros and Euthydemos, given 'local' rank in Sicily, (iv) Demosthenes and Eurymedon as generals-designate. In a matter of such practical importance it is safer not to give too much weight to constitutional procedure.

εἴκοσι ⟨καὶ ἑκατὸν⟩ τάλαντα: H alone has καὶ ἑκατόν, but is supported by Valla (centum viginti), Diod. xiii. 8. 7 (ἑκατὸν τεσσαράκοντα), and probability; twenty talents would not have gone very far.

17. 2. περὶ τὴν Πελοπόννησον - - - εἴκοσι ναῦς: since (a) the purpose of this contingent, to prevent the sending of troops from the Peloponnese to Sicily, is attributed in § 4 to τὴν ἐν τῇ Ναυπάκτῳ φυλακήν, (b) when the force at Naupaktos is next mentioned (19. 5) it consists of twenty ships, (c) the Corinthian ships which assembled at Leukas (vi. 104. 1) do not seem to have been worried about Athenian interception, and (d) no other action 'around the Peloponnese' is attributed to the contingent now dispatched, Naupaktos must be its destination and Konon its commander (cf. 31. 4); it also follows that no standing force had been maintained there.

4. πρὸς τὴν ἐν τῇ Ναυπάκτῳ φυλακήν: cf. § 2 n. above.

18. 1. ὥσπερ τε προυδέδοκτο αὐτοῖς: cf. vi. 93. 2 n. on the Spartan delay. One consideration on which Thucydides is silent here—but his Alkibiades is not (vi. 90. 2 ff.), and cf. viii. 2—is the revival in Sparta of the old fears of the Athenian domination which would result from an Athenian victory in Sicily (cf. Andrewes, CQ N.S. ix [1959], 230). Perhaps the Spartans were not decisively convinced by the picture which Alkibiades painted, but the prospect of the arrival of very large Athenian reinforcements in Sicily now made the whole question more urgent and impelled them to execute the plan which they had formulated.

ὅπως δὴ ἐσβολῆς γενομένης διακωλυθῇ: the total number of Athenian hoplites sent to Sicily was not large, and their absence from Attica would not increase the Spartans' chances of capturing the Long Walls; and Spartan chances of provoking the Athenians to a full-scale battle on land were actually diminished. It was the absence of ships which mattered. With most of her ships away, Athens could not inflict reprisals on the Peloponnese which would console her for the losses she was suffering in Attica or seriously deter the Peloponnesians; recognizing this—as the Peloponnesians thought— she might hesitate to denude herself by sending reinforcements to Sicily.

ἐδίδασκε τὴν Δεκέλειαν τειχίζειν: cf. vi. 93. 2 n.

2. ἐγεγένητό τις ῥώμη: here, as in 42. 2; the 'confidence' which results from favourable developments, not the '(sc. material) strength' which may be part of such developments. Cf. vi. 31. 1 n.

ἐν γὰρ τῷ προτέρῳ πολέμῳ: 'in the previous fighting'; the expression does not reflect any weakening in Thucydides' 'one war' view. Cf. 28. 3 and de Romilly, *Imp.*, 189 n. 1.

σφέτερον τὸ παρανόμημα μᾶλλον γενέσθαι: the Theban attack on Plataia in 431 was not initiated by Sparta or by any decision of the Peloponnesian League, but by having Thebes as an ally Sparta shared her guilt.

αὐτοὶ οὐχ ὑπήκουον ἐς δίκας προκαλουμένων τῶν Ἀθηναίων: Sparta did indeed send envoys to Athens ἐγκλήματα ποιούμενοι (i. 126. 1) at the end of 432; but according to Thucydides' account this was done not in order to open the way to arbitration, as Archidamos had proposed (i. 82. 1, 85. 2), but after the decision to fight had already been taken (86 f., 125), and it was done in a manner designed to provoke refusal (139. 1, 140. 2, cf. 144. 2) and in the hope of gaining a moral advantage from that refusal (126. 1).

εἰκότως δυστυχεῖν: the belief that the gods punish the breaking of oaths is one of the oldest and firmest in Greek theology. The parties to an international agreement swore oaths that they would keep it; if they broke it, they must expect divine punishment. Since Thucydides was at least unconventional in theology, and may well have been an atheist, his matter-of-fact statements about the religious motivation of states must be taken seriously. The Spartans were not the only people to interpret misfortune as a sign of divine displeasure; in 421 the Athenians restored the population to Delos ἐνθυμούμενοι τάς τε ἐν ταῖς μάχαις ξυμφορὰς καὶ τοῦ ἐν Δελφοῖς θεοῦ χρήσαντος (v. 32. 1). Cf. 77. 2 ff. and Popp, 11 ff.

3. ταῖς τριάκοντα ναυσὶν ἐξ Ἄργους ὁρμώμενοι: vi. 105.

ἐληστεύοντο: ἐλῄστευον B: the passive is *lectio difficilior*, sc. οἱ Λακεδαιμόνιοι, but cf. vi. 18. 6 n. on change of subject.

ἐς δίκας προκαλουμένων τῶν Λακεδαιμονίων οὐκ ἤθελον ἐπιτρέπειν: we have heard nothing of this in book v in connection with the disputes arising from the peace treaty (cf. vi. 10. 2 n.), and the Spartan 'summons' is perhaps to be dated later than the events of vi. 104.

4. σίδηρόν τε - - - καὶ τἆλλα ἐργαλεῖα: iron for the clamps and dowels which would hold the masonry of the fort, and 'the (sc. necessary) tools also' for cutting the blocks and building the walls. προσηνάγκαζον: allies who had sworn to 'follow where Sparta led' could naturally be treated as under an obligation to provide material for a military project which Sparta proposed to lead; cf. ἀναγκαστός in 13. 2 and 58. 3 and προσαναγκάζειν of a commander's exercise of authority over those liable for military service (vi. 72. 4, 91. 4).

YEAR 19: 413–412 B.C. (CC. 19–viii. 6)

19–20. Operations in Greece

19. 1. ἡγεῖτο δὲ ῏Αγις ὁ Ἀρχιδάμου: according to Diod. xiii. 9. 2 (contra, Plu. Alc. 23. 7) Alkibiades came with Agis on this occasion. If this is true, and if there is any historical foundation for Satyros' remarks (ap. Ath. 534 b) on Alkibiades' adaptability in Thebes and Thessaly (cf. vi. 92. 5 n.), this may be the occasion on which Alkibiades visited those places, acting as an ambassador for Agis; so H. D. Westlake, JHS lviii (1938), 31 ff., but cf. Hatzfeld, 214 n. 1.

2. ἀπέχει δὲ ἡ Δεκέλεια - - - καὶ ἀπὸ τῆς Βοιωτίας: Dekeleia is 18 km. from Athens by the shortest route, so that 150 m. is the value of the stade implied here (cf. pp. 467 f.). On the other hand, from Dekeleia across Parnes to the edge of the Boeotian plain is less, 9–10 km. Thucydides is speaking, presumably, of the main route via Oropos (which was Athenian until the end of 412, cf. viii. 60. 1), not of the isolated traveller, much less of the crow's flight.

ἐπιφανὲς μέχρι τῆς τῶν Ἀθηναίων πόλεως: X. HG i. 1. 35 describes how later in the war Agis, standing at Dekeleia, could see the corn-ships coming into Peiraieus.

3. τῶν τε Εἱλώτων - - - καὶ τῶν νεοδαμώδων: the Βρασίδειοι con-stituted a precedent for the dispatch of a Helot force without any Spartan ingredient except its commander (iv. 80. 5, v. 34. 1, 67. 1). On νεοδαμώδεις cf. v. 34. 1 n.

καὶ Ἡγήσανδρος Θεσπιεύς: the elements in Thespiai unfriendly to Thebes had been disposed of after their premature rising in the spring of 414 (vi. 95. 2).

4. τοὺς δὲ προσμισθωσάμενοι Ἀρκάδων: thus there were Arkadians on both sides; cf. 57. 9.

Σικυώνιοι: cf. 58. 3. Sikyon had evidently been of doubtful loyalty to Sparta at the time of the Mantineia campaign, for Sparta inter-vened in the winter of 418/17 and established a stronger oligarchy (v. 81. 2).

5. αἱ τοῦ χειμῶνος πληρωθεῖσαι: cf. 17. 4.

20. 1. περί τε Πελοπόννησον: co-ordinated (τε B solus) with § 2 καὶ τὸν Δημοσθένη, κ.τ.λ.

Χαρικλέα τὸν Ἀπολλοδώρου: it is reasonable, though not inevitable, to identify him with the notorious Charikles (of tribe VI, assuming that the list in X. *HG* ii. 3. 2 is in tribal order) who later became so powerful a member of the Thirty (cf. X. *Mem.* i. 2. 31, And. i. 101) but in 415 was, with Peisander, a ζητητής and εὐνούστατος τῷ δήμῳ (And. i. 36).

2. ἑξήκοντα μὲν ναυσίν, κ.τ.λ.: cf. vii. 42. 1 for the total accumulated by the time Demosthenes arrives in Sicily. In Diod. xiii. 9. 2 the Athenians vote for sending eighty triremes and 5,000 hoplites, and Demosthenes arrives (11. 2) with 'more than eighty ships'.

καὶ νησιωτῶν: cf. 5. 3 and 82. 1; in the latter passage it is implied that the majority of the allied troops under Athenian command are islanders (vi. 68. 2 is also relevant). Presumably the Aegean islands, having no land frontiers to defend and carrying in some cases a population larger than they could support, had become the handiest and most abundant source both of sailors and of troops.

εἴ ποθέν τι εἶχον ἐπιτήδειον ἐς τὸν πόλεμον: sc. ξυμπορίζειν.

21–25. *The Fall of Plemmyrion*

21. 1. ἄγων - - - στρατιάν: cf. 7. 2.

3. ὁ Ἑρμοκράτης: it is not clear whether he had now been reinstated in any military office (cf. vi. 103. 4); the way in which his actions are related in c. 73 suggests that he had not, but at any rate his influence is now of some weight.

τοῦ ταῖς ναυσὶ μὴ ἀθυμεῖν ἐπιχειρῆσαι πρὸς τοὺς Ἀθηναίους: if this text is right (τοῦ om. GM) τοῦ - - - μή appears to have a final sense: 'Hermokrates joined Gylippos in urging them (sc. to attempt a naval battle) in order that they might not despair of attacking the Athenians at sea'. This is a little inappropriate; we would expect rather 'persuaded them not to despair'; and it is possible that τοῦ - - - μή does not in fact have a final sense. In Lys. viii. 17 ᾤμην γὰρ ἀπόθετος ὑμῖν εἶναι φίλος, τοῦ μηδὲν ἀκοῦσαι κακὸν δι' αὐτὸ τοῦτο, διότι πρὸς ἐμὲ τοὺς ἄλλους ἐλέγετε κακῶς, τοῦ virtually = ὥστε and the final sense is negligible; cf. Th. viii. 39. 4 ἀγγελίαν ἔπεμπον ἐπὶ τάς - - - ναῦς τοῦ ξυμπαρακομισθῆναι (where B has χάριν after ναῦς). ἀθυμεῖν is constructed with an infinitive on the analogy of φοβεῖσθαι. Herbst's explanation (ii. 115 ff.) that μὴ ἀθυμεῖν here takes a genitive on the analogy of ἐπιθυμεῖν is less attractive. For πρός with ἐπιχειρεῖν instead of the usual dative cf. the equally rare ἐπί in Pl. *Mx.* 241 d ὡς ἐπιχειρήσων πάλιν ἐπὶ τοὺς Ἕλληνας.

χαλεπωτάτους ἂν [αὐτοῖς] φαίνεσθαι: if πρὸς ἄνδρας τολμηρούς is taken closely with ἀντιτολμῶντας, αὐτοῖς with χαλεπωτάτους φαίνεσθαι is

neither ungrammatical nor tautological. Cf. vi. 82. 2 and X. *Cyr.*
ii. 3. 4 τοῖς μὴ θέλουσιν ἑαυτοῖς προστάττειν ἐκπονεῖν τἀγαθὰ ἄλλους
αὐτοῖς ἐπιτακτῆρας δίδωσι (sc. ὁ θεός).

καὶ σφᾶς ἂν τὸ αὐτὸ ὁμοίως τοῖς ἐναντίοις ὑποσχεῖν: τὸ αὐτό refers
to 'that by which the Athenians frighten their enemies', which is
explained as 'daring' (LSJ s.v. ὑπέχειν I. 2 is badly astray), and
θάρσος ὑποσχεῖν τοῖς ἐναντίοις would be lit. 'hold daring under the
enemy', hence 'show a bold face to their enemies', 'confront their
enemies with boldness'. I know no exact parallel; certainly Pi. *O.*
2. 54 πλοῦτος - - - βαθεῖαν ὑπέχων μέριμναν ἀγροτέραν is not one.
ὑπάρχειν (Hᵃᶜ) in respect of meaning suits the context much better
since its participles are used absolutely of aggression or initiative;
cf. Pl. *Grg.* 456 e ἀμυνομένους, μὴ ὑπάρχοντας and D. xix. 280 διὰ τὰς
εὐεργεσίας ἃς ὑπῆρξαν εἰς ὑμᾶς. It is not found with an accusative
object before the late fourth century; yet the passive occurs with
a neuter pronoun as subject (with reference to help or benefaction)
in the fifth (Ant. v. 58). τὸ αὐτὸ ὑπάρχειν, advocated by Linwood,
may thus be admissible Thucydidean Greek.

4. καὶ Συρακοσίους εὖ εἰδέναι ἔφη, κ.τ.λ.: 'he said that he was sure
that if the Syracusans ventured to fight the Athenian fleet, which
would be contrary to the Athenians' expectations, the advantage
which they would gain over the enemy, who would be taken aback
by such an occurrence, would be greater than any harm which the
enemy could inflict by his skill upon the Syracusans, inexperienced
as they were.'

22. 1. παρεσκευάσατο: if this (ABCEFGM) is right, it is the sole
reference to Gylippos as having a say in preparations for fighting
at sea (cf. 2. 1 n., and contrast his purely hortatory role in c. 21).
παρεσκεύαστο (Hψ) removes the anomaly.

ἐκ τοῦ μεγάλου λιμένος - - - ἐκ τοῦ ἐλάσσονος: cf. 3. 5 n.

[καὶ] περιέπλεον: καί om. Hψ, perhaps rightly, though μέν/δέ(- - -)
καί (adverbial) is permissible (cf. Denniston, 305) and here even
desirable, given πέντε μέν - - - ἐπέπλεον, αἱ δέ - - - περιέπλεον (cf.
E. Chambry, *RPh.* xxi [1897], 106).

23. 1. ἅμα τῇ ἕῳ: Gylippos, having brought his force round from the
north of Epipolai and across the Anapos ὑπὸ νύκτα (§ 1), attacks the
forts on Plemmyrion at dawn. The movement of the ships must
have taken place περὶ ὄρθρον (which precedes ἅμα ἕῳ in vi. 101. 3),
not necessarily in conditions of good visibility; the Athenians are
likely to have had patrols out in the direction of the Syracusan
harbours, and they were, after all, able to put to sea in time.

2. ὑπὸ τριήρους μιᾶς καὶ εὖ πλεούσης: either (i) 'by one ship which
was a trireme and, moreover, fast' (cf. Denniston, 291 f.), or (ii) 'by

one fast trireme', cf. πολλά καὶ ἀγαθά (ibid. 290); but there is no parallel for insertion of καί between εἷς and another adjective; or (iii) 'by one very fast trireme', καὶ εὖ being used (as it does not seem to be used elsewhere) like καὶ πάνυ, καὶ μάλα, etc. (ibid., 317 f.), or (iv) 'by a trireme which was by itself' (sc. and thus favourably placed for pursuit) 'and fast'. None of these solutions is altogether easy, and it is possible that a word or phrase meaning 'separate from the others' or 'ahead of the others' is lost after μιᾶς.

24. 1. τὰ δὲ δύο ἐπισκευάσαντες ἐφρούρουν: we learn later (§ 3) that they also kept some triremes there, which would maintain their communications with the city.

2. ὥστε γὰρ ταμιείῳ χρωμένων - - - τοῖς τείχεσι: B has ἅτε for ὥστε, and Josephus *Ant.* xviii. 9. 1 ἐχρῶντο ὥσπερ ταμιείῳ ταῖσδε ταῖς πόλεσιν suggests a further variant ὥσπερ. ὥστε, whether taken (as ἅτε would be) with the participle or (= ὥσπερ) with ταμιείῳ, can be paralleled from poetry and from Herodotos (cf. vi. 40. 1 n.), but from nowhere else in Attic prose; it probably originated in a conflation of two variants, ἅτε and ὥσπερ, just as ὥσπερ in E at 25. 1 seems to originate in a conflation of ὅπως (B) and οἷπερ (ACEGHM) and ὥσπερ and ὅπως are vv.ll. at X. *Cyr.* viii. 3. 46.

ἱστία τεσσαράκοντα τριήρων: the main sails were, if possible, stored on land when action was expected (cf. X. *HG* vi. 2. 27), and the Athenian triremes at Syracuse had to be ready for action continuously.

3. κατάπληξιν παρέσχε: sc. ἡ λῆψις, probably; but cf. vi. 46. 4 n.

25. 1. Ἀγάθαρχον: cf. 70. 1.

γέμοντα χρημάτων: not necessarily, or even probably, money; cf. 24. 2, 27. 3; and as late as [D.] lvi. 8 χρήματα is used to mean 'cargo' in a context in which the distinction between money and cargo is important.

2. ξύλα ναυπηγήσιμα ἐν τῇ Καυλωνιάτιδι: the politics of Kaulonia at this time are unknown. For the comparative abundance of shipbuilding timber in Italy cf. vi. 90. 3.

3. μία τῶν ὁλκάδων τῶν ἀπὸ Πελοποννήσου: cf. 19. 3 ff.

5. ἐν τῷ λιμένι: cf. 3. 5 n.

6. ναῦν μυριοφόρον: technical terms are rarely self-explanatory, and though a μυριοφόρος ship (cf. μυριαγωγός in Str. 151) was clearly meant to hold (approximately) ten thousand units of something, we do not know what units, or of what commodity; probably amphorae of liquid or μέδιμνοι of grain (cf. H. T. Wallinga, *Mnemosyne* 1964, 22 f.). Translation from Roman sources shows that the numerals compounded with -φόρος there refer sometimes to Roman amphorae, sometimes to modii (Wallinga, 13). Talents are another possibility (cf. iv. 118. 5). Hdt. i. 194. 3 speaks of ships on the Euphrates which could carry a 5,000-talent load, and vast rafts on the Nile (ii. 96. 5) 'some of which carry many thousands of talents', but he regards these as remarkable, and they are, after all, river barges. The data given by Ath. 208–9 on Hieron II's *Syrakosia* must be treated with the same reserve as other numerical data found in Athenaios. Whatever the unit, a ship which could carry 10,000 of them was obviously a big ship by fifth-century standards; it is equally obvious that Thucydides expected his readers to know how big, and could not foresee the perplexities to which centuries of linguistic change would give rise.

ἔκ τε τῶν ἀκάτων ὤνευον ἀναδούμενοι τοὺς σταυροὺς καὶ ἀνέκλων: the size and shape of these ἄκατοι (for the word in general cf. Lübeck, *RE*, s.v.) is not certain. In Hdt. vii. 186. 1 τοῖς σιταγωγοῖσι ἀκάτοισι seems to be synonymous with 191. 1 σιταγωγῶν ὁλκάδων: in Luc. *VH* i. 5 an ἄκατος conveys fifty men on an ocean voyage, but needs to be 'strengthened' for the purpose. Thucydides' ἄκατοι must have been big enough for a substantial crew of oarsmen, for without their exertions tying a cable round a stake and winching it in would be more likely to bring the boat to the stake than the stake out of the water (Gomme, ms. note, observed this problem). A. Breusing, *Die Nautik der Alten* (Bremen, 1886), 84, conjectured ἀκατείων (sc. ἱστῶν), 'foremasts' (cf. ἀκατίων BˢHψ); his description of the winching operation may sound somewhat implausible, but he knew more about sailing ships than any commentator on Thucydides. ἀνέκλων may mean 'bent' rather than 'broke off'; ἀνάκλασις is used in Hp. *Fract.* 2 of the movement of the limbs from the joints.

9. Κορινθίων καὶ Ἀμπρακιωτῶν καὶ Λακεδαιμονίων: with πρέσβεις, not with πόλεις, for we see from 32. 1 that the embassy went to the west and south of Sicily, and that one of them, at least, was a Corinthian (32. 2 n.); for Spartans and Ambrakians in Gylippos' force cf. 7. 1, vi. 104. 1.

26. *Demosthenes and Charikles at Kythera*

26. 1. τῷ τε Χαρικλεῖ: cf. 20. 1.

παραλαβόντες τῶν Ἀργείων ὁπλίτας: cf. 20. 1. These Argives were to co-operate only in the attack on Lakonia, and would not be taken to Sicily (§ 3).

2. τῆς Ἐπιδαύρου τι τῆς Λιμηρᾶς: cf. iv. 56. 2 n.

ἐς τὰ καταντικρὺ Κυθήρων: Kythera itself was occupied by the Athenians in 424 (iv. 54. 4). Its evacuation was required by the peace treaty (v. 18. 7), but since Κυθήριοι were present in the Athenian force at Syracuse (57. 6) it had evidently not been evacuated by 413. Demosthenes and Charikles will have landed somewhere in the bay of Boiai; Paus. iii. 22. 9 mentions a temple of Apollo in the agora of Boiai, but Thucydides is clearly not speaking of a town.

ἰσθμῶδές τι χωρίον: the most conspicuous places of this kind 'opposite Kythera' are the strip of land (now shallow water) separating Onugnathos (Paus. iii. 22. 8, Strabo 363 f.) from the mainland, and the neck of the rocky peninsula which projects from the SE. coast of Onugnathos itself (cf. Philippson, iii. 496 f.), but there has been much subsidence on that coast since ancient times, and identification is hazardous. The Athenian fort was abandoned in the winter of 413/12 (viii. 4).

ἵνα δὴ οἵ τε Εἵλωτες - - - αὐτομολῶσι: helots had deserted to Pylos when it was in Athenian hands (v. 14. 3), and Messenians and Helots constituted its garrison except between its evacuation in 421 (v. 35. 6 f.) and the replacement of this garrison in 419 (v. 56. 3). The area of Boiai may seem to us an odd choice as a reception point for helots or as a base for raids on Lakonian farms, but Demosthenes knew more about that than we do; the very fact that Boiai and Pylos were in opposite directions from Sparta made matters more troublesome for the Spartans, and the point chosen had to be both accessible to the Athenians and inconveniently remote from Sparta.

ὥσπερ ἐκ τῆς Πύλου: cf. vi. 105. 2.

27–28. *The Effect of Dekeleia*

For ease of reference it is necessary to subdivide the traditional paragraphs. I refer to 28. 3 μάλιστα δ' αὐτούς - - - ἀκούσας as 28. 3a, to τὸ γὰρ αὐτούς - - - ἐκ Πελοποννήσου as 28. 3b, to 28. 4 δι' ἃ καὶ τότε - - - τοῖς χρήμασιν as 28. 4a, and to καὶ τὴν εἰκοστήν - - - ἀπώλλυντο as 28. 4b.

The sequence of thought in these chapters is notoriously obscure. Their essential framework is:

A. They proposed to send the Thracian force home, as they could not afford it (27. 2).

B. The reason was that the occupation of Dekeleia inflicted severe losses on them (27. 3–28. 2).

C. And they were fighting a war on two fronts (28. 3).

D. Therefore they were bankrupt (28. 4).

E. Therefore they sent the Thracians home (29. 1).

The date of the dispatch of the Thracians cannot be determined with exactitude. Demosthenes no doubt set sail as early in the summer as he could; the Peloponnesian army had entered Attica and had begun to construct the fort at Dekeleia at the very beginning of spring (19. 1), i.e. in March. Demosthenes on his way to Sicily stopped opposite Kythera, spent some time assembling troops and ships at Kerkyra, and also had dealings with states in South

Italy; he had been at Syracuse perhaps two or three weeks, perhaps more, by the time the moon was eclipsed on 27 August; and the Sicilian campaign ended in disaster within a month after that. The dispatch of the Thracians might be dated to the end of June, or even the beginning of July, by which time the Athenians had suffered for three months from the effects of Dekeleia.

Yet when we begin to read Stage (B) of the exposition we receive an impression that Thucydides is describing the situation as it existed considerably later than the middle of the summer of 413. At the outset we are presented with the antithesis 'fortified *in this summer* and occupied by a *succession* of garrisons' (27. 3), and again (27. 4) 'sometimes larger numbers, sometimes the bare garrison'. In 27. 5 we are told 'more than 20,000 slaves had deserted'. By when? If Thucydides had said 'great numbers of slaves had deserted' there would be no problem, but a precise number implies that he has a certain point of time in mind. It appears from 28. 1 that he is thinking of a time at which the Athenians still possessed Euboea, which they lost for good in the autumn of 411 (viii. 95. 7); but the description of the sufferings inflicted on them by Dekeleia ends with an implicit reminder that he is looking beyond the summer of 413: 'they suffered in summer and winter alike'. It appears, then, that Stage (B) contains digressive elements, prompted by the statement in 27. 2 'they thought it too expensive to keep the Thracians' but going beyond the time at which this decision was taken; looking ahead, in fact, at least to the following winter.

At the end of the list of Athenian troubles comes the statement (28. 3a) 'what caused them more difficulty than anything was the fact that they were fighting two wars at once'. As our attention has been diverted, in the course of reading 27. 3–28. 2, to 413/12–411, it is natural that we should interpret 'two wars' as referring to (i) the unbroken hostilities in Attica itself, τὸν ἐκ τῆς Δεκελείας πόλεμον, and (ii) naval operations in Asia Minor. That situation, however, hardly deserves the name of 'two wars' in comparison with the early years of the Archidamian War, and even less in comparison with the summer of 413, when Athens was fighting two really separate wars at a great distance from each other, in Attica and in Sicily; cf. the passages in book vi (e.g. 36. 4) on 'the war here' and 'the war there', and the last clause of 28. 3b. It then becomes clear that this is what Thucydides means by 'two wars at once', for he continues 'their determination to win was such as no one would have thought possible, before it came into being' and amplifies this (τὸ γάρ, κ.τ.λ.) by reference to (i) their refusal to evacuate Sicily even when threatened in Attica, and (ii) the fact that they had attacked Syracuse sixteen years after the start of hostilities with the Peloponnesians. Thus Stage (C) first refers explicitly to 413 and then glances back to 415.

This stage of the argument continues, however, with a return to 413:
δι' ἃ καὶ τότε (28. 4a) 'they became bankrupt'. καὶ τότε is contrasted
with 'sixteen years after the first Peloponnesian invasion' in the
previous sentence; δι' ἃ refers to 'two wars at once' and 'their determination to win', for they could have avoided bankruptcy if they
had brought themselves to withdraw from Sicily (cf. 28. 3a n.). Then
finally: 'About this time they imposed the 5 per cent tax on seaborne traffic in place of the tribute.' 'This time' must mean, in the
light of the previous sentence, where καὶ τότε is contrasted with 415,
the summer of 413. A normal re-assessment of tribute was due in the
autumn of 414, if the procedure laid down in 425/4 was followed
(*ATL* A9. 26; cf. Meritt, *AFD* 15 ff.) and the first payments under
the re-assessment were due in the spring of 413. If a 5 per cent tax
was substituted for tribute in the assessment of 414, there is no great
linguistic difficulty in 'about this time'—Thucydides would simply
be looking back a few months—but one of the reasons given for the
substitution is that 'their revenues were diminishing'. As a statement
about 414, this is inexplicable (cf. L. Ćwikliński, *Hermes* xii [1877],
70 f.), and it is hard to avoid the conclusion that the change was
actually made in the autumn of 413, some time after the first year's
payments under a normal assessment had come in.

If Thucydides wrote the whole of this digression as we have it and
himself put it at this point in his narrative, we must say that in
Stage (B) he was describing a state of affairs of which all the significant effects were already apparent by midsummer 413 but was also
looking ahead to the full development of these effects. Nothing that
he says requires him to be looking further ahead than the winter of
413/12, with the possible exception of '20,000 slaves had deserted',
and there are three possible interpretations of that sentence:

(i) They had deserted by midsummer 413. I see no historical
objection to this (cf. viii. 40. 2). It means that his attention is really
fixed on 413 throughout, as 28. 3 would suggest, despite his occasional
(imprecise) references to later developments.

(ii) They had deserted by a certain later date of which Thucydides
gives no clear indication. In that case, his attention is not on 413,
but on that other date; why, then, does he put the passage here rather
than at the appropriate point in book viii, and why does he revert,
without warning, to the summer of 413 in 28. 3a?

(iii) They had deserted by the end of the war, i.e. 20,000 was the
total number of desertions. The pluperfect tense raises no difficulty;
if he is describing *as a whole* a state of affairs which began in 413 and
lasted for eight years, 'they lost by desertion 20,000 slaves', a statement applicable strictly to the end of the period, can form part of
such a description as easily as 'they were deprived of all their land'
and 'all the livestock were lost', which apply strictly to the beginning.

But the reference to Euboea in 28. 1 shows that Thucydides is *not* thinking of the period as a whole, and the problem raised by the ending of the list in 28. 3a with μάλιστα δέ is even less tractable than on hypothesis (ii).

It thus seems that if Thucydides wrote the digression, as it stands, for its present place, he intended to describe the situation as it was in the summer of 413, and that his references to later developments in 'a succession of garrisons', 'sometimes a larger force and at other times the bare garrison', and 'summer and winter alike' are simply asides. Thucydides is, of course, willing to glance aside from strict chronological sequence in order to keep together points which belong together logically, but passages which have been adduced to demonstrate his indifference to chronological strictness (Erbse, *RhM* xcvi [1953], 38 ff. adduces i. 56-9. 1 and iv. 80 f.) are different in character from the present digression, and the possibility of interpolation must now be considered.

Interpolation may be of two kinds: the work of an 'editor' inserting Thucydides' own notes, or free composition not based on anything of Thucydides' own. Moreover, we cannot in this connection treat the digression as a whole, but must consider each of its major sections separately (27. 3-28. 2, 28. 3, 28. 4, or 27. 3-28. 2, 28. 3-4a, 28. 4b).

Nothing in the language of any part of the digression points to freely composed interpolation. ἐξ ἀνάγκης in 27. 4 and ποιούμενοι in 28. 2 are equally difficult whoever wrote those passages, and the syntactical difficulties of 28. 3b are more naturally attributable to Thucydides himself than to anyone else. Positive resemblances to Thucydides' undoubted usage abound, e.g. 27. 3 ἐν τοῖς πρῶτον - - - ἐκάκωσε τὰ πράγματα ~ 24. 3 μέγιστόν τε καὶ ἐν τοῖς πρῶτον ἐκάκωσε τὸ στράτευμα, 28. 3a μάλιστα δ' αὐτοὺς ἐπίεζεν ὅτι, κ.τ.λ. ~ 18. 2 μάλιστα δέ - - - ἐγεγένητό τις ῥώμη, διότι, κ.τ.λ. and viii. 96. 3 μάλιστα δ' αὐτούς - - - ἐθορύβει, εἰ, κ.τ.λ., 28. 3a ἐς φιλονικίαν καθέστασαν τοιαύτην ~ viii. 76. 1 ἐς φιλονικίαν καθέστασαν. This very fact has been adduced to prove interpolation (Ćwiklinski, loc. cit., 73), but rather inappropriately in an author of Thucydides' stylistic habits. Equally, nothing can be found in the digression which is historically objectionable. Schwartz (346, cf. Ullrich, 119 n. 137) regarded ἦλθον ἐς Σικελίαν ἤδη τῷ πολέμῳ κατὰ πάντα τετρυχωμένοι as nonsense, but the contrast with vi. 26. 2 is not as important as he thought; the Athenians in 415 *had* suffered terrible losses in lives and property and money in the previous sixteen years, and in any case κατὰ πάντα τετρυχωμένοι is not a wholly objective statement by the writer but is coloured by the general opinion (cf. vi. 16. 2) which 28. 3b is designed to explain. As for 28. 4b, it will be proved to be a post-Thucydidean interpolation if it is ever discovered that the substitution of the 5 per cent tax for the tribute occurred in 414; on present evidence, we have no adequate grounds for dating the tax earlier than 413.

If 27. 3–28. 2 were interpolated, 28. 3a must have been remodelled by the interpolator, for the opening words μάλιστα δέ presuppose a preceding 'catalogue' (cf. vi. 6. 2, vii. 18. 2, 50. 3) and do not carry straight on from 27. 2. But why did the interpolator design a passage which looks forward to later events and insert it in a context entirely concerned with the situation in 413, when viii. 1 or viii. 2 was a much more inviting context? 27. 3–28. 3a cannot have been interpolated, for 28. 3b logically presupposes, and syntactically requires, 28. 3a. In one respect 28. 3ab or 28. 3b by itself is a more plausible interpolation: 28. 4 follows very nicely after 28. 2, δι' ἅ referring to 27. 3–28. 2 as a whole and καὶ τότε bringing the reader unambiguously back to 413 after the forward references. Yet the elaborate Thucydidean language and syntactical audacity of 28. 3 go further than anything to guarantee its authenticity.

There remains Schwartz's hypothesis that the digression consists of a series of Thucydides' own notes incorporated in the text, and in part amplified and remodelled, by an 'editor'. One of Schwartz's main premisses (202), that the 'digression has nothing to do with the episode of the Thracians', is a surprising judgement from any man who has read vi. 1–6 and vi. 53–60, and Schwartz's argument irritates by alternate excesses of subtlety and crudity. It avoids, by admitting the essentially Thucydidean language and character of most of the digression, some of the criticisms which may be brought against the hypothesis of 'free' interpolation, but it is still vulnerable to the most important criticism of all: why did the 'editor' insert 27. 3–28. 2 here? It is one thing to suppose that Thucydides himself glanced ahead chronologically in the course of a digression in which his attention was primarily focused on 413, but another thing to suppose that his editor chose the summer of 413 as the appropriate context in which to insert a passage which must have looked to him like a description of 412 or 411.

On balance, probabilities are in favour of those who maintain that the whole digression was written by Thucydides in this context. Gomme noted in the margin of his copy of Schwartz: 'One might say (1) that Thuc. wrote about effects of Decelea some time after 413, and (2) that he would not have left it as it stands; not that he did not put it where it is.' (1) at least is non-controversial, and (2) is an illuminating suggestion. If Thucydides had revised book viii, I do not believe that he would have enlarged on the effects of Dekeleia in vii; he wrote about them when they were in his mind. The content of 28. 3–4, on the other hand, can belong only to vii, and he would have left that where it is, no matter what opportunities he had to revise viii.

27. 1. Θρᾳκῶν τῶν μαχαιροφόρων τοῦ Διακοῦ γένους: cf. ii. 96. 2, where Thucydides gives the name Dioi to the 'mountain Thracians' who inhabited the Rhodope range and were αὐτόνομοι (i.e. not controlled by the Odrysian king) and μαχαιροφόροι. They must not be confused with the Dies of Dion in Chalkidike, who were at this time in revolt from Athens (v. 82. 1) and in any case were hardly Thracians (iv. 109. 3 f.).

2. διενοοῦντο αὐτούς - - - ἀποπέμπειν: 'made plans for sending them home', cf. 56. 1.

4. βραχεῖαι γιγνόμεναι αἱ ἐσβολαί: the invasion of 430, which lasted forty days, was the longest (ii. 57. 2). The contrast between the early invasions and the occupation of Dekeleia is depicted vividly by *Hell. Oxy.* 17 Bart. (12 G–H). 5; however, iii. 26. 3 suggests that the olive plantations must have suffered very great damage by 427.

καὶ ὁτὲ μὲν καὶ πλεόνων ἐπιόντων: 'more' by contrast with the number described in the next clause. Steup suggests that Thucydides had in mind occasions such as viii. 71. 1, but then the additional forces are summoned in readiness for a possible entry into the Long Walls, not for more extensive destruction.

ὁτὲ δ' ἐξ ἀνάγκης τῆς ἴσης φρουρᾶς καταθεούσης, κ.τ.λ.: 'the equal garrison' is strange Greek for 'the normal (*or* constant) garrison', and if the point of ἐξ ἀνάγκης is that it was impossible for the Peloponnesians to keep the garrison above a certain strength all the time there is a curious shift from the Athenian to the Peloponnesian standpoint in this clause. The text is certainly corrupt; perhaps Thucydides wrote τῆς ἐξ ἀνάγκης φρουρᾶς, meaning either (*a*)= ἀναγκαστοῦ, the garrison which the allies were compelled to provide (cf. 48. 5 ἐπικουρικὰ μᾶλλον ἢ δι' ἀνάγκης) or (*b*) = ἀναγκαίας, the minimum garrison (cf. vi. 37. 2 ἀναγκαίας παρασκευῆς, and for ἐξ ἀνάγκης = ἀναγκαῖον cf. D. lii. 5 ἐξ ἀνάγκης γάρ μοι ἐστὶν ἁπάντων Ἡρακλεωτῶν ἐπιμελεῖσθαι). This greatly diminishes the shift of standpoint; itacistic dittography of -ης will have been the origin of the corruption (cf. Poppo ad loc. and J. U. Powell, *CQ* xxi [1927], 176; and in D. xxi. 149 ταύτης τῆς τιμῆς and τῆς ἴσης τιμῆς are variants).

5. ἀνδραπόδων πλέον ἢ δύο μυριάδες ηὐτομολήκεσαν, καὶ τούτων τὸ πολὺ μέρος χειροτέχναι: for discussion of the bearing of this datum on the question of the total slave population of Attica cf. W. L. Westermann, *The Slave Systems of Greek and Roman Antiquity* (Philadelphia, 1955), 7 f. (there are important corrections in the review by G. E. M. de Sainte Croix, *CR* N.S. vii [1957], 54 ff.). Lys. xii. 8 ~ 19, D. xxvii. 9, 24, Aeschin. i. 97, provide illustrations of the number of slaves which might be employed in privately owned 'factories', and those slaves would certainly be regarded as χειροτέχναι, 'trained to a craft' (cf. vi. 72. 3 n.), but τέχνη is wider than our 'craft'. Slaves listed in the confiscated property of the Hermokopidai are often designated as specialists, though their specialities vary greatly in skill, e.g. τραπεζοποιός (*SEG* xiii. 13. 74), ὀνηλάτης (ibid. 13. 76), ὀβελισκοποιός (ibid. 17. 20), χρυσοχοῦς (ibid. 13. 77), σκυτοτόμος (ibid. 17. 21 f.). Cf. Aeschin. (loc. cit.) γυναῖκα ἀμόργινα ἐπισταμένην ἐργάζεσθαι - - - καὶ ἄνδρα ποικιλτήν. There is no reason to suppose that most of the 20,000 were slaves who worked in the mines at Laureion, though no doubt a high proportion of the mine-workers were included in the 20,000 (X. *Vect.* 4. 25; cf. S. Lauffer, *AMAW* 1956, 904 ff.). Alkibiades in his speech (vi. 91. 7) attached importance to the silver mines, but we are not told anywhere that Agis made them a special objective. It is understandable that a slave should desert when his circumstances are so bad that any change must be for the better (cf. Ar. *Eq.* 20 ff., *Nu.* 6 f.), and that there should be mass desertions from a state in which it was customary to punish slaves harshly (cf. viii. 40. 2, where 'the majority' of the slaves on Chios desert to the Athenians and Thucydides thinks it worth while to explain this), but surprising that the slaves of Attica should as a whole expect a better life in Peloponnesian ownership. No doubt the enemy found it politic to make a fuss of deserted slaves and even to make them lavish promises of eventual liberation.

28. 1. ἥ τε τῶν ἐπιτηδείων παρακομιδὴ ἐκ τῆς Εὐβοίας: in 431 the Athenians transferred their livestock to Euboea (ii. 14. 1), and thereafter the security of supplies from Euboea was of supreme importance; cf. viii. 96. 2. It is not easy to estimate whether sea-traffic was necessarily more costly than land-traffic; no doubt shipowners made the most of the situation, and fodder would have to be bought for animals carried alive by sea, but one ship can carry more produce than a long train of pack-animals. H. D. Westlake, *CR* lxii (1948), 2 ff., therefore suggests that Thucydides means: (i) supplies had to come from Euboea by sea, *and* (ii) the volume of traffic from Euboea was now greatly increased. θάσσων οὖσα, in antithesis to πολυτελής, implies 'and therefore cheaper'.

τῶν τε πάντων ὁμοίως ἐπακτῶν ἐδεῖτο ἡ πόλις: Athens had long relied on imported grain (vi. 20. 4); now she needed to import *all* commodities.

2. πρὸς γὰρ τῇ ἐπάλξει, κ.τ.λ.: although ἔπαλξις literally means the parapet on a fortification-wall, παρ' ἔπαλξιν in ii. 13. 6 has the general sense 'on duty in defence of the walls', and πρὸς τῇ ἐπάλξει must be general here, including both those posted on the walls (ἐπὶ τοῦ τείχους) and the reserves in support of them; cf. viii. 69. 1 οἱ μὲν ἐπὶ τείχει, οἱ δ' ἐν τάξει, τῶν ἐν Δεκελείᾳ πολεμίων ἕνεκα ἐφ' ὅπλοις.

οἱ μὲν ἐφ' ὅπλοις †ποιούμενοι†: ποιούμενοι makes no sense (if Thucydides had meant us to understand τὴν φυλακήν, as Dobree thought, from φυλάσσοντες, he would have said τοῦτο ποιοῦντες), but που (B) does: 'some under arms somewhere', i.e. stationed with their arms in one part or another of the area enclosed by the city walls and Long Walls, 'and others on the wall' (cf. Badham, *Mnemosyne* 1876, 139). Possibly Thucydides wrote ποι, with τεταγμένοι or some such word in mind, the inevitable variant που (cf. 73. 1, viii. 27. 3, 55. 1) was conflated with it, giving ποιου, and this was 'corrected' to ποιούμενοι. The numerous emendations which take ποιούμενοι as their starting-point all disregard the fact that που makes sense.

3. καὶ ἐς φιλονικίαν καθέστασαν τοιαύτην ἣν πρὶν γενέσθαι ἠπίστησεν ἄν τις ἀκούσας: φιλονικία, to the Greek way of thinking, is not something which one chooses, but something of which one becomes a victim, like love, fear, and grief; cf. Pl. *La.* 194 a ἀλλά τίς με καὶ φιλονικία εἴληφεν πρὸς τὰ εἰρημένα, *Ly.* 215 d φθόνου τε καὶ φιλονικίας καὶ ἔχθρας ἐμπίμπλασθαι, and de Romilly, *Imp.*, 326, 333, on the 'pathology' of imperialism. In Plu. *Alc.* 2. 1 τὸ φιλόνικον is reckoned among the πάθη of Alkibiades, and Th. vi. 24. 3 καὶ ἔρως ἐνέπεσε τοῖς πᾶσιν ὁμοίως ἐκπλεῦσαι has many later echoes such as Diod. xiv. 18. 7 τοσαύτη σπουδὴ τοῖς πλήθεσιν ἐνεπεπτώκει; cf. Müri, *MH* iv (1947), 262 ff. Hence so far from punctuating strongly after εἶχον (V. Bartoletti, *SIFC* N.S. xiv [1937], 233 n. 1) and thus giving καί the sense of καίτοι, we need no punctuation at all after εἶχον; the φιλονικία of the Athenians is one of the things which ἐπίεζεν αὐτούς and is included in the reference of δι’ ἅ in 28. 4. Isoc. viii. 84 f., in which the spirit of 413 is blamed, not admired, has: εἰς τοῦτ’ ἀφροσύνης ἦλθον ὥστε τῶν προαστείων τῶν οἰκείων οὐ κρατοῦντες Ἰταλίας καὶ Σικελίας ἄρξειν προσεδόκησαν. Aeschin. ii. 75 f. uses ἄκαιρος φιλονικία with the same reference, but characteristically dates the *sending* of the Sicilian expedition ('to help Leontinoi') *after* the occupation of Dekeleia.

τὸ γάρ - - - ἐκ Πελοποννήσου: the sentence explains the nature of the incredible φιλονικία; it is expressed in the infinitive because it is a statement not simply of what happened but also of what would have been rejected as impossible by anyone to whom it had been put in hypothetical terms. Cf. Pl. *Phd.* 99 b πολλὴ ἂν καὶ μακρὰ ῥᾳθυμία εἴη τοῦ λόγου· τὸ γὰρ μὴ διελέσθαι οἷόν τ’ εἶναι, κ.τ.λ. ('it would be an inability to distinguish . . .'). For γάρ introducing a statement of content cf. Hdt. i. 82. 7 τὰ ἐναντία τούτων ἔθεντο νόμον· οὐ γὰρ κομῶντες πρὸ τούτου, ἀπὸ τούτου κομᾶν (Hude, *Hermes* xxxvi [1901], 313 ff. and Denniston, 67 f.). Schwartz's emendation τὸ γάρ - - - ἀντιπολιορκεῖν - - - [καὶ] - - - ἐποίησε, κ.τ.λ. (346) seems to rest on ignorance of syntax.

καὶ τὸν παράλογον τοσοῦτον ποιῆσαι - - - ὅσον - - - ἐνόμιζον - - - ὥστε - - - ἦλθον, κ.τ.λ.: if τοσοῦτον and ὥστε are correlative and the ὅσον-clause parenthetic, the sequence of thought, lit. 'they made the unexpectedness so great (in so far as everyone thought . . .) that they attacked Sicily . . .', makes sense; if τοσοῦτον and ὅσον are correlative and the ὥστε consequential, lit. 'they made the unexpectedness as great as everyone's expectation . . . and so attacked Sicily . . .', the sense is dubious. Against this must be set the fact that τοσοῦτον/ὅσον is so natural and so common that any Greek reader would suppose that to be the essential relationship in this sentence; cf. Marchant, *CR* vi (1892), 303 f. But the hearer is more important than the reader; the spoken word can make quite clear what is parenthetic and what is not, and if we assume that Thucydides thought of what he wrote as sounds, not as marks on papyrus, we need not have recourse to the hypothesis that the sentence is careless and unrevised (Pohlenz, *NGG* 1919, 97 n. 1) or that both ὅσον and ὥστε pick up τοσοῦτον (Chambry, *RPh.* xxi [1897], 106 f.) or that ὅσον is corrupt (H. Richards, *CQ* viii [1914], 80, conjectures ὧν, cl. X. *HG* i. 3. 9, where a papyrus has ὡνπερ for ὅσονπερ). A further important consideration is that παράλογος does not mean 'miscalculation', but 'unexpectedness' (cf. 55. 1 and ii. 61. 3), and this disposes of Bartoletti's emendation of ὥστε to ὡς ὅτε (*SIFC* N.S. xiv [1937], 231), which in any case would debilitate the rhetorical effect of the passage.

οἱ μὲν ἐνιαυτόν, οἱ δὲ δύο, οἱ δὲ τριῶν γε ἐτῶν οὐδεὶς πλείω χρόνον ἐνόμιζον περιοίσειν αὐτούς: 'and of the rest (sc. although some thought that they would survive three years) no one thought that they would survive *more* than three years'. τῶν δέ - - - οὐδείς would have been normal syntax, and supported by Thucydides' apparent dislike of οἱ μέν / οἱ δέ / οἱ δέ (cf. vi. 35. 1 n.), but he has a tendency to avoid the juxtaposition of genitives with different reference (cf. vi. 4. 6 n.), and τῶν δὲ τριῶν γ' ἐτῶν would be misleading. Schwartz's οἱ δὲ δύο, οὐδὲ τριῶν, κ.τ.λ. has a parallel in 77. 1, but 'A οὐδὲ B' = 'A B δ' οὔ' is very rare in Attic prose and should not lightly be introduced by emendation (cf. Denniston, 190). οἱ δὲ δύο, τριῶν δ' ἐτῶν οὐδείς would be unobjectionable linguistically, but γε is wanted for the sense, and δέ γε in Thucydides is an adversative, not 'and . . . at least'. Altogether, it is hard to see how Thucydides could have expressed what he meant except by writing what the MSS. give us.

4. καὶ τὴν εἰκοστήν - - - ἐποίησαν: on the date cf. p. 402. Comparison of the tribute collected from the Aegean Islands in 417/16 and 416/15 (*ATL*, Lists 38. 4 ff., 39. 8 ff.) with the assessments of those same states in 425/4 (*ATL*, A9. 61 ff.), when the assessment of the whole empire amounted to 1,460T, suggests that the annual tribute of the whole empire during the assessment period 418/17–415/14 amounted to *c.* 900T (after making allowance for the inclusion in the assessment of 425/4 of states from which no tribute was ever actually collected). It follows that the Athenians estimated that the annual value of the seaborne traffic on which they could hope to collect the tax exceeded 18,000 talents. D. xxiii. 110, in the middle of the fourth century, estimates at 200 talents the annual revenue of the Thracian king Kersebleptes from the coastal emporia under his control.

αἱ δὲ πρόσοδοι ἀπώλλυντο: internal revenue, that is; there was nothing to interfere with external revenue until the fleet had been lost in Sicily.

29–30. *The Thracians at Mykalessos*

29. 1. Διειτρέφει: probably the man who was appointed to command in the Thracian area in 411 and was active in the oligarchic cause (viii. 64. 2). Pausanias (i. 23. 3 f.) saw in Athens a brazen statue depicting Dieitrephes struck with arrows. We have no other evidence on how, when, or where Dieitrephes died, and clearly Pausanias had none, for he associates the statue with the fight at Mykalessos and expresses surprise at the arrows—a weapon, as he says, used by no Greeks except the Cretans.

2. ἔς τε τὴν Τάναγραν: i.e. in the territory of Tanagra; the city itself lay well inland.

ἐπὶ Μυκαλησσόν: the modern Ritsona, in Strabo's time (Str. 404) κώμη τῆς Ταναγραϊκῆς; cf. R. M. Burrows and P. N. Ure, *ABSA* xiv (1907–8), 226 ff., Fiehn, *RE* xvi. 1005 ff., and Philippson, i. 515.

3. τοῦ τείχους ἀσθενοῦς ὄντος καὶ ἔστιν ᾗ καὶ πεπτωκότος: possibly any attempt to repair the walls would have incurred the displeasure of Thebes, which in 423 had demolished the city-wall of Thespiai; cf. iii. 33. 2 n. on Athenian policy towards her subjects in Asia Minor.

5. οὐδεμιᾶς ἥσσων μᾶλλον ἑτέρας ἀδόκητός τε ἐπέπεσεν αὕτη καὶ δεινή: 'this (disaster which) fell upon the whole city (as an) exceptionally unexpected and horrible (one) (was a) disaster second to none.' For the type of sentence cf. vi. 31. 1 and 54. 5. So far from being objectionable (μᾶλλον ἑτέρας secl. Heilmann), the juxtaposition of οὐδεμιᾶς ἥσσων and μᾶλλον ἑτέρας ἀδόκητός τε - - - καὶ δεινή is deliberate; the former makes the primary point that Mykalessos had never suffered a greater disaster, the latter the point that the disaster was of an exceptionally horrid kind. The element of tautology present in i. 138. 3 διαφερόντως τι - - - μᾶλλον ἑτέρου ἄξιος θαυμάσαι and iv. 3. 3 διάφορόν τι - - - ἑτέρου μᾶλλον is absent here.

30. 1. ἐπὶ τὸν Εὔριπον καὶ τὴν θάλασσαν: 'to the sea at the Euripos'; the construction is logically the converse of vi. 103. 1 ἀπὸ τῶν Ἐπιπολῶν καὶ τοῦ κρημνώδους = 'from the precipitous edge of Epipolai' but formally identical.

2. καὶ ἀποκτείνουσιν αὐτῶν ἐν τῇ ἐσβάσει τοὺς πλείστους: τοὺς πλείστους refers to the majority of the 250 who were killed, not the majority of the total force of 1,300; cf. iv. 44. 2.

ἔξω τοξεύματος: so Hᵖᶜψ: cf. Valla, *extra ictum sagittarum*. ἔξω τοῦ ζεύ(γ)ματος (cett.) could only refer to a pontoon bridge across the Euripos, which would make little sense in this context, and an Athenian general stirring up trouble in Boeotia would not have regarded a bridge from Boeotia to Euboea as a desirable construction.

προεκθέοντές τε καὶ ξυστρεφόμενοι ἐν ἐπιχωρίῳ τάξει: this not very illuminating description probably means that the main body, as it moved towards the Euripos, would send out detachments to the flanks to keep the pursuers at bay and would continuously relieve these detachments at high speed. Hdt. ix. 62. 3, describing Persian tactics at Plataia, has little relevance, since the Persians who 'charged into the Spartans singly or in small groups συστρεφόμενοι' all perished.

3. τῶν βοιωταρχῶν: cf. iv. 91, v. 38. 2 n.

ὀλοφύρασθαι ἀξίῳ: the massacre at Mykalessos must have aroused much bitterness among the enemies of Athens, especially when linked to rumours of Athens' willingness to employ barbarians against Greeks (ii. 101. 4, vi. 90. 3). Interesting parallels are to be found in the use of Red Indians by British, French, and Americans in the late eighteenth and early nineteenth centuries. No firm inference on Thucydides' values can be drawn from the fact that he expresses a sympathy for Mykalessos which he denies to Melos; it is simply that his emotions are rather more in evidence in this book (cf. 86. 5) than in the other books, and the Melians had the opportunity to avert the fate which they had done something to provoke.

31. *Demosthenes and Eurymedon at Naupaktos*

31. 1. μετὰ τὴν ἐκ τῆς Λακωνικῆς τείχισιν: cf. 26. 2.

ἐν Φειᾷ τῇ Ἠλείων: combination of the description of this locality in ii. 25. 3 ff. (see notes) with Strabo 343 shows that Pheia was on the west side of the beginning of the promontory which now has Katákolo on its east side.

ἐν ᾗ οἱ Κορίνθιοι ὁπλῖται - - - ἔμελλον περαιοῦσθαι: cf. 19. 4.

2. ἐς τὴν Ζάκυνθον καὶ Κεφαλληνίαν: these two islands had been Athenian allies since the beginning of the war (ii. 7. 3, 30. 2).

τῶν Μεσσηνίων: cf. 57. 8 n.

ἐς Ἀλυζιάν τε καὶ Ἀνακτόριον, ὃ αὐτοὶ εἶχον: Alyzia is the modern Kandýla, two miles inland from the beach and anchorage at Mýtikas (Philippson, ii. 389). Anaktorion, a Corinthian colony at the southeast corner of the bay between Actium and the modern Vónitsa (cf. i. 55. 1 n. and Philippson, ii. 380), was captured by the Athenians and Akarnanians in 425 and was thereafter occupied by the Akarnanians (iv. 49); this, however, does not sufficiently account for the wording '(the Athenians) themselves held it' (cf. viii. 95. 6). In the summer of 421 Corinth regarded its return (to the original colonists, presumably) as being within the power of Athens; cf. v. 30. 2 n. For Demosthenes' relations with the Akarnanians cf. 57. 10 n.

3. τότε τοῦ χειμῶνος: cf. 16. 2. Eurymedon had taken the best part of six months (cf. 34. 3 n.) to sail from Athens to Syracuse and back to Kerkyra. However much allowance we make for the difficulties of travel by sea during the first three of those months (cf. vi. 21. 2 n.), he cannot have been sheltering from storms all this time; presumably he took part in the fighting at Syracuse, or busied himself on diplomatic or logistic activity in Italy, or both, until he judged that Demosthenes was on his way to Kerkyra. The news of the capture of Plemmyrion had, after all, caught up with him.

4. ἀφικνεῖται δὲ καὶ Κόνων παρ' αὐτούς: this is the first appearance of the famous general in history and his only appearance in Thucydides.

αἱ πέντε καὶ εἴκοσι νῆες τῶν Κορινθίων: cf. 17. 4 and 19. 5.

οὔτε καταλύουσι τὸν πόλεμον ναυμαχεῖν τε μέλλουσιν: if the text is right, it means 'so far from going home without a fight' (or 'so far from abandoning their hostile attitude') 'they were ready for a naval battle', but the wording is extraordinary; contrast iii. 115. 4 ἡγούμενοι θᾶσσον τὸν ἐκεῖ πόλεμον καταλυθήσεσθαι, 'in the belief that the war in Sicily would be more swiftly brought to a (sc. successful) conclusion'. Madvig (i. 329) was almost certainly right in deleting τὸν πόλεμον; in v. 23. 1 intransitive καταλύειν = 'cease hostilities', and cf. its common use = 'stop', 'stay' (with a person or at a place) at the end of a journey.

ὡς οὐχ ἱκανὰς οὔσας - - - ναυμαχεῖν: sixteen years earlier Phormion, based on Naupaktos, had confidently attacked and defeated 47 Peloponnesian ships with 20 Athenian (ii. 83 f.). Now the situation is very different, and Konon will not pit 18 against 25; but no doubt when the needs of the force in Sicily had been met Konon and other commanders of small detachments were left with inferior ships and crews, while every year of training and experience saw an improvement in the Peloponnesian fleets. See, however, 34. 7 for an indication of high Athenian morale. We are not told why the 20 Athenian ships at Naupaktos (19. 5) are now down to 18.

5. πέντε καὶ δέκα τε ναῦς πληροῦν κελεύσας αὐτοὺς καὶ ὁπλίτας καταλεγόμενος: since 427 (iii. 75. 1 f.) Kerkyra had been a full ally (cf. 33. 6 n.).

ξυνῆρχε γὰρ ἤδη Δημοσθένει ἀποτραπόμενος: the point is in ξυν-, not in -ῆρχε; the fleet now had the joint command assigned to it in the previous winter. ἀποτραπόμενος suggests 'turning *aside*', sc. from a return route to Athens on learning that Demosthenes was already at Kerkyra, not simply 'having returned sc. from Sicily'.

32–33. 3. *Sikeliot Help for Syracuse*

32. 1. οἱ - - - τότε - - - πρέσβεις οἰχόμενοι ἐς τὰς πόλεις: cf. 25. 9.
Κεντόριπάς τε καὶ Ἁλικυαίους καὶ ἄλλους: on the Kentoripes cf.
vi. 94. 3 n. (H)alikyai is located by Steph. Byz. (s.v.) between Lily-
baion and Entella, i.e. inland northwards from Selinus; this location
is consistent with the part it played in Dionysios' campaigns in
the west of Sicily (Diod. xiv. 48. 4 f. and 55. 7; cf. Ziegler, *RE* xiv.
2265 f.). Diodoros in both passages explicitly (and rightly, see below)
distinguishes it from the Sikan tribes. It is surprising that a people
so far to the west should be in a position to attack the force travelling
to Syracuse; but if the force set out from Selinus already knowing
the Akragantines' refusal to allow a passage through their territory,
it might well strike north-eastwards into the interior. This would
encourage the Halikyaioi (we do not know how far eastwards their
territory extended—possibly even to the east of Entella) to follow
it until an attack could be concerted with Sikels coming from Kentoripa 'and others'. *SEG* x. 68 records a treaty between Athens and
ἁλι]κυαίοις Ἐλ[ύμοις: this treaty, to be dated *c.* 433/2 (cf. Raubitschek, *TAPhA* lxxv [1944], 10 ff. and A. G. Woodhead, *Hesperia* xvii
[1948], 59 f.), was inscribed on the same stele as the treaty with
Segesta of 458/7 (*IG* i². 19, ML 37; cf. M. T. Manni Piraino, *Kokalos* vi
[1960], 58 ff., who questions ἐλ[ ). Kahrstedt, *WJA* ii (1947), 28,
argues that there must be two different Halikyai, since the ambassadors did not go as far as Selinus; but we are not in a position to
say how far they went, and on Halikyai and Kentoripa as western
and eastern termini of an inland route cf. Raubitschek ad loc.
ὅπως μὴ διαφρήσωσι τοὺς πολεμίους: διαφρήσουσι cj. Dobree, -ωσι
Stahl, = 'let pass' (cf. Ar. *Av.* 193); διαφήσουσι or -ωσι (codd.)
would mean 'dismiss' (or 'release') 'in different directions', a common
word in Polybios.
Ἀκραγαντῖνοι γὰρ οὐκ ἐδίδοσαν διὰ τῆς ἑαυτῶν ὁδόν: this is our first
news of the attitude of Akragas. Its neutrality (33. 2) is one of the
facts which must affect our judgement of Alkibiades' original plan
(vi. 48). Akragas was presumably among 'all the Dorian cities except
Kamarina' which supported Syracuse against Leontinoi in 428/7
(iii. 86. 2), despite an earlier war between Akragas and Syracuse
assigned by Diodoros xii. 8 to 446/5, but it welcomed Phaiax's mission
in 422/1 (v. 4. 6). Diodoros xiii. 4. 2 represents Akragas as declaring
for Athens in the summer of 415, but this may well be an epitoma-
tor's error; in the same passage he even makes Katane declare for
Syracuse.
2. διέφθειραν ἐς ὀκτακοσίους μάλιστα: Diod. xiii. 8. 4 turns this affair
into an attack on a body of 3,000 Himeraians and Sikans brought by
Gylippos; this is simply a conflation of Thucydides' narrative with

a doublet of Gylippos' original journey from Himera to Syracuse (Diod. xiii. 7. 7).

πλὴν ἑνὸς τοῦ Κορινθίου: the sequence of letters could perhaps be interpreted as πλὴν ἑνός του Κορινθίου (Herwerden, *Mnemosyne* 1880, 297 f.); but 25. 9 πρέσβεις - - - Κορινθίων, κ.τ.λ. cannot be pressed to mean that there was more than one envoy of every nationality mentioned. Cf. Lys. ix. 8 f., where ἔτι πλέονας καὶ νόμους καὶ ἄλλας δικαιώσεις παρασχήσομαι is followed by a single νόμος and a variety of δικαιώσεις. Cf. also Hdt. ii. 101. 1 πλὴν ἑνὸς τοῦ ἐσχάτου αὐτῶν Μοίριος.

33. 1. καὶ οἱ Καμαριναῖοι ἀφικνοῦνται: news of the capture of Plemmyrion achieved what rhetoric could not.

2. σχεδὸν γάρ τι ἤδη πᾶσα ἡ Σικελία πλὴν Ἀκραγαντίνων (οὗτοι δ' - - -) οἱ δ' ἄλλοι - - - ἐβοήθουν: there is neither corruption nor incoherence in the sentence; cf. *ATL* ii. D17 (*IG* i². 39). 52 ff. τὸς δὲ χσένος - - - ὅσοι οἰκôντες μὲ τελôσιν Ἀθέναζε - - - τὸς δὲ ἄλλος τελêν ἐς Χαλκίδα. 'Except Akragas' is not a complete amplification of 'almost', for Messene did not help Athens (cf. vi. 74. 1) and is not recorded in c. 58 as helping Syracuse. The prophecies of Hermokrates (vi. 33. 4) and Athenagoras (vi. 37. 2) are now fulfilled.

33. 3–6. *Demosthenes and Eurymedon at Thurioi*

33. 3. ἔκ τε τῆς Κερκύρας καὶ ἀπὸ τῆς ἠπείρου: cf. 31. 2.

ἐπ' ἄκραν Ἰαπυγίαν: cf. vi. 30. 1 n.

4. ἐς τὰς Χοιράδας νήσους: these must be the small islands lying off the harbour of Taras.

τῷ Ἄρτᾳ - - - ἀνανεωσάμενοί τινα παλαιὰν φιλίαν: the origin of this relationship is not known; it may be pre-war, or it may be one of the details which Thucydides warns us he has omitted (iii. 90. 1) in his account of the fighting in the West in 427–424; cf. vi. 75. 3 n. παλαιάν does not imply 'immemorial'; Leontinoi in 427 considered herself an Athenian ally κατὰ παλαιὰν ξυμμαχίαν (iii. 86. 3), but the alliance can hardly have been of more than twenty years' standing (cf. Meritt, *CQ* xl [1946], 85 f.).

Μεταπόντιον τῆς Ἰταλίας: Ἰταλία is used here in the restricted sense 'Bruttium and Lucania'; Taras is in 'Iapygia', Kyme in 'Opikia' (vi. 4. 5). Thucydides is following the usage of Antiochos (F 3), though elsewhere he uses Ἰταλία in its later, wider sense, e.g. vi. 42. 2 ~ 44. 2, and no doubt it always has the wider sense in rhetorical passages such as vi. 90. 2 f. Cf. van Compernolle, 479 ff.

5. κατὰ τὸ ξυμμαχικόν: the origin of this alliance too is unknown.

τοὺς τῶν Ἀθηναίων ἐναντίους ἐκπεπτωκότας: Thurioi rebuffed Gylippos (vi. 104. 2). There has been no previous mention of a significant anti-Athenian faction, but cf. Diod. xii. 35. 1 ff., where strife between the Athenian and Peloponnesian elements within the city is assigned to 434/3, and on the attitude of Thurioi generally cf. A. J. Graham, *The Greek City and its Colonies* (Manchester, 1964), 198 f.

6. τοὺς αὐτοὺς ἐχθροὺς καὶ φίλους τοῖς Ἀθηναίοις νομίζειν: in i. 44. 1 this type of 'full' alliance, according to which A must help B if B chooses to attack C, is explicitly distinguished from a defensive alliance (ἐπιμαχία) according to which A helps B only if B is attacked by C. As a 'full' ally of Athens Thurioi would be committed, on request from Athens, to participation in the Athenian attack on Syracuse. Although Thurioi did contribute hoplites and other troops (35. 1), Thucydides does not tell us whether she actually took the oath of full alliance.

34. Naval Battle at Naupaktos

34. 1. οἱ ἐν ταῖς πέντε καὶ εἴκοσι ναυσίν: cf. 17. 4, 19. 5, and 31. 4. **καὶ προσπληρώσαντες ἔτι ναῦς ὥστε ὀλίγῳ ἐλάσσους εἶναι αὐτοῖς τῶν Ἀττικῶν νεῶν**: with 31. 4 in mind, the reader naturally thinks of the Athenian fleet as totalling 28, but it was by now larger, as § 3 below tells us.

κατὰ Ἐρινεὸν τῆς Ἀχαΐας ἐν τῇ Ῥυπικῇ: if the text of Paus. vii. 22. 10 is sound and its substance correct, Erineos (-on?), 170 stades by sea from Patrai and 60 from Aigion, was the bay on which the modern village Lembíri lies (26 km. east of Patrai), west of the mouth of the river Salmeníko. His figures are protected by his sequence Patrai—Cape Rhion (cf. Th. ii. 86. 3 f.)—Panormos (ibid. 86. 1, 4)—Athenasteichos—Erineos—Aigion; cf. Strabo 387, who places Rhypes, already uninhabited in his day, between Cape Rhion and Aigion, Bölte, *RE* iiA. 1288 ff. and Philippson, iii/1. 189. The coastline of the 'crescent-shaped place', which is well inside the Gulf and out of sight of Naupaktos, runs south-east and east, and a line of ships anchored in it ἐμφάρξασαι (§ 2) would have to turn through 100° to face an enemy sailing into the Gulf from Naupaktos. This is not so strange a station as it might seem. The purpose of the Corinthian ships was to prevent the Athenians from interfering with the departure of troopships from Elis; they could achieve this purpose by lying well to the east of the narrows, for the Athenians would be unwilling (as is shown by their taking the initiative in attack) to search westwards for the troopships so long as the Corinthians could sail out of the Gulf behind them and attack Naupaktos.

2. Πολυάνθης Κορίνθιος: a Corinthian Polyanthes is among those alleged by X. *HG* iii. 5. 1 to have accepted Persian gold in 395.

3. τριάκοντα ναυσὶ καὶ τρισίν (ἦρχε δὲ αὐτῶν Δίφιλος): Konon had 18 ships, Demosthenes had added 10 to these (31. 4 f.), and Konon would need one ship for his journey home; therefore Diphilos had brought 6 with him. The natural explanation of this relief is that Konon was one of the generals of 414/13, Diphilos one of those of 413/12, and that Diphilos arrived at Naupaktos shortly after Prytany I. 1 of 413/12, i.e. in the middle of July (cf. pp. 264–70).

5. ἀντίπρωροι ἐμβαλλόμεναι καὶ ἀναρραγεῖσαι τὰς παρεξειρεσίας ὑπό - - - παχυτέρας τὰς ἐπωτίδας ἐχουσῶν: ἐπωτίδες, which the Corinthians strengthened, were anchor-blocks (cf. E. *IT* 1351 f.) fixed one each side of the bows (cf. Strabo 138)—the ears (ὦτα), as it were, of the trireme seen head-on or from above; cf. Köster, Abb. 28, and App. *BC* v. 119, where ships in a battle collide αἱ μὲν εἰς τὰ πλάγια, αἱ δὲ κατ' ἐπωτίδας, αἱ δὲ ἐπὶ τοὺς ἐμβόλους. παρεξειρεσία is not 'that which is past the rowing', i.e. the bows, from which it is distinguished in Poll. i. 124, but 'the rowing which is along and outside', i.e. an outrigger. Polyainos iii. 11. 14 describes how Chabrias fitted to each trireme a spare pair of rudders, which διὰ τῆς παρεξειρεσίας κατὰ τὰς θρανίτιδας κώπας παρετίθει; cf. ibid. 11. 13. Arr. *Peripl. Eux.* 3. 3 describes how in a rough sea water came in μὴ κατὰ τὰς κώπας μόνον, ἀλλὰ καὶ ὑπὲρ τὰς παρεξειρεσίας. No two modern writers agree in detail on the nature and structure of this outrigger (G. S. Sale, *CR* xii [1898], 347 f.; Köster, 107 f.; F. Brewster, *HSCPh* xliv [1933], 209 ff.; W. W. Tarn, *The Mariners' Mirror* xix [1933], 61; J. S. Morrison, ibid. xxvii [1941], 29, and *CQ* xli [1947], 122 ff.). The strengthened anchor-block would sheer away the outrigger on one side of the enemy ship, taking with it the unfortunate θρανῖται and no doubt much of the attached superstructure. One such blow would not make a ship totally ἄπλους, but would make it an easy victim for further blows; yet so long as it was not rammed on the waterline it would stay afloat; cf. 40. 5.

7. ἐνόμιζον ἡσσᾶσθαι ὅτι οὐ πολὺ ἐνίκων: cf. 31. 4 n., and, for Athenian attitudes to victory and defeat, i. 70. 7.

8. ἀπέχον τοῦ Ἐρινεοῦ - - - ὡς εἴκοσι σταδίους: not as far west as Athenasteichos, which was 90 stades from Erineos (Paus. vii. 22. 10).

35. Demosthenes and Eurymedon Arrive at Rhegion

35. 2. ἐπὶ τῷ Ὑλίᾳ ποταμῷ: this river is mentioned nowhere else, and the eastern limit of the territory of Kroton is not known.

ἐπὶ Πέτραν τῆς Ῥηγίνης: Petra, otherwise unknown, may be another name for Leukopetra, but that does not help us much, since Leukopetra is (i) vaguely, *promunturium agri Regini*, Cic. *Phil.* i. 7, (ii) more exactly, a promontory 50 stades south of Rhegion (Strabo 259), i.e. Punta di Pellaro, which projects westwards towards Sicily, (iii) a promontory 15 Roman miles from Rhegion and 51 from Lokroi

(Plin. *NH* iii. 43 and 74), i.e. Capo dell'Armi, which is conspicuously light-coloured, (iv) *Tarentinorum*, Cic. *Att.* xvi. 6. 1. Cf. Philippson, *RE* xxiii. 2286, and Vallet, pl. III. As we next hear of Demosthenes and Eurymedon when they arrive at Syracuse (42. 1), it seems that they crossed to Sicily from Petra and did not go to Rhegion itself, where the first expedition had met so unfriendly a reception.

36–41. *Naval Battles at Syracuse*

36. 2. τὰς πρῴρας τῶν νεῶν ξυντεμόντες - - - τὰς ἐπωτίδας ἐπέθεσαν - - - παχείας: cf. 34. 5 n. Shortening and squaring off the bows no doubt reduced the speed of the ship, but speed was not the most important consideration in fighting in a restricted space (cf. § 3).

ἀντηρίδας ἀπ' αὐτῶν πρὸς τοὺς τοίχους ὡς ἐπὶ ἓξ πήχεις ἐντός τε καὶ ἔξωθεν: since the axis of each anchor-block was at right angles to the bows, a head-on collision would tend to force it backwards and break it off from its base. To prevent that, a heavy strut was inserted behind it to take the strain of collision. As these struts are described as being 'about six cubits long *inside and outside*', they must have extended not only from the anchor-blocks *to* (πρός) the sides of the ship but also *through* apertures in the sides, bearing at the rear on a main transverse beam. Cf. X. *Cyr.* vi. 1. 30 προσέθηκε δὲ καὶ δρέπανα σιδηρᾶ - - - πρὸς τοὺς ἄξονας. G. S. Sale, *CR* x (1896), 7 f., argues that the ἀντηρίδες were not struts at right angles to the anchor-blocks but extra pieces of timber passing through the bows and fastened both to bows and to anchor-blocks. But the word elsewhere has too wide a range of meanings to permit any precise inference; it is used of 'stretchers' in a net (X. *Cyn.* 10. 7), buttresses (Vitr. vi. 11. 6 and x. 16. 9), and struts for supporting a ladder which is pivoted at the bottom and raised from a horizontal position by ropes and pulleys (Plb. viii. 6. 6).

4. οὔτε περίπλουν οὔτε διέκπλουν: cf. ii. 83. 5 n. The defence against διέκπλους (on which Plb. i. 51. 9 and xvi. 4. 14 tell us more than anything in Thucydides), as the Syracusans perceived, is close array, which on the open sea would invite περίπλους but in a restricted space is practicable.

5. τὸ ἀντίπρωρον ξυγκροῦσαι: the text (*PHamb.* 164. 10 has τό) is probably sound; though the defence of it by Herbst–Müller (ii. 66 ff.) is on wrong grounds and makes excessive claims for the freedom of the 'absolute' neuter article. The true parallel is 67. 1 τῆς δοκήσεως προσγεγενημένης τὸ κρατίστους εἶναι εἰ τοὺς κρατίστους ἐνικήσαμεν, where the content of the δόκησις is expressed by τό *c. inf.*, not by a strictly concordant apposition, and perhaps also viii. 87. 3 καταβοῆς ἕνεκα - - - τὸ (τῷ AB) λέγεσθαι ὡς οὐκ ἀδικεῖ and Antiphon i. 28 θαυμάζω - - - τῆς τόλμης τοῦ ἀδελφοῦ καὶ τῆς διανοίας(,) τὸ διομόσασθαι, κ.τ.λ. These seem to be a natural extension from such expressions as X. *Cyr*. vii. 5. 52 ἡ δεινὴ ἀγγελία, τὸ πάντας - - - συλλέγειν; cf. Hess, *RM* lxxxvii (1938), 95. A head-on ramming with ordinary bows and rams was ἀμαθής because no one could be sure of inflicting on the enemy greater damage than he would suffer himself.

6. σφῶν ἐχόντων τὴν ἐπίπλευσιν ἀπὸ τοῦ πελάγους τε καὶ ἀνάκρουσιν: as the position of τε shows, the Syracusans reckoned that only a Syracusan ship could (*a*) turn in the open sea and row back into the harbour, choosing its point and angle of engagement, and (*b*) withdraw backwards in any direction and to virtually any point of the harbour.

37. 2. οἱ ἀπὸ τοῦ Ὀλυμπιείου: cf. p. 480.

γυμνητεία: cf. vi. 31. 3 n. on ὑπηρεσία.

3. τούς - - - κατὰ τάχος χωροῦντας ἱππέας τε πολλοὺς καὶ ἀκοντιστάς: the slower-moving hoplites (§ 2) will have been advancing behind this screen.

38. 2. πρὸ τοῦ σφετέρου σταυρώματος: whether this was semicircular, or a pair of converging lines of stakes, or three sides of a rectangle, it must have had several substantial exits, for a single narrow exit into the waters of the harbour would have caused impossibly difficult and dangerous delays in putting to sea against a Syracusan attack and would have rendered the barrier now described unnecessary. It is even possible that the σταύρωμα was simply a pair of parallel breakwaters, one each side of the beach occupied by the Athenians; but this depends on the interpretation of 41. 2, see note.

3. διαλειπούσας δὲ τὰς ὁλκάδας ὅσον δύο πλέθρα: the reason for the effectiveness of this barrier becomes apparent in 41. 2.

39. 2. Ἀρίστων ὁ Πυρρίχου Κορίνθιος: Plu. *Nic*. 25. 4 attributes to him the chief responsibility for the tactics described in c. 36 above (cf. Diod. xiii. 10. 2) and records his death in the final battle in the harbour.

τὴν ἀγορὰν τῶν πωλουμένων παρὰ τὴν θάλασσαν μεταστῆσαι κομίσαντας: lit. 'the market-place of things (sc. normally) sold', clearly distinguished from ὅσα τις ἔχει ἐδώδιμα, i.e. the private stores of individuals not normally for resale. αὐτοῖς refers to all the people who would then be selling food, retailers and private individuals alike; there is no point in Stein's αὐτοί, 'they themselves', and no necessity for Badham's αὐτόσε (*Mnemosyne* 1876, 140).

40. 3. ἐξαίφνης δὲ οἱ Συρακόσιοι πληρώσαντες τὰς ναῦς ἐπέπλεον αὖθις: according to X. *HG* ii. 1. 22 ff. Lysander owed his victory at

Aigospotamoi to a refinement on this stratagem; and Charidemos employed it to good effect (D. xxiii. 165).

4. ἀλλ' ἐπιχειρεῖν ὅτι τάχιστα: Plu. *Nic.* 20. 4 ff. represents Nikias as unwilling to fight this battle but urged into it by Menandros and Euthydemos.

5. ἀνερρήγνυσαν τὰς τῶν Ἀθηναίων ναῦς ἐπὶ πολὺ τῆς παρεξειρεσίας: cf. 34. 5 n.

οἱ ἀπὸ τῶν καταστρωμάτων: the Athenians were afterwards compelled to imitate this feature of Syracusan tactics, peculiarly suited to sea-fighting in a restricted space; cf. 62. 2 ff., 67. 2.

ἔς τε τοὺς ταρσοὺς ὑποπίπτοντες - - - καὶ ἐς τὰ πλάγια παραπλέοντες: in fourth-century naval inscriptions (e.g. *IG* ii². 1604. 23) ταρρός is a collective noun, 'oars', and in Hellenistic writers, 'bank of oars', e.g. Plb. xvi. 3. 12 ἀπέβαλε τὸν δεξιὸν ταρσὸν τῆς νεώς. All its other usages are intelligible as referring to plaiting or close packing in rows, e.g. 'wing', 'eyelash', 'roots', etc., and even its epic sense 'foot', where the row of toes is the point of resemblance. Hence Hdt. viii. 12. 1 τοὺς ταρσοὺς τῶν κωπέων ἐτάρασσον = 'threw the banks' (not 'blades') 'of the oars into confusion', i.e. prevented the oars from moving in ordered unison. The Syracusan boats were evidently rowed into contact with the sides of stationary Athenian triremes and even, where necessary, between and beneath the oars. On λεπτοῖς πλοίοις cf. 52. 1 n.

41. 2. αἱ κεραῖαι ὑπὲρ τῶν ἔσπλων αἱ ἀπὸ τῶν ὁλκάδων δελφινοφόροι ἠρμέναι: a 'dolphin-bearing spar' is a spar from which a fish-shaped weight of iron was suspended; when an enemy ship came close, the spar was swung round over it and the iron weight was dropped, with the intention that it should fall straight through the bottom of the ship. This odd but effective (§ 3) device was not peculiar to the campaign at Syracuse, but is twice referred to in Comedy; Ar. *Eq.* 762 'before he attacks . . . raise your dolphins', and Pherecr. fr. 12 δελφινοφόρος τε κερούχος, 'which will descend on the bottom of their ship, cut through it, and sink them'. Cf. Diod. xiii. 78. 4, where Konon protects the passages into the harbour at Mytilene by means of ὁλκάδες λιθοφόροι and, for full discussion of these tactics, Müller, 197 ff. In saying (38. 3) that the merchant ships were 200 feet apart Thucydides probably does not mean that an expanse of 200 feet of water was protected by the dolphins of two ships—that would imply κεραῖαι of prodigious size, strength, and weight—but that the passages through the line of stakes (ἔσπλοι), each passage being protected by a dolphin, were 200 feet apart. Each dolphin-ship naturally protected itself against ramming; cf. Müller, 200.

42–45. *Arrival of Demosthenes and Eurymedon; Night Attack on Epipolai*

42. 1. ναῦς τε τρεῖς καὶ ἑβδομήκοντα μάλιστα: Demosthenes started with 65 (20. 2), ordered 15 from Kerkyra (31. 5), and gave 10 to Konon (ibid.) ; Eurymedon sailed to Sicily with 10 (16. 2), and when he returned to meet Demosthenes at Kerkyra must have left 9 of those 10 in Sicily. On the voyage along the Italian coast they collected 2 from Metapontion. If μάλιστα (om. Bψ, probably through homoeoteleuton with ἑβδομήκοντα) is right, it means not 'about' but 'I calculate' (sc. 'assuming the correctness of the data from which the total is calculated'; cf. pp. 204 f.). ξύν here = 'including'.

καὶ ὁπλίτας - - - καὶ τὴν ἄλλην παρασκευὴν ἱκανήν: for the recruitment of allied troops cf. 31. 2, 5, and 33. 4 ff.

2. κατάπληξις - - - οὐκ ὀλίγη ἐγένετο: the control of entrance to the harbour, which the capture of Plemmyrion helped the Syracusans to achieve (36. 6) did not extend to the exclusion of Demosthenes' powerful fleet, which according to Plu. *Nic.* 21. 1 sailed in with impressive flamboyance.

εἰ πέρας μηδὲν ἔσται σφίσι τοῦ ἀπαλλαγῆναι τοῦ κινδύνου: 'as they felt that they were never going to succeed in putting themselves out of danger'; cf. D. xl. 40 τί ἂν ἦν πέρας ἡμῖν τοῦ διαλυθῆναι; and Kühner–Gerth, i. 264 f.

3. ἰδὼν ὡς εἶχε τὰ πράγματα - - - ἐκπλήξει: the formal resemblance of this sentence to vi. 64. 1 γιγνώσκοντες - - - (τοὺς γὰρ ἂν φιλούς - - -) τοιόνδε τι οὖν - - - μηχανῶνται, is less important than its formal difference ; there, the whole parenthesis is expressed in the accusative and infinitive of indirect thought (cf. vii. 51. 1), whereas here it is expressed in finite tenses and includes (ἦν οὐδ' ἂν μετέπεμψαν, κ.τ.λ.) a statement of what might have happened in certain circumstances. We must therefore regard the parenthesis as expressing Thucydides' own judgement, not merely his report of Demosthenes' judgement, though the two may largely have coincided (cf. G. Donini, *Hermes* xcii [1964], 116 ff.). ii. 13 provides the clearest example of parenthetic γάρ-clauses 'glossing' a report of another's speech (Wade-Gery and Meritt, *Hesperia* xxvi [1957], 193 ff. ; note especially ii. 13. 7, which by its nature cannot be part of what Perikles told the Athenians in 431), and iii. 113. 6, viii. 87. 4, 96. 4 are examples of Thucydides' hypothetical judgements on the past. vii. 6. 1 is intermediate in character—νομίζοντες - - - (ἤδη γάρ - - -) ἀντεπῆσαν οὖν, κ.τ.λ.— since the first part of its parenthesis is a statement of objective fact while the second part (εἰ προέλθοι, ταὐτὸν ἤδη ἐποίει, κ.τ.λ.) is a judgement in which Thucydides concurs with those whose thought he is reporting.

Thucydides, then, blames Nikias primarily for spending the winter in Katane and not 'laying siege to Syracuse at once', and secondarily,

by implication, for allowing Gylippos to reach Sicily. If we had lost
book vi and knew only that the Athenian expedition arrived in
Sicily during the summer of 415, we should infer from this passage
that there was no attack on Syracuse until the spring of 414. As it is,
two interpretations of the passage are open to us:

(i) He is condemning the failure of Nikias—and of Lamachos, who
was not killed until the summer of 414—to press the advantage they
gained by their surprise landing and victory in the harbour, described in vi. 64–71. This interpretation makes the clearest contrast
with 'spent the winter in Katane'. It necessitates reference of
ἀφικόμενος to the landing in the harbour, not to the Athenians'
arrival in Sicily.

(ii) He is condemning the adoption by the three generals of
Alkibiades' plan instead of Lamachos' (vi. 49). This accords well (cf.
vi. 49. 2) with ἀφικόμενος - - - φοβερός and with his representation of
Demosthenes' insistence on the importance of seizing the initiative
while the enemy's morale is still affected by his arrival. ὑπερώφθη
also accords well with the description (vi. 63. 2) of how the Syracusans'
courage revived *before* the landing in the harbour. But it means that
'spent the winter in Katane' is a compressed and misleading way of
saying 'established a summer base at Katane with the intention of
returning there for the winter' (hence διεχρόνιζεν cj. J. Weidgen,
RhM lxxvii [1928], 385 f.). Neither interpretation is in tune with
vi. 71, where we are given the impression that the Athenians would
have established themselves at Syracuse after their victory if only
the enemy cavalry had not proved so formidable; there, Thucydides makes no comment on the generals' decision to withdraw
(Luschnat, 78 n. 2, infers that he thought the Syracusan cavalry
overrated and the withdrawal unnecessary). Neither, again, ab-
solves Thucydides from a charge of rhetorical distortion (both are
unjust to Nikias, in so far as they ignore the responsibility of his
colleagues, but this injustice is determined by the context, where the
issue is essentially between Demosthenes and Nikias). The distortion
is much less gross in the former interpretation than in the latter. To
say that the Syracusans 'would have thought that they were a match
for Nikias, and by the time they discovered that they were not they
would have been walled off' is just, since Syracusan morale was
broken not (vi. 72 f. and 75) by their defeat by the Helorine road but
by the Athenian victories and siege-walls in 414 (vi. 103. 3, cf. Plu.
Nic. 17. 1 ff.), and they were dissuaded from capitulation by the
arrival of Gongylos in the nick of time (vii. 2. 1) just as they were
saved from circumvallation by Gylippos (2. 4).

The tone of the whole passage strongly suggests that Thucydides
believed that Lamachos was right in his initial plan, and, therefore,
that Alkibiades was wrong. Yet this conclusion has to be reconciled

with ii. 65. 11, where the failure of the expedition is attributed to the recall of Alkibiades. Reconciliation may be achieved by the hypothesis that Thucydides changed his mind, vii. 42. 3 representing his opinion at the time he wrote book vii, ii. 65. 11 his opinion after the end of the war, under the influence of the activities of Alkibiades in 411–407, so highly praised in vi. 15. 3 f. (on this hypothesis, a later insertion into the narrative of the Sicilian expedition). I am not sure, however, that a fundamental change of opinion is a necessary hypothesis; it is rather a question of two different strands of opinion. It was quite possible for Thucydides to believe simultaneously that (a) Lamachos put forward the best plan at the start of the campaign, (b) even though the wrong plan was adopted, victory was still possible, as his own narrative of the events of 414 makes plain, (c) if Alkibiades had been present at the Athenian victory by the harbour, he would have persuaded his colleagues to press on with the siege at once, and (d) even if he had failed to do that, he would have accelerated operations after the death of Lamachos (cf. Freeman, ii. 230 ff.) and would have taken more effective steps to prevent the arrival of Gylippos in Sicily.

It would, however, be correct to speak at least of a change of emphasis: considerations (a) and (b) seem to have been prominent in Thucydides' mind at the time of writing vii. 42. 3, while (c) and (d) were apparent at the time of writing vi. 15. 3 f.

οὐχ οἷόν τε εἶναι διατρίβειν οὐδὲ παθεῖν ὅπερ ὁ Νικίας ἔπαθεν: 'not possible to waste time or (sc. desirable) to incur the difficulties which Nikias had incurred' (cf. 61. 2 and Isoc. v. 24 μή - - - ἀποστῆς - - - μηδὲ πάθης ταὐτὸν τοῖς ἐπιτηδείοις τοῖς ἐμοῖς), rather than (Marchant and Steup) 'not possible to waste time without incurring (sc. as a consequence of wasting time) . . .'. Cf. Hp. Aer. 9 οὐ γὰρ οἷόν τε ἕτερον ἑτέρῳ ἐοικέναι ὕδωρ, ἀλλὰ (sc. ἀνάγκη) τὰ μὲν γλυκέα εἶναι, κ.τ.λ.

ἀφικόμενος γὰρ τὸ πρῶτον ὁ Νικίας φοβερός: not 'when Nikias arrived he at first inspired fear', sc. ἦν, for that would require ὡς ⟨δ'⟩ to follow; 'Nikias having at first inspired fear' (sc. ὢν or γενόμενος) is possible, but it is better to take φοβερός closely in sense with ἀφικόμενος, τὸ πρῶτον being pleonastic as in vi. 46. 2 (cf. n.). Hence: 'For when Nikias, whose first arrival inspired fear, did not at once . . .'

τῇ πρώτῃ ἡμέρᾳ μάλιστα δεινότατος: μάλιστα can accompany a superlative, as in Hdt. i. 171, but it is also possible (pace Steup) to treat it as part of a progressive intensification: 'at that time, on the first day, more than (= and not) at any other time, most formidable'.

τῇ παρούσῃ τοῦ στρατεύματος ἐκπλήξει: 'the consternation caused (sc. in Syracuse) at this moment by his force'; cf. 47. 3 n.

43. 1. κατεκαύθησάν τε - - - αἱ μηχαναί: cf. Aen. Tact. 33. 1 f. on the ways of setting fire to siege-engines.

2. τοξευμάτων τε: τοξεύματα occurs elsewhere in Thucydides only = 'arrows' (e.g. iv. 34. 1), but here it is better interpreted as 'corps of archers', as in Hdt. v. 112. 2 οὔτε ἵππου (= 'cavalry') ὑπαρχούσης οὔτε τοξευμάτων.

τὴν πᾶσαν στρατιάν: Plu. Nic. 27. 1 says τὴν πεζὴν στρατιάν, and Diod. xiii. 11. 3 10,000 hoplites and 10,000 light-armed troops. Nothing in Thucydides' narrative suggests that any troops but the hoplites took part in the fight (e.g. 44. 2, 45. 1 f.), but he has just told us that archers were included in the force; presumably the light-armed troops were held back at the foot of the ascent to Euryelos, ready to be brought forward in daylight as a protection against cavalry attacks when the hoplites had mastered the counter-wall and the forts.

3. τὸ πρῶτον ἀνέβη: cf. vi. 97. 2.

4. ἐν προτειχίσμασιν: cf. p. 478.

καὶ τοῖς ἑξακοσίοις τῶν Συρακοσίων: the body of 600 picked men, constituted in 414 (vi. 96. 3), suffered very heavily in its first encounter with the Athenians (vi. 97. 4), but evidently had been reconstituted.

5. ὅπως τῇ παρούσῃ ὁρμῇ τοῦ περαίνεσθαι ὧν ἕνεκα ἦλθον μὴ βραδεῖς γένωνται: περαίνεσθαι appears to be passive, since the middle is nowhere attested except in composition with δια-, and it is easier to relate τοῦ περαίνεσθαι to βραδεῖς (cf. ὕστερος, ὑστερεῖν, and ἐλλιπής, c. gen.) than to ὁρμῇ: 'so that they might not be slow, with the impetus of the moment, in the accomplishment of the purpose for which they had come'. Cf. Pl. Grg. 454 c τοῦ ἑξῆς ἕνεκα περαίνεσθαι τὸν λόγον ἐρωτῶ, X. An. iii. 2. 32 ἵνα ἔργῳ περαίνηται = 'to get the job done'. An alternative syntactical analysis, with little difference of meaning, is to take μὴ βραδεῖς = 'quick' and τοῦ c. inf. = ὥστε c. inf.; cf. 21. 3 n. Herwerden characteristically, but perhaps rightly, deleted ὅπως and μὴ βραδεῖς γένωνται as an interpolated explanation of the 'infinitive of purpose'.

ἀπὸ τῆς πρώτης τὸ παρατείχισμα - - - ᾔρουν: 'others began by capturing the counter-wall', sc. instead of pressing on to defeat the main body of the enemy. Cf. i. 77. 3 ἀπὸ πρώτης ἀποθέμενοι τὸν νόμον = 'setting the law aside to begin with', sc. instead of circumventing it later; given the parallel, we can hardly understand ὁρμῆς, as Herbst, ii. 125 ff., suggested. τό (transp. Göller) before παρατείχισμα is indispensable; τό before ἀπό (codd.) is a matter of indifference.

7. οἱ Βοιωτοί: cf. 19. 3 and 25. 3.

44. 1. οὐδ' ἀφ' ἑτέρων: cf. v. 26. 5 and pp. 466 f.

ἐν μὲν γὰρ ἡμέρᾳ σαφέστερα μέν - - - μόλις οἶδεν: 'for in (a battle by) day (men know what happened) more clearly, but even that those who have taken part do not (know) completely, except each individual, with some difficulty, knows (what happened in) his own part of the field.' For the singular verb, accommodated to the nearer ἕκαστος rather than to the further οἱ παραγενόμενοι, cf. vi. 65. 2. In i. 22. 3 Thucydides complains more generally of the adverse effects of partiality and uncertain memory on all eye-witness accounts; the present passage is unique in raising this general point in the course of the narrative, but cf. v. 68. 2 and Schmid, 156 f.

ἔν γε τῷδε τῷ πολέμῳ: from 431 to the time of writing; night battles in the Greek world were not so common as to make the point that this was the only night battle in the Sicilian campaign worth emphasizing. In 408, according to Diod. xiii. 72. 2–73. 2, Agis approached Athens with a very large force under cover of a moonless night, but the Athenian defenders of the walls were alerted in time, and there was no νυκτομαχία.

2. ἦν μὲν γὰρ σελήνη λαμπρά: Plu. Nic. 21. 10 says that the moon was setting behind the Athenians during the battle. This is highly unlikely, since they needed to approach Euryelos in darkness and advance across Epipolai as the moon rose behind their enemies—conditions which would best be satisfied, at that time and place, in the second week of August (Busolt, iii/2. 1372 f. n. 4).

τὴν μὲν ὄψιν τοῦ σώματος προορᾶν, τὴν δὲ γνῶσιν τοῦ οἰκείου ἀπιστεῖσθαι: lit., 'to see the sight of the body beforehand, but the knowledge of what is one's own to be mistrusted', i.e. 'one sees that someone is there before there can be any assurance that he is on one's own side'.

4. σημῆναι: 'give an order', as commonly; cf. 50. 3.

5. ὥστ' εἰ μὲν ἐντύχοιέν τισι - - - διεφθείροντο: 'so that if they (sc. Athenians) encountered, in superior force, a body of the enemy, they (sc. the enemy) got away from them (sc. the Athenians), knowing the Athenian password, but if the Athenians themselves did not answer (sc. when challenged in similar circumstances by Syracusans, etc.) they were killed.'

ἐπιστάμενοι τὸ ξύνθημα: to judge from the lack of imagination shown in Greek passwords (X. An. i. 8. 16, vi. 5. 25, Cyr. iii. 3. 58, vii. 1. 10) it must sometimes have happened that opposite sides had the same password.

6. ἔβλαψε καὶ ὁ παιανισμός· ἀπὸ γὰρ ἀμφοτέρων παραπλήσιος ὢν ἀπορίαν παρεῖχεν: the singing of the paean as a prayer before a battle or expedition (vi. 32. 2) or as a hymn of thanks after a victory was a universal Greek custom, but in Thucydides the paean as a war-cry in battle or as a signal to attack is Boeotian (iv. 96. 1), Peloponnesian (ii. 91. 2), Corinthian (iv. 43. 3), Kerkyrean (i. 50. 4), and Syracusan (vii. 83. 4), never Athenian or Ionian. In this passage it is Dorian in general; Thucydides' point is not that there were peoples of similar dialects on both sides, but that there was no paean at all from the Athenians and Ionians.

8. [οἱ] πολλοὶ ῥίπτοντες ἑαυτούς: if οἱ is sound, it must mean 'the majority of those who were killed' (cf. 30. 2 n.), not 'the majority of the Athenian force'. Plu. Nic. 21. 11 suggests that Plutarch's text had οἱ here and that he drew a wrong inference from it in conjunction with 45. 2: 'of those who survived' (sc. the battle) 'few got away safely with their arms.'

45. 2. ἀπέθανον δὲ οὐκ ὀλίγοι αὐτῶν τε καὶ τῶν ξυμμάχων: 2,000 in Plu. Nic. 21. 11, 2,500 in Diod. xiii. 11. 5.

ψιλοὶ [ἄνευ τῶν ἀσπίδων]: as ψιλός in 78. 3, iii. 27. 2, etc. means 'without a hoplite's armour', the words ἄνευ τῶν ἀσπίδων are unnecessary and may be rightly deleted (by Pluygers, *Mnemosyne* 1862, 95, following Haacke) as an explanatory interpolation.

46–50. Aftermath of the Battle on Epipolai

46. ἐς μὲν Ἀκράγαντα στασιάζοντα: on the politics of Akragas cf. 32. 1 n.

Σικανὸν ἀπέστειλαν: elected general in the autumn of 415 (vi. 73. 1), deposed the following summer (103. 4), and now back in favour; cf. 52. 2 n. and 70. 1.

47. 1. πρὸς τὴν παροῦσαν - - - κατὰ πάντα ἀρρωστίαν: κατὰ πάντα and the details which follow show that ἀρρωστία here has a general sense, 'weakness' or 'impotence' (cf. iii. 15. 2 ἀρρωστία τοῦ στρατεύειν), not (as LSJ) 'loss of morale'.

2. καὶ τὸ χωρίον ἅμα - - - ἑλῶδες καὶ χαλεπὸν ἦν: they may have fallen victim, like other armies after them, to the malaria of the coastal regions of Sicily; and, like other armies in all ages, they knew that marshy ground was unhealthy without knowing why. But it is uncertain how far that part of the Mediterranean at that period was malarial, and fly-borne intestinal diseases must have flourished in the conditions in which the Athenians were compelled to live.

τά τε ἄλλα ὅτι ἀνέλπιστα αὐτοῖς ἐφαίνετο: if the text is sound, νόσῳ is co-ordinated with ὅτι: 'they were oppressed (*a*) by disease . . . , and (*b*) because . . .'; cf. Lüdtke, 35 f. With Reiske's plausible conjecture ὅτι ἀνελπιστότατα, the co-ordination is different: '(*a*) they were oppressed by disease . . ., and (*b*) everything else . . .'.

3. ἀπιέναι ἐψηφίζετο καὶ μὴ διατρίβειν: the repetition of (μὴ) διατρίβειν (42. 3 and 43. 1) conveys, and is meant to convey, the passion with which Demosthenes strove to make Nikias see the situation as it was; cf. the repetition of αἰσχρόν in viii. 27. 2 f., giving in reported

speech the effect of passionate scorn which is given in direct speech
by (e.g.) Ar. *Lys.* 430 ff.

ἕως ἔτι τὸ πέλαγος οἷόν τε περαιοῦσθαι καὶ τοῦ στρατεύματος ταῖς
γοῦν ἐπελθούσαις ναυσὶ κρατεῖν: lit, 'while it was still possible for
them to be conveyed across the sea' (i.e. before bad weather made
a return voyage impracticable) 'and, of their forces, they had the
upper hand at least with the ships which had come as reinforcements'.
As it is still August (50. 4 n.) it is remarkable that Demosthenes
should be thinking of the onset of winter storms, but the words
leave no doubt of this—he speaks of crossing the sea, not of escaping
from Syracuse—and the position of τοῦ στρατεύματος points to a distinction between the two elements on which the issue turned, nature
and arms, both at that time in their favour. Demosthenes had
formed a strong impression of Nikias' capacity for delay, and may
well have thought that if a decision to withdraw were not taken now
he could not persuade Nikias to reconsider it until the winter was
at hand.

4. πρὸς τοὺς ἐν τῇ χώρᾳ σφῶν ἐπιτειχίζοντας: the fact that Demosthenes could use this argument is a strategic vindication of the
Spartan occupation of Dekeleia.

48. 1. ψηφιζομένους μετὰ πολλῶν: how large a body Nikias has in
mind is not clear; he may possibly have contemplated putting the
issue to the vote of the whole Athenian component of his forces,
but he does not seem to envisage that in § 4, and even if only taxiarchs
(as in 60. 2) and trierarchs were brought into the discussion, enough
men would be involved to make it certain that the decision would
become generally known. On the problem of Thucydides' sources
for these two chapters, cf. vi. 46. 5 n.

λαθεῖν γὰρ ἄν, ὁπότε βούλοιντο, τοῦτο ποιοῦντες πολλῷ ἧσσον: probably 'for (sc. if they voted at a meeting for retreat) they would be
much less able to do this (= retreat) without the enemy's knowledge
when they wished to' rather than 'for if they did this (= voted at
a meeting) they would be much less able to escape the enemy's
notice (sc. in retreating) when they wished (sc. to retreat)', as γάρ
commonly = 'for thus'.

2. καὶ ἦν γάρ τι - - - ἐπεκηρυκεύετο ὡς αὐτόν: the identity, strength,
and motives of this 'fifth column' are unknown to us; cf. 49. 1 n.
and 55. 2 n. Probably some of the wealthy citizens of Leontinoi
who in 422 had become citizens of Syracuse and had not broken
away among the earlier malcontents (v. 4. 3 f.) were now hankering
after an independent Leontinoi. (Diod. xiii. 18. 5 says that the
Athenians believed that the message delivered after the last battle
[73. 3] came from Leontinians.) These men, in order to retain the
help of a powerful ally, their only hope, would not have hesitated

to deceive Nikias, and perhaps themselves too, by an exaggerated picture of Syracusan difficulties (cf. Alkidas' Ionian friends [iii. 31. 1]; and the conduct of emigrés in our own day provides parallels), but Thucydides does not deny (49. 1) that Syracuse was short of money.

3. Ἀθηναῖοι σφῶν ταῦτα οὐκ ἀποδέξονται: Nikias and his colleagues were dispatched αὐτοκράτορες (vi. 8. 2); but this would not save them from their country's anger if they were held to blame for failure. A striking example is afforded by Andokides and his fellow envoys in 392/1: Philoch. F 149 a ~ And. iii. 33.

καὶ γὰρ οὐ τοὺς αὐτοὺς ψηφιεῖσθαί τε - - - καί - - - γνώσεσθαι: Nikias is not thinking primarily (as an Athenian general might sometimes think) of the situation in which men sit in judgement, as a jury, on a man under whose command they have served as soldiers, but of the majority of citizens, who will not have been at Syracuse, and (§ 4) of the extent to which even the minority which has been there will fall in with the prevailing mood and seek a scapegoat for its own military failure.

4. ὑπὸ χρημάτων καταπροδόντες: for 'betrayal' by generals cf. vi. 103.4 and the fate of the Athenian generals who returned from Sicily in 424 (iv. 65. 3).

ἐπιστάμενος τὰς Ἀθηναίων φύσεις: cf. 14. 4 n.

τοῦτο παθεῖν ἰδίᾳ: death under sentence from a jury would be δημοσίᾳ, because the decision would be taken by the state; ἰδίᾳ therefore means 'on his own initiative', 'at a time, and in a manner, of his own choosing'. Nikias' pride and consequent cowardice in the face of personal disgrace lead him to put forward as disgraceful a proposition as any general in history: rather than risk execution, he will throw away the fleet and many thousands of other people's lives, and put his country in mortal peril. Even Grote's condemnation (vi. 145 f.) of his 'guilty fatuity' on this occasion may be thought unduly temperate.

5. τά τε Συρακοσίων ἔφη ὅμως ἔτι ἥσσω - - - εἶναι: ὅμως = 'in spite of everything', cf. 1. 2 n.

6. τρίβειν οὖν ἔφη χρῆναι προσκαθημένους: in view of τρίβειν αὐτούς in 49. 2, where Demosthenes is referring explicitly to Nikias' arguments (αὐτούς is emended there to αὐτοῦ by Krüger, followed by more recent editors, but cf. Haacke ad loc. and Fraenkel on A. Ag. 1055), the meaning must be 'wear down (sc. Syracuse) by a siege'; cf. viii. 46. 4 τρίβειν οὖν ἐκέλευε πρῶτον ἀμφοτέρους. There is no certain example of intransitive τρίβειν = διατρίβειν.

καὶ μὴ χρήμασιν, ὧν πολὺ κρείσσους εἰσί, νικηθέντας ἀπιέναι: ὧν B : ᾧ f : ὣ ψ: ὡς cett. In ii. 60. 5 χρημάτων κρείσσων = 'incorruptible', and Danielsson, Eranos xiii (1913), 237 f., suggests that the expression χρήμασιν - - - νικηθέντας is deliberately chosen in order to compare

426

withdrawal through fear of expenditure to corruption. ὧν could have the sense 'in which'; cf. i. 80. 4 ἀλλὰ τοῖς χρήμασιν; ἀλλὰ πολλῷ ἔτι πλέον τούτου ἐλλείπομεν. But ᾧ is supported by 62. 3, and in this context corruption of ᾧ to ὧν or ὡς is so much more likely than the reverse as to make it almost certain that Thucydides wrote ᾧ. Cf. Pl. Smp. 182 c οὐ - - - συμφέρει - - - φρονήματα μεγάλα ἐγγίγνεσθαι - - - οὐδὲ φιλίας - - - ὃ δή - - - φιλεῖ - - - ὁ ἔρως ἐμποιεῖν, X. Cyr. vii. 5. 56 ἑστίας, οὗ (v.l. ἧς) οὔτε ὁσιώτερον χωρίον, κ.τ.λ. Nikias betrays a certain obsession with the financial aspect of war (cf. 83. 2), and this may explain some of the weaknesses of his strategy; he underrated the other half of the Periclean dictum (ii. 13. 2) τὰ δὲ πολλὰ τοῦ πολέμου γνώμῃ καὶ χρημάτων περιουσίᾳ κρατεῖσθαι. Cf. Bender, 40.

49. 1. αἰσθόμενος - - - κρατήσειν: the long-winded recapitulation of 48 is surprising, and 48 is itself repetitious (§ 2 ~ § 5). Possibly a further revision would have shortened 48–9; cf. 27. 3–28 n.

καὶ ὅτι ἦν αὐτόθι πολὺ τὸ βουλόμενον τοῖς Ἀθηναίοις γίγνεσθαι τὰ πράγματα: it was τι in 48. 2; πολύ is Linwood's conjecture (JKPh. viii [1862], for που B: om. cett.). J. U. Powell, CR xxvi (1912), 123, added ⟨ὑπό⟩ before τοῖς, cl. Hdt. vii. 11. 3 ἵνα - - - ὑπὸ ῞Ελλησι ἤ - - - ὑπὸ Πέρσῃσι γένηται, and H. Richards, CQ vi (1912), 228, suggested that ὑπό, misplaced, >που. But Plu. Nic. 20. 5 has ἄνδρες οὐκ ὀλίγοι, which suggests that he read πολύ, surprising though this may seem.

καὶ ἅμα ταῖς γοῦν ναυσὶ μᾶλλον ἢ πρότερον ἐθάρσησε κρατήσειν: B has θαρρῶν (om. cett.), for which Herwerden conjectured μᾶλλον; then ἐθάρσησε B, θαρσήσει cett., and at the end κρατηθείς codd., κρατήσειν Herwerden. Since θαρσεῖν is never used with the constructions of verbs of thinking in Thucydides, and hardly ever in Attic elsewhere, while θαρρῶν (note -ρρ-) looks like an intrusive gloss designed to 'regularize' the characteristic Thucydidean inconcinnity αἰσθόμενος - - - καὶ ἅμα - - - ἐθάρσησε, I propose ταῖς γοῦν ναυσὶν ἐθάρσησε, πρότερον κρατηθείς. For ταῖς ναυσί cf. 55. 2 ταῖς ναυσὶν ἐκρατήθησαν = 'they lost superiority at sea' and D. xix. 253 οὔτε κατὰ γῆν παρελθὼν οὔτε ναυσὶ κρατήσας. For the layout of the sentence cf. vi. 16. 2 μείζω ἡμῶν τὴν πόλιν ἐνόμισαν - - -, πρότερον ἐλπίζοντες, κ.τ.λ., iii. 81. 2 τούς τε Μεσσηνίους ἐς τὴν πόλιν ἤγαγον, πρότερον ἔξω ὄντας and X. HG v. 4. 1 ὑπ' αὐτῶν μόνων τῶν ἀδικηθέντων ἐκολάσθησαν πρῶτον, οὐδ' ὑφ' ἑνὸς τῶν πώποτε ἀνθρώπων κρατηθέντες. For the processes by which Thucydides' words were transformed into what the MSS. present, cf. the remarkable situation at ii. 96. 3.

2. ἀλλὰ τρίβειν αὐτοῦ: so Krüger, but cf. 48. 6 n.

ἐν στενοχωρίᾳ, ἢ πρὸς τῶν πολεμίων μᾶλλόν ἐστι: cf. 36. 3, 67. 3.

3. καὶ μὴ μέλλειν: cf. 47. 3 n.

καὶ ὁ Εὐρυμέδων αὐτῷ ταῦτα ξυνηγόρευεν: on the absence of Menandros and Euthydemos from these deliberations cf. 16. 1 n.

50. 1. ὁ δὲ Γύλιππος καὶ ὁ Σικανὸς ἐν τούτῳ παρῆσαν: cf. 46.

ἡ τοῖς Συρακοσίοις στάσις [ἐς] φιλία ἐξεπεπτώκει: ἐς (del. Bauer) is clearly impossible; ἡ τοῖς Συρακοσίοις στάσις is not Greek for 'the pro-Syracusan faction', nor ἐς φίλια (neut. plur.) for 'into friendly territory'. On the stasis at Akragas cf. 46.

τοὺς ἐκ τῆς Πελοποννήσου - - - ἀποσταλέντας: 19. 3 f.

2. δόντων Κυρηναίων: Kyrene, as a colony of Thera (and thus ultimately of Sparta), could reasonably be expected to help Peloponnesians.

Εὐεσπερίταις - - - ξυμμαχήσαντες: Euesperides is the later Berenike, the modern Benghazi. Gomme (ms.) remarks that the Athenians were not the only people who spent precious time on peripheral military activities.

ἐς Νέαν πόλιν, Καρχηδονιακὸν ἐμπόριον: it appears from Strabo 834, Plin. *NH* v. 24, that this place was on the east coast of Cape Bon, and the modern Nabeul is the obvious identification; the distance from Nabeul to Selinus is 230 km., so that the average speed implied by Thucydides' datum is rather less than 6·5 km.p.h. (cf. vi. 1. 2 n.). It is interesting that the Peloponnesians preferred this circuitous route, which brought them eventually to the wrong end of Sicily, to a direct voyage from Euesperides to Syracuse, which would not have taken much longer than from the Peloponnese to Syracuse; possibly the direct route from Cyrenaica was little used and the distance exaggerated.

3. ἀλλ' ἢ μὴ φανερῶς γε ἀξιῶν ψηφίζεσθαι: cf. 48. 1 n.

προεῖπον - - - ἔκπλουν ἐκ τοῦ στρατοπέδου πᾶσι, καὶ παρασκευάσασθαι ὅταν τις σημήνῃ: 'issued to everyone, as secretly as they could, a warning order (προ-) for departure from their position and (sc. ordered them in advance) to prepare (sc. to depart) when the order should be given'. παρεσκευάσθαι (Abresch) makes a slight difference to the sense: 'to be prepared by the time the order should be given' rather than 'to prepare (sc. now) for when . . .', but is unnecessary. For προεῖπον - - - ἔκπλουν cf. Pi. *O.* 7. 32 f. ὁ χρυσοκόμας - - - ναῶν πλόον εἶπε.

4. ἡ σελήνη ἐκλείπει: 27 August 413 (Boll, *RE* vi. 2355).

οἵ τε πλείους ἐπισχεῖν ἐκέλευον τοὺς στρατηγούς: later writers, from Diodoros (xiii. 12. 6) to the present day, have tended to blame Nikias for his unenlightened superstition and (by implication) to exonerate the majority of the Athenians who, according to Thucydides here, made the eclipse a matter of religious scruple (cf. 18. 2 n.). Philochoros F 135, a seer himself (T1, cf. F 76–88), asserts that the omen was misinterpreted; Plu. *Nic.* 23, using and citing Philochoros, offers the excuse for Nikias that his trusted seer Stilbides was dead, but (like Diodoros) he attributes to Nikias personally, not to the professional seers, the insistence on a delay of 27 days. Thucydides'

criticism of Nikias is not that he was more superstitious than the
men whom he commanded but that as an educated man in a responsible position he should have paid less attention to seers (θειασμός, wrongly translated by LSJ, is utterance which claims to reveal
through a human medium the intentions of the gods; cf. viii. 1. 1)
and should have recognized eclipses as a natural phenomenon.
Possibly Demosthenes, left to himself, would have succeeded in persuading the men to disregard the seers' warning; cf. Pl. *La.* 198 e
on the need for a general to be master, not servant, of his seer (Bender, 42), the anecdote (attached to an occasion on which we know
that in fact there was no eclipse) about Perikles in Plu. *Per.* 35. 2,
and the attitude of Dion and his seer Miltas (Plu. *Dion* 24. 1 ff.).
Thucydides himself, who was not well disposed towards seers and
oracles (cf. ii. 54. 2 f., v. 26. 3 f.; de Romilly, *Imp.*, 292), was not
unique among his contemporaries in preferring scientific to theo-
logical explanations; cf. especially Hp. *Aer.* 3 ἃ νομίζουσι τὸ θεῖον
ποιεῖν, κ.τ.λ. He made an empirical statement about solar eclipses
(ii. 28) and may have known that a lunar eclipse can occur only
when the moon is full (cf. the argument of W. K. Pritchett and B. L.
van der Waerden, *BCH* lxxxv [1961], 17 ff., for Thucydides' scientific
interest in the calendar); but γάρ in ἐτύγχανε γὰρ πανσέληνος οὖσα
may make only the simple point that the visible event which we call
a lunar eclipse was able to happen on this occasion because there
was a substantial amount of moon to be eclipsed.

τρὶς ἐννέα ἡμέρας μεῖναι: the phraseology is oracular; cf. v. 26. 4.

51–54. *Naval Battle at Syracuse*

51. 2 κατά τινας πύλας: πύλαι here, as commonly (e.g. ii. 2. 2 and
4. 5), is used of a single gate.

ἵππους τε ἑβδομήκοντα ἀπολλύασι: they abandoned their horses in
order to escape into their fortifications on foot.

52. 1. ἓξ καὶ ἑβδομήκοντα: 74 in Diod. xiii. 13. 1. It was in this battle,
according to Plu. *Nic.* 24. 1 ff. (from Philistos?), that Syracusan boys
in fishing-boats were in the fray. Diod. xiii. 14. 4 refers to the last
battle in the harbour. Busolt (*Hermes* xxxiv [1899], 285 f.) may well
be right in associating the incident with the λεπτὰ πλοῖα of 40. 5.

ἓξ καὶ ὀγδοήκοντα: before the arrival of their reinforcements the
Athenians had put 75 ships to sea (37. 3), of which 'one or two' were
sunk on the first day's fighting (38. 1), 'seven sunk and many
damaged' on the second day (41. 4). Thereupon Demosthenes and
Eurymedon arrived with 73 (42. 1); but the majority of these ships
were carrying troops (cf. vi. 43 n. and Busolt, iii/2. 1370, 1379), and
apart from the technical problem of reconverting troop-carriers in

a hurry the number of spare crews cannot in any event have exceeded the number of ships lost or put out of action, and human casualties would have made it smaller.

2. ἔχοντα τὸ δεξιὸν κέρας: Diod. xiii. 13. 2 puts Euthydemos on the left wing and Menandros in the centre, and on the opposing side Agatharchos on the right, Sikanos on the left, and Pythen in the centre; that may be based on the order of names in 70. 1, but cf. 53. 4 n. Diod. xiii. 39. 4 similarly reverses the right and left of the Athenian fleet as described by Th. viii. 104. 3 at the battle of Kynossema. In the present battle I imagine the Athenian line as running NW.–SE., facing NE.; Eurymedon sailed so close to Ortygia that he found himself eventually facing NNW., and was isolated in the northern end of the harbour.

ἐν τῷ κοίλῳ καὶ μυχῷ τοῦ λιμένος: cf. p. 480.

καὶ τὰς μετ' αὐτοῦ ναῦς ἐπισπομένας: seven were lost, according to Diod. xiii. 13. 4.

53. 1. ἐπὶ τὴν χηλήν: cf. p. 484.

2. οἱ Τυρσηνοί: cf. 57. 11 n.

ἐς τὴν λίμνην τὴν Λυσιμέλειαν καλουμένην: cf. p. 484.

4. ἐμπρῆσαι βουλόμενοι: Sikanos' suggestion, according to Diod. xiii. 13. 6.

55–56. *Syracusan Strategy*

55. 1. γεγενημένης δὲ τῆς νίκης - - - λαμπρᾶς: almost 'decisive'—via 'outstanding'—as in 71. 5 ἐπικείμενοι λαμπρῶς.

2. μόναις ἤδη ὁμοιοτρόποις: Thucydides returns to this theme in viii. 96. 5.

δημοκρατουμέναις τε, ὥσπερ καὶ αὐτοί: we have seen Syracusan democracy in operation; cf. vi. 32. 3–41. Some difficulty is caused by the statement in Arist. *Pol.* 1304ᵃ27 that after the defeat of the Athenians ἐν Συρακούσαις ὁ δῆμος - - - ἐκ πολιτείας εἰς δημοκρατίαν μετέβαλον. Aristotle explains elsewhere what he means by πολιτεία: it is ἐκ τῶν ὁπλιτευόντων (1265ᵇ26); it is a mixture between oligarchy and democracy, 'but they are accustomed to give the name πολιτεία to those πολιτεῖαι which incline towards democracy' (1293ᵇ33); 'democracy is a παρέκβασις of the πολιτεία - - - πρὸς τὸ συμφέρον τὸ τῶν ἀπόρων' (1279ᵇ4). His statement on Syracuse is corroborated by Diod. xiii. 34. 6, who dates after certain events of 412 the adoption of the proposal of Diokles, 'the most influential of the demagogues at Syracuse', that appointment to office should be made by lot and that a commission of νομοθέται should be set up (an anecdote in Plu. *Reg. Imp. Apophth.* 175 c–d presupposes use of the lot in determining order of speaking in the assembly at the time of Dionysios'

rise to power). The truth may be that until the reforms of Diokles—
for which 412 would be too early a date; Hermokrates and his colleagues in the Aegean were not sentenced to exile until 411/10 (X.
HG i. 1. 27, cf. Th. viii. 85. 3; Hüttl, 85 ff.)—appointment to office
was by election, and, the voting habits of the Greek electorate being
what they were, the well-to-do were usually elected, so that political
influence was essentially in the hands of the upper classes. It is
important that elsewhere (Pol. 1316ª33) Aristotle says that the
tyranny 'of Gelon' (i.e. of the Deinomenid family) was followed by
democracy, and Diod. xi. 68. 6, referring to the end of the tyranny,
says that the Syracusans 'preserved their democracy for nearly sixty
years, down to the tyranny of Dionysios'. It is even more important
that Syracuse seemed to Thucydides democratic enough, in the
Athenian sense, to justify the point which he makes here. These few
words of Thucydides demolish the thesis of H. Wentker, 52 ff., that
Syracuse was not a democracy in 415–413; cf. the review of Wentker
by P. A. Brunt in CR N.S. vii (1957), 243 ff.

καὶ μεγέθη ἐχούσαις: 'developed on a large scale'; cf. Hp. Fract. 2
ἀπὸ τῶν τοιούτων - - - ἀφεσίων - - - ταχεῖαι καὶ αἱ ἰσχύες καὶ τὰ μήκεα
γίγνονται and Aer. 15 τά τε μεγέθεα μεγάλοι, τὰ πάχεα δ' ὑπερπάχητες.
οὐ δυνάμενοι ἐπενεγκεῖν οὔτ' ἐκ πολιτείας τι μεταβολῆς τὸ διάφορον
αὐτοῖς, ᾧ προσήγοντο ἄν, οὔτ' ἐκ παρασκευῆς πολλῷ κρείσσονος:
'when they were unable to bring anything to bear upon them (a) by
means of a change in political structure or (b) by means of greatly
superior force' clearly describes the consequences of the two
respects in which Syracuse was like Athens. The interpretation of
τὸ διάφορον is difficult. (i) If it refers only to political difference, lit.
'to bring to bear upon them something from a change of constitution,
(I mean) the (political) difference (between them), by which they
were accustomed to bring (an enemy) over', the separation of
αὐτοῖς from ἐπενεγκεῖν is extraordinary, for it is thrust into the
middle of a parenthesis which explains τι. (ii) If, on the other hand,
τὸ διάφορον refers to difference in general, the position of αὐτοῖς is
less abnormal (cf. ὑμῖν 64. 1), τι will be an 'internal accusative' with
the verbal noun μεταβολῆς (on verbal nouns in Thucydides cf. vi.
82. 4 n.), and προσάγεσθαι will cover the inducement of surrender both
by the promise of political change and by the threat of destruction,
lit.: 'to bring to bear upon them (= to use as a weapon against them)
the difference (between them), by which they were accustomed to
induce (an enemy) to surrender, either as a result of a (promised)
change, in some respect, of constitution, or as a result of much greater
forces'. No one will pretend that (ii) is easy Greek, but the objection
to (i) seems to me decisive. On the importance of Syracusan democracy as an obstacle to Athenian plans cf. Nikias' warning in vi.
20. 2 and de Romilly, Imp., 206 n. 2.

56. 2. τοὺς μὲν ἐλευθεροῦσθαι, τοὺς δὲ φόβου ἀπολύεσθαι: the co-ordination of these words with futures (φανεῖσθαι, ἔσεσθαι, θαυμα-σθήσεσθαι) shows that they are prophetic (cf. vi. 91. 3) and do not imply that the Syracusans believed that the Athenian empire was already dissolving.

4. τοῦ ξύμπαντος λόγου: since λόγος means 'total' in fourth-century inscriptions of Epidauros (e.g. *IG* iv (i). 109. I. 130, II. 152), 'propor-tionate amount' in Herakleitos fr. 31 (cf. Kirk, *Heraclitus*, 325, 331 f.), and very commonly 'account' or 'reckoning', there is no good reason why ὁ ξύμπας λόγος in Thucydides should not mean 'the reckoned total', 'the whole list' (so Haacke); cf. English 'count' = 'counted total', and 'the whole *tale*' (Arnold).

ἐν τῷδε τῷ πολέμῳ: here at least the reference of this expression to the whole war from 431 to the time of writing cannot be questioned. Cf. 44. 1 n. and vi. 17. 5 n.

57–59. 1. *The Catalogue*

The catalogue is organized thus:

(I) 57. 2–11. Athens and her allies. Criterion of division: geographical.

  (A) 57. 2–10. From Greece and the Aegean. Criterion: status.

    (i) 57. 2. Athens and her colonies.

    (ii) 57. 3–10. Allies. Criterion: status.

      (*a*) 57. 4–6. Subjects. Criterion: racial.

        (1) 57. 4. Ionians, plus Karystos.

        (2) 57. 5. Aeolians.

        (3) 57. 6. Dorians.

      (*b*) 57. 7–8. Formally independent. Criterion: not apparent.

        (1) 57. 7. Islands of the north-west.

        (2) 57. 8. Messenians; Megarian exiles.

      (*c*) 57. 9–11. Essentially independent. Criterion: not ap-parent.

      Argives, Mantineans, etc.

  (B) 57. 11. From Italy and Sicily. Criterion: racial.

    (i) Greeks.

    (ii) Non-Greeks.

(II) 58. 1–3. Syracusan allies. Criterion: geographical.

  (A) 58. 1–3. From Sicily. Criterion: racial.

    (i) 58. 1–2. Greeks. Criterion: geographical.

      (*a*) 58. 1. South coast.

      (*b*) 58. 2. North coast.

    (ii) 58. 3. Non-Greeks.

(B) 58. 3. From Greece. Criterion: geographical.
   (i) From the Peloponnese and Peloponnesian colonies.
   (ii) Boeotia.

It is clear that Thucydides does not treat any one criterion as fundamental, but classifies unpredictably, at different levels, by location, race, or political status. The fact that the racial criterion is employed at all shows that racial sentiment, no matter how often or how flagrantly it was violated, was none the less a reality and not a rhetorical commonplace (cf. vi. 77. 1 n.). De Romilly, *Imp.*, 83 f., exaggerates, I think, Thucydides' subordination of this element in his catalogue, and E. Will, *Doriens et Ioniens* (Strasbourg, 1956), 65 ff., does not seem to regard the Catalogue as relevant to the subject. Thucydides in fact comments throughout when members of the same race are arrayed against each other (57. 5, 6, 7, 9 *ter*), but only if they are Greeks; the fact that there are Sikels on both sides (57. 11, 58. 3) passes without comment.

The complexity of classification in (I) (A) follows from the point which is made in 57. 1: the states which fought as allies on either side did so not so much κατὰ δίκην or in accordance with the claims of kinship as because they were subjects and had no choice or because it was in their interest to fight on one side rather than the other. To fight κατὰ δίκην is to fight for the redress of a grievance (cf. vi. 89. 3 n., δικαίως), or in response to the demand of an ally; unfortunately, the expression does not occur at any point in the Catalogue itself, and the only states whose participation seems to be treated as κατὰ δίκην are Plataia (57. 5 εἰκότως κατὰ τὸ ἔχθος), Kerkyra (57. 7 κατὰ ἔχθος τὸ Κορινθίων), and the Etruscans (57. 11 κατὰ διαφορὰν Συρακοσίων). Similarly, few states are represented as participating solely from racial sentiment: the Athenian colonies (57. 2) and Leukas and Ambrakia (58. 3). Mercenaries are presumably regarded as participating κατὰ τὸ ξυμφέρον. The theme of ἀνάγκη is much more prominent; the Ionians among the allies of Athens fight on the side which one would expect from their race, but they follow the Athenians ὑπήκοοι ὄντες καὶ ἀνάγκῃ, and the other subjects of Athens, whatever their race, are naturally no less 'compelled' to fight. Internal ἀνάγκαι are responsible for the participation of Thurioi and Metapontion (57. 11), and Sikyon fights for Syracuse ἀναγκαστοί (58. 3). There are, of course, degrees of ἀνάγκη, and that is why the element of 'justice' in fulfilment of an ally's obligations achieves no mention in the Catalogue; the formalities of alliance are subordinated to the reality, which is the extent to which an ally is free to fight or not. Hence the Kephallenians and Zakynthos, though formally independent allies of Athens, have no real choice (57. 7), and Kerkyra, in the same area, apparently pretends that she has no choice (ἀνάγκῃ ἐκ τοῦ εὐπρεποῦς

57. 7), though in her case the ἀνάγκη would no doubt be represented as the need to fulfil her obligations, not as subjection to Athens. The last category of Athenian allies from Greece and the Aegean is those of whom ἑκούσιος μᾶλλον ἢ στρατεία ἐγίγνετο (57. 9). It is as if Thucydides envisaged a man informed that the Greek world gathered for battle at Syracuse and inferring, from his knowledge of racial affinities and colonization and traditional enmities, who was on which side; such a man would make many mistakes, because it was the situation of the moment (τῆς ξυντυχίας 57. 1), and the relation of each state to that moment, which essentially determined the alignment.

The importance attached to compulsion lies behind the distinctions of status drawn among the Athenian allies. The category 'subjects', described in 57. 4 as ὑπήκοοι καὶ φόρου ὑποτελεῖς, includes two partial exceptions: Chios, which is οὐχ ὑποτελεῖς φόρου, ναῦς δὲ παρέχοντες αὐτόνομοι, and Methymna, which is ναυσὶ καὶ οὐ φόρῳ ὑπήκοοι (in 57. 5 ὑποτελεῖς, with which ναυσὶ ὑπήκοοι is contrasted, = φόρου ὑποτελεῖς; cf. de Romilly, *Imp.*, 87 n. 6). It might appear from this that Chios enjoyed some degree of independence which Methymna did not, and that αὐτόνομοι is in this instance used in a special sense and does not denote anything conflicting with the classification of Chios in the category of ὑπήκοοι in the general sense. Perhaps, for example, Chios remained bound to the ἡγεμονία of Athens by the original oaths of the League but was exempted from some of the enactments by which Athens intensified her control over her empire as a whole. Perhaps she had some juridical privilege, though the reference to her in *IG* i². 16 (ML 31). 10 f. (καθάπερ X]|ίοις, καί, κ.τ.λ.) hardly tells us enough to justify such a supposition (Wade-Gery, 187 ff.). Again, during the quarter-century which followed the enforced adoption of Athenian coinage throughout the empire (*ATL* ii. D14), Chios continued to strike her own silver coins; but so did Samos and several other states, none of which is classed by Thucydides as αὐτόνομοι (E. S. G. Robinson, *Hesperia* Suppl. viii [1949], 324 ff., 330). Now, in vi. 85. 2 no distinction is made by Euphemos between Chios and Methymna; both are νεῶν παροκωχῇ αὐτονόμους, as opposed to the allies who are controlled χρημάτων βιαιότερον φορᾷ. Similarly the Mytilenean speaker in iii. 10. 5 (Mytilene, of course, lost her privileged status after the suppression of her revolt, and Methymna alone among the communities of Lesbos retained it) refers to Lesbos and Chios together as the two formal exceptions (αὐτόνομοι δὴ ὄντες καὶ ἐλεύθεροι τῷ ὀνόματι) to the general subjection (ἐδουλώθησαν) of the empire. It therefore seems improbable that there was any formal difference in status between Chios and Methymna; both were αὐτόνομοι in so far as they contributed ships and paid no tribute and suffered comparatively little Athenian interference in their internal affairs, but the word αὐτόνομοι is used of Chios in the present passage and not of Methymna because Chios was a large and powerful state while Methymna was small and weak, so that Athens exercised a less rigorous control over Chios than over Methymna.

There are four pointers in the Catalogue to its date of composition: 57. 2 Αἰγινῆται, οἳ τότε Αἴγιναν εἶχον, 57. 8 οἱ Μεσσήνιοι νῦν καλού- μενοι ἐκ Ναυπάκτου καὶ ἐκ Πύλου τότε ὑπ᾽ Ἀθηναίων ἐχομένης, 58. 1 Ἱμεραῖοι δὲ ἀπὸ τοῦ πρὸς τὸν Τυρσηνικὸν πόντον μορίου, ἐν ᾧ καὶ μόνοι Ἕλληνες οἰκοῦσιν.

(a) The reference to Himera, which may be thought to antedate its destruction in 409, does not permit a firm conclusion, for the reasons given in vi. 62. 2 n., and must be interpreted in the light of (b)–(d) below.

(b) The Messenians were expelled from Naupaktos after the end of the war (Paus. iv. 26. 2, x. 38. 10); according to Diod. xiv. 34. 2, not at once after Aigospotamoi—Lysander's expulsions of Athenians from Aigina and Melos, mentioned in X. *HG* ii. 2. 9, were incidental to his voyage from the Hellespont to Athens—but in 401/0, after the conclusion of Sparta's war against Elis (Diod. xiv. 17. 4 ff., 34. 1, cf. X. *HG* iii. 2. 21, 25, 30 f.). Thereafter Μεσσήνιοι as a state ceased to exist. If it is assumed that οἱ Μεσσήνιοι νῦν καλούμενοι means 'that community which now (exists and) is called Μεσσήνιοι' rather than 'that community which (formerly existed and) is now referred to as Μεσσήνιοι (when we speak of the past)', 400 is the lower terminus for the Catalogue. The assumption is reasonable, given that Thucy- dides elsewhere does not normally mean the inhabitants of Messenia when he says Μεσσήνιοι; in i. 101. 2 he thinks it necessary to comment on the use of this term in reference to the helots by reminding us of their ancestry, and cf. iv. 3. 2, 41. 2.

(c) Aigina was occupied by Athenians from 431 (Th. ii. 27. 1) to 405 (X. *HG* ii. 2. 9). τότε might imply either a contrast with the period before 431 or a contrast with the period after 405 (cf. Genesis 12. 6, 'And the Canaanite was then in the land', the implications of which exercised Jewish scholars even in the Middle Ages). But it is unlikely that Thucydides, writing κτῆμα ἐς αἰεί between those two dates, would assume that when the war was over the Athenians would give up Aigina and restore its original inhabitants; and if he wrote these words before 405 and meant to indicate the difference between the period before 431 and the period after, he would more naturally have said νῦν ἔχουσιν. These words, then, were probably written after 405 (cf. Schmid, 135 n. 3; *contra*, Andrewes, *Historia* x [1961], 9 [who, however, would now prefer conclusion (ii) below]).

(d) Had he written before the evacuation of Pylos, he might well have said, as he does, τότε ἐχομένης, assuming that it would have been evacuated, in consequence of the end of the war, before future generations read his history. The reference to Pylos therefore has no chronological significance of its own, and must be interpreted in the light of (c).

The two possible conclusions are: (i) that the entire Catalogue was written between 405 and 400, and the present tense in 58. 1 is due to the survival of some Ἱμεραῖοι, or (ii) that the Catalogue was drafted before 409, revised between 405 and 400, and 58. 1 escaped revision.

The judgement of C. Meyer, *Die Urkunden im Geschichtswerk des Thukydides* (Munich, 1955), 12 n. 1, that 'Amtliche Verzeichnisse (Urkunden) sind zweifellos . . . verwendet' does scant justice to Thucydides' (or any reasonable historian's) ability to extract data from informants and co-ordinate them in notes.

57. 1. ἐπὶ Σικελίαν - - - περὶ Σικελίας - - - ἐπὶ Συρακούσας ἐπολέμησαν 'against Sicily and in defence of Sicily' is unobjectionable, but ἐπὶ Συρακούσας, which would most naturally be understood as 'to gain Syracuse' (cf. στρατεύεσθαι ἐπί c. acc., etc. and X. *An.* iii. 4. 46 ἐπὶ τὴν Ἑλλάδα - - - ἁμιλλᾶσθαι = 'fight to regain Greece') is a most awkward addition, and should be either deleted (Classen) or replaced by an expression meaning simply '*at* Syracuse'. This is ἐν Συρακούσαις in Pl. *Ep.* 7. 329 c al., but with the idea of *coming* to Sicily so conspicuous in this context ἐς Συρακούσας is a distinct possibility. ἐπὶ Συρακούσαις (Bauer) has too strong a flavour of purpose.

ὡς ἑκάστοις τῆς ξυντυχίας - - - ἔσχεν: Bⁱ has ἕκαστοι, and ψ have ἔσχον; no MS. has both, but since impersonal ἔχειν does not occur elsewhere in Thucydides, and the closest parallel to this clause as a whole is i. 22. 3 ὡς - - - τις εὐνοίας ἢ μνήμης ἔχοι, he probably wrote ἕκαστοι - - - ἔσχον here: 'according to each nation's relation to the events of the time'.

2. καὶ αὐτοῖς - - - ἄποικοι ὄντες ξυνεστράτευσαν: the essential distinction, as part of the sequence 'Athenian initiative—ties of blood—subject status—alliance', is between ἑκόντες ἦλθον and ἄποικοι ὄντες ξυνεστράτευσαν. Lemnos became an Athenian possession c. 500 (Hdt. vi. 136. 2; cf. Wade-Gery, 163). Imbros, which is constantly paired with Lemnos in the historians (e.g. iii. 5. 1; cf. X. *HG* iv. 8. 15, v. 1. 31), may well have become Athenian at exactly the same time, and presumably Athenian settlement of both islands was early. '*Still* using the same dialect and institutions as the Athenians' seems worth saying of Lemnos and Imbros, on the assumption of this early settlement, but hardly worth saying of Aigina, which had been Athenian only since 431 (cf. p. 435), or of Hestiaia, which was settled after the suppression of the Euboean Revolt in 445 (i. 114. 3). Perhaps, however, it seemed to Thucydides worthy of remark that the institutions of Aigina and Hestiaia were still Athenian, given that a colony might turn its back on its mother-city (as Amphipolis did) within a generation of its foundation. It is hardly possible to divide the sentence after *Ἴμβριοι* and translate 'and the Lemnians and Imbrians (sc. came too) . . .; and the Aiginetans . . . and Hestiaians . . . joined in the expedition as colonists'. This would deprive καὶ ἔτι of its cumulative effect, blur the distinction which seems fundamental to the sentence as a whole, and, by restricting ἄποικοι to Aigina and Hestiaia, implicitly deny that the Lemnians and Imbrians were ἄποικοι. There is some reason to believe that the Lemnians included both 'colonists' in the normal sense (i.e. citizens of the communities Ἡφαιστιῆς and Μυριναῖοι [cf. Hdt. vi. 140. 2 and ATL i. 511]) and cleruchs settled there during the Pentekontaetia (cf. ATL iii. 289 ff. and P. A. Brunt, *Ehrenberg Stud.* 80 and n. 38); the Imbrians may have been similarly composite. Yet it is hard to believe that Thucydides intended his readers to understand, simply from the attachment of ἄποικοι ὄντες to the Aiginetans and Hestiaians, that the Lemnians and Imbrians were not *exactly* ἄποικοι; his language, when he speaks of settlement, is not so precise, and his contemporaries must have thought of Lemnos and Imbros as ἀποικίαι of Athens (cf. Ehrenberg, *CPh.* xlvii [1952], 143 ff., and Brunt, 77 ff.). It is suggested in ATL iii. 291 f. that the sentence is divided after εἶχον, so that ἦλθον is understood with Lemnos, Imbros, and Aigina, and only the Hestiaians are the subject of ξυνεστράτευσαν. The disadvantages of this division are that, like division after *Ἴμβριοι*, it obscures Thucydides' point; it classes Aigina with Lemnos and Imbros, against Hestiaia, although the language used by Thucydides of Aigina and Hestiaia is very similar (ii. 27. 1 τὴν Αἴγιναν - - - πέμψαντας ἐποίκους ἔχειν· καὶ ἐξέπεμψαν - - - τοὺς οἰκήτορας ~ i. 114. 3 Ἑστιαιᾶς δὲ ἐξοικίσαντες αὐτοὶ τὴν γῆν ἔσχον); and it poses the problem why Thucydides did not write something much less cumbrous in the last part of the sentence, e.g. οἱ ἐς Ἑστίαιαν τὴν ἐν Εὐβοίᾳ οἰκισθέντες. αὐτοῖς should be taken primarily with τῇ αὐτῇ, but it foreshadows ξυνεστράτευσαν: it is not, as stated by Ehrenberg (148), 'emphatic', for αὐτ- in Thucydides commonly follows καί (e.g. 34. 2), as σφι does in Herodotos.

The colonial contingent in the Athenian force fell short of a complete round-up (there is no mention of Poteidaia, Melos, or Skyros), and the principle of inclusion is obscure; Lemnos and Imbros were tributary cities, whereas Aigina and Hestiaia, like Poteidaia, paid no tribute after Athenian settlement. Possibly Skyros was insignificant, the Athenians of Melos understandably busy, and those of Poteidaia more useful *in situ*, since so much of the northern Aegean coast was in a lasting state of rebellion.

3. οἱ μὲν ὑπήκοοι, οἱ δ' ἀπὸ ξυμμαχίας αὐτόνομοι: cf. p. 434.

4. Τήνιοι: so B: Τήϊοι cett.: the reading of Π¹⁸ is doubtful. Τήϊοι is impossible; the compilers of the tribute-lists naturally included Teos in Ionia, not in 'the Islands'.

καὶ τὸ πλεῖστον Ἴωνες ὄντες οὗτοι πάντες καὶ ἀπ᾽ Ἀθηναίων - - - ὑπήκοοι δ᾽ ὄντες καὶ ἀνάγκῃ ὅμως Ἴωνές γε ἐπὶ Δωριᾶς ἠκολούθουν: Thucydides' point is threefold: the states listed in § 4 (i) constituted the greater part of the Athenian force (this point is missed by Gomme, *Historia* ii [1953/4], 7, and Wade-Gery and Meritt, *Hesperia* xxvi [1957], 191 f.), (ii) were all, except Karystos, Ionian, and (iii) therefore, although subject, were nevertheless 'natural' allies of Athens against their common racial enemy. Points (i) and (ii) are simply stated by making (i) the main clause, τὸ πλεῖστον - - - οὗτοι - - - ἠκολούθουν, and (ii) a participial clause within it, Ἴωνες ὄντες - - - πάντες; lit., 'these followed as the greatest part, being all Ionian'. The relation between (ii) and (iii) is obscured by something which is either a textual corruption or slipshod writing (not surprising in so concentrated a sentence). ἀνάγκῃ must qualify ἠκολούθουν, since ὑπήκοοι ὄντες καὶ ἀνάγκῃ = 'being subjects and under compulsion' is not Greek. So then must ὑπήκοοι ὄντες qualify ἠκολούθουν, as an adverbial participial clause; and since a sentence of the form Ἴωνες ὄντες, ὑπήκοοι δ᾽ ὄντες ὅμως Ἴωνες ἠκολούθουν is not Greek either, δ᾽ after ὑπήκοοι is suspect and must be either attributed to a confusion in Thucydides' sequence of thought ('Ionians, but subjects' superimposing itself on 'although subjects, Ionians') or transposed to follow ὅμως. The text of *POxy.* 1376, which looks as if it had δέ twice, supports the second hypothesis: υπηκ[οοι|δο]ντ[ε]σκαιαν[α]γκηομωσ| [..ιων]εσγε κ.τ.λ.

οὗτοι δ᾽ εἰσὶ Δρύοπες: Hdt. viii. 46. 4 classifies the people of Styra and Kythnos as Dryopes, but nowhere expresses any opinion on Karystos. According to Paus. iv. 34. 6 Styra was not proud of its possible Dryopian origin, and evidently Thucydides accepted an alternative tradition which made it Ionian.

5. ναυσὶ καὶ οὐ φόρῳ ὑπήκοοι: cf. p. 434.

τοῖς κτίσασι Βοιωτοῖς ⟨τοῖς⟩ μετὰ Συρακοσίων: the insertion of ⟨τοῖς⟩ (Lindau) is necessary for the sense; otherwise the words would mean that the Lesbians fought on the side of Syracuse. On the tie of sentiment between Boeotia and Lesbos, cf. iii. 2. 3.

μόνοι εἰκότως κατὰ τὸ ἔχθος: i.e. 'the only people you would expect to find fighting against their own race, because of their long-standing enmity to Boeotia'. It is hardly less to be expected that Kerkyreans should fight against Corinth, but where they are mentioned (§ 7) a more complicated point is made.

6. Κυθήριοι: cf. 26. 2 n.

Ῥόδιοι δὲ Ἀργεῖοι γένος: cf. vi. 43. In *Il.* ii. 653 ff. Tlempolemos, leader of the Rhodian contingent in the Trojan War, is a son of Herakles; Pi. *O.* 7. 19 ff. gives the myth of the foundation of Rhodes from Argos.

Γελῴοις δὲ καὶ ἀποίκοις ἑαυτῶν οὖσι: cf. vi. 4. 3.

7. **Κεφαλλῆνες μὲν καὶ Ζακύνθιοι**: cf. Euphemos' reference to these free but vulnerable allies, vi. 85. 2; cf. also 31. 2 n.

κατὰ ἔχθος τὸ Κορινθίων: cf. i. 38.

8. **οἱ Μεσσήνιοι νῦν καλούμενοι**: cf. p. 435.

Μεγαρέων φυγάδες: cf. vi. 43 n.

Μεγαρεῦσι Σελινουντίοις οὖσι: cf. vi. 4. 2.

9. **Ἀργεῖοι - - - Μαντινῆς δὲ καὶ ἄλλοι Ἀρκάδων μισθοφόροι**: cf. vi. 22 n., 43, and vii. 19. 4 n.

Κρῆτες δὲ καὶ Αἰτωλοί: the Aitolians last appeared in Thucydides' narrative as enemies of Athens, iii. 94. 3 ff.; Demosthenes must have recruited these Aitolians when he was at Kerkyra, cf. 31. 2, 5, 33. 3. **τὴν Γέλαν Ῥοδίοις ξυγκτίσαντας**: cf. vi. 4. 3.

10. **Δημοσθένους φιλίᾳ καὶ Ἀθηναίων εὐνοίᾳ**: a product of Demosthenes' highly successful campaign in 426/5, which resulted in profitable gains for the Akarnanians (iii. 94-8, 100-2, and 105-14).

11. **Θούριοι καὶ Μεταπόντιοι ἐν τοιαύταις ἀνάγκαις τότε στασιωτικῶν καιρῶν κατειλημμένοι**: on the situation at Thurioi cf. 33. 5 f. Metapontion contributed to the force under Demosthenes and Eurymedon (33. 4 f.), but nothing is said in that context of its internal politics. στασιωτικὸς καιρός is a stage or moment in a process of conflict, and the point of τοιαύταις is 'of such a kind as to lead to their being on the Athenian side'. Hence: 'Thurioi and Metapontion took part on the Athenian side, as was inevitably imposed upon them by the state which their internal conflicts had at that time reached.' Cf. Isoc. xiv. 38 τοιαῦται γὰρ αὐτοὺς ἀνάγκαι κατειλήφασιν ὥστε, κ.τ.λ. and Hp. Art. 30 οὐ μάλα καταλαμβάνουσι τοιαῦται ἀνάγκαι βρωμάτων ὥστε τὸν ἄνθρωπον χανεῖν μεῖζον ἢ ὅσον δύναται.

Ἐγεσταῖοί: the cavalry referred to in vi. 98. 1.

καὶ Σικελῶν τὸ πλέον: cf. vi. 88. 4 n. The Sikels' contribution in money was substantial; cf. SEG xvii. 7. 9 f. Σικε[λοὶ - - -]| ⊢ Ⱶ𐅅𐅁[- -, 13 f., 19 f.

Τυρσηνῶν τέ τινες: cf. vi. 88. 6, where 'some cities' of Τυρσηνία take the initiative in offering help to Athens. Pindar's prayer after Hieron's victory at Kyme (P. 1. 73) that henceforth 'the Etruscan war-cry may stay at home' was not fulfilled, for we hear of a war of sea-raiding between Etruscans and Syracuse in 453 (Diod. xi. 88. 4 f.). (Meyer, GdA iv. 519, wished to identify the Τυρσηνοί mentioned here and in 53. 2 with the Campanian mercenaries who according to Diod. xiii. 44. 2 were 'enrolled by the Chalkideans'—i.e. Kyme?—and sent, too late, to help the Athenians; cf. M. O. B. Caspari, CQ v [1911], 113 ff. The basic premiss of both Meyer and Caspari was that the Etruscans at this period were too preoccupied with their own troubles in Campania [Livy xxxvii. 1 f.] to send help to the enemies of Syracuse.)

καὶ Ἰάπυγες μισθοφόροι: cf. 33. 4.

58. 1. Καμαριναῖοι: cf. vi. 67. 2, 75. 3, and vii. 33. 1 n.
Γελῷοι οἰκοῦντες μετ' αὐτούς: cf. vi. 67. 2, vii. 1. 5, and 33. 1. 'after them' is said from the point of view of a man travelling outwards from the focus of interest, not from the bird's-eye view of a man reading a map.
Ἀκραγαντίνων ἡσυχαζόντων: cf. 32. 1, 33. 2, 46, and 50. 1.
Σελινούντιοι: cf. vi. 65. 1, 67. 2, and vii. 1. 3 ff.
2. Ἱμεραῖοι: cf. c. 1 and p. 435.
3. Σικελοὶ - - - ὅσοι μὴ ἀφέστασαν πρὸς τοὺς Ἀθηναίους: cf. vi. 88. 4 n., vii. 1. 4 f., and 57. 11.
ἡγεμόνα: if there were no other evidence, we should naturally take this to mean simply that the commander of the contingent of *Λακεδαιμόνιοι* was a Spartiate, the men under his command *νεοδαμώδεις* and helots. If we take into account vi. 91. 4 and vii. 2. 1, we see—as in both those passages—an ambiguity. It is, however, possible that Thucydides believed that vi. 91. 4 removed the possibility of ambiguity in any reference which he might make thereafter to the status of Gylippos.
νεοδαμώδεις: cf. v. 34. 1 n. As Thucydides has used the word several times already (last in 19. 3) it is unlikely that he would first explain it here, especially with so vague an explanation; hence E. Portus's deletion of *δύναται - - - εἶναι* is extremely plausible. I doubt whether any critical inference can be drawn from Σ^ABCF *νεοδαμώδης ὁ ἐλεύθερος παρὰ τοῖς Λακεδαιμονίοις*, which can be a *σημείωσις* on our MSS.' text.
Λευκάδιοι καὶ Ἀμπρακιῶται: cf. vi. 104. 1 and vii. 7. 1.
Σικυώνιοι ἀναγκαστοὶ στρατεύοντες: in 417 the Spartans intervened in Sikyon to restore their own control of her politics (v. 81. 2); but since *προσηνάγκαζον* is used in 18. 4 above of Sparta's relation to the Peloponnesian League as a whole, and there is no suggestion of any special subjection of Sikyon in 19. 4, it is probable that here the contrast intended is between *ἀναγκαστοί* (cf. 57. 1 *ἀνάγκῃ*) and *μισθοφόροι*.
4. κατὰ πάντα: 'in all arms', amplified by *καὶ γὰρ ὁπλῖται πολλοί, κ.τ.λ.*

59. 2–60. 4. *Preparations for Battle*

59. 3. ἔκλῃον οὖν τόν τε λιμένα εὐθὺς τὸν μέγαν: completed in three days, according to Diod. xiii. 14. 2. Cf. 69. 4 n.
ὀκτὼ σταδίων μάλιστα: the distance from the rocks at the southern tip of Ortygia to the little island (Scoglio Castelluccio) off the tip of Plemmyrion is 1·04 km., and to the western projection (C. Farruggia) of Plemmyrion 1·24 km. Cf. pp. 467 f.

60. 2. καὶ οἱ ταξίαρχοι; cf. 48. 1 n. Normally ten taxiarchs were elected annually, one for each *φυλή*; it is hard to believe that all ten were sent to Sicily, and however the force at Syracuse was divided into contingents (cf. vi. 98. 4 n.) I presume that the commander of each contingent had, as it were, the 'local' rank of taxiarch.

ἀπολαβόντες διατειχίσματι ὅσον οἷόν τε ἐλάχιστον: cf. p. 484.

3. ἡλικίας μετέχων: 'provided he was not too old or too young'. Since all the soldiers and sailors would naturally be ἡλικίας μετέχοντες, the reference must be to slaves.

4. δέκα μάλιστα καὶ ἑκατόν: cf. 52. 1 n. According to Diod. xiii. 14. 4, the Athenians manned 115 ships.

ἐξ ἀναγκαίου τε καὶ τοιαύτης διανοίας: either (a) 'as their circumstances dictated' (cf. ἐξ ἴσου) 'and in accordance with' (i) 'a plan which reflected that stress' (cf. 57. 11 n.), or (ii) 'a plan of the kind described' (i.e. involving the use of archers, etc.)—in these two interpretations we have virtual zeugma with ἐκ—or (b) 'in accordance with a plan which was forced upon them by circumstances and was of the kind described' (for feminine ἀναγκαῖος cf. i. 2. 2). In either case the point is that in the circumstances they were compelled to fill their decks with archers; (a) (ii) is perhaps the least peculiar way of saying that. ὅσα (for ὡς) in B and the presence of καὶ ὡς after ἦν in Π¹⁸ reveal some uncertainties in the textual tradition, but not a helpful answer.

60. 5–64. Speech of Nikias

61. 2. τὴν ἐλπίδα τοῦ φόβου ὁμοίαν ταῖς ξυμφοραῖς ἔχουσιν: 'the expectation which their fear' (sc. arising from their previous defeats) 'engenders is (lit.) like their misfortune', i.e. 'does not rise above their misfortune'. Nikias cannot pretend that the Athenian situation is not a ξυμφορά; he can only try to encourage optimism (cf. 77. 3 f.).

3. καὶ τὸ τῆς τύχης κἂν μεθ' ἡμῶν ἐλπίσαντες στῆναι: τὸ τῆς τύχης is the contribution of chance to the situation (cf. 62. 2 τὸ τῆς ἐπιστήμης), here virtually personified (στῆναι), as more plainly in 68. 1.

62. 1. ἃ δὲ ἀρωγὰ ἐνείδομεν ἐπὶ τῇ τοῦ λιμένος στενότητι πρὸς τὸν μέλλοντα ὄχλον τῶν νεῶν ἔσεσθαι: ἐπί = 'given'; ἔσεσθαι goes with μέλλοντα; and for ἐνείδομεν cf. 36. 2, where again it refers to seeing possibilities in a situation.

πάντα καὶ ἡμῖν - - - ἡτοίμασται: the preceding τὴν ἐκείνων - - - παρασκευήν gives point to καί: 'we too (sc. like the Syracusans) have made preparations'.

2. ναυμαχίαν μὲν ποιούμενοι ἐν πελάγει: the order of words indicates not 'if we were fighting a sea-battle on the open water' but 'if we were fighting a (sc. real) sea-battle, on the open water', contrasting

441

ναυμαχίαν with τῇ ἐνθάδε - - - πεζομαχίᾳ and denying the name of ναυμαχία to the coming battle.

3. καὶ πρὸς τὰς τῶν ἐπωτίδων αὐτοῖς παχύτητας - - - χειρῶν σιδηρῶν ἐπιβολαί: cf. 34. 5 n., 36. 2 ff. For καί = 'including especially' cf. W. J. Verdenius, *Mnemosyne* 1953, 179 f.

4. τῆς γῆς - - - πολεμίας οὔσης: π. ἐσομένης (B) is rhetorically less suitable to the context.

63. 2. τῷ πεζῷ ἐπικρατεῖν: the fighting described in 53. 2 f. gave some substance to this optimistic generalization.

3. τοῖς δὲ ναύταις παραινῶ: the previous words, καὶ ταῦτα τοῖς ὁπλίταις, κ.τ.λ., show that the tactical advice and encouragement of 62–63. 1 have been primarily directed to the sailors, including the trierarchs and officers, and the last part of 63. 1 makes this doubly clear. Now Nikias returns to the ναῦται in the narrow sense, the oarsmen, to give them moral encouragement rather than tactical instructions.

ἐκείνην τε τὴν ἡδονὴν ἐνθυμεῖσθαι: Nikias treats the sailors, without restriction or qualification, as non-Athenians, culturally and linguistically atticized (there may well be rhetorical exaggeration here) but not as subjects of Athens, as § 3 ἔς τε τὸ φοβερὸν τοῖς ὑπηκόοις and § 4 κοινωνοὶ μόνοι ἐλευθέρως ἡμῖν τῆς ἀρχῆς show. Again in 64. 1 f. the Athenian contribution is treated as ships and soldiers, not as sailors. Either, then, these men came from subject-allies, and the ὑπήκοοι in whom they 'inspired respect' were their own fellow citizens, or—and this is, I think, an easier interpretation—they were essentially mercenaries (Gomme, ms.). If Thucydides was right in regarding the great majority of the Athenian sailors at Syracuse in this light, the Corinthian reproach ὠνητὴ ἡ Ἀθηναίων δύναμις μᾶλλον ἢ οἰκεία (i. 121. 3) had come half-true by 413—the other half depends on what one regards as οἰκεῖον—and the words attributed to Perikles in 432/1, κυβερνήτας ἔχομεν πολίτας (i. 143. 1), not to mention calculation of the number of sailors needed to man a hundred triremes, imply that they were true to the same extent even before the war. We have no clue to the original nationalities of these men; probably all the over-populated regions of the Greek world were represented among them, and many are likely to have been born at Athens and to have known no other home. Chios and Methymna could, of course, be described rhetorically as κοινωνοί - - - τῆς ἀρχῆς, but since they contributed their own ships their nationals are not likely to have been strongly represented among the rowers of the Athenian ships. For a later date, *IG* ii². 1951 is instructive: the rowers of one ship include men from Aphytis, Chios, Keos, Naxos, Rhodes, Samos, and elsewhere (230 ff.) and in another the ναυπηγός is simply μέτοικος (102) and the αὐλητής a Siphnian (100). Cf. Amit, 37 ff. and *Athenaeum* N.S. xl (1962), 157 ff.

καὶ τῆς ἀρχῆς τῆς ἡμετέρας οὐκ ἔλασσον - - - πολὺ πλέον μετείχετε: if the text is right: 'your share in our empire has been no less'— either sc. 'than our own' or sc. 'than your share in our culture'—'so far as the benefits are concerned' (i.e. but not in responsibility, expense, or danger), 'in inspiring our subjects with respect and, far more important, in immunity from wrong'. I can see no decisive ground for choice between the two possible interpretations of οὐκ ἔλασσον. Yet πολὺ πλέον looks as if it belongs with μετείχετε, 'you had a much larger share' (cf. vi. 40. 1) and may be an intrusive variant (del. Krüger) on οὐκ ἔλασσον; in any case 'inspiring our subjects with fear' and 'immunity from wrong' are somewhat similar, and the addition of 'more important' to the latter only makes the tautology more conspicuous.

4. δικαίως [ἂν] αὐτὴν νῦν μὴ καταπροδίδοτε: either ἂν must be omitted (ψ) or we must read καταπροδίδοιτε (f); for the former, 'be just and do not betray it now', cf. iv. 62. 3 μὴ χαλεπῶς σφαλλέσθω 'let him not resent his defeat'.

ἕως ἤκμαζε τὸ ναυτικὸν ἡμῖν: cf. 12. 3 and 14. 1 n.

ἑτέρας εὐτυχούσης ῥώμης: ῥώμης is primarily contrasted with ἀσθενείας—a further contrast with ἐπιστήμη is superimposed—and εὐτυχούσης with ξυμφορῶν.

64. 1. τούς τε Ἀθηναίους ὑμῶν πάλιν αὖ καὶ τάδε ὑπομιμνήσκω: τε (not δέ) might suggest that it is to the Athenians among the *sailors* that he is speaking; but since the Athenian hoplites have so far been given no moral encouragement of the kind offered in 63. 3–64, τοὺς Ἀθηναίους ὑμῶν should embrace both soldiers and sailors.

οὔτε ὁπλιτῶν ἡλικίαν: sc. τοῖσδε ὁμοίαν.

εἴ τε ξυμβήσεταί τι ἄλλο ἢ τὸ κρατεῖν ὑμῖν: the euphemism for defeat is more elaborate, and seems in its context more artificial, than the common euphemism ἐάν τι πάθω = 'if anything happens to me'.

τούς τε ἐνθάδε πολεμίους εὐθὺς ἐπ' ἐκεῖνα πλευσομένους: cf. vi. 10. 1 n.

οἷς αὐτοὶ ἴστε οἵᾳ γνώμῃ ἐπήλθετε: since their position is admittedly desperate, Nikias' point is not that it would be shameful for so proud an enterprise to be defeated, but that they can expect no mercy from an enemy whose independence they had proposed to destroy. Nothing that Thucydides himself says of the Athenian plans suggests that they had a more sinister intention, the massacre and enslavement of the population of Syracuse, but he represents the Syracusan generals (68. 2 n.) as inflaming their troops by assuming that Athens did have these intentions, and Diod. xiii. 2. 6 represents it as a secret decision of the Athenian generals and the council; cf. ibid. 2. 2 κατακληρουχεῖν ἤλπιζον τὴν Σικελίαν and Strasburger, *Hermes* lxxxvi (1958), 29 n. 1.

2. καθ' ἑκάστους τε καὶ ξύμπαντες: cf. vi. 39. 1 n.

οἱ ἐν ταῖς ναυσὶν ὑμῶν νῦν ἐσόμενοι καὶ πεζοὶ τοῖς Ἀθηναίοις εἰσὶ καὶ νῆες, κ.τ.λ.: 'you that will be on these ships are the army and navy of Athens' (Gomme, ms.). The logic of the sentence has been imprudently impugned by commentators ('how can people on ships be ships?', etc.).

καὶ τὸ μέγα ὄνομα τῶν Ἀθηνῶν: cf. D. xx. 69 τούτου τὴν δόξαν τὸ τῆς πόλεως ὄνομα καρποῦται.

65–68. Syracusan Speech

65. 3. παρεκελεύσαντο ἐκείνοις οἵ τε στρατηγοὶ καὶ Γύλιππος: cf. i. 72. 2, where the Athenians at Sparta in 432 παρελθόντες - - - ἔλεξαν τοιάδε. In both cases, either one speech was made by one representative whom Thucydides cannot name, or the one speech which Thucydides presents is compounded of several speeches made by several people. Thucydides' formula does not make plain which he intends us to think; cf. 69. 1. The sentiment and standpoint throughout are Syracusan (e.g. 68. 2, cf. Freeman, ii. 347) and we are not to think of Gylippos as the speaker. This manner of presentation is a warning against too rigid a defence of the historical fidelity of all Thucydidean speeches.

66. 2. ἔπειτ' - - - καὶ τῆς Πελοποννήσου καὶ τῆς ἄλλης Ἑλλάδος: cf. vi. 90. 3.
τὴν δ' ἐκ τοῦ εἰκότος νῦν νικήσετε: 'and you have every reason to expect that you will win the battle now impending'; a translation involving 'probability' would be inappropriate to the occasion.
3. καὶ τῷ παρ' ἐλπίδα τοῦ αὐχήματος σφαλλόμενοι καὶ παρὰ ἰσχὺν τῆς δυνάμεως ἐνδιδόασιν: 'when their pride is cast down by the unexpected outcome' (or 'by events which falsify their proud hopes') 'they collapse more quickly than the strength of which they are capable warrants'.

67. 1. τὸ κρατίστους εἶναι: cf. 36. 5 n.
2. οἳ οὐδ' ὅπως καθεζομένους χρὴ τὸ βέλος ἀφεῖναι εὑρήσουσι: lit., 'who will not find even how positioning themselves they must discharge the missile', i.e. 'who will not be able to find positions suitable for the discharge of their missiles'. For καθέζεσθαι = 'station oneself' cf. viii. 90. 4.
4. τὸ δ' ἀληθέστατον γνῶτε ἐξ ὧν ἡμεῖς οἰόμεθα σαφῶς πεπύσθαι: what has preceded is speculation and prediction; now the speaker refers in τὸ ἀληθέστατον to an existing fact, the Athenian decision to retreat. 'I will tell you the one thing which is certain, in the light of what we are confident we have discovered without doubt'; cf. vi. 17. 6 and Pl. Cri. 43 d ἥξει τήμερον, ἐξ ὧν ἀπαγγέλλουσιν ἥκοντές τινες.

οὐ παρασκευῆς πίστει μᾶλλον ἢ τύχης ἀποκινδυνεῦσαι: the MSS. have ἀποκινδυνεύσει (cf. v. 100 τὴν παρακινδύνευσιν ποιοῦνται): 'they are reduced to desperation, in staking everything on fortune, in the only way they can, with no confidence in their arms, in order to break out . . .' Duker's ἀποκινδυνεῦσαι gives an infinitive somewhat loosely dependent on ἐς ἀπόνοιαν καθεστήκασιν: but cf. vi. 80. 2, and the resulting sense is greatly superior: 'they are reduced to the desperate expedient—trusting to fortune, not to their arms—of taking a supreme risk in the only way they can, in order to break out . . .'

68. 1. καὶ τύχην ἀνδρῶν ἑαυτὴν παραδεδωκυῖαν πολεμιωτάτων: cf. 61. 3 n., and on the role of chance in Thucydides cf. Herter, *RM* xciii (1949/50), 133 ff., Müri, *MH* iv (1947), 253 ff., and Radford, 40 f. The rhetorical personification of τύχη (as distinct from a cult of Τύχη) is much older than Thucydides; cf. A. *Ag.* 664 τύχη (Τύχη?) δὲ σωτὴρ ναῦν θέλουσ' ἐφέζετο.

ὡς ἐπὶ τιμωρίᾳ τοῦ προσπεσόντος δικαιώσωσιν ἀποπλῆσαι τῆς γνώμης τὸ θυμούμενον: custom and morality sanctioned revenge; cf. Adam on Pl. *R.* 331 f., Dodds on E. *Ba.* 877, and Page on *Md.* 809.

ἅμα δὲ ἐχθροὺς ἀμύνασθαι ἐκγενησόμενον ἡμῖν καὶ τὸ λεγόμενόν που ἥδιστον εἶναι: 'and, secondly, that to punish enemies' either (*a*) 'which will be possible for us, is, as the saying goes, the greatest of delights', or (*b*) 'will be possible for us, and is, etc.'. A participial construction after νομίζειν is everywhere rare, and unexampled in Thucydides; this fact favours (*a*), in which ἐκγενησόμενον ἡμῖν is parenthetic and καί adverbial. Yet τὸ λεγόμενόν που is certainly parenthetic, and two parentheses in one short clause are objectionable; this consideration favours (*b*), in which ἐκγενησόμενον is co-ordinated with εἶναι by καί, and the whole complex co-ordinated with νομιμώτατον εἶναι - - - οἳ ἄν, κ.τ.λ., in order to achieve variety. For a parenthesis or subordinate clause after adverbial καί cf. 85. 1 n., Hp. *Reg.* 48 ἀτὰρ καί, περὶ οὗ ὁ λόγος ἦν, ὅτι, κ.τ.λ.: subordinate clauses immediately after conjunctive καί are normal. Whereas Greek poetry and tradition agree that revenge is νομιμώτατον, and we have several bloodthirsty prayers (e.g. Theognis 341 ff.) relating to particular circumstances, they seldom say outright, as a general maxim, that it is also ἥδιστον. Nevertheless, Thucydides appears to be referring to an actual proverb or proverbial verse, of the type κάλλιστον τὸ δικαιότατον, κ.τ.λ.

2. ἀνδράσι μὲν ἂν τάχιστα προσέθεσαν, κ.τ.λ.: he means that, as happened at Melos (v. 116. 4), the men would have been killed, the women and children enslaved, and the site of the city would have passed into alien hands (cf. 64. 1 n.); the αἰσχίστη ἐπίκλησις is probably ἀνάστατος (cf. vi. 76. 2).

445

69–71. *Athenian Attempt to Break Out*

69. 2. πατρόθεν τε ἐπονομάζων καὶ αὐτοὺς ὀνομαστὶ καὶ φυλήν: lit., 'naming (*sc.* them) from their fathers and themselves by name and their tribe', i.e. 'calling upon them by their fathers' names and by their own and their tribes'. Cf. Pouilloux, *Recherches* . . . *Thasos* (Paris, 1954), i. 371, no. 141. 7 f. ἀναγράφειν δὲ αὐτῶν τὰ ὀνόματα πατρόθεν. To praise or exhort a man by addressing him as his father's son was a commonplace. Nikias reminded each trierarch of his tribe, not of his deme, because the eponymous hero of each tribe was a paradigm of valour, whereas few demes (the Acharnians are a notable exception) were felt to have martial traditions of their own. D. lx. 27 ff., taking each tribe in turn, professes to describe how the legends about its eponymous hero inspired its contemporary members to self-sacrifice. This passage of Thucydides has no bearing (*pace* Kolbe, *Philologus* lviii [1899], 531 f. and Wilamowitz *Aristoteles und Athen*, ii. 171, n. 3) on the organization of trierarchies and naval divisions.

καὶ τῆς ἐν αὐτῇ ἀνεπιτάκτου πᾶσιν ἐς τὴν δίαιταν ἐξουσίας: ii. 37 is the most famous expression of this characteristic (more remarkable by Greek standards than by ours) of Athenian society; cf. nn. ad loc. An appeal on the eve of battle to the liberal organization of society represents a great advance on a simple appeal to ἐλευθερία, which in Greek eyes was consistent with the tyranny of law and custom.

καὶ ὑπὲρ ἀπάντων παραπλήσια - - - προφερόμενα: the structure of the sentence as a whole is: πατρίδος τε ὑπομιμνῄσκων ||| ἄλλα τε λέγων || ὅσα ἄνθρωποι | οὐ φυλαξάμενοι εἴποιεν ἄν | ἀλλ' ἐπιβοῶνται. ὑπομιμνῄσκων and λέγων are co-ordinated by τε / τε; καί before ὑπὲρ ἀπάντων cannot be co-ordinated with ἄλλα τε, making παραπλήσια a second object of λέγων, for the superimposition of the antithesis οὐ - - - εἴποιεν ἄν / ἀλλ' ἐπιβοῶνται upon this co-ordination is impossible, and ὑπὲρ ἀπάντων παραπλήσια, 'things in similar form' (cf. i. 22. 4) 'for all occasions', must refer to general practice, not to Nikias on one occasion. καί = 'including especially'; cf. 62. 3 n. The type of appeal which Thucydides has in mind is exemplified by A. *Pe.* 403 f., ἐλευθεροῦτε δὲ παῖδας γυναῖκας θεῶν τε πατρῴων ἕδη θήκας τε προγόνων. ἀρχαιολογεῖν (absurdly translated by LSJ, apparently with reference to this passage, as 'discuss antiquities or things out of date') is 'say what has always been said'; cf. Dobree, *Adversaria*, ad loc., Hudson-Williams, *CQ* xlii (1948), 79 f., and Luschnat, 99. ἀρχαιολογεῖν is precisely what Thucydides avoids in the speeches which he gives in full; the Funeral Speech is strikingly different from conventional examples of the genre (note especially ii. 36. 4).

3. ὡς ἐπὶ πλεῖστον ἐδύνατο: cf. p. 484.

4. οὗτοι γάρ - - - στρατηγοὶ ἐπέβησαν: cf. 16. 1 n.

πρὸς τὸ ζεῦγμα τοῦ λιμένος καὶ τὸν παραλειφθέντα διέκπλουν: the ζεῦγμα is the chain of boats described in 59. 3; nothing is said there of any gap, but one was clearly necessary for the Syracusans' own transference of ships to and from the Little Harbour. ψ have καταληφθέντα, which Valla translates: *fauces portus praeoccupatas praeclusasque*; that makes no sense, but καταλειφθέντα (B) does, cf. X. *An.* iv. 2. 11 οὐ κύκλῳ ἀλλὰ καταλιπόντες ἄφοδον τοῖς πολεμίοις, εἰ βούλοιντο φεύγειν.

70. 1. ναυσὶ παραπλησίαις τὸν ἀριθμὸν καὶ πρότερον: i.e. about 76 (52. 1); since the Athenians have 110 (60. 4), the figure agrees with the statement (70. 4) that the total of the two fleets was 'not far short of 200'.
Σικανὸς μὲν καὶ Ἀγάθαρχος ... Πύθην δέ: cf. vi. 104. 1 n., vii. 25. 1, 46 n., and 52. 2 n.

2. ἐπειδὴ δὲ οἱ ἄλλοι Ἀθηναῖοι προσέμισγον τῷ ζεύγματι: οἱ ἄλλοι does not appear to be contrasted, either retrospectively or prospectively, with any other portion of the Athenian force. If it is correct (B omits it, but it appears as καὶ οἱ ἄλλοι in Dion. Hal., *Thuc. Jud.* 875. 1, and E also has καί), it can hardly mean 'one of the several detachments', for whereas οἱ ἕτεροι can mean 'one of the two detachments' no comparable use of οἱ ἄλλοι is attested. Affinity with the idiom 'A καὶ οἱ ἄλλοι B' = 'A and also B' can be ruled out; nor can Ἀθηναῖοι be an intrusive gloss on οἱ ἄλλοι, for Thucydides does not say 'the others' = 'the opposing side' in any of his numerous descriptions of battles. It is possible that if πανταχόθεν σφίσι τῶν Συρακοσίων - - - ἐπιφερομένων was regarded by Thucydides as a statement not of what the Syracusans did but of what the Athenians experienced (cf. Arnold), οἱ ἄλλοι is anticipatory (cf. vi. 50. 4) and contrasted implicitly with all the rest of the Athenian ships, upon which the enemy fell; but this is not an easy interpretation, and οἱ ἄλλοι may be displaced from before οἱ Κορίνθιοι in the previous line.

4. αἱ μὲν ἐμβολαί - - - ὀλίγαι ἐγίγνοντο: ἐμβολαί = 'ramming attacks' (CE, cf. Σ^Patm. ἔμβολοι) is the obvious contrast to προσβολαί = 'collisions', and ἐκβολαί (ABFM Dion.) has no meaning suitable to the context.

6. τὰ μὲν ἄλλοις ἐμβεβληκέναι, τὰ δὲ αὐτοὺς ἐμβεβλῆσθαι: 'that on one quarter they had rammed an enemy ship, while on another quarter they had themselves been rammed'.

7. κατά τε τὴν τέχνην καὶ πρὸς τὴν αὐτίκα φιλονικίαν: the exercise of their duty required them to give technical orders, but they also shouted encouragement in response to the emotional demands of the situation. Cf. Isoc. iv. 97 (on Salamis) τοὺς θορύβους - - - καὶ τὰς κραυγὰς καὶ τὰς παρακελεύσεις, ἃ κοινὰ πάντων ἐστὶ τῶν ναυμαχούντων:

and on the history of κελευστής cf. E. von Leutsch, *Philologus* xi (1856), 716 ff.

νῦν, εἴ ποτε καὶ αὖθις, προθύμως ἀντιλαβέσθαι: the correct punctuation is (Classen) νῦν, εἴ ποτε, καὶ αὖθις - - -, 'now again, if ever (sc. before)' ; cf. 64. 2, iv. 20. 1, 55. 2, A. *Ag.* 520 f. εἴ που πάλαι, - - - δέξασθε, κ.τ.λ., and Diod. xiii. 15. 1 εἰ καὶ πρότερον, [ἢ] τὸ νῦν ἀντιλαβέσθαι τῆς - - - ἐλπίδος.

8. τῆς οὐ δι' ὀλίγου πόνου κεκτημένης θαλάσσης: without πόνου (which, however, is presented by the formidable combination of B, Σ^Mcf, and Dion. Hal., loc. cit.) the meaning would be 'possessed for so long' (cf. vi. 11. 4 n.). For Athenian 'possession' of the sea cf. ii. 62. 2.

71. 1. πολὺν τὸν ἀγῶνα καὶ ξύστασιν τῆς γνώμης εἶχε: Plu. *Mor.* 347 b has ἰσορρόπου τῆς ναυμαχίας καθεστηκυίας ἄλαστον ἀγῶνα καὶ σύνταξιν (sic) τῆς γνώμης, and Σ^Mcf points to ξύντασιν by the paraphrase ἰσχυρῶς ἠγωνίων καὶ τὰς διανοίας συνετέταντο. Yet ξύστασιν 'conflict' (cf. Hdt. vi. 117. 2) makes better sense than ξύντασιν 'effort' (in Pl. *Smp.* 206 b and *Phlb.* 46 d σύστασις and σύντασις are vv.ll.) and is supported here by Dio xlix. 9. 3 ἀντιπάλου γὰρ ἐπὶ πολὺ τῆς μάχης γενομένης - - - ἰσορρόπῳ καὶ αὐτοὶ συστάσει τῆς γνώμης συνέσχοντο (cf. Barrett on E. *Hp.* 983). As for ἄλαστον (an epic and lyric epithet of grief and trouble), although πολύς can have strong emotive overtones in Thucydides (cf. ii. 85. 2 ἐδόκει - - - πολὺς ὁ παράλογος εἶναι, vi. 24. 2, vii. 31. 5 n.), so that a more colourful word is not demanded here, it cannot be said that Thucydides, especially in so highly wrought a passage, would eschew a purely poetic word; κατήφεια in 75. 5 is a most striking example, and cf. C. F. Smith, *TAPhA* xxxi (1900), 69 ff. There is a serious possibility that Thucydides here wrote, not ἄλαστον, but ἀλίαστον, an epic epithet of war explained as = πολύς by Σ^D Hom. *Il.* ii. 797 and Σ *Ap. Rh.* i. 1326. Vollgraff, *Mnemosyne* 1906, 426, points out an alternative process of corruption: καθεστη-κυιασαλιαστοντον > καθεστηκυιαστον followed by conjectural insertion of πολύν.

2. διὰ τὸ ⟨ἀνώμαλον⟩ τῆς ναυμαχίας ἀνώμαλον καὶ τὴν ἔποψιν ἐκ τῆς γῆς ἠναγκάζοντο ἔχειν: the MSS. have διὰ τὸ ἀνώμαλον καὶ τὴν ἔποψιν τῆς ναυμαχίας ἐκ τῆς γῆς, κ.τ.λ., for which the simplest remedy is the supposition that τὸ ἀνώμαλον and τῆς ναυμαχίας belong together (for the sense cf. Hp. *Progn.* 3 τὰ σκέλεα ἀνωμάλως διερριμμένα) and that an adjective referring to τὴν ἔποψιν is lost. Wölfflin (*Hermes* xvii [1882] 176) transposed τῆς ναυμαχίας ; for the missing adjective, some such word as ἀσαφῆ is stylistically preferable, but ἀνώμαλον (Bauer) affords an easy explanation of the corruption : ανωμαλοντησναυμαχιασ ανωμαλονκαιτηνεποψιν > ανωμαλονκαιτηνεποψιν > (through collation) ανωμαλονκαιτηνεποψιν sscr. τησναυμαχιασ > ανωμαλοντησναυμαχιασκαιτηνεπσψιν. Steup's conjecture ἀνώμαλον ⟨τῶν γιγνομένων⟩ ⟨ἀνώμαλον⟩ καὶ τὴν ἔποψιν τῆς ναυμαχίας explains the corruption even more simply, but only by introducing a pleonasm.

4. ἦν τε - - - πάντα ὁμοῦ ἀκοῦσαι: the resemblance to E. *Ba.* 1131 ff. ἦν δὲ πᾶσ' ὁμοῦ βοή, ὁ μὲν στενάζων - - - αἱ δ' ἠλάλαζον is probably fortuitous; ὁμοῦ is a favourite word of Thucydides in this book (e.g. 84. 5, 87. 2), and for the form of the sentence as a whole cf. § 7 ἦν τε - - - ἔκπληξις.

νικῶντες κρατούμενοι: cf. X. *Cyr.* vii. 1. 40 κατεῖδε μεστὸν τὸ πεδίον ἵππων ἀνθρώπων ἁρμάτων φευγόντων διωκόντων κρατούντων κρατουμένων, but Thucydides' language is characteristically bolder: 'wailing and yelling, winners and losers'; cf. D. xxiii. 185.

5. καὶ ἐπικείμενοι λαμπρῶς: cf. 55. 1 n.

6. οὐκέτι διαφόρως: by contrast with the conflicting and alternating emotions described in § 4.

7. προσαπώλλυντο αὐταῖς καὶ οἱ ἐν τῇ νήσῳ ἄνδρες διαβεβηκότες: cf. especially iv. 14. 5, 15. 1.

72–74. *Aftermath of the Battle; Athenian Plans for Retreat*

72. 2. νεκρῶν μὲν πέρι ἢ ναυαγίων οὐδὲ ἐπενόουν αἰτῆσαι ἀναίρεσιν: for the recovery of wrecks under truce cf. ii. 92. 4: 'they recovered the dead and the wrecks on their own shore, and gave the enemy his (τὰ ἐκείνων) under truce.' In the immediate aftermath of a battle it would be, in the main, from the wrecks that the dead would be collected; dead bodies in the water would not yet have risen to the surface (cf. A. W. Platt, *JPh.* xxxiii [1914], 276 f.).

3. ἦσαν γὰρ τοῖς μὲν Ἀθηναίοις περίλοιποι ὡς ἑξήκοντα, τοῖς δ' ἐναντίοις ἐλάσσους ἢ πεντήκοντα: it follows that the Athenians had lost 50 ships, the Syracusans 30; cf. 60. 4, 70. 1, and 52. 1. Diod. xiii. 19. 1 says that the Syracusans captured 50 ships which the Athenians left behind; cf. 74. 2 and 60. 4 n.

4. καὶ ξυγχωροῦντος Νικίου τῇ γνώμῃ: now, at least, Nikias is not in a dilatory or obstructive mood, but the initiative still lies with Demosthenes. The chronology of the last stage of the campaign is not precise enough in Thucydides for us to be certain that the Athenian attempt to break out was made before the 'thrice nine days' enjoined by the seers (50. 4) had elapsed. We have to fit in the 'sufficient number of days' devoted to naval practice by the Syracusans (51. 2), the two days' battles which followed (51. 2–54), the closing of the harbour mouth (59. 2 f. n.), and the Athenian evacuation of the 'upper fortifications' and construction of a διατείχισμα (60. 2 f.). This does not sound like the work of as long a period as 27 days; it follows that Nikias agreed to attempting the breakout despite his original refusal (50. 4) 'to take any decision about the possibility of moving', and it now seems that he did not regard the failure of the first attempt as such clear evidence of divine displeasure that he was unwilling to make a second attempt. Probably the seers reconsidered their interpretation of the eclipse when the Syracusans closed the harbour.

οἱ ναῦται οὐκ ἤθελον ἐσβαίνειν: cf. 14. 2 n., but, more important, 73. 2 n.

73. 1. τοῖς ἐν τέλει οὖσιν: in this case, at least the generals, and perhaps other magistrates as well, = οἱ ἄρχοντες of § 3; cf. vi. 88. 10 n.

λέγων ταῦτα ἃ καὶ αὐτῷ ἐδόκει: (so *POxy.* 1376 as well as the MSS.). The reference is clearly to the reflections described in ὑπονοήσας, κ.τ.λ. above. We should expect καί with λέγων, rather than in the subordinate clause, to make the sense 'what he thought, he also expressed' clearer; but cf. Denniston, 295 f., and for the order ἃ καὶ αὐτῷ ἐδόκει cf. ibid. 326 f.

2. τοὺς δὲ ἀνθρώπους - - - οὐ δοκεῖν ἂν ῥᾳδίως ἐθελῆσαι ὑπακοῦσαι: sc. ἔφασαν from ἐδόκει: 'but (they said) they did not think that the men' (for οἱ ἄνθρωποι = 'the rank and file' cf. 50. 3) 'would be readily disposed to obey.' Despite the intervening clause ὑπὸ γάρ - - - ἐν τῇ ἑορτῇ, where the subject of the infinitive is τοὺς πολλούς, the understood subject of ἐλπίζειν is again the authorities: 'and the last order in which they would expect the men to obey them' (lit. 'expected that the men would obey them') 'was to take up arms at such a time and march out.' It is interesting to observe that the Syracusan army in victory was just as recalcitrant as the Athenian army in defeat; the sacrifice to Herakles is relevant, but the chief impediment to resolute military action that night was probably not piety but alcohol (cf. Polyain. i. 43. 2 and Popp, 120 ff.).

3. ἦσαν γάρ τινες τῷ Νικίᾳ διάγγελοι τῶν ἔνδοθεν: cf. 48. 2 n. The gender of τῶν ἔνδοθεν is in doubt; 'certain men, among those in the city, who brought him news' (cf. Pl. *Smp.* 174 e παῖδά τινα τῶν ἔνδοθεν) or 'certain men who brought him news of the events in the city' (cf. iii. 36. 3 ἄγγελον τῶν δεδογμένων).

74. 1. νομίσαντες οὐκ ἀπάτην εἶναι: they must have had some doubts, recollecting the trick they had played on the Syracusans two years earlier (vi. 64. 2 ff.); but they may have thought it would in any case be easier for them to fight their way through a well-established blocking force in daylight than through a hastily organized force in the dark. Cf. also 48. 2 n.

καὶ ἐπειδὴ καὶ ὡς οὐκ εὐθὺς ὥρμησαν: let us call the day of the battle 'Day 1', the following day 'Day 2', and the day of their departure (τρίτῃ ἡμέρᾳ, 75. 1) 'Day 3'. The decision here described (ἔδοξεν) was taken either during the night of Day 1 or on the morning of Day 2. If it was taken during the night of Day 1, καὶ ὣς must mean 'in spite of their original intention', περιμεῖναι 'wait *during*', and τὴν ἐπιοῦσαν ἡμέραν (cf. p. 276) Day 2. On this interpretation καὶ ὣς is both vague and otiose—though we might compare ὅμως in 48. 5 and 77. 3—and the aorist aspect of περιμεῖναι a little surprising. If the decision was taken on Day 2, καὶ ὣς means 'in spite of their intention to depart that morning', οὐκ εὐθὺς ὥρμησαν 'they did not succeed in getting away promptly' (why, Thucydides leaves to our imagination), περιμεῖναι 'wait *for*' (cf. v. 7. 3, 64. 4, vi. 56. 2, and viii. 16. 3, al.), and τὴν ἐπιοῦσαν ἡμέραν Day 3. If we are content not to be told just why they could not get away promptly on the morning of Day 2, we can be satisfied with the second interpretation, and have no need to emend. If we are not content, and so fall back on the first interpretation, we may remove one of its difficulties by Stahl's καὶ ὣς for καὶ ἐπειδὴ καὶ ὣς (cf. 7. 3 n.).

2. ὥσπερ διενοήθησαν: 60. 2; cf. 72. 3 n.

75. *Departure of the Athenians*

75. 2. δεινὸν οὖν ἦν οὐ καθ᾽ ἓν μόνον τῶν πραγμάτων: καθ᾽ ἕν, lit. 'one at a time' or 'in one respect' (cf. Pherekr. fr. 248 πανταχῇ λυπηρόν, οὐ καθ᾽ ἓν μόνον and Lys. xviii. 3 ὧν καθ᾽ ἓν ἕκαστον πολὺ ἂν ἔργον ἂν εἴη λέγειν) may function as subject or object of a verb, like καθ᾽ ἑκαστ-; cf. 8. 1 ἀγγέλλων - - - καθ᾽ ἕκαστα τῶν γιγνομένων, D. ix. 22 καθ᾽ ἕνα - - - περικόπτειν καὶ λωποδυτεῖν τῶν Ἑλλήνων. A distinction is drawn between their actual situation (πράγματα), of which every aspect (amplified in ὅτι, κ.τ.λ.) was discouraging, and the moral effect of abandoning their camp.

3. πολὺ τῶν τεθνεώτων τοῖς ζῶσι λυπηρότεροι ἦσαν καὶ τῶν ἀπολωλότων ἀθλιώτεροι: 'more distressing (sc. in sight and sound) than the dead to the living, and less fortunate than those who had perished'; τεθνεώτων describes dead men as objects, ἀπολωλότων describes them as beings whose capacity to do and suffer is ended.

4. οὐκ ἄνευ ὀλίγων ἐπιθειασμῶν καὶ οἰμωγῆς ὑπολειπόμενοι: ὀλίγων, 'few' (not, as in English, '*a* few = 'some'), strikes a false note in this scene. οὐκ ἄνευ in Classical prose is not equivalent to 'with'—were it so here, οὐκ ἄνευ ὀλίγων would mean 'without not few' = 'without many', cf. 79. 1 οὐκ ἐπ᾽ ὀλίγων ἀσπίδων = 'many shields deep'— but implies inevitability or indispensability. The point is that the sick and wounded did not lightly accept their fate, and their adjurations and lamentations were the price which the able-bodied had to pay for leaving them behind (cf. Pl. *Smp.* 174 d πορεύεσθαι ὑπολειπόμενον and Ar. *Ra.* 1091 f. ἔθει - - ὑπολειπόμενος, 'falling behind'). It is thus unlikely that Thucydides, intending to say 'not without not few', fell into the same trap as so many reputable authors who have used double negative expressions. Valla's *non sine multis* points to πολλῶν (cj. Meineke, *Hermes* iii [1869], 360, following Poppo); the later use of οὐκ ἄνευ = μετά (cf. Dio xli. 15. 4 καταδρομήν - - - οὐκ ἄνευ ἀρῶν ἐποιήσατο = 'he attacked them and cursed them too') produced a corruption of a simple psychological type (H. Richards, *CQ* viii [1914], 81, notes that ὀλίγων and πολλῶν are vv.ll. in Arist. *Rh.* 1356ᵇ13). For discussion of this and other passages which appear to say the opposite of what they mean cf. Herbst, ii. 132 ff., Herbst–Müller, iii. 27 ff., Lange, *Philologus* lvi (1897), 661 f., H. Herter, *RhM* xcii (1944), 174 ff., and Jebb on S. *Ant.* 4. Stahl suggested οὐκ ἄνευ ὀλολυγῶν, on which ἐπιθειασμῶν would be a gloss (cf. Usener, *RhM* lv [1900], 480 f.), but the only other occurrence of ὀλολυγή in Thucydides (ii. 4. 2) indicates that it would be inappropriate to the mournful situation described here.

5. μυριάδες γὰρ τοῦ ξύμπαντος ὄχλου οὐκ ἐλάσσους τεσσάρων ἅμα ἐπορεύοντο: the figure of 40,000 men 'lost in Sicily' recurs in Isoc. viii. 86 (together with 240 triremes, a figure irreconcilable with Thucydides' data), but it has been questioned, e.g. by Busolt, iii/2. 1370 f., n. 3. Thucydides appears to have calculated the number from vi. 43, vii. 16. 2, and 42. 1, on the assumption that 40 ships in the original expedition and the same number in the second were troop-carriers (cf. vi. 8. 1 n. and vi. 43 n.). If he has not simply disregarded casualties —and it would be strange if he did—he has included slaves in his round figure on the assumption that the number of slaves left was roughly equal to the number of soldiers and sailors killed, left behind, or missing. Cf. 82. 3 n. and 87. 4 n.

ἔφερον - - - καὶ οἱ ὁπλῖται καὶ οἱ ἱππῆς παρὰ τὸ εἰωθὸς αὐτοὶ τὰ σφέτερα αὐτῶν σιτία: this is perhaps the clearest evidence we have of the extent to which a hoplite force in the field used servants.

6. καὶ μὴν ἡ ἄλλη αἰκία καὶ ἡ ἰσομοιρία τῶν κακῶν ἔχουσά τινα ὅμως τὸ μετὰ πολλῶν κούφισιν οὐδ' ὡς ῥᾳδία ἐν τῷ παρόντι ἐδοξάζετο: if the text is right, we have a complicated hendiadys: 'The impartial distribution of misery in the rest of their degradations' (sc. apart from doing without servants), 'though it lightened the burden somewhat —"in company...", as they say—even so was not easily borne at such a time.' It is, however, more probable that Thucydides wrote καὶ τῇ ἰσομοιρίᾳ or καὶ ἰσομοιρίᾳ (cj. Dobree, followed by Steup, cl. ἡ ἰσομοιρία [*sic*] B): 'The rest of their degradation, even though lightening the burden somewhat by the impartial distribution of misery . . .'

7. [τῷ] Ἑλληνικῷ στρατεύματι: τῷ is impossible, and its insertion was perhaps occasioned by οἷς, for which ('. . . to a Greek army; for *this* army . . .') cf. 44. 1 ἐν νυκτομαχίᾳ, ἥ - - - (= 'and *this* one . . .'). The qualification Ἑλληνικῷ is necessary; Thucydides has in mind disasters which befell Oriental armies.

76–77. *Speech of Nikias*

76. βοῇ τε χρώμενος ἔτι μᾶλλον ἑκάστοις καθ' οὓς γίγνοιτο ὑπὸ προθυμίας καὶ βουλόμενος - - - ὠφελεῖν τι: ὑπὸ προθυμίας and βουλό-μενος ὠφελεῖν τι give the two reasons why Nikias raised his voice (cf. i. 49. 3 ὑπό τε τοῦ πλήθους - - - καί - - - πιστεύοντες, κ.τ.λ.). Either, then, τε is displaced from its original place after ὑπὸ προθυμίας, or it must be deleted altogether, or 'spoke as follows', linked by τε to ἐθάρσυνέ τε καὶ παρεμυθεῖτο, must be inserted; since Thucydides nowhere else omits such words at the beginning of a speech, the latter solution is the most probable (Steup). ἔτι μᾶλλον, 'even more' has no point of reference except the previous occasion on which Nikias addressed his army, which is now impossibly remote. It must be emended to ἀεί τι μᾶλλον, 'more and more' (J. Weidgen, *RhM* lxxvii [1928], 388)—ἔτι μᾶλλον cannot have that meaning, *pace* LSJ s.v. βιάζομαι on Hdt. i. 94. 5—or ἤ must be inserted, so that ἔτι μᾶλλον ἑκάστοις ⟨ἤ⟩ καθ' οὓς γίγνοιτο will mean 'even more, to each group (cf. X. *Cyr.* vii. 1. 12 κατ' ἄλλους δὲ αὖ τοιάδε [sc. εἶπεν] - - - κατ' ἄλλους δ' αὖ, κ.τ.λ.) than was appropriate to (sc. the numbers of) those before whom he stood' (Dover, *CR* n.s. iv [1954], 201 ff.). For the comparative with ἔτι and ἤ κατά cf. 45. 2, and for the 'double duty' of κατά cf. the genitive in Pl. *Phlb.* 16 b οὐ καλλίων - - - ἧς ἐγὼ ἐραστής εἰμι and perhaps πρός in vi. 31. 6 στρατιᾶς πρὸς οὓς ἐπῆσαν ὑπερβολῇ and ii. 65. 11 γνώμης ἁμάρτημα - - - πρὸς οὓς ἐπῆσαν.

77. 1. μηδὲ καταμέμφεσθαι ὑμᾶς ἄγαν αὐτούς - - - ταῖς παρὰ τὴν ἀξίαν νῦν κακοπαθίαις: it would have been in keeping with the traditional picture of Nikias as a deeply religious man if Thucydides had made him say: 'No doubt our sufferings are due to divine displeasure; but now we are punished enough, and we can look forward to divine help.' But his actual argument is more complicated: 'Your sufferings are *undeserved*' (i.e. such a strong force ought not to be defeated, unless it has offended the gods, as we have not); 'I suffer terribly; yet I have deserved well; therefore the question of desert does not yet arise.' There is nothing to suggest any doubt on the part of the speaker that the sufferings of the Athenians are παρὰ τὴν ἀξίαν. Superimposed on this logical exposition is the assurance that desert does matter in the end: 'I have deserved well; therefore I am confident of the future; and if we have offended, surely we have been punished enough.' This second argument actually overlaps the first in § 3, giving: 'I have deserved well; therefore I am confident of the future; and it is not in terms of desert that our disasters are alarming.' The order of words shows that the disasters *are* alarming, and δή rejects the idea that ἀξία has anything to do with them. (Schwartz's insertion [355] of ⟨αἱ⟩ before οὐ, approved by Luschnat

[103], makes Nikias say: 'But, I admit, our undeserved setbacks do frighten me.') Nikias' confidence for the future is not too confidently expressed: 'perhaps our sufferings may abate . . .' and his estimate of the gods' pity is linked (τε / καί) with the more practical 'Consider how strong you still are.' If Nikias had hitherto believed that piety was an insurance against disaster, events at Syracuse had compelled him to assign a bigger role to human will and error and to accident. At the same time, just as Solon (1. 25 ff.) assures his hearers that though the wicked prosper their descendants will be punished in the end, so Nikias is sure (rather like the Melians in v. 104) that *in the end* desert will count. At all costs he has to check the spread of a belief in his army that it is god-forsaken. His logic is not impeccable, but logic is a bleak consolation to a demoralized army.

2. καίτοι πολλὰ μὲν ἐς θεοὺς νόμιμα δεδιῄτημαι, πολλὰ δὲ ἐς ἀνθρώπους δίκαια καὶ ἀνεπίφθονα: cf. 86. 5 n.

3. οὐ κατ' ἀξίαν δή: cf. § 1 n.

ἱκανὰ γὰρ τοῖς τε πολεμίοις ηὐτύχηται καί - - - ἀποχρώντως ἤδη τετιμωρήμεθα: with the idea that they have been adequately punished for any respect in which they may have incurred divine anger (recollection of heroic legend must have made Nikias wonder in his heart whether one can judge what a god will think adequate) Nikias blends another common idea, that complete success in itself provokes divine resentment (he does not suggest that the Syracusans have committed impieties). Cf. Hdt. iv. 205, where Pheretime, having achieved complete revenge on Barke, dies a hideous death, demonstrating ὡς ἄρα ἀνθρώποισι αἱ λίην ἰσχυραὶ τιμωρίαι πρὸς θεῶν ἐπίφθονοι γίνονται.

4. ἀνθρώπεια δράσαντες ἀνεκτὰ ἔπαθον: the traditional antithesis δρᾶσαι / παθεῖν suggests crime and punishment, and the argument requires ἀνθρώπεια to mean 'acts such as men, prone to error, commit'; cf. iii. 40. 1 ἁμαρτεῖν ἀνθρωπίνως and X. *Cyr.* vi. 1. 37 (spoken to a ruler, not to a god) συγγνώμων τῶν ἀνθρωπίνων ἁμαρτημάτων. This is more appropriate to the context than 'acts which it is reasonable to expect men to commit', as in i. 76. 2, where the context shows that οὐδ' ἀπὸ τοῦ ἀνθρωπείου τρόπου means 'motivated by love of honour, fear of enemies, and desire to improve one's own situation'.

ἀπὸ τοῦ θεοῦ: as Nikias is the speaker, Krüger's emendation θείου is inept. When a Greek says ὁ θεός in a context where there is no reference to the recognizable functions of some particular god, he may mean Zeus, or he may mean 'whatever god is concerned with this'; cf. Antiphon iv. β. 8 τούτοις μὲν οὖν ὁ θεὸς ἐπιθείη τὴν δίκην.

οἴκτου γὰρ ἀπ' αὐτῶν ἀξιώτεροι ἤδη ἐσμὲν ἢ φθόνου: in E. *El.* 1329 f. one of the Dioskuroi says, in justification of his exclamation of distress at Orestes' plight, ἔνι γὰρ κἀμοὶ τοῖς τ' οὐρανίδαις οἶκτοι θνητῶν πολυμόχθων. In general, Greek gods are not prone to pity, except for one who is wronged by man and appeals to them for redress; none the less, a man in misery naturally (though not often) appeals to them for pity. The treatment of Pity (ἔλεος) as a divinity and the history of the 'altar(s) of Pity' are an entirely different question; cf. R. E. Wycherley, *CQ* N.S. iv (1954), 143 ff.

6. σπουδὴ δέ - - - ἔσται τῆς ὁδοῦ: in the circumstances these words are a promise by the generals rather than an order to the troops.

οὗτοι γὰρ ἡμῖν διὰ τὸ Συρακοσίων δέος ἔτι βέβαιοί εἰσιν: the Athenians were to have no opportunity of discovering whether the friendship of the Sikels would survive defeat; cf. 80. 5 n.

7. ἄνδρες γὰρ πόλις: this famous sentiment is at least as old as Alkaios fr. 112. 10 ἄνδρες γὰρ πόλιος πύργος ἀρεύιος. Cf. Meister, 33.

78-85. *Retreat and Destruction of the Athenians*

Thucydides' data are as follows:

Day	Distance Travelled	Location	Reference
1	c. 40 stades	Cross Anapos.	78. 1-4
2	c. 20 stades	Cross plain. Arrive at valley leading to Akraion Lepas.	78. 4-5
3	0	Fighting in valley.	78. 6
4	0	Fighting in valley.	79. 1-5
5	5-6 stades	(S. of valley? see below.)	79. 5-6
5/6	?	Towards the sea. Nikias and Demosthenes separated.	80. 1-4
6	(Nikias) 50+ stades	Arrive at the sea. Cross R. Kakyparis. Demosthenes surrenders. Nikias crosses R. Erineos.	80. 5-82. 3
7	0	South of R. Erineos.	83
8	?	Arrive at R. Assinaros.	84

The Athenians must have crossed the Anapos where it flows NW.–SE. before turning eastwards to the sea in its lowest reach, and then gone westwards towards the modern Floridia, which lies in a fertile tract 10 km. west of Syracuse and 30 km. east of Akrai. The valley leading from the plain to the Akraion Lepas has traditionally been identified with the Cava di Culatrello (Lupus, 152 f. and Holm, ii. 399 f.), of which the entrance lies 2·3 km. west of Floridia; this is a steep-sided gorge which suits the description of 78. 5, but not a place in which the Syracusan cavalry could have attacked the Athenians from the flanks (Holm, *Verh. d. 36 Samml. deutscher Philol.* [1882], 267). A route further south, through the area now called Contrada

Raiana (A. Leone, *Paideia* [Arona] viii [1953], 177 ff.), suits Thucydides' description of the Syracusan tactics better but his description of the ground less well. Certain identification is precluded by Thucydides' characteristic lack of precision in his account of the fighting; the cavalry may have attacked the Athenians only as they approached and entered the valley, not after they were in it.

On Day 3 the Athenians were trying to fight their way up the valley, but made little progress and ended the day where they had begun it. On Day 4 they reached the Syracusan barrier at the head of the valley (79. 1), prevented Gylippos from erecting another barrier behind them (79. 4), and again withdrew for the night πρὸς τὸ πεδίον (79. 5), far enough out of the valley to escape the danger that a barrier would be built behind them during the night. Their movement on Day 5 was an advance (προυχώρουν and προελθόντες), and this must have been an attempt to by-pass the valley. Thucydides can hardly have described a third attempt to force the valley in fundamentally different terms from those of 78. 6–79. 5; it is noteworthy that they were attacked on all sides (κύκλῳ) during this day, but nothing is said of any attempt on their part to storm a barrier or a hill, and at the end of the day they rested (ἀνεπαύοντο; contrast ἀνεχώρησαν 78. 6 and ἀναχωρήσαντες 79. 5) in the plain. As they were able to reach the sea during the following night the direction which they took in their attempt to by-pass the valley must have been southwards or south-eastwards.

Striking towards the sea from the plain around Floridia, and naturally taking care not to reappear in the neighbourhood of Syracuse, they would reach the sea north-east of the river Cassibile, which rises near Palazzolo Acreide (the ancient Akrai), and this river is undoubtedly the Kakyparis. The modern road from Syracuse to the site of Heloros comes very close to the sea at the mouth of the Cassibile, having previously run well inland. Between the Cassibile and the Tellaro—the ancient Heloros, close by the ruins of the town—there is now only one true river, which flows past Noto and into the sea 11 km. south of the mouth of the Cassibile. This river, named 'Falconara' in Baedeker and nineteenth-century maps, is called 'Asinaro' 'n its upper reaches and 'Fiumara di Noto' in the lower (M. Margani, *RF* N.s. viii [1930], 195 ff.). Either, then, (*a*) the Assinaros and the Heloros are the same river, the modern Tellaro, the Erineos is the Fiumara di Noto, and the name 'Asinaro' has been wrongly attached to the upper reaches of the latter, or (*b*) the Assinaros is the Fiumara di Noto, and the Erineos is one of the seven watercourses, normally dry in summer, between the Cassibile and the Fiumara di Noto. Pais identified the Assinaros as in (*a*) (*Ricerche storiche e geografiche* [Torino, 1908], 189 ff.); he cited examples of rivers which have borne more than one name, derived

'Tellaro' from 'Assinaros' via one of its local forms, 'Atiddáru', accepted the column called 'La Pizzuta', 1 km. north of the Tellaro, as a Syracusan victory monument, and identified the Erineos as the now dry Cavallata. The column, however, is not a monument of Classical antiquity at all (Margani, 198 ff.). Just south of Avola—a town 9 km. south-west of the Cassibile and 4·5 km. north of the Fiumara di Noto—is a watercourse called 'Cava Mammaledi', which dried up after the great earthquake of 1693. This was undoubtedly the river called 'Miranda' by Fazello in the mid-sixteenth century and Clüver in 1619 and identified by them, rightly, with the Erineos; 'Miranda' is now the name of a spring which waters Avola (Margani, 194 ff.). It therefore seems that Demosthenes surrendered not far south of the Cassibile, and Nikias crossed the Cava Mammaledi later on the day of the surrender.

Clearly both detachments reached the sea: 'They became disordered; Nikias' force stayed together and drew far ahead, while Demosthenes' . . . was separated from Nikias' and its movement was less disciplined. Nevertheless (ὅμως) they arrived at the sea at dawn' (80. 4 f.). When Demosthenes was heavily attacked and was on the point of being surrounded, Nikias was 50 stades ahead of him (81. 2 f.), and on the same day Nikias crossed the Erineos (82. 3). 50 stades amount to something between 7 and 9 km. (cf. pp. 467 f.).

78. 2. τὸ δὲ ἐχώρει ἐν πλαισίῳ τεταγμένον: τὸ δέ refers to the whole στράτευμα. On πλαίσιον cf. vi. 67. 1 n. In the present case it travels across country in two portions; each portion would be a column of which the outer files were hoplites and the inner files carriers and light-armed troops, with a stiffening of hoplites at the 'mouth' and at the 'tail'. Cf. X. *Cyr.* vi. 3. 3 διὰ μέσου ποιούμενοι τὰ σκευοφόρα ἔνθεν καὶ ἔνθεν ἐπορεύοντο οἱ ὁπλοφόροι, and *An.* iii. 2. 36. ἐν διπλασίῳ (ACEFGM), which is not Greek, is a corruption of an unfamiliar to a familiar word; Heitland's ingenious conjecture ἐν διπλαισίῳ (*JPh.* xxiv [1895], 25 ff., cl. διστάδιον etc.; the attribution of διπλαισίῳ to ACEFM in Kleinlogel, *Geschichte des Thukydidestextes im Mittelalter*, 79 n. 69 is, I assume, a misprint) is not required, for ἐν πλαισίῳ means not 'in a πλαίσιον' but 'in πλαίσιον formation'.

3. ἐπὶ τῇ διαβάσει τοῦ Ἀνάπου ποταμοῦ: cf. p. 455.

4. ἐς χωρίον ἄπεδόν τι: cf. p. 455.

5. ἐκαλεῖτο δὲ Ἀκραῖον λέπας: cf. p. 455.

79. 1. στενὸν γὰρ ἦν τὸ χωρίον: the words explain (γάρ) why it was possible for the Syracusans to defend the position in such depth.

3. ἐνόμιζον ἐπὶ τῷ σφετέρῳ ὀλέθρῳ καὶ ταῦτα πάντα γίγνεσθαι: cf. vi. 70. 1 n.

5. τῇ δ᾿ ὑστεραίᾳ προυχώρουν: cf. p. 456.

80. 2. ἦν δὲ ἡ ξύμπασα ὁδὸς αὕτη οὐκ ἐπὶ Κατάνης, κ.τ.λ.: before the last battle in the harbour the Athenian intention was to go to Katane if their ships could break out, but otherwise to take whatever route would most quickly lead to friendly territory, 'Greek or foreign' (60. 2). Nikias in 77. 4 ff. says nothing of Katane, but reveals that notice of the retreat had been sent to Sikel tribes, and 80. 5 shows that the intended rendezvous with the Sikels was on the upper Kakyparis, i.e. in the area of Akrai. So far, then, Thucydides has given us no indication of their destination, nor even told us that they had at this stage a nameable destination in mind. It is therefore unlikely that he now means 'their destination was now *no longer* Katane, but the south-west coast', and if he did mean that it is surprising that he did not also say it. (Diod. xiii. 18. 2, 18. 6–19. 2, certainly represents their original destination as Katane, but one must have reservations about the accuracy with which his source interpreted the evidence.) The point of Thucydides' words is 'their destination was not Katane, as you might expect from their turning back towards the sea, but the south-west coast'. ἡ ξύμπασα ὁδός is the over-all journey, as distinct from any particular stage in it. But there is still a doubt whether he means by 'this' the whole journey from the first day onwards or only the journey now beginning with their escape during the night. If the former, then they did have a destination in mind from the first, and Thucydides only now reveals it, having implicitly denied it in his account of Nikias' last speech. If the latter, then they formulated a plan when they found that progress past Akraion Lepas was impossible, and their intention to march up the Kakyparis (80. 5) to a rendezvous with the Sikels must have been in harmony with this new plan. On balance, the demonstrative αὕτη and Thucydides' previous silence on their plans suggest that the plan to aim for the south-west coast was a new one (one wonders what they intended to do when they got there) and that their original plan did not look beyond a rendezvous with the Sikels in the area of Akrai.

3. καὶ αὐτοῖς, οἷον φιλεῖ καὶ πᾶσι στρατοπέδοις - - -, φόβοι καὶ δείματα ἐγγίγνεσθαι, - - - ἐμπίπτει ταραχή: 'as is wont to happen— panic and fear, I mean, are wont to arise—'. The passage bears a singular resemblance to X. *An.* ii. 2. 19 τοῖς Ἕλλησι φόβος ἐμπίπτει, καὶ θόρυβος καὶ δοῦπος ἦν οἷον εἰκὸς φόβου ἐμπεσόντος γενέσθαι.

5. ἐσβάντες ἐς τὴν ὁδὸν τὴν Ἑλωρινὴν καλουμένην: cf. p. 456.
ἐπὶ τῷ ποταμῷ τῷ Κακυπάρει: cf. p. 456.
οὓς μετεπέμψαντο: cf. 77. 6. If the original rendezvous was near Akrai, following the Kakyparis upstream would certainly have brought them to it.
6. φυλακήν τινα τῶν Συρακοσίων: a product of the activity described in 74. 2.

πρὸς ἄλλον ποταμὸν τὸν Ἐρινεόν: cf. pp. 456 f.
ταύτῃ γὰρ οἱ ἡγεμόνες ἐκέλευον: guides; cf. 50. 2.

81. 1. ἑκόντα ἀφεῖναι τοὺς Ἀθηναίους: it would be interesting to know their interpretation of Gylippos' motives. Possibly they thought that he as a Spartan—all his training and military instincts would have dissuaded him from fighting an unnecessary battle—was content with decisive victory, while they were in the mood for spectacular revenge. More probably, however, the 'pan-Sikeliot' sentiment encouraged by Hermokrates manifested itself, in a moment of disappointment, in a suspicion that there might exist a similar bond of sentiment between their Spartan general and their enemy; Nikias, too, was regarded as having close relations with Sparta (86. 3). Cf. 86. 2 ff. and Freeman, ii. 384. No doubt natural jealousy aggravated the situation, though according to Plu. *Nic.* 19. 6 Philistos gave all the credit for victory to Gylippos.

3. καὶ πεντήκοντα σταδίους: Bψ have ἑκατὸν καὶ πεντήκοντα σταδίους, for which there is no room in Π¹⁸; nor is so high a figure reconcilable with the topography of the retreat, on any value of the stade; cf. pp. 467 f.

4. ἔς τι χωρίον ᾧ κύκλῳ μὲν τειχίον περιῆν, ὁδὸς δὲ ἔνθεν καὶ ἔνθεν: cf. X. *Cyr.* vi. 1. 30 πρὸς τοὺς ἄξονας ἔνθεν καὶ ἔνθεν. Plu. *Nic.* 27. 1 (from Philistos?) specifies the place as περὶ τὴν Πολυζήλειον αὐλήν, which is of no help to us.

5. καὶ ἅμα φειδώ τέ τις ἐγίγνετο - - - μὴ προαναλωθῆναί τῳ: if the Athenians had not had so far to go, discipline could still have saved them from complete disaster—Pl. *Smp.* 221 b, referring to the retreat from Delion, remarks that a victorious enemy in a pursuit keeps clear of a fugitive who looks ready to hit back—but hunger and thirst and desperate fatigue were having their effect by now.
ταύτῃ τῇ ἰδέᾳ: by herding them together and shooting them down περισταδόν.

82. 1. τῶν νησιωτῶν: cf. 20. 2 n.
καὶ ἀπεχώρησάν τινες πόλεις οὐ πολλαί: cf. 63. 3 f. and (on the organization of the Athenian force) vi. 98. 4 n.
2. καὶ μὴ ἀποθανεῖν μηδένα - - - τῆς ἀναγκαιοτάτης ἐνδείᾳ διαίτης: yet Demosthenes himself died βιαίως (86. 2; cf., however, 86. 5 n.), and the ration of food and water given to the Athenians imprisoned in the quarries (87. 2) fell short of a reasonable or humane minimum.
3. ἑξακισχίλιοι: since (*a*) the total number which left the camp six days before was 'not less than 40,000' (75. 5), (*b*) slaves cannot have constituted more than 10–20 per cent of this total (cf. 75. 5 nn.), (*c*) Demosthenes had 'half or more' of the total (80. 4), i.e. at least 20,000 men, and (*d*) not many contingents of 'islanders' took

advantage of the Syracusan offer, it seems that they suffered casualties on a much greater scale than Thucydides' narrative, or other retreats in Greek history, would have led us to expect. Cf. 87. 4 n.

83. 3. οἱ δὲ Συρακόσιοι καὶ Γύλιππος οὐ προσεδέχοντο τοὺς λόγους: ἄνδρες γὰρ πόλις. The Syracusans, like Nikias, knew that Athens could raise money, and would raise as much of it as possible from her subjects, but soldiers and sailors were not so easily replaceable.

84. 2. πρὸς τὸν Ἀσσίναρον ποταμόν: cf. pp. 456 f.

85. 1. τοῦ δὲ καί, εἴ τι διαφύγοι, ὑπὸ τῶν ἱππέων: the sense requires 'and the rest—such of it as escaped—by the cavalry', and the punctuation of Stuart Jones is correct; cf. 68. 1 n.

πιστεύσας μᾶλλον αὐτῷ ἢ τοῖς Συρακοσίοις: cf. 81 n.

3. οὐ πολὺ ἐγένετο: cf. 87. 4 n.

ἅτε οὐκ ἀπὸ ξυμβάσεως - - - ληφθέντων: Demosthenes' surrender had been negotiated, so that the Syracusan state was responsible for the men who surrendered—responsible, among other things, for preserving their lives—but it entered into no such agreement with Nikias' men; hence those who surrendered were the booty of individuals, who could keep or sell them as they pleased.

4. τῶν ἐν τῷ [Σικελικῷ] πολέμῳ τούτῳ: these words depend on οὐδενὸς ἐλάσσων; πλεῖστος is not tautologous, but means 'more than at any other stage of the retreat'. Σ^Mcf, drawing attention to 87. 5, expresses the opinion that Thucydides wrote Ἑλληνικῷ, not Σικελικῷ, and Dobree deleted the word altogether. The positive suggestion is faulty, since Ἑλληνικῷ would be a curious addition to τῷ πολέμῳ τούτῳ, and 87. 5 is no help at all, but the suspicion is just, and Dobree was right to delete; demonstratives encourage glosses.

τούτοις δ' ἦν ἀναχώρησις ἐς Κατάνην: among them was the speaker of [Lys.] xx, who says (24 f.): 'When our force had been destroyed and I had succeeded in saving myself and reaching Katane, I took part in raids based on Katane and inflicted losses on our enemies, with the result that a good 30 mnai were paid as a tithe to Athena and for the redemption of those of our soldiers who were in enemy hands. When Katane insisted that we should serve as cavalry, I did so, and in that too there was no perilous undertaking in which I failed to play my part.' This man was back in Athens by 410, when the speech was delivered. Paus. vii. 16. 4 f. tells the story of one Kallistratos son of Empedos, an Athenian hipparch; charging through the enemy at the Assinaros, he got to Katane, returned to Syracuse to harry the Syracusans who were (still, according to the story) plundering the Athenian camp, and was killed in that action.

86–87. *The Fate of the Athenian Prisoners*

86. 2. ἐς τὰς λιθοτομίας: the great quarries east of the theatre, which now plunge down from the slope of the plateau, are described by Cic. *II Verr.* v. 68 (when three and a half centuries of quarrying had passed since the days of Hermokrates) in the words *nihil tam clausum ad exitum, nihil tam saeptum undique, nihil tam tutum ad custodiam nec fieri nec cogitari potest.*

Νικίαν δὲ καὶ Δημοσθένη ἄκοντος τοῦ Γυλίππου ἀπέσφαξαν: this event provided material for historical controversy and rhetorical invention in later times. Philistos (F 55) followed Thucydides; Timaios (F 101) said that Hermokrates gave the Athenian generals the opportunity to escape the disgrace of execution by suicide. The story of Plu. *Nic.* 28. 3 and Diod. xiii. 19. 5, that Hermokrates was opposed to the execution and advocated τὸ καλῶς χρῆσθαι τῇ νίκῃ (Plutarch) or τὸ τὴν νίκην ἐνεγκεῖν ἀνθρωπίνως (Diodoros), is almost certainly from Timaios (F 101). In Plutarch the proposal for the execution is made by 'Eurykles' ὁ δημαγωγός; certainly a mistake for Diokles (cf. the misprinting of Ἑρμοκράτους as Ἑρμοκρέοντος in Jacoby's text of Philistos F 55), who is the proposer in the full-dress debate of Diod. xiii. 20–32. On the attitude of Gylippos Plutarch accords with Thucydides; Diodoros makes him support Diokles. There existed in the fourth century a highly elaborate rhetorical exercise, attributed to Lysias by Theophrastos (Dion. Hal. *Lys.* 14), which represented a speech by Nikias to his captors.

3. τὸν δὲ διὰ τὰ αὐτὰ ἐπιτηδειότατον: cf. v. 16. 1, 43. 2, and vi. 89. 2.

4. ὅτι πρὸς αὐτὸν ἐκεκοινολόγηντο: cf. 48. 2 n.

ὅτι πλούσιος ἦν: Lys. xix. 47 and X. *Vect.* 4. 14 are our earliest evidence after Thucydides for the tradition of Nikias' great wealth.

5. διὰ τὴν πᾶσαν ἐς ἀρετὴν νενομισμένην ἐπιτήδευσιν: the words πᾶσαν ἐς ἀρετήν are provided by B and Σᴹᶜᶠ; without them, the meaning would be 'because of the conduct which he had practised', which cries out for further qualification. No one who has read this history up to the present point is likely to have formed a very favourable view of Nikias. His one consistent characteristic is his obsessive anxiety to preserve his own reputation as a successful general. His behaviour in the face of Kleon's challenge over Pylos gave us a foretaste of this anxiety (iv. 28. 1), and Thucydides brings it into prominence in describing the negotiations which led to the Peace of Nikias (v. 16. 1). It remains prominent in his speeches on the Sicilian expedition (vi. 9. 2 and 23. 3), is reflected in the cool disloyalty of his confidential proposal to his fellow generals that they should not attempt to realize the main object of the expedition (vi. 47), and culminates in his obstinate resistance to his colleagues' demand for withdrawal (vii. 48. 1), his magnification of inadequate

reasons for prolonging the campaign (48. 2, 5, 50. 4), and his readiness
to sacrifice the whole expedition provided that he can die honourably
in battle and escape the disgrace of trial and execution (48. 4). He
must at one time have been a resourceful general; the operation at
Kythera (iv. 53 ff.) was a success, and there is no reason to see
sarcasm in Ar. *Av.* 361 f. εὖ γ' ἀνηῦρες αὐτὸ καὶ στρατηγικῶς· ὑπερακοντίζεις σύ γ' ἤδη Νικίαν ταῖς μηχαναῖς (cf. the similar idea of
Phrynichos fr. *22*, from the same year); success (however 'lucky')
is a recommendation, and the Athenians did not commonly elect
incompetents to high command or reward mediocrity by repeated
election. The successes achieved by the Athenians at Syracuse in the
autumn of 415 and the early summer of 414 (eight victories, by the
reckoning of the ἐπικήδειον composed by Euripides after the loss of
the expedition [Plu. *Nic.* 17. 4]) may not all be attributable to
Lamachos. Nikias was prompt enough, even when sick, in saving
the Athenian fort on Epipolai from capture when it was horridly
exposed (vi. 102. *2* f.). During the critical period when he was left in
sole command he was inept, dilatory, and querulous, and how far
these characteristics were the product of sickness is, and must remain, an open question; Thucydides makes no excuses for him in
vii. 42. *3*. In extreme adversity his technical competence re-asserted
itself; he knew how to organize a fast retreat (80. 4)—by no means
a negligible military virtue—and at the last he redeemed his earlier
preoccupation with his own good name by surrendering to save his
men from slaughter (85. 1). If it is meaningful to compare him with
generals of modern times, he seems to have alternated between the
ill-organized and ineffective conscientiousness of Raglan and the
attitude which Weygand revealed by exclaiming, when he was
called from Syria to take command of the French armies in May
1940, 'If I had known the situation was so bad I would not have
come!'

If Thucydides had said that Nikias did not deserve to fail, or even
that he did not deserve to die, that would have been a surprising
judgement in the absence of any comparable expression of sympathy
for Demosthenes. What Thucydides actually says, however, is that
Nikias did not deserve the great misfortune of being executed in
cold blood by the enemy to whom he had surrendered. Harsher
critics than Thucydides are at liberty to agree with that judgement
without believing (any more than Thucydides believed) in a divinely
organized system of rewards and punishments and without dissenting from the reason which Thucydides gives (cf. H. D. Westlake,
CQ xxxv [1941], 59). Nikias had a conscience, however curious we
may find its limitations on occasion, he had tried to meet his obligations to gods and men, just as he is made to claim in 77. 2, and such
a man can be thought to deserve to be treated with equal scruple by

other men, even by an enemy. Thucydides was certainly aware of the negative character of Nikias' virtues and of his failure to understand what the situation demanded (cf. H. A. Murray, *BICS* viii [1961], 33 ff., 41 ff.).

Some commentators (e.g. A. W. Platt, *JPh.* xxxiii [1914], 277) have discerned irony in Thucydides' judgement. The judgement, however, formally resembles others in which irony is out of the question, e.g. viii. 97. 2 οὐχ ἥκιστα δὴ τὸν πρῶτον χρόνον ἐπί γε ἐμοῦ - - - εὖ πολιτεύσαντες· μετρία γάρ, κ.τ.λ. Yet it is not wholly free from ambiguity of expression. The Greeks did not speak of 'the virtues' (cf. Schwartz, 351 ff.), but πᾶσα ἀρετή in the sense 'complete virtue' (and it would be hair-splitting, in the present context, to distinguish that from 'every virtue') is a recognized expression; cf. *GVI*, i. 488 (Peiraieus), 544 (Athens), and 1962 (Athens), fourth-century epitaphs in which πάσης ἀρετῆς ἐπὶ τέρμα μολεῖν is a formula. We can, however, be fairly confident that νενομισμένην does not agree with ἀρετήν, for the resulting expression τὴν ἐς ἀρετὴν ἐπιτήδευσιν is unlike its nearest parallel, τῆς ἀνθρωπείας τῶν μὲν ἐς τὸ θεῖον νομίσεως τῶν δ' ἐς αὐτοὺς βουλήσεως (v. 105. 1), in so far as its sense could be expressed not only easily, but better, by τὴν ἀρετῆς ἐπιτήδευσιν. Although νενομισμένην suggests the practice of a whole society rather than of an individual (cf. the common νενόμισται = 'it is customary', and H. Richards, *CQ* viii [1914], 82), there are such passages as A. *Ch.* 1001 φιλήτης ἀνήρ - - - ἀργυροστερῆ βίον νομίζων and E. fr. 87. 3 ἡμᾶς - - - τοὺς νομίζοντας τέχνην. If Thucydides had really wanted to distinguish traditional concepts of goodness from some more original concept, he could have made the distinction by writing ἀρετὴν τὴν νενομισμένην, and what the MSS. have does not make any such distinction apparent. In any case, the definition of ἀρετή implied in v. 105. 4 (cf. n.) indicates that Thucydides would not have wanted to deny the name of goodness to the sustained effort to be just and conscientious in fulfilling one's obligations. Hence lit., 'through his practice all observed into goodness', i.e. 'because he had ordered his whole life by high moral standards'. Cf. Bender, 49 f.

According to Paus. i. 29. 3, Nikias' name was omitted from the casualty list at Athens, and Pausanias gives as the reason for this the alleged fact (cited from Philistos [F 53]) that Nikias had surrendered of his own free will, whereas Demosthenes, while surrendering his troops, had exempted himself from the agreement and tried to commit suicide. I see no good grounds for disbelieving Pausanias' datum or denying that effective διαβολή of Nikias and glorification of Demosthenes at the time when the casualty list was erected may have given currency to the story which Philistos records. But this was a temporary phase. Nikias' character and even his military reputation were secure in the fourth century. The attractive portrait of him in Plato's *Laches*, where he appears as a patient, serious, honest man, is from the pen of a writer who was not afraid to hold unpopular opinions, and Lys. xviii. 2 f., 'Nikias did you great service when he followed his own judgement, and the blame for our failure in Sicily must be put upon those who persuaded you to go there, against Nikias' advice', may be regarded as a partisan statement, coming as it does from a speech on behalf of Nikias' brother, but in D. iii. 21 Nikias is named with Aristeides and Perikles among the great men of old 'whom all praise but none imitate', and *Ἀθ. π.* 28. 5. represents a high opinion of Nikias as 'agreed by almost everyone'. Plutarch, who claims (*Nic.* 1. 5) to have taken some trouble to collect material illustrative of the man's character, amplifies the traditional picture with a wealth of anecdotal detail, enlarging on Nikias' generosity (4. 3), severe dedication to public duty (5. 1 ff.), strict religious observance (4. 1 f. and 5. 4), and a courtesy which amounted in Plutarch's view to pusillanimity (2. 4 ff.); all of which accords very well with Th. vii. 77. 2.

87. 1. τῇ μεταβολῇ ἐς ἀσθένειαν ἐνεωτέριζον: cf. διὰ τὴν μεταβολήν (§ 2). The effects of sudden changes in temperature, humidity, diet, or habits were taken very seriously in medical theory (cf. Hp. *Reg.* 35 αἱ μέγισται μεταβολαὶ τῶν περὶ τὰς φύσιας ἡμέων καὶ τὰς ἕξιας συμβαινόντων μάλιστα νοσοποιοῦσιν, *Aer.* 2, and *VM* 10), and among laymen also; cf. X. *Cyr.* vi. 2. 27 ἐπὶ μὲν τῷ σίτῳ νῦν εὐθὺς ἀρχώμεθα πίνειν ὕδωρ· τοῦτο γὰρ ἤδη ποιοῦντες οὐ πολὺ μεταβαλοῦμεν --- ἡ γὰρ κατὰ μικρὸν παράλλαξις πᾶσαν ποιεῖ φύσιν ὑποφέρειν τὰς μεταβολάς, and Plu. *Nic.* 6. 3 on the Plague.

2. ἐπὶ ὀκτὼ μῆνας: since many were sold after 70 days (§ 3), this figure refers to the Athenians and the others who remained. Presumably at the end of eight months all these were sold.

κοτύλην ὕδατος καὶ δύο κοτύλας σίτου: recent finds of measures (cf. especially O. Broneer, *Hesperia* vii [1938], 222 ff., Suzanne Young, ibid. viii [1939], 278 ff., H. A. Thompson, ibid. xxiv [1955], 69 f.) confirm traditional calculation; a liquid κοτύλη was 0.27 litres, a dry κοτύλη 270–275 c.c. Under the terms of the truce at Pylos (iv. 16. 1) the Spartans had been allowed to supply even the slaves on Sphakteria with four κοτύλαι of flour per man per day.

4. οὐκ ἐλάσσους ἑπτακισχιλίων: since 6,000 were captured with Demosthenes (82. 3), it follows that only 1,000 of Nikias' contingent (originally nearly 20,000 [75. 5 ~ 80. 4]) were brought to Syracuse as prisoners. The number is remarkably small, but 85. 3 f. give us some warning of it.

5. ἔργον τοῦτο ['Ελληνικόν]: given ὧν ἀκοῇ 'Ελληνικῶν ἴσμεν (cf. 75. 7), 'Ελληνικόν is stylistically objectionable (secl. Krüger) and is probably in origin a gloss on τόνδε; cf. 85. 4 n.

YEAR NINETEEN: SUMMER—413 B.C. VII. 87. 6

6. πανωλεθρίᾳ δὴ τὸ λεγόμενον - - - οὐδὲν ὅτι οὐκ ἀπώλετο: H. Strasburger's suggestion (*Hermes* lxxxvi [1958], 39 n. 3) that Thucydides
had in mind Hdt. ii. 120. 5 on the fall of Troy, τοῦ δαιμονίου παρα-
σκευάζοντος ὅκως πανωλεθρίῃ ἀπολόμενοι καταφανὲς τοῦτο τοῖσι ἀνθρώποισι ποιήσωσι ὡς τῶν μεγάλων ἀδικημάτων μεγάλαι εἰσὶ καὶ αἱ τιμωρίαι
παρὰ τῶν θεῶν, seems to me refuted by τὸ λεγόμενον. I suspect that
if Thucydides had recalled the Herodotean passage he would have
taken some trouble to avoid the appearance of subscribing to its
theology.

H h

APPENDIX

THE TOPOGRAPHY OF SYRACUSE AND THE SIEGE

THIS appendix is based on the following material:

1. Inspection of the terrain in 1960 and photographs taken then.

2. Sheet 274 II SW of the 1/25,000 Italian military map, revised from aerial photography up to 1943; the 1/10,000 map published by the Azienda Autonoma Turismo at Syracuse (n.d., but obtained in 1960); and sheet 4058 of the 1/10,000 U.S. Hydrographic Office chart, revised up to 1957.

3. Discussions of the topographical question in:

> F. S. Cavallari, A. Holm, and C. Cavallari, *Topografia antica di Siracusa* (Palermo, 1883).
>
> B. Lupus, *Die Stadt Syrakus im Altertum* (Strassburg, 1887), a German version of Cavallari–Holm.
>
> E. Odermann, *Der Festungskrieg vor Syrakus in den Jahren 414–413 v. Chr.* (Leipzig, 1927), and more briefly, in *RE* viiA. 1405 f.
>
> K. Fabricius, *Das antike Syrakus* = *Klio*, Beiheft xxviii (1932).

(Other articles are mentioned in the appendix where relevant. It should be noted that the maps and sketches in existing editions of Thucydides are in many respects inaccurate, and in certain respects have become progressively less accurate since the early nineteenth century.)

Map 1 shows Syracuse as it is today; map 2 shows the location of the Syracusan and Athenian fortifications in 415–413 as I believe them to have been.

Thucydides does not tell us whether or not he himself had seen Syracuse. The belief that he had is an article of faith with some editors and historians (and in Freeman's case clearly a focus of emotion), but it has no firmer rational basis than the fact that although he is vague or silent on many of the topographical points on which the reader most needs enlightenment, and although it is quite possible that on some questions of importance he is ignorant or mistaken, there is no problem which is conclusively solved solely by the assumption of ignorance or error on his part.

None of his descriptions of what was said and done and thought in Syracuse before and during the siege imply that he had been there. His information on the night battle on Epipolai came 'from

466

both sides' (vii. 44. 1); but Peloponnesian and Boeotian troops were present in substantial numbers on that occasion, not to mention the Arkadian mercenaries who fought on both sides, and Syracusan ships, commanded by Hermokrates and other men who had taken a prominent part in the events of 415–413, formed part of the Peloponnesian fleet in the Aegean from the autumn of 412 onwards (viii. 26. 1, etc.). There had also been some coming and going of envoys during 414–413 between Syracuse and Sparta and Corinth.

He writes at times as if both he and his readers were familiar with places and objects in the neighbourhood of Syracuse; this is notably true of his references to the Olympieion, Daskon, the Anapos, and the Helorine Road in vi. 64–6, Temenites in vi. 75. 1, and Euryelos, Labdalon, and the fig-tree (or 'Syke'; see below) in vi. 97–8. The same observation is applicable to vi. 100. 1, 'the stockade in the region of the pyramid' (B¹H), where the reading πυλίδα (Bˢ cett.) is harmless ('the stockade in the region of its gate') but a banal corruption; cf. Schwartz, 343 ff. (The definite article in vi. 99. 2 τοῖς σταυροῖς is difficult on any hypothesis save that of corruption; v. ad loc.) Now, he cannot consciously have assumed that his readers, to whom on other occasions he gives topographical information on Attica, were familiar with the environs of Syracuse; his elementary description of the position and nature of Epipolai (vi. 96. 2) shows that when he gave his attention to the matter at all he made precisely the opposite assumption. If he had been to Syracuse himself, we should have expected him to display his knowledge, as he displays his knowledge of Thrace (ii. 95 ff.), and such a display is conspicuously absent from vi–vii; the contrast with v. 10. 6 (on Amphipolis) is interesting. His apparent assumption of our familiarity with places and objects rests on his own familiarity with them as recurrent elements in the many individual narratives on which he based his history, and has little or no bearing on the question of autopsy; it is noteworthy that in describing the beginnings of the Athenian fortifications on Epipolai he says (vi. 98. 2) ἐτείχισαν τὸν κύκλον, i.e. 'they built *the* circle' (sc. 'which is to figure in the rest of my story'), referring in this case to a purely temporary feature of the landscape.

It is necessary now to examine certain passages which may reflect his own ignorance of the relevant topography:

(i) vii. 59. 3, where the harbour mouth is described as 'about eight stades wide'. This passage is inconclusive; as the distance is 1,040 m. from the southern tip of Ortygia to the Scoglio Castelluccio off Plemmyrion, the datum, if correct, presupposes a stade of *c.* 130 m. This is not significantly different from the equation '1 stade = 140 m.' presupposed by vi. 1. 2 (cf. n.), but diverges a little more from that of vii. 19. 2 (120 stades = 18 km.) and is irreconcilable with viii.

85. 3, where the distance by sea from Oropos to Eretria (10·5 km.) is given as 60 stades, and with ii. 13. 7, where the Long Walls of Athens (6·35 km.) are 40 stades long. An even greater difficulty is raised by iv. 3. 2, where the distance from Sparta to Pylos, *c.* 90 km., is given as 400 stades (Gomme ad loc. calls this 'approximately correct', but this judgement seems to assume a stade of *c.* 225 m.). iv. 8. 6, where the length of Sphakteria is given as 15 stades, is a problem of another order and belongs with the other topographical difficulties in Thucydides' description of Sphakteria (cf. vol. iii, pp. 482 ff.). 'Stade' is a somewhat subjective term in Greek historians (cf. 'block' in rural as well as urban America), and on present evidence we cannot know whether Thucydides measured the mouth of the Grand Harbour inaccurately with his own eye, or measured it correctly but was misinformed about distances in other parts of the world, or accepted information which he was given by Syracusans (who would naturally aim high in their estimate, to magnify their own achievement in closing the harbour, whereas an Athenian would aim low in order to magnify the difficulty of escaping).

(ii) vi. 97. 1. Leon, where the Athenians landed in 414, is described as 'six or seven stades from Epipolai'. Since the Athenians actually ascended the plateau at Euryelos, one would expect the distance given to be the distance from their place of ascent; but no point of the coast is nearer than 3·5 km. to that. Presumably, therefore, Leon was six or seven stades from the nearest point of Epipolai; but Livy xxiv. 39. 13 places it five Roman miles from 'Hexapyla' (= Scala Greca, see below). If that is correct, it cannot have been less than 7 km. from the nearest point of Epipolai. Obviously one cannot draw any firm conclusion from this hopeless conflict except that either Livy or Thucydides is wrong, and as it is highly unlikely that the Athenians would land so far from Epipolai as Livy's Leon it seems more probable that Livy is wrong.

(iii) vi. 99. 3. The first Syracusan counter-wall is described as being 'below the Athenian circle', but we are not told whether it ran along the edge of the plateau or on the substantial tract of firm sloping ground between the plateau and the marsh. Since Thucydides goes on to speak of 'the precipitous ground above the marsh' (vi. 101. 1) it is possible that he simply did not know of the firm tract. If he did, his vagueness on the course of the first counter-wall is lamentable.

(iv) Similarly, his failure to give us the slightest indication of the direction and terminal point of the third counter-wall, or of the location of the three προτειχίσματα which played so important a part in the night battle, is most charitably imputed to ignorance.

(v) The meaning of the statement that Epipolai is ἐπιφανὲς πᾶν

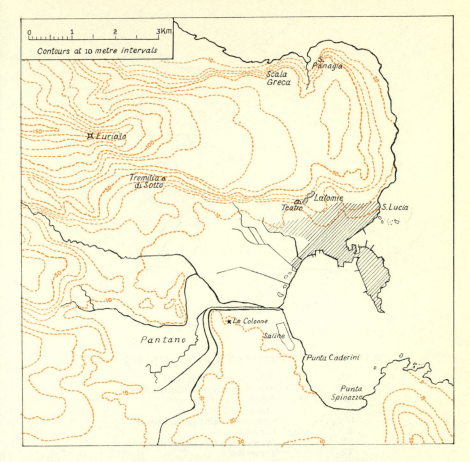

MAP I. SYRACUSE AS IT IS TODAY

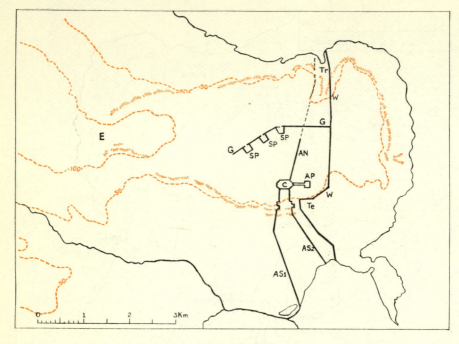

MAP 2. THE FORTIFICATIONS IN 415–413 B.C.

AN	Athenian northern wall
AP	Athenian advance fortification
AS1 . . . AS2	Athenian southern walls
C	Athenian 'Circle'
G . . . G	Syracusan Third Counter-wall
E	Euryelos
SP	Syracusan advance fortifications
Te	Temenites
Tr	Trogilos
W . . . W	Syracusan wall built in winter 415/14

Omitted from map: Labdalon, Leon, and the crosswall between the Athenian southern walls ἔσω (vi. 96. 2) is discussed below. If it means that most of the surface of the plateau is visible from the Island or from the mainland town adjoining the Island, it is untrue.

It is unfortunate that excavation has revealed no traces of walls which can be referred to the period of the siege, with the possible exception of a small piece immediately south of the Roman amphitheatre (Fabricius, 9 f.), which could be part of the Temenites wall (see below). The great wall which lies in, and south of, the eastern end of the modern cemetery (*NSA* 1888, 145 ff. and Fabricius, 10 f.) is too far west to be part of the Syracusan fortifications of 415–413 and too massive to be an Athenian siege-wall.

I. *The Plateau*

As one approaches Syracuse from Leontinoi, the town and harbour are hidden by a plateau which has its roots in Monte Climiti away to the west, rises to the village of Belvedere in the south-west, and thence extends eastwards to the sea. Three roads now mount and cross this plateau from the north. One approaches it from the north-east, mounts it at its 'waist', where it is high (140 m. above sea-level) and narrow, and there forks westwards to Belvedere and southwards to the descent of the plateau on the other side. The second road, further to the east, approaches the plateau from the north-west, mounts it at Scala Greca, within 400 m. of the sea, crosses it at its widest part, on a course running from north-north-west to south-south-east, and descends into the north-west environs of the town. The third road, further east still, crosses the plateau on a north to south course from the little inlet called Santa Panagia and joins the road from Scala Greca a short distance north-west of the town.

Immediately to the east of the Waist lies the great Hellenistic fort (cf. A. W. Lawrence, *JHS* lxvi [1946], 99 ff.) which stands at 150 m. above sea-level. From this fort the plateau descends eastwards; from the fort due east to the middle of the Scala Greca road is a distance of 4·8 km. and a gradual descent of 90 m. The centre of the Santa Panagia road, 460 m. east of the Scala Greca road, is slightly lower, but beyond it to the east the plateau again rises to a considerable tract at 60–65 m. before descending to the sea. The over-all distance from the fort due eastwards to the sea is 7·3 km. The surface of the plateau is rough and rocky, though covered with vegetation and increasingly inhabited and cultivated in its eastern parts. Its edges are steep, and in parts precipitous, but not continuously so; on the northern edge, between the fort and Scala Greca, there are many points at which a man walking recklessly in a straight line would break his legs, but comparatively few where he would break his neck. The north-eastern and eastern edges are interrupted by some deep gullies, among which the most impressive is that which leads down to the cove of Santa Panagia. At the south-east edge, on the northern outskirts of the town, is a deep re-entrant (complicated by quarrying); the road from Santa Panagia descends along the western side of this re-entrant, uniting with the road from Scala Greca. The broad spur which constitutes the western flank of the re-entrant slopes gradually down south-south-eastwards into the town, reaching the 5 m. contour 400 m. from the northern end of the Great Harbour. The Roman amphitheatre is situated on the western side of this spur, and the Greek theatre lies north-west of that. From the Greek theatre westwards the south edge of the plateau is abrupt but not, for the most part, precipitous (its average gradient is 1 in 5) for a distance of *c.* 800 m. Further west it is severely precipitous at some points, notably about Tremilia di sotto (2·2 km. south-east of the Waist and 3·1 km. west of the theatre), and also north-west of the modern cemetery, 1·1 km. west of the theatre.

The southern edge of the plateau does not at any point rest directly on the very low ground which lies in the north-western region of the harbour. West of the Spur, and bounded on the north by the edge of the plateau and on the south by the low-lying ground, is a fertile tract of gently sloping ground, measuring 500–650 m. from north to south and about 1·5 km. from the Spur to the gully on the western side of the cemetery, which may be regarded as its natural boundary. Its average gradient from north to south is a descent of 1 in 30, but it also slopes down from north-west to south-east, so that its eastern end forms a kind of trough from which the ground rises comparatively steeply to the Spur and the theatre. This trough, the centre of which is 7 m. above sea-level, does not appear to need any unusual amount of drainage, and can hardly have been marshy in antiquity. We may call this whole area 'Fusco' after the most important estate in it.

Epipolai was the name either of the whole plateau (see below) or of that part of it which lay west of the Santa Panagia road.

Euryelos. When the Athenians first ascended the plateau in force, coming from the north, they did so κατὰ τὸν Εὐρύηλον (vi. 97. 2). For the attack on the third Syracusan counter-wall they ascended at exactly the same place (vii. 43. 3), coming this time from the south. These data alone suffice to put Euryelos in the neighbourhood of the Waist (it may, strictly speaking, have been the name of the hill on which Belvedere now stands, but that does not affect the fact that the Athenians ascended via the Waist). The fort which now stands just east of the Waist is clearly the Euryalus described by Livy xxv. 25. 2: *tumulus est in extrema parte urbis* (on this phraseology, see below) *auersus a mari uiaeque imminens ferenti in agros mediterraneaque insulae*; Marcellus (ibid. 25. 5) did not regard its capture by assault as practicable.

City Walls of Syracuse. There is no archaeological support for the belief generally held from the Renaissance until comparatively recent times that the city wall of Syracuse before 415 included any part of the plateau. The so-called 'Gelonian Wall', which lies east of the Santa Panagia road, is in fact a line of rock from which blocks have been quarried (Fabricius, 13 f.). Moreover, if the city wall had run south to north across the plateau the Syracusan addition, in the winter of 415/14, of a wall 'along all that part which faces towards Epipolai' (vi. 75. 1), i.e. a wall west of the city wall and parallel to it, could not have been thought much more likely than the existing wall to achieve the purpose of 'preventing them from being walled off at close quarters'. I therefore assume that in the summer of 415 the city wall ran roughly in an arc from the northern end of the Great Harbour to the shore in the area of Santa Lucia.

Later writers, regarding the entire area brought within walls by Dionysios' fortification of the plateau as 'the city', refer to the components of this area indifferently as 'cities' or as 'parts of the city'. One of these components is the Island; the others are 'Neapolis', 'Tyche', and 'Achradina', names which nowhere occur in Thucydides. Achradina (which has no etymological connection with ἄκρα; on the Hellenistic dedication πεδιακρα[. . .]η[- - [*SEG* xv. 579] cf. J. and L. Robert, *RÉG* lxvi [1953], 211) is unquestionably the part which adjoins the Island (Diod. xi. 67. 8, Livy xxv. 30 f., al.) and forms a substantial part of the modern town; the traditional assumption that it spread as a continuous built-up area on to the plateau is in no way justified by the evidence (F. Haverfield, *CR* iii [1889], 110 f., xi [1897], 363, and Fabricius, 28). At the time of Marcellus' attack Achradina had its own fortification-wall separating it from the 'outer city', Neapolis, and Tyche (Plu. *Marc.* 18. 6, cf. Diod. xi. 73. 1 f. [anachronistic]), it had προάστεια (Diod. xi. 68. 4 and xiv. 63. 1), and part, at least, of its wall was directly assailable from the sea (Plb. vii. 4 f.). On Neapolis, identifiable as the area of the Spur, see below. Tyche was probably the south-eastern area of the plateau, north-east of Neapolis and north of Achradina, since Marcellus, who entered the fortified area from the north and controlled most of the plateau, *inter Neapolim et Tycham—nomina ea partium urbis et instar urbium sunt—posuit castra, timens ne, si frequentia intrasset loca, contineri ab discursu miles auidus praedae non posset* (Livy xxv. 25. 5).

Syracusan Wall of Winter 415/14. During the winter of 415/14 the Syracusans 'built, adjoining their city, bringing Temenites inside, a wall along all the part which looked towards Epipolai, so that, in the event of a defeat, it would not be easy to wall them off at close quarters' (vi. 75. 1). Literary evidence associates Temenites with the western part of the city; Cic. *II Verr*. iv. 119 says that Neapolis contains both the theatre and *signum Apollinis qui Temenites uocatur*, and in Plu. *Dio* 27. 3 ~ 29. 1 Dion, approaching from Akrai, enters by Τεμενίτιδες πύλαι. Recent excavation has revealed an archaic sanctuary immediately west of the theatre, and its identification as the sanctuary of Apollo Temenites appears extremely plausible from the summary accounts so far published (*FA* vii [1954], no. 1605 and B. Neutsch, *AA* lxix [1954], 595 f. and 604 f.). The ἄκρα Τεμενῖτις, where Gylippos took up his position during the fighting in front of the Athenian wall (vii. 3. 3), will be the top of the Spur; and the τέμενος in which the Syracusans chopped down the olive trees for wood (vi. 99. 3) will have lain in the Trough.

The Winter Wall therefore included at least part of the Trough—and necessarily the Spur—and the southern edge of the plateau for at least 50 m. west of the theatre. The rest of its course is uncertain. If there were already ancient quarries on the site of the Paradiso and Santa Venera quarries, just east and north-east of the theatre, one would expect the wall to turn towards these, so that the greatest use could be made of the considerable defensive potentialities of quarries; and, since the wall round Temenites is described in vi. 100. 2 as a προτείχισμα (περιπροτείχισμα B), presumably it formed three sides of a quadrilateral projecting from the main line of the wall. Once past the quarries, we should expect the wall to go eastwards to the sea, in a line roughly parallel to the existing city wall; that is the prima facie interpretation of Thucydides' words. There are, however, two objections to this. One is that such a wall could not have been thought by the Syracusans to present anything like so formidable an obstacle to an enemy siege-wall as the alternative possibility of building northwards across the plateau to Santa Panagia (Haverfield, *CR* iii [1889], 111 f. and A. Rehm, *Philologus* lxxxix [1934], 156); the second is that the description of the fighting in vii. 5 f. is difficult, perhaps even impossible, to explain except on the hypothesis that the Winter Wall ran from south to north and the Syracusan third counter-wall was built westwards from it (see below, and Rehm, loc. cit.). I therefore posit that the Winter Wall ran from the upper part of the Spur north-eastwards, and then northwards, to the coast just east of the cove of Santa Panagia, utilizing the natural defensive strength of the gully which runs down to the cove. This hypothesis necessitates the interpretation of 'Epipolai' in vi. 75. 1 as the plateau exclusive of its eastern quarter, i.e. the plateau from the Santa Panagia road westwards to Euryelos. Such an interpretation is by no means at variance with the nature of the ground and the impression one receives in walking over and around it; and it has the advantage of justifying the statement (vi. 96. 2) that Epipolai 'slopes down right to the city and is all visible inside (ἔσω)', since from the old city and the island most of the surface of the plateau is hidden behind a false crest at a height of 60 m. or less, whereas from the slightly elevated ground east of the Santa Panagia road the visibility westwards across the surface is excellent. It is therefore necessary to interpret 'inside' as referring to the city as it was after the building of the Winter Wall, and to interpret 'from the city' in vii. 4. 1 similarly (cf. Rehm, loc. cit. 153). This interpretation is facilitated if we suppose that by 415 there was already some settlement and cultivation of the area east of the Santa Panagia road.

The Athenian Circle. vi. 98. 2 : 'The Athenians advanced towards the fig-tree' (or 'Syke'), 'where they took up their position and built the Circle (ἐτείχισαν τὸν κύκλον) quickly.' This Circle (which was not necessarily circular; the word is used of a wall which constitutes the perimeter of a city, e.g. ii. 13. 7, Isoc. xviii. 45, and D. xviii. 300) was intended to be their central fortified position, the base of their main force and their stores, from which they could extend their siege-walls. The aorist tense in vi. 98. 2 rules out the possibility that κύκλος could mean the entire siege-wall, i.e. the wall which would cut off Syracuse on the landward side. Therefore vi. 99. 1 ἐτείχιζον - - - τὸ πρὸς βορέαν τοῦ κύκλου τεῖχος means 'they began to build the wall north of the Circle'; cf. ii. 96. 4 οἰκοῦσι δ' οὗτοι πρὸς βορέαν τοῦ Σκόμβρου ὄρους. Given the Athenian plan, one would expect the Circle to lie well to the south of the crest of the plateau, so that it would be equally convenient as a base for operations in the plain below and on the plateau. This expectation is confirmed by vi. 101. 1 ἀπὸ τοῦ κύκλου ἐτείχιζον - - - τὸν κρημνὸν τὸν ὑπὲρ τοῦ ἕλους, where the insertion of ⟨πρὸς⟩ (Stahl) before τὸν κρημνόν may not be necessary; if the Circle lay near the edge, it is possible that the building of a pair of nearly parallel walls southwards from it (they certainly built two walls from the edge to the sea, as vi. 103. 1 informs us, and it would be safer to begin them both from the Circle) could be described by the words ἀπὸ τοῦ κύκλου ἐτείχιζον τὸν κρημνόν. ἀπό here has almost its mathematical sense 'on', as in Pl. *Meno* 83 c and 85 b; but 101. 3 τὸ πρὸς τὸν κρημνόν - - - ἐξείργαστο tells rather in favour of Stahl.

It is also noteworthy that Labdalon, on the north edge of the plateau (vi. 97. 5), was invisible from the position in which the Athenians were drawn up to defend themselves against Gylippos (vii. 3. 4); indeed, the implication of the latter passage is that even a movement of enemy troops towards Labdalon was invisible to them, and this is most easily intelligible if the Circle lay well to the south of the centre of the plateau. If in vii. 2. 4 τῷ δὲ ἄλλῳ τοῦ κύκλου - - -

APPENDIX

λίθοι τε παραβεβλημένοι τῷ πλέονι ἤδη ἦσαν the meaning were 'the rest of the Circle . . .' the passage would be in conflict with the interpretation which we have seen to be required by vi. 98. 2; but the Greek for 'the rest of the Circle', at least in Thucydides, is ὁ ἄλλος κύκλος (the only exception to this involves a pronoun, not a noun: viii. 25. 4 ὡς ἑώρων τὸ ἄλλο σφῶν ἡσσώμενον). The passage is therefore corrupt, and the obvious way to mend it is to delete τοῦ κύκλου as an interpolation (we shall see below that two other passages in the neighbourhood appear to have suffered interpolation of practically the same kind, and all three interpolations can be attributed to the same source) and take τῷ δὲ ἄλλῳ as 'the rest of the wall', in antithesis to the double wall to the harbour mentioned in the previous part of the sentence.

Syke. συκῆ = 'fig-tree'; a tree of exceptional size, shape, or antiquity may often have the status of a place in terms of which directions are given, and 'Syke' is not mentioned again in antiquity. There was, however, an ancient theory which conflated συκῆ and Τύχη; this is reflected in the reading of f, Τυκήν, at vi. 98. 2, and in the reading of the MSS. at Diod. xi. 68. 1 μέρος τῆς πόλεως κατελάβοντο τὴν ὀνομαζομένην Ἰτύκην, where we should expect Τύχην, as Achradina and the Island have been mentioned in the previous part of the sentence. Cic. *II Verr.* 4. 119 precludes the identity of συκῆ and Τύχη: *tertia est urbs quae, quod in ea parte Fortunae fanum antiquum fuit, Tycha nominata est.*

Labdalon. Nothing more is known of its location than is mentioned above.

Trogilos. From the Circle the Athenians λίθους καὶ ξύλα ξυμφοροῦντες παρέβαλλον ἐπὶ τὸν Τρωγίλον καλούμενον ἀεί, i.e. laid the material in a line which reached, or was designed to reach, Trogilos (cf. vii. 2. 4), 'where their siege-wall would follow the shortest route from the Great Harbour to the other sea' (vi. 99. 1). Trogilos was therefore in the region of Scala Greca and Santa Panagia; geometrical precision in the interpretation of 'shortest' is out of place, since any point in that region could be described as the terminus of the 'shortest route' by contrast with the coast further north-west and north. Livy xxv. 23. 10 (cf. Plb. viii. 3. 6) suggests that *Portus Trogilorum* was not very far from 'Hexapyla' (which plainly = Scala Greca; cf. Diod. xvi. 20. 1 f., al.), and there is no 'harbour' in the region which so clearly merits a name of its own as the cove of Santa Panagia (cf. H. W. Parke, *JHS* lxiv [1944], 100 ff.). The gully down to the cove is also the most striking physical feature of the region, and if Τρωγίλος is connected with τρώγειν and τρώγλη it is a very apt name for the gully (Parke, loc. cit. 102). Military considerations also indicate the west side of the gully as a much stronger position for the Athenian wall than any point further to the west. It is therefore probable that Trogilos is the gully and cove of Santa Panagia.

First Syracusan Counter-wall (map 3). The Syracusans built this wall κάτωθεν τοῦ κύκλου τῶν Ἀθηναίων (vi. 99. 3). Whether κάτωθεν means 'on the seaward side', i.e. between the circle and the harbour, or 'on lower ground' (I greatly doubt whether any Greek would take it to mean 'south') Thucydides does not reveal whether he means between the circle and the edge of the plateau or below the plateau, across Fusco. Since the second counter-wall is described simply as 'across the marsh', and the edge of the plateau is 'above the marsh' (vi. 101. 1), the imprecision of κάτωθεν τοῦ κύκλου is one of the strongest grounds for suspicion that Thucydides had not seen Syracuse and was unaware of the existence of the Fusco tract. From a tactical point of view one might have expected the Syracusans to build their first counter-wall on the plateau, close to the edge, for thus they would have a wall which could be attacked from one side only, whereas a wall across Fusco could be attacked from both. Yet a wall on the plateau was hardly a practical proposition. The Syracusans planned (vi. 99. 2) to protect their work against interference by first occupying 'the routes by which it could be attacked' (τὰς ἐφόδους) with stakes, and this they evidently succeeded in doing. Now, a wall being built along the south edge of the plateau could be attacked from the north or west at *any* point, and we have the impression that the plateau as a whole was under Athenian control. Therefore the Syracusans would have had to succeed at one stroke, before the Athenians could interfere, in planting a palisade which would run parallel to the south edge for some distance and then converge on it. This is neither realistic nor in harmony with the suggestion of the expression τὰς ἐφόδους that the Athenian approaches to the building of the counter-wall were several and separate. It is thus more probable that the Syracusans built their first counter-wall westwards over Fusco from the sanctuary of Apollo, planting sections of palisade at various points low on the edge of the plateau, wherever descent was easiest, and across Fusco, from the edge southwards to the marsh, at its western end. The Athenians attacked the finished work on a tactical plan which remains obscure (vi. 100. 1) no matter where we locate the wall. A picked group attacked with all speed in the direction of the counter-wall and captured the palisade, the guards of which fled (100. 2) into τὸ προτείχισμα τὸ περὶ τὸν Τεμενίτην. The main Athenian army advanced in two separate parts: one towards 'the stockade where it ran past the pyramid' (or, with BˢACEFGM, 'where it ran past the gate' or 'in the area of its gate'), and the other 'towards the city, in case the Syracusans should try to intervene'. The Syracusan tribal contingent which was guarding the counter-wall (100. 1), as distinct from the guards of the palisade, is not mentioned as having fought at all; nor does any part of the Athenian army seem to have fought, except the assault party, some of whom briefly forced their way into the προτείχισμα. I suggest that the assault party attacked southwards, straight down to the edge of the plateau, one section of the main army attacked from the west, to deal with the largest section of the palisade, and the other section moved towards the city north-east of Temenites, to head the Syracusans off from the region of the counter-wall and also to block any diversionary attack towards their own walls.

Third Syracusan Counter-wall. Reasons have already been adduced for the supposition that the Winter Wall ran south to north across the plateau, and this supposition necessarily entails an east-to-west course for the third counter-wall, beginning from the Winter Wall at a point somewhere north-east of the Circle. This course is indicated on its own merits by the passages which follow, independently of any arguments about the Winter Wall.

vii. 4. 1 ἐτείχιζον - - - διὰ τῶν Ἐπιπολῶν ἀπὸ τῆς πόλεως ἀρξάμενοι ἄνω πρὸς τὸ ἐγκάρσιον τεῖχος ἁπλοῦν. I see no objection to interpretation of πρὸς τὸ ἐγκάρσιον as 'towards that point at which it would be ἐγκάρσιος to the Athenian wall', i.e. 'at a right angle'; the expression is not exactly similar to X. *HG* iv. 3. 23 πρὸς τὸ σιμόν, 'to where the slope grew steeper' or to A. *Ag.* 130 πρὸς τὸ βίαιον, 'taking force as the standard of action', i.e. 'by force', but similar enough to both to be acceptable with a sense of πρός which lies between the two. It is not necessary (with Rehm, loc. cit. 134 ff.) to make ἐγκάρσιον agree with τεῖχος and assume that Thucydides left a blank after πρὸς τό, intending to fill it in when he had the necessary information (how could he have guessed that the name which he did not at the moment know would be neuter in gender?).

7. 1 ξυνετείχισαν τὸ λοιπόν - - - μέχρι τοῦ ἐγκαρσίου τείχους. The meaning cannot be that the counter-wall had passed (6. 4) the Athenian wall on a parallel course and now changed course and was completed up to the point at which it crossed the line of the Athenian wall at a right angle (W. S. Scarborough, *TAPhA* xxx [1899], vii f.), for that would not be good enough; the Syracusans wanted a wall which would go further west than that and finally preclude the Athenian continuation. Therefore we cannot discard τείχους as a gloss and take the words μέχρι τοῦ ἐγκαρσίου together; τοῦ ἐγκαρσίου τείχους must go with τὸ λοιπόν. Either, then, (i) Thucydides gave a topographical indication after μέχρι and this has been omitted, ousted by a misplacement of τοῦ ἐγκαρσίου τείχους, or (ii) μέχρι is the remnant of a gloss based on a guess or on information from

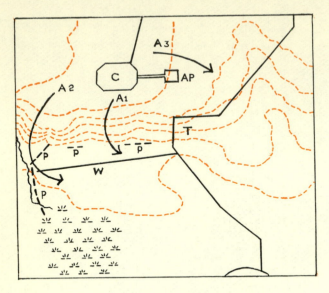

MAP 3. FIRST SYRACUSAN COUNTER-WALL

A1   Athenian assault detachment
A2   Part of Athenian main force
A3   Part of Athenian main force
AP   Athenian advanced fortification
C   The Circle
P   Syracusan palisades
T   Temenites
W   Syracusan First Counter-wall

another historical source (cf. Holm, ii. 394 f. and F. Bindseil, *ZfGymnw*. xxx [1876], 747), or (iii)—which may well be the case—Thucydides left a blank after μέχρι (Rehm, loc. cit. 135 f.), in which case τοῦ ἐγκαρσίου τείχους could be genuine, or an unintelligent interpolation to give μέχρι a construction, or an intrusive gloss on τὸ λοιπόν.

5. 1. Gylippos in building the counter-wall used 'the stones which the Athenians had deposited in readiness for their own use', and in challenging the Athenians to fight he drew up his own troops πρὸ τοῦ τειχίσματος.

5. 2. He attacked the Athenians and fought μεταξὺ τῶν τειχισμάτων, 'where there was no opportunity to use the Syracusan cavalry'.

5. 3. Worsted, he confessed that he had been to blame for fighting ἐντὸς λίαν τῶν τειχῶν.

6. 2. He led his hoplites ἔξω τῶν τειχῶν μᾶλλον ἢ πρότερον and posted his cavalry and javelin-men ἐκ πλαγίου - - - κατὰ τὴν εὐρυχωρίαν, ᾗ τῶν τειχῶν ἀμφοτέρων αἱ ἐργασίαι ἔληγον. The cavalry attacked the Athenian left wing and won the battle.

6. 3. That night the Syracusan counter-wall, which had almost passed 'the end of the Athenian wall' already (6. 1), was taken right past and so deprived the Athenians of all hope of completing their siege-wall.

The crucial fact in this sequence of events is that at the time of the battle the end of the Syracusan wall had *nearly* passed the Athenian. If the two walls converged at an acute angle, the nearer Gylippos took his troops to the point 'at which the construction of both walls ended' the *more* restricted the space; the further he fought 'within the walls', the *less* restricted. If the two walls ran parallel, and yet so close that one night's work sufficed to bring one of them round past the other, all battles between the two were equally restricted, and there was no 'more' or 'less'. The remaining possibility—which is, after all, the strongest *a priori*—is that they converged at a right angle or an obtuse angle, and that the Syracusan wall at the time of the battle was on the point of crossing the projected line of continuation of the Athenian wall at some distance from the northern end of the *completed* Athenian wall. 'Beginning from the city' in vii. 4. 1 is in accord with the interpretation of ἔσω (vi. 96. 2) offered above.

Thucydides never tells us where the third counter-wall ended. It was possible for the Athenians to attack it frontally with siege-engines (vii. 43. 1) from their own position on the plateau, but to get behind it they had to approach it from Euryelos. Military considerations would suggest that once it had passed the line of the Athenian wall it should turn south-west, in order to restrict Athenian freedom of movement (from the Circle) on the plateau as much as possible.

When the Athenians attacked it at night, having captured a Syracusan fort at Euryelos (vii. 43. 3), they encountered and defeated the special force of 600 'who guarded Epipolai in this region' (43. 4), and not only reached but began to demolish the counter-wall (43. 5) before being effectively opposed by the Syracusans and allies who were stationed in three προτειχίσματα (43. 4, 6). The battle is described as taking place ἐν στενοχωρίᾳ (44. 2). Now προτειχίσματα would have been placed either on the side of the wall from which attack was most likely or so as to protect it from attack in any direction; the one thing of which we can be certain is that they would not all have been placed on the side from which attack seemed least likely. Therefore they were not on the north side of the wall; and clearly (from Thucydides' description of the sequence of events) they did not all lie between the wall and Euryelos. It follows that they were either all on the south side of the wall or disposed in a triangular layout around its end. We must bear in mind the facts that (i) the Athenians naturally wanted to get north of the wall, (ii) the Syracusans naturally wanted above all to prevent the Athenians from advancing eastwards, for they could not know in the dark how large a proportion of the Athenian forces were committed, and must have feared a concerted attack from the Circle, and (iii) if the προτειχίσματα were disposed around the end of the wall, and yet the Athenians reached the wall before meeting the enemy from them, the Syracusans must have been able to attack the leading Athenian detachments in the rear; but in the vivid picture of confusion which Thucydides draws that is the one element which is conspicuously absent, for the Athenians, as they advance, fight a succession of actions with an enemy in front of them, until they are pushed back, and their disintegration stems from that. Again, if the προτειχίσματα were south of the wall and separated from it, the troops from them would have had to come round the end of the wall, and would have taken the leading Athenian detachments in rear. If, however, the προτειχίσματα were projections from the south side of the wall, with egress to the north side, all these difficulties are removed. The description of the battlefield as στενοχωρία suggests by itself that the wall ran nearer to the northern edge of the plateau than we would otherwise have postulated; but no hypothesis makes στενοχωρία fully intelligible except as an erroneous subjective impression communicated to Thucydides by some participants in the battle.

II. *The Harbour Area*

The area Pantanelli is low-lying, the 2-m. contour being at some points nearly 1 km. from the sea. It is drained by three main channels into the Harbour, and it seems to be the northern end, due south of the modern cemetery, which requires the most thorough drainage. Its shore is sandy, and there are large permanent pools of water (Hobbes's map is the first, I think, to show them) immediately behind the southern half of the shore.

The Anapos has high artificial banks. It is joined at its mouth by two parallel channels, which also have high banks; these are the Ciane and the Mammiabica, which have been constructed in modern times to drain the large low-lying area Pantano. The Ciane originally flowed into the Anapos 5 km. from the sea, and is so represented in maps from the seventeenth to the nineteenth centuries.

South of the river the shore is flat and sandy for 900 m., and thereafter rocky, with a low cliff, to a point 500 m. south of Punta Caderini. The modern salt-pans, 700 × 300 m. in extent, lie immediately behind this shore. A tract of flat land, irregular in shape, is enclosed on the north by the Mammiabica, on the east by the saltpans and the shore, and on the south, west, and south-east by rising ground. On the west and south-west this rise is abrupt, stepped, and in places precipitous; the remains of the temple of Zeus stand at its highest point (Le Colonne). On the south-east the rise is also abrupt, though slight in extent, so that the shore from the lighthouse to Punta Caderini forms a low, narrow spur. Between the base of this spur and the beginning of the higher ground to the south-west there is only a gentle slope; modern sketches which mark a continuous line of precipitous ground here are wrong.

From 500 m. south of Punta Caderini to 250 m. south of Punta Spinazza the shore is predominantly sandy, but thereafter rocky.

It is doubtful whether there has been any significant change in the land-level since ancient times.[1] Around the Island and Plemmyrion submersion of up to 1 m., but hardly as much as much as 2 m., would be reconcilable with the results of recent underwater exploration (cf. N. Flemming, *Nature* cciii [1964], 1060); and at the northern end of the Harbour the pipe which the builders of the Roman gymnasium intended as a drain from the gymnasium into the sea has come in course of time to introduce sea-water into the gymnasium (Cavallari–Holm, 403 ff., and Lupus, 309). But at the same time the river has deposited alluvium, and this process has counteracted submersion in many parts of the Harbour; at one point in the north-west a tract by the edge of the sea dried out and became cultivable in the nineteenth century (Cavallari–Holm, 26, and Lupus, 21). Off the river-mouth the 2-m. sounding lies 500 m. out, in the north-west over 250 m. out, and in the south over 100 m. out.

[1] I am grateful to Dr. Flemming and to Dr. L. Bernabò Brea for discussion of this matter. If I have misrepresented the current state of the problem, the fault is not theirs. Investigation of historical changes in the relation between land and sea levels in Sicily and southern Italy is proceeding.

Olympieion. Even today the remains of the temple dominate the skyline as one enters the Great Harbour from the sea or looks across from Ortygia. In the summer of 415 the Syracusans put a garrison ἐς τὸ ʼΟλυμπιεῖον (vi. 70. 4), which was not disturbed by the Athenians, and during the following winter established a φρούριον (vi. 75. 1) afresh. During the Athenian occupation of Plemmyrion, Syracusan cavalry were securely based ἐπὶ τῇ ἐν τῷ ʼΟλυμπιείῳ πολίχνῃ (vii. 4. 6), and later in the summer of 413 this force was augmented by other arms (vii. 37. 2 f. and 42. 6). A πολίχνη is more than a fort; the word occurs as a place-name in several parts of the Aegean (cf. viii. 14. 3 n., and *ATL* i. 382 ff. and 541), and Pl. *R.* 370 d refers to his ideal city in an early stage as πολιχνίον. When Strabo (270) says that Syracuse τὸ παλαιὸν πεντάπολις ἦν, the Olympieion is probably the fifth component which he has in mind (the other four being the Island, Achradina, Tyche, and Neapolis, the four of Cic. *II Verr.* iv. 119) ; and ἡ καλουμένη Πολίχνα of Diod. xiii. 7. 5. and xiv. 72. 3 seems from the latter passage to be the Olympieion, despite the impossibility of reconciling the former with anything in Thucydides. There must then have been a walled inhabited locality at the Olympieion; in vii. 4. 6 Thucydides is thinking of the village and the sanctuary as distinct, but in other passages he treats τὸ ʼΟλυμπιεῖον as the name of the locality as a whole, just as a town could be called Διὸς ἱερόν and its citizens Διοσιρῖται (viii. 19. 2 and *ATL* i. 266 f., 483).

Daskon. This place is mentioned by Thucydides only in vi. 66. 2 παρά τε τὰς ναῦς σταύρωμα ἔπηξαν καὶ ἐπὶ τῷ Δάσκωνι, ἔρυμά τε, ᾗ εὐεφοδώτατον ἦν τοῖς πολεμίοις - - - ὤρθωσαν : 'They planted a palisade along by their ships and ἐπί Daskon, and erected a strongpoint where it was easiest for the enemy to attack them' ; ἔρυμά τι, conjectured by Krüger and found in ψ, gives the sense 'they planted a palisade along by their ships, and ἐπί Daskon they erected a strongpoint, where it was easiest for the enemy to attack (sc. them, or Daskon?)'. In Diod. xiii. 13. 3 Daskon is a bay (κόλπος) where Eurymedon was cut off by Syracusan ships and killed after he had led the right wing too far forward and round in an attempt to encircle the enemy fleet. Th. vii. 52. 2, describing this incident, says that Eurymedon was killed ἐν τῷ κοίλῳ καὶ μυχῷ τοῦ λιμένος, and were it not for Diodoros we should most naturally refer this description to the northern end of the harbour. Diodoros is very probably mistaken about the location of Eurymedon's death, but that does not mean that he was wrong in believing Daskon to be the name of something in the centre of the Harbour. The coast between Punta Caderini and Punta Spinazza is sufficiently distinctive in shape to merit a name, and Daskon may well have been the name of this

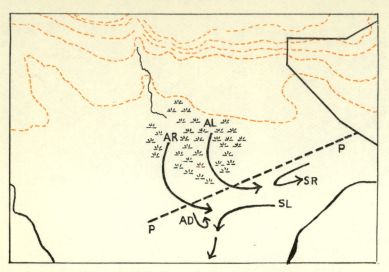

MAP 4. SECOND SYRACUSAN COUNTER-WALL

AD	Athenian fast detachment	SL	Syracusan left wing
AL	Athenian left wing	SR	Syracusan right wing
AR	Athenian right wing	P	Palisade

MAP 5. ATHENIAN LANDINGS IN 415 B.C.

A	Athenian landings	O	Olympieion
B	Bridge destroyed by Athenians	P	Athenian palisade
E	ἔρυμα	S	Syracusan army
L	Standing water		

stretch of coast and the fertile land behind it; this would be consistent with Diod. xiv. 72. 3 τὸ πρὸς τῷ Δάσκωνι χωρίον and 73. 2 πρὸς τὸ κατὰ Δάσκωνα μέρος. ἐπί with the dative is not always distinguishable in sense from 'on' or 'at' (cf. vi. 97. 5) but it may also have the sense 'to protect' or 'to neutralize' (the common factor is 'having in view'), and could properly be used of a palisade planted between the spur of Caderini and the rising ground to the west in order to impede an enemy attack from the south.

Second Syracusan Counter-wall (Map 4). (This is discussed before the details of the Athenian landing in 415, as it admits of fewer alternative reconstructions and helps to give us a picture of the Pantanelli area.) The second Syracusan counter-wall consisted of a palisade and ditch διὰ μέσου τοῦ ἔλους (vi. 101. 2). One cannot plant a palisade or dig a ditch through a lake; therefore the area called ἔλος did not consist uniformly of standing water, but contained both water and firmer ground. The Athenians came down from Epipolai in the dark ἐς τὸ ὁμαλὸν καὶ διὰ τοῦ ἔλους, ᾗ πηλῶδες ἦν καὶ στεριφώτατον, by putting down flat boards to tread on, and captured the palisade at dawn (101. 3). Therefore there were muddy areas north of the palisade, and, indeed, watery tracts, with which the 'firmest' parts are contrasted. In the battle the Syracusan right wing fled towards the city, the left wing (or part of it) παρὰ τὸν ποταμόν (101. 4). A fast Athenian detachment headed for 'the bridge', to prevent the Syracusans from crossing the river; but this detachment was repulsed and forced back into the Athenian right wing (101. 4 f.). Thereupon Lamachos came to the rescue from the Athenian left wing, but was killed, and the Syracusans got his body 'across the river into safety' before the Athenians could intervene (101. 6).

This narrative prompts one conclusion which may have important consequences in other connections: that the river, even at the height of summer, was not one which a body of troops could cross wherever it wished.

Secondly: 'towards the city' and 'along the river' must have been divergent courses. If the battle took place close to the river, where it runs towards the south-east before turning east towards the sea, the Syracusan left wing will have fled downstream in order to cross over to the Olympieion. But, if Thucydides' visualization of the terrain is correct, (i) this argues a remarkably long palisade, extending a good 3 km. from the city; (ii) the Athenians would not have needed to cross a marshy or muddy tract to reach any point in the western half of such a palisade; (iii) at such a distance from the city, why should the Syracusan left wing have so quickly abandoned hope of getting back to the city and escaping envelopment by the advance of the Athenian left? It seems probable—again, on the

I i

assumption that Thucydides visualized correctly—that the battle took place rather nearer the city, which would make intelligible both the Athenians' crossing of the mud and the Syracusan left wing's fear of envelopment. But then, either (*a*) the river-mouth lay further north than it does now, and the Syracusan left wing fled upstream, south-west and west, past the Athenians who were pushing them back, and the fast Athenian detachment tried to overtake them; or (*b*) παρά is a misleading word, and the Syracusans actually fled not 'along' but towards the river, with the intention of going along it, when they had reached it, to the bridge. The first alternative not only involves us in moving the river, but even then does not yield an entirely realistic picture of events. The second alternative is therefore preferable, although it involves either a slight incongruity of language or the abandonment of the assumption that Thucydides' picture is correct, and it has an important implication: if Thucydides thought of the Syracusans as fleeing *towards* the river, the passage does not reveal whether or not he regarded the river as a serious obstacle, for he may have thought of the bridge as being by chance near the point at which they were aiming.

Athenian Landing in 415 (Map 5). In 415 the Athenians landed 'opposite (κατά) the Olympieion' in an area where they would be least vulnerable to cavalry attacks 'both during and before the action', since 'one way they were protected by walls and houses and standing water (λίμνη) and along the other (*or* another) side by precipitous ground (κρημνοί)' (vi. 66. 1). After landing they protected themselves by fortifications at, or in the direction of, Daskon (see above) and 'broke down the bridge over the Anapos' (66. 2).

Some obvious military considerations control our speculation about the location of this landing. The Syracusans, important though it was that they should challenge and defeat the Athenians quickly, would not be so foolhardy as to put the Athenian army between themselves and their city; nor would the Athenians, unless their generals were very much more confident than Nikias sounds (68), want to get between the Syracusan army and Syracuse. Nor again would the Athenians want to put the Syracusan army between themselves and their ships. Thus the axis of the Athenian advance must have lain between north-west and north-east.

1. If the Athenians landed north of the river, and broke down the bridge to protect themselves against possible attack from the south, Thucydides' description of the site is nonsense. There were no κρημνοί on either side of the Athenians; if there was a λίμνη on their left, their right was protected by the sea; and if the λίμνη was on their right, between them and the sea, they had chosen a peculiarly awkward place to land and had put an obstacle between themselves

and their ships. Moreover, a landing north of the river could hardly be described as 'opposite the Olympieion'; and what and where, north of the river or on it, was Daskon?

2. If the Athenians landed south of the river, Daskon can be satisfactorily placed, but how did the Syracusans cross the river to fight them (the bridge being destroyed), why did the Syracusans fight with the barrier of the river between themselves and the city, and why is the river never mentioned in the course of the battle as an impediment either to the Syracusan retreat or to the Athenian advance? Also: if the Athenians were facing west or north-west, they had precipitous ground on their left but the river, not a lake, on their right; and if they were facing north, then, again, they had precipitous ground on their left but the sea, not a lake, on their right (and cf. above on the unlikelihood of their landing where a lake sat just behind the shore).

The hypothesis that they both landed and fought south of the river seems to demand the assumption that the river was no obstacle at all to the movement of troops, and that the destruction of the bridge was a formality. This assumption is reconcilable, as we have seen, with Thucydides' account of the loss of the second counter-wall, but it is not an assumption which anyone can happily make without a serious effort to find an alternative hypothesis. Such an alternative seems to present itself in the hypothesis that the Athenians landed mainly south, but also north, of the river, and fought the battle north of it. This hypothesis implies: (i) The bridge which they destroyed—if it was where the road to Heloron crossed the river, it could well be called *the* bridge—was some distance upstream, but they used another bridge near the mouth and perhaps built others alongside it. (ii) The lake lay just north of the river-mouth, separated from the river and from the sea by a spit of land (cf. below on vii. 53); P. Clüver, *Sicilia Antiqua* (Leyden, 1619), 174, says that standing water is to be seen in his own day at the mouth of the Anapos in wet weather, but I doubt if he means more than the pools which are there now. Thus in saying τῇ μέν - - - λίμνη, παρὰ δὲ τὸ κρημνοί Thucydides does not mean that the Athenians were perfectly protected on each flank, but that enemy movement was in some degree restricted, on the south-west of the occupied area by precipitous ground and on the north-east by a lake. Daskon will be the area south of Punta Caderini, and the palisade will have been planted across the slope west of Punta Caderini; the ἔρυμα, on the other hand, could be right at the other end of the beachhead.

For the sake of completeness we ought to consider the possibility that the river-mouth was not where it is today, though this possibility does not yield any better result than has already been obtained.

3. If the river-mouth was further north, and the Athenians landed and fought south of it, we can keep the lake where we have just put it, but it will now be south of the river. The difficulty remains that the river, despite the destruction of the bridge, was no impediment to the approach of the Syracusans or to their retreat.

4. If the river-mouth was further south, and the Athenians landed and fought north of it, we can again keep the lake in the same place, but Thucydides' words παρὰ δὲ τὸ κρημνοί, referring to precipitous ground which will now be beyond the river from the Athenians, would be pointless—unless, again, the river were negligible as an obstacle, and that would bring us back once more to the question why the Athenians should destroy a bridge which did not matter.

Thus by moving the river-mouth we gain no advantage over the hypothesis that the Athenians landed mainly south, but also north, of the present river-mouth and fought north of it.

Lysimeleia. At the end of the battle in which Eurymedon was killed some Athenian ships went aground 'outside the palisades and their own camp' (vii. 53. 1). Gylippos took some troops 'on to the spit' (χηλή) to seize these ships; but the Etruscans, 'who were manning the Athenian perimeter in this region', attacked his troops and 'forced them into the lake called Lysimeleia' (53. 2). Since Lysimeleia must lie either between the eastern Athenian wall and the city or between the western Athenian wall and the river, and, whereas there is nowhere any mention of a lake or marsh in the former location, we have already seen reason to place a lake in the latter, it seems that Lysimeleia is identical with the lake which the Athenians had on one side of them when they landed 'opposite the Olympieion' in 415. Gylippos will have crossed the river by a bridge, coming from the Olympieion, and the 'spit' will be a strip of land between Lysimeleia and the sea (cf. Holm, ii. 396).

Athenian Southern Walls. From Lysimeleia to the northern end of the Harbour the Athenians had available at the most 1·2 km. of shore. How much of that they used, we do not know; it depends on how many triremes at a time they reckoned to draw up on shore, and in how many ranks. The area of the southern walls was marshy (vii. 47. 2), but obviously cannot all have been actual marsh, or the continuation of the wall through it would never have been contemplated.

ADDENDA

Book v

p. 32 (v. 33. 1). Dr. J. Roy draws my attention to the late fifth-century list of Delphic thearodokoi, Daux, *RÉG* lxii (1949) 6, where the reading of ll. 5–8 is not in doubt, ἐ|[ν Μ]εθυδρίοι Δ|[αμ]οτέλεος πα|[ῖδ]ες; and to the Methydrians in X. *An.* iv. 1. 27 and elsewhere. The inscription shows that Methydrion had this much independent existence at a date later than, but not far removed from, 418; the question is, whether Pausanias' συντελούντων is compatible with this degree of independence. Dr. Roy may be right to see in the Pausanias passage evidence for the expansion of Orchomenos in the early fourth century, not in the fifth.

p. 47 (41. 3). It should have been made clear that this passage, taken by itself, suggests a date for the Hyakinthia much earlier in the year than the late June or July imposed by the other evidence (see viii. 10. 1 n.). The negotiations described in c. 41 may have begun later and lasted longer than one would have guessed from Thucydides' narrative; and cf. 46. 4 n.

p. 49 (43. 2). For further ostraka see E. Vanderpool, *Hesperia* xxxvii (1968), 117–18; and on the stemma, ibid. 398.

p. 87 (61. 1). On πρὶν δή, see Denniston, 220.

p. 104 (67. 1). On the *Arkadikon* coinage see R. T. Williams, *Num. Notes and Monographs* 155 (1965), 'The Confederate Coinage of the Arcadians in the Fifth Century B.C.'. He effectively demolishes the theory that this coinage was minted at Heraia: his positive conclusions, though in the main approved by Jennifer Warren in *JHS* lxxxviii (1968), 245–6, seem to me much more fragile, especially the identification of one Zeus in the series as Zeus Meilichios on the strength of the *phiale* he holds.

p. 114 (68. 3). For οἱ πατριλόχοι in Hesych. s.v. μόρα, Latte prefers to restore οἵ ποτε λόχοι. It is not clear that this is an improvement, but it makes no difference to the argument here.

p. 143 (79. 4). For ἐρίζειν cf. the second 'Table of Herakleia', *DGE* 63. 26–7, καὶ τοὶ μὲν ἐρίξαντες ἀπέσταν, τοῖς δὲ ἐδικαξάμεθα δίκας τριακοσταίας. The details of the procedure are not clear, but it looks as if ἐρίζειν here represents a disagreement which may *not* issue in litigation.

p. 168 (97). For doubts about the dating of *GHI* 62 (now ML 67) and about Melos' contribution to Alkidas in 427, see Lewis in ML, p. 184.

ADDENDA

p. 170 (101). For the early senses of σωφροσύνη see Helen North, *Sophrosyne* (Cornell, 1966), 3–4: ' "prudence" or "shrewdness" in one's own interest—a meaning that it never entirely loses, in spite of the much more extensive range of connotations it subsequently acquired'. For Thucydides' use of the word, ibid. 100–15.

p. 185 (113). But see also W. Liebeschuetz in *JHS* lxxxviii (1968) 73–7, who takes a realistic view about the general workings of Thucydides' mind, but believes that he meant to represent the Athenians as mistaken about their own true interest.

Book vi

p. 209. See now J. N. Coldstream, *Greek Geometric Pottery* (London, 1968), 324 f., on the relative dating of the earliest pottery from Megara and the earliest from Syracuse; ibid. 326, on Gela.

p. 214 (vi. 2. 6). Cf. Coldstream, op. cit. 388, on the Phoenicians.

p. 216 (4. 1). Cf. Coldstream, op. cit. 368 ff., on the Lelantine War and Euboean pottery in the West.

pp. 218 f. (4. 6). On Pausanias iv. 23. 6 ff. and Rhianos see now H. T. Wade-Gery in *Ehrenberg Studies*, 289 ff.

p. 219 (5. 3). Dunbabin, 106 f., refers in fact to the excavation of graves, not, strictly speaking, to the site of the city, and draws inferences from the number and continuity of burials.

p. 220 (6. 1) *and p.* 228 (8. 2). Cf. K. von Fritz, *Die griechische Geschichtsschreibung* i (Berlin, 1967), 724 f., on the εὐπρέπεια of the expressed Athenian aims.

p. 230 (8. 4). See von Fritz, op. cit. 739 ff., for objections to de Sanctis's view of Nikias.

p. 263 (25. 2). Decision between the variants is affected by the consideration mentioned below (on p. 309).

pp. 268 f. On the chronology of the sales of the property of the men condemned for impiety see D. M. Lewis, *Ehrenberg Studies*, 181 f., 186. He also points out (p. 188) that confiscation of the estates of some fifty Athenians of the highest social class must have made a significant difference to the financing of the war.

p. 268, n. 1. The letter which stood after the disputed φ, and is now unreadable through damage to the stone, was read as θ when it was visible.

p. 297 (32. 3). For the general forward reference of τοιοίδε cf. Theocr. 6. 4 ff. τοιάδ᾽ ἄειδον. πρᾶτος δ᾽ ἤρξατο Δάφνις, ἐπεὶ καὶ πρᾶτος ἔρισδε. "βάλλει τοι κτλ."

p. 307 (40. 1). The emendation ὧνπερ receives some support from the documentary formula μετέχειν πάντων ὧνπερ . . . μετέχουσιν. Note

486

ADDENDA

especially *ASAA* xxii/xxiii (1944/5), 68, no. 36. 8 ff. μετέχοντας πάντων ὧνπερ καὶ τοὶ ἄλλοι Καλύμνιοι μετέχοντι ~ 60, no. 28. 24 ff. μετέχοντας πάντων ὧνπερ καὶ τοὶ ἄλλοι Καλύμνιοι.

p. 308 (41. 4). For τὰ δέ cf. also Pi. *O.* 9. 95, 13. 55, *Paean* 8. 28.

p. 309 (43). On all matters relating to the structure, manning, and handling of triremes see now J. S. Morrison and R. T. Williams, *Greek Oared Ships 900–322 B.C.* (Cambridge, 1968).

Ibid., on troopships. The alternative interpretations of the terms στρατιῶτις and ὁπλιταγωγός offered on p. 309 are not exhaustive; in the light of i. 116. 1 ἐναυμάχησαν . . . ναυσὶν ἑβδομήκοντα, ὧν ἦσαν αἱ εἴκοσι στρατιώτιδες (cf. viii. 25. 1), we must also consider the possibility that a troopship could and did fight without structural modification, but was at something of a disadvantage.

p. 313 (46. 5). On Alkibiades as a source of information cf. E. Delebecque, *Thucydide et Alcibiade* (Aix-en-Provence, 1965); but cf. the criticisms of Delebecque's thesis by von Fritz, op. cit. 327 ff. H. D. Westlake, *Individuals in Thucydides* (Cambridge, 1968), 175, regards it as 'beyond reasonable doubt that other officers must have attended', and suggests Menandros as a possible informant of Thucydides.

pp. 315 f. (50. 1). Delebecque, op. cit. 15 n. 1, treats Lamachos in this debate as 'le porte-parole des idées de Thucydide', but offers no good reason for doubting that Lamachos expressed the view which Thucydides says he expressed.

pp. 320 f. On Aristotle's account of the Peisistratidai see now C. W. Fornara, *Historia* xvii (1968), 400 ff.

p. 336 (59. 4). C. W. Fornara, *Philologus* cxi (1967), 294, argues that the words ὑπὸ Λακεδαιμονίων καὶ Ἀλκμεωνιδῶν τῶν φευγόντων must mean 'by the Spartans and those of the Alcmaeonids who were in exile'. If he is right in believing that a Greek reader would have taken them so and that Thucydides must have known that they would be taken so, then, of course, he is right in contending that to interpret them otherwise in the light of Hdt. v. 62. 2 is to beg the question of agreement between Thucydides and Herodotos on the Alkmeonidai. But (i) on the analogy of 31. 3, τοῖς θρανίταις τῶν ναυτῶν καὶ ταῖς ὑπηρεσίαις, it would seem that 'the Alkmeonidai among the exiles' is linguistically possible (for the absence of the definite article before the expression Ἀλκμεωνίδαι cf. Hdt. v. 62. 2), and (ii) if Thucydides believed that all the Alkmeonidai were in exile together and if he had no reason to think that anyone alleged or believed the contrary, it may not have occurred to him that any reader could take his words to mean 'those of the Alkmeonidai who were in exile'.

pp. 339 f. (62. 2). K. Ziegler, *Gymnasium* lxxiv (1967), 327 ff., argues strongly for a date of composition before the destruction of Greek cities in Sicily by the Carthaginians.

Book vii

p. 382 (vii. 3. 3). As de Romilly points out (*Histoire et Raison*, 36), the identity of wording with vi. 98. 3 serves to emphasize the difference between Gylippos' reaction and the Syracusan generals'.

p. 386 (9). On Euetion and Melesandros cf. W. E. Thompson, *Hesperia* xxxvi (1967), 105 f.

pp. 386 f. Westlake, op. cit. 192, points out that just as in 27–8 Thucydides puzzles us by looking ahead to the situation as it was some months after the events which he professes to be describing, so in Nikias' letter he looks ahead to a situation worse than that in which Nikias actually found himself at this time.

p. 392 (16. 1). On Menandros, to X. *HG* ii. 1. 16 add i. 2. 16.

p. 395 (18. 4). It is noteworthy that nothing is said of any conference of the Peloponnesian League at this point; cf. the Spartan procedure in 419, when Argos threatened Epidauros (v. 54. 1 n.), and it may also be the case that when Lakonia itself had been attacked the Spartans were not interested in any reservations which their allies might have had about resumption of war with Athens.

p. 396 (20. 1). On Charikles cf. also Arist. *Pol.* 1305^{b}25 f.

p. 406 (27. 5). On the massive desertion of slaves from Attica cf. M. I. Finley, *Historia* viii (1959), 159 f.

p. 409 (29. 1). On the family of Dieitrephes see now E. Vanderpool, *Hesperia* xxxvii (1968), 118 f.

pp. 419 ff. (42. 3). W. Liebeschuetz, *Historia* xvii (1968), 289 ff. (especially 299–302), argues: (i) It is by no means certain that the Athenians could have taken Syracuse before the arrival of Gylippos, let alone before the end of 415, no matter what tactical plan they had adopted. (ii) This is made plain by the indications given throughout the narrative. (iii) Therefore the long parenthesis in 42. 3 cannot express Thucydides' own judgement. This argument, however, does not take adequately into account the most important formal characteristic of the long parenthesis, its finite tenses. Either Thucydides' judgement on the military practicability of the expedition was at variance with his data, or he expressed someone else's judgement in a form from which his readers could hardly fail to conclude that it was his own judgement. Liebeschuetz by implication chooses the latter alternative; is it necessarily preferable to the former?

p. 434. On the coinage of Samos at this time see now J. P. Barron, *The Silver Coins of Samos* (London, 1966), 80 ff., esp. 86.

pp. 435 f. See on pp. 339 f.

p. 439 (57. 11). On the Campanians, see M. W. Frederiksen, *Dialoghi di Archeologia* ii (1968), 12 ff., who points out that (*a*) they were cavalrymen, and (*b*) either they arrived too late to take part in the fighting or they were subsumed by Thucydides' informant under Naxos and Katane (the 'Chalcidians' of Diodoros).

p. 459 (81. 1). See Westlake, op. cit. 285 ff., for a fuller discussion of the standing of Gylippos in the last stages of the campaign and afterwards.

pp. 461 ff. (86. 5). Cf. Westlake, op. cit. 209 ff., for Thucydides' judgement on Nikias.

INDEXES

I. GENERAL

Accusative case, 216, 235, 386, 428, 431.
Achaia, 70, 150, 212.
Achradina (Syracuse), 471.
Adonia, Athenian festival, 224, 271.
Aeschylus, on Athens and Argos, 50.
Agesippidas, of Sparta, 68, 77 f.
Agis II, king of Sparta, 74, 81–5, 89–91, 97–103, 119–21, 124, 127, 145, 395.
Aigina, 73, 77; Athenian colonists, 127, 435–7; at Thyrea, 47; coinage, 56, 90.
Aigytis (Peloponnese), 33 f., 104.
Ainianes, 68.
Aitolia, 439.
Akarnanians, 26, 410 f.
Akragas, foundation, 203 f., 206 f.; politics, 412, 424, 428.
Akrai (Sicily), 203 f., 456, 458.
Akraion Lepas (Sicily), 455 f.
Alesion, Mt. (Mantineia), 94, 96 f., 99 f.
Alkibiades Phegusios, 280, 282, 286.
Alkibiades, son of Kleinias, ancestors, 49 f., 246, 361; date of birth, 48 f., 236 f.; generalships, 13, 52, 69, 78 f., 88, 155, 225; policy in Peloponnese, 30, 51 f., 76, 87 f., 128, 147, 151 f., 232, 242, 248, 290; expeditions to Peloponnese, 69–71, 77; victory at Olympia, 246 f.; Melos, 190 f.; mysteries, 271–88; Sicilian strategy, 228, 242 f., 314, 339, 420 f.; exile, 242–5, 360, 366; later career, 242–5.
    Position at Athens, 49, 283, 289; rivalry with Nikias, 51–3, 76, 128, 240 f.; oratory, 246; wealth, 246 f.; as source of Thucydides, 313, 487.
Alkmeonidai, 325, 330, 336, 362, 487.
Alliances, general character, 23, 44 f., 221, 253, 312, 414, 433; joint command, 56, 105, 142; Sparta and Athens, 5, 21 f., 43 f., 54; Argos, Elis, and Mantineia, 55 f., 63 f., 139; these with Athens

(Quadruple Alliance), 54–63, 75–7, 88, 139, 148, 248. *See also under individual cities.*
Alliteration, 230.
Alpheios, R., 31–3, 66, 104.
Alyzia, 410.
Anaktorion, 26, 410.
Anapos, R., 371, 479, 481–4.
Anaxilas, of Rhegion, 218 f.
Andokides, of Athens, 52, 271–82, 286 f., 337.
Androkles, of Athens, 283.
Andromedes (Andromenes), of Sparta, 47.
Androsthenes, of Mainalos, 64.
Anthene (Kynouria), 47.
Antiochos, of Syracuse, 200–5, 212.
Antithesis, 239, 245.
Apollo Archegetes, 214 f.; Daphnephoros (Athens), 158; Lykeios (Argos), 61; Parrasios, 32; Pythaieus, 71 f., 80; Pythios (Athens), 331; Temenites (Syracuse), 472.
Apposition, 416 f.
Arbitration, 28, 142–4, 394.
Archers, 155, 294, 346, 409, 422.
Archias, of Corinth and Syracuse, 215.
Archippos, of Athens, 277, 281.
Archonides, of Herbita, 379 f.
Archon-list, at Athens, 330–3.
Argos, earlier treaty with Sparta, 23 f., 46, 50; proposed general alliance, 23, 39, 41 f., 45; *see also* Alliances; war with Epidauros, 71, 75, 77; campaigns of 418 B.C., 80–8, 123 f., 126–8; agreement with Sparta, 131 f., 136–9, 141 f., 145, 147; oligarchy and counterrevolution, 149–52, 154; later operations, 8, 152, 155, 189, 222, 377 f., 399.
    Allies, 106 f., 139, 141; connection with Macedon, 146; army, 105 f., 121–5, 149; constitution, 58 f., 84, 86 f., 121–3.
Aristogeiton, *see* Harmodios.
Aristokles, of Sparta, 120.

491

Aristomenes, of Athens, 277, 281.
Ariston, of Corinth, 417.
Aristoteles, of Athens, 287.
Aristotle, on the Peisistratidai, 320 f.
Arkadia, mercenaries in Sicily, 258, 395; Spartan allies, 79, 91; topography, 31–4, 73, 81, 91–101, 109 f. *See also under individual cities and tribes.*
Artas, Messapian ruler, 413.
Article, definite, 232, 239, 258, 307 f., 315, 342, 344 f., 365, 407, 416 f., 424, 467.
Asea (Arkadia), 32, 34, 92.
Asine (Argolid), 71.
Asine (Messenia), 367.
Asopos, R. (Peloponnese), 81, 107 f.
Aspect of verbs, 9 f., 15, 24, 47, 66 f., 71, 82, 121, 212, 333, 371, 432.
Assinaros, R. (Sicily), 455–7.
Asyndeton, 102, 301.
Athenagoras, of Syracuse, 296 f., 301, 348.
Athenian Empire, formation, 186, 252 f., 350, 354; Athens' relations with, 36 f., 165–7, 174, 184, 186, 345, 353 f., 388, 434 f., 438, 442 f.; coinage decree, 434; tribute, 402 f., 408 f.; use of allied forces, 433 f., 438; of rowers and ships, 310, 388, 434, 442; of land troops, 155, 157, 168, 293, 396, 419.
Athens, position in 421 B.C. and after, *see* Alliances, Peace of Nikias; relations with Argos, 50, 146 f., 151 f., 155; with Corinth, 31, 72 f., 188; campaigns of 418 B.C., 83, 86–8, 123 f., 128 f.; Thraceward area, 37, 43, 153 f., 176; objectives in Sicily, 197, 228 f., 241, 256, 443, *see also* Sicilian expedition; final defeat, 166 f., 242–5.
　　Character and traditions, 177, 231, 253, 255; colonies, 167 f., 350, 432, 436 f.; economy, 229 f., 406; finance and taxation, 236, 263, 266, 268 f., 365 f., 400–2, 408 f.; military organization, 372, 425, 440 f., 446, *see also* Generalship; naval organization, 442, *see also* Triremes; political organization, 51–3, 57 f., 239 f.; internal politics, 78 f., 87 f., 128 f., 229 f., 240 f., 289, 361 f.
Athos, 36 f., 150.
Autokles, Athenian general, 78.

Barbarians, Greek attitude towards, 235 f., 410, 432 f.
Belmina (Peloponnese), 33 f., 91 f.
Boeotia, relations with Athens, 11, 31, 69, 188; with Sparta, 6, 29, 31, 39–46, 68 f., 188; campaign of 418 B.C., 79 f., 83; in Sicily, 422, 438.
　　Constitution, and federal league, 30, 41 f.; state stable, 67.
Boiai (Lakonia), 400.
Brachylogy, 145, 355, 359, 391.
Brasideioi, 34–6, 79, 112 f.
Bryas, of Argos, 150.

Calendars, Greek, equations with Julian, 11 f., 264–71, 276; irregularities, 18 f., 75; manipulation, 75, 129 f., 151.
Campanians, 439, 489.
Carthage, 241, 298.
Cavalry, in Greek warfare, 80, 124, 346; Athenian, 83, 257, 310, 429; Boeotian, 83, 85; Sicilian, 344, 346, 422, 456; Spartan, 104 f.
Chalkideis, Chalkidike, 29, 37, 42, 139, 146, 223, 232.
Chalkis (Euboea), 214–16, 350.
Charadros, R. (Argos), 86.
Charikles, of Athens, 284, 396, 488.
Charmides, of Athens, 277, 281, 283, 287.
Charmos, of Athens, 333 f.
Charoiades, Athenian general, 197.
Charon, of Lampsakos, 324.
Chios, 310, 434 f.
Choirades Is. (Italy), 413.
Clubs, 286.
Comparatives, 232, 312, 329, 357.
Concord, grammatical, 238, 358, 423.
Conflation of variants, 89, 385, 398, 407.
Corinth, colonization, 215; attack on Kleonai, 107; earlier relations with Epidauros, 72 f.; reaction against Peace of Nikias, 5 f., 23, 26, 31, 232; reconciliation with Sparta, 39–41, 52, 63 f., 70, 75 f., 128; in campaign of 418 B.C., 82 f.; later attitudes, 152, 188, 222; relations with Syracuse, 376, 399, 413.
　　Internal affairs, 41; pottery, 208 f.
Corinth, Gulf of, 70.
Crete, 139, 217 f., 263 f., 310.

Daskon (Syracuse), 480–3.
Dative case, 219, 237, 245, 255, 299, 354.
Dekeleia, 177, 367, 395, 400 f., 405, 425.
Delion, battle of, 126.
Delos, 30.
Delphi, 120, 214 f., 218.
Democracy, general character of, 301, 304 f., 430 f., 446.
Demonstratives, 210, 222, 460.
Demosthenes, Athenian general, 129, 146 f., 392 f., 411, 419 f., 424 f., 457, 460, 463.
Demostratos, of Athens, 224, 263.
Desertion, 387–9, 406.
Diagoras, of Melos, 59.
Dieitrephes, Athenian general, 409, 488.
Dio, imitating Thucydides, 237 f., 258, 386.
Diodoros, narrative differing from Thucydides, 52, 68, 80, 88, 91, 105 f., 124 f., 149, 155, 172 n., 190, 412, 430; numbers different, 86, 308, 372, 380, 393, 396, 422, 429, 441, 449.
Dioi (Thrace), 405.
Diokleides, of Athens, 273–88.
Dion (Athos), 36 f., 150.
Dionysia (Athens), 22, 54.
Diphilos, Athenian general, 414 f.
Diplomacy, Greek style and procedure, 52, 135, 161, 220, 228.
Discipline, 390, 426, 450.
Disease, 387, 424.
Dispatches, 385.
Dolopes, 68.
Dorians, 71, 74, 121, 155, 217 f., 412, 423. See also Race.
Dryopes, 71, 438.

Earthquakes, 53, 67, 369.
Eïon, 129.
Elis, quarrel over Lepreon, 26–9, 36, 88; alignment after Peace of Nikias, see Alliances; Olympia of 420 B.C., 64–7, 148; campaigns of 418 B.C., 83, 88, 128; later relations with Sparta, 148 f., 360 f.
    Constitution, 60 f.; control of Olympia, 64.
Ellipse, 118, 131, 231, 253.
Elymians, 200, 203, 212.
Embezzlement, 237.
Endios, of Sparta, 50 f.

Ephoros of Kyme, on Sicily, 197 f., 207, 209 f., 214; information independent of Thucydides, 68, 106; divergences from Thucydides, 149 f., see also Diodoros.
Epidauros, earlier relations with Corinth, 72 f.; Athenian expedition of 430 B.C., 293; quarrel with Argos, 71–8, 129 f., 136–8, 145, 147; campaign of 418 B.C., 85.
Epigrams, 336.
Epipolai (Syracuse), 370 f., 469–73.
Epomphes, of Athens, 192.
Erasinides, of Corinth, 384.
Erineos (Achaia), 414 f.
Erineos, R. (Sicily), 455–7.
Eryx, temple of, 312 f.
Eryximachos, of Athens, 278, 281, 283 f., 287 f.
Etruscans, 439.
Euboea, 406; pottery, 216.
Euesperides, 428.
Euetion, Athenian general, 386, 488.
Eukles, Syracusan general, 376.
Eukrates, brother of Nikias, 278, 287.
Euphamidas, of Corinth, 76.
Euphemism, 288 f., 443.
Euphemos, of Athens, 186, 350, 353 f.
Euphemos, son of Telekles, of Athens, 276, 278, 284.
Euphiletos, of Athens, 278, 281, 286.
Euripides, on Athens and Argos, 50; on Orestes in Arkadia, 93; on Alkibiades' Olympic victory, 246 f.
Euripos, 409 f.
Eurotas, R. (Lakonia), 33, 91–3.
Euryelos (Syracuse), 469–71, 477 f.
Eurymedon, Athenian general, 156 n., 393, 411, 419, 480.
Eusebios, 201 f., 206 f.
Euthydemos, Athenian general, 129, 153, 391 f., 418, 427.
Exiles, 236, 342, 366.

Fortifications, 360, 373, 395, 400, 471, 473 f., 482; Long Walls, 70, 151 f.
Future tense, 46, 455.

Gela, 200, 203–8, 217, 344.
Gelon, of Syracuse, 202, 204, 216, 219.
Generalship, Athenian, 13, 57, 224, 228, 261 f., 308, 391–3, 426.
Generalship, Syracusan, 348, 371.
Generations, chronology by, 203–8.

Genitive case, 84, 119, 219, 221, 222, 228, 235, 245, 317, 340, 386, 396, 408, 422.
Geometric pottery, 209.
Gongylos, of Corinth, 380.
Grain, 98, 222, 257, 259, 368.
Gylippos, of Sparta, 8, 364 f., 367, 380 f., 384, 440, 444, 459, 461, 477, 489.
Gymnopaidiai (Sparta), 150 f.

Halikyai (Sicily), 412.
Harmodios and Aristogeiton, 317–35.
Harpine (near Olympia), 66.
Hegesistratos, son of Peisistratos, 333.
Hellanikos, of Lesbos, on Peisistratidai, 321–3, 326, 328; on Rome, 212; on Sicily, 199–203.
Hellanodikai, 60 f., 66.
Helots, 34–8, 79, 93, 395, 400, 440; see also Messenians.
Heraia (Arkadia), 104.
Heraion (Epidauros), 130.
Herakleia Trachinia, 68 f.
Herakleides, Syracusan general, 376.
Herakleion (Mantineia), 94, 98 f., 101.
Herbita (Sicily), 380.
Hermokrates, of Syracuse, age, 304; character, 347; diplomacy, 351; oratory, 350; politics, 296 f., 348, 431, 461; as source of Thucydides, 467; strategy, 299, 396.
Herms, mutilation of, 271–89.
Herodotos, chronology, 205; on the Peisistratidai, 320 f.
Hesiod, on the West, 210 f.
Hestiaia (Euboea), 436 f.
Hexapyla (Syracuse), 474.
Himera, destruction, 339, 435; foundation, 200, 219; Sicilian expedition, 379.
Himeraion (Thrace), 386.
Hipparchos, archon at Athens, 332.
Hipparchos, son of Charmos, 333 f.
Hipparchos, son of Peisistratos, 317–35.
Hippias, son of Peisistratos, 317–37.
Hippoklos, of Lampsakos, 336.
Hippys, of Rhegion, 199 f.
Homer, on the West, 210 f.
Horse-breeding, 237.
Hostages, 88, 135 f.
Hyakinthia (Sparta), 47 with addenda, 54.

Hybla Geleatis, 340 f.
Hylias, R. (S. Italy), 415.
Hysiai (Argolid), 152 f., 186.

Iapygia, 291.
Ietai (Sicily), 382.
Imbros, 436 f.
Inachos, R. (Argolid), 81, 107–9.
Inessa (Sicily), 369.
Infinitive constructions, 123, 254, 353, 355 f., 367, 396, 407, 416 f., 419, 422, 445.
Intensification, 421.
Intermarriage, between states, 220 f.
Interpolation, 306 f., 403 f., 411, 424, 476 f.
Ionian Sea, 239, 299.
Ionians, 167 f., 350, 354 f., 438. See also Race.
Ionic dialect, 199.
Iophon, son of Peisistratos, 333.
Islanders, 155, 157, 188, 344, 384, 396.
Italiots, 311.
Italy, 375, 391, 411.

Josephus, imitating Thucydides, 398.

Kakyparis, R. (Sicily), 455–8.
Kallias, son of Hyperochides, 333.
Kallistratos, Athenian general, 154.
Kamarina, destruction, 219; foundation, 203 f., 206; Sicilian expedition, 316 f., 349, 353, 357, 486.
Karneia, Karneios month, 69, 74 f., 127 f., 129.
Karyai (Peloponnese), 33, 76, 91.
Karystos (Euboea), 438.
Kasmenai, 203 f.
Katane, foundation, 202 f., 206; Sicilian expedition, 316, 342 f., 420, 458, 460.
Katavóthres, 97 f.
Kaulonia (Italy), 398.
Keloussa, Mt. (Argive border), 81, 107.
Kentoripa (Sicily), 369, 412.
Kephallenia, settlement of Messenians, 37 f.; Sicilian expedition, 410.
Kephisodoros, metic at Athens, 334.
Kerameikos (Athens), 334.
Kerkyra, foundation, 206 f.; Sicilian expedition, 291, 411, 433 f.

Kleandridas, father of Gylippos, 367, 377.
Klearidas, of Sparta, 22, 29.
Kleisthenes, archonship, 330.
Kleoboulos, Spartan ephor, 38–41.
Kleomedes, Athenian general, 158, 189.
Kleon, and Skione, 30, 153; imperial policy, 167, 183 f.
Kleonai (Peloponnese), 81, 106 f., 139, 369.
Knossos, 139.
Konon, Athenian general, 393, 411, 414 f., 418.
Kontoporeia, from Kleonai to Mycenae, 81.
Kranioi (Kephallenia), 37, 188.
Kritias, of Athens, 278, 287.
Kroton, 201, 206 f., 311.
Kyme (Cumae), 206, 208 f., 218.
Kynouria (Peloponnese), 47, 108–10, 145.
Kypsela (Arkadia), 32.
Kyrene, 428.
Kythera, 145, 399 f.

Labdalon (Syracuse), 473 f.
Laches, Athenian general, 78, 87, 99, 129; in Sicily, 197, 221, 317, 349.
Laispodias, Athenian general, 378.
Lamachos, Athenian general, 7 f., 223 f., 314 f., 374, 420 f.
Lamis, of Megara, 215.
Lampsakos, 336.
Laodokeion (Arkadia), 32, 92.
Larisa (Argos), 71, 107.
Lawcourts, Athenian, 365.
Lelantine War, 216, 486.
Lemnos, 436 f.
Leogoras, of Athens, 278, 281, 287 f.
Leokoreion (Athens), 334.
Leon, of Sparta, 50.
Leon (near Syracuse), 468.
Leontinoi, foundation, 202–4, 209; Sicilian expedition, 220–2, 228, 236, 356, 425 f.
Lepreon (Peloponnese), 26–8, 36, 65–7, 88, 148.
Letter-forms, Attic, 331 f.
Leukopetra (Italy), 415 f.
Leuktra, Leuktron (Arkadia), 33 f., 73, 92.
Lichas, of Sparta, 66 f., 131.
Light-armed troops, 374, 422.
Ligurians, 211.

Lokris, 30, 94, 144.
Lokroi (Italy), 311, 379.
Lot, 308.
Luck, of generals, 249, 375 f.
Lykaion, Mt. (Arkadia), 32, 73.
Lykomedes, of Athens, 158.
Lykomidai, of Athens, 158.
Lykosoura (Arkadia), 33.
Lyrkeia (Argolid), 107 f.
Lyrkeion, Mt. (Argolid), 108–10.
Lysimeleia (Syracuse), 484.

Macedon, 153 f., 222 f.
Mainalioi (Arkadia), 32, 34, 64, 81, 93, 104, 136, 148.
Malaria, 424.
Maleatis (Arkadia), 33 f., 73.
Malians, 68.
Mantineia, subjects in Arkadia, 24 f., 32, 81, 104, 136; position after Peace of Nikias, see Alliances; campaigns of 418 B.C., 80, 87 f., 91–127, 248; position after defeat, 148, 152, 290, 310.
  Constitution, 59 f.; numbers, 80 f., 112.
Maps, absence of, 313, 440.
Marathon, date of battle, 337.
Marmor Parium, 206, 215, 321–3.
Medical theory, 255, 464.
Megalopolis, plain of, 32, 73, 92 f.
Megara (Greece), 30, 42, 188, 217, 310.
Megara (Sicily), 202–10, 215–17, 315, 368.
Mekyberna (Thrace), 11, 43.
Meletos, of Athens, 279, 281.
Melos, connection with Sparta, 157, 161 f., 172 f., 181, 187 f.; previous relations with Athens, 156–8, 161 f., 168, 183; siege and surrender, 155 f., 188–90; execution, 158, 167, 186 f., 190 f.
  Melian Dialogue, date, 166 f.; form, 159, 182, 186; purpose, 157, 162, 182–8; Thucydides' sympathies, 168, 171 f., 183–7, 410; forward references to Sicilian expedition, 171 f., 177 f., 181–3; to fall of Athens, 165–7.
Menandros, Athenian general, 391 f., 418, 427.
Mercenaries, 258, 263, 310, 386, 400.
Messene (Sicily), 218 f., 314, 349.
Messenia (Peloponnese), 32, 34, 92.

Messenians (Peloponnese), 37 f., 188, 218 f., 400, 435.
Metapontion (Italy), 212, 439.
Methone (Pieria), 222 f.
Methydrion (Arkadia), 32, 81, 485.
Methymna (Lesbos), 434 f.
Miltiades, archonship, 330.
Mines, 406.
Morale, 386 f., 415, 420, 454.
Movement, by land, 83, 91–3, 395.
Movement, by sea, 83, 197 f., 258, 284, 411, 425, 428.
Mycenae, 58, 81 f., 107.
Mykalessos (Boeotia), 409 f.
Myletidai (Himera), 219.
Mysteries, 271–85.
Mytilene, 157, 177; Athenian debate, 181–5.

Naupaktos, 70, 393, 414 f., 435.
Naxos (Sicily), destruction, 215; foundation, 202–10, 214; Sicilian expedition, 316.
Neapolis (Africa), 428.
Neapolis (Syracuse), 471.
Negatives, 451 f.
Nemea, 81–5, 106 f.
Night fighting, 423.
Nikias, and Melos, 156, 190; policy towards Sparta, 53 f., 76, 78 f., 87, 147; proposed expedition to the north, 153 f.; views on Sicilian expedition, 230, 260 f., 285, 314; strategy, 314, 419 f.
    Character, 461–4; easily discouraged, 344, 386 f., 418, 461 f.; illness, 375, 462; nervous of Athenian character, 231, 390 f., 425 f.; piety etc., 428 f., 449 f., 453 f.; luck, 249; wealth, 461.
    See also Peace of Nikias.
Nikodoros, of Mantineia, 59.
Nikostratos, Athenian general, 78, 87 f., 99, 129.
Nisaios, of Athens, 279, 287.
Nominative ad sensum, 262.

Oaths, 25, 51, 57, 61, 137, 394.
Oinobios, Athenian general, 14 f.
Oitaioi, 68.
Oligarchy, general character of, 159, 235, 337, 362.
Olives, 405.
Olympia, 54, 60–2, 64–7, 93, 204, 246 f.

Olympieion (Syracuse), 346, 479–82.
Omens, 345.
Optative mood, 143, 371.
Oracles, 12, 172, 197.
Oral tradition, 205, 323.
Oratory, 159, 162, 229, 231, 235 f., 251, 299, 303, 356, 391; gesture, 231, 260; tone of voice, 256, 260.
Orchomenos (Arkadia), 32, 79, 85, 88, 94, 135 f.
Oresthasion, Orestheion (Arkadia), 91–3.
Orneai (Argolid), 81, 107–10, 139, 222.
Ostracism, 287, 332.

Paean, 423 f.
Pallantion (Arkadia), 32, 92–5, 101.
Pammilos, of Megara, 216 f.
Panaitios, of Athens, 279, 282.
Panakton (Attic border), 37, 40 f., 43, 45 f., 48.
Panathenaia, 266–70, 273 f., 335 f.
Parallelism, 249, 253.
Parenthesis, 40, 220, 232, 419, 431, 445.
Parrasioi (Arkadia), 31–4, 88, 93.
Participles, 222, 231, 431, 445.
Passwords, 423.
Patrai (Achaia), 69 f., 151 f.
Pay, 56, 228, 293–5.
Peace of Nikias, signatories, 26, 147, 157, 172; terms, 28 f., 67; Spartan attitude, 30, 53, 232; uncertainty, 15, 252, 349; breaches, 77 f., 188, 377 f.; duration, 6–8, 37.
Peisandros, of Athens, 283 f.
Peisistratidai, 317–37.
Peisistratos, son of Hippias, 331 f.
Pelagos wood (Mantineia), 94–6, 100 f.
Pellene (Achaia), 150.
Peloponnesian League, membership, 31, 43 f., 148, 172; procedure, 24–6, 28 f., 74 f., 85, 138–42; fleet, 231 f., 411.
Perdikkas, king of Macedon, 145 f., 153 f., 223, 386.
Perikles, imperial policy, 167, 170, 179, 184 f., 254 f.
Persian Wars, 161, 163, 173, 178 f., 354 f.
Petra (Italy), 415 f.
Phaiax, of Athens, 287 f.
Pharax, of Sparta, 124.
Pheia (Elis), 410.

Pherekles, of Athens, 279, 281 f.
Philistos, of Syracuse, 206 f., 346, 380, 429, 459, 461, 463.
Philocharidas, of Sparta, 50.
Philokrates, Athenian general, 189.
Philoktetes, 212.
Phleious, 80–2, 85, 107, 153, 369, 378.
Phlya (Attica), 158.
Phoenicians, 214, 313, 486.
Phokians, 30 f., 94, 144, 212 f.
Phyrkos (Elis), 65.
Pisatis, 27, 66.
Plataia, Theban attack, 12, 18 f.; relations with Athens, 30; in Sicily, 433; topography, 94.
Pleistoanax, king of Sparta, 31, 120, 127.
Plemmyrion (Syracuse), 8, 383, 397.
Pleonasm, 421.
Plutarch, additions to and divergences from Thucydides, 51 f., 190 f.
Polyanthes, of Corinth, 414.
Population, transplantations of, in Sicily, 249 f.
Poseidon Hippios (Mantineia), 95 f.
Proverbs, 97, 445.
Pulytion, metic at Athens, 279, 282, 287.
Punctuation, 103, 388, 407, 448, 460.
Pylos, Spartan anxiety to recover, 43, 145; Athenian raids from, 77 f., 188, 377 f., 400, 435.
Pythen, of Corinth, 376.
Pythodoros, Athenian general, son of Isolochos, 197.
Pythodoros, Athenian general in 414 B.C., 378.

Race, 146, 220, 351, 356, 384, 432 f., 438.
Ransom, 65.
Religion, 72, 136 f., 173 f., 369, 394, 428 f., 453 f., 462 f.
Repetition of words, 91, 222, 424 f.
Rhegion (Italy), 218, 312, 352, 415 f.
Rhion (Achaia), 70 f.
Rhodians, 217, 310, 438.
Rhypes (Achaia), 414.

Sacrilege, 346; see also Herms and Mysteries.
Samians, 218.
Saminthos (Argolid), 82.
Saronic Gulf, 72, 77.

Scholia, paraphrases in, 89, 103, 123, 144, 153, 171, 180, 247, 300 f., 307, 329, 338, 341, 357, 363.
Scouts, 100 f., 104.
Secretaries, Athenian, 387.
Security, military, 300, 313 f., 348.
Segesta, 212 f., 220–2, 228, 236, 312 f., 339 f.
Selinus, 202–10, 216 f., 256, 339 f., 344, 353, 379.
Ships, large, tonnage of, 399.
Sicilian expedition, chronology, 266, 271–6, 400 f., 415, 423, 428, 449–51; strategy of, 220, 228 f., 339, 418–21, 471 f.
Sicilian Sea, 239.
Siege-engines, 421, 477.
Sigeion, 336 f.
Sikanos, Syracusan general, 424.
Sikanos, R. (Spain), 211.
Sikans, 200 f., 213 f., 339 f., 412.
Sikels, migration, 200 f., 203 f., 212 f.; in Sicilian expedition, 298, 311, 340, 359 f., 379 f., 412, 433, 439, 455, 458.
Sikyon, 94, 107 f., 148 f., 395, 440.
Simonides, 336.
Skione, 30, 153, 181 f., 185–7.
Skiritai, 32–4, 103 f., 120.
Skyllaion, C., 73, 83.
Slaves, 162 f., 365, 388, 401–3, 405 f., 441, 452, 460.
Sollion (Akarnania), 26.
Sophistry, sophists, 162–4, 166, 174, 178, 182, 246, 366.
Sparta, 421 B.C. and after, see Alliances, Boeotia, Corinth, Elis, Peace of Nikias; relations with Argos, 8, 23 f., 39–41, 47, 86, 89, 130–45, 149–52; campaigns of 418 B.C., see Agis, Argos, Mantineia; relations with allies, 5 f., 21 f., 25 f., 30, 104 f., 384, 395, see also Peloponnesian League; Dekeleia, 367, 393–5; help to Syracuse, 367. See also Herakleia Trachinia, Melos.
    Kings, 74, 85, 89–91, 127; ephors, 38, 74, 84, 135, 361; assembly, 134 f.; see also helots, ξύμβουλοι, τέλος.
    Army organization, 103, 111–17; command in field, 91, 103, 119, 124 f.: polemarchs, 84, 103, 113; age-groups and call-up, 74, 93; perioikoi in army, 33, 73 f., 117;

K k

Sparta (*cont.*)
cavalry, 104 f.; 'hippeis', 112, 121; supply, 91–3, 97; military traditions, 102, 118 f., 121, 125. Calendar, 38; dialect, 132–4; music, 118; religion, 394; reputation, 24, 70 f., 127 f., 142; secrecy, 110 f., 127; concept of virtue, 175 f., 187.
Sphakteria, 102, 115, 127.
Stasis, 36, 251 f.
Stesichoros, 211 f.
Stockades, 342 f., 373, 417, 475 f.
Stymphalos (Arkadia), 94, 108.
Styra, 438.
Subject, change of, 82, 255, 357, 394.
Subjunctive mood, 143, 257, 371.
Superlatives, 85, 126, 292.
Supply, military, 257, 259, 391, 417.
Sybaris, 201.
Syke (Syracuse), 473 f.
Symaithos, R. (Sicily), 343, 369.
Syracuse, allies, 342, 344, 353, 432 f.; army, 371, 374, 476; constitution, 303, 307, 348 f., 430 f.; diplomacy, 298, 352; foundation, 201–10, 215; harbours, 382 f., 478 f.; navy, 388, 397; politics, 296 f., 348, 375, 382, 387, 425 f., 430 f., 450; hostility of other Sikeliots, 298, 352; Sikels, 256 f.; walls, 468–76, 481.

Tabula Iliaca, 211 f.
Tactics, military, 120 f., 343, 346, 374, 383, 410, 417, 422, 476–8.
Tactics, naval, 397 f., 415–18, 430, 444, 447, 449, 480.
Tanagra, 409; battle of, 126.
Taras, 299.
Taureas, of Athens, 280, 287.
Tautology, 255, 291 f., 390, 397, 409.
Taxation, 329 f., 408 f.
Taygetos, Mt. (Lakonia), 32 f., 92.
Tegea, 32, 46, 88–91, 94 f., 98–101, 104 f., 119, 145.
Teisias, Athenian general, 158, 189.
Teisimachos, of Athens, 158.
Temenites (Syracuse), 469, 471 f.
Tenos, 437.
Terias, R. (Sicily), 316, 368.
Terina (Italy), 377.
Thapsos (Sicily), 215 f.
Thebes, 67 f., 166, 369 f., 394.

Theron, of Akragas, 204.
Theseion (Athens), 338.
Thespiai, 369 f., 395.
Thessalos, son of Kimon, 283.
Thessalos, son of Peisistratos, 320, 333.
Thessaly, 68.
Thrace, Thraceward area, 13 f., 24, 29, 36 f., 42 f., 129, 153 f., 176, 386, 405, 409 f.
Thrasonides, of Corinth, 384.
Thrasylos, of Argos, 84, 86 f.
Thucydides, birth, 12 f.; generalship, 13; exile, 13–15; possible signs of presence in Peloponnese, 85 f., 101 f., 111, 125 f., 202; in Sicily, 198, 466 f., 475; death, 13, 16; politics, 149, 183 f., 186, 229 f.; religion, 12, 172, 394, 429; science and philosophy, 19, 174, 265 n., 429; views on chance, 171, 185, 243.
Stages of composition,* 5, 9, 16 f., 21, 24 f., 37, 63 f., 127, 131 f., 175, 197, 215, 242–5, 325–9, 339 f., 347, 404, 421, 423, 427, 432, 435 f., 476, 488; editor, 16, 327, 403 f.; 'notes', 9, 16 f., 30, 127; special character of book v, 16 f., 43, 63, 154, 192.
Sources, 101 f., 111, 123, 127, 147, 313 f., 323–5, 348, 423, 466 f., 487; information from Athens during exile, 76, 79, 83, 125, 128, 192; use of documents, 62 f., 131–3, 324 f., 333, 436; narrative technique, 73, 110, 119, 345; digressions, 198, 317, 321 f., 325–9, 401, 403 f.; speeches, 159, 182 f., 297, 349, 367, 444, 446, 453; chronology, 6–9, 11 f., 18–22, 54, 149, 154, 181, 337, 402 f.; on strategy, 197, 346, 419–21, 488; topography, 94, 101 f., 126, 440, 466–84; generalization, 183, 185, 187 f., 341; omissions and possible omissions, 27, 36, 101, 131, 154, 156–8, 183, 191, 312, 380, 394, 451; errors and possible errors, 45, 53, 67, 117, 123, 377; exaggeration, 274, 328, 331, 408, 420 f.; reticence and allusiveness, 35, 66, 72 f., 75 f., 86, 169, 172 f., 179 f., 199, 216, 339, 456, 467 f.
Style, 350, 403 f., 448; *see also*

* We hope to include in vol. v an appendix dealing with the evidence for this.

GENERAL

Alliteration, *and many other headings*.
Thukles, of Chalkis, 200, 206, 214.
Thurioi, 338, 376, 413 f.
Thyrea (Kynouria), 47, 109, 153, 369.
Thyssos (Athos), 37.
Timaios, of Athens, 280, 282.
Timaios, of Tauromenion, 206 f., 461.
Timber, 363, 375, 398.
Trade, volume of, in Athenian empire, 408.
Tradition, Athenian, on Peisistratidai, 322 f., 327–9.
Transport, cost of, 406.
Treachery, Greek conception of, 375.
Treaties, frequency of renewal, 221.
Tretos road (Argolid), 81.
Trierarchs, 293 f.
Triremes, 293–5, 342, 388, 416, 447 f., 487.
Trogilos (Syracuse), 474 f.
Troopships, 263, 308–10, 429 f., 487.
Trotilon (Sicily), 215.
Twelve Gods, altar at Athens, 331.

Tyche (Syracuse), 471.
Tylissos (Crete), 139.
Tyranny, 303, 321–3, 337, 362.

Valla's translation, 177, 180, 231, 233 f., 236, 301, 308, 341, 359, 371, 374, 393, 447, 452.
Variation, stylistic, 179, 236, 249, 408, 424, 445.

Walls, *see* Fortifications.
Weather, 258, 345 f., 411, 425.
West Greek dialects, 132–4, 136.
Word order, 55, 65, 119, 162, 178, 222, 295 f., 341, 352, 358, 374, 388, 431.

Xenares, of Sparta, 38–41, 52, 68.

Zakynthos, 224, 410.
Zankle, 218.
Zeugma, 386, 441.
Zeus Lykaios (Arkadia), 32; Soter (Mantineia), 61.

II. AUTHORS AND PASSAGES DISCUSSED

Figures in larger type indicate the pages of this volume; those in smaller type the references to authors.

Andokides, i. 11–65, 273–82; 42, 276; iv, 287 f.; iv. 22, 190.
Antiphon, ii. β. 6, 337 f.
Aristophanes, *Av.* 186 with Σ, 189 f.; *Lys.* 387 ff., 223 f.; *Pax* 250 f., 364; *V.* 684 f., 293.
Aristotle, Ἀθ. π. 16. 4, 329; 16. 10, 325.

Bacchylides, fr. 4, 71.

Diodoros, xii. 75. 7, 105 f.; 77. 4, 68; 78. 1–4, 80; 78. 6, 91; 79–80, 106; 79. 5–7, 124; 80. 2–3, 149; 80. 3, 150; 80. 4, 30; 80. 5, 190; 81. 2, 155; 81. 5–82. 1, 155; xiii. 8. 4, 412 f.; 13. 2, 430; 13. 3, 480 f.
Dionysios of Halikarnassos, *AR* i. 22. 2, 201, 214; 22. 5, 201.

Eupolis, fr. 8. Ib. 8 Dem., 87.
Euripides, *Epinikion*, 246 f.; *Hcld.*, *Supp.*, 50.

Herodotos, iv. 148. 4, 27; v. 75. 2, 127; viii. 73. 3, 108 f.
Hesychios, s.v. δαμώδεις, 35.

Inscriptiones Graecae, i². 76 (= ML 73), 270; 86 (= GHI 72), 54–7, 61 f.; 98/99 (= ML 78), 224–7; 295 (= ML 61), 293; 302 (= ML 77), 86 f., 129, 153 f., 156, 189, 266, 369; 761 (= ML 11), 331 f.; xii. 3. 1187, 192.
Isaios, vi. 14, 271.
Isokrates, iv. 100, 109, 30, 187, 191; xii. 62–6, 30, 191; xvi. 15, 69; xvi. 34, 246.

Lysias, xiv. 41, 281.

Marcellinus, *Vit. Thuc.* 32, 14 f.; 34, 13.
Meiggs and Lewis, 42, 58 f., 122, 139; *see also Inscriptiones Graecae, Supplementum Epigraphicum Graecum*.

INDEXES

Pausanias, i. 23. 9, 14; ii. 20. 2, 106,
150; 25. 5–6, 107 f.; viii. 10–11,
94–6; 27. 3–4, 32–4.
Pindar, *O*. 2. 93, 205.
Plato, *Mnx*. 243 d, 244.
Plutarch, *Alc*. 14–15, 51 f.; 15. 4–5,
151 f.; 16. 5–6, 190 f.; *Lys*. 14. 8,
135; *Nic*. 10, 51 f.; 20. 5, 427;
21. 11, 424; *Pel*. 17. 4, 113.
Poetae Melici Graeci, 893, 895, 336.

Strabo, viii. 6. 17, 376, 108.

*Supplementum Epigraphicum Grae-
cum*, x. 104, 151; x. 227 (= ML 72).
79, 268 n.; x. 352 (= ML 6),
330 f.

Timaios, *FGrH* 566 F101, 461.

Xenophon, *HG* ii. 2. 19, 166 f.; iii. 2.
23, 135, 361; iv. 5. 11–17, 113, 116;
v. 2. 2, 148; 3. 10, 127; 4. 37, 24 f.;
vi. 4. 2, 135; *Lac. Pol*. 11. 4, 111,
114–17.

III. GREEK

ἅδε, 144.
ἀδεής, 358.
ἀδικεῖν, 54, 77, 161 f.
ἀϝρήτευε, 59, 122.
αἰσχρός, 175, 178 f.
αἰτεῖσθαι, 313.
ἄκατος, 399.
ἀκολασία, 362.
ἀκριβής, 165, 328, 355, 390.
ἄλλος, 447, 474.
ἀμείνων, 230.
ἄμιπποι, 79 f.
ἀμόθι, 138.
ἄν, 71, 86, 262, 341.
ἀναγκαῖος, 441.
ἀναγκαστός, 388, 440.
ἀνάγκη, 87, 162–4, 405, 433 f.
ἀναπαύεσθαι, 373.
ἀναψηφίζειν, 239 f.
ἀνδραγαθία, 170.
ἀνθρωπείως, 171 f.
ἀντηρίς, 416.
ἀπάγειν, 90.
ἀπαρτᾶν, 258.
ἀπό, 391, 473.
ἀποδεικνύναι, 358.
ἀποδιδόναι, 340.
ἄποικος, 217, 437.
ἀποκρύπτω, 99.
ἀποστέλλειν, 214.
ἀρετή, 175 f., 235, 461–3.
ἀρρωστία, 424.
ἀρτῦναι, 58 f.
ἀρχαί, 57–9, 159.
ἀρχαιολογεῖν, 446.
αὐτοκράτωρ, 23, 228.
αὐτόνομος, 23, 138, 174, 389, 424.
αὐτοπόλιες, 141.
αὐτός, 17 f., 221 f., 232, 330, 354 f., 437.

βιάζεσθαι, 341.
βοτάμια, 72.
βούλεσθαι, 349, 355.
βραχύς, 390.

γάρ, 407, 419, 425.
γε, 261.

δέ, 413.
δέ γε, 408.
δελφινοφόρος, 418.
δεχήμερος, 11, 31, 223.
δή, 87, 233.
δημιουργός, 58–60.
δημοτικός, 289.
διαβατήρια, 74.
διαλύειν, 154.
διάνοια, 235, 342.
διατιθέναι, 245.
διέκπλους, 416.
δίκαιος, 138, 160, 162–5, 172, 361.
δίκας διδόναι, 142 f.
δι’ ὀλίγου, 234.
δουλεία, 160.
δύνασθαι, 301 f.

ἐγγύς, 198–200, 204 f., 342.
εἰ, 25, 291, 359.
εἰ δέ (sc. μή), 137.
εἰ (. . .) καί, 337 f.
εἶδος, 351.
εἰκάζειν, 295.
εἰκός, 165, 167, 213.
εἶναι, 236.
εἰρημένον, εἴρηται, 25, 28 f., 44 f.
εἰσιών, ἐπιών, 276.
ἐκκλησία, 134.
ἐκπίπτειν, 370.
ἐκπλήσσεσθαι, 102 f.

ἐλλείπειν, 171.
ἐμβολή, 447.
ἐνωμοτάρχης, 103.
ἐξαρτᾶν, 370 f.
ἐξισοῦν, 359.
ἐπαγωγός, 159.
ἔπαλξις, 406.
ἐπί, 289, 436.
ἐπιβάτης, 296, 310.
ἐπιμαχεῖν, ἐπιμαχία, 23, 63 f.
ἐπιμέλεσθαι, 386.
ἐπισπονδαί, 31.
ἐπιστολή, 385.
ἔποικος, 217.
ἐπωτίς, 415.
ἐργασία, 288.
ἐρίζειν, 143 f., 485.
ἔρις, 295.
ἔρυμα, 368.
ἐς, 316, 436.
ἔτης, 144 f.
εὔλογος, 350.
ἔχειν, 210, 386, 436.
ἐχόμενος, 199.
ἐχυρός, 12.

ἡγεμών, 440.
ἤπειρος, 233.
ἤπερ, 307.

θειασμός, 429.
θεράπων, 388.
θεσμοφύλακες, 61.
θεωροί, 60.
θρανίτης, 294 f.
Θρινακίη, 211.

-ίδαι, 219.
ἰδίᾳ, ἴδιος, 26, 43 f., 426.
ἰδιώτης, 348.
ἴσος, 162-4, 170.
Ἰταλία, 200 f., 413.

καί, 51, 88, 217, 234, 262, 310, 342, 397 f.,
    409, 442, 445 f., 460.
κακουργεῖν, 351 f.
κατακλήειν, 153 f.
κατάλογος, 264, 295.
καταλύειν, 27, 411.
κατασχεῖν, 261.
κατοικίζειν, 207.
κατορθοῦν, 238.
κενός, 293 f.
κοινόν, 228.
κόλπος, 239.

κρατεῖν, 235.
κρίνειν, 141.

λῆν, 136 f.
λόγος, 338, 432.
λύειν, 239 f.

μάλιστα, 198 f., 204 f., 419, 421.
Μεγαρεῖς, 216, 368.
μέλλησις, 103, 189.
μέν, 84, 164 f.
μέν/δέ, 263, 391.
μετά, 118.
μετέωρος, 233.
μυριοφόρος, 398 f.

ναύτης, 388.
νεοδαμώδεις, 35 f., 79, 112 f., 116, 440.
νόμος, 118, 163, 174 f., 239 f., 285.

ξυγχωρεῖν, 47.
ξυμβολαί, 142-4.
ξύμβουλοι, 90, 103, 119, 124 f.
ξυμμαχία, 34, 43 f., 172 f., 221, 353.
ξύμμαχοι, 155, 221.
ξύμπας, 458.
ξύν, 419.
ξύνεδροι, 159 f.
ξυνθήκη, 28 f., 61.
ξύντασις, ξύστασις, 448.

οἴκαδε, 140.
ὁλκάς, 343.
ὅμως, 379, 426.
ὄρθριον, 82.
ὅριον, 349.
ὅσιος, 172.
ὅσον, 407 f.
ὅστις, 199.
ὅτι, 54.
οὐδέ, μηδέ, 258, 384, 387, 408, 421.

παρακελευστός, 238.
παράλογος, 408.
Πάραλος, 388.
παρανομία, 285.
παραρρήγνυσθαι, 123 f.
παρεξειρεσία, 415.
παρωνύμιον, 333.
πάτρια, 138, 143 f.
Πελοπόννησος, 249.
περί, 69.
περιγίγνεσθαι, 168, 228 f.
περιορᾶν, 29.
περίπλους, 416.

INDEXES

πίστις, 51.
πλαίσιον, 343, 457.
πλοῖον, 343.
πόλεμος, 10 f., 221, 252, 347 f.
πόλις, 364.
πολιτεία, 250.
πρίν, 87, 485.
πρό, 39 f.
προ-, προσ-, 119, 220, 254.
πρός, 476.
πρόσωπον, 288 f.
προτείχισμα, 472, 478.
πρόφασις, 26, 71, 220, 230, 389.

ῥύεσθαι, 90.
ῥώμη, 291, 394.

σαφῶς, 365.
σιτοποιός, 259.
σκηνή, 349.
στάδιον, 198, 467 f.
στρατηγός, 391 f.
στρατιώτης, 262.
σφεῖς, 54, 64 f., 341.
σωτηρία, 160.
σώφρων, 169 f., 486.

ταρσός, 418.
τε, 220, 223, 240 f., 338, 370, 396, 417, 453.
τέλος, ἐν τέλει, 23, 52, 60, 84, 134 f., 361, 450.
τέχνη, 405 f.
τοίνυν, 160, 173.
τοιόσδε, 297, 486.
τοξεύματα, 422.
τότε, 435.
τρίβειν, 426.
Τρινακρία, 211.

ὑπέρ, 72.
ὑπέχειν, 397.
ὑπήκοος, 434.
ὑπηρεσία, 294.
ὑποπτεύειν, 357.
ὑποτελής, 434.

φιλία, 352.
φύσις, 173 f., 185.

χρήματα, 398.

ὡς, 291, 364.
ὥστε, 167, 398, 407 f.

PRINTED IN GREAT BRITAIN
AT THE UNIVERSITY PRESS, OXFORD
BY VIVIAN RIDLER
PRINTER TO THE UNIVERSITY